Doing Feminist Theory

From Modernity to Postmodernity

SUSAN ARCHER MANN

New York Oxford
OXFORD UNIVERSITY PRESS

Oxford University Press, Inc., publishes works that further Oxford University's objective of excellence in research, scholarship, and education.

Oxford New York
Auckland Cape Town Dar es Salaam Hong Kong Karachi
Kuala Lumpur Madrid Melbourne Mexico City Nairobi
New Delhi Shanghai Taipei Toronto

With offices in
Argentina Austria Brazil Chile Czech Republic France Greece
Guatemala Hungary Italy Japan Poland Portugal Singapore
South Korea Switzerland Thailand Turkey Ukraine Vietnam

For titles covered by Section 112 of the US Higher Education Opportunity Act, please visit www.oup.com/us/he for the latest information about pricing and alternate formats.

Published by Oxford University Press, Inc.
198 Madison Avenue, New York, New York 10016
www.oup.com

Library of Congress Cataloging-in-Publication Data

Mann, Susan Archer.
Doing feminist theory : From Modernity to Postmodernity / Susan Archer Mann. — 1st ed.
p. cm.
Includes bibliographical references and index.
ISBN 978-0-19-985810-1
1. Feminist theory—History. 2. Feminism—History. I. Title.
HQ1190.M356 2012
305.4201—dc23
2011032276

The image on the front cover is taken from a 1914 International Women's Day poster.

Dedicated with love to my mother
Hannah Grashl Mann

CONTENTS

ACKNOWLEDGMENTS

Social theory has been my passion and my life's work. Writing this text was like writing my intellectual life as it represents the culmination of thirty years of reading, writing, and teaching. It is a privilege to have spent my adult life doing work that I love. It also is a privilege to have had the emotional, material, and intellectual support of many dear friends, family members, and colleagues. Among my earliest mentors, Emily Blumenfeld and Gordon Welty not only taught me the value of critical, analytical thought, they also introduced me to feminist theory and to the rich theories of the Old and New Left. Michael Grimes and James Dickinson gave me invaluable emotional, material, and intellectual support throughout the years. They read voluminously in diverse areas of critical thought, and I tapped into their vast knowledge at many points in the writing of this text. The love of my life, my son Joshua Mann Sartisky, kept me grounded in the realities of everyday life and taught me the immense joys of mothering. For the gift of good mothering, I thank my own mother, Hannah Grashl Mann, a strong and generous woman to whom this book is dedicated. My brother, Hunter Mann III, was always there for me, and I am grateful that his love, like mine, transcends our politics. Even the words of my deceased father spurred me on. His frequent reminders that the Bible was written faster than I ever completed a book echoed for years in my mind.

Feminism provided a community of women who intellectually and politically fed and nourished me. I am particularly grateful to the women involved in the University of New Orleans Women's Center and Women and Gender Studies Program—especially Linda Coleman and Marina Heung—who taught me so much while we were founding a home for women at our university. Several scholars and close friends—Jane Ward, Rachel Luft, D'Lane Compton, Dimitra Cupo, Sara Crawley, Valerie Gunter, Alison Griffith, Alice Kemp, Phyllis Raabe, Madelon Powers, Beth Blankenship, Martha Kegel, Peter Graham, Susan Dumais, and Jenson Jeng—enhanced my understanding of feminist theory and my appreciation for the value of good friends and colleagues. Some of their contributions are visible in this volume, while others are less visible but equally noteworthy.

My colleagues in the UNO Department of Sociology always provided me with intellectual and emotional sustenance. My chair, H. David Allen, along with the UNO College of Liberal Arts and UNO Office of Research contributed much institutional support. My superb grant writing colleagues Pam Jenkins, Vern Baxter, and Shirley Laska also were generous in providing material and intellectual support. Innumerable students in my classes over the past three decades taught me to craft and refine my pedagogical skills. Among them, Nicole Gillies and Jessie Jacobs deserve special thanks for developing the timeline for this text. Several graduate and undergraduate students—Ashly Patterson, Nicole Gillies, Kristen Schwartz, Laura Dean Shapiro, and Kristen Lewis—endured the less pleasant tasks of creating the glossary, the indices, and the reference section. Claude Teweles deserves thanks for initially accepting my proposal to write this text and for taking a risk on a little known author.

I thank the following reviewers, in addition to several anonymous reviewers, who commented on versions of this manuscript and provided helpful feedback:

- Deirdre M. Condit, Virginia Commonwealth University
- Sara Crawley, University of South Florida
- Hawley Fogg-Davis, Temple University
- Cecilia Herles, University of Georgia
- Erika Kuhlman, Idaho State University
- Marie Laberge, University of Delaware
- Emily Lutenski, Bowling Green State University
- Amy Lynch, George Washington University
- Kelly Pemberton, George Washington University
- Christine Talbot, University of Northern Colorado

In turn, I thank the copyeditors who did an amazing job of carefully correcting the errors in my unruly manuscript. Finally, I am grateful to my editor Sherith Pankratz and her assistant Cari Heicklen at Oxford University Press for their various roles in enhancing this text. I especially appreciate Cari's patience and persistence in obtaining the permissions and Sherith's thoughtful advice and sound judgment. While the insights and support of all of these people contributed immensely to the construction of this text, its failures and limitations are mine alone.

INTRODUCTION

Toward a history of the vanishing present . . .
—Gayatri Chakravorty Spivak

To live in the new milleneum is to live in a digitized and globalized world unlike any previously known to human history. While this new world order offers unprecedented opportunities to improve the human condition, it is plagued by explosive conflicts, controversies, and catastrophes. Our major political battles today reflect the inequalities of a postcolonial and postmodern world, yet they often appear as culture wars rooted in ancient worlds and scriptures as religious fundamentalisms flourish both at home and abroad. The turbulent social processes that ushered in the twenty-first century entail contradictory, ambiguous, hopeful, and threatening features that are being played out each day on the political, economic, social, and cultural global landscape. Like any social theory text, this text asks big questions: "What is going on just now? What is happening to us? What is this world, this period, this precise moment in which we are living?" (Foucault quoted in Best and Kellner 2001: 5).

To answer these questions, readers are provided with a diverse array of theoretical perspectives that attempt to understand and to analyze the social world we live in and how it came to be. Because this is a *feminist* theory text, attention centers on what these various social transformations mean for gender relations and for women of different classes, races, sexualities, and global locations. These different social locations present a multiplicity of lenses for viewing the world, and each theorist provides insights into her or his own "vanishing present" that helps us to better understand our own (Spivak [1999] 2006).[1] Having taught feminist theory and sociological theory for almost three decades, I am well aware of the trepidation with which many students approach social theory as an intimidating subject and/or as an unnecessarily abstract and irrelevant one. Consequently, I have organized this text in a number of specific ways to make feminist thought more accessible to readers and to help them understand its value.

USING THIS TEXT TO NAVIGATE FEMINIST THOUGHT

The title of this text, *Doing Feminist Theory*, was chosen to highlight the social agency involved in theory production—how constructing theory is a social practice and a form of labor. Just as textile workers weave yarn and thread to create fabrics, feminist theorists weave concepts and ideas to better understand the gendered fabric of social life. While all knowledge is socially constructed, doing feminist theory is a *critical* social practice directed toward better understanding and improving the position of women in diverse social locations. Hence, feminist theory is intrinsically political and cannot be separated from its role as a political practice designed to foster social change.

The subtitle highlights how this text is organized so that readers can more clearly see *paradigm shifts from modernity to postmodernity.* It is designed to enable readers to compare and contrast two distinct forms of feminist thought that have characterized U.S. feminism by counter posing modern feminist approaches to feminist perspectives that have taken the postmodern turn. A comparison between these two modes of social thought—the modern and the postmodern—holds the key to some of the major conflicts and debates within feminism today. The modern perspectives examined in this text include: liberal feminisms; radical feminisms; Marxist, socialist, and anarchist feminisms; and intersectionality theories. Although the names given to some of these theoretical frameworks did not enter the feminist lexicon until late modernity, precursors of these perspectives are discussed in each chapter. For example, even though the term *intersectionality theory* was not coined until the 1980s, this chapter examines precursors to this theoretical approach in the nineteenth and early twentieth centuries as well as contemporary theorists' works.

The feminist perspectives examined in this text that embrace a postmodern epistemology include postmodernism, poststructuralism, queer and transgender theories, postcolonial theories, and the third wave agenda of the younger generation of U.S. feminists. Analytical distinctions between modern and postmodern epistemologies are briefly addressed in chapter 1 and then explored in greater depth throughout the text. The final chapter summarizes the major paradigm shifts that have taken place in U.S. feminist thought in recent decades. Each chapter is written so that it can stand on its own. While this format means that readers will encounter some repetition of ideas, it enables professors to select certain chapters for their classes without assigning the entire text.

Designed for upper-level undergraduate and graduate courses in feminist theory, this text is interdisciplinary in format. Materials from both the social sciences and the humanities are interwoven to explore feminist thought from the late eighteenth century to the present. While the focus is on U.S. feminist thought, feminist theories from abroad that have substantially impacted U.S. feminism are included. A major goal is to highlight the multiplicity of feminisms that have constituted feminist thought over this time period. Particular attention is paid to the diversity of feminist voices and vantage points by race, ethnicity, class, sexuality, and global location. Within this diversity, the sites of conjunction, consensus, and agreement that analytically distinguish major feminist perspectives are specified. However, this text is not simply descriptive. Rather, a critical, analytical approach is used to reveal the underlying assumptions of major theoretical perspectives and to highlight their strengths and weaknesses.

Most existing feminist theory texts and anthologies are organized in one of three ways: by chronology, by theoretical perspectives, or by topics. *Doing Feminist Theory* synthesizes these approaches by employing three different levels of organization. Below I discuss how this threefold approach maintains the advantages of each of its distinct levels of organization as well as how other features of the text are designed to aid students in navigating the world of feminist thought.

The first level of organization is historical in that the text covers feminist thought from the late eighteenth century to the present. The advantages of an historical approach are that readers can see how theories are constructed over time and how they often develop in response to concrete historical conditions as well as to other perspectives and the debates they engender. Theories often build on the strengths of earlier approaches and correct or, at least address, previous weaknesses. A historical approach also enables readers to compare and contrast the different concerns of feminists in different historical eras. Most important, it illuminates how theories are not "free floating ideas" but are grounded in social, economic, and political conditions that influence their form and content (Morton 2003: x). Such historical grounding is not meant to suggest that theory develops in a cumulative, progressive, or linear fashion. Rather, it enables us to see the "dynamics of persistence and change within feminism" that have been given voice by feminist theorists in different time periods and from different social locations (Delmar 1986). Later in this text some of the problems associated with linear models of social change and with a linear history of ideas are examined (Kuhn 1962, Spivak [1999] 2006). In turn, alternative ways of viewing history that point to the uneven and contingent features of social and theoretical development will be discussed.

No doubt, many histories of U.S. feminism have employed a linear, wave approach. While there are debates over the actual timing of different waves, there is general consensus that the **first wave** designates the surge of women's rights activism beginning in the 1830s and culminating around the campaign for woman suffrage that ended or at least went into abeyance in 1920 with passage of the Nineteenth Amendment to the U.S. Constitution (Taylor 1989). The **second wave** denotes the resurgence of women's organizing in the 1960s and ends—or at least suffers major setbacks—with the defeat of the Equal Rights Amendment (ERA) in 1982. The **third wave** refers to the resurgence of feminist activism in the 1990s, especially by younger feminists who came of age after the second wave (Siegel 1997a). Although women's rights advocates of the first wave rarely used the term *feminist* (Cott 1987: 13–14), I will take the liberty of using it throughout the text.

At times, these different waves will be referred to in this text. However, I chose not to foreground this oceanography of feminism for a number of reasons. First, wave approaches too often downplay the importance of individual and small-scale collective actions as well as indirect and covert acts. Second, they ignore feminist writings and activities before and between the different waves. Third, wave approaches generally draw attention to the common themes that unify each wave and focus on the largest and most hegemonic feminist organizations. Hence, they tend to obscure the diversity of competing feminisms *within* each wave as well as the contributions of more politically radical feminists and of women activists and theorists marginalized within each wave.

By contrast, *Doing Feminist Theory* is careful to highlight the diversity and multiplicity of feminist visions and voices by race, ethnicity, social class, and sexual orientation within each wave. It also examines a wide array of perspectives that cross the political spectrum of feminist thought. It recognizes that "waves of feminism" are not synonymous with the history of U.S. feminism. Rather, just as ocean waves crest and subside, waves of feminism simply refer to those historical eras when the U.S. women's movement rose to a crest by successfully mobilizing a large *activist mass-base*. Consequently, this text includes feminist theories written prior to these crests, during these crests, and in the periods of subsidence between the various waves. I will even argue that some of the most influential works that have shaped contemporary feminist thought were written between the second and the third waves.

The second level of organization highlights the diversity and multiplicity of feminist political perspectives that have characterized U.S. feminist thought. The importance of organizing the text in terms of political perspectives lies in the fact that *feminism is not simply a body of thought; it is a politics directed toward social change.* This level of organization highlights the relationship between theory and political practice. It enables readers to see the similarities and differences between these theoretical perspectives and their political strategies for social change. It also makes visible which perspectives were dominant in each historical era and which were more marginalized. In addition, it highlights the diversity of feminisms within each era since different political concerns often reflect the different standpoints or social locations of women theorists/activists in terms of their race, ethnicity, social class, sexual orientation, and global location. It will readily become apparent that "feminism is not a monolithic theory, that all feminists do not think alike, and that, like all other time-honored modes of thinking, feminist thought has a past as well as a present and a future"(Tong 1998: 1).

Because the emphasis is on the *political*, the organization of this text differs from more conventional texts. For example, a separate chapter on psychoanalytic feminisms is usually found in other feminist theory texts. By contrast, this text places liberal psychoanalytical feminisms within the chapter on liberal feminisms and Marxist or radical feminist psychoanalytic approaches within their respective chapters. The point here is to highlight the *political implications* of different feminist perspectives because a central tenet of this text is that politics is the *raison d'etre* of feminist theory.

The third level of organization focuses on theory applications or how feminist theories have addressed specific topics over historical time. This is done in two different ways. First, rather than having a separate chapter on ecofeminism, I show how each feminist political perspective addresses the links between the domination of women and the domination of nature. In this way, ecofeminist theories are threaded throughout the text and readers will be able to see how the ecofeminist approaches rooted in radical feminism differ from the ecofeminist perspectives employed by Marxist feminists or anarchist feminists. Even though the term *ecofeminism* was not coined until 1974, this text will examine how environmental concerns were addressed by feminists throughout the history of the U.S. women's movement.

The second way in which readers are introduced to theory applications is to hold the topic constant and explore how different feminisms have addressed this topic over historical time. The last section of this text is devoted entirely to exploring feminist approaches to global issues. Global social relations have been salient to the history of the United States from its beginnings as a colony to its current role as a global superpower. Therefore, readers can see how feminists addressed this issue from the first through the third waves of U.S. feminism. Because the area we now call the United States has been both a colony and a colonizer, the ways in which these mutually constitutive roles have affected women of different races, ethnicities, classes, sexualities, and nations also will be examined.

The choice of this topic and the space devoted to it in this text reflect the importance and urgency of understanding gender relations using a global perspective. Globalization is now ubiquitous. As the new world order becomes increasingly integrated, the privileges and oppressions of women in the United States are tied increasingly to the privileges and oppressions of women across the globe. Thus, it becomes ever more important for feminists to recognize and to understand the links between the global and the local (Jaggar and Rothenberg 1993: xiii). Although U.S. feminists today exhibit greater sensitivity to diversity by race, class, and sexuality than did their predecessors, our gaze still continues to be too inwardly myopic and U.S.-centered. This nation-centered gaze has deflected attention from calls by feminists from other global locations to decenter U.S. and other Western-inspired feminisms. While it is impossible to decenter U.S. feminist thought in a book devoted to this topic, the last section of the text will explain what this call for decentering means and why it arose.

Holding the topic of globalization constant enables readers to see how questions of colonialism and imperialism were important to nineteenth- and early-twentieth-century suffragists—a history that is not well-known (Hoganson 2001, Sneider 2008, Mann 2008). This excavation of earlier feminist global writings and activism not only serves to legitimize feminist anti-imperialist struggles as serious and ongoing struggles; it also unearths theories and practices that have been ignored in more conventional histories. Holding the topic of globalization constant also enables us to see how feminists from diverse political perspectives addressed this issue and how feminist thought on this topic has changed over time. In this way analytical distinctions between feminist approaches and paradigm shifts in feminist thought over historical time should become more visible.

The larger goal of this feminist theory text is to help readers develop the critical, analytical skills necessary to understand and to analyze new social conditions as they unfold. Such critical skills also assist us in questioning conventional wisdoms about innumerable features of social life that we so often take for granted. By using these skills, we are left with a deeper understanding of what we already know, as well as new ideas and imperatives for social change. Indeed, what is theory if not the endeavor to know how and to what extent it is possible to think otherwise? (Foucault 1986: 8–9)

NOTE

1 "Toward a History of the Vanishing Present" is the subtitle of Gayatri Chakravorty Spivak's *Critique of Postcolonial Reason* ([1999] 2006).

CHAPTER 1

Doing Feminist Theory

> Making this theory is the challenge before us. For in its production lies the hope of our liberation, in its production lies the possibility of naming all our pain—of making all our hurt go away.
>
> —Bell Hooks

INTRODUCTION

As a feminist, I was both saddened and heartened by an editorial written by Leonard Pitts, an African-American columnist for the *Miami Herald*. I was saddened by his tale and heartened by his response to it. His editorial begins: "Brace yourself. I'm going to use a word that offends folks. I'm talking the 'F' word. Feminist." (Pitts 2008: B-7). Pitts was distressed that his seventeen-year-old daughter responded with a "mildly horrified no" when he asked her if she was a feminist.[1] He then discussed the "I'm-Not-a-Feminist-but Syndrome" where many women—young and old—embrace and espouse feminist politics, such as equal pay for work of equal value and the importance of struggles against rape and domestic violence, but refuse to call themselves "feminists."[2]

> We have, I think, lost collective memory of how things were before the F-word. Of the casual beatings. Of casual rape. Of words like "old maid" and "spinster." Of abortion by coat hanger. Of going to school to find a man. Of getting an allowance and needing a husband's permission. Of taking all your spirit, all your dreams, all your ambition, aspiration, creativity, and pounding them down until they fit a space no larger than a casserole dish. "I'm not a feminist, but . . .?" That's a fraud. It's intellectually dishonest. And it's a slap to the feminists who prepared the table at which young women sup.

Doing Feminist Theory is designed to revive our collective memory. It revisits the history of the U.S. women's movement and highlights the major theoretical perspectives that guided this movement and that were engendered by it so that we can better understand our own lives within this rich and vibrant history.

DECONSTRUCTING THE "F-WORD": WHAT IS FEMINISM?

Doing Feminist Theory covers feminist perspectives from the late eighteenth century to the contemporary era. However, the term *feminism* was rarely used in the United States before the early twentieth century. Originating in France in 1837, the first use of *feminisme* is attributed to Charles Fourier, a utopian socialist philosopher who discussed how the extension of liberty to women was a general principle of social progress in his *Theory of Four Movements* (Offen 1988). According to feminist historian Nancy Cott (1987), Hubertine Auclert, founder of the first woman suffrage society in France, also used the term *feminism* in the 1880s.

Over the next decade, the term migrated to England, though it was mainly used by detractors to criticize how "unwanted Continental doctrines" were having an impact in England. The earliest reported use of the term *feminist* in the United States is attributed to a 1906 article about Madeleine Pelletier—a socialist feminist who initiated "militant" tactics borrowed from French suffragists (Cott 1987: 14–15). Prior to that, U.S. feminists referred to themselves as suffragists or used the awkward term *women's righters*. Nineteenth- and early-twentieth-century women's rights activists also referred to their political concerns as the "Woman Question," intentionally using the singular "woman" to denote the unity women shared in their political cause and social movement (3). After 1910, feminist became more frequently used in the United States.

Today feminism not only is used in academic and political discourses but also is part of everyday discourse. Yet in everyday discourse *feminism*—whether used as a negative label to dismiss this *-ism* or as a positive label to empower women—too often is portrayed as a single entity. By contrast, *this text highlights the multiplicity of feminisms existing today and rejects the notion that feminism is a single or monolithic "ism."* Yet, precisely because there are many and diverse feminist perspectives, the term *feminism* defies any simple explanation. Indeed, it is quite common for contemporary feminist texts to evade or elide the question of what feminism means—a situation that can be frustrating for students. This evasion is not the result of limited knowledge, since hundreds of pages of feminist texts are spent discussing what various feminist perspectives mean by the term. Most feminist texts today deliberately refuse to define this term to avoid the dangers of prescribing what feminism means and/or speaking for other feminists who may have different and equally viable definitions of feminism. While this evasion may appear as a weakness of feminism, it can reflect one of its strengths—namely a commitment to openness and inclusiveness.

In place of precise definitions, feminist texts often offer a number of other paths to enable students to better understand what feminism is. One of these well-traversed paths is for texts to provide a list of definitions used by a variety of feminists. This practice is illustrated in Box 1.1, which presents excerpts from Cheris Kramarae and Paula Treichler's *The Feminist Dictionary* (1985). Definitions that represent the voices of first and second wave feminists from a range of political perspectives have been selected. *The Feminist Dictionary* even has blank pages at the end of the book so that readers can make their own contributions and send them for possible future publication.

BOX 1.1

What Is Feminism?

"Has as its goal to give every woman 'the opportunity of becoming the best that her natural faculties make her capable of.'"

Millicent Garret Fawcett, 1878

"I myself have never been able to find out precisely what feminism is: I only know that people call me a feminist whenever I express sentiments that differentiate me from a doormat."

Rebecca West, 1913

"Is that part of the progress of democratic freedom which applies to women."

Beatrice Forbes Robertson Hale, 1914

"Mother, what is a Feminist?"
A Feminist, my daughter,
Is any woman now who cares
To think about her own affairs
As men don't think she oughter'.
Alice Duer Miller, 1915

Feminism is a method of analysis as well as a discovery of new material. It asks new questions as well as coming up with new answers. Its central concern is with the distinction between men and women, with the fact of this distinction, with its meanings, and with its causes and consequences.

Juliet Mitchell and Ann Oakley, 1976

Feminism is the political theory and practice to free all women: women of color, working-class women, poor women, physically-challenged women, lesbians, old women, as well as white economically privileged heterosexual women. Anything less than this is not feminism but merely female self-aggrandizement.

Barbara Smith, 1979

It is an entire worldview or gestalt, not just a laundry list of 'women's issues'. Feminist theory provides a basis for understanding every area of our lives, and a feminist perspective can affect the world politically, culturally, economically, and spiritually.

Charlotte Bunch, 1983

Well, I'm convinced that many frustrated and crabby women are merely feminists in restraints.

Diane F. Germain, 1983

From Cheris Kramarae and Paula A. Treichler, eds., *A Feminist Dictionary* (London: Pandora, 1985), pp. 158–161).

No doubt, reading definitions created by feminists in different eras is enlightening and fun. However it leaves the impression that people can pick and choose what definition of feminism best applies to their own concerns and interests—kind of a grab bag or "do-it- yourself" approach to defining feminism. Just find what feminism fits you and wear it or design one yourself.

This grab bag approach does not sit well with all feminists. Brief definitions such as those presented in Box 1.1 are clever and interesting, but they reduce the subtleties of a complex field to neat slogans that can distort this complexity by their very simplicity. Although there is good reason to be wary of rigid definitions of what feminism means, the term is not entirely up for grabs. Even though feminism is a fluid and ever-changing practice that means different things to different women, it does have some contours, if not boundaries (Rothfield 1990). In an insightful book on this topic titled *What Is Feminism?* Chris Beasley (1999: 21) wonders

> if feminism's distinctive characteristics are *so* unimportant or insubstantial—its diversity so limitless or ineffable—perhaps the label itself should be abandoned? . . . Indeed, feminism would be a peculiarly empty terminology, a critical stance without critique, if it were so limitless that it could not be somewhat more specifically characterized. In this context, I suggest that the precarious project of delineating feminism's characteristics cannot be entirely evaded. (Her emphasis)

As Beasley points out, to avoid such a limitless approach to defining feminism some authors resort to taking the path of minimalist definitions. Such minimalist definitions assert at least some contours or boundaries to feminism while simultaneously being broad and inclusive. As the term "minimalist" suggests, such a definition pares down feminism to its most basic practices without which it could not exist. Box 1.2 provides examples of such minimalist definitions.

BOX 1.2

Minimalist Definitions of Feminism

In its broadest use the word refers to everyone who is aware of and seeking to end women's subordination in any way and for any reason. . . . Feminism originates in the perception that there is something wrong with society's treatment of women.

Encyclopedia of Feminism, 1987

For any viewpoint to count as feminist it must believe that women have been oppressed and unjustly treated and that something has to be done about this. But it does not follow from this that consensus is available as to the precise forms this oppression or injustice takes, or as to how they should be remedied.

Jean Grimshaw, 1986

It is certainly possible to construct a base-line definition of feminism. . . . Many would agree that at the very least a feminist is someone who holds that women suffer discrimination because of their sex, that they have specific needs which remain negated and unsatisfied, and that the satisfaction of these needs would require a radical change . . . in the social, economic and political order.

Rosalind Delmar, 1986

Excerpts from Chris Beasley, *What Is Feminism? An Introduction to Feminist Theory* (1999: 27–28).

Readers will note that "women" appears in all of the minimalist definitions in Box 1.2. However, in recent years even this term has come under scrutiny by feminists who consider *women* to be an unstable and fluid category. For example, in the deconstruction practices of postmodernists and poststructuralists, the question is no longer who or what is woman but, rather, how the category called women is socially constructed and what the effects of this construction are. The argument is that any attempt to define either "women" or "feminism" is to prescribe or establish a definition that inevitably leaves out or excludes "differences" between women (see chapter 6). Consequently, these theorists depict feminism as a form of "critical endeavor" in the realm of sexual politics. Here the only normative or prescriptive element that is conceded is that feminism is defined as a "critical" practice or stance, the term "critical" implying "an imperative toward change" (Beasley 1999: 28–29).

DECONSTRUCTING *WOMEN* AND RECOGNIZING DIFFERENCE

Because readers might wonder how any feminist practice could argue that the category of "women" is unstable and fluid, let us move from an abstract to a more concrete discussion. Historically, feminists have tended to argue that sex is biological while gender is socially learned.[3] Today many feminists view both sex and gender as socially constructed. Chapter 6 elaborates on the poststructural assumptions underlying this new position. Yet one does not have to be a poststructuralist to grasp the instability and socially constructed nature of both sex and gender. For example, most of us realize that biological technologies today have advanced to a stage where the chromosomal makeup of human beings can be determined. In "Are There Only Two Sexes?" (1998)—an article that was widely circulated in both academic circles and the mass media, feminist biologist Ann Fausto-Sterling discusses how, based on her study of patterns of X and Y chromosomes, the chromosomal makeup of human bodies indicates that there are five rather than two sexes. Her analysis suggests that we could replace our binary male/female system with a five-sex category scheme. In *Sexing the Body: Gender Politics and the Construction of Sexuality* (2000: 101) Fausto-Sterling concludes:

> I imagine a future in which our knowledge of the body has led to resistance against medical surveillance, in which medial science has been placed at the service of gender variability, and genders have multiplied beyond currently fathomable limits. . . . Ultimately, perhaps, concepts of masculinity and femininity might overlap so completely as to render the very notion of gender difference irrelevant.

Another concrete example that saturated local, national, and international media in the summer of 2009 was when South African track star and gold medal winner Caster Semenya was forced to undergo "gender testing" to prove she was a girl. Overnight Semenya's case became an international cause celebre and evoked a wide range of impassioned responses as well as claims of racism and gender policing.[4] Box 1.3 provides a poststructuralist analysis of such gender policing that highlights the instability of sex/gender categories and calls for their demise.

BOX 1.3

The Unforgiveable Transgression of Being Caster Semenya

World champion runner Caster Semenya returned to a hero's welcome in her native South Africa last month, where the public denounced the "gender testing" she was forced to undergo after her gold medal in Berlin. Outraged by the racist and sexist comments of rivals who told journalists that you could tell she was a man just by looking at her, the president of South African athletics, Leonard Chuene, resigned from the International Association of Athletic Federations (IAAF). "This girl has been castigated from day one, based on what?" he told the *LA Times* "You denounce my child as a boy when she's a girl? If you did that to my child, I'd shoot you."

As in Semenya's case, female masculinity is often associated with forms of disguise and deceit (the stigma of "doping" and of South African Athletics perhaps trying to "pass off" a male runner as a woman is clearly relevant here). But it is also associated, and for related reasons, with the extraordinary. . . . We are drawn to the virtuoso . . . but it is that very intensity of response that can lead to the kind of panicked rush to quarantine virtuosity, or explain it away as plain freakishness. Female masculinity like that of Semenya . . . can be thought of as a virtuosic performance of gender. . . .

The long sordid history of considering transgender embodiment an intrinsic hoax is still relevant, regardless of whether one wants to claim Semenya as a trans figure. It reflects the essentialist conviction that bodies must have a stable sex that presents itself in appropriate dress, voice, attitude and behavior, and that anybody who does not must by definition be engaged in a deception. This essentialist imperative to expose, examine and fix the transgressive body is also what is motivating the IAFF's panic around Semenya. It represents the latest intensification of gender essentialism, in which the body itself—its genetic makeup, hormonal levels, etc.—is taken to participate in a kind of self-deception; one that, we are told, will take weeks if not years to fully unravel. The threat hanging over Semenya—to be "stripped" of her medal—is a clear giveaway that the logic remains one of a deceit demanding forcible public exposure.

The real challenge when an ugly, gender-disciplinary inquisition like the one the IAAF has started crops up is not to allow ourselves to be blackmailed into simplistic reassertions of gender normativity for the sake of the vulnerable child. . . . And instead of insisting upon the naturalness of her gender, how about turning the question around and denaturalizing the world of gender segregated, performance-obsessed, commercially-driven sports, a world that can neither seem to do with or without excessive bodies like Semenya's and their virtuosic performances?

"The Unforgiveable Transgression of Being Caster Semenya," posted by Tavia Nyong'o on September 8, 2009 at http://bullybloggers.wordpress.com/tag/caster-semenya.

Along with such deconstructive practices, a focus on *differences between women* has become a hallmark of contemporary U.S. feminisms. As discussed in chapter 5, U.S. women of color have been critical of how the first and second waves of the U.S. women's movement too often reflected the concerns of white, middle-class women. Many second wave African–American feminists chose to use the term **womanist** to distinguish their perspective from white feminisms. In her book *In Search of Our Mother's Garden: Womanist Prose* (1983) Alice Walker defines this term as follows:

> WOMANIST: 1) From *womanish.* (Opposite of "girlish" i.e. frivolous, irresponsible, not serious.) A black feminist or feminist of color. From a colloquial expression of mothers to daughters "You're acting womanish," i.e. like woman. Usually referring to outrageous, audacious, courageous or *willful* behavior. Wanting to know more and in greater depth than is considered "good" for one. Interested in grown-up doings. Acting grown-up. Interchangeable with other colloquial expression: "You're trying to be grown," Responsible. In charge. Serious. . . . 2) Also: . . . Herstorically capable, as in "Mama, I'm walking to Canada and I'm taking you and a bunch of other slaves with me." Reply: "It wouldn't be the first time." (Quoted in Smith 1983: xxvi–xxv; her emphasis)

Walker concludes by saying: "Womanist is to feminist as purple is to lavender" (xxv). Clearly, purple is a more powerful color than lavender and historically it has been associated with royalty. Yet purple is also the color of a bruised body. In her award-winning book *The Color Purple* (1982) Walker describes the bruised and torn vagina of a rape victim as purple and the swollen face of a battered woman as the color of eggplant. One of the turning points in the novel is when two of the main women characters find beauty in a field of purple flowers despite the trials and tribulations of their lives. Like the "color purple" the term "womanist" represents for Walker the ability to find strength and beauty in the face of subjugation particularly through relationships with other women (Fiske 2008).

Many of the new generation of third wave, African–American feminists also developed their own distinct label. As Joan Morgan explains in *When Chickenheads Come Home to Roost* (1999: 21–22), they often prefer the term "hip hop feminist" to distinguish themselves from white feminists and their African–American second wave predecessors:

> As a child of the post-Civil Rights, post-feminist, post-soul hip-hop generation, my struggle songs consisted of the same notes but they were infused with distinctly different rhythms. What I wanted was a [feminism] *for colored girls* . . . of my own. The problem was that I was waiting for someone else to write it. . . . Relying on older heads to redefine the struggle to encompass our generation's issues is not only lazy but dangerous. (her emphasis)

Although Morgan expresses her "mad love and respect" for the theoretical writings of her black foremothers (22), she wants a feminism that speaks to young black women, the way hip hop does. She writes: "If feminism is to have any relevance in the lives of the majority of black women . . . it has to rescue itself from the ivory towers of academia" (quoted in Henry 2004: 76). Morgan finds that second wave writings by women of color too often focused on their domination by white people (including white feminists) and black men. She wants "a feminism that would explore who we are as women—not victims. One that claimed the powerful richness and delicious complexities inherent in being black girls now—sistas of the post-Civil Rights, post-feminist, post soul, hip hop generation" (Morgan 1999: 56–57).

Both second and third wave women of Hispanic/Latina descent chose a number of different labels that they preferred, such as "Hispanas," "Latinas," "Mestizas," "Chicana Feminists," and/or Xicanistas (Lugones and Spelman [1983] 2005, Anzaldúa 1987, Castillo 1994, Maatita 2005). Consider the words of this third wave xicanista:

> I remember reading somewhere about womanists and I thought that I would consider myself a womanist. I was at a conference and I was talking to some Black girl and I told her I was a womanist. She was all, "You can't be a womanist. 'Womanist' is for Black women." Then I thought, "Okay, maybe I'm not a womanist after all because I am not Black." Then I hear about Ana Castillo's *xicanista*. I read a little about it and I guess I would call myself a *xicanista*. I'm not a feminist. I'm not a womanist. I'm a *xicanista*. That to me says that I'm for women and I'm *mujer*. I guess that makes me a *xicanista*. I like that word better anyway." (Quoted in Maatita 2005: 30)

The term *xicanista* is designed to encompass the postcolonial histories of Mexican-American, Latina, and Hispanic women in the United States and their affinities with other women of color/ethnicity (Castillo 1994: 40). Not only does it reflect the indigenous mestiza roots of many contemporary xicanistas, but also it implies that they will ally with men in their community to fight racism or ethnic chauvinism. It further recognizes the more complicated family roles—especially the respectful daughter role—experienced by and expected of xicanistas. As Florence Maatita (2005) points out, this search for new political labels reflects the complex issues entailed in finding a language to connect one's brand of feminism with one's racial/ethnic identity.

That feminists today are sensitive to differences between women is exemplified in the following response from third wave feminist Jee Yeun Lee:

> These days, whenever someone says the word "women" to me, my mind goes blank. What "women"? What is this "women" thing you're talking about? Does that mean me? Does that mean my mother, my roommates, the white woman next door . . . half of the world's population? (Quoted in Siegel 1997a: 57–58)

HOW FEMINISTS DO THEORY AND FOR WHOM

Having interrogated the terms *women* and *feminist*, I will now examine the word *theory*. To put it simply, because people want to make sense of the worlds in which they live, they develop concepts, discourses, and theories designed to organize what they perceive as reality in ways that make it intelligible. **Concepts** are simply abstractions designed to categorize or group similar individual features of social reality. **Discourses** are historically variable ways of specifying knowledge that link together concepts into ideas that enable writing, speaking, thinking, and acting. **Theories** are developed discourses that offer a general account of how a range of phenomena are systematically interconnected. Theories place individual items within a larger context to understand both the whole and the parts constituting that whole. Feminism is "incipiently theoretical" to the extent that it understands the plights of individual women as connected with each other, as instances of *systemic subordination* rather than as the results of individual, accidental, or coincidental misfortune (Jaggar and Rothenberg 1993: 75).

To translate the scholarly language above, I shall use a rather silly example that, nevertheless, has been painful for some women. *Blonde* is a concept that represents in abstract form a certain color of hair that is different from, say, a brunette or a redhead. The concept *blonde* is an abstraction because it could categorize a range of different hair colors observed to be light colored, such as platinum blonde or strawberry blonde. *Fun* is another abstraction that refers to people enjoying themselves. However, determining what is meant by fun is a much more difficult task. As soon as we try to define what fun means, we realize that it could mean something different in diverse times and places, just as it could mean something different to diverse groups of people—such as people of different ages or people of different religions and levels of religiosity. Let us sidestep this dilemma and examine a discourse on beauty constructed for a hair coloring advertisement that circulated widely in U.S. magazines and on television in the post–World War II era that stated: "blondes have more fun."[5]

Feminists could develop complex theoretical analyses based on this simple statement. For example, feminists might analyze how this discourse "blondes have more fun" is a *gendered* discourse. Indeed, even though this statement never explicitly says so, it is understood that this discourse is directed at women not men. Feminists might go further to discuss how more general issues of beauty and appearance are gendered and even document how women in place X at time Y spend far more time, money, and effort on beauty and appearance than do their male counterparts. A Marxist feminist might chime in that this gender inequality is the result of women using their appearance more often than men to gain power and wealth because women have been excluded historically from control over property and/or access to certain occupations. An intersectionality theorist or a postcolonial theorist might join this theoretical chorus to argue that the discourse "blondes have more fun" reflects not only gender and class issues but also racial and global privilege given how women of Western European descent both locally and globally are more likely to have blonde hair. In turn, a queer theorist might interrogate the heterosexual assumptions that underlie this discourse. I will stop here, but readers can see how this simple statement could be spun into various theories that address gender, as well as race, class, sexuality, and global issues.

In the Introduction to this text, I argued that "doing feminist theory" is a critical and intrinsically political practice because it is directed toward both understanding and improving the position of women. Yet the questions of how we do theory and for whom are not simple and have been the focal points of intense debates among feminists. Some critics argue that feminists have foolishly "climbed out on a limb of academic theory that is all but inaccessible to the uninitiated" (Denfeld 1995: 5). Others say we should abandon theory altogether because it is divorced from the real world and exists in, of, and for itself (Roiphe 1993). Still others highlight how theories are powerful discourses or objectified forms of knowledge that empower some people and silence others (Grimshaw 1993). Some authors even choose not to describe their works as "theory" but, rather, as "critical practices," "critical stances" or "critical inquiries" (Beasley 1999: 29). My point here is that we cannot even begin to address the question of what is theory without visiting a number of competing and conflicting views among feminists on this subject.

ACCESSIBILITY AND MULTIPLE SITES OF THEORY PRODUCTION

A key issue in the debates over how we do feminist theory and for whom is the *accessibility of feminist theory*. If feminist theory is a tool for social and political change, should it be accessible and understandable to the average person? While reading this text, students should keep in mind how many women are excluded from academic training and/or lack the time and resources to construct academic theory. In the United States, only about 30 percent of women twenty-five years and older have obtained a four-year college degree, and an even smaller percentage of women take gender studies courses (Macionis 2011). Moreover, if one looks through a global lens, the percentage of women receiving a college education would be minute. Thus, the very practice of reading this college-level text suggests relative privilege.

Some of the most influential feminist theoretical perspectives today—such as feminist postmodernism, poststructuralism, and postcolonial theory—use very difficult scholarly language. Among their ranks are scholars who challenge the notion that feminist theory should be written in a style accessible to all. For example, postcolonial theorist Gayatri Spivak's writings (which map the effects of different colonial legacies on the way we think about gender) are presented in a complex language and style that are difficult to understand. This abstruse style would appear to contradict the political aim of Spivak's work: to articulate the voices and political agency of oppressed subjects in the Third World (Morton 2003: 5). Yet Spivak challenges the commonsense assumption that clear, transparent language is the best way to analyze oppression. She suggests the opposite, that transparent systems of representation through which things are known and understood are also the systems which control and dominate people. Her writings emphasize the limitations of linguistic and philosophical representations and their potential to mask real social and political inequalities in the contemporary world:

> When I am pushed these days with the old criticism—"Oh! Spivak is too hard to understand!"—I laugh, and I say okay. I will give you, just for your sake

> a monosyllabic sentence and you'll see that you can't rest with it. My monosyllabic sentence: We know plain prose cheats. (Quoted in Morton 2003: 6)

Spivak's reply sounds like a simple play on words; however, her point is more serious. Her essays and books carefully link disparate histories, places, and methodologies in ways that often refuse to adhere to the conventions of western linear thought. Such a refusal is a conscious rhetorical strategy calculated to engage the reader in the critical interrogation of how we make sense of literary, social, and economic texts in the aftermath of colonialism. For Spivak both the form and the content of her approach are designed to spark critical engagement (6).

In contrast, feminists from another equally influential, contemporary theoretical approach—intersectionality theory—level scathing critiques against theorists who use language that is only accessible to the few. For example, Patricia Hill Collins views the difficult language of postmodernism as exclusive and elitist—a means of keeping marginalized peoples from speaking for themselves—a view shared by other critics (Christian 1988: 71; Di Stefano 1990):

> The new language of postmodernism has become a new form of cultural capital in the academic marketplace. By performing a powerful gatekeeping function for those who lack access to the exclusionary language of postmodernism, the rhetoric of deconstruction can be used to maintain the status quo. . . . To me this is the ultimate postmodernist irony. The ability to manipulate exclusionary language becomes yet another standard used to exclude Black women from legitimated intellectual work. (Collins 1998: 142)

Other intersectionality theorists have distinguished between those who view theory as a democratic tool that should be widely accessible and those who engage in theory bashing or anti-intellectualism that treats theory as something that only an elite and not ordinary people produce. In "Theory as Liberatory Practice" from her book *Teaching to Transgress* (1994), bell hooks[6] directly addresses this issue. hooks (1994: 59) describes how she came to theory because she was desperate to comprehend what was happening around and within her. She found theory to be "a location for healing"—a sanctuary where she could imagine possible futures and places where life could be lived differently. Yet hooks makes clear that theory is not inherently healing, liberatory, or revolutionary. It fulfills these functions only when we direct our theorizing toward these ends (61). She criticizes theories that use difficult language where readers are left "stumbling bleary-eyed" and "feeling humiliated" (64–65). Nevertheless, she knows that theories entail important ideas that, if used differently, could serve a healing, liberatory function.

hooks also criticizes those who "trash" theory and who promote a "false dichotomy between theory and political practice" (65). She discusses how she has witnessed many women who dismiss intellectuals, put down theory, and praise speaking from the gut rather than in the abstract. In contrast, she argues that feminists must actively work to call attention to the importance of producing theory:

> Making this theory is the challenge before us. For in its production lies the hope of our liberation, in its production lies the possibility of naming all our pain—of

> making all our hurt go away. If we create feminist theory, feminist movements that address this pain, we will have no difficulty building a mass-based feminist resistance struggle. There will be no gap between feminist theory and feminist practice. (bell hooks 1994: 75)

Along with debates over the accessibility of theory, many *feminists have called for a broader description of the activity that customarily qualifies as theoretical—pointing to multiple sites of theory production both inside and outside of the academy* (Siegel 1997a). Consider Bettina Aptheker's *Tapestries of Life: Women's Work, Women's Consciousness, and the Meaning of Daily Life* (1989: 39), where she points to the importance of socially lived knowledge or the "dailiness" of women's lives.

> By the dailiness of women's lives I mean the patterns women create and the meanings women invent each day and over time as a result of their labors and in the context of their subordinated status to men. . . . The search for dailiness is a method of work that allows us to take the patterns women create and the meanings women invent and learn from them. If we map what we learn, connecting one meaning or invention to another, we begin to lay out a different way of seeing reality. This way of seeing is what I refer to as women's standpoint.

In "The Race for Theory" (1988: 52), Barbara Christian argues that "people of color have always theorized—but in forms quite different from the Western form of abstract logic":

> Our theorizing (and I intentionally use the verb rather than the noun) is often in narrative forms, in the stories we create, in riddles and proverbs, in the play with language, since dynamic rather than fixed ideas seem more to our liking.

Similarly, in "Poetry Is Not a Luxury," Audre Lorde explains how poetry is a "distillation of experiences" that can serve as an emancipatory project for women where emotions and feelings are used as a means of understanding the world in which we live. Recognizing how her views clash with the rational rules undergirding more conventional views of theory, Lorde contrasts her insights with the "European mode" preferred by "the white fathers" (see Box 1.4 below).

BOX 1.4

"Poetry Is Not a Luxury"

When we view living in the European mode only as a problem to be solved, we rely solely upon our ideas to make us free, for these were what the white fathers told us were precious.

But as we come more into touch with our own ancient, noneuropean consciousness of living as a situation to be experienced and interacted with, we learn more and more to cherish our feelings and to respect those hidden sources of our power from where true knowledge and, therefore, lasting action comes.

At this point in time, I believe that women carry within ourselves the possibility for fusion of these two approaches so necessary for survival, and we come closest to this combination in our poetry. I speak here of poetry as a revelatory distillation of experiences, not the sterile wordplay that, too often, the white fathers distorted the word *poetry* to mean, in order to cover a desperate wish for imagination without insight.

For women, then, poetry is not a luxury. It is a vital necessity of our existence. . . . Poetry is the way we help give name to the nameless so it can be thought. The farthest horizons of our hopes and fears are cobbled by our poems, carved from the rock experiences of our daily lives. . . .

The white fathers told us: I think, therefore I am. The Black mother within each of us—the poet—whispers in our dreams: I feel, therefore I can be free. Poetry coins the language to express and charter this revolutionary demand, the implementation of that freedom."

Audre Lorde, "Poetry Is Not a Luxury," in *Sister/Outsider* (Trumansburg, NY: Crossing Press, 1984), pp. 37–38.

In further defense of multiple sites of theorizing, some feminists have warned against a metonymic view of the production of theory where one aspect of theory construction is taken to represent the whole (Siegel 1997b: 59). In "Producing Sex, Theory, and Culture: Gay/Straight Remappings in Contemporary Feminism" (1990: 89), third wave feminist Katie King criticizes how the academy privileges certain types of theory and leaves other types unacknowledged or deemed as lesser:

> An error feminists make over and over is to mistake the part of a particular theoretical reading, especially a published reading, for the whole of the many forms theorizing takes: active thinking, speaking, conversation, action grounded in theory, action producing theory, action suggesting theory, drafts, letters, unpublished manuscripts. . . . It's not that all human actions are equivalent to theorizing, but rather that a particular product of many forms of theorizing should not be mistaken for the processes of production itself.

Today many feminists view theory and theorizing as an activity that extends well beyond the classroom, the seminar paper, and the academic journal. In short: "The assumption that all theory takes place in the academy—is epistemologically naïve, historically inaccurate, and ultimately misinformed" (Siegel 1997a: 49).

GROUNDING THEORIES IN SOCIAL HISTORY

This text emphasizes how concepts, discourses, and theories are influenced by the social, economic, and historical conditions under which they were created. It is designed to give students more knowledge of history and to enable them to place theories within their larger social contexts. It should help readers better understand why particular issues dominated feminist thought at certain points in history and how feminist ideas often were responding to changing social, economic, and historical conditions. Grounding feminist theories in their social context also should enable us to better understand the *paradigm shifts in feminist thought* that have taken place in recent decades.

A **paradigm shift** refers to a fundamental change in the theoretical assumptions underlying an entire school of thought or worldview. For example, the shift from Newtonian physics to Einstein's relativity theory exemplifies a paradigmatic shift in the natural sciences. It resulted not simply in different scientific conclusions, but rather the entire conceptual framework for understanding physics was transformed (Kuhn 1962). The notion of paradigm shifts in feminist thought is not unique to this text. A number of feminists have discussed a marked divide between the content of modern feminist thought and the postmodern feminisms that have become more prominent in recent decades. This transformation has been referred to as a "paradigm shift" (Brooks 1997), a "theoretical shift" (Alcoff 1997), and a theoretical "gulf" (Zalewski, 2000). In *Destablizing Theory: Contemporary Feminist Debates* (1992: 1–2), Michele Barrett and Anne Phillips discuss this transformation as follows:

> In the past twenty years the founding principles of contemporary western feminism have been dramatically challenged, with previously shared assumptions and unquestioned orthodoxies relegated almost to history. *These changes have been of the order of a "paradigm shift", in which assumptions rather than conclusions are radically overturned.* (Emphasis added)

Before the major underlying assumptions of modern and postmodern thought can be examined, this analysis must first be historically grounded by a discussion of the major differences in social, economic, and political conditions that characterize modernity and postmodernity.

What Is Meant by Modernity?

A central concept in the works of major Western social theorists of the nineteenth and twentieth centuries is the concept of **modernity**. Some historians and theorists discuss the rise of modernity as beginning with the increase in mercantile trade and the emergence of a world market beginning in the 1400s (Aries 1962, Wallerstein 1974). In this text, I use a more conventional definition of modernity *as reflecting the social conditions that accompanied the rise of industrialization.* Here modernity is an umbrella term used to describe the social patterns set in motion by the Industrial Revolution that began in Western Europe in the mid-eighteenth century. The term *modernization* refers to this complex process of industrialization and the political, social, and cultural changes that accompanied it, such as urbanization, the increasing use of science and technology, the rationalization and secularization of social life, the rise of the nation state, and an increasing focus on the individual.

Clearly, different societies modernized at different times in history. Because the area we now call the United States was initially a colony whose industrialization process was thwarted by its British colonial masters, industrialization occurred a bit later than in Western Europe. Our "founding fathers" tended to be landowners and slaveowners rather than burgeoning merchants or industrial entrepreneurs. Although development in the United States was certainly influenced by the first industrial revolution, it was not until the mid-nineteenth century that the United States began to join the ranks of the major industrial powers. From the mid-nineteenth century to the turn of the twentieth century, social and economic conditions in the United States were transformed so radically that some observers have referred to this era as the "second industrial revolution" (Luke 1999: 219). A few examples will illustrate the changes that catapulted the United States into becoming one of the most powerful societies of the modern era. Whereas in 1860 the United States trailed England, France, and Germany in the total value of its manufactured output, by the mid-1890s the value of U.S. manufactures almost equaled those of England, France, and Germany combined. Before the Civil War, U.S. industrial, wageworkers were outnumbered by slaves; by the mid-1890s, the industrial, working class in America was the largest in the world. In 1870, half of the nation's manufacturing establishments were still powered by water and steam. By the early twentieth century, coal, electricity, and later petroleum were fueling much of America's industry (221–222). This rapid increase in urbanization and industrialization not only ushered in significant growth in the production capacity of the United States; it also introduced a host of new social problems.

Many Western social theorists compared and contrasted modern, industrial societies to premodern, agrarian societies in order to highlight the *dramatic social changes that accompanied modernization*. Some theorists discussed how modernization weakened the fabric of social life that previously had been provided by small, cohesive communities and fostered a process of "individualization" where individual interests took priority over social groups (Durkheim [1893] 1964, Berger 1977). Others saw the major thrust of modernization as promoting a more secular, rational, and scientific worldview as superstition, magic, and tradition lost their hold over everyday life. Although social progress was attributed to the greater efficiency and calculability of rational social forms, modernity was depicted as a cold, impersonal, disenchanted world in which social life was narrowly specialized and increasingly dehumanized (Weber [1921] 1968).

Karl Marx highlighted how a particular mode of production—capitalism—rather than modernization itself was the culprit behind the weakening of social ties, an increasingly specialized and dehumanized division of labor and the predominance of a formally rational but substantively irrational world view. By this he meant that while the means used in industrial capitalist societies—such as science and technology—were rational, the goals to which they were directed—the accumulation of private rather than public wealth—were irrational. For him, the rise of wage labor, market economies, and the commoditization of social life were key factors that distinguished modernity from premodern social formations (Marx [1867] 1967).

Despite their different analyses all of these modern Western theorists viewed *industrialization and modernization as ultimately leading to social progress*[7]—at least in terms of providing the economic growth and material abundance that could enhance the standards of living of the vast majority of people. The immense technological advances that were a hallmark of the modernization process portended the possibility of eradicating major social ills, such as poverty, illiteracy, hunger, and disease. In turn, release from the constraints of tradition was seen as signaling the victory of scientific rationalism and political liberalism as well as a move toward greater freedom, tolerance, and democracy. Today critics refer to this composite of beliefs as the "**Western narrative**" or the "**Euro-American Master Narrative**" of modernization and development (Smart 1993).

By contrast, critics highlight how this Western narrative is simply a dominant discourse that represents particular historical and political choices, interests, and practices that are not in any way inevitable (McMichael 1996: 18). Rather than a natural, historical evolution of societal development, critics see it as a particular path taken by Western societies that is used to underscore their superiority. For example, postcolonial theorists argue that the very idea of "modernity" was one of the "central tropes" through which the more industrially, developed West constructed itself as the center and the rest of the world as its more backward, periphery (Mary Louise Pratt in Spurlin 2006: 23; see chapter 10).

What Is Meant by Postmodernity?

The term *postmodernity* is controversial and has generated debates over whether the seismic transformations in social conditions over the past half century are substantial enough to speak of a qualitatively new social era.[8] Theorists who agree with this assessment use the terms "information societies," "postindustrial societies" or "postmodernity" to refer to this qualitatively new social era (Featherstone 1991, Smart 1993). Those who disagree with this assessment argue that we are simply witnessing the unfolding or unraveling of a later stage of modernity that they term "high modernity," "radicalized modernity," "late capitalism," "fast capitalism," or "flexible capitalism" (Giddens 1990, Agger 1998, Harvey 1989). Because this particular debate is less relevant to the concerns of this text than is the question of *how contemporary feminist theorists address these recent transformations in social life*, I will sidestep this controversy and take the liberty of interweaving these various terms throughout the text.

In this text, **postmodernity** refers to new social, economic, political, and cultural conditions that arose over the past half century. Among the most important of these developments is the rapid increase in globalization and its impacts locally. While many features of the globalization process are discussed in chapters 8, 9, and 10, suffice it to say here that between 1960 and 1980 direct foreign investments by U.S. corporations increased more than tenfold (Thurow 1996: 42). As a consequence of these developments, the United States experienced a period of rapid **deindustrialization** as many corporations moved their manufacturing abroad in search of cheaper labor. Between 1965 and 1985, the manufacturing share of total U.S. employment dropped from 60 percent to 26 percent, while the share of employment in the service sector rose from 40 percent to 74 percent (Stacey 1991: 18). In turn, real wages for men fell—a reduction that had never before occurred in U.S. history over a two-decade period when real per capita gross domestic product (GDP) was advancing (Thurow 1996: 224). *The gender, race, and ethnicity of the*

U.S. labor force dramatically changed as women entered the workforce in record numbers to buttress their households in the face of falling male wages, while the increase in low-paying service jobs opened doors to the employment of immigrants and minorities. Moreover, immigration into the United States in the final decades of the twentieth century entailed more racial diversity—particularly from Asia and Latin America—than did the largely European immigration of the nineteenth century.

We shall see how many feminist theorists today place less emphasis on social class and more emphasis on other forms of difference, such as gender, race, ethnicity, and global location than did earlier feminisms. While the decreasing emphasis on class mirrors the decentering of the first world industrial working class, the increasing focus on gender, race, and ethnicity mirrors the changing composition of the labor force at home and the increasingly global nature of the division of labor (see chapters 9 and 10). Since these processes are interwoven, many theorists today recognize that a full understanding of gender, class, race, and ethnicity in the United States must be related to social, economic, and political developments on a world scale (Kandal 1995: 156).

In turn, contemporary feminist theorists often highlight how the operation of global forces have blurred, dispersed, and unsettled geopolitical boundaries (see chapter 10). Theorists now speak more fluidly of scapes, circuits, and networks. The term **transnational** has virtually replaced the term *international* to highlight how new social forms transcend or fail to correspond to the boundaries of the nation-state. Examples of this process include the rise of transnational forms, such as the European Union (EU) for global economic positioning; the rise of transnational combatants, such as Al Qaeda, for global warfare; and the rise of transnational social services, such as Doctors without Borders, to deal with global social problems.

These global developments were made possible by the *growth of the new digital, microchip and satellite technologies* that compressed time and space (Harvey 1989). These new technologies have significantly transformed not only economic and political institutions but also mass culture and mass consumerism. Culture critics view the ideologies embedded in mass culture today as far more complex and subtle than in the past, appearing almost as "silent argument" (Agger 1998: 125). The new electronic media dramatically quicken the distribution of ideas such that they flash by with a speed that makes them difficult to unpack. The ability of these new technologies to create simulations and virtual realities further blurs the lines between artifice and reality (Baudrillard 1983). In such a swirling sea of signs and symbols, it is no wonder that in many contemporary feminist theories *discourse* appears to have inordinate power or that a major device used to decode such messages—*deconstruction*—has become a buzzword in contemporary social thought (Agger 1998: 125).

However, even though recent technological developments have been ingenious, science and technology have been placed under far more critical scrutiny by social theorists in postmodernity. These rational means that modernists claimed would promote social progress have created some of the major risks that plague our planet today, such as environmental pollution and nuclear arms—risks that were unknown to or unanticipated by nineteenth- and early-twentieth-century modern theorists (Giddens 1990).[9] It was only in late modernity that there was growing public awareness of the impact of nuclear warfare and the increasing devastation of the earth's atmosphere, climate, water, soil, flora (Merchant 1999: 153). Perhaps it took such world-scale damage to make people critically aware of the dangers of continuing with a blind faith in the ability of science and technology to fix all social problems. Given these new earth-threatening risks, a common trope used by some theorists to refer to postmodernity is the "new risk society" (Beck 1992). Accordingly, feminist theorists today also focus more attention on these new risks, such as environmental degradation.

Whether or not we have entered a qualitatively new era in human history, these seismic transformations of social life have resulted in equally seismic paradigm shifts in social thought. Recent decades have witnessed a virtual explosion of criticisms leveled against the epistemological assumptions of modern science. This juncture in the history of social thought has been referred to as the "Big Bang" in that *former trends toward seeking universal "truths" and theoretical convergence have given way to multiple "truths" and theoretical pluralism* (Cheal 1991: 153). No doubt these paradigm shifts have destabilized feminist theory and engendered new conflicts and debates within contemporary feminism (Barrett and Phillips 1992: 1–2). However, they have not resulted in unbridgeable gulfs. Some of the most influential and cutting edge feminist perspectives today employ features of both modern and postmodern thought.

To aid readers in understanding important distinctions between modern and postmodern thought, their epistemological underpinnings are examined below. Professors may choose to save these epistemological discussions for later in their courses because they involve complex issues that might be more easily understood after students become acquainted with a number of feminist approaches.

EPISTEMOLOGICAL UNDERPINNINGS OF FEMINIST THEORIES

The term **epistemology** simply refers to the study of who can be a knowledge producer and how knowledge is produced. Because there is not one, but many feminisms, feminists do not always agree on epistemological positioning. What they do share is a focus on challenging hierarchical modes of creating and distributing knowledge (Hesse-Biber, Leavy, and Yaiser 2004). Some major analysts of feminist epistemologies have divided them into three major camps—feminist empiricist epistemology, feminist standpoint epistemology, and feminist postmodern epistemology (Hesse-Biber, Leavy, and Yaiser 2004, Harding 2004, Hekman 2004).[10] A signal work that highlighted these epistemic underpinnings of feminist thought was Sandra Harding's 1986 article "From the Woman Question in Science to the Science Question in Feminism," which I draw from below.

Empiricist Epistemology

Modern empiricist epistemology is rooted in the ideas of Enlightenment thought, which arose in the eighteenth century alongside the development of modern, industrial societies. As discussed in chapter 2, the term *Enlightenment* comes from the idea that this body of thought could lift the world from an age of darkness, ignorance, and superstition into a world of science and rational thought. Enlightenment thinkers set about the task of creating a new world based on reason and science.

For feminist empiricists, theories are *privileged discourses* when they are based on rational means for their construction, such as logic and/or empirical science. By privileged, I mean that they are given more status, credibility, and power than other forms of knowledge, such as intuition or common sense. By *rational*, I mean that they adhere to certain formal rules of procedure similar to those that undergird the scientific method. In science, there are rules regarding what counts as empirical evidence as well as what counts as reliable, valid, and/or representative data. For example, when one refers to **empirical** data, this simply means that evidence must be capable of being observed through the senses (sight, sound, smell, or touch) by other individuals. Such rules are both inclusive and exclusive in the sense that certain data—such as the supernatural—lie outside of the domain of scientific theories or practices. Theories are judged in terms of whether they adhere to such rational rules, and they can be undermined or viewed as untenable if they lack logic or clash with empirical data.

Thus, logic and empirical evidence provide the bases for determining the greater truth or falsity of different knowledge claims and/or the success or failure of certain political policies or practices. Logic and science are used not only to develop feminist theory; but also to empirically challenge alternative claims that women are inferior to or less capable than men and to document existing inequalities between men and women. Theory construction based on feminist empiricism has done much to expose the **androcentric** or male bias in conventional studies. The many feminist empiricist studies that "added women" resulted in major reassessments of the concepts, theories, and methods employed within and across academic disciplines (Hesse-Biber, Leavy, and Yaiser 2004).[11] For these reasons, *modern, feminist empiricists view theory as potentially empowering and as providing the basis for reforming or transforming society in the interests of greater freedom and equality.* For them, the relationship between theory and research, as well as the relationship between theory and political practice, hold the potential for more freedom rather than more control.

A modern empiricist view of theory construction is exemplified by Charlotte Bunch's article "Not by Degrees: Feminist Theory and Education" [1979] (2005). Bunch highlights how "theory is not just a body of facts or a set of personal options"; rather, "it involves explanations and hypotheses that are based on available knowledge and experience" (12). A major difference between her view and more conventional empiricist discussions of theory is that Bunch argues that "no theory is totally 'objective' because it reflects the interests, values and assumptions of those who created it" (13). For Bunch, feminist theory is designed to "aid the liberation of women" and, thereby, is "not an unengaged study of women" (13). More conventional feminist empiricist approaches argue that it is possible to undertake feminist research as a detached, objective or value-neutral observer (Chavetz 1990, Sprague and Zimmerman 1993).

Bunch analytically distinguishes four interrelated parts to feminist theory. The first is *description*—gathering and interpreting "facts about women" in order to 'substantiate our assertions" (14). The second is *analysis*, which she describes as determining the origins of women's oppression and the reasons for its perpetuation. In her view, this is the most "complex task of theory" because it entails "sorting out how the forms of oppression change over time" or "probing how they vary in different cultures" (14). The third part is *vision*, which refers to determining what should exist and establishing principles or goals for attaining this vision. Bunch argues that in taking action to bring about social change people operate out of certain assumptions about what is just and fair as well as what a more equal society would look like. Fourth is *strategy* or determining the most effecting policies or practices that can bring about the visions or goals that have been set. This means considering various "tools for social change" (such as protests, demonstrations, and/or legislative actions) and determining which of these tools are most effective in a given situation. Bunch's view of feminist theory highlights the relationship between theory and research as well as the relationship between theory and political practice. However, it also reflects a certain type of theorizing that was characteristic of the goals of modern feminism particularly during the second wave when feminists generated a number of comprehensive or grand theories. Critics often refer to these theories as **masternarratives** or **totalizing theories** because of the generalizing and comprehensive features of their analysis (Foucault [1976] 1980).

One of the major features of comprehensive or totalizing feminist theories is that they attempt to account for the origins or historical causes of women's subordination and use these understandings of origins to develop a systematic account of women's oppression over historical time. Those who embrace this form of theorizing assume that understanding the roots of women's oppression is a necessary prerequisite for developing effective political strategies to liberate women. They fear that without developing an understanding of historical roots and their manifestations in different cultures and historical eras, feminist political strategies will address only symptoms rather than the underlying causes. Such comprehensive theories attempt to explain all the various features of women's oppression using one overarching theoretical framework. They implicitly assume there is only one correct theory that can be universalized to all situations or cases.

Attempts by feminists to develop comprehensive or totalizing theories of women's oppression often utilized concepts and approaches first developed by male theorists to address other forms of oppression. Chapter 2 examines how liberal feminists drew from the works of male theorists, such as John Stuart Mill. Chapter 4 discusses how Marxist and socialist feminisms were informed by the works of Karl Marx and Friedrich Engels. Because these male theorists had developed comprehensive theories that provided the bases for major political social movements, feminists thought that similar theories were needed to foster feminist movements and to guide feminist political practice. When feminists included women's issues while still leaving existing "malestream"[12] theories largely in tact, critics disdainfully described this as an "add Mary Wollstonecraft and stir" approach (Grimshaw 1986: 10–11; Beasley 1999: 5). However, many feminists refigured and reshaped "malestream" theory in fundamental ways (Clark and Lange 1979: xvii; Tong 1998: 1). No longer were women marginalized or analyzed from a male vantage point. The *centering of women* positioned their concerns and social locations as critical for generating analytical thought and knowledge (Delmar 1986).

Overall, feminist empiricists see emancipatory possibilities in developing theories that are buttressed by logic and scientific evidence. They view theories as powerful tools for increasing our understanding of social reality and for guiding political practice. For them, scientific facts are subversive because they can undermine patriarchal assumptions about women. The main tasks of feminist theorists are to accurately describe the social realities of women's existence and subordination, provide a deep explanation of how those realities came to be, offer an alternative vision of how the social world could be better for women, and guide political strategies for ending or at least reducing women's subordination (Jaggar and Rothenberg 1984: xvi).

Standpoint Epistemology

Beginning in the late 1970s and early 1980s, feminists expressed increasing skepticism about the desirability and even possibility of a theory that aimed to produce broad generalizations about women's subordination. This skepticism arose both within and outside of U.S. feminism. From *within* the United States, inadequacies with existing feminist theorists were voiced primarily by those feminists who had been marginalized or silenced in the past because of their own subordinate social locations in terms of race, class, and sexuality. At times calling themselves "sister/outsiders," these critics exposed how generalizations about women qua women were usually false (Lorde 1984). They argued that different groups of women experience subordination in very different ways, depending on their race, class, and sexuality. What may appear to some women as the most important or urgent issues facing feminism were not seen as the most important concerns of other women. Consider the words of bell hooks (1984: 5–6):

> Feminist emphasis on "common oppression" in the United States was less a strategy for politicization than an appropriation by conservative and liberal women of a radical political vocabulary that masked the extent to which they shaped the movement so that it addressed and promoted their class interests.

These critical insights clashed with earlier modern feminisms that focused on the similarities shared by women and that developed generalizations based on these similarities. To earlier feminist theorists, highlighting the common oppressions shared by all women was empowering precisely because it served to unify women in collective action. In such slogans as SISTERHOOD IS POWERFUL or SISTERHOOD IS GLOBAL, the "sisterhood" or feminist "we" simply assumed that all women shared similar problems, concerns, and oppressions (Morgan 1970 and 1984). As discussed in chapter 5, these generalizations are often criticized today as a form of **essentialism** that attributes essences, attributes, or behaviors to *all* members of a group. For example, a feminist essentialist argument might argue that women share similar attributes because of their ability to bear children or because they are psychologically prone to be more nurturing than men. In the face of an onslaught of criticisms of essentialism, earlier assumptions about commonalities shared by women had to be critically reexamined, rethought, and refigured (Spelman 1988).

A powerful critique of essentialism can be found in Maria Lugones and Elizabeth Spelman's "Have We Got a Theory for You! Feminist Theory, Cultural Imperialism, and the Demand for 'The Woman's Voice'" [1983] (2005). By interweaving Spanish and English, as well as counterposing the vantage points of white women and Hispanas, both the form and content of their article illustrate their critical points. As the Hispana voice argues:

> But you theorize about women and we are women, so you understand yourselves to be theorizing about us, and we understand you to be theorizing about us. Yet none of the feminist theories developed so far seems to me to help Hispanas in the articulation of our experience. We have a sense that in using them we are distorting our experiences. (20)

Lugones and Spelman highlight how, by speaking for other women without understanding their lives and experiences, many feminist theorists from privileged social locations ended up using an imperial we. This imperial, feminist we colonizes the visions and voices of women in less privileged social locations. While a **colonialist stance** is discussed in more depth in chapter 10, suffice it to say here that it refers to representations that employ a type of "missionary framework" in which women from subordinate social locations are viewed as victims who are unable to represent themselves and, therefore, must be rescued from their own cultural traditions (Narayan 1997: 48–49).

Such criticisms of essentialism raise the following questions: if theory moves from the specific to the general and if we cannot speak of women as a group who share common interests—does this mean the end of feminist theory? For most feminists the answer is no. Rather, these critical insights are seen as enriching feminist theory rather than abandoning it. They do, however, require feminists to be *sensitive to difference and dominance* and *accountable* for their analyses. They have to consider how their ideas are influenced by their own social locations and take responsibility for how their work affects other people (Jaggar and Rothenberg 1993: 113–114).

Today, most feminists recognize that there is no generic woman—every woman has some specific class, race, sexuality, and global location; hence, gender is always inflected by race, class, sexuality, and global location. Armed with this new understanding of gender, political concerns moved away from considering women in general toward exploring the specificities of gender relations and the ways in which gender is necessarily shaped and practiced in conjunction with other systems of domination (xvi). Feminist scholarship turned away from both general foundational issues, such as determining the origins of women's oppression and developing universal, comprehensive theories, in favor of **historical specificity** or concrete analyses of a specific time and place. Earlier debates over which form of oppression—class, race, gender, sexuality, or nation—was the most fundamental, oppressive, or urgent—gave way to an understanding of forms of oppressions as simultaneous and interlocking (Smith 1983). Accordingly, the metaphor of feminist lenses often replaced the notion of feminist frameworks. Because lenses can be superimposed on one another, this metaphor better conveyed how perceptions are enriched when we examine women's oppression through several different lenses or vantage points (Jaggar and Rothenberg 1993: xv–xvii).

Standpoint epistemologies were among the first feminist approaches to highlight how knowledge was socially situated. In her many works on the science question in feminism, Sandra Harding provides the following contrasts between standpoint epistemologies and conventional views of theory and research. First, rather than viewing scientific knowledge as value-free or neutral, standpoint approaches view all knowledge as socially situated and influenced by the knower's social location. No one—including scientists—can "erase the fingerprints that reveal this production process" (Harding 1993: 57). The term **God trick** is used to refer to claims by conventional scientists that through science the world can be viewed in a detached or impartial manner and that their one view of reality is the correct one. In contrast, standpoint theorists advocate a **reflexive approach to knowledge** through which researchers acknowledge their own roles in constructing knowledge and how their social locations might influence the results of their studies.

Second, standpoint theorists highlight the differential privilege given to certain groups in knowledge production. For Harding, the starting point of standpoint theory is the recognition that in societies stratified by race, class, gender, and sexuality, "one's social situation enables and sets limits on what one can know" (54–55). Hence, the activities of those in dominant social locations both organize and set limits on what people can understand about themselves and the world around them. As such, the experiences and lives of marginalized people are often "devalued or ignored" as sources of so called "objective" knowledge (54):

> standpoint theorists have criticized conventional sciences for their arrogance in assuming that they could tell one true story about the world that is out there. . . . Without listening to women's accounts or being aware that accounts of nature and social relations have been constructed within men's control of gender relations. (Harding 1991: 141)

Historically women, like other marginalized people, have been excluded from knowledge production because they were viewed as biologically and/or intellectually inferior (140). Consequently, the standpoint of women is just one of many social locations that offer critical insights for research problems and agendas.[13] To avoid rewriting the other's world from the one's own vantage point, standpoint theorists advocate starting social inquiry from the lived experiences of women and others who traditionally have been outside of the institutions in which knowledge about social life is generated and classified. However, for Harding, it is not the subjective views of the marginalized per se but, rather, their *social locations* that generate critical questions about the way the world is organized (Harding 1993: 62).[14]

Standpoint epistemology shares some similarities with postmodern epistemoloy in that it recognizes the relationship between knowledge and power, as well as the socially situated nature of knowledge. Although Harding sometimes refers to her's as a "postmodern standpoint approach," she does not take the postmodern turn to embrace **judgmental relativism**—the notion that, because all views are relative to one's social location, one vantage point cannot be given epistemic privilege or judged as more valid than another. Rather Harding takes the modernist stance that feminists must be able to adjudicate between competing knowledge claims in order for theory to guide political practice. She (1993: 61) highlights how judgmental relativism opens up a Pandora's box for any and every viewpoint to claim legitimacy—even those that are harmful to the interests of women or other oppressed groups:

> Judgmental (or epistemological) relativism is an anathema to any scientific project, and feminist ones are no exception. It is not as equally true as its denial that women's uteruses wander around in their bodies when they take math courses, that only Man the Hunter made important contributions to human history . . . that sexual molestation and other physical abuses children report are only their fantasies—as various sexist and androcentric scientific theories have claimed.

Harding argues that feminists do not have to choose between "the evils of the Charybdis of scientific realism or the Scylla of social relativism," as one observer put it (Keller 1992: 9). Rather, she views standpoint theories as fostering "strong objectivity" or "strengthened standards of objectivity" for a number of reasons (Harding 1991: 142). First, unlike conventional science, standpoint epistemologies do not arrogantly dismiss the vantage points of those who are treated as lesser or who have been excluded from knowledge production. Second, knowledge produced from the standpoint of subordinated groups may offer stronger objectivity due to the increased motivation for these groups to understand the perspectives of those in positions of power. Third, standpoint approaches must explain and account for the differences between situated vantage points and the findings of conventional objectified knowledge. This should lead to a fuller appreciation of the power dynamics involved in knowledge production (142).

An insightful article that articulates well the power dynamics involved in knowledge production is Kum-Kum Bhavani's "Tracing the Contours: Feminist Research and Feminist Objectivity" (2004). Bhavani asks the important question: what makes a research project "feminist"? She argues that just because a research project is done by women and/or addresses women's concerns does not necessarily mean it is a feminist project. She suggests that for a research project to be a feminist project, three major criteria should be met: First, *feminist analyses should not reinscribe dominant representations of inequality*. This does not mean providing romanticized view of subordinated peoples; it means that feminist researchers must pose the question as to whether their analyses are complicit with or reinforce subjugation. Second, *feminists must expose the micropolitical processes that are in play during the conduct of their own research, analyses, and theory construction.* They must ask what relationships of domination and subordination the researchers have confronted and negotiated in the process of doing their analyses. Third, Bhavani argues that *feminists must query whether they have dealt adequately with differences between people.* Are differences and diverse vantage points acknowledged? Is there recognition of the situated and partial nature of knowledge claims? Together these questions foster a reflexive approach to knowledge that critically interrogates and strengthens objectivity.

Bhavani also employs a method referred to today as the **new historicism** to encourage inquiries into the political economy of knowledge production. Historicising social thought means to place social theorists and their works within their historical and social locations to better understand why they are addressing various issues. *Rather than assuming an ahistorical and universal scientific method that reveals truths that transcend cultures and historical time, the historical and social contexts of ideas are used to reveal the power relations hidden behind different theories and methods.* The focus is not on the truth or falsity of knowledge claims but, rather, on the sociohistorical context of power relations entailed in the construction of knowledge.

The new historicism is frequently used by standpoint theorists as well as in postcolonial theory and critical cultural studies to illustrate the importance of historically situating knowledge (see chapter 10). Thus it is a method that bridges modern and postmodern thought. For example, Bhavani (2004: 65) calls our attention to how "scientific" studies of the relationship between cranium or brain size and intelligence arose in Western societies in the late nineteenth century as feminist movements were gaining headway. Scientists compared the size and weight of men's and women's craniums and brains (often using data obtained from autopsies) to provide "scientific evidence" of men's greater intelligence. One critic of these practices referred to it as the "wide hats and narrow minds" theory of intelligence (Gould 1980: 145). Such examples illustrate how revealing the history of "scientific" methods and claims also reveals the gendered, racial, and class-based subtexts and inequalities embedded in the creation of knowledge.

In summary, the primary goal of standpoint epistemologies is to reveal the relations of power that are hidden in conventional knowledge production processes. They claim that when greater attention is paid to the social location of knowledge producers, a more transparent rendering of the relations of ruling can be obtained. In chapter 4, the standpoint approaches of Nancy Hartsock, Dorothy Smith, and Donna Haraway are examined, while in chapter 5, the standpoint epistemologies underyling Patricia Hill Collins's "outsider-within stance" and bell hooks's call for feminist theory to "move from margin to center" are explored. These theorists all highlight the value of **polyvocality** or the inclusion of many and diverse feminist voices. While these new polyvocal standpoint feminisms bridge modern and postmodern thought, overall they maintain a foothold in modernism. They abandon neither theory and its integral relationship to scientific research and political practice nor the notion of structural, hierarchical *group* forms of oppression, such as race, class, gender, sexuality, and nation that explain how and why certain social locations generate different standpoints.

Postmodern Epistemology

Postmodern epistemology is an umbrella term that incorporates insights derived from postmodernism, poststructuralism, and postcolonial theory (Hesse-Biber, Leavy, and Yaiser 2004). Given its heavy theoretical debt to Michel Foucault's poststructuralist approach, queer theory also embraces a postmodern epistemology. In addition, I argue that many third wave feminisms take a postmodern turn in their epistemological stance. While these perspectives are addressed in more depth in chapters 6, 7, and 10, suffice it to say in this introductory chapter that a major contribution of these postmodern epistemologies is their emphases on the relationship between knowledge and power. They confront new questions about the social construction of knowledge, the positioning of the knower, and even the viability of group concepts, like women, women of color, or working-class women.

Postmodern epistemologies are the most wary of totalizing theories which they view as power moves for domination rather than as tools for liberation. They also are the most careful in pointing out how the power of discourses can both silence and empower and how the vantage points of both the subjugated and the privileged are mutually constructed in this process. For example, postcolonial theorists explore how the vantage points of both the colonizers and the colonized are mutually constructed in distorted ways by the process of colonization (see chapter 10). Here again the focus is not on the truth or falsity of knowledge claims but, rather, on the sociohistorical context of power relations entailed in the construction of knowledge. Thus a complex level of reflexivity is entailed in postmodern epistemologies.

Perhaps the hallmark of postmodern epistemologies is that they reject the modern assumption that reality has an inherent order or structure objectively discernible through scientific inquiry. Postmodern epistemologies emphasize that what becomes culturally legitimated as knowledge and as rational is the result of specific exercises of social power. Thus reason and the scientific method are merely a set of variable cultural conventions licensing or legitimating certain rules of discourse over others (Jaggar and Rothenberg 1993: 76–77). Using a postmodern lens, social reality is open to a multitude of possible interpretations or situated knowledges that are rooted in different social locations of varying degrees of power and privilege. There is no way to adjudicate between these partial perspectives. Science and history—the evidentiary bases of modern thought—are all just narratives, just stories that silence some and give voice to others. In short, reality is discourse-dependent (see chapter 6).

If discourse is the foundation of our notions of reality, than what can be known is only known through the interpretations and narratives of diverse social actors. Such notions of discourse highlight how different ways of specifying knowledge and truth can both restrict and enable writing, speaking, thinking, and acting. Thus, discourses and theories—even liberatory discourses and theories—can both empower and constrain. Many examples of this are provided in this text. As noted above, many U.S. women of color viewed hegemonic feminist theories of the first and second waves as blind to their concerns and deaf to their voices. Today, many third wave feminists view second wave feminisms as restrictive and disciplinary (see chapter 7). However, postmodern epistemologies go further to highlight how power lies *within* these discourses and the truths they claim—regardless of who makes them. "Truth is never outside power" (Foucault quoted in Rainbow 1984: 73). Rather the very notion of truth becomes multiple and suspect. There is no single truth, but many different truths situated in different discourses, some of which are more dominant than others (see chapter 6).

The postperspectives also highlight how there is no uniquely privileged social location, standpoint, or vantage point from which a final or authoritative feminist theory can be constructed. They reject the notion that anyone (including scientists) can be a detached or neutral observer. Rather than moving feminist theory "from margin to center" as standpoint theorists argue, the postperspectives position themselves forever on the margins in order to provide more critical insights into how power is imbricated in knowledge and discourses (see chapter 6). They engage in a process of *continual critical deconstruction* that advocates "jamming the theoretical machinery" not in order to construct an alternative view of the social world which would itself be a power move but, rather, to unravel the social processes that have constructed visions of the social world in hierarchical ways (Irigaray [1977] 1985: 78). Such jamming practices are ways of "creating resistance to dominant knowledge and allowing that resistance to disrupt the social system thereby necessitating social change" (Hesse-Biber; Leavy, and Yaiser 2004: 19).

Jane Flax's article "The End of Innocence" (1992) highlights the issues at stake in debates about postmodern epistemologies. For example, modern feminists argue that postmodern epistemologies are apolitical because their relativism and failure to adjudicate between different truth claims make any political stance "impossible to justify" (446). For postmodernists, conflicts cannot be resolved by references to facts or validity; they can only be resolved "through the raw exercise of power" (445). In contrast, modern feminisms assume that their writings "must generate and sustain a notion of truth so that we can adjudicate conflicts among competing ideas and legitimate the claims of (some) feminist theorists and activists" (446).

In defense of postmodernism, Flax addresses the modernist claims that postmodernism is incompatible with feminism. Her article, while difficult, is still one of the clearest explanations of why postmodern epistemologies are valuable to feminism. The title—"The End of Innocence"—refers to how those who embrace a modern empiricist epistemology have an innocent faith in the Enlightenment ideas of a universal scientific method and a singular notion of truth:

> By innocent knowledge I mean the discovery of some sort of truth which can tell us how to act in the world in ways that benefit or are for the (at least ultimate) good of all. . . . A central promise of Enlightenment and Western modernity is that conflicts between knowledge and power can be overcome by grounding claims to and the exercise of authority in reason. Reason both represents and embodies truth. . . . The Enlightenment hope is that utilizing truthful knowledge in the service of legitimate power will assure both freedom and progress. (447).

For Flax this "innocent knowledge" is a "fantasy" or "dream" that cannot be realized because "there is no stable, unchanging, and unitary Real against which our thoughts can be tested" (453). Modern thought simply creates an illusion of unity and stability by "reducing the flux and heterogeneity of the human and physical worlds into binary and supposedly natural oppositions. Order is imposed and maintained by displacing chaos into the lesser of each binary pair, for example culture/nature or male/female" (453). Consequently, postmodernists call for the demise of binary or dualistic thinking. Their goal is to reveal these category schemes as fictive, as simply the creations of objectified knowledge. They also expose how it is only the "rules of a discourse" that enable people to make certain sorts of statements and to make truth claims. Truth claims are in principle "undecidable" outside of or between discourses. "There is no trump available which we can rely on to solve all disputes" (452).

Postmodernists' deconstruction of thought's ability to mirror or to represent reality and their related critique of truth claims are profoundly unsettling because they radically question and change the background assumptions and contexts within which debates about such questions are usually conducted (446 and 455). Flax notes how modernists (including those who she deems among the "most persuasive") assume rather than demonstrate that there are necessary connections between truth, knowledge, emancipation, and justice. They also assume that truth and domination are opposites (456 and 457). In contrast, Flax believes that modern notions of truth hide attempts to dominate. Thus, she urges us to rethink all concepts and "let them float freely, and explore their differences" (457).

For Flax, one of the "dangerous consequences" of universal notions of truth, justice, and knowledge is that they release us from taking full responsibility for our actions. Rather, she thinks modernists "remain children" waiting for these "higher authorities" to save us from the consequences of our acts (459). Feminists must face the "end of innocence"; we must "take responsibility and firmly situate ourselves within contingent and imperfect contexts, to acknowledge differential privileges of race, gender, geographic location, and sexual identities and resist the delusory and dangerous hope of redemption by science and logic" (460). Overall, those who embrace postmodern epistemologies are skeptical that science and rational techniques necessarily lead to social progress. They point to how science and technology have ushered in some of the worst nightmares of the twentieth century, such as the ability to destroy our planet through nuclear or environmental disasters.

> At its best, postmodernism invites us to engage in a continual process of disillusionment with the grandiose fantasies that have brought us to the brink of annihilation (460).

CONCLUSION

A primary goal of this text is to provide a better understanding of the multiplicity and diversity of feminisms by presenting reflexive, dynamic, and inclusive notions of doing feminist theory. Another major goal is to expose the falsity of the dichotomy between theory and practice by constantly reminding us that feminist theorizing is a political act and that the point of this theorizing is political transformation. The most vital legacy feminism has to offer is its insistence on joining theoretical analysis with political practice (Siegel 1997a: 69; Kauffman 1989: 3).

Doing Feminist Theory highlights how all feminist discourses and theories simultaneously give voice and silence, empower and constrain. Every theoretical position presented in this text has contributed valuable insights to feminist theory and political practice. However, every feminist perspective examined here also has blind spots and limitations. By presenting these feminist frameworks in a way that demonstrates the continuities and contrasts between them, I hope to inspire a critical evaluation of each perspective's strengths and weaknesses. A major lesson to be learned from reading this text is the development of critical thought. By sharpening our critical skills we can move together to navigate feminist thought and feminist practices in ways that enable us to chart the contours of a world that is less structured by centers and margins or by domination and subordination.

NOTES

1 It is risky to begin the first chapter of a feminist theory text with a father admonishing his daughter for her failure to identify as a feminist. However, this text is designed to provoke critical thought and to query whether feminism is a political stance that any person can embrace and practice.
2 The "I'm-Not-a-Feminist-but Syndrome" is critically examined in chapter 7.
3 Although first wave feminists did not use the term *gender*, their writings at least recognized the difference between anatomical/biological sex and socially learned masculine and feminine gender roles.
4 Female athletes have long suffered from gender policing. For example, the only woman to make ESPN's list of the top ten U.S. athletes of the twentieth century was the 1932 Olympic track star and pro-golfer Mildred "Babe" Didrikson, who faced similar accusations in her era (Cayleff 1995).
5 As shall be shown throughout this text, if messages are replicated often enough from a variety of different media outlets they often come to be viewed as true regardless of their veracity.
6 bell hooks is the pen name of Gloria Jean Watkins. She prefers that this pen name be typed lowercase to highlight the content of her writings rather than herself as author.
7 Raymond Williams (1988), who charted the development of the word *modern* from its early French and Latin roots, stresses that it was not until the nineteenth and twentieth centuries that the term *modern* became virtually synonymous with *improved*. In earlier eras it was viewed unfavorably in comparison with the traditional.
8 Parts of this section first appeared in S.A. Mann and D.J. Huffman, "Decentering Second Wave Feminism and the Rise of the Third Wave," *Science and Society*, 2005, 69 (1): 56–91. The author wishes to thank Guilford Press/Publications for providing permission to print them.

9 See chapter 4 for some exceptions here, such as Max Horkheimer and Theodor Adorno's *Dialectic of Enlightenment* ([1944] 1972).

10 It may be more accurate to pluralize "epistemologies" here so as to highlight the differences *within* as well as between these different camps.

11 For example, just the exclusion of women from research questions and research samples have been shown to bias the findings of many disciplines. By "restoring women to history," historian Joan Kelly has argued that the Renaissance, while a period of greater freedom and intellectual awakening for men, was an era of greater repression for women (Kelly 1984). Similarly, through examining the voices of women, psychologist Carol Gilligan (1982) found that women have different moral standards for judging behaviors than do men (see chapter 2).

12 Political philosopher Mary O'Brien coined the term "malestream thought" to describe the masculine, taken-for-granted assumptions of social thought in most disciplines (O'Brien 1981; Marshall 2000: 28).

13 Harding's more recent book *Sciences from Below: Feminisms, Postcolonialities, and Modernities* (2008), begins with the intriguing question of whether science itself is multicultural.

14 Harding devotes an entire section of her article "Rethinking Standpoint Epistemology: What is 'Strong Objectivity'? (1993) to explaining how her position differs from other feminist approaches that privilege the knowledge of the oppressed. For a more detailed discussion of this topic see chapters 4 and 5.

SECTION I

Modern Feminist Thought

CHAPTER 2

Liberal Feminisms

The true republic—men, their rights and nothing more; women, their rights and nothing less.

—Susan B. Anthony

INTRODUCTION

The most popular and hegemonic feminist perspective in the United States from the American Revolution to the present era has been liberal feminism. While this feminist framework has undergone significant changes over this lengthy time period, it has been the theoretical and political framework that guided the largest women's rights organizations in American history. During the first wave, the **National American Woman Suffrage Association (NAWSA)** was the largest women's rights organization in the United States. By the turn of the twentieth century, NAWSA could boast around seventeen thousand members (Deckard [1979] 1983: 277).[1] From the second wave to the present day, the **National Organization for Women (NOW)** has been the largest feminist organization in the United States. Today NOW has more than 500,000 contributing members and over 500 local and campus affiliates in all fifty states and the District of Columbia.[2]

This chapter focuses on the contributions of liberal feminisms to the U.S. women's movement. In the eighteenth century, liberal ideas were revolutionary. They sparked the overthrow of absolute monarchy in France and fostered the demise of Britain's colonial rule of the American colonies. However, once democratic republics were established, liberal feminists embraced a reform-oriented politics that advocated working within the system through legitimate electoral, legislative, and judicial processes. They did not argue that women's emancipation required qualitative changes in the economic or political system. They neither called for the demise of capitalism nor challenged the basic assumptions of a democratic republic so long as women enjoyed the same rights as men. Consequently, for most of American history they favored reform over revolution.

Because England was the birthplace of the industrial revolution and entered the modern world before its colony that later became the United States of America, some of the earliest statements of liberal feminism were penned by British feminists. Among the most influential British works are *A Vindication of the Rights of Woman* (1792) by Mary Wollstonecraft and "Early Essays on Marriage and

Divorce" (1832), "Enfranchisement of Women" (1851), and "The Subjection of Women" (1869) by Harriet Taylor Mill and John Stuart Mill.[3] While these important writings will be discussed below, to understand the roots of liberal feminism we must delve deeper into the history of ideas. Liberal feminism has its deepest theoretical roots in Enlightenment thought—a body of thought that shook the foundations of social life in Europe and the American colonies in the eighteenth century.

THE "WOMAN QUESTION" AND ENLIGHTENMENT THOUGHT

More than theorists of any preceding age, Enlightenment thinkers, such as John Locke (1632–1704), Jean-Jacques Rousseau (1712–1778) and Voltaire[4] (1694–1778), held firmly to the conviction that the human mind could comprehend the universe and subordinate it to human needs. In this "Age of Reason," Enlightenment thinkers set about the task of creating a new world based on rational thought and scientific truth. They argued that, if science could reveal the laws of the physical world, than similar laws could be discovered in the social world. They investigated all aspects of social life, analyzing economic, political, religious, and social institutions by subjecting them to merciless criticism from the standpoint of reason. They demanded change in social forms they found to be irrational—which often meant traditional values and institutions—and waged war against the irrational using criticism as their major weapon (Zeitlin 1981).

The very term *Enlightenment* comes from the idea that this body of thought could lift the world from an age of darkness and ignorance into a world of science and rational thought. The Enlightenment thinkers fought against superstition and bigotry. They called for an end to censorship, demanded freedom of thought, and struggled against the prerogatives of the old feudal classes whose traditional and customary rules constrained the burgeoning new merchant and industrial classes. They also called for a more secular world, which was blasphemy in a feudal order steeped as it was in religion and superstition. One of the Enlightenment thinkers most admired by the masses and feared by the ruling classes was Voltaire, whose famous work *Candide* (1759) used wit and humor to expose the feudal aristocracy and the church as corrupt institutions.

Enlightenment ideas provided the ideology and slogans of some major political revolutions of the late eighteenth century—namely the American Revolution and the French Revolution. To many people living under the rule of absolute monarchies, these revolutions served as exemplars of the success of Enlightenment thought. For example, the American Declaration of Independence, as well as the U.S. Constitution and its Bill of Rights, exemplify the Enlightenment idea of a social contract theory of the state. This concept, derived from the work of such theorists as Rousseau and Locke, argued that to form governments citizens should have a written contract that specifies the rights and responsibilities of both the government and its citizens, as does the U.S. Constitution. As compared with absolute monarchies, the revolutionary features of this contract meant that citizens could not be governed without their consent and that citizens could overthrow their government if it abrogated their rights or its responsibilities.

Enlightenment thinkers focused on the individual and maintained that citizens had "natural and inalienable rights," such as freedom of speech and freedom of assembly. Another radical idea for that era was John Locke's notion that people are born as tabula rasas or clean slates.[5] This opened a Pandora's box for political activists to highlight not only how *all* people are influenced by the rationality or irrationality of their social environments but also how *all* people are born equal. While most Enlightenment thinkers viewed citizenship as inclusive only of free men with property, these same ideas would later be voiced by many subjugated groups—including women. The point is that these Enlightenment ideas made the progress of women toward equal membership in society "thinkable" (Taylor 2010: 38).

A hallmark of Enlightenment thought was the belief in progress. By using science, technology, rational thought, and political movements, people could use human action to improve society. They could attain ever greater degrees of freedom and ever greater degrees of perfection by transforming and improving social institutions. The notion of the "perfectability of man" was one of their key ideas, and they did mean "man" here. In regard to the "Woman Question," Enlightenment thinkers were far less progressive than their critical ideas would suggest (Knott and Taylor 2005, O'Brien, 2009). Indeed, many male Enlightenment intellectuals held conservative ideas about women's roles—ideas that Mary Wollstonecraft would decry as "sentimental nonsense" and "empty words" that only fostered women's subordination (quoted in Taylor 2010: 38). Such conservative views are evident in John Adams's response to his wife Abigail's request to "remember the ladies" when he was composing the Declaration of Independence. Abigail Adams's letter is one of the earliest U.S. feminist statements, written on the eve of the American Revolution. Excerpts from the Adamses' letters can be found in Box 2.1.

BOX 2.1

Selected Letters from the Adams Family Correspondence, 1776

The following excerpts are from correspondences between Abigail and John Adams written on the eve of the American Revolution:

From Abigail Adams to John Adams, March 31, 1776:

I long to hear that you have declared an independency—and by the way in the new Code of Laws which I suppose it will be necessary for you to make I desire you would Remember the Ladies and be more generous and favourable to them than your ancestors. Do not put such unlimited power into the hands of the Husbands. Remember all Men would be tyrants if they could. If perticuliar care and attention is not paid to the Laidies we are determined to foment a Rebelion, and will not hold ourselves bound by any Laws in which we have no voice, or Representation.

From John Adams to Abigail Adams, April 14, 1776:

As to your extraordinary Code of Laws, I cannot but laugh. We have been told that our Struggle has loosened the bands of Government every where. That Children and Apprentices were disobedient—that schools and Colledges were grown turbulent—that Indians slighted their Guardians and Negroes grew insolent to their Masters. But your Letter was the first Intimation that another Tribe more numerous and powerfull than all the rest were grown discontented.—This is rather too coarse a Compliment but you are so saucy, I won't blot it out.

Depend upon it, We know better than to repeal our Masculine systems. Altho they are in full Force, you know they are little more than Theory. . . . We are the subjects. We have only the Name of Masters, and rather than give up this, which would compleatly subject us to the Despotism of the Peticoat, I hope General Washington, and all our brave Heroes would fight.

"Selected Letters from the Adams Family Correspondence," pp. 10–11 in *The Feminist Papers: From Adams to de Beauvoir*, edited by Alice S. Rossi (New York: Bantam, 1974). Both letters reproduced as in the original.

John Adams's reply that he "cannot but laugh" at Abigail's "extraordinary" and "saucy" request no doubt rankles feminists today. However, his views on voting rights were typical of Enlightenment thinkers and reveal how issues of gender, class, and race were imbricated in their refusal to grant women the vote. In a letter to James Sullivan dated May 26, 1776, John explains why property ownership must be a qualification for voting. He states that, without this qualification, all people—even those in dependent positions would desire equal rights. For John, people who are without property are "too dependent upon other men to have a will of their own" (quoted in Butterfield, Friedlaender, and Kline 1975: 375). He continues:

> Depend on it, Sir, it is dangerous to open so fruitful a source of controversy and altercation as would be opened by attempting to alter the qualifications of voters; there will be no end to it. New claims will arise; women will demand a vote; lads from twelve to twenty-one will think their rights not enough attended to; and every man who has not a farthing, will demand an equal voice with any other, in all acts of state. It tends to confound and destroy all distinctions, and prostrate all ranks to one common level. (375; reproduced as in the original)

John's letter to Sullivan highlights how many liberals of this era did not embrace the notion that *all* people are born equal. Rather the focus was on free and independent citizens. Although Adams himself did not own slaves, many of the founding fathers were slaveholders as well as landowners, and in their eyes, property ownership was the key to independence (in thought and action) and to citizenship. Thus, while Enlightenment thought was radical for its era, many people were excluded from the citizenship rights it so proudly proclaimed.

THE RISE OF THE U.S. WOMEN'S MOVEMENT IN EARLY MODERNITY

Because most of our founding fathers agreed with John Adams that only property-owning, free men could be citizens with inalienable rights, women were excluded from the freedoms heralded by the U.S. Constitution and its Bill of Rights. The inability to own property and/or to control their own income or wealth were major issues that galvanized nineteenth-century, free women's support for women's rights. One of the most serious obstacles to attaining these rights was the **doctrine of coverture**, which governed marriage laws across most of the country.[6] This doctrine held that once a man and woman were married, they were one in front of the law. This "one" was the man, and he controlled the property and income of the household. This doctrine also gave husbands the right to chastise or punish their wives and children. The temperance movement of the late nineteenth century was a direct response to these gender inequalities. Alcohol abuse was a serious issue not only because it was associated with domestic violence but also because wives feared their husbands would drink up their households' income. For these reasons, many women's rights activists of this era also were members of the temperance movement.

However, the abolitionist movement was the major trigger for the rise of the nineteenth-century women's movement, and this is why historians often date the beginnings of the first wave in the 1830s. Through their involvement in this movement to end slavery, women quickly learned that they could not function as equals alongside their male abolitionist counterparts. Not only were women barred from membership in some abolitionist organizations, but they also had to battle simply to speak in public. Among the first white, liberal feminists to fight this battle were Sarah and Angelina Grimké, daughters of a South Carolina slaveholding family. In order to promote the abolitionist cause, the Grimké sisters moved to the North and began to write and to speak out publicly against slavery. The unceasing attacks on these women both for their abolitionist stance and for speaking publicly convinced them that the issues of freedom for slaves and freedom for women were inextricably intertwined.

As early as 1838, in her "Letters on the Condition of Women in the United States Women," Sarah Grimké raised a number of issues that would continue to be voiced by feminists a century later. She observed how women in the "fashionable" (i.e., wealthy) class are "miserably deficient" in education and are taught that marriage is "the only avenue to distinction"; she describes them as "vacuous of mind" and frivolous "pretty toys" (Grimké [1838] 2005: 69) When she bemoans how their "chief business" is "to attract the notice and win the attentions of men by their external charms," she sounds much like Betty Friedan describing the "feminine mystique" more than a century later (69). When Grimké discusses working-class women, she criticizes "the disproportionate value set on the time and labor of men and women." She also points to how men hold the top positions even in areas of work where women predominate, such as teaching or sewing—what second wave feminists would call sex-segregated occupations (70). In her letters Grimké expresses the deepest sorrow for the plight of slave women. She vividly describes the tyranny they suffer as well as the floggings and "brutal lust" of slave owners that these women endured:

> Can any American woman look at these scenes of shocking licentiousness and cruelty, and fold her hands in apathy, and say, "I have nothing to do with slavery"? *She cannot and be guiltless.* (70; her emphasis)

Notably, Sarah Grimké, unlike many other first wave liberal feminists, was careful to point out class differences in the life experiences of women. Indeed, one of the major strategies that white, middle-class liberals used to advance their feminist demands was to highlight the *similarities* between their own lack of freedom and that of slaves. This is exemplified in an 1872 speech given by Susan B. Anthony at a trial after she and fifteen other women were arrested for trying to vote in a presidential election. Here Anthony discusses how neither free women nor slaves could own their own property, control their own incomes, keep their own names, or have custody of their children. Black women's rights activists often were angered by this comparison, given that they were far more subjugated than white women both before and after the Emancipation (see chapter 5).

Nevertheless, even *within* the abolitionist movement, white and black women experienced second-class status. Often they were relegated to the galleries and prohibited from participating in meaningful ways in movement events and proceedings. Such experiences at the 1840 World Anti-Slavery Convention held in London led Lucretia Mott and Elizabeth Cady Stanton to vow to hold a women's rights convention after they returned to the United States. Eight years would pass, however, before these soon-to-be luminaries of the U.S. suffrage movement fulfilled their vow (Hole and Levine 1979).

The Seneca Falls Declaration of Sentiments

The first women's rights convention in U.S. history was held at Seneca Falls, New York, in 1848. Three hundred women and men attended this convention, which approved the famous **Seneca Falls Declaration of Sentiments**. This document was drafted by Elizabeth Cady Stanton and modeled on the Declaration of Independence to highlight the contradictions between the rights espoused there and the failure of women to attain these rights. It states: "We hold these truths to be self-evident: that all men and women are created equal; that they are endowed with certain inalienable rights." (Stanton [1848] 2005: 71). The Declaration of Sentiments enumerated over a dozen ways that men established "tyranny" over women, such as "depriving her of her inalienable right to elective franchise"; "taking from her all right to property, even to the wages she earns"; and "making her, if married, in the eye of the law, civilly dead" (72). The only resolution not accepted unanimously was the right to suffrage, which suggests that these women were more interested in access to education and employment, the right to control their property and earnings, and easier divorce laws (Hole and Levine 1979: 548). They also strove for guardianship of their children since, at that time, men received custody after divorce.

Their concern with these more immediate demands made sense in the social context of their era. From the mid- to late nineteenth century, many necessities of everyday life were increasingly being produced in factories (Zaretsky 1976). What was once homemade could now be purchased so that women no longer had to produce such items as bread, butter, cheese, soap, candles, or clothing. By the early 1900s, four-fifths of the production processes carried on in the average home in 1850 had departed never to return (Ehrenreich and English 1978: 143–144). Alongside this industrialization of women's work a new discourse emerged which romanticized women's roles as housewives, homemakers, and mothers—often referred to as the "**cult of domesticity**" or the "**cult of true womanhood**" (Welter 1973). This discourse entailed a "**doctrine of separate spheres**," which deemed the private realm of the household as women's sphere and the public realm outside of the home as men's sphere (Baca Zinn and Eitzen 1993: 56). While there is some evidence that the cult of true womanhood trickled down to the less well-to-do classes,[7] it remained an ideal rather than a reality for most women. Indeed, the extent to which women's lives conformed to this ideal varied according to their social class and race (Lerner 1979: 190–192).

The industrialization of women's work freed many middle-class women from arduous labor and enabled them to engage in philanthropic activities. While political activism was not considered appropriate for women under the doctrine of separate spheres, freedom from producing many of the necessities of everyday life at least provided the material grounds for more widespread feminist activism. Thus, it is not surprising that the early U.S. women's movement was led by middle-class women and that its ranks swelled in the latter part of the nineteenth century.

Some Seneca Falls demands were more easily achieved than others. For example, the right to participate fully in religious activities has not been granted by some religions today. By contrast, in the field of education free women gained some of their earliest rights. As early as the 1830s, much ground-breaking work in education had been done by women's rights activists, such as Emma Willard and Frances Wright. One of the more notable successes achieved before the Seneca Falls Convention occurred in 1833, when Oberlin College became the first college in the United States to open its doors to women (Hole and Levine 1979: 544). However, access to education continued to be a feminist demand because many universities and occupations remained only open to men.

From the Seneca Falls Convention until the beginning of the Civil War, women's rights conventions were held every year in different cities across the country. A signal event of this era was when the ex-slave Sojourner Truth spoke at a women's rights convention in 1851. The white, middle-class women speakers at this convention were heckled by men in the audience who jeered at the idea that men were masters given how women were put on a pedestal. Here again John Adams's claim that "men were only masters in theory" reappeared some seventy-five years later. Sojourner Truth went to the podium and gave her famous "Ain't I a Woman?"

speech, which boldly stated how she had never put on a pedestal; rather, she had "plowed and fenced" like a man and even withstood the whip. Truth's stirring speech quickly silenced the male hecklers and is viewed today as one of the earliest statements of black feminist thought that poignantly highlighted differences between women based on race and class (see chapter 5).

When the Civil War began in 1861, women's rights advocates were urged to abandon their cause and support the war effort, which they did with some hesitation. After the war, the emancipation of slaves was guaranteed by the Thirteenth Amendment to the U.S. Constitution. However, white women's rights activists were alarmed to learn that sex would not be included in the Fourteenth or Fifteenth Amendments. The Fourteenth Amendment prohibited discrimination on the bases of race, religion, and nation of origin, whereas the Fifteenth Amendment gave black men the right to vote. That sex had been left out of these amendments caused schisms within the U.S. women's movement, deeply dividing it along racial lines. While a few black feminists, like Sojourner Truth, refused to support the Fifteenth Amendment, arguing that it would make black men masters over black women, the vast majority of African–Americans supported this amendment (Terborg-Penn 1998a; see chapter 5). In contrast, most white suffragists did not support the Fifteenth Amendment, and some began campaigns to place literacy restrictions on voting. The racism underlying these campaigns is evident in Elizabeth Cady Stanton's 1866 remarks below:

> In view of the fact that the Freedmen of the South and the millions of foreigners now crowding our shores, most of whom represent neither property, education, nor civilization, are all in the progress of events to be enfranchised, the best interests of the nation demand that we outweigh this incoming pauperism, ignorance and degradation, with the wealth, education, and refinement of the women of the republic. (Quoted in Frost-Knappman and Cullen-Dupont 2005: 398).

Because restrictions like literacy requirements also limited the voting rights of poor whites, such demands reflected class interests as well as racial and ethnic privilege. As will be shown in the Theoretical Applications section of this text, many white middle-class suffragists, including Stanton, favored literacy requirements for suffrage even in the new colonies and territories that the United States acquired in the late nineteenth and early twentieth centuries. As ironic as it may seem, once the colonized became colonizers, they wanted to maintain their privilege in regard to their global location as well. Stanton was not alone here. Similar colonialist views were held by other famous liberal feminists, such as John Stuart Mill[8] and Susan B. Anthony (see chapter 8).

LIBERAL FEMINISTS ON LOVE, MARRIAGE, AND SEX IN EARLY MODERNITY BY JANE WARD AND SUSAN MANN

Although during the first wave women were denied many of the legal and economic rights granted to men, middle- and upper-class women could achieve some degree of social recognition in exchange for their accomplishments in regard to beauty, fashion, style, chastity, and moral stewardship. Liberal feminists were divided on the issue of whether women possessed a superior moral sense to men. Those who embraced this notion argued that women's suffrage was not only fair but would also contribute to a more virtuous society. Those who rejected this assumption viewed such notions as romanticizing women and as setbacks to attaining the equality.

Social Reformers

In *A Vindication of the Rights of Woman* (1792), Mary Wollstonecraft boldly challenged the view that women, by nature, are more moral than men. Rather than view these qualities as inherent to women's nature, she viewed them as the result of prevailing gender norms and women's lack of access to education. She emphasized the need for cultural and economic reforms that would allow women to choose or to cultivate moral righteousness and, concomitantly, to access their authentic selves and their true sexuality. For Wollstonecraft, women gained only superficial status by asserting themselves as the natural possessors of innocence and delicacy. In this way, she offered a prescient feminist critique of the social construction of gender in her era.

Unlike most of her contemporaries, Wollstonecraft did not shy away from directly discussing the sexual implications of men's preference for frail and undereducated women. Interestingly, her arguments addressed men by highlighting male sexual self-interests: If men really want "enthusiastic affection" from women, they must seek love based on companionship and mutual respect, not on women's fragility, beauty, or ignorance of reciprocal passion. Wollstonecraft called for a reconceptualization of women's virtue that would place emphases on the Enlightenment values of knowledge and reason. She assigned great significance to women attaining rationality, self-determination, and strong bodies (traits usually associated with masculinity) and saw little value in reclaiming domestic femininity or other qualities historically assigned to women (Martin 2001).

Wollstonecraft's writings were not as revolutionary as those of her anarchist and socialist feminist peers (see chapter 4). Rather, her perspective exemplified a thread of eighteen- and nineteenth-century feminist theorizing about sexual practices that could be termed **sexual reformism.** Proponents of sexual reform focused on women's right to make sexual choices based upon rationality, dignity, and self-determination rather than out of fear of their husbands or conformity to the prevailing scripts that governed feminine virtue or coquettishness. Writing a half century later, British social reformers Harriet Taylor Mill and John Stuart Mill also declared that marriages would be much happier if heterosexual affections were based on friendship and equality. Yet Harriet and John Mill viewed sex within marriage as more violent and oppressive than did Wollstonecraft.

> However brutal a tyrant [a wife] may unfortunately be chained to—though she may know that he hates her, though it may be his daily pleasure to torture her, and

> though she may feel it impossible not to loathe him—he can claim from her and enforce the lowest degradation of a human being, that of being made the instrument of an animal function contrary to her inclinations. (Mill [1869] 1970: 160)

Given this oppressive view of marriage, as well as their long, platonic love affair before Harriet's first husband died, it is not surprising that Harriet and John wrote extensively about the importance of reforming marriage, divorce, and child custody laws. The Enlightenment idea of reason controlling the "lower," "base," or "animal instincts" permeates these writings (Rossi 1970: 49).

In "The Subjection of Women" (1869), John had a terse response to the claim that there were "natural" differences between the sexes which precluded full equality for women. He wrote: "No one can know the nature of the sexes as long as they have only been seen in their present relation to each other. . . . What women are is what we have required them to be" (quoted in Rossi 1970: 60). He challenged his opponents to open the doors of education and public life to women. If women were naturally inferior, they would show themselves to be so. However, without such equal opportunities, no one could judge what women were like or what they could become.

While Harriet and John shared the view that women should enjoy the same political, economic, and educational opportunities as men, they diverged over the issue of mothers working outside the home. In the "Enfranchisement of Women" (1851) Harriet described how few educated women would likely be satisfied with motherhood and child rearing. She also made clear that women could not be the true equal of men without contributing to the material support of the family (Rossi 1970: 23). John, on the other hand, assumed that women would choose family over career:

> Like a man when he chooses a profession, so, when a woman, marries, it may in general be understood that she makes choice of the management of a household, and the bringing up of a family, as the first call upon her exertions, during as many years of her life as may be required for the purpose; and that she renounces not all objects and occupations, but all which are not consistent with the requirements of this (Mill [1869] 1970: 179).

Neither Harriet nor John questioned whether women should be the primary child rearers. For them, child bearing went hand-in-hand with child rearing. John thought married women voluntarily would devote themselves to child rearing and discussed communal child rearing only as a solution to child rearing after divorce (Rossi 1970: 23). Harriet's only answer for women who worked outside of the home was to rely on "a panoply of domestic servants" for child rearing, reflecting her own upper-middle class vantage point (Eisentein 1986: 131).

As noted earlier, Sarah Grimké's ideas extended beyond the horizons of her own social location. She highlighted gender, racial, and class oppressions in her discussion of sexual relations. Although Grimké drew more heavily from Christian beliefs than from Enlightenment thought, she exposed the hypocrisy of American gender relations. How could American men be virtuous while treating white women as "pretty toys or as mere instruments of pleasure" or subjecting black women slaves to brutal sexual violence and torture? And how could white women be virtuous in a society in which they witnessed and normalized their husbands' frequent "crimes of seduction and illicit intercourse" with women slaves? (Grimké [1838] 2005: 70–71).

Overall, sexual reformers viewed sexual relations and sex itself (though few spoke of sexual practices specifically) as a direct reflection of women's political, economic, and social subordination to men. Because many of these reformers presented sexual violence as a symptom of the larger problem of unequal gender relations, they laid a crucial foundation for later feminist analyses of domestic violence and sexual assault. Most nineteenth-century women's rights activists, including such major leaders as Elizabeth Cady Stanton and Susan B. Anthony, did not support birth control or abortion but rather demanded the right to **voluntary motherhood**. This meant that women should be free to abstain from having sexual relations with their husbands—today we would call this freedom from marital rape. Overall, in the eyes of most nineteenth-century women's rights advocates, sex for Victorian women appeared to be largely synonymous with danger and victimization rather than with sexual pleasure and agency.

Free Love Advocates

Most women's rights activists of this era provided little insight into women's positive experiences of sexuality. Only a few made the then-radical claim that women should be able to experience sexual pleasure outside of marriage. Although the concept of free love is often linked to the sexual revolution of the 1960s and 1970s, the free love movement actually began in the nineteenth century. **Free love** or **sex love** in this earlier era referred to the right to have sex *with someone you loved* whether inside or outside of marriage. It did not refer to indiscriminate or casual sexual relations.[9] The "high priestess of free love" among U.S. liberal feminists of this era was Victoria Claflin Woodhull.[10] For Woodhull, sex "based upon mutual love and desire" that provided "reciprocal benefit" was simply not possible within the institution of legal marriage at that time since marriage was an economic necessity for most women. Indeed, Woodhull viewed marriage as no different from prostitution—as a site of women's captivity and servitude. For her, free love was rooted in the rights to refuse compulsory marriage and to be held to prudish sexual mores as well as in the individual's right to pursue sexual fulfillment. Using classic liberal terminology, Woodhull proclaimed in a speech at New York's Steinway Hall on November 20, 1871:

> Yes, I am a Free Lover. I have an inalienable, constitutional, and natural right to love whom I may, to love as long or as short a period as I can; to change that love every day if I please, and with that right neither you nor any law can frame any right to interfere (Quoted in Frisken 2004: 40).

Proponents of free love also pointed to women's lack of access to accurate information about their bodies and sexuality. Victorian physicians commonly diagnosed women with hysteria if they complained that sex with their husbands was painful, uncomfortable, or otherwise unfulfilling. The word *hysteria* is derived from the Latin for womb, and in that era, hysteria was defined as "a faulty reproductive system." Its treatment included massage of female patients' genitalia by male physicians, a procedure that physicians reported to be tedious and time-consuming to administer. Hysteria and other gendered diagnoses of that era glossed over the social factors influencing the quality of women's sexual experiences and instead suggested that women who did not enjoy sex possessed a physiological abnormality. Such assumptions led Woodhull to describe women's widespread sexual dissatisfaction as "sickening." Her 1873 speech titled "The Elixer of Life" depicts women's sexuality in the most solemn of terms: "I know fully one-half of the world is undergoing sexual starvation; dying either for want of intercourse or for lack of the proper kind" (Woodhull [1873] 2005: 97).

Given that she had what then were considered quite radical lifestyle views, it may appear odd to place Woodhull in the liberal feminist camp. However, she was not a political revolutionary like her socialist and anarchist peers who were advocates of free love (see chapter 4). Although her childhood was spent in poverty, Woodhull made a fortune as the first women to own an investment firm and was a free-market enthusiast. She also embraced political reform within the system and was the first women to run for president of the United States in 1872.[11] Because of her views on free love, she was referred to as "the prostitute who ran for President" (Goldsmith 1998: 16). During this era, any woman who lived in intimate relationships outside of marriage was referred to as a prostitute. At most Woodhull was a lifestyle radical. Her other key interests included spiritualism (where she relayed messages to and from loved ones to the dead), homeopathic medicine, vigorous exercise, and healthy diets that included no alcohol, caffeine, meat, or lard (Goldsmith 1998). These ideas were not only unconventional, they also were way ahead of their time.

The vast differences in the positions held on sexual relations by liberal women's rights advocates should make us wary of making too many generalizations about distinct feminist positions during the Victorian era. Nevertheless, it remains useful to note the ways in which ideas about sexuality, womanhood, and moral purity converged under the name of social reform for liberal feminists during this period.[12] As will be shown in later chapters, women's social locations and vantage points in terms of class and race mattered during this era. Socialist and anarchist women's rights activists who worked as labor organizers were more likely to support birth control and abortion as well as free love (see chapter 4). In contrast, activist women of color focused less on women's sexual oppression in the domestic sphere and more on the sexual double standard used to justify both the brutal lynching of men of color and the pervasive, white racist assumption that sexual relations between people of color—male and female—were more animalistic, lascivious, and promiscuous. Such negative stereotypes led activist women of color to practice what later would be called a "politics of respectability" (see chapter 5).

Although liberal feminists of the late nineteenth and early twentieth centuries shared a focus on social reform, they were not a homogenous group. Like today, liberalism included perspectives that ranged from moderate to left. The moderates more readily supported issues directly related to their own middle- or upper-class interests (such as the demand for literacy requirements for voting). Left-wing liberals were more likely to be involved in the Progressive Movement for social reform that sought to curb the excesses of rapid industrialization, particularly evident in the squalid living conditions of poor and working-class people in this era—particularly those who were immigrants and/or people of color.

DIVERGENT PATHS OF LIBERAL FEMINISTS IN EARLY MODERNITY

Left–Liberal, White Reformers

As compared to moderate liberal feminists who worked mainly with people of their own social classes, the left–liberal white suffragists of this era often worked in settlement houses and/or initiated various experiments in collective forms of living as well as communal kitchens and child care (Hayden 1982) Because the settlement houses were located in neighborhoods of poor and working-class people, these middle-class reformers came face-to-face with the dire effects of poverty and squalor. Hull House in Chicago founded by Jane Addams is the most famous settlement house, and Hull House women's activism took many and diverse forms. Not only were these women strong women's rights activists, but they also conducted social research and collected data on myriad urban problems. They provided poor and working-class families with health care, child care, and adult education and struggled for the rights of working-class people to unionize.

The Hull House women were heavily involved also in addressing environmental issues during this era.[13] Because the doctrine of separate spheres dictated that women's place was in the home, women who participated in environmental activism in the nineteenth and early twentieth centuries had to defend their activities as extensions rather than as rejections of the traditional roles of wife and mother. As historian Carolyn Merchant (1995) points out, the term **municipal housekeeping** was used to describe this environmental activism, and thousands of women mobilized under the banner of municipal housekeeping to address the environmental problems engendered by modernization and industrialization, such as air and water pollution, sanitation issues, safe food, and occupational safety (see Box 2.2).

BOX 2.2

The Municipal Housekeeping Movement

The concerns of the municipal housekeeping movement were diverse; they included air and water pollution, garbage and sanitation issues, safe food, as well as industrial health and safety. Sources of power like coal belched smoke and soot onto town and city landscapes as Rebecca Harding Davis' social realist novel, *Life in the Iron Mills* (1861) so vividly described.[14] Women were particularly active in the antismoke campaigns not only because smoke affected their families' health but also because it affected their ability to uphold standards of cleanliness (Merchant 1995). Household refuse and industrial pollution were other serious environmental concerns. It was not unusual in the nineteenth century for household garbage to be thrown out into alleys, where it piled up, causing dreadful odors and serious health hazards. Water supplies were affected by household waste, and industrial pollution had even more far-reaching consequences. By the 1870s, years of abuse and neglect had so fouled the waterscapes of urban America that public concern had galvanized around the issue of clean water. Many women and women's clubs got involved in local, state, and national committees to address these environmental concerns. The rationale for their involvement lay in the effects of environmental pollution on every American home: pure water, clean air, and safe food meant health; impurities meant disease and death (Merchant 1995: 140).

Scientist Ellen Swallow Richards (1842–1911) is viewed as the founder of the municipal housekeeping movement. Although she never supported suffrage,[15] her contributions to environmental activism were many. A graduate of Vassar College and the first woman enrolled at the Massachusetts Institute of Technology (MIT), she was the first scientist to conduct stream-by-stream water surveys, and her research on food products led to the first food inspection laws in the country. Richards studied heating and ventilation and made significant advances in home and workplace ventilation. In her book *Euthenics* (1910), she explicitly called for women to engage in municipal housekeeping and to make connections between the household, the municipality, and the natural environment. In 1892, Richards developed the new field of oekology. Derived from the Greek word *oikos*, meaning house, this field was envisioned as fostering a more scientific relationship between the environment and the home. It became known as home ecology and, later, home economics. Richards founded the American Home Economics Association and became its first president in 1909. However, with the passage of time and the success of key goals of this movement, such as safer food, air, and water, many people lost sight of this field's original connection with environmental issues (Merchant 1995: 139–140).

Jane Addams was the first woman to be appointed as a municipal sanitary inspector, and the Hull House Women's Club undertook systematic studies of the city's system of garbage collection, providing the health department with mountains of data on the hazards involved (Elshtain 2002: 172). Mary McDowell, a self-taught sanitation engineer, was renowned for her efforts to clean up Bubbly Creek—a major source of drinking water that literally bubbled from stockyard animal refuse dumping (Washington 2005: 102). Water-related infections, such as cholera, yellow fever, and typhoid proved especially deadly in the nineteenth century.[16] Feminist and pioneer epidemiologist Alice Hamilton (1869–1970), sister of renowned classicist Edith Hamilton, provided scientific evidence for Hull House reforms to deal with typhoid and other "filth diseases" (Merchant 2007: 126).[17] While these activities speak to some of the domestic reforms fostered by left-liberal suffragists in the United States, their global endeavors included formation of the Women's Peace Party (WPP) as well as the International Committee of Women for Permanent Peace (ICWPP), both in 1915 (see chapter 8).[18]

Left–Liberal Black Women's Clubs

African–American women contributed significantly to passage of the Nineteenth Amendment as well as to municipal housekeeping movement. Black suffragists tended to be more educated than other women of their race. However, they often crossed class lines to address the concerns of poor and working-class women (Lerner 1979: 93; Gordon 1995: 463). According to historian Rosalyn Terborg-Penn (1998a), the first generation of black suffragists grew slowly out of a small group of reformers within the abolitionist movement. Among the more prominent black suffragists of the antebellum era were Mary Ann Shadd Cary, Harriet Forten Purvis, Margaretta Forten, Sarah Remond, Francis Harper, and Sojourner Truth (Lerner 1979, Giddings 1984, Shaw 1995, Terborg-Penn 1998a). As noted earlier, passage of the Fifteenth Amendment after the Civil War created serious rifts between white and black suffragists, as many white feminists, such as Elizabeth Cady Stanton, began to call for educated suffrage rather than universal suffrage. Although Black suffragists continued working with the major white suffrage organizations, they also organized separately—especially through their own black women's clubs.

In the 1890s, black women's clubs in a number of cities began to form federations, and by 1896 the three largest federations were unified in the **National Association of Colored Women (NACW)**. The NACW included over one hundred local women's clubs and predated the founding of the National Association for the Advancement of Colored People (NAACP) (Lerner 1979: 83; Shaw 1995: 441). While the white women's club movement largely comprised conservative, well-to-do women many of whom did not support women's suffrage, the black women's clubs played a major role in mobilizing for suffrage in the late nineteenth and early twentieth centuries (Terborg-Penn 1998a, Lerner 1979, Giddings 1984). Terborg-Penn (1998a: 106) argues that mobilization for suffrage had a "snowballing effect" among black clubwomen, as more and more women's organizations joined the movement.

Many attempts by black suffragists such as Josephine St. Pierre Ruffin, Fannie Barrier Williams, and Mary Church Terrell to foster interracial cooperation for suffrage were rebuked or went unheeded. The National American Woman Suffrage Association (NAWSA) vacillated between placating white suffragists in the south and courting black feminists in the north (Terborg-Penn 1998a). For example, black suffragists reported being asked not to march with white suffragists, but to walk with their own race at the end of parades or demonstrations, and many were prohibited from joining local suffrage organizations (122–123). When Terborg-Penn examined existing copies of the *Suffragist*—journal of the National Woman's Party's (NWP)—from the years 1914–1919, she found only two items referring to the contributions made to suffrage by African–Americans and numerous derogatory references to them. The cover of a 1917 issue featuring the jailing of NWP members, for example, read: "Refined, intelligent, society women act as pickets and are thrown into the workhouse with negroes and criminals" (133). Perhaps most disheartening was how passage of the Nineteenth Amendment did not necessarily mean that African-American women could vote in practice. Southern blacks—male and female—remained virtually disfranchised as southern states continued to circumvent the amendment through poll taxes, literacy requirements for voting, and sheer terror.

However, the black women's clubs did far more than just work for suffrage. They also provided important aid to African-Americans—especially those who were moving en masse to northern cities. In the early decades of the twentieth century, during what is called the Great Migration, hundreds of thousands of African-Americans migrated from the rural south to the urban north ,seeking refuge from Jim Crow policies and escalating violence in the south and lured by the job opportunities afforded by industrialization and the production demands of World War I.[19] Ida B. Wells-Barnett, internationally renown for her antilynching campaigns (see chapter 5), organized the first black women's club in Chicago as well as the first black settlement house—the Negro Fellowship League—to aid migrants from the south. Barnett came to be known as the "Jane Addams among the Negroes," though the origin, shape, and destiny of these two women's work were quite different (Schechter 2001: 170). The League could not seek government contracts or social services in the same way as Hull House because it functioned in such a racially hostile city. It also did not have access to the patronage available to the wealthy Hull House women and their social networks. Consequently, the League, like other black settlement houses, operated as a mutual aid society and suffered a shorter life span.

Race mattered in terms of the political options available to African-Americans as contrasted to poor and working-class whites. Because the Progressive Party, as well as most trade unions and settlement houses, were segregated in this era, these avenues for urban reform were not open to African-Americans (172 and 230). Rather they were forced into more violent paths of resistance. This was evident when the rapid influx of black migrants into urban areas created intense competition not only for jobs but, also, for urban space. Space—especially housing—was among the important factors underlying America's bloodiest race riot, the Chicago race riot of 1919. Over the four days in which this riot took place, 38 people were killed, 537 were injured, and 1,000 were left homeless[20] (Washington 2005: 134 and 141).

Black women club members were far more successful than white women club members in crossing class lines to address the concerns of poor and working-class women. Historian Paula Giddings explains this difference by pointing to how these middle-class black women recognized that *all* black women were perceived in the light of those who had the least resources. Mary Church Terrell, one of the wealthiest and most highly educated black women of that era, wrote that club members "have determined to come into the closest possible touch with the masses of our women . . . through whom the womanhood of our people is always judged" (quoted in Giddings, 1984: 98). Other scholars concur that there was less class distance "between the helper and the helped"; less chronological distance, since many middle-class black women's upward mobility had been so recent; and less geographical distance, since black women of all classes lived in segregated areas (Gordon 1995: 463).

The black women's clubs' municipal housekeeping activities were more akin to the white settlement houses than to the white women's clubs. They undertook neighborhood and home cleanup campaigns and worked to reduce the spread of diseases arising from unsafe air and water (Lerner 1979: 89; Mann 2011). One of the more remarkable institutions created during this era was the Atlanta Neighborhood Union—the black women's organization most similar to Hull House during this era (Lerner 1979: 88–90). Organized in 1908 under the leadership of Lugenia Burns Hope, it established a nursery, a kindergarten, and a medical center to treat tuberculosis and other filth-related diseases. By the late 1920s, nearly one thousand children were being examined annually (Giddings 1984: 136). Given their focus on women's issues and the environmental concerns of poor and working-class people as well as people of color, these activists deserve mention as pioneers of ecofeminism and environmental justice (Mann 2011).[21]

Overall, the black women's club movement had more serious problems to deal with than those of their white counterparts. Because local governments and social welfare institutions neglected or excluded blacks, this pushed black women's work beyond traditional charity work to community development (Shaw 1995: 440). Not only were health conditions perilous in the black shanty towns and ghettoes of apartheid America, but issues like child care were far more compelling for the vast majority of black women. As Olivia Davidson remarked, most black women not only were "overworked and underfed" but also "suffered to a greater or lesser degree from sheer physical exhaustion" (quoted in Giddings 1984: 100). Black clubwomen dealt with social problems that spanned the life cycle from day nurseries to old age homes. Their activities helped compensate for poorly funded black schools, hospitals, and clinics. Fannie Barrier Williams captures well the differences between the white and the black women's clubs:

> The club movement among colored women reaches into the sub-social conditions of the entire race. . . . Among white women the club is the forward movement of the already uplifted. (Quoted in Giddings 1984: 98)

Moderate–Liberal Women's Rights Advocates

Noticeable divisions existed among the moderate or more mainstream liberal feminists of the nineteenth and early twentieth centuries. Many moderates believed that there were essential differences between men and women that included physical capabilities as well as emotional and cultural differences. Some moderate suffragists embraced the notion that women possessed a superior moral sense to men. They highlighted women's roles as mothers—as nurturers and as moral educators of children—to win the vote. They further argued that through voting women's greater morality would contribute to a more virtuous society. Liberal feminists who rejected this assumption held the view that men and women were more similar than different. For them, such notions of essential female characteristics were simply romantic illusions and only set back women's attempts to attain equal rights with men. Elizabeth Cady Stanton, for example, thought it was a mistake to argue for suffrage on any ground other than social justice and rejected such views of women's essential nature as romantic nonsense (Sneider 2008: 92; Griffith 1984: 109).

Divisions among moderate liberal feminists were evident also in the political differences of the various suffrage organizations. In the nineteenth century, the two major suffrage organizations were the National Woman Suffrage Association (NWSA) and the American Woman Suffrage Association (AWSA). The AWSA was more moderate, focusing only on suffrage and pursuing a slower, state-by-state path to winning the vote. The NWSA, led by Stanton and Anthony, did not limit its activism to suffrage, but included other demands expressed in the Seneca Falls Declaration of Sentiments. It also worked at the state and federal levels to change state constitutions and to pass a woman suffrage amendment to the U.S. Constitution. By 1890 it was clear that the moderate, single-issue approach garnered more public support, and the two organizations merged to form the **National American Woman Suffrage Association (NAWSA)** (Hole and Levine 1979).

After the turn of the century, a new generation of more militant suffragists came of age. Under the leadership of Alice Paul, in 1913 these suffragists formed the Congressional Union, which later became known as the **National Woman's Party (NWP).** These activists worked exclusively for a federal woman suffrage amendment using a wider array of tactics that Paul had learned from her contact with militant British suffragists. The NWP organized parades and demonstrations. They picketed the White House and even engaged in hunger strikes. At the time, such activities were considered militant, and on several occasions these women were arrested and jailed.

As Judith Hole and Ellen Levine (1979) point out, the various forms of liberal activism undertaken to attain the vote were impressive and incredibly time-consuming. Over seventy years passed between the Seneca Falls Convention and the victory of women's suffrage with passage of the Nineteenth Amendment in 1920. Not even counting the numerous meetings, speeches, petitions, parades, pickets, demonstrations, and cross-country campaigns by automobile and railroad, Carrie Chapman Catt, a former president of NAWSA, estimated that it took:

> 56 campaigns of referenda to male voters; 480 campaigns to get Legislatures to submit suffrage amendments to votes; 44 campaigns to get State constitutional conventions to write woman suffrage into state constitutions; 277 campaigns to get State party conventions to include woman suffrage planks; 30 campaigns to get presidential party conventions to adopt woman suffrage planks in party platforms, and 29 campaigns with 19 successive Congresses. (Quoted in Hole and Levine 1979: 554)

After passage of the Nineteenth Amendment, Alice Paul called for a new campaign to pass the Equal Rights Amendment (ERA) to the Constitution. Yet, by 1920 so much energy had been expended in achieving the vote that the woman's movement virtually collapsed with exhaustion (Hole and Levine 1979). While many individuals and groups would continue to work for women's rights, the mass-based activism that characterized the first wave went into abeyance (Taylor 1989). It would take more than four decades before a second wave of mass activism by U.S. feminists crested in the 1960s.

ADVANCES AND SETBACKS BETWEEN THE WAVES

Even given the demise of mass-based activism after the passage of the Nineteenth Amendment, women made some important strides in the period between 1920 and 1930. Among the advances that received the most publicity was the so-called sexual revolution of the 1920s, during which barriers to sexual pleasure were slowly eroding for heterosexuals (Cott 1987). According to John D'Emilio's and Estelle Freedman's *Intimate Matters: A History of Sexuality in America* ([1988] 1997), among the more significant changes during this era were the redefinition of womanhood to include eroticism and less public reticence about sex. D'Emilio and Freedman point out that, by 1920, the separate spheres so critical to the construction of nineteenth-century, middle-class sexual mores were beginning to collapse. Women were engaged in the public world as workers, consumers, and voters. Forms of entertainment shifted—especially for middle-class couples. The heterosexual world of commercialized amusements that working-class youth had long enjoyed was spreading to the middle class. Cabarets and nightclubs attracted middle-class couples and allowed men and women to interact informally outside of a domestic setting. The motion picture traveled uptown, out of the working-class neighborhoods in which it was first housed (231). In previous decades, a woman's participation in public amusements marked her as disreputable. By the 1920s, however, many women viewed such activities as simply part of modern life. No doubt, the sexual revolution of the 1920s lacked the explicitness and pervasiveness that would characterize the sexual revolution of the 1960s. Nevertheless, the gulf between the public and the private narrowed considerably (233–234).

Historian Nancy Cott describes how the achievements of individual women in areas generally considered the prerogative of men also were much publicized in the 1920s, such as when Gertrude Ederle swam the English Channel in 1926, Amelia Earhart crossed the Atlantic by air in 1928, and Mary Pickford rose meteorically from film star to corporate partner in United Artists (1987: 215). Such publicity broadened notions of women's capabilities and chipped away at the notion that women's place was only in the private sphere of the home. While the lives of these celebrities did not reflect the opportunities available to most women, there were important changes afoot—especially for middle-class women.

In particular, Cott points to significant advances made in educational attainment and in the professions. A staggering 40 percent of students who received college degrees in 1930 were women, a percentage twice as high as in 1900. While this percentage would remain about the same in the 1940s and 1950s, the percentage of doctorates awarded to women rose and then declined sharply during the first half of the twentieth century. In 1920 and 1930, women were awarded approximately 15 percent of all doctorates, as contrasted to both 1910 and 1950, when the number was closer to 10 percent (219).[22] She attributes women's educational advances in the 1920s to the expansion of higher education and the professions during this era. She explains women's advances relative to men's by the fact that "brains and commitment" were the only prerequisites for professional expertise, unlike in business and politics, where wealth and social connections were more important (216). However, traditional areas of women's work—such as nursing and teaching—explain much of the increase in women's professional roles between the waves. In terms of advanced degrees, the fields of psychology and anthropology were most welcoming to women.[23] As will be shown below, significant works were written by women in these academic disciplines between the waves.

New Directions in Psychoanalytic Thought

Among the more influential works written by women between the first and second waves were the psychoanalytic theories of Karen Horney and Melanie Klein. Although Horney was German-born, in the 1920s she immigrated to the United States where she practiced psychiatry for the rest of her life. She was the first woman to present a paper on gender differences in psychology, and her writings on this topic can be found in *Feminine Psychology* (1932). A recurring theme in her work is how both men and women have a need for self-actualization. She discusses how cultures worldwide encourage women to be dependent on men and how women develop a will to please and overly esteem men. Horney viewed women's focus on charm and beauty as being at variance with their self-actualization, but she thought childbirth enabled women to satisfy this need.

Horney's views on gender differences were based on significant revisions of the theories of Sigmund Freud. Although she acknowledged and agreed with Freud on many issues, she disagreed with several of his key ideas. She criticized his theory of penis envy, arguing that women's envy or jealousy simply reflected men's greater power in the world and that womb envy was equally present among men. She viewed men's focus on occupational achievements as reflecting their attempts to compensate for their inability to give birth to children. She also revised Freud's oedipal complex to argue that men's "dread of the vagina" is far deeper than their dread of castration by the father.

> I think it is probable that the masculine dread of the woman (the mother) or of the female genital is more deep-seated, weighs more heavily, and is usually more energetically repressed than the dread of the man (father). (Horney [1932] 2005: 155)

Horney attributed this "vagina dread" to the boy child judging his penis as too small for his mother's genitalia: "his original dread of women is not castration anxiety at all, but a reaction to the menace to his self respect" (157). For her, it is present in all males and is evidenced in dream analysis. It is a deeply held secret that is "energetically repressed" by forms of denial reflected in men's objectification of women as well as in the various ways they disparage women as being "too ridiculous" to dread (154–155). Horney also used this vagina dread to explain male homosexuality.

Although Horney's critique of Freud's notion of penis envy was embraced by many feminists, Melanie Klein's psychoanalytic work had a greater impact on feminist thought. Klein, like Freud, was born in Austria but immigrated to England in the 1920s. Freud and his psychoanalyst daughter Anna followed a decade later as fascism gained political hegemony in Austria. In London, protracted debates ensued between Kleinians and Freudians, and these divisions within the field of psychoanalysis were exported to the United States.

Many of Klein's writings can be found in *Love, Guilt and Reparation: And Other Works, 1921–1945* (1975). Unlike Freud, whose ideas concerning children were derived primarily from his work with adult patients, Klein worked directly with children and analyzed their play as a form of emotional communication. She also was a cofounder of objects relations theory, which explores the dynamic process of developing psychological orientations as one grows in relation to others—particularly mothers. The objects in this theory are both real others in one's world as well as one's internalized images of others. Klein argued that object relations are initially formed during early interactions with primary caregivers and that they exert a strong influence throughout one's life. Although Klein's work was not a feminist analysis, it heavily influenced second wave feminist psychoanalytic frameworks (as will be shown later in this chapter).

Cross-Cultural Contributions on Sex and Gender

Anthropologist Margaret Mead's work gained widespread professional and media attention because of its focus on sexual practices and gender roles. Her first book, *Coming of Age in Somoa* (1928), discussed how young Samoan women deferred marriage for many years while enjoying casual sex. Mead's reports of healthy and permissive attitudes toward sex in the South Pacific earned her a reputation as champion of liberal sexual practices.[24] Her later book, *Sex and Temperament in Three Primitive Societies* (1935), documented how gender roles were culturally relative and socially learned. Based on her ethnographic studies of three different tribes in New Guinea, she showed how none of these tribes had gender roles that were typical of those found in the United States or other Western, industrial societies. The Arapesh people were pacifists who rarely engaged in warfare; both men and women took on gender roles that in the West were considered feminine. Among the Mundugumor, the opposite was the case; both men and women were aggressive and warlike, taking on roles that Westerners perceived as masculine.

In the third tribal group studied by Mead, the Tchambuli, men spent their time decorating themselves while the women worked at more instrumental tasks—thus reversing what in the West would be considered traditional gender roles. As Mead ([1935] 2005: 157–158) writes:

> Each of these tribes had, as has every human society, the point of sex-differences to use as one theme in the plot of social life, and each of these three peoples has developed that theme differently. In comparing the way in which they have dramatized sex-difference, it is possible to gain a greater insight into what elements are social constructs, originally irrelevant to the biological facts of sex-gender.

By showing how gender is socially constructed and culturally variable, Mead's work became a classic of the U.S. women's movement.

Shakespeare's Sister

Another important influence on feminist thought between the first and second waves was the work of British novelist and essayist Virginia Woolf. She was a founding member of the Bloomsbury group in London—one of the most famous salons of the twentieth century. **Salon culture** flourished in Europe during and after the Enlightenment as intellectual, social, political, and cultural elites gathered to exchange ideas. Salons provided important venues for women in societies where men defined and controlled intellectual life. Women were responsible for selecting guests and deciding whether the salon would be primarily social, literary, or political. Before higher education was open to women, salons served almost like informal universities where women and men were able to read their own works, engage in critical analyses, and be introduced to the works and ideas of other intellectuals. For example, Elizabeth Montagu's eighteenth-century salon became known as the Blue Stocking Society. Later **bluestockings** was used as a pejorative term for educated women[25] (Bodek 1976; Goodman 1994).

While Woolf's novels like *Mrs. Dalloway* (1925) and *To the Lighthouse* (1927) garnered her a place as one of the few women writers included in the canon of great literature, her nonfiction work *A Room of One's Own* (1929) spoke more directly to feminist issues. Here Woolf articulated feminists' frustrations about how "great literature" was too often written from a male vantage point:

> "Chloe liked Olivia," I read. And then it struck me how immense a change was there. Chloe liked Olivia perhaps for the first time in literature. . . . And I tried to remember any case in the course of my reading where two women were represented as friends. . . . But most often without exception they are shown in their relation to men. It was strange to think that all the great women of fiction were, until Jane Austen's day, not only seen by the other sex, but seen only in relation to the other sex. And how small a part of a women's life that is. (Woolf [1929] 2005: 152)

In one of the most famous selection's from *A Room of One's Own,* Woolf introduces **Shakespeare's sister**—a "poor poet who never wrote a word" and who "was buried at the crossroads" without fame or fortune precisely because women of that era were precluded from opportunities for education and writing. Yet Woolf argues that Shakespeare's sister "still lives"—"she lives within you and in me, and in many other women who are not here tonight" (154). Here begins Woolf's clarion call for women to take up the pen, to make their voices heard and to write their way into history. Later feminists criticized Woolf for her upper-middle-class vantage point that ignored the plight of poor and working-class women—especially women of color (Lorde 1984). However, in this piece Woolf does not entirely ignore the material prerequisites for literary activism. Along with the "habit of freedom" and the "courage to write exactly what we think" she also includes as prerequisites for writing "five hundred pounds" (economic independence) and "a room of one's own" (a place free from interruptions and the demands of everyday life) (Woolf [1929] 2005: 154). For Woolf, women's relegation to work in the home—to "washing up dishes and putting children to bed"—posed serious obstacles to literary production (154).

Although some nineteenth-century women authors could boast greater commercial success than Charles Dickens, breaking the glass ceiling of the academic canons of literature was another matter. The term *canon* historically referred to sacred religious texts. In academia, it denotes the most essential and highest quality texts of an academic discipline. Such disciplinary canons confer excellence, and historically women authors have been excluded from them. Nathaniel Hawthorne's frequently quoted claim that he left the United States to get away from "that mob of damned scribbling women" suggests how women's writings were deemed lesser. A revealing account of this problem can be found in Annette Kolodny's "Dancing through the Minefield: Some Observations on the Theory, Practice, and Politics of a Feminist Literary Criticism" (1980). Written a half century after *A Room of One's Own*, Kolodny's work echoes Woolf's frustrations in describing the obstacles faced by women writers. Kolodny laments:

> We [feminists] find ourselves endlessly responding to the *riposte* that the overwhelmingly male presence among canonical authors was only an accident of history—and never intentionally sexist—coupled with claims to the "obvious" aesthetic merit of those canonized texts. It is as I say, a fruitless exchange . . . dragging us, again and again, through the minefield. (25)

POLITICAL CHANGES IN LIBERAL FEMINISMS IN THE TWENTIETH CENTURY

Like their Enlightenment predecessors, liberal feminists in early modernity *focused on the individual rather than on groups* and viewed individuals as the masters or mistresses of their own fate. Having overthrown an absolute monarchy, these early liberals were skeptical of a strong, activist government and wanted freedom from government intervention in their lives. Such demands as the right to bear arms or the right to privacy were designed to protect citizens from a powerful and abusive government. Moreover, many first wave liberal feminists did not view all people as equal. Among moderate liberals, there were feminists who viewed men and women as differently endowed, just as there were many feminists who held classist and racist views. Only left–liberal feminists in early modernity appeared willing to grant all people—irrespective of race, class, or ethnicity—equal rights and equal opportunities. Yet, even these left–liberals only supported formal equality.

Formal equality means that citizens have equal civil rights in front of the law, but it does not mean that they all start from the same location. Formal equality ignores the impact of ascribed statuses on individuals' life chances and only rewards individuals for **achieved status** or status attained through individual merit. By contrast, *substantive equality* recognizes both achieved and ascribed statuses. **Ascribed statuses** are positions acquired at birth, such as one's race, gender, and the social class into which one is born. While ascribed statuses are accidents of birth and no fault of the individual, they can heavily impact life chances. They also affect *groups* rather than simply individuals. For example, ascribed statuses affect such basic resources as whether one's parents are literate or whether they have sufficient income to provide for a child's health, education, and welfare. Ascribed statuses also have been used to exclude people from certain occupations or positions in society—as in the cases where race and gender have historically precluded people from attending universities or holding government offices. Ascribed statuses entail even more subtle differences, such as the presence or absence of social networks that enhance upward mobility. Thus not all children start at the same place when bodily inscriptions, such as race and gender, or social privileges, such as inheritance (material, cultural, and social), can play a major role in life chances. This is why children born into wealthy families are often said to be born on third base and require fewer individual achievements to hit a home run in life. In short, ascribed statuses reflect *persistent and systemic social structural inequalities.*

One of the major transformations of liberal feminism in the twentieth century was the increasing recognition of the role played by ascribed statuses and social structural inequalities. Liberal politics began to change with the Great Depression and the New Deal of President Franklin Roosevelt. The new twentieth-century liberalism, often referred to as *welfare liberalism*, holds that the forces of government should be marshaled to protect the rights of minorities and to provide some means of social support for those who fall through the cracks when the free market system fails. Unlike nineteenth-century liberals who feared too much government intervention in individuals' lives, welfare liberals were willing to expand government involvement in social life.

The new social movements of the post–World War II era, such as the civil rights movement and the women's movement, furthered liberal feminists' recognition of the need for legislation to protect racial/ethnic minorities and women. Consequently, during the second wave, liberal feminists began embracing protective legislation that was designed to make up for past discrimination based on ascribed statuses, such as **affirmative action**—legislation which gave preferential hiring or selection to qualified women of all races and to qualified men from racial minorities. Like their first wave predecessors, second wave liberal feminists continued to criticize male dominance in major social institutions, such as education, religion, government, and the economy. However, they developed far more serious critiques of the inequalities in interpersonal life when they addressed women as mothers, wives, and lovers. This focus on interpersonal relations was accompanied by an increasing role given to therapy as well as demands for men to be more involved in child rearing. Second wave liberal feminists would make the personal political in many other ways, such as their far greater success in establishing laws to deal with reproductive rights and domestic violence.

LIBERAL FEMINISMS IN LATE MODERNITY

World War II not only lifted the U.S. economy from the depths of the Great Depression, it also jettisoned vast numbers of women into the wartime economy and into occupations traditionally held by men. While Rosie the Riveter is the iconic example of this transformation, women also entered many white collar occupations formally dominated by men. Yet when male soldiers returned home in the immediate postwar era, clear preference was given to them in both hiring and advanced education because they were viewed as the major breadwinners. Married and/or pregnant women often were forced by both private and public hiring policies to leave their jobs in favor of men (Cott 1987: 225). Not surprisingly, the immediate postwar era also witnessed a revival of the "cult of domesticity" that idealized the role of homemaker. However, many women remained in or entered the paid work force in the postwar decades due the rapid growth of the U.S. economy. Indeed, women workers as a percentage of all workers increased steadily from 1940 to 1970 (Deckard [1979] 1983: 306).

Yet powerful images of the postwar, intact nuclear family with stay-at-home moms and breadwinner dads continue to beam into our living rooms in countless reruns of 1950s television sitcoms. The *Leave it to Beaver* and *Father Knows Best* families portrayed on these sitcoms are often romanticized as the types of families that were typical of American society in earlier decades. However, as feminist scholars of U.S. family life point out, families of the 1950s were not only subject to problems of alcohol abuse and family violence in an era when divorce was more difficult to obtain, but they also were "a historical fluke, based on a unique and temporary conjuncture of economic, social, and political factors" (Coontz 2000: 28). These factors included an incredibly prosperous economy[26] given the devastation that World War II had wrought on America's global economic competitors as well as the enhanced roles that the U.S government played in providing job training, educational subsidies, low-interest home loans, and the highway and sewer construction that enabled suburban development (28–29). Although intact, traditional (homemaker/breadwinner) nuclear families became the yardstick or standard by which other family forms were deemed deficient (Smith 1993b), they were the product of unique historical conditions that were beginning to erode in the mid-1970s, as Americans became to feel the impact of deindustrialization and globalization. Nevertheless, it was during the so-called heyday of American family prosperity that the gender inequalities hidden in the household began to be revealed.

One of the early triggers for the rise of a second wave liberal women's rights movement was President John F. Kennedy's establishment in 1961 of the Presidential Commission on the Status of Women (created at the urging of Esther Peterson,[27] director of the Women's Bureau). Some feminists argue that this was Kennedy's way of repaying hundreds of women who had worked in his campaign without giving them high-level government jobs (Deckard [1979] 1983: 320). This short-lived commission documented American women's second-class citizenship and established fifty state commissions to address these inequalities.

Dissatisfied with the lack of progress made on their recommendations, many women involved in this work joined Betty Friedan in 1966 to found the **National Organization for Women (NOW)**—the first feminist organization to be established in the United States in almost fifty years (Freeman 1979). At NOW's second national conference in 1967, the major order of business was drawing up the NOW Bill of Rights. The eight demands that were finally agreed upon can be found in Box 2.3.[28]

BOX 2.3

1968—National Organization for Women (NOW) Bill of Rights

WE DEMAND:

I. That the United States Congress immediately pass the Equal Rights Amendment to the Constitution to provide that "Equality of rights under the law shall not be denied or abridged by the United Sates or by any Sate on account of sex," and that such be immediately ratified by the several States.

II. That equal employment opportunity be guaranteed to all women, as well as men, by insisting the Equal Employment Opportunity Commission enforces the prohibitions against sex discrimination in employment under Title VII of the Civil Rights Act of 1964 with the same vigor as it enforces the prohibitions against racial discrimination.

III. That women be protected by law to ensure their rights to return to their jobs within a reasonable time after childbirth without loss of seniority or other accrued benefits, and be paid maternity leave as a form of social security and/or employee benefit.

IV. Immediate revision of tax laws to permit the deduction of home and child care expenses for working parents.

V. That child care facilities be established by law on the same basis as parks, libraries, and public schools, adequate to the needs of children from the pre-school years through adolescence, as a community resource to be used by all citizens from all income levels.

VI. That the right of women to be educated to their full potential equally with men be secured by Federal and State Legislation, eliminating all discrimination and segregation by sex, written and unwritten, at all levels of education, including colleges, graduate and professional schools, loans and fellowships, and Federal and State training programs, such as the Job Corps.

VII. The right of women in poverty to secure job training, housing, and family allowances on equal terms with men, but without prejudice to a parent's right to remain at home to care for his or her children; revision of welfare legislation and poverty programs which deny women dignity, privacy and self-respect.

VIII. The right of women to control their own reproductive lives by removing from penal codes laws limiting access to contraceptive information and devices and laws governing abortion.

Excerpted from Judith Hole and Ellen Levine, *Rebirth of Feminism* (New York: Quadrangle, [1971] 1975), pp. 439–440

NOW's 1968 political platform was criticized by lesbian feminists for failing to address heterosexism and lesbian issues. One of the more famous demonstrations against the invisibility of lesbian issues in NOW's policies was called the Lavender Menace protest—because as president of NOW Betty Friedan refused to address lesbian issues and referred to lesbians as the "lavender herring" of the women's movement (Deckard [1979] 1983: 340; see chapter 3). When Rita Mae Brown resigned from NOW over this issue she stated: "Lesbianism is the one word which gives the New York NOW Executive Committee a collective heart attack" (quoted in Deckard [1979] 1983: 341). In 1971, after repeated protests, NOW changed its position and included pro-lesbian resolutions in its political platform (343).

NOW's 1968 Bill of Rights was criticized also for not adequately addressing racial issues. Critiques of liberal feminism by women of color are discussed later in this chapter and in chapter 5. However, it should be noted that, from its inception, NOW welcomed women of color into the organization. One of the cofounders was Pauli Murray—a famous African-American civil rights advocate, lawyer, writer, poet, and ordained priest. Murray also founded the *Women's Rights Law Reporter*, the first legal periodical to focus exclusively on women's rights. She contributed to the NAACP's litigation strategy in *Brown v. Board of Education* (which in 1954 mandated the desegregation of public schools) and was the first African-American woman ordained as an Episcopal priest in the United States.

In 1971, congresswomen Bella Abzug, Elizabeth Holtzman, Shirley Chisholm, and Patricia Schroeder joined Friedan and feminist writer Gloria Steinem to form the National Women's Political Caucus, an organization designed specifically to elect women to political office. The following year, Chisholm (the first African-American congresswoman) made a credible run in the Democratic presidential primaries, thereby breaking barriers both as a woman and an African-American. That same year witnessed the creation of a new magazine called *Ms.*, and its initial, trial run of 300,000 sold out in only eight days (Gosse 2005: 162). As a women's magazine, it could boast a number of novel acts. ***Ms.* magazine** was the first U.S. women's magazine to feature prominent women demanding the repeal of laws that criminalized abortion, to advocate for the ERA, to rate presidential candidates on women's issues, to commission a national study on rape, and to put domestic violence and sexual harassment on the cover of a women's magazine.

Other influential liberal feminist organizations include the League of Women's Voters, the Women's Equity Action League, and the organization of Federally Employed Women (FEW). These national organizations are formally, hierarchically, and bureaucratically organized, with elected officers, boards of directors, and bylaws (Freeman 1979), and have numerous local branches. A major liberal organization that focuses on constitutional rights—the American Civil Liberties Union (ACLU)—often provided feminists with legal services and waged their legal battles in the courts. The ACLU assisted in one of the second wave's major victories—the U.S. Supreme Court's 1973 decision in *Roe v. Wade*, which established a constitutional right to privacy, a woman's right to control her body, and the legalization of abortion.

From the "Feminine Mystique" to the "Feminist Mystique"

Many U.S. feminists view Betty Friedan's *The Feminine Mystique*, first published in 1963, as sparking the second wave of the U.S. women's movement. Friedan's focus was on white, college-educated, heterosexual, middle-class women who had achieved what in the post–world War II era was considered as the "American Dream" for women. That is, they were stay-at-home moms with children, breadwinner husbands, homes of their own, and sufficient disposable income to live comfortably. Nevertheless, Friedan documented how many of these women were experiencing deep and persistent depression. Some medical journals referred to this phenomenon as "housewives' syndrome" or "housewives' fatigue." However women had a difficult time articulating the source of their depression, as did other observers and experts. Therefore Friedan called this phenomenon **"the problem that has no name"**:

> The problem lay buried, unspoken, for many years in the minds of American women. It was a strange stirring, a sense of dissatisfaction, a yearning that women suffered in the middle of the twentieth century in the United States. Each suburban wife struggled with it alone. As she made the beds, shopped for groceries, matched slipcover material, ate peanut-butter sandwiches with her children, chauffeured Cub Scouts and Brownies, lay beside her husband at night—she was afraid to ask even of herself the silent question—"Is this all?" (Friedan [1963] 2005: 198).

Friedan rooted this "problem" in the lack of individual fulfillment these educated women found in being housewives and mothers. While earlier socialist feminist writings, such as Charlotte Perkins Gilman's "The Yellow Wallpaper" (1892) and Simone de Beauvoir's nonfiction work *The Second Sex* (1952), had pointed to a similar problem (see chapter 4), these works were not well known to women in postwar America—especially given how the cold war and McCarthyism had suppressed radical thought.

Although Friedan's book was not as radical as these earlier works, it led many women to question the constraints of gender roles in the United States. For example, Friedan documented how by the end of the 1950s the average age of marriage for American women had dropped while the birthrate had increased. She contrasted how "a century earlier women had fought for higher education," whereas in the 1950s they went to college not to get a doctorate, but "to get a husband" (Friedan [1963] 2005: 198). She sarcastically suggested that a new college degree had been established for women—the Ph.T.—an acronym for putting their husbands through college. She lamented how young women were taught to pity "unfeminine" women who wanted to be poets, physicians, or presidents. "Truly feminine" women did not want careers, higher education, political rights, or the independence and opportunities that the first wave struggled to achieve. Friedan called this notion of femininity that crippled women's aspirations the **"feminine mystique"** and blamed it not simply on socialization, but on a more systemic, gendered worldview that formed the normative core of U.S. society:

> In the fifteen years after World War II, this mystique of feminine fulfillment became the cherished and self-perpetuating core of contemporary American culture. Millions of women lived their lives in the image of those pretty pictures of the American suburban housewife, kissing their husbands goodbye in front of the picture window, depositing their stationwagonsful of children at school, and smiling as they ran the new electric waxer over the spotless kitchen floor. . . . Their only dream was to be perfect wives and mothers. . . . They had no thought for the unfeminine problems of the world outside the home; they wanted the men to make the major decisions. They glorified in their role as women, and wrote proudly on the census blank: "Occupation: housewife." (199)

Friedan reported that by the early 1960s, "the doors of all those pretty suburban houses opened a crack" as magazines, newspaper columns, and books began discussing how thousands of American housewives felt "empty," "incomplete," or "as if they did not exist" (200–201). Women received advice from marriage and family counselors as well as from psychotherapists and psychologists on how to adjust to their role as housewives. Friedan argued that "the problem could not be understood in the generally accepted terms by which scientists have studied women, doctors have treated them, counselors have advised them and writers have written about them." (202). Rather *the problem was rooted in deeply ingrained assumptions about men's and women's gender roles that experts and laypeople had not questioned.* "We can no longer ignore the voice within women that says: "I want something more than my husband and my children and my home" (203).

Friedan's writings came under attack by second wave women of color who were angered by the white, middle-class focus of *The Feminine Mystique* (see chapter 5). As intersectionality theorist bell hooks (1984: 1–2) writes of Friedan:

> She did not discuss who would be called in to take care of the children and maintain the home if more women like herself were freed from their house labor and given equal access with white men to professions. She did not speak of the needs of women without men, without children, without homes. She ignored the existence of all non-white women and poor women. She did not tell readers whether it was more fulfilling to be a maid, a babysitter, a factory worker, a clerk, or a prostitute, than to be a leisure class housewife.

A number of feminists also protested the "ideology of competitive, atomistic liberal individualism" that permeates Friedan's book (hooks 1984: 8). In the sarcastically titled article "Why Can't a Woman Be More Like a Man?" Jean Bethke Elshtain (1981: 251) criticized liberal feminists for singing "a paean of praise to what Americans themselves call the 'rat race'" and for suggesting that women should emulate traditional masculine values. Anarchist feminist Carol Ehrlich echoed similar criticisms:

> Women need to know . . . that feminism is not about dressing for success or becoming a corporate executive. . . . It is not being able to share a two career marriage and take skiing vacations and spend huge amounts of time with your husband and two lovely children because you have a domestic worker who makes all this possible for you, but who hasn't the time or money to do it for herself. (Quoted in hooks 1984: 7–8)

Even Friedan came to realize that this competitive, male model of success was a mistake. In *The Second Stage* (1981), published almost two decades after **The Feminine Mystique**, Friedan coined the term "the feminist mystique" to discuss how 1980s "superwomen" were no less oppressed than the 1960s "stay-at-home" moms had been. Concerned that her daughter's generation "ran themselves ragged in the name of feminism trying to be fulltime career women as well as housewives and mothers," Friedan reversed the theoretical underpinnings of her liberal feminism (Tong 1998: 27–29). Whereas *The Feminist Mystique* argued that men and women were essentially the same, *The Second Stage* argued that men's and women's orientations to social life were different. In this theoretical reversal, Friedan reverted to a more psychological approach, employing the notion of "alpha" and "beta" styles to distinguish between men's and women's orientations to social life ([1981] 1988: 236). The former described a task-oriented, instrumentally rational "masculine" orientation, while the latter referred to a more fluid, flexible and interpersonal "feminine" sensitivity. Her 1963 book had encouraged women to become more like men, while her 1981 book called for women to rediscover the family circle and "the power of the women's sphere" as the "basis of their identity" (249). Her hope was for an androgynous future where men and women adopted both "masculine" and "feminine" traits. Nevertheless, by citing feminists' major failure as their "blind spot about the family" (43), *The Second Stage* provided ammunition for the pro-family antifeminists who defeated the ERA. Yet contrary to the claims of both Friedan in regard to feminists' "blind spot" and the antifeminists who portrayed feminism as "anti-family," a number of feminist theorists—particularly those who embraced psychoanalytic approaches—focused heavily on the important role of mothering.

Liberal Psychoanalytic Feminisms

It has been argued that second wave liberal feminists did not view men and women as fundamentally different but, rather, as the same in terms of their ability to participate as equals in modern societies (Nicholson 1997: 3).Yet, while liberal feminists did not believe in biological essentialism, they did foster a form of socially constructed essentialism that was deeply rooted in early childhood socialization processes. Not only can distinct male and female psychological orientations be found in Friedan's *The Second Stage*, but this type of essentialism is evident also in liberal psychoanalytic feminist analyses of gender and intimacy.

A left–liberal psychoanalytic analysis is presented in *Intimate Strangers: Men and Women Together* (1984), written by psychotherapist Lillian Rubin.[29] Rubin's central question was: what is the effect on gender relations that women mother? Building on Melanie Klein's psychoanalytic theory, Rubin uses object-relations theory to argue that deep-seated, psychosocial orientations are created in the process of an infant's/child's separation from his or her primary object of affection—the mother. For Rubin mothering refers to the primary care of the infant/child; it does not have to be done by the biological mother or even by a woman. To be mothered implies to be nurtured in the most elemental sense—to be cared for in numerous ways that range from physical bodily care to emotional and psychological care (Rubin 1984: 42).

While it may be comforting to think that there is some innate maternal instinct or biological imperative to mothering, Rubin points out how history suggests otherwise. Even if we simply look at Western societies, family historians have documented how mothering practices varied immensely. Edward Shorter (1975) described how it was common practice among upper-class families in eighteenth-century France to send their newborns away for the first few years of life to live with wet nurses. Lawrence Stone (1977: 114) concluded that from the sixteenth to the eighteenth centuries, English mothers were "often almost as remote and detached from their infant children as fathers" and described how the streets of London were littered with abandoned babies. Moreover, in earlier centuries the maternal death rate was so high that many children were raised by stepmothers or other relatives. History suggests that mothering is a social construction and that the bond between mother and child that we speak of today may itself be a product of modernity. Nevertheless, Rubin's major point is that mothering—whether done well or not—has historically been done by women. It is a woman who is the object of our first attachment to another human being, and for Kleinian-inspired psychoanalytic feminisms this is a profound attachment.

All infants and toddlers must separate from their primary caregivers in order to begin the process of becoming separate selves. However, girls and boys experience this separation differently according to Rubin. Because boys have to separate from their mothers to take on adult male gender roles, this leads them to break the ties between affect (emotion) and role learning. They compartmentalize their emotional lives and become more independent and autonomous social actors. In contrast, because girls, like their mothers, enact adult female gender roles, the tie between affect and role learning is maintained. Thus, girls' identification processes are relational—a girl's self-concept is embedded in social relations, and she defines herself in relationship to others.

According to Rubin, the most significant difference between girls and boys is the degree to which they view themselves as separate or connected. Her reference is to deep-seated and often unconscious processes, a "child within" who continues to affect one's intimate relationships throughout life:

> Thus, in adulthood, when we find ourselves in an intimate relationship, we each experience again, even if only in highly attenuated form, those early struggles around separation and unity—the conflict between wanting to be one with another and the desire for an independent, autonomous self. (Rubin 1984: 52)

The data on which Rubin's *Intimate Strangers* are based are the result of years of psychotherapy with heterosexual couples, and a few examples will illustrate her findings. She describes how her women patients frequently voiced complaints that men distanced themselves from their emotional lives. Men were described as being "closed off from what they're feeling," as "being too rational" and "intellectualizing" rather than "verbalizing their feelings" (70–71). Differences in relational views of self also were evident in gender-specific responses to the concept of independence. Whereas men generally associated independence with freedom, control, power, self-sufficiency, and happiness, women in general had more negative associations with the word. Even women who associated positive features with independence tended to qualify their remarks by saying that the concept also elicited feelings of fear and loneliness. Overall, women tended to think in terms of interpersonal relationships, whereas men rarely used the term *independence* in such relational contexts (120–121). Such mismatched interests, concerns, and behaviors are the reasons why Rubin titled her book "intimate strangers."

Over the next decade, more popularized versions of these findings appeared in self-help books, and such best-selling nonfiction as John Gray's *Men Are from Mars, Women Are from Venus* (1992). Instead of calling men and women "intimate strangers," Gray suggests that they live on different planets. Liberal feminist Deborah Tannen's *You Just Don't Understand: Women and Men in Conversation* (1990) is more scholarly that Gray's account, but it too is written in an accessible style and topped the charts as a best-selling work of nonfiction. Tannen does not discuss intragalactic estrangement but, rather, portrays men and women as living in different cultures and speaking different languages—a "different words, different worlds" approach (23). Both authors suggest a moderate–liberal approach to solving gender and intimacy problems. They urge men and women to understand and to empathize with their respective gendered differences. In short, better communication is their key to bridging the different cultures and different worlds of gender relations.

Critics argue that both Gray and Tannen fail to theorize how power relations at the structural level are re-created and maintained at the interactional level as a result of these gendered differences (Crawford 1995: 96; Mann, 2000: 490–491). For example, Tannen provides numerous examples throughout her work of how men dominate conversations—especially in public spheres. She even admits that she might be accused of "copping out" or "of covering up real domination with a cloth of difference" (Tannen 1990: 209). However, she nonetheless chooses to see understanding as the key to social change:

> Understanding style differences for what they are takes the sting out of them.... You can ask for or make adjustments without casting or taking blame.... Understanding the other's ways of talking is a giant step toward opening lines of communication. (298)

In contrast, Mary Crawford (1995: 106) argues that this type of rhetoric makes everyone—and no one—responsible. For similar reasons, other critics have characterized Tannen's work as "depoliticized" (Cameron 1992: 467; Freed 1992: 1–2). At the very least, Tannen's liberal feminist approach calls for individual rather than institutional change.

Unlike Tannen's focus on the individual, Rubin's left–liberal approach focuses on how systemic gender inequalities are created and reproduced by these deep-seated gender differences. Rubin argues that these gender inequalities will continue to be reproduced so long as it is only women who "mother." While psychoanalytic therapy provides a means by which individuals can come to understand and to better cope with the problems that arise from these deep-seated, psychosocial orientations, *transcending these inequalities requires that both men and women mother.* On the societal level, this would necessitate a number of significant reforms, such as establishing paid maternity and paternity leaves, providing family-friendly policies in the workplace, and ensuring that day care centers and other forms of early childhood education are staffed by both men and women. In addition, equal pay and part-time or flexible employment opportunities would be required to enable women and men to financially provide for their families while both are mothering.

A slightly different marriage of psychoanalytic theory and feminism is undertaken by Carol Gilligan in her influential work *In a Different Voice: Psychological Theory and Women's Development* (1982). Gilligan focuses on the topic of moral development and especially on Freud's essay "On Narcissism," first published in 1914. Here Freud traces the development of the capacity to love, which he equates with maturity and psychic health. He locates its origins in the contrast between love for the self and love for mother. However, as Gilligan describes, in dividing the world of love into narcissism and "object" relationships, he finds that while men's development becomes clearer, women's becomes increasingly mysterious and difficult to discern. For Freud, men develop morality and a clear sense of self, while women's psychology is a "dark continent" for psychoanalysis (Gilligan 1982: 313).

Gilligan argues that Freud's theory of moral development is male-centered and gender-blind. She finds a similar male-centered approach to moral development in writings on this topic by psychologist Lawrence Kolhberg.[30] Kolhlberg had theorized six stages of moral development that ranged from an immature egocentric understanding of fairness to his most mature stage, which rests on the freestanding logic of equality and reciprocity (stages 5 and 6). However, in developing these stages of moral development Kolhlberg had used only male subjects.

Gilligan was the first to consider gender differences in moral development. She found that when girls made moral decisions they were more concerned with relationships with other people than were boys. She concluded that girls are more oriented toward an "ethic of care" while boys are more oriented toward an "ethic of justice." For Gilligan, the morality of care that emphasizes interconnectedness emerges to a greater degree in girls owing to their early connection in identity formation with their mothers. The morality of justice emerges from masculine identity formation that requires separation and individuation from the mother. For boys, this separation heightens their awareness of the difference in power relations between children and adults and engenders a more intense concern over inequalities and justice. For girls, their continued attachment to their mothers fosters an understanding of morality viewed within a context of social relations and connectiveness.

The feminist psychoanalytical approaches discussed above root distinct differences in the psychosocial development of males and females to the gendered consequences of women mothering. In turn, they all have been criticized for their essentialist approach to gender that attributes common or essential attributes to *all* women and ignores important differences between women, such as those by race, class, or sexual orientation. For example, a study on African-American men and women did not find the same patterns of female "connection" versus male "autonomy" described by these feminist psychoanalytic approaches (Grimes, Mann, and Shavor 1998).[31] Nevertheless, they had a signicant impact on both academic and popular thought.

Liberal Ecofeminisms

As will be shown throughout this text, ecofeminism is not a monolithic or homogeneous body of thought but, rather, encompasses a diverse array of theoretical perspectives, discourses, and political practices. The fundamental feature that the various ecofeminisms share is that they *link the domination of nature and the domination of women.* Whether these links are conceptualized as socially constructed or biological often distinguishes different types of ecofeminism. To explain as well as to distinguish different ecofeminist approaches, I draw heavily from the works of two major historians of ecofeminism, Vera Norwood's *Made from This Earth* (1993) and Carolyn Merchant's *Earthcare* (1995), *Ecology* (1999) and *American Environmental History* (2007).

It was not until the post–World War II era that the environmental destruction inflicted by and on human societies began to *encompass the entire earth.* Nonrenewable fuels, such as coal, oil, and gas, upon which modern, industrial societies were so dependent, were being exhausted, as were many mineral resources. Although the replacement of natural raw materials by synthetics began in the early decades of the 1900s, over the long term these synthetic fibers resulted in an abundance of nonbiodegradable waste. The toxic wastes and by-products of urbanization, industrialization, and militarization were plaguing not just local communities but also communities across the globe. In two hundred years, industrial societies had done more damage to the natural environment than all previous civilizations combined (Balbus 1982: 362–363). Perhaps it took such world-scale damage to make people critically aware of the dangers of continuing on the path of environmental destruction. However, this also meant a very late start for mobilizing mass-based movements that could confront the highly developed forms of production, consumption, and warfare that imposed intolerable burdens on the planet's ecosystem.

As Carolyn Merchant points out, it is notable that works by women launched two social movements in the United States that would eventually come together to struggle for environmental sanity. Rachel Carson's *Silent Spring* (1962) caused a not-so-silent uproar by making the question of the care of the earth a public issue. Carson's vivid prose and dire warnings of the deadly effects of chemical insecticides, such as DDT, that progressively accumulated in the soil and contaminated the human food chain captured the attention of the nation and is credited with launching the U.S. environmental movement (see Box 2.4). A year later Betty Friedan's *The Feminine Mystique* (1963) triggered the second wave of the women's movement in the United States. Although the environmental movement and the women's movement emerged separately, many women participated in both (Merchant 1995: 140).

BOX 2.4

Rachel Carson's *Silent Spring*: A Feminist Awakening Story

Rachel Carson's *Silent Spring* (1962) is credited with sparking environmental activism in the 1960s. This book rallied large numbers of women to question the safety of the chemical pesticides used in their homes, gardens, and municipalities. Women figured prominently in lawsuits filed to stop local spraying of pesticides (Norwood 1993). Newspapers were quick to make headlines of women's key role in this public outcry. Coincidentally, the same year that *Silent Spring* was published, a woman physician, Frances Kelsey, was a key figure in well-publicized debates over the U.S. ban of the birth defect–causing drug thalidomide. As one newspaper reported, "Men may dominate the sciences, but women are making the headlines" (168).

The public furor generated by *Silent Spring* led many men of science to publicly vocalize their sexist views. They attacked Carson's personal life to try to invalidate her findings and appealed to prevalent sexist stereotypes. The science editor of *Time* magazine wrote a scathing review of *Silent Spring*, accusing its author of being "hysterically overemphatic." Other reviewers used the word "hysterical" and suggested that women were incapable of truly understanding science (169). In the face of this sexist backlash, Carson began linking environmental issues to women's issues and called on women to take "positive action" for redirecting the research agendas of government, science, and industry away from harmful policies and toward ensuring that the world remained fit for future generations (170). Thus, Carson's role in mobilizing women for environmental activism in late modernity was similar to Ellen Swallow Richards's role in mobilizing the municipal housekeeping movement in early modernity (Merchant 1995: 140).

The theoretical connections between these two movements came to be known as **ecofeminism**. First coined in 1974 by French feminist Françoise d'Eaubonne, the term *ecofeminism* (écologie-féminisme) describes the diverse range of women's efforts to save the earth as well as transformations in feminist thought that have resulted in new conceptualizations of the interrelationships between women and nature (Diamond and Orenstein 1990: ix). U.S. feminists were quick to pick up on and extend the links d'Eaubonne made between women and nature. The first U.S. conference on Women and the Environment was held in 1974 in Berkeley, California. In 1980, spurred by the Three Mile Island catastrophe in 1979, a number of feminists organized another major conference, Women and Life on Earth, in Amherst, Massachusetts. Later that same year, mass support for the Women's Pentagon Action to protest nuclear war and weapons hallmarked the emergence of ecofeminism as a social movement in the United States (Merchant 1995: 150 and 157).

Contemporary liberal ecofeminism is grounded in the Enlightenment-inspired belief that both men and women are rational social actors and that rational means, such as science and technology, can advance social progress. For liberal ecofeminists, the notion of reason is even used to distinguish humans from animals and other forms of nature. For them, human potential for rational thought makes human beings superior to nature. Thus, they take an **anthroprocentric** or homocentric approach to the environment in which humans are viewed as superior to other natural forms and nature is viewed as an object that exists to provide for the needs of human beings. Any intrinsic value to nature derives only from a human perspective. Conversely, any abuse or degradation of nature is viewed in terms of its negative outcomes for human beings (Merchant 1995: 8–9).

For liberal ecofeminists, social progress is achieved through human control of nature. Often described as a **technocratic approach,** this approach relies on the use of science and technology to fix social and environmental problems (85). For example, Rachel Carson's solution to environmental pollution from pesticides was not to abandon science or technology but, rather, to develop biological rather than chemical methods of insect control. The basic underlying assumption here is that technological solutions exist or can be created to correct socially or naturally induced problems (Balbus 1982: 364). Because liberal ecofeminists view men and women as more similar than different, women, if given equal opportunities to education and occupations, can contribute just like men to rationally fostering ecological progress .

Often ignored by this technocratic approach is that rational means can create more serious problems than they can fix. The premier example of this is the development of nuclear power—a scientific advance that won the Nobel Prize when it was first developed. Critics of this technocratic approach point to the divergence between formal rationality (rational means) and substantive rationality (rational goals) and the recognition that the technocratic mentality, itself, could be a major source of environmental problems. In contrast, liberal ecofeminists view environmental problems as primarily resulting from the overly rapid use and misuse of natural resources as well as the failure of local, state, and national governments to regulate hazards and pollutants (Merchant 1995: 9). Increased environmental education and stricter laws and regulations are their major demands. Moreover, liberal ecofeminists do not view environmental degradation as historically specific to any one type of society but, rather, as a problem that could occur in any type of society, be it capitalist, socialist, or even premodern. Liberal ecofeminists are not anticapitalist, as are many of their radical counterparts, but neither do they advocate laissez-faire approaches to the economy, as conservatives do. Instead, they champion a more active role by citizens and governments to curb environmental excesses and to foster environmentally sustainable alternatives. Merchant cites organizations, such as the Sierra Club and the Greenbelt Alliance, where U.S. liberal ecofeminists have played important roles (9).

A SHORT HISTORY OF GENDER ANALYSES

A major contribution of second wave liberal feminists was to make gender a core concept in feminist analysis. By highlighting the distinction between biological sex and socially learned gender, they focused on how gender roles could be socially transformed through conscious social and political action to foster a more egalitarian society. In turn, by identifying the various ways in which gender differences are learned and reinforced by social institutions they fostered a rethinking of many disciplinary frames. Although first wave feminists recognized how masculinity and femininity were socially learned, they did not use the term gender. They simply alluded to these differences or used other concepts, such as Mary Wollstonecraft's "femininity" or Charlotte Perkins Gilman's "excessive sex distinctions" (see chapter 4).

The term *gender* was first introduced between the first and second waves by medical and psychoanalytic research on sexual pathologies. The term *gender identity* referred to a person's subjective, self-understanding of his or her sex and was used to deal with cases where individuals' self-understandings differed from their biological anatomies (Marshall 2000: 21). Prior to and during the early second wave, social scientists were slow to use gender as a concept, more frequently using **"sex roles"** (Komarovsky 1946 and 1953; Parsons and Bales 1955; Maccoby 1966; Astin, et al. 1975). Though feminists, such as Mirra Komarovsky (1946; 1953) and Eleanor Maccoby (1966) pointed to contradictions and inequalities in sex roles, the more conservative structural functionalist approach of Talcott Parsons and Robert Bales (1955) prevailed in academia in the 1950s and early 1960s. Unlike the individualistic and subjective nature of gender in earlier psychological literature, the concept of sex roles shifted the focus to the normative structure of society and highlighted how individuals as social actors learned and performed socially prescribed or socially appropriate roles (Marshall 2000: 23; Hess and Ferree, 1987). Here attention focused on sex role socialization, sex role maintenance, and sex role strain.

Feminist critiques of this normative framing of sex roles were many. Even when employed by feminist scholars, sex role theory was tainted by the hegemony of functionalist analyses in which male and female sex roles were viewed as functional and complementary to the workings of modern societies. Equally pervasive at this time in the social sciences was the view that the intact nuclear family was the "normal" and most functional family form in modern, industrial societies (Parsons 1965: 1). It was argued that **expressive roles**—emotional, people-oriented, caretaking roles played by women—complemented **instrumental roles**—impersonal, task-oriented roles played by men. Together these gender-specific roles fostered a functional sexual division of labor between husbands and wives within nuclear families and positive role models for children.

As many feminists pointed out, such a gendered division of labor simply gave theoretical legitimation to the doctrine of separate spheres where the private world of the home was deemed women's sphere and the public world outside of the home was deemed men's sphere. Depicting these sex roles as functional and complementary ignored not only class differences between women (given that many women worked of necessity outside of the home) but also the structural inequalities *within* the household that accompanied such a gendered separation of private and public spheres. Feminist critics highlighted the inequalities entailed when housework and child rearing done by housewives/mothers were unpaid while work outside the home by husbands/fathers earned income, as the term *breadwinner* describes. This meant that homemakers were dependent on the benevolence of breadwinners for their income and financial security. Moreover, by emphasizing women's roles as expressive roles, women's emotional labor of love was highlighted while the physical labor involved in cooking, cleaning, and child care was as invisible as it was unpaid. Feminist critics argued that these sex roles were not complementary and equal; rather, they were separate and unequal (see domestic labor debates in chapter 4).

Whether the terms sex roles or gender roles were used, the very concept of roles ignored power, privilege, and inequality. As Barbara Marshall (2000: 24) points out, role theorists rarely used the terms "class roles" or "race roles" because they recognized the structural inequalities involved. By contrast, sex roles were made to appear natural despite the claim that such roles were socially learned. In turn, while other roles reflected specific areas of social life, such as parental roles or occupational roles, males and females performed sex roles in *all* spheres of their life. An important contribution of these feminist critiques was to insist on the gendered dimensions of *all* aspects of social life, which the concept of "role" failed to reflect.

More left-wing feminist critics of sex role theory highlighted how gender relations were power relations that were found at all levels of social analysis from the individual, to the cultural, to the institutional. Joan Acker focused on the gendered nature of different institutions—particularly bureaucratic workplaces and formal organizations (Acker 1992: 566). Through such efforts, gender analysis was transformed from a focus on social roles that individual actors play to a social structural phenomenon that affects all areas of social life. Similarly, Judith Lorber (1994: 1) discussed gender as a social institution that "establishes patterns of expectations for individuals, orders the social processes of everyday life, is built into the major social organizations of society, such as the economy, ideology, the family, and politics, and is also an entity in and of itself." Lorber also discussed the integral relationship between **social structure** and **social agency** by illuminating how the patterned social relationships that form the institutional architecture of social structures are constructed through everyday social acts or practices—such as the way we dress or the way we wear our hair (Lorber 1994). In this way the individual and society, as well as the micro and macro levels of society, were better linked

Candace West and Don Zimmerman's influential article "Doing Gender" (1987) was one of the earliest articles to highlight how gender is an ongoing social practice or accomplishment. Their analysis came out of the field of ethnomethodology—a field that not only prides itself on making the social practices of everyday life its focus but also highlights how people construct the worlds in which they live through their practices. As West and Zimmerman so aptly put it:

> Our purpose in this article is to propose an ethnomethodologically informed, and therefore *distinctively sociological, understanding of gender as a routine, methodical, and recurring accomplishment*. . . . When we view gender as an accomplishment, an achieved property of situated conduct, our attention shifts from matters internal to the individual and focuses on the interactional and, ultimately, institutional arenas. . . . Rather than as a property of individuals, we conceive of gender as an emergent feature of social situations: both as an outcome of and a rationale for various social arrangements and as a means of legitimating one of the most fundamental divisions of society. (125, my emphasis)

A more recent text that follows a distinctively sociological, social constructionist path is *Gendering Bodies* (2008) by Sara Crawley, Lara Foley, and Constance Shehan. Among the beauties of this text are its accessibility and student-friendly explanations of how gender constructs the body and what is meant by "doing gender." As will be shown in chapter 6, treating gender as a verb and viewing the subject as produced by their gender performances is characteristic of feminist postmodern, poststructural and queer analyses. In short, social constructionist approaches to gender that take both modern and postmodern forms are more prevalent in feminism today.

In summary, over time feminist analyses shifted from the position that gender was a subjective identity or internalized norm that led social actors to act in certain ways to the position that gender practices produce or constitute the subject and identity. As such, gender moved from being the cause of certain behaviors or practices to being the effect of these practices. In turn, earlier feminist claims that sex is biological while gender is social also eventually became passé—as the more radical constructionist feminisms that emerged on the heels of the second wave would treat both sex and gender as socially constructed (see chapter 6). Readers who prefer a more detailed history of gender analyses should see *Revisioning Gender* (2000) by Myra Marx Ferree, Judith Lorber, and Beth Hess.

DEFEAT OF THE EQUAL RIGHTS AMENDMENT

> Equality of rights under the law shall not be denied or abridged by the United States or by any State on account of sex.

The simple statement above was the proposed Equal Rights Amendment (ERA). After a long and difficult battle, the defeat of the ERA in 1982 was a crushing blow to the second wave. The political climate had significantly changed since the 1960s and early 1970s. By the late 1970s the Moral Majority's so-called family values campaigns had captured the national limelight, and conservative Republicans were beginning to enjoy a sweep of electoral victories. These right-wing political successes were due in large part to how Ronald Reagan's 1980 presidential campaign and the **STOP-ERA movement** led by Phyllis Schlafly adeptly united fundamentalist Christians and secular conservatives. The Reagan and George H. W. Bush victories in the 1980s transformed the composition of the U.S. Supreme Court and federal district courts that in the 1970s had been quite friendly to second wave feminist demands. A successful backlash to the women's movement was under way.

Susan Marshall's analyses of the defeat of the ERA in "Keep Us on the Pedestal: Women against Feminism in 20th Century America" [1989] (1995) draws parallels between the antifeminist campaign against suffrage in the late nineteenth and early twentieth centuries and the antifeminist campaign against the ERA in the 1970s and early 1980s. Marshall discusses how three major themes—God, country, and family—were utilized in both of these antifeminist movements. Relying on Scripture to argue for women's subordination was a tactic of both campaigns and sparked first wave feminist Elizabeth Cady Stanton's efforts to write *The Women's Bible* (1898). For Schlafly, the antitheses of a God-fearing, democratic society were feminism and socialism. She frequently portrayed advocates of either -ism as undermining religious doctrines and as "seditious radicals who agitate and demonstrate and hurl demands at society" (Schlafly 1977: 10). Because many second wave feminists had been involved in the anti–Vietnam war movement (see chapter 9), Schlafly viewed feminists as unpatriotic allies of socialism. She also made much of how the ERA would require women to go into combat and sparked fears that this would undermine the military. In these ways, the themes of God and country were used against feminists and helped forge an alliance between fundamentalist Christians and more secular, pro-war conservatives.

Marshall argues that the most effective tactic of the STOP-ERA movement was how they used the theme of family against the second wave. In particular, this movement criticized feminists for "deliberately degrading the homemakers" (Schlafly 1977: 86). In *The Power of the Positive Woman* (1977), Schlafly even quoted Betty Freidan to buttress her claims that feminism ignored the family. For her, the ERA was "an elitist upper-middle class cause" whose destructive antifamily stance would harm men, women, and children (125). One of her more compelling points was how working-class women would never find work outside of the home more appealing that being a homemaker:

> If you think diapers and dishes are never-ending, repetitive routine, just remember that most jobs outsides of the home are just as repetitious, tiresome and boring. Consider the assembly-line worker who pulls the same lever, pushes the same button or inspects thousands of identical pieces of metal or glass or paper, hour after weary hour; the stenographer who turns out page after page of typing . . . it is ludicrous to suggest that they are more self-fulfilling than the daily duties of a wife and mother in the home. (125)

Even the title of her movement—STOP-ERA—cleverly highlighted these issues. In this antifeminist acronym, STOP stood for Stop Taking Our Privileges (meaning the privileges of being a stay-at-home mom), while ERA referred to the Extra Responsibilities Amendment (the extra responsibilities women would shoulder if they had to work both inside and outside of the home).

This critique of feminism clearly struck a chord with white, working-class women. Although the data from the small number of empirical studies on the antifeminist movement of the 1970s and early 1980s is inconclusive, they suggest that the STOP-ERA movement received much of its support from white, working-class homemakers (Marshall [1989] 1995). It appears that the second wave ignored how the economic prosperity of the postwar era had made it possible for many U.S. white, working-class women to be stay-at-home moms for the first time in their families' histories. For these women, "occupation housewife" was clearly a privilege as compared to blue collar and lower level white collar work, even though this brief window of prosperity was soon coming to an end. Marshall's analysis points to the failure of second wave feminists to address the concerns of these working-class women. In contrast, during their successful campaign for suffrage, the first wave had done a better job of organizing across class lines.

Second wave feminists' support for reproductive rights also was construed by conservatives as being antifamily. Their pro-choice stance on abortion proved to be one of the most contentious political issues in the second half of the twentieth century. The 1973 Supreme Court decision in *Roe v Wade* that legalized abortion sparked the mobilization of the antifeminist religious right and undermined passage of the ERA. Feminist support for sex education and accessible birth control only added fuel to the fire. These heated political battles over reproductive rights continue to be waged today.

Overall, the STOP-ERA movement made significant headway by chastising feminists for being antifamily despite the important work the second wave did on family issues. While conservatives criticized feminists' pro-choice stance on abortion and their support for birth control and sex education, they failed to mention the attention the feminist movement had given to child bearing and child rearing. They did not discuss how the feminist self-help movement had fostered major improvements in childbirth and lactation. Women who gave birth in the

1940s and 1950s often were anesthetized during the birthing process and had few of the options available today for natural childbirth or prenatal birthing classes (Baumgardner and Richards 2000). Even as late as 1970 it was rare for fathers and other loved ones to participate in births. The feminist self-help movement made great strides in improving the birthing process and enabling both mothers and fathers to participate in this process. The second wave also made the availability and quality of day care key issues. Conservatives did not discuss how a Republican President—Richard Nixon—vetoed feminist and bipartisan efforts to enhance government support for day care or how Schlafly's Eagle Forum had lobbied against this legislation (Mann 1986: 242).[32]

CONCLUSION: FROM REFORM-ORIENTED TO REVOLUTIONARY FEMINISMS

To pave the way for the following chapters, it is important to point out that most histories of the second wave in the United States characterize it as originating from two different groups of women who had distinct politics and who embraced different forms of political organization—the Women's Rights Movement and the Women's Liberation Movement (Freeman 1979, Deckard [1979] 1983, Nicholson 1997). This chapter focused primarily on the Women's Rights Movement and its predecessors given its focus on liberal feminisms. Chapters 3, 4, and 5 focus on the Women's Liberation branch and its predecessors in early modernity. Jo Freeman's article "Women's Liberation Movement: Its Origins, Organizations, Activities, and Ideas" (1979) describes the major differences between these branches, and I draw from her work below.

The activists in the Women's Rights branch were older and tended to be professional women. They worked within traditional democratic venues and used established legal, political, and media institutions to pursue primarily legislative and judicial victories at the state and national levels (Freeman 1979). They established large national organizations that were formally, hierarchically, and bureaucratically administered, with elected officers, boards of directors, and bylaws.

By contrast, the younger and more radical branch of the second wave prided itself on its lack of formal, hierarchical organization. They developed in an amoebic rather than a formally organized fashion, except in some cities that had coordinating committees (Freeman 1979: 559). The various groups in this radical branch maintained links to each other through pamphlets, journals, newsletters, conferences, and overlapping memberships, as well as through joint protests and demonstrations. Their pamphlets and practices often took underground and do-it-yourself (DIY) forms so prevalent in the third wave today. This younger branch also focused more on the local, community level. They developed women's bookstores, rape crisis and battered women's shelters, and independent presses that produced and distributed much of the second wave's early theoretical writings. They also were central in developing women's culture by fostering women's music, art, literature, and poetry.

Many of these younger women had cut their political teeth not in electoral politics, but in social movements, such as the civil rights movement and the anti–Vietnam War movement. Like their first wave predecessors in the abolitionist movement, these women became disillusioned with the sexism they experienced within these larger social movements. Infamous examples include how a paper written in 1965 by two feminists in the Student Non-Violent Coordinating Movement (SNNC) elicited catcalls as well as storms of ridicule and verbal abuse or how feminists demanding that attention be given to women's issues at the 1966 Students for a Democratic Society (SDS) convention were pelted with tomatoes and thrown out of the convention (Deckard [1979] 1983: 327). Many of these women left these male-led movements to develop their own feminist organizations.

In concluding, it is important to emphasize that the initiatives undertaken by the Women's Rights branch often were supported by the Women's Liberation branch. Many feminists were members of both branches, and the vast majority of second wave feminists supported reform even if they did not think these reforms went far enough. Indeed, *one of the hallmarks of second wave feminism was its ability to mobilize mass-based, collective action*. After the defeat of the ERA, this mass-based activism subsided, but the production of feminist theory continued and even flourished in the final decades of the twentieth century. As the following chapters will show, the women's liberation branch of the U.S. women's movement produced the most feminist theory both during and after the second wave (Nicholson 1997: 10).

Additional writings by liberal feminists on global issues are examined in chapters 8 and 9.

CRITICISMS OF LIBERAL FEMINISMS

1. That many liberal feminists (particularly in the nineteenth century) ignore the role played by ascribed statuses acquired at birth because they focus on formal equality (equal civil rights in front of the law) and support meritocracy (rewards based on individual merit or achievement). However, ascribed statuses heavily impact life chances and affect groups rather than simply individuals (Pease, Form, and Rytina 1970).

2. That liberal feminism is based on an ideology of competitive individualism that not only ignores the plight of women who are not winners in this competition but also implies that for women to succeed they should emulate traditional masculine values of aggression and competition (Elshtain 1981).

3. That liberal feminists' political concerns represent a white, middle-class vantage point that ignores the plight of women marginalized by race or class. Critics assert that liberal feminists take an essentialist approach to feminism which suggests that all women share the same concerns and interests and fail to recognize differences between women (hooks 1984).

4. That because liberal feminists are reform-oriented and work only within the system to pursue primarily legislative and judicial victories they have no critique of the role that capitalism plays in gender inequality and are unable to critique how the overall patriarchal system must be transformed for women's liberation (Hartmann 1981).

NOTES

1 Barbara Deckard ([1979] 1983: 277) provides data to show that by the time the Nineteenth Amendment was passed, the NAWSA had about two million members, but these data are rough estimates.

2 See www.now.org.

3 The general consensus is that John and Harriet coauthored "Early Essays on Marriage and Divorce" and that Harriet wrote "Enfranchisement of Women." "The Subjection of Women" was written by John after Harriet died. Nevertheless, John claimed that everything he wrote after 1840 were "joint productions" based on ideas shared by both of them (Rossi 1970: 39). For an interesting discussion of the debates over the authorship of these works as well as Harriet's intellectual contributions, see Rossi 1970.

4 Although known as Voltaire, his name was Jean François-Marie Arouet. He added Voltaire later.

5 Locke wrote: "Let us suppose the mind to be, as we say, white paper, void of all characters, without any ideas."

6 A similar law called the head and master law prevailed in Louisiana because Napoleonic law, rather than English common law, was the basis of this state's legislation.

7 See Mann 1990b

8 John Stuart Mill worked for the East India Company and held similar views on the need for literacy requirements in colonies. See Rossi 1970.

9 Mary Wollstonecraft's unmarried intimate relationships with men and women led many of her critics to associate her with the free love movement (see chapter 3).

10 Her sister Tennessee Claflin also was a well-known women's rights advocate who embraced many of Victoria's views.

11 Although her name did not appear on the ballot, Woodhull was nominated to run for president by the Equal Rights Party.

12 Marge Piercy provides a fictional account of first wave debates over sexual practices and reproductive freedom that interweaves the lives of Stanton, Anthony, Woodhull, and Anthony Comstock (founder of the Society for the Study of Vice) in her novel *Sex Wars: A Novel of Gilded Age New York* (2005).

13 Parts of this section on first wave environmental activism first appeared in S. A. Mann, "Pioneers of Ecofeminism and Environmental Justice," *Feminist Formations* 23, no. 2 (2011): 1–25. Copyright © 2011 Feminist Formations. Reprinted with permission by The Johns Hopkins University Press.

14 Davis (1831–1910) was a journalist in the iron mill town of Wheeling, West Virginia, and drew inspiration for her novels from her firsthand accounts of people's lives. She sought not only to improve women's position but also to effect social change for blacks, immigrants, Native-Americans, and the working class in general. Below, Davis ([1861] 1995: 198) describes the danger of smoke in a town dominated by coal-burning industries:

> The idiosyncrasy of this town is smoke. It rolls sullenly in slow folds from the great chimneys of the iron-foundries and settles in black, slimy pools on the muddy streets. . . . Smoke everywhere! . . . breathing from infancy to death an air saturated with fog and grease and soot, vileness for soul and body.

15 Some contemporary feminists argue that Richards's focus on enhancing the scientific skills involved in domestic labor glorified housework and failed to challenge women's relegation to the home (Eherenreich and English 1978: 153–154, 161 and 164). Others point to women involved in the white settlement houses and in the black women's clubs as more deserving of the title pioneers of ecofeminism (Mann 2011).

16 For example, the worst yellow fever epidemic in U.S. history occurred in 1878, during which more than five thousand people died in Memphis while twenty thousand deaths were reported in the whole of the Mississippi Valley (Humphreys 1999)

17 For a discussion of other women associated with Hull House, see Lengermann and Niebrugge-Brantley 1998.

18 These early-twentieth-century groups referred to themselves as "international" organizations. However, they only included representatives from countries in Europe and North America (Ferree and Tripp 2006).

19 During the first two decades of the twentieth century, approximately 770,000 blacks migrated to the North (Taylor 2002: 25).

20 From July of 1917 to March of 1921, bombings occurred on average once every twenty days (Washington 2005: 134).

21 Even environmental historians who are the most sensitive to issues of race, class, and gender often fail to include the black women's clubs in their discussions of environmental activism in the nineteenth and early twentieth centuries (Mann 2011).

22 The Great Depression reduced women's options, as preference was given to men (presumably the primary breadwinners) in both occupational and advanced educational opportunities. The striking pattern of women's slippage in professional fields in the 1930s underlines how women worked under a systemic economic disadvantage in competition with men (Cott 1987: 225).

23 For example, women constituted 18 percent of the American Psychological Association's membership in 1923 and reached a peak of 34 percent in 1928 (Cott 1987: 223).

24 Although she was married three times, her daughter's biography of Mead hints at an intimate relationship between Benedict and Mead. In turn, Mead spent her final years in a close personal and professional relationship with anthropologist Rhoda Metraux, and letters between the two also suggest that their relationship was intimate. Although Mead never identified herself as lesbian or bisexual, she did believe that people's sexual orientations evolved throughout their lives.

25 As a pejorative term, *bluestockings* was equivalent to calling these educated women dowdy or frumpy. A reference to the worsted wool stockings worn by men, bluestockings were considered unfashionable as compared to black silk stockings. See www.encarta.msn.com/dictionary_1861591415/bluestocking.html (last accessed October 10, 2010).

26 Per capita income increased by 35 percent, and consumer spending skyrocketed. Food expenditures rose by 33 percent in the five years following World War II, clothing expenditures rose by 20 percent, and purchases of household furnishings and appliances climbed by 240 percent. By 1960, 87 percent of American families had a television and 75 percent possessed a car (Coontz 2000: 24–25).

27 Esther Peterson (1906–1997) was a leading activist in the labor movement, the women's movement, and the Consumer's League. She served as a labor organizer for the American Federation of Teachers and as a lobbyist for the AFL-CIO and was president of the Consumer's League. During the administration of President John F. Kennedy she directed the first President's Commission on the Status of Women and served as an assistant secretary of labor.

28 It was not until the late 1970s that NOW chose to focus its energies on passing the Equal Rights Amendment (ERA) to the virtual exclusion of its other concerns.

29 It is possible that Lillian Rubin's politics are even further left than her book *Intimate Strangers* suggests. Rubin wrote a number of important books on gender and class, including *Worlds of Pain: Life in the Working-Class Family* (1976) and *Families on the Fault Line* (1994).

30 Kolhberg was famous for his revisions and extensions of Jean Piaget's theory of moral development. Hence, in her work Gilligan is indirectly critiquing the views of a number of famous psychologists.

31 The author thanks Jean Ait Belkhir, editor of *Race, Gender, & Class* for providing permission to reprint sections of "Gender and Intimacy: Do Race and Class Matter?" *Race, Gender &, Class* 1998;5 (2):54–77 by Michael Grimes, Susan Mann and James Shavor in this section of the text.

32 The Comprehensive Child Development Act had passed both the House and the Senate in 1971. Nixon vetoed this act claiming that day care would "Sovietize" American children (Mann 1986: 242).

CHAPTER 3

Radical Feminisms

> Sexism is the foundation on which all tyranny is built. Every social form of hierarchy and abuse is modeled on male-over-female domination.
>
> —Andrea Dworkin

INTRODUCTION

Of all the feminist perspectives that arose in late modernity during the second wave of the U.S. women's movement, radical feminism made the greatest strides in bridging the personal and the political. Radical feminists were foremost among second wave feminists for emphasizing how women's emancipation required that women understand, protect, and control their own bodies. They also were key voices in the second wave that drew attention to lesbian issues as well as to various oppressions that had previously been relegated to the private realm of interpersonal life, such as rape, domestic violence, and sexual harassment. Indeed, whether they were highlighting the dangers or the pleasures associated with sexual practices, radical feminists exposed and analyzed women's issues that previously had been closeted or hidden in the household.

The phrase **the personal is political** was first coined in 1969 by radical feminist Carol Hanisch and soon became a slogan embraced by second wave feminists from a wide array of political perspectives. Like a double-edged sword, "the personal is political" has both emancipatory and disciplinary features. It is emancipatory in that it can empower women by illuminating how many gender-related "personal" problems should be addressed not at the individual level but, rather, collectively as problems rooted in social and political institutions. Prior to the modern women's movement, issues like rape, domestic violence, and sexual harassment were treated as personal problems that should be dealt with privately and individually. Battered women often were told they provoked the violence or that they "made their bed" now they "should sleep in it." Rape victims often were made to feel that they were to blame—that they had somehow provoked or enticed their rapist. By claiming that the personal is political, feminists in the late 1960s and 1970s argued that these so-called personal problems were political issues and demanded that they be addressed collectively by the women's movement as important political concerns. Thus, solutions were sought at the macrostructural or institutional level rather than at the microinterpersonal or household level.

The disciplinary side of the "the personal is political" enjoined feminists to live their politics in their everyday lives—to practice what they preached. If they were engaged in personal lifestyle choices that undermined feminist politics, they should make every effort to change their lives so that their personal practices were consistent with their political views. Chapter 7 will show how third wave feminists often rail against this disciplinary feminism of the second wave. However, at this point I want to highlight its positive features. Together the emancipatory and disciplinary dimensions of "the personal is political" were a powerful duo. They linked the macro and micro levels of society as well as social structure and human agency and called for a feminism that transformed both the individual and society.

PRECURSORS TO RADICAL FEMINISM IN EARLY MODERNITY BY JANE WARD AND SUSAN MANN

It is difficult to say who would best stand as precursors to radical feminism in early modernity. Radical feminism entails a woman-centered, revolutionary politics that is conscious of how men in particular and patriarchal institutions in general benefit from *control over women's lives and bodies.* This radical feminist stance is, in part, visible in the gender politics of anarchist and socialist feminists, such as Emma Goldman and Margaret Sanger, who fought for women's access to birth control and abortion under penalty of arrest or deportation and in the radical sexual and lifestyle politics of Victoria Woodhull. However, these feminists were aligned with political movements in which women were committed to working closely with men to achieve their political goals.

Perhaps a more women-centered example is Josephine Butler's "Letter to My Countrywomen, Dwelling in the Farmsteads and Cottages of England," written in 1871. Butler highlights how the Contagious Diseases Acts passed in England in the late 1860s were designed primarily for the military to protect soldiers and sailors from venereal diseases. This legislation required all prostitutes to be periodically examined by doctors. Failure to do so was grounds for arrest. If found to be diseased, women were sent to hospitals, where they remained until police were given certificates of their clean health. In "Letter to My Countrywomen" Butler calls these hospitals "prisons" because a woman could be "kept against her will for any length of time, not exceeding nine months" and could be forced to do "any work which the governor and nurses may think fit to demand of her" (Butler [1871] 2005: 90). Moreover, while hospitalized, accused prostitutes were not allowed to see their friends, clergy, or even their own lawyers without permission.

The Contagious Diseases Acts provided police with excessive powers of surveillance over women. Any woman (or girl) who was accused or simply suspected of being a prostitute could be ordered to submit to these medical procedures and "doomed to sin and shame for life" (88). There was no penalty for false accusations and no penalty for any man who used the services of prostitutes. The sworn oath of one policeman was sufficient cause, and anyone could write to the police and not be called upon to provide evidence. This made women vulnerable to blackmail and extortion by anyone angry with them. Indeed, just to be seen out late at night or "larking" about the streets and talking with men was sufficient grounds for suspicion (89). Butler highlights how these arbitrary laws were unjust and how they "encouraged men in vicious habits" (89). These laws also were heavily class-biased, making poor and vagrant women most vulnerable to accusation and arrest. As will be discussed in chapter 8, some late-nineteenth-century U.S. feminists criticized similar prostitution laws established by the U.S. military in U.S. overseas territories, adding a global dimension to these early modern, Western feminist concerns.

There also were women in early modernity who committed their personal and sexual lives to relationships with other women. However, because lesbianism was a modern social construction, it remained largely invisible in earlier eras. The focus of chapter 2 was changes in women's heterosexual practices. The following sections of this chapter will focus on lesbianism in early modernity and between the waves.

Lesbianism as a Modern Social Construction

The late nineteenth century witnessed some major institutional and economic changes that expanded women's sexual possibilities in addition to the circulation of ideas about free love and the feminist critiques of sexual practices within marriage noted in the previous chapter. The proliferation of women's colleges in the United States during the late 1800s opened the door for educated, upper-middle-class women to form intimate bonds with other women and to remain independent of financial and legal ties to men. Whether women went to college together, engaged in professional careers, or lived together as "kindred spirits" or "spinsters," freedom from marriage enabled many women to engage in intimate, romantic, and sexual relationships with other women and for such relationships to go relatively unnoticed. While women's sexual pleasure was a controversial subject in the nineteenth century, even more unimaginable was the idea that women might experience sexual pleasure with one another. Hence, such relationships generally remained under the radar of moralists and others who later would become sharply critical of homosexuality. In fact, it was not until 1869 that the term *homosexual* appeared in scientific literature and not until much later that the concept of homosexual or heterosexual identity was fully introduced to the general public. Although there is a wealth of historical evidence that both women and men have engaged in same-sex sexuality for as long as sex itself has existed, Victorian cultural and religious ideology linking sex with marriage and reproduction rendered these relationships either invisible or simply "friendly."

Furthermore, patriarchal conceptualizations of sex as a male-controlled and phallus-centered activity made sex between women unfathomable prior to the late nineteenth century. This heteropatriarchal construction of sex carried not only costs but arguably also some benefits, for women engaged in sexual relationships with women. As historian Lillian Faderman has illustrated in her research on the history of lesbian sexuality, the presumed impossibility of "love without a penis" meant that women "were allowed to demonstrate the most sensual behavior towards one another without suffering stigma" (Faderman 1981:149) What we now refer to as lesbian sex or desire hardly registered as sexual through much of the nineteenth century.

By the late 1800s, some journalistic accounts hint at the emergence of fears that allowing women access to education and to intimacy with other women might have negative consequences for heterosexuality in general and for marriage in particular. These concerns were not unfounded. American women who attended college were less likely than their counterparts to marry men and more likely to pursue professional careers and long-term partnerships with other women, sometimes referred to as "Boston marriages" (190). "Romantic friendships" between women were especially common in the context of women's colleges, one of few environments in which young women could form close relationships outside of families. Women's colleges were the site of romantic all-women dances and other social activities as well as places in which young women found academic and athletic role models among female professors, many of whom lived on campus as couples. Although the extent to which women students had sexual relationships with one another is uncertain, several indictors suggest that it was likely. A column in an 1873 Yale student newspaper describes college romances between women, also known as "smashes," "crushes," or "spoons":

> When a Vassar girl takes a shine to one another, she straightaway enters upon a regular course of bouquet sendings, interspersed with tinted notes, mysterious packages of "Ridley's Mixed Candies," locks of hair perhaps, and many other tender tokens, until at last the object of her attention is captured, the two women become inseparable, and the aggressor is considered by her circle of acquaintances as—smashed. (Quoted in Faderman 1991: 19)

According to Faderman, social conditions in the late nineteenth century were ideal for women to be able to express sexual desire for other women: "How could such excitements not lead to passionate loves," asks Faderman, "at a time when there was not yet widespread stigma against intense female same-sex relationships?" (20).

While wealthy white women were beginning to have access to colleges in the 1800s, women of color and poor white women were more likely to attempt to "pass" as men in order to gain some degree of access to the public sphere. For example, Terry Lovell (2000) points to over a hundred cases of women who successfully passed as soldiers in earlier eras before military medical exams precluded this possibility. The vast majority of these women were working-class women. Lovell suggests that because these women engaged in arduous labor not so different from the labor of working-class men it might have been easier for these women to pass as men.

Many of the concerns taken up by white, middle-class feminists in the nineteenth century—access to the public sphere, freedom of employment, free love, restrictive beliefs about female frailty or weakness—reflected these feminists' own racial and socioeconomic privileges. The nineteenth-century logic of separate spheres suggested that white, middle-class women required protection from the heartless, male-dominated, and sexually volatile public realm, yet women slaves, poor women, and prostitutes were not included in the narrow category of woman upon which such logic relied. Black women slaves and women factory workers (across various racial groups) engaged in backbreaking work as difficult as any manual labor undertaken by men, and women slaves and prostitutes were frequently subjected to the most brutal forms of sexual violence and torture. These abuses reflected a contradiction in Victorian gender ideology, one that would carry forward into the current era. White women, especially white middle- and upper-middle-class women were imbued with chastity, purity, and great maternal importance, while women of color and poor women of all races were regularly subjected to demeaning forms of sexual violence and social control (see chapters 4 and 5).

Consequently, even though we know little about the same-sex desires of nineteenth- and early-twentieth-century women, those we know about tend to be white, middle- or upper-class women and working-class women who were literate. Despite this race and class bias, it is worth noting that some of the most compelling examples of same-sex desire in this era come from prominent feminist activists. At the turn of the century, Jane Addams openly considered herself married to philanthropist Mary Rozet Smith, with whom she bought a house and shared a bed and to whom she wrote letters expressing great love and longing during her travels. Jane wrote to Mary: "You must know, dear, how I long for you all the time, and especially during the last three weeks. There is reason in the habit of married folks keeping together" (Quoted in Faderman 1991: 26). Emma Goldman, who refused identification with lesbianism when the label later entered public awareness, shared a very "romantic" vacation in the country with a female admirer and prostitute named Almeda Sperry. In letters to Goldman dated 1912, Sperry recalled Goldman's "beautiful throat that I kissed with reverent tenderness," "your sweet bosom, unconfined," the "rhythmic spurt of your love juice," and the moment when "you reached the climax . . . the moment I had complete possession of you" (34). Although Charlotte Perkins Gilman married, her first love was Martha Luther, and after her divorce she had several passionate affairs with women (Lengermann and Niebrugge-Brantley 1998: 108–109). The record is less clear for late-eighteenth and early-nineteenth-century feminists, such as Mary Wollstonecraft, who ultimately married but also wrote and spoke about her intimate and possessive relationships with women (Faderman 1981: 138–142).

At the same time that some prominent women activists were cultivating passionate relationships with one another in Europe and the United States, European male sexologists, such as Richard von Kraft-Ebing Havelock Ellis, had begun to theorize about the origins and characteristics of homosexuality, then known as "inversion." As John D'Emilio and Estelle Freedman discuss in *Intimate Matters: A History of Sexuality in America* ([1988] 1997), while Ellis's books were the object of censorship in his English homeland, his *Studies in the Psychology of Sex* (six volumes printed between 1897 and 1910) quickly found an American readership.

For Ellis, sex was "wonderful and lovely"—the "chief and central function of life." He did not think that sexual indulgence posed a threat to health or character and encouraged sexual gratification. He questioned the institution of marriage and advocated a period of "trial marriage" before couples made a lasting commitment and recognized that people might need a variety of sex partners. He wrote approvingly of masturbation and called for the removal of the stigma attached to homosexual behavior. For him, "sexual inversion" was a congenital condition and as "natural" as heterosexual behavior. While Ellis rejected the notion that women were passionless, he did discuss male and female orientations to sex as being distinctly different. He characterized men as active, aggressive, and sexually insistent and women as needing more attention and stimulus to be aroused (D'Emilio and Freedman [1988] 1997: 224).

As Michel Foucault pointed out, the homosexual subject was literally produced by scientific and medical discourses of the nineteenth century (Foucault [1976] 1980). Beginning in the 1880s, U.S. physicians began documenting cases of "contrary sexual impulse." Initially this was viewed as an acquired form of insanity, but as Ellis's writings became better known, medical opinion began to shift toward a congenital model. As D'Emilio and Freedman ([1988] 1997: 226) point out, it was not until the 1920s, when "Freudianism swept competitors from the field," that "the pendulum swung back to the position that homosexuality was an acquired condition" as well as a pathology. Moreover, according to many sexologists of this era, female inversion—including androgyny, sexual desire for women, and interest in activities associated with men—was not unrelated to the problem of feminism, which encouraged women to seek autonomy and to emulate men.

Sigmund Freud first discussed homosexuality in *Three Essays on the Theory of Sexuality* (1905). Unlike Ellis, Freud did not think sexual drives were inherited. Rather he thought all children were born "polymorphously perverce"—that is, that their sexual drives could be drawn to any object. It was childhood experiences that caused children's sex drive to be directed to members of the opposite or the same sex. This analysis fostered a psychiatric tradition of labeling nonheterosexual sexualities as perversions and aberrations. Indeed, one section of *Three Essays* gave parents tips on how to rear children to "normal" heterosexual adjustment. This equation of homosexuality with pathology would dominate American psychiatry until the 1970s.

Notably, long before second wave feminists would critique Freud, Charlotte Perkins Gilman saw his work on sex and sexuality as proof of the intertwining of patriarchal culture, morbid sexuality, and domination—part of a backlash against women's gains in economic independence. Her views of his work are prescient:

> The perverted sex-philosophy of Freud . . . seems to embody the last effort on the part of man to maintain his misuse of the female. . . . Not since the phallic religions of antiquity has sex-worship so strongly appeared. (Quoted in Lengermann and Niebrugge-Brantley 1998: 127).

In summary, theories of female homosexuality and any link between lesbianism and feminism received little popular or feminist attention until the early decades of the twentieth century. First wave feminists had few reasons to theorize lesbianism since the label and the stigma it would later carry was relatively unknown to them. Hence, our record of feminist thought on same-sex desire appears less in the form of educational speeches or essays and more in the form of personal correspondences between women who had little reason to hide their emotional and sexual attachments to one another. Historian Nancy Cott describes how, when young women rejected feminism in the 1920s, in part they did so because of the newly created association between feminism and lesbianism advanced by the new fields of psychoanalysis and sexology (Cott 1987: 279). It appears to have taken a few decades for the power of these new scientific discourses on sexuality to trickle down to the masses.

LESBIAN SEXUAL POLITICS BETWEEN THE WAVES

As John D'Emelio and Estelle Freedman point out in *Intimate Matters: A History of Sexuality in America* ([1988] 1997: 289), World War II created "substantially new erotic opportunities for the articulation of a gay identity and the rapid growth of a gay subculture." The war years fostered large migrations of people away from their families and away from small towns and rural areas. Cities provided more options for sexual expression, but residential segregation and the strictures placed on movements of people of color within white-controlled space meant that racism restricted these options (Collins 2004a: 109). Nevertheless, both the military and wartime factory work placed gays and lesbians of all races in more densely populated areas (and often in sex-segregated settings) where they were able to meet others with similar feelings and sexual interests. Some historians have described World War II as something of a "nationwide 'coming out' experience" (D'Emelio and Freedman [1988] 1997: 289).

These changes set in motion by the war continued after demobilization, as many lesbians and gay men did not return to their prewar geographic locations. Rather, they often stayed in cities and created gay institutions to bolster their identity. D'Emelio and Freedman discuss, for example, how gay bars began to be established in cities across the country in the 1940s, although they are careful to point out gendered differences in the ability to establish gay spaces. Not only did gay men make more income, but they also had greater access to public entertainment spaces without the "disreputable" connotations often associated with bar life for women. Gay men developed more gay bars, more neighborhood enclaves, and more bathhouses. The lesbian subculture was smaller and more hidden—especially for lesbians of the working and lower classes—though, unlike their wealthier counterparts, they too developed their own bar culture. Ironically, black lesbians were less likely to frequent these bars because of racial segregation, even though many were located in their own neighborhoods (Collins 2004a: 111).

By contrast, wealthy lesbians were able to provide private gay spaces modeled on the salon culture described in chapter 2. Among the more famous lesbian writers of the salon culture between the waves were Gertrude Stein and Alice

B. Toklas. While both Stein and Toklas were Americans, they lived most of their adult lives in Europe. Stein is author of some of the earliest coming-out stories, such as the short story "Miss Furr and Miss Skeene" (1922) and *Q.E.D.*, the latter written in 1903 but not published until 1950 under the title *Things as They Are*. Her book *The Autobiography of Alice B. Toklas* (1932)—which actually is Stein's autobiography—is well known in lesbian, gay, bisexual and transgender (LGBT) literature. Alice B. Toklas (often referred to as Stein's wife and the manager of her affairs) is probably best known for her own memoir, *The Alice B. Toklas Cookbook* (1933), which included a recipe for marijuana brownies that received far more publicity than her memoir.[1] The most famous lesbian novel written between the waves was Radclyffe Hall's *The Well of Loneliness* (1928). Although the main character's attitude toward her sexuality is anguished, the novel presents lesbianism as natural and makes a plea for greater tolerance. The novel is not sexually explicit but was nonetheless the subject of an obscenity trial in Britain, where attempts were made to have it banned and all copies destroyed. Publication in the United States was not allowed until 1949, after a long series of court battles.

The repression and surveillance of homosexuality in the United States from the early to mid-twentieth century accompanied its growing visibility. While more permissive attitudes toward heterosexual sex were gaining ground between the waves, restraints on lesbians and gay men increased. As homosexuality became named and studied, local, state, and federal governments mobilized against what was viewed as an underground world of sexual perversion, a homophobic onslaught that reached its peak during the 1950s and early 1960s.

Social scientific research on sexuality, such as Alfred Kinsey, et.al.'s *Sexual Behavior in the Human Male* (1943) and *Sexual Behavior in the Human Female* (1953) received much publicity in the popular press. Although these works were not intended for repressive purposes, their findings in regard to the unexpectedly high incidence of homosexual behavior were unsettling to mainstream mores. However, according to D'Emelio and Freedman, it was during the cold war period of the fifties and sixties that the greatest repression of homosexuals occurred. Politicians first latched onto the issue of homosexuality in February 1950—the same month that Senator Joseph McCarthy charged that the U.S. State Department was riddled with communists. Homosexuals within the government were deemed threats to national security. They were considered perfect targets for communist counterespionage due to their lack of "emotional stability" and "moral fiber" as well as the ease with which they could be blackmailed (D'Emelio and Freedman [1988] 1997: 292). Thus, the Red Scare was accompanied by a lavender scare, and Republican politicians jumped onto the anticommunist and antigay bandwagon. In 1950, the Republican national chairman sent a letter to seven thousand party workers warning them that "sexual perverts . . . have infiltrated our Government" and that homosexuals were "perhaps as dangerous as actual Communists." In June 1950 the Senate authorized a formal inquiry into the employment of "homosexuals and other moral perverts" in government (292).

The response to this panic over homosexuals in government was immediate and far-reaching. Dismissals from civilian posts increased twelvefold over the pre-1950 rate. After President Dwight D. Eisenhower was inaugurated, he issued an executive order barring gay men and lesbians from all federal jobs. The federal government's harsh stance encouraged local police to harass gays and lesbians with impunity. The FBI initiated a widespread system of surveillance, and the armed forces purged homosexuals from its ranks. One study in the mid-1950s estimated that over 12.6 million workers—more than 20 percent of the labor force—faced some type of loyalty-security investigations as a condition of employment.[2] For lesbians, who faced the same constricted employment options that all women faced in the post–World War II era, this cold war employment discrimination posed serious hardships (293). Leslie Feinberg's *Stone Butch Blues* (1993) highlights the violence and discrimination faced by lesbians in the cold war era. Feinberg's novel became an underground hit before it surfaced as mainstream literature. While it specifically portrays butch–femme culture, it is generally regarded as a groundbreaking work on gender and a classic of LGBT literature.[3]

While there were a number of small riots and demonstrations by lesbian and gay activists during the immediate post–World War II decades,[4] the **Stonewall riots** that took place in 1969 at a gay bar (the Stonewall Inn) in New York City often are cited as the defining event that marked the beginning of the lesbian and gay rights movement. Within two years after the spontaneous and violent Stonewall demonstrations, lesbian and gay rights groups had been established in many American cities. However, lesbian feminists at times found themselves in conflict with the gay rights movement. Many found gay men's attitudes and behaviors to be patriarchal and chauvinistic. Moreover, the issues most important to gay men—entrapment and public solicitation—were not shared by lesbians (D'Emelio and Freedman [1988] 1997: 294). Many left the lesbian and gay rights movement to form their own radical feminist groups.

The routes to radical feminism were many for both lesbians and heterosexual women. Some, such as Andrea Dworkin, came out of the New Left and the anti–Vietnam war movement. Dworkin was jailed for her antiwar activism, and among her first efforts to end violence against women were her protests against the sexual abuse of prisoners. Others initially worked in NOW until they felt forcibly pushed out by Betty Friedan's attempts to distance this organization from lesbian issues in the 1960s. It was not until 1971, after such radical feminists as Rita Mae Brown and Ti-Grace Atkinson had staged a number of protests at national women's conferences, that NOW finally began to address lesbian issues (Deckard [1979] 1983: 341–342). Brown's famous poem "Sappho's Reply" is reproduced in Box 3.1. Sappho was an ancient Greek poet whose writings centered on passion and love for all things beautiful, including people of both genders. The word *lesbian* derives from the island of her birth—Lesbos. "Sappho's Reply" pays tribute to those who have had the courage to live a lesbian life amid much suffering as well as to those who continue the struggle against lesbian oppression.

BOX 3.1

"Sappho's Reply"

My voice rings down through thousands of years.
To coil around your body and give you strength,
You who have wept in direct sunlight,
Who have hungered in invisible chains,
Tremble to the cadence of my legacy:
An army of lovers shall not fail.

"Sappho's Reply," by Rita Mae Brown. From *Poems* (Freedom, Calif.: Crossing, 1971). Reprinted on p. 580 in Linda Wagner-Martin and Cathy N. Davidson, eds., *The Oxford Book of Women's Writing in the United States* (New York: Oxford University Press, 1995).

RADICAL FEMINISMS IN LATE MODERNITY

The "Dialectic of Sex"

One of the earliest and most influential statements of radical feminism was Shulamith Firestone's *Dialectic of Sex* published in 1970. Firestone had been a key activist in founding the group Radical Women in New York. Their protest against the Miss America Pageant in 1968 was the first feminist demonstration of the second wave to get front-page coverage in the national press (Deckard [1979] 1983: 329). At this protest a sheep was crowned Miss America and a "Freedom Trash Can" was provided for women to throw away "women's garbage," such as "bras, girdles, curlers, false eyelashes and wigs" (329). Most likely this event contributed to the legendary labeling of second wave feminists as bra burners (the actual burning of bras was never documented). The tone and political stance of radical feminists in these early years is captured well in *The "BITCH Manifesto"* (1968) written by Joreen [Jo Freeman] (see Box 3.2).

BOX 3.2

Excerpts from "The Bitch Manifesto"

BITCH is an organization which does not yet exist. The name is not an acronym. It stands for exactly what it sounds like. . . .

BITCH does not use this word in the negative sense. A woman should be proud to declare she is a Bitch, because Bitch is Beautiful. It should be an act of affirmation by self and not negation by others. . . .

The most prominent characteristic of all Bitches is that they rudely violate conceptions of proper sex role behavior. They violate them in different ways, but they all violate them. Their attitude towards themselves and other people, their goal orientations, their personal style, their appearance and way of handling their bodies, all jar people and make them feel uneasy. Sometimes it's conscious and sometimes its not but people generally feel uncomfortable around Bitches. They consider them aberrations. They find their style disturbing. So they create a dumping ground for all who they deplore as bitchy and call them frustrated. Frustrated they may be, but the cause is social, not sexual. . . .

Therefore, if taken seriously, a Bitch is a threat to the social structures which enslave women and the social values which justify keeping them in their place. She is living testimony that woman's oppression does not have to be, and as such raises doubts about the validity of the whole social system. . . .

Bitches have to learn to accept themselves as Bitches and to give their sisters the support they need to be creative Bitches. Bitches must learn to be proud of their strength and proud of themselves. . . . Bitches must form together in a movement to deal with their problems in a political manner. They must organize for their own liberation as all women must organize for theirs. We must be strong, we must be militant, we must be dangerous. We must realize that Bitch is Beautiful and that we have nothing to lose. Nothing whatsoever.

"The BITCH Manifesto," by Joreen [Jo Freeman] (1968). Copyright by Jo Freeman, www.jofreeman.com. Reprinted on pp. 213–217 in *Feminist Theory: A Reader*, 2nd ed., edited by Wendy K. Kolmar and Frances Bartkowski (Boston: McGraw Hill, 2005).

Firestone states at the beginning of *The Dialectic of Sex* ([1970] 1981: 5) that her aim is "to develop a materialist view of history based on sex" in order to achieve for women's oppression what Karl Marx had achieved for class oppression. Rather than the social relations of production driving history as in Marx's theory, biological relations of reproduction drive history in Firestone's "dialectic of sex."[5] A major claim made by Firestone that became a central tenet of radical feminism is that *women's oppression is the earliest and most fundamental form of oppression and provides the model for all later forms of oppression*, such as those based on class, race, or sexual orientation.

Unlike other feminist frameworks that root women's oppression in sociohistorical conditions, Firestone ([1970] 1981: 8) *roots women's oppression in biology*:

> Women throughout history before the advent of birth control were at the continual mercy of their biology—menstruation, menopause, and "female ills", constant painful childbirth, wetnursing and care of infants all of which made them dependent on males for survival.

Firestone adds to this list the long gestation period of the human fetus and the even longer period that human infants are dependent on adults as part of her argument that biology is destiny (8). In her view, the sexual division of labor in the earliest human societies was simply a reflection of these biological differences. She sees this "first division of labor based on sex" as the "origins of all further division into economic and cultural classes and is possibly even at the root of all caste" (9). Firestone also *directly links child rearing and child bearing*—a connection critically questioned by those feminists who highlight how child rearing can be done by either sex.

For Firestone, this *biologically based sexual division of labor is "the root" of major cultural differences between men and women* (175). She defines culture as "the attempt by man [*sic*] to realize the conceivable in the possible" and refers to these cultural differences as the "male technological mode" and the "female aesthetic mode" (174). The technological mode refers to a type of cultural response where "the contingencies of reality" are overcome through "the mastery of reality's own workings" (174). Examples of this include the use of science, technology, and rational thought to master the vagaries of the natural and social worlds. By contrast, the aesthetic mode refers to a cultural response through which the individual denies the limitations and contingencies of reality "by escaping from it altogether, to define, create, his [*sic*] own possible" or ideal (175).[6] Examples of this aesthetic mode include poetry, music, and philosophy. Thus biological sex differences are the foundation for the material base in Firestone's theory while gendered cultural orientations form its superstructure.

Given that the root of women's oppression is innate and biological, little room is left for social change. According to Firestone, the true liberation of women would have to wait until the new reproductive technologies were sufficiently developed to transcend women's biological imperatives and to enable reproduction to take place outside of the human body. With such technological advances, ex-utero reproduction could replace childbirth and heterosexual intercourse would become just one of many kinds of sexual experiences, no longer being so important for procreation. Then people could experience many erotic experiences and reclaim the "polymorphously perverse" sexualities they were born with,[7] what she sometimes calls "pansexuality" (11). The

> end goal of the feminist revolution must be . . . not just the elimination of male *privilege* but of the sex *distinction* itself; genital differences between human beings would no longer matter culturally." (11; her emphasis)

At the end of *The Dialectic of Sex*, Firestone argues that "the most important characteristic to be maintained in any revolution is *flexibility*" (227; her emphasis). Once women were freed from their biological chains, gender roles and lifestyles could be many and diverse; people would be encouraged to mix and match feminine and masculine traits in whatever combination they wished. Not only could humans evolve into androgynous persons, but all of culture could become androgynous. Unlike the early Friedan, Firestone considers any image of "drafting women into a male world rather than the elimination of the sex class distinction altogether" as part of a "1984 nightmare."[8] She does not want a society in which "women have become like men, crippled in the identical ways" (210–211). Rather, Firestone is among the earliest second wave feminists to call for **androgyny** as integral to women's liberation.

The major theoretical assumptions of Firestone's radical feminist theory are captured in Marge Piercy's feminist's novel *Women on the Edge of Time* ([1976] 1997). In this fictional, radical feminist utopia, one finds pansexuality, androgynous persons, and ex-utero reproduction. Piercy's characters practice many and diverse sexualities, such as the celibate character Magdalena or the heterosexually promiscuous Jack Rabbit. All of her characters are androgynous. One of the more masculine-looking characters, the bearded Barbarossa, is breastfeeding. In the background, fetuses are gestating in enormous breeding tanks. As one character explains:

> It was part of women's long revolution. When we were breaking up all the old hierarchies. Finally there was one thing we had to give up too, the only power we ever had. . . . The original production: the power to give birth. Cause as long as we were biologically enchained, we'd never be equal . . . we all became mothers. Every child has three. To break the nuclear bonding. (98)

In both Firestone's theory and Piercy's novel, *the nuclear family is viewed as a major site of women's oppression.* In their visions for the future the nuclear family is eliminated as a procreative unit, as an economic unit, and as the primary unit of socialization for young children. In its place there is communal child rearing and multiple mothers (of no particular sex), and all children are viewed as precious responsiblities of the entire community (Firestone [1970] 1981: 206). Notably, Firestone writes quite a lot about children. She uses historian Philippe Ariès's well-received book *Centuries of Childhood* (1962) to document how children in pre-modern societies were not excluded and shielded from adult life. She argues that modern societies have suffered from separating children from the adult world.[9] One of Firestone's major demands was for the total integration of women and children into all aspects of the larger society. In particular, she believed that "the modern school must be destroyed" ([1970] 1981: 208). She wanted children to be introduced into the adult world by a more hands-on approach to education, one that does not isolate children from the knowledge and skills of adults.[10]

Similarly, in Piercy's novel there are no schools, and children learn directly from adults as they practice their various occupations. Children in the novel also engage in sexual activities with the full blessing of adults, which was also one of Firestone's demands (236). This integration of children into the adult world is portrayed positively as suggested by the following quote: "I think growing up is less mysterious with us since the adult world isn't separate" (Piercy [1976] 1997: 124). Moreover, despite their communal lifestyles, children are taught to be autonomous and independent individuals.

Diversity reigns in both Firestone's theory and Piercy's novel. Not only is the uniqueness of individuals lauded but so, too, is cultural diversity. In *Woman on the Edge of Time*, the community makes efforts to maintain cultural identities, but racism is eliminated through gene mixing in the breeding machines:

> We decided to hold on to separate cultural identities. But we broke the bond between genes and culture, broke it forever. We wanted there to be no chance of race hate again. But we didn't want the melting pot where everyone ends up with thin gruel. We wanted diversity, for strangeness breeds richness. (Piercy [1976] 1997: 97)

Neither Firestone nor Piercy suggest that individuals should conform to any singular vision or that people should be the same. Rather, "Beautiful is many" (Piercy [1976] 1997: 90).

Both of these radical feminists' visions for the future are predicated on advanced technology. Firestone ([1970] 1981: 196) recognizes that technology can liberate or control people but argues that "who" controls technology is the key. Not only does she predicate women's liberation on the new reproductive technologies, but in her chapter "Feminism in the Age of Ecology," Firestone envisions a "man-made" [*sic*] ecological balance as a product of the "total mastery of nature" by science and technology (192–193). One of the most serious ecological problems, in her view, is "the population explosion," and she looks to new methods of fertility control to address it (193–199). In turn, cybernation is the key to transforming the workplace—"altering man's [*sic*] age-old relation to work and wages" (200). This **technocratic mentality**—the view that science and technology can fix all problems—can be found also in Piercy's fictional utopia, where advanced technology makes ex-utero reproduction possible and enables people to live comfortably in a communal lifestyle. Everyone in the novel appears to use their artistic or craft skills to realize themselves in non-exploitative labor that is socially useful and interesting:

> We dumped the jobs telling people what to do, counting money and moving about, making people do what they don't want or bashing them for doing what they want. (Piercy [1976] 1997: 121)

In this feminist utopia there are no problems feeding, clothing, or sheltering the community. Everyone works; they have "high productivity" coupled with short working hours (121). How and where the advanced technology is produced that makes such a pleasant and comfortable life possible is not revealed.

Other radical feminists criticized Firestone's theory for embracing a technocratic mentality and for not celebrating the positive features of women's lives and culture (Daly 1978). However, whether radical feminists agreed with Firestone that women had to await the new reproductive technologies to free them from their biological chains or rejected her biological determinism and took a more social constructionist approach, many called for feminist separatism as the path women should take to challenge and resist the impact of patriarchy in their everyday lives.

Feminist Separatism and the Woman-Identified Woman

Feminist separatism refers to women's conscious and willful separation from various forms of patriarchal control. Among the most radical statements of feminist separatism was Charlotte Bunch's essay "Lesbians in Revolt," first published in 1972 in the lesbian feminist journal *The Furies*. While Bunch shares Firestone's views on the origins of women's oppression and the sexual division of labor as the major root of women's oppression, her major theoretical contributions lie in her discussions of feminist separatism and what she called **the woman-identified woman**:

> The woman-identified woman commits herself to other women for political emotional, physical, and economic support. Women are important to her. She is important to herself. (Bunch [1972] 1993: 174)

Bunch contrasts the "woman-identified woman" to women who give their primary commitments to men. In her view, "giving support and love to men over women perpetuates the system that oppresses her" (175). She discusses how heterosexuality separates women from each other, forces women to compete for men, and encourages them to define themselves through men. She also discusses how heterosexual women "gain a few privileges" as compensation for their loss of freedom. They are "honored" as mothers, they are socially-accepted as wives or lovers, and they often receive some economic and emotional security as well as "protection on the street" (176). In her view, these privileges give heterosexual women a personal and political stake in maintaining the status quo. So long as heterosexual women receive these privileges they cannot be trusted and will at some point "betray their sisters, especially Lesbian sisters who do not receive those benefits" (178). According to Bunch, "Lesbians must become feminists and fight against woman oppression, just as feminists must become lesbians if they hope to end male supremacy" (175). For Bunch, "Woman-identified lesbianism, is, then, more than a sexual preference; *it is a political choice*" (175; emphasis added).

The view that lesbianism is a political act also was expressed in an early statement by the Radicalesbians titled "The Woman-Identified Woman," first published in 1970. This group grew out of the Lavender Menace protest in New York—a protest against the invisibility of lesbians in the women's movement and especially in the National Organization of Women (NOW). As noted in chapter 2, the term "lavender menace" referred to Betty Friedan's remark that lesbianism was a "lavender herring" and NOW's refusal to address lesbian issues. By contrast, the Radicalesbians [1970] 2005: 239) portrayed lesbianism as a woman's courageous efforts "to act in accordance with her inner compulsion to be a more complete and freer human being than her society cares to allow her."

> A lesbian is the rage of all women condensed to the point of explosion. . . . Lesbian is the word, the label, the condition that holds women in line. When a woman hears this word tossed her way, she knows she is stepping out of line. She knows that she has crossed the terrible boundary of her sex role. . . . Lesbian is a label invested by the Man to throw at any woman who dares to be his equal, who dares to challenge his prerogatives . . ., who dares to assert the primacy of her own needs. (239)

At this time it was not uncommon for lesbian feminist writers to emphasize that lesbianism should not be viewed simply as a sexual or "bedroom issue." I highlight this point because later feminists criticized Bunch and the Radicalesbians for taking the "sex" out of lesbianism (see chapter 7). However, these early radical feminists had important reasons for downplaying sexual practices in this historical context. For Bunch ([1972] 1993: 175), defining the question of "whom one sleeps with" as a "private" issue ignored the more serious "public" issues of power and domination entailed in heterosexuality; in short, it "sidetracks our understanding of the politics of sex."

> As long as straight women see lesbianism as a bedroom issue, they hold back the development of politics and strategies that would put an end to male supremacy and they give men an excuse for not dealing with their sexism. (177)

These writings exacerbated one of the most serious splits in the second wave women's movement—the gay versus straight split—first initiated by Friedan's "lavender herring" statement in 1966. Bunch's call for all feminists to become lesbians and her claim that only heterosexual women who "cut their ties with male privilege can be trusted to remain serious to the struggle against male dominance" added fuel to the fire (177). Readers can imagine the debates that arose over these issues. Were feminist mothers to separate from their male children? Should heterosexual feminists refuse to sleep with the enemy? To this day, these debates continue in regard to one of the premier cultural activities initiated by radical feminists—the Michigan Womyn's Music Festival [the "y" removes the "men" from women]. This festival refuses entry to males over the age of twelve and to transsexuals, as indicated on its 2009 website:

> Since 1976, the Michigan Womyn's Music Festival has been created by and for womyn-born womyn, that is, womyn who were born as and have lived their entire life experience as womyn. . . . the Festival remains a rare and precious space intended for womyn-born womyn.[11]

Diverse Voices within Radical Feminism

A number of radical feminists attempted to heal the gay/straight divisions within the U.S. women's movement. Unlike Bunch. whose feminist separatism required women to disengage from any relations with men, for other radical feminists, separatism took more moderate forms. According to Marilyn Frye's "Some Reflections on Separatism and Power" (1978), separatism can involve avoiding close relationships with men, excluding someone from your company, withdrawing from participation in certain activities and institutions, and withholding support or commitment to certain people. In short, Frye makes clear that feminist separatism included a wide range of possible actions as part of a conscious strategy for liberation. Most feminists, she argues, already practice some separation from sexist people and activities. Because Frye's examples range from serious, life-altering refusals, such as refusing to work for or to live with men, to more minor refusals, such as not listening to music with sexist lyrics, her article reduced some of the tensions between gay and straight feminists.

Perhaps the major healer of the gay/straight split was radical feminist poet Adrienne Rich. In her widely read piece "Compulsory Heterosexuality and Lesbian Existence" ([1980] 2005), Rich argued that the notion of "women-identified women" entailed a spectrum of female-to-female relationships, which she referred to as the **"lesbian continuum"** (349). Here woman-to-woman relationships ranged from sexual intimacy with women to mother-daughter relations, sister-to-sister relations, and best friend relations—relationships that all women could have with other women. Not only did Rich's continuum describe lesbianism as more than a bedroom issue, but her view of women-identified women also *fostered common ground for politically unifying lesbian and straight women.*

The foundation of Rich's argument is that *gender is more important than sexual orientation*, thus implicitly urging lesbians to ally with heterosexual feminists rather than with gay males. She highlighted the privileges enjoyed by both straight and gay males—such as higher incomes and earning power. She pointed to "qualitative differences in female and male relationships," citing how males engage in more "anonymous sex" while females are more relationship-oriented. She criticized gay males for a number of sexual practices, such as pedophilia and sadomaschism, as well as "the pronounced ageism in male homosexual standards of sexual attractiveness" (349). For Rich, being woman-oriented and woman-born is a "profoundly female experience." Hence, she argued that "equating lesbian existence with male homosexuality because each is stigmatized is to erase female reality once again" (349). She writes:

> Just as the term *parenting* serves to conceal the particular and significant reality of being a parent who is actually a mother, the term *gay* may serve the purpose of blurring the very outlines we need to discern, which are of crucial value for feminism and for the freedom of women as a group (349)

Overall, Rich's approach to radical feminism is distinctly different from that of Firestone. Rather than biological determinism driving her writings, Rich takes a *social constructionist approach to gender and sexuality*. For Rich, heterosexuality is not a natural emotional and sensual inclination but, rather, is "forcibly and subliminally imposed on women" (350 and 351). **Compulsory heterosexuality** refers to how heterosexuality has been created and rigidly enforced by various institutional, ideological, and normative means in order to achieve women's subservience through emotional and erotic loyalty to men. Using examples that cut across class, race, and cultural lines, Rich points to how historically many women have resisted heterosexuality at great costs, such as imprisonment, physical torture, psychosurgery, social ostracism, and poverty (351). She asks, if heterosexuality is natural, why do societies need such violent strictures to enforce it?

Rich also laments the *invisibility of lesbian existence*. She sees the destruction of records, memorabilia, and letters documenting the realities of lesbian lives as an indication of the serious "means of keeping heterosexuality compulsory for women" (349). Through this destruction, all women are denied knowledge of the joys, sensuality, and courage of lesbians as well as their loneliness, guilt, and pain. Here again, her social constructionist approach is evident in her portrayal of history as an ongoing and creative process that both gives voice and silences by its inclusions and its omissions.

In *Of Woman Born: Motherhood as Experience and Institution* [1976] (1977), Rich also takes a different approach to childbirth and mothering from that of Firestone. Rich highlights the trials and tribulations, as well as the sheer joy, entailed in biological gestation, childbirth, nursing, and nurturing children:

> My children cause me the most exquisite suffering of which I have any experience. It is the suffering of ambivalence: the murderous alternation between bitter resentment and raw-edged nerves, and blissful gratification and tenderness. . . . Their voices wear away at my nerves, their constant needs, above all their need for simplicity and patience, fill me with despair at my own failures, despair too at

> my fate, which is to serve a function for which I was not fitted.... And yet at other times I am melted with the sense of their helpless, charming and quite irresistible beauty.... *I love them.* But it's in the enormity and inevitability of this love that the sufferings lie. (Rich 1976 [1977]: 1–2; her emphasis)

This emotional and socially lived approach to motherhood contrasts sharply with Firestone's rather cold, analytical, and impersonal call for women to be freed from the chains of biological reproduction—a freedom not likely to be relished by many women, including feminists.

Rich also rejects Firestone's view that women's biology is simply restrictive. In women's bodies she sees a radical potential to bring forth and nurture life as a "field of contradictions" (Rich [1980] 1977: 90). She also highlights how women's bodies are a "resource" that women should control and celebrate rather than renounce:

> I have come to believe... that female biology—the diffuse, intense sensuality radiating out from clitoris, breasts, uterus, vagina... has far more radical implications than we have come to appreciate. Patriarchal thought has limited female biology to its own narrow specifications. The feminist vision has recoiled from female biology for these reasons; it will, I believe, come to view our physicality as a resource, rather than a destiny. In order to live a fully human life we require not only control of our bodies (though control is a prerequisite); we must touch the unity and resonance of our physicality, our bond with the natural order, the corporeal ground of our intelligence. (21)

Rich's views on mothering are different also from liberal feminist psychoanalytical approaches to mothering, which posit as the primary solution to sexual inequality having men share equally in child rearing responsibilities (see chapter 2). Rich argues that this transformation would not be sufficient to radically alter the balance of male power in a male-identified society. She points to other dimensions of male power that would still need to be addressed: the denial of women's right to free sexual expression, the exploitation of women's labor, and the withholding of large areas of society's knowledge and cultural attainments from women ([1980] 2005: 348).

As the subtitle of Rich's *Of Woman Born* [1976] (1977) suggests, she distinguishes between two meanings of motherhood—first, motherhood as experience or the "potential relationship" of any women to her powers of reproduction and to her children; and second, motherhood as a "patriarchal institution" which aims at ensuring that this potential remains under male control (xv). Rich makes clear that she is critiquing motherhood as a patriarchal institution; she is not calling for an end to women's role in childbearing or child rearing (xvi).

In contrast, many radical feminists directed their attacks against men rather than against patriarchal institutions. Consider the following quote from the "Redstockings Manifesto" written in 1969:

> Attempts have been made to shift the burden of responsibility from men to institutions or to women themselves. We condemn these arguments as evasions. Institutions alone do not oppress; they are merely tools of their oppressors (Redstockings [1969] 2005: 221).

Redstockings was a short-lived radical feminist organization that reclaimed the pejorative label *bluestockings* used for educated women in the nineteenth century with the color red to signify their radical politics. Members of this group viewed all men as benefiting from women's oppression and all men as oppressors. Contrary to contemporary claims by third wave feminists that the second wave ignored differences between women (Henry 2004), the Redstockings Manifesto discusses the "economic, racial, educational, or status privileges" that divide women. It rejects, however, the notion that women can oppress men. The entire manifesto can be found in Box 3.3.

BOX 3.3

"Redstockings Manifesto"

I. After centuries of individual and preliminary political struggle, women are uniting to achieve their final liberation from male supremacy. Redstockings is dedicated to building this unity and winning our freedom.

II. Women are an oppressed class. Our oppression is total, affecting every facet of our lives. We are exploited as sex objects, breeders, domestic servants, and cheap labor. We are considered inferior beings, whose only purpose is to enhance men's lives. Our humanity is denied. Our prescribed behavior is enforced by the threat of physical violence.

Because we have lived so intimately with our oppressors, in isolation from each other, we have been kept from seeing our personal suffering as a political condition. This creates the illusion that a woman's relationship with her man is a matter of interplay between two unique personalities, and can be worked out individually. In reality, every such relationship is a class relationship, and the conflicts between individual men and women are political conflicts that can only be solved collectively.

III. We identify the agents of our oppression as men. Male supremacy is the oldest, most basic form of domination. All other forms of exploitation and oppression (racism, capitalism, imperialism, etc.) are extensions of male supremacy: men dominate women, a few men dominate the rest. All power structures throughout history have been male-dominated and male-oriented. Men have controlled all political, economic and cultural institutions and backed up this control with physical force. They have used their power to keep women in an inferior position. All men receive economic, sexual, and psychological benefits from male supremacy. All men have oppressed women.

IV. Attempts have been made to shift the burden of responsibility from men to institutions or to women themselves. We condemn these arguments as evasions. Institutions alone do not oppress; they are merely tools of the oppressor. To blame institutions implies that men and women are equally victimized, obscures the fact that men benefit from the subordination of women, and gives men the excuse that they are forced to be oppressors. On the contrary, any man is free to renounce his superior position, provided that he is willing to be treated like a woman by other men.

We also reject the idea that women consent to or are to blame for their own oppression. Women's submission is not the result of brain-washing, stupidity or mental illness but of continual, daily pressure from men. We do not need to change ourselves, but to change men.

The most slanderous evasion of all is that women can oppress men. The basis for this illusion is the isolation of individual relationships from their political context and the tendency of men to see any legitimate challenge to their privileges as persecution.

V. We regard our personal experience, and our feelings about that experience, as the basis for an analysis of our common situation. We cannot rely on existing ideologies as they are all products of male supremacist culture. We question every generalization and accept none that are not confirmed by our experience.

Our chief task at present is to develop female class consciousness through sharing experience and publicly exposing the sexist foundation of all our institutions. Consciousness-raising is not "therapy," which implies the existence of individual solutions and falsely assumes that the male-female relationship is purely personal, but the only method by which we can ensure that our program for liberation is based on the concrete realities of our lives.

The first requirement for raising class consciousness is honesty, in private and in public, with ourselves and other women.

VI. We identify with all women. We define our best interest as that of the poorest, most brutally exploited woman.

We repudiate all economic, racial, educational, or status privileges that divide us from other women. We are determined to recognize and eliminate any prejudices we may hold against other women.

We are committed to achieving internal democracy. We will do whatever is necessary to ensure that every woman in our movement has an equal chance to participate, assume responsibility, and develop her political potential.

VII. We call on all our sisters to unite with us in struggle.

We call on all men to give up their male privilege and support women's liberation in the interest of our humanity and their own.

In fighting for our liberation we will always take the side of women against their oppressors. We will not ask what is "revolutionary" or "reformist," only what is good for women.

The time for individual skirmishes has passed. This time we are going all the way.

"Redstockings Manifesto." Issued as a mimeographed flyer in New York City on July 7, 1969, the manifesto was designed for distribution at women's liberation events. Further information about the Manifesto and other source materials from the rebirth years of feminism in the 1960s are available from Redstockings Women's Liberation Archives for Action, at www.redstockings.org; or at P.O. Box 14017 Gainesville, FL 32604.

Another influential approach to radical feminism in the 1970s was Gayle Rubin's "The Traffic in Women: Notes on the 'Political Economy' of Sex" ([1975] 2005). Rubin coined the phrase "sex/gender system," which she defined as "the set of arrangements by which a society transforms biological sexuality into products of human activity, and in which these transformed sexual needs are satisfied" (287). Her analysis of the sex/gender system is a unique, synthetic work. She builds on the writings of Karl Marx and Friedrich Engels to understand the economic basis of gender relations (see chapter 4) but argues that this economic analysis must be accompanied by a more thorough understanding of marriage and the family. Here she draws from the work of Claude Lévi-Strauss to show how the incest taboo and the "exchange of women" forged bonds between groups through marriage and kinship. Lévi-Strauss's notion of "gift exchanges" was used also by Rubin to broaden anarchist feminist Emma Goldman's earlier notion of the "traffic in women" (see chapter 4). In Rubin's analyses, the "traffic in women" referred to the various ways women are "given" in marriage, "taken in warfare," or "exchanged" for tribute throughout history (277).

To illuminate the "deep structures" or psychosocial roots of both sexist and heterosexist oppression, Rubin drew from the works Sigmund Freud and Jacques Lacan. This latter analysis entailed a deconstruction of both heterosexual and homosexual relations that was to earn her a reputation as an early precursor to queer theory. Her later writings, such as "Thinking Sex: Notes for a Radical Theory of the Politics of Sexuality" (1984), and her work on leather culture place her more firmly in the poststructuralist camp and as a major voice in queer theory (see chapter 6). Notably, Rubin also was a key voice on the pro-sex side of the so-called sex wars waged among feminists of the second wave.

The "Sex Wars"

The term *sex wars* has been used to describe heated debates that took place within the second wave of U.S. feminism from the late 1970s through the mid-1980s. These debates focused on the implications of various sexual practices for women's liberation. Feminists argued over pornography, sexwork, censorship, sadomasochism, and other erotic practices in terms of what constituted nonpatriarchal forms of sex or whether there should even be such a notion (Henry 2004: 89). The pro-sex side of this debate rejected any form of censorship or restrictions on sexual practices in the interests of more openness and freedom. In contrast, their opponents—often referred to today as victim feminists—highlighted the violence and danger associated with certain sexual practices and had quite definite opinions about what constituted patriarchal and nonpatriarchal forms of sex. While feminists from a wide array of feminist perspectives participated in these debates, the focus below will be on the voices and visions of radical feminists. Not only were they among the most vocal on *both* sides of this debate, but radical feminism became fractured from *within* during these intense, internecine battles.

Sex as a Realm of Pleasure

As was shown above, both Firestone and Piercy embraced a pro-sex approach in their call for freedom of sexual expression for women and children as well as a vision of polymorphous or pansexuality as integral to women's liberation. Another prominent feminist on the pro-sex side of the sex wars is Anne Koedt, who, with Firestone, founded the New York Radical Feminists (NYRF) in 1969. Koedt is best known for her article "The Myth of the Vaginal Orgasm" (1970), in which she discussed how women had been socialized into believing the "myth" that orgasm occurs in the vagina rather than in the clitoris. She argued that the importance of the clitoris to female orgasms had been hidden to ensure women's dependence on men and to reinforce heterosexuality. Koedt's article had a major effect on feminist discourses on sexuality because the clitoral orgasm potentially removed men as necessary to women's sexual pleasure. Feminists also lauded her work for taking into account mutual sexual enjoyment. However, Koedt's criticisms of the heterosexual experiences of women were mocked by a number of prominent feminists. Germaine Greer, the Australian feminist and author of *The Female Eunuch* (1971), wrote, "One wonders just whom Miss [*sic*] Koedt has gone to bed with;" while Betty Friedan called "those strangely humorless papers about clitoral orgasms that would liberate women from sexual dependence on a man's penis" a "joke" (both quoted in Henry 2004: 83).

Gayle Rubin, discussed above, is another key voice in the pro-sex chorus. In the 1960s and 1970s, Rubin argued that one of the keys to both women's liberation and human liberation was ending sexual repression. In "Thinking Sex: Notes for a Radical Theory of the Politics of Sexuality" originally published in 1984, her analysis moves in a poststructuralist direction to attack all ideologies of sexual repression—whether they come from the left, the right, or from feminists themselves. In particular, Rubin studied the hierarchies of sexual values institutionalized in religious, medical, psychiatric, and popular discourses on sexuality. She argued that within such hierarchies there appears to "be a need to draw and maintain an imaginary line between good and bad sex"—a line that stands between "sexual order and chaos" (282). Rubin stood steadfast against any ideologies that attempted to describe sex in terms of sin, disease, neurosis, pathology, decadence, pollution, or the decline and fall of empires (278). Convinced that sexual repression was one of the most irrational ways for civilizations to control human behavior, she viewed sexual permissiveness as in the best interests of both women and men. In her view, it was misguided for feminists to dictate which types of sex were patriarchal or nonpatriarchal. Sexual repression was repression regardless of who made the rules.[12] For more second wave pro-sex positions, see *Carol Vance's* anthology *Pleasure and Danger: Exploring Female Sexuality* (1984) based on papers presented at a conference held at Barnard College in 1982.

Sex as a Realm of Danger

It must be emphasized that the second wave radical feminists who undertook to delineate what types of sex were violent and/or patriarchal were motivated by their desire to end unequal power relations and violence against women. They were not victim feminists in the sense of highlighting the dangers of sex simply to present women as passive or weak victims in the face of these dangers.[13] On the contrary, they named certain sexual practices as violent and patriarchal to illuminate injustices so that women would refuse to be victims any longer. As Deborah Siegel (1997b: 76) so aptly points out—this type of victim feminism is an articulation of strength, not of weakness.

The slogan of radical feminists that "the personal is political" made violence against women a more central focus of feminist activism than it had been during the first wave. This slogan led feminists whose politics crossed the political spectrum to address such issues as battering, rape, incest, sexual harassment, and pornography—issues that previously had been treated as individual, personal problems too often hidden behind closed doors. Not only did they establish rape crisis and battered women centers, but they also challenged and revised laws that dealt with these issues. In turn, events like the first "**Take Back the Night**" march held in Pittsbugh in 1977 dramatized "women's insistence on their right to enjoy public space in safety" and drew feminists of various political stripes to a protest that continues to be held annually in many cities (Lederer 1980: 15). While different feminists had different solutions to violence against women, second wave feminists were at least united in the urgent need to address violent acts against women.

Two major issues divided the second wave and caused deep splits within radical feminism: (1) whether feminists should legislate that certain sexual practices constituted patriarchal and/or violent forms and (2) whether feminists should censor violent and degrading images or just concern themselves with violent acts and behaviors. While Adrienne Rich's writings on lesbianism and mothering had helped to heal splits within the second wave, her judgmental analysis of sexual practices divided feminists—including those who shared other aspects of her radical feminist approach. As noted above, Rich pointed to qualitative differences between female and male sexual relations, lauding the nurturing and commitment-oriented relationships she associated with females, while criticizing the aggressive and indiscriminate sexual practices she associated with males. She also explicitly described a number of sexual practices, such as pedophilia, sadomasochism, prostitution, and pornography, as reflecting "male power" and forcing male sexuality on others (Rich [1980] 2005: 348–349). Robin Morgan drew similar lines between patriarchal and non-patriarchal sexual practices when she critiqued "the male style" as follows:

> Every woman knows in her gut the vast differences between her sexuality and that of any patriarchally trained male's - gay or straight . . . That the emphasis on genital sexuality, objectification, promiscuity, emotional non-involvement, and, of course, invulnerability was the *male style*, and that we, as women,placed greater trust in love, sensuality, humor, tenderness, commitment." (Morgan 1977: 181 her emphasis).

Although other radical feminists such as Rubin, Firestone, and Koedt rejected the notion of feminists legislating "good" and "bad" sexual practices, the issue of censoring sexual images created the most conflict. Various actions had been taken by feminists in the 1960s and 1970s to protest degrading images of women. In 1976, members of Women against Violence against Women (WAVAW) defaced billboards and demonstrated against various media images of women they found degrading. That same year, in San Francisco, Women against Violence in Pornography and Media (WAVPM) was established (Berger, Searles, and Cottle 1991: 32). Yet while second wave feminists had few objections to protests and demonstrations, censorship was a more divisive issue.

One of the earliest radical feminists to call for the censorship of pornography and to treat pornography as form of violence against women was Kate Millett in her book *Sexual Politics* (1970). Like her radical feminist counterparts, Millett argued that women's oppression is the paradigm for all other power relationships. She addressed brute forms of power—like rape—as well as more subtle forms—like the use of misogynist language. She pointed out how patriarchal sexual politics entailed power over heterosexual women as well as over homosexual males and females. A significant portion of *Sexual Politics* was devoted to exposing the patriarchal ideology embedded in Western societies. Millett attacked the patriarchal assumptions in various academic theories, such as Freud's, as well as the sexism and heterosexism of the modern novelists D. H. Lawrence, Henry Miller, and Norman Mailer. She referred to them as "literate pornographers" and cited numerous examples of "pornography" in their literature.[14]

While Millett shared with Firestone the vision of an androgynous future, she shared with Rich definite views on which traits and behaviors were compatible with women's liberation. For example, in her vision of the future androgynous person Millett included neither the "aggressiveness" traditionally exhibited by men nor the "obedience" traditionally exhibited by women. She also called for censorship of pornography and had strong views on the "patriarchal" and "pernicious" behaviors that must be "eliminated" to achieve feminist liberation (42).[15]

In the 1980s, the most vocal feminists on the topic of pornography were Andrea Dworkin and Catharine MacKinnon. Dworkin's *Pornography* (1981) and *Intercourse* (1987), along with MacKinnon's *Pornography and Civil Rights* (1988), were among the most widely read feminist books on this topic. These radical feminists placed pornography "at the center of a cycle of abuse" and viewed it as a "core constitutive practice" that helped to institutionalize and legitimize gender inequality by creating a social climate in which sexual assault and abuse were tolerated (MacKinnon 1988: 47). Other radical feminists had similar views but focused more on pornography as an ideology that fostered violence. For example, Kathleen Barry's analysis in *Female Sexual Slavery* (1979) viewed pornography as the embodiment of "cultural sadism"—an ideology that depicts sexual violence as normative and pleasurable for men and women. She argued that pornography was the principal medium through which cultural sadism is diffused into the mainstream culture and integrated into the sexual practices of individuals. Radical feminist Robin Morgan (1977: 5) put it more succinctly: "Pornography is the theory, and rape is the practice"—a political stance also espoused by Susan Brownmiller in her influential work *Against our Will: Men, Women and Rape* (1975).

Antipornography feminists, such as Gloria Steinem, founder of *Ms.* magazine, often made distinctions between "erotica" as images of mutually pleasurable sexual expression between equal and consenting subjects and "pornography" as objectifying women and portraying sex as violent, degrading, or dehumanizing (Steinem 1980). However, these dividing lines proved too fuzzy for opponents of censorship and were rejected by pro-sex advocates because they still entailed rules governing sexual practices. To the opponents of censorship, Dworkin and MacKinnon argued that pornography was not merely a fantasy, a simulation, or an idea. Rather, it was a concrete discriminatory social practice that institutionalizes the inferiority and subordination of one group to another (Berger, Searles, and Cottle 1991: 37). Hence, they demanded that laws be passed to deal with pornography in the same way that laws had been set up to deal with racial discrimination.

When the first of antipornography civil rights ordinance (based on the work of Dworkin and MacKinnon) was introduced in Minneapolis in 1983, conflicts within the second wave became the most heated and polarized. The Minneapolis ordinance did not ban pornography, but it gave women the option of filing a civil suit against those whose involvement with pornography caused harm to women. While critics argued that this would increase state control over sexual practices, Dworkin and MacKinnon argued that this was not so. Rather, in their view such ordinances would empower women by giving them the ability to initiate civil litigation. The Minneapolis ordinance was revoked later by a higher court, but the writings of MacKinnon and Dworkin were used to establish antipornography ordinances in neighboring Canada.[16] While Dworkin and MacKinnon saw the antipornography movement as revitalizing feminism in the wake of the ERA's defeat, critics saw it as leading to internecine battles that would further fragment the feminist movement (7).

Feminists against censoring pornography responded by forming the Feminist Anti-Censorship Taskforce (FACT). Anticensorship feminists came from many and diverse perspectives. Liberal feminists generally opposed censorship, viewing it as a violation of freedom of speech and the right to privacy (Duggan, Hunter, and Vance 1985). Although they worked to change images of women that were objectifying or degrading, censorship was not part of the liberal feminist toolbox.

Other feminisms within the second wave were more divided on this issue. Some women of color discounted feminists' concerns about pornography as a misplaced outrage that only white, middle-class women could afford—concerns that paled in comparison to other problems they faced (Tong 1998: 219). Other womanists of color argued that pornography should be addressed because its negative imagery reinforced sexual stereotypes that had plagued people of color historically. Alice Walker, for example, criticized how the black man "is defined solely by the size, readiness, and unselectivity of his cock" while the black woman has historically been viewed as a Jezebel or slut, and she called on women of color to address the issue of pornography (Walker 1980: 103). Audre Lorde made a strong plea for the "replenishing" and empowering force of the erotic and described pornography as its opposite—as the "direct denial of the power of the erotic" that "emphasizes sensation without feeling" (1980: 296). Many of these feminist perspectives on pornography can be found in Laura Lederer's anthology *Take Back the Night: Women on Pornography* (1980).

Radical feminists, Marxist feminists, and socialist feminists were divided among themselves on this issue. While some supported antipornography campaigns, others embraced a pro-sex position and viewed censorship as antithetical to liberation. The latter feared that restrictions on pornography would foster a climate of repression, strengthen oppressive sexual norms, and inhibit women's ability to discover sexual pleasure. They also saw pornography as flouting conventional sexual mores in favor of more sexual freedom (Ferguson 1984, English, Hollibaugh and Rubin 1981). Because many feminists of the second wave placed value on empiricism for validating their theoretical and political positions (see chapter 1), debates ensued over research that studied whether violent images led to violent actions or if pornography could have a cathartic effect that reduced viewers' sexually aggressive behaviors (McCormack 1978; Lederer 1980). In turn, pro-sex feminists of the second wave refused to view women as passive victims of pornography but highlighted women's agency and their ability to negotiate this terrain for their own purposes (Snitow, et al. 1983, Vance 1985).

Because censorship of pornography caused divisions *within* many feminist political perspectives, it is difficult to place feminist positions on pornography on a conventional right-wing to left-wing political spectrum. Indeed, radical feminists who called for censorship of pornography often ended up with strange political bedfellows since their allies were often conservative, right-wing antifeminists who were more interested in how pornography harmed the moral fabric of society than how it harmed women. Although radical feminists transformed campaigns against pornography from debates over morality to debates over gender violence, uniting the second wave around laws that prohibited sexual practices and censored sexually degrading images did not happen. In this sense, the pro-sex side of the sex wars won.

The only issue on which there was more agreement across the second wave was sexual harassment in the workplace. Most sexual harassment laws on the books today are based on MacKinnon's legal work. In *Sexual Harassment of Working Women: A Case of Sex Discrimination* (1979), MacKinnon distinguished two types of sexual harassment: quid pro quo, from the Latin phrase meaning "one thing in return for another," and creating a hostile environment, meaning that sexual harassment is a persistent condition of the workplace. The latter can entail a range of comments, gestures, and physical contacts interpreted as sexual in nature that are deliberate, repeated, and unwelcome. While creating a hostile environment entails more ambiguities than quid pro quo harassment, both types are generally included in sexual harassment legislation.

Radical feminists also were major voices in the struggle to end violence against women internationally (see chapter 9). For example, MacKinnon represented Croatian and Muslim women and children who were seeking justice in international courts for the mass rapes and sexual atrocities they experienced during the ethnic conflicts in the former Yugoslavia in the early 1990s. Charlotte Bunch founded the Center for Women's Global Leadership (CWGL) that became a leading organization in the global movement for women's human rights. Her coauthored book *Demanding Accountability: The Global Campaign and Vienna Tribunal on Women's Human Rights* (1994), is a classic on this topic. Robin Morgan's *Sisterhood Is Global* (1984) was described by Western reviewers as a global feminist encyclopedia and "the definitive text on the international women's movement" (Morgan [1984] 1996: vii). Although radical feminist writings on international issues often were criticized for their essentialism (see chapters 9 and 10), they played an important role in fostering U.S. feminists to think globally and to make links between the local and the global.

THE RADICAL FEMINIST ROOTS OF CULTURAL AND SPIRITUAL ECOFEMINISMS

The major ecofeminist perspectives that have roots in radical feminism are cultural ecofeminism and spiritual ecofeminism. Both forms of ecofeminism developed in the 1970s, and both are **essentialist** in terms of arguing that all women share certain intrinsic traits. In particular, they argue that *women are closer to the natural world than men because of their embodiment as women and potential mothers.* Just as the earth gives birth to natural resources, women have the potential to give birth to social life. Rather than denigrate this relationship between women and nature as patriarchal cultures historically have done, they *celebrate it as a source of female power.*

Both cultural and spiritual ecofeminists *focus heavily on the symbolic and cultural connections between women and nature.* They portray women as oriented toward nurturing and caring and, thereby, as potentially providing a more symbiotic relationship between humans and nature. In contrast, men are portrayed as more rationally oriented and more prone to uncritically use science and technology to dominate women and nature. Whereas patriarchal cultures historically have used the binary polarizations of men/women, mind/body, rational/irrational, and culture/nature to argue for the subordination of women, cultural and spiritual ecofeminists invert these dualisms and herald women's traits as sources of their empowerment and ecological sensitivity. By inverting the binaries of patriarchal thought, they simply reverse the attribution of superiority but do not transcend this type of thinking.

Such dualistic thought is exemplified in the works of cultural ecofeminists Mary Daly and Susan Griffin. Daly's *Gyn/Ecology* (1978) and Griffin's *Woman and Nature* (1978) are among the most influential ecofeminist writings of their time. Daly and Griffin were both wordsmiths who wrote in a clever and provocative style to illustrate how the relationship between women and nature was deeply ingrained in patriarchal cultures and how these cultures denigrated women and their bodies by identifying them with nature. An excerpt from Griffin's *Woman and Nature* is presented in Box 3.4. Interweaving powerful images of man's conquest of women and nature, it illustrates how language and culture buttress patriarchal oppression.

Key figures in the development of spiritual ecofeminism are Charlene Spretnak, Starhawk, and Carol Christ. In contrast to the negative, critical approach used by Daly and Griffin to expose how patriarchal cultures exploit women and the environment, these spiritual ecofeminists employ a positive, functional approach to women and nature. They call for recapturing the symbolism of premodern eras when goddesses were worshipped and reviving ancient rituals centered on natural cycles, such

BOX 3.4

"Use"

He breaks the wilderness. He clears the land of trees, brush, weed. The land is brought under his control; he has turned waste into a garden. Into her soil he places his plow. He labors. He plants. He sows. By the sweat of his brow, he makes her yield. She opens her broad lap to him. She smiles on him. She prepares him a feast. She gives up her treasures to him. She makes him grow rich. She yields. She conceives. Her lap is fertile. Out of her dark interior, life arises. What she does to his seed is a mystery to him. He counts her yielding as a miracle. . . . He is determined to master her. He will make her produce at will. He will devise ways to plant what he wants in her, to make her yield more to him.

He deciphers the secrets of the soil. (He knows why she brings forth.) He recites the story of the carbon cycle. (He masters the properties of chlorophyll.) He recites the story of the nitrogen cycle. (He brings nitrogen out of the air). . . . He increases the weight of kernels of barley with potash; he makes a more mealy potato with muriate of potash, he makes the color of cabbage bright green with nitrate, he makes onions which live longer with phosphates, he makes the cauliflower head early by withholding nitrogen. His powers continue to grow. . . .

And he has devised ways to separate himself from her. He sends machines to do his labor. His working has become as effortless as hers. He accomplishes days of labor with a small motion of his hand. His efforts are more astonishing than hers. No longer praying, no longer imploring, he pronounces words from a distance and his orders are carried out. Even with his back turned to her she yields to him. And in his mind, he imagines that he can conceive without her. In his mind he develops the means to supplant her miracles with his own. In his mind, he no longer relies on her. What he possesses, he says, is his to use and to abandon.

From Susan Griffin, *Woman and Nature: The Roaring Inside Her* (New York: Harper Colophon, 1980), pp. 52–54.

as those of the moon or women's reproductive cycles. Especially popular were rituals from premodern cultures that were matrilineal or that were based on a specific female deity. Native-American traditions inspired many U.S. spiritual ecofeminists, as have Celtic and ancient Greek cultures. For spiritual ecofeminists, reclaiming such ceremonies, rituals, and beliefs fosters a revolution in symbolic structures to counter the hegemony of patriarchal religions and cultures (Merchant 1995: 11).

By unearthing pagan rituals and their histories feminists have learned that women charged with witchcraft in premodern and early modern societies often posed threats to male authority or would not submit to the patriarchal norms of their communities (Starhawk 1979, Daly 1978). For example, a number of women deemed to be witches in eighteenth- and nineteenth-century America were actually midwives or lay practioners who used herbal medicines to attend to lower-class patients who could not afford the services of certified medical doctors (Ehrenreich and English 1973: 15–18). Yet because many premodern rituals are pagan, spiritual ecofeminism generated strong reactions from supporters of dominant religions. For example, when ecofeminist and self-identified witch Starhawk spoke at a public lecture at a Catholic university in New Orleans in 1989, the university came under attack by angry protesters for ostensibly supporting witchcraft.

Both cultural and spiritual ecofeminists embrace an **ecocentric approach** to the environment whereby human beings are viewed as just one of many parts of the natural world—not as morally or ethically superior to nonhuman forms of nature.[17] As contrasted to liberal ecofeminists, who focus on rules, rights, and utilities, cultural and spiritual ecofeminists employ an ethic of care, love, and trust. The future envisioned by cultural and spiritual ecofeminists is highly decentralized and democratic and organized around nonsexist, nonracist, and communitarian principles (Merchant 1999: 16–17). This vision of the future sounds similar to the depictions in Firestone's *Dialectic of Sex* (1970) and Piercy's *Women on the Edge of Time* (1976). A major difference is that Firestone and Piercy embraced science and technology, whereas cultural and spiritual ecofeminists view them as male-centered means of domination over women and nature. Hence, cultural and spiritual ecofeminisms take a decidedly antitechnology and antirational turn.

"The Myth of Gaia" from Charlene Spretnak's *The Spiritual Dimension of Green Politics* (1986) exemplifies this antirational turn. Gaia is one of the major icons of spiritual ecofeminism. In *Lost Goddesses of Ancient Greece* (1978: 30–31) Spretnak explains how Gaia (also called Ge) is the ancient earth-mother who brought forth the world and the human race from the gaping void Chaos. Spretnak's efforts to reclaim Gaia as an earth-mother were part of many feminist attempts to create a new earth-based form of spirituality rooted in ancient traditions that revered both the earth and female deities (Merchant 1995: 3). By incorporating the Gaia myth into ecofeminism, spiritual feminists created a new cultural framework that countered male-dominated cultures and religions and fostered the idea of living symbiotically with the earth.

Carol Christ's article "Why Women Need the Goddess" (1999) highlights four major reasons for the importance of the Goddess symbol to women. First, this symbol acknowledges the legitimacy of female power and stands in sharp contrast to the portrayals of female dependence on and inferiority to men that predominate in dominant religions and cultures. Second, the Goddess symbol is an affirmation of the female body and its life cycles, a sharp contrast with the frequent denigration of female bodies expressed in cultural/religious taboos surrounding menstruation, childbirth, and menopause. Third, the Goddess symbol represents the positive valuation of women's will. Unlike more individualistic portrayals of will, within the Goddess framework an individual will can be achieved only through harmonic exercise with nature and other human beings. Fourth, Goddess symbolism encourages women to reevaluate their bonds and heritage. This woman-identified focus is meant to unify women through respecting and celebrating their woman-to-woman relationships (Merchant 1999: 16).

The 1980s was a period of significant growth in cultural and spiritual ecofeminisms within the U.S. women's movement. Some observers claim that their ideas "injected new life" into the ecofeminist movement during the 1980s and were an "integral part" of what sustained the women's movement after the defeat of the Equal Rights Amendment (Whittier 1995: 211–212; Merchant 1995: 4). Other feminists view cultural and spiritual ecofeminisms as irrational and politically reactionary. To these critics, they romanticize women's bodies and lives in ways that foster conservative notions of women that historically have been used to exclude women from educational and occupational opportunities. A more rational approach is frequently voiced by liberal and Marxist ecofeminists (see chapters 2 and 4). Early anarcha-ecofeminists also embraced a rational approach, but later their perspective shifted toward melding the rational and the spiritual (see chapter 4). Environmental justice activists criticize spiritual ecofeminists primarily for their insensitivity to women of color. On the one hand, pagan religions are offensive to many African–Americans who work in close partnership with churches for their civil rights and environmental justice campaigns (Taylor 2002). On the other hand, Native–Americans view spiritual ecofeminists as appropriating their ancient traditions in an "imperialist" manner that uses them out of context and distorts them without giving back to Native communities (Smith 1997; see chapter 5).

THE "UNHAPPY MARRIAGE" OF FEMINIST THEORY AND LESBIAN THEORY

As is discussed in chapters 6 and 7, a shift from radical feminist lesbian theory to queer theory took place in the 1990s as many U.S. feminists began to criticize second wave lesbian theories and embrace queer politics. Cheshire Calhoun's "Separating Lesbian Theory from Feminist Theory" (2003) provides a conceptual bridge between these modern and poststructuralist camps. Although Calhoun stays within the modernist camp, she argues not only that radical feminist lesbian theory desexualized and sanitized lesbian theory but also that it swallowed up lesbian politics. Her description of the situation, what she calls the "unhappy marriage of feminist theory and lesbian theory," alludes to the inequalities entailed in marriage law under the common law doctrine of coverture whereby when a man and woman married they became one but not equal under law, as the man retained legal power over his wife. Calhoun argues that wedding feminist theory with lesbian theory resulted in feminist theory subsuming and dominating lesbian theory.

To her credit, Calhoun places these nuptials in their historical context. She understands that second wave lesbian feminists were, in part, downplaying sex in lesbian relations in order to highlight the shared concerns of lesbians and heterosexual women. This was important not only to counter the homophobia of that era but also to mend the gay–straight split in the women's movement (336). Nevertheless, she argues that joining lesbian theory with feminist theory submerged the power of heterosexism. She points to how patriarchy and heterosexism are two analytically distinct systems of oppression and how lesbians are more oppressed by heterosexism:

> Being a woman and being oppressed as a woman are often not the most important facts in a lesbian's life. Being a lesbian and being oppressed as a lesbian often matter more (344)

Calhoun also questions the earlier claim by lesbian feminists that lesbianism is a "paradigm for feminists" (Radicalesbians 1970) because lesbians rarely live with or do domestic labor for males. For Calhoun, this "escape from male dominance" is a feminist paradigm only from the vantage point of a heterosexual woman. A lesbian may be free from an individual man in her personal life, but she is not free from *systemic heterosexism*. The coercive forces brought to bear on lesbians are witnessed in numerous situations not faced by heterosexual women. Lesbians often are denied custody of their children, punished for public displays of affection, and lose jobs if they are "outed":

> To refuse to be heterosexual is simply to leap out of the frying pan of individual patriarchal control into the fire of institutionalized heterosexual control. (Calhoun 2003: 338)

For Calhoun, a heterosexual vantage point also underlies many second wave feminists' criticisms of certain lifestyle and sexual practices. She argues that it is only from a heterosexual vantage point that butch/femme and sadomaschism are seen as emulating patriarchal roles or power dynamics. From a lesbian vantage point, the "identification" with masculinity that appears as butch is not a simple assimilation of lesbianism back into the terms of heterosexuality. Rather it is a dissonant juxtaposition that enables butch to deconstruct and denaturalize masculinity and femininity. Within a lesbian context, sadomaschism need not involve oppressive forms of power but, rather, can be sexually playful and enhance eroticism. Practices that are repressive from a heterosexual vantage point may be forms of resistance to normalizing sexual regimes in a nonheterosexual context. In these ways Calhoun shares with queer theorists an appreciation for how "subversive performances" can contest or resist the status quo (Butler 1990: 128). Nevertheless, given her binary analysis of oppression, her affirmative lesbian identity politics, and her standpoint epistemology, her theoretical perspective remains within the modernist camp (Calhoun 2003: 343–344).

CONCLUSION

This chapter has pointed to a diverse array of radical feminisms generated by the U.S. women's movement. Other commentators have analytically distinguished between these different forms of radical feminism in various ways. Some have divided them on the basis of whether they view sex as pleasure or sex as danger. Others have focused on whether they highlight cultural differences between males and females or material and/or biological differences. Still others have mixed and matched these foci to divide radical feminism into two camps: radical libertarian feminists versus radical cultural feminists (Tong 2009: 90–95). Overall, I find the various radical feminisms of the second wave too diverse and nuanced for such precise categorizations. For example, the work of Shulamith Firestone could be placed in a number of these categories. She was a libertarian in that her perspective lauded sexual freedom and pansexuality. She was a materialist feminist in terms of rooting women's oppression in a biologically based sexual division of labor. She also employed cultural feminism in discussing the "female" aesthetic and the "male" technological cultural forms.

Perhaps the more fundamental distinction between different branches of radical feminism is between those who employ a biological determinist framework and those who embrace social constructionism. Given the important role that social constructionism is playing in feminism today, this may be a better predictor of which radical feminisms will have a longer life span. Overall, the common ground that radical feminists share is a fairly narrow isthmus. They share the view that women's oppression is the earliest and most fundamental form of oppression that serves as a model for all other forms of oppression. They hierarchicalize oppressions by deeming women's oppression as the most important form of oppression. They also tend to essentialize women and argue that there are core traits (whether biological, social, or cultural) shared by all women. Thus, they have been heavily criticized for ignoring differences between women by race, class, and global location (Lorde 1984; Mohanty 1984; see chapters 5, 9, and 10). Nevertheless, radical feminists developed the most woman-centered perspective of all of the second wave feminist frameworks.

Another hallmark of second wave, radical feminisms is their concern with women's bodies. On the one hand, they drew the most attention to how women's bodies were objectified, used, and abused in patriarchal societies. They did an extraordinary amount of work on violence against women—whether it took the form of physical, emotional, or symbolic violence. On the other hand, they did the most to celebrate women's bodies—to argue that we should love our bodies, our natural cycles, our blood, and our tears despite the derogatory and demeaning messages we received from the patriarchy. While many younger feminists are quick to call radical feminism a classic example of second wave victim feminism because it focused so much on women as victims of both institutional and individual patriarchy (Roiphe 1993, Wolf [1993] 1994, Denfeld 1995), the aim of radical feminism was quite the opposite. By naming women's victimization and recognizing it as a political rather than a personal issue, they encouraged women to collectively empower themselves to end such abuse. They were the strongest second wave advocates of how women must understand, protect, and control their own bodies.

Their other positive contributions were many. Although their movement is often castigated today, their essentialist slogans, such as SISTERHOOD IS POWERFUL and SISTERHOOD IS GLOBAL, helped build community and collectivity among women. Radical feminists also provided a better understanding of the cultural dimensions of women's lives by simultaneously critiquing how patriarchal culture dominated women and celebrating women's culture. Their voices were central in drawing U.S. feminists' attention to compulsory heterosexuality as well as to those oppressions that previously had been relegated to the private realm of personal problems, such as rape, incest, domestic violence, and sexual harassment. Indeed, whether they were highlighting the dangers of sexual violence or the pleasures of sexual freedom they made great strides in making the personal political.

Additional writings by radical feminists on global issues can be found in chapter 9.

CRITICISM OF RADICAL FEMINISMS

1. That because radical feminists hierarchicalize oppressions by treating gender oppression as the most fundamental and important form of oppression, they ignore the simultaneous and interlocking nature of multiple oppressions, such as those of race and social class (Smith 1983).

2. That radical feminists are guilty of essentialism because they treat all women as having common attributes, traits, and concerns and, therefore, ignore important differences between women (Lorde 1984).

3. That radical feminists fail to analyze how women also can dominate or oppress others, such as when women with race or class privilege dominate both men and women who are marginalized by their racial or class locations (Collins 1990).

4. That radical feminists often take a colonialist stance in dealing with women from third world countries. They tend to homogenize third world women as passive victims of backward, traditional cultures who are unable to represent themselves and who must be rescued by modern, Western feminists (Mohanty 1984).

NOTES

1 For example, Arlo Guthrie's famous song "Alice's Restaurant" (1966) as well as the 1968 Peter Sellers movie *I Love You, Alice B. Toklas* both made much of her cannabis brownies. Some commentators claim that the slang term "toke" for inhaling majiuana is derived from her last name.

2 For more on federal and local crackdowns on homosexuals and other erotic communities see Gayle Rubin's discussion in "Thinking Sex" (1984).

3 *Stone Butch Blues* won the Stonewall Book Award in 1994.

4 For example, gay and transgender people staged a small riot in Los Angeles in 1959 in response to police harassment, while in San Francisco in 1966 a riot ensued when police tried to arrest drag queens, hustlers, and transvestites sitting in Compton's Cafeteria. This latter event is often cited as marking the beginning of transgender activism (Faderman and Timmons 2006; Stryker 2008).

5 While Firestone dedicates her book to Simone de Beauvoir, she criticizes her for taking an idealist approach by positing a priori categories of thought and existence—"otherness"—that fail to realize how these philosophical categories grow out of history (Firestone [1970] 1981: 7–8).

6 Sometimes Firestone ([1970] 1981: 195) contrasts these two approaches by calling them the "scientific" versus the "idealistic."

7 Firestone references Freud's theory here, though she criticizes his theory in another chapter, claiming it reflects the "power psychology" created by the patriarchal family [1970] 1981: 42–43).

8 Firestone is referring here to the totalitarian, repressive, and bleak social world portrayed in George Orwell's dystopian novel *1984* (Firestone [1970] 1981: 238).

9 Ariès's *Centuries of Childhood* points out how children in the premodern era were not separated from adult life. They witnessed childbirth and death; they worked alongside their parents. Children of the elite were often represented in portraits as little adults, and according to Ariès, there was no sense of childhood (no children's clothes or toys) until early modernity. Firestone highlights the positive features of this integration of children into the adult world, but ignores the negative sides, such as violence against children and the exploitation of child labor.

10 Here Firestone discusses the kibbutz model as well as Summerhill—a popular model of liberal education in that era developed by A. S. Neill. However, neither of these models is sufficiently radical for her.

11 See www.lesbianlife.about.com/od/lesbianactivism/a/TransatMich.htm (last accessed May 17, 2009).

12 Rubin's analysis here is very similar to the Foucaultian-inspired article "Missionary Feminism" by third wave feminist Gina Dent (1995) (see chapter 7). Both authors suggest how feminism itself can act as a disciplinary discourse or what Dent calls a "missionary feminism" that judges and evaluates the politically correct sexual practices for feminists.

13 See chapter 7 for various third wave feminists (often called the "dissenting daughters") who criticized second wave feminism for being a form of "victim feminism" and who used this term in a pejorative way (Wolf 1993, Roiphe 1993, Denfeld 1995).

14 For example, Millett provided the following quote from a work by Norman Mailer: "He took pleasure in degrading her. I could scarcely blame him for it, she was such a prim, priggish bitch in her street clothes. You'd swear she didn't own a cunt the way she carried herself in the street. . . . Once he played her a dirty trick. . . . He had her worked up to such a state that she was beside herself. Anyway, after he had almost polished the ass off her with his back-scuttling he pulled out for a second, as though to cool his cock off . . . and shoved a big long carrot up her twat" (quoted in Millett 1970: 400).

15 Millett contrasts the works of these "literate pornographers" to the deconstructionist plays of the homosexual author Jean Genet. She (1970: 42) writes: Sex is deep at the heart of our troubles, Genet is urging, and unless we eliminate the most pernicious of our systems of oppression, unless we go to the very center of the sexual politic and its sick delirium of power and violence, all our efforts at liberation will only land us again in the same primordial stews.

16 In *R. v. Butler*, [1992] 1 S.C.R. 452, known as the *Butler* decision, the Supreme Court of Canada largely accepted the arguments made by MacKinnon and Dworkin. Ironically, this law was used by Canadian customs to seize shipments of Dworkin's book *Pornography*. It also was used to prosecute gay and lesbian bookstores for selling the lesbian sadomasochistic magazine *Bad Attitude*.

17 This approach led many cultural and spiritual ecofeminists to become vegetarians and animal rights activists. It also melds well with their interests in earlier forms of spirituality, such as totemism and animism.

CHAPTER 4

Marxist, Socialist, and Anarchist Feminisms

If voting changed anything, they'd make it illegal.

—Emma Goldman

Woman continues to be a domestic slave, because petty housework crushes, strangles, stultifies and degrades her, chains her to the kitchen and to the nursery, and wastes her labor on barbarously unproductive, petty, nerve-racking, stultifying and crushing drudgery.

—V. I. Lenin

INTRODUCTION

One of the more disturbing observations about contemporary U.S. feminist scholarship is that while race, ethnicity, gender, sexuality, and global location have come to the forefront of feminist analyses, social class has received far less attention. For more than a decade, Jean Ait Belkhir (1998: 18), editor of the journal *Race Gender & Class*, has been vigilant in pointing out this shortcoming: "Despite its place in the now familiar list of race, class and gender—class is often the last addressed of these issues. Belkhir points to the paucity of selections on class and the lack of working-class voices in major texts in race, class, and gender studies. Moreover, there has been no institutionalization of working-class studies comparable to developments in women's studies, gay and lesbian studies, or the racial/ethnic foci of Africana, Latina, and Native-American studies (5–6). Other scholars have criticized the "theoretically impoverished concepts of class" employed by authors who claim to do race, gender, and class analyses (Kandal 1995 143; Mann and Grimes 2003). In short, class appears to be the weakest link in the frequently voiced trilogy of race, class, and gender. As will be shown below, this paucity of class analysis was not the case during the first and second waves of U.S. feminism.

This chapter examines how the Old and New Left have influenced U.S. feminist thought from early modernity to the present. Marxism and anarchism were the major **Old Left** theoretical perspectives that impacted U.S. feminism in the nineteenth and early twentieth centuries. Marxism highlighted social class—specifically the battle between the **proletariat** (wage laborers) and the **bourgeoisie** (the capitalist business owners who hired them)—as the primary axis of oppression in modern societies and championed the industrial working class as the major agent of revolutionary social change. While anarchists sought to rid the world of all forms of domination, they too focused primarily on class conflict and the struggles between labor and capital in this period. The **New Left** refers to the new social movements of late modernity, such as the civil rights movement, the women's movement, the gay and lesbian rights movement, and the anti–Vietnam war movement. Along with a focus social class, the New Left addressed the conflicts and cleavages generated by inequalities of race, gender, sexuality, and global location that tore at the fabric of American society in that era. Historian Van Gosse (2005: 5) refers to the New Left as a "movement of movements" that encompassed all of the struggles for fundamental change from the 1950s roughly to 1975.

Although the distinction between Marxist feminism and socialist feminism did not become part of the feminist lexicon until the second wave, there were some precursors to socialist feminism in the first wave, as will be shown below. Also explored in this chapter is how anarchist theory injected a radical thrust into the women's movement that was distinct from Marxism. The term *anarchism* derives from the Greek word *anarchos*, meaning "without rulers," and, unlike Marxists, anarchists reject all forms of hierarchy and domination, especially all forms government (including socialist governments). While Pierre-Joseph Proudhon is considered the founder of modern anarchist theory, more revolutionary anarchist politics were developed by the Russian theorists Mikhail Bakunin ([1876] 1991) and Peter Kropotkin ([1914] 2005) in the nineteenth and early twentieth centuries. These revolutionary anarchists advocated a spontaneous, militant, direct action form of politics and were less willing to engage in reformist measures on their path to revolution. Given these Russian roots, it is not surprising that the most famous anarchist feminist in the United States during the first wave was the Russian immigrant Emma Goldman.

Marxists, including Marx himself, engaged in bitter disputes with anarchist theorists to win the working class over to their politics. Feminists inspired by these Old Left theories also engaged in heated theoretical battles. Yet, despite their differences, Marxist, socialist, and anarchist feminists *all share a heavy focus on class and gender*. By contrast, the postmodern turn taken by feminist scholars in recent decades included a rejection of Marxism as a totalizing theory and an underdevelopment of class analysis. No doubt, such shifts in feminist scholarship away from class analyses also reflect important local and global social, economic, and political developments over the past few decades. The implosion of the Soviet Union in the late 1980s and the opening up of many former socialist/communist societies to capitalism (or at least to more mixed economies) certainly played a role in reducing the credibility of both Marxism and socialism as providing paths for future emancipatory projects. In turn, the erosion of class in the realm of theory mirrored the decline of the industrial working class in the advanced industrial nations as corporations increasingly moved manufacturing abroad in search of cheaper labor and less restrictive working conditions. This **deindustrialization** of the West has had dramatic implications for changing the gender, race, and ethnic composition of the workforce and for *increasing inequalities* within the United States.

Because the **third world** or **global South** is becoming the center of industrial manufacture, some of the major contributions of contemporary Marxist and socialist feminists have been their analyses of women's work in third world societies and the local/global linkages this entails. Chapters 8 and 9 of this text include numerous examples of Marxist, socialist, and anarchist feminist analyses of imperialism and globalization. In turn, the integration of Marxism into the new feminist paradigms of postmodernity is most explicitly found in postcolonial theory. As discussed in chapter 10, postcolonial theory is the most influential contemporary feminist perspectives to locate its roots in a synthesis of Marxism and poststructuralism.

MARXIST, SOCIALIST, AND ANARCHIST FEMINISMS IN EARLY MODERNITY

The Origins of Women's Oppression

It was rare in the late nineteenth and early twentieth centuries for male theorists to address women's oppression. Aside from John Stuart Mill (discussed in chapter 2), the other male theorists who made the most significant contributions during this era were Marxists. Most noteworthy were the writings by Karl Marx and Friedrich Engels who provided a general conceptual framework for understanding forms of oppression as well as a specific analysis of the origins of women's oppression. Engels's *Origin of the Family, Private Property, and the State* ([1884] 1972), which was based on Marx's *Ethnological Notebooks* ([1880–1882] 1986),[1] is an enduring classic of nineteenth-century feminist thought. Other famous feminist works by male Marxists in the early twentieth century include August Bebel's *Women under Socialism* (1904),[2] V. I. Lenin's writings collected in *The Emanicpation of Women* ([1934] 1995), and the works of Leon Trotsky, which can be found in *Women and the Family* (1973). While all of these writings inspired later feminists, the focus here will be on the contributions of Marx and Engels.

In *Origin of the Family, Private Property, and the State* ([1884] 1972), Engels located the roots of women's oppression not in biology but, rather, in sociohistorical developments. He argued that women's oppression had not always existed but arose alongside the origins of class oppression in ancient agricultural societies that had developed a notion of private property as well as in their state systems that enforced property rights and patriarchal dominion. According to Engels, the earliest human societies—hunting and gathering societies—did not have such developed systems of stratification either by class or by gender. Rather they were organized in matrilineal clans in which both men and women had significant roles providing economic subsistence. Because hunting and gathering is more risky and vulnerable to the vagaries of nature than agricultural production (where people at least control how much is planted), he argued that hunting and gathering societies entailed more sharing of foodstuffs or what anthropologists today call "mutual aid" than did later modes of production. Because of this sharing and the relative absence of class and gender inequalities, Engels referred to hunting and gathering as the primitive communist mode of production. His analysis was based on existing anthropological data, such as Lewis Henry Morgan's research on Native-American tribes. Morgan's work was familiar to American suffragists, who also were interested in the gender equality found in these tribes (Landsman 1992; see chapter 8).

Engels argued that hunters and gatherers who lived off wild vegetation and wild game had no interests in private property in land (the major source of subsistence at that time) because they were nomadic and needed to move across open spaces in search of their economic subsistence. These tribes or clans were matrilineal, meaning that lineage was traced through the mother rather than the father. Although there was a sexual division of labor where women primarily gathered and men primarily hunted, for Engels this was not equivalent to sexual oppression or patriarchy. Rather because gathering brought in a substantial amount of the food used by hunters and gatherers, women's role in production was extremely important. Engels claimed that women's more equal role in production gave them more equal social and political rights than women in later class-based, patriarchal modes of production. (See chapters 8 and 9 for works by Native-American feminists who discuss the greater gender equality enjoyed by their female ancestors).

By contrast, farmers—especially in agrarian modes of production based on large-scale grain production, such as wheat or rice—required political and economic systems that recognized private property in land. Unlike hunting and gathering, agriculture could provide a controlled economic surplus where people produced more than they consumed and the entire population did not have to be engaged constantly in foraging for food. This socially controlled surplus not only enabled people to engage in other activities, such as crafts or mining, but it also provided the material conditions for the development of class systems. That is, some people could live off the labor of others by virtue of owning income-producing property.[3] This *appropriation of the surplus labor of others* was the basis for Marx's notion of class exploitation (Mandel 1970: 39–45).

To *reproduce class systems over generational time* required that private property be passed down to one's children or heirs, and for Engels, this required control over women's sexuality. To put it simply, women know who their children are because they give birth to them. However, men have greater uncertainty of paternity, particularly men in ancient societies where paternity could not easily be verified. Thus biological differences play some role in Engels's theory but *only* in certain historical eras characterized by property-based modes of production. To ensure that males passed down property to their own children, institutionalized forms of patriarchy were developed to control women's sexuality. Examples include how women in propertied classes were restricted to the household and required chaperones if and when they were allowed to venture into more public spaces. Ancient agrarian societies also established patriarchal laws, such as those that punished women but not men for adultery. For Engels, *women's relegation to the home and to domestic activities originally arose to protect property rights and class privilege.* In turn, the rise of the state and the privatized family—as opposed to the more communal clans in hunting and gathering societies—were major institutions that reinforced women's inequality.

In Engels' theory, **patriarchy**—meaning institutionalized male dominion over women and children (which he also refers to as the "decline of mother right")—began with the rise of agricultural societies, developed systems of stratification, and private property. These ancient agrarian societies (like those described in the Hebrew Bible) were generally based on private property in land and slaves. Under these class-based modes of production, private property and inheritance required the institutions of the family and the state to control women, hence the title of Engels's book. In this way, Engels tied the rise of women's oppression to the rise of class oppression. Based on this understanding of the origins of women's oppression, the Marxist path to women's emancipation included: the abolition of privately owned, income-producing property through a socialist revolution; the overthrow of patriarchal domination in the family and in state laws; the entry of women into the workplace and the polity on an equal footing with men; and the transformation of work in the home through the industrialization and socialization of housework and childrearing.

The question of the origins of women's oppression generated one of the signal debates of the early second wave. The intensity of these debates suggests how important feminists at this time viewed understanding the origins of women's oppression as a prerequisite to understanding how to transform and end that oppression. These debates were especially heated between second wave Marxist feminists and radical feminists. As discussed in chapter 3, some radical feminists argued that women's oppression had existed throughout human history because it was rooted in biology. On this basis they claimed that women's oppression was the earliest and most fundamental form of oppression; hence, gender trumped class as their focus of revolutionary struggle. Following Engels, Marxist feminists argued that women's oppression was rooted in social rather than biological causes and only arose in history with the rise of agricultural societies and class stratification. Here class and not gender was the focal point of struggle. During the second wave, special journal issues were devoted to this debate, and feminist anthropologists were called on to provide up-to-date data on the topic. Among the second wave Marxist and socialist feminists who contributed to this debate were anthropologists Kathleen Gough (1961), Rae Lesser Blumberg (1978) and Eleanor Leacock (1972).[4] A brief and accessible discussion of Engels's theory and the debates between second wave feminists over the origins of women's oppression can be found in Evelyn Reed's "Women: Caste, Class, or Oppressed Sex?" (1984).

Women's Work in the Home

Charlotte Perkins Gilman's *Women and Economics* (1898) provided the most substantial feminist analysis of housework and child care written in the nineteenth century. Gilman's writings differed from most first wave writings in two fundamental ways. First, suffragists of this era rarely criticized women's responsibility for housework and child care. Indeed, some women's rights activists pointed to their roles as mothers and caretakers of the next generation to argue for the right to vote (Sneider 2008: 70). On the other hand, most first wave feminist writings are largely descriptive. By contrast, Gilman believed in the critical role of social theory and wrote *Women and Economics* in "the voice of a grand theorist"—an analytical and theoretical style more common to male theorists of her era (Lengermann and Niebrugge-Brantley 1998: 113 and 124).

Gilman was involved in the Progressive movement of this era, but her work was inspired by utopian and Fabian socialism. These types of socialism embrace cooperative and collective forms of social life but reject revolutionary approaches to social change. However, they share with Marxism the view that labor is fundamental to the existential well-being of human beings. Marx discussed how labor gave intrinsic meaning to human life because humans could realize themselves in the products they produced and imprint themselves on the world through their labor. Gilman embraced a similar idea. The crux of her work is an examination of how gender arrangements in modern, industrial societies distort the nature of women's work and, thereby, the well-being of women. For her, the distorted nature of existing gender arrangements results in false consciousness through which women come to think primarily in personal rather than sociopolitical terms. Gilman uses the term "excessive sex distinctions" instead of gender, but the meaning is similar. She calls these distinctions "excessive" because they corrupt social life far beyond anything entailed in biological sex differences and because they draw attention away from the common qualities men and women share as human beings (116 and 125).

Like Marx, Gilman assigns much weight to human labor in giving meaning to human life. The relationship between the individual and the economy, what she calls the "sexuo-economic relation," provides the conceptual framework of *Women and Economics*. Gilman ([1898] 1966: 22) points to how the unequal "sexuo-economic" relation where females are economically dependent on men exists only among human beings: "We are the only animal species in which the female depends on the male for food, the only animal species in which the sex-relation is also an economic relation." For Gilman, it is the relegation of women to domestic labor in the home that denies them economic independence: "It is not motherhood that keeps the housewife on her feet from dawn till dark: it is house service, not child service" (20). That is, women are serving men in a relationship of subordination and domination:

> Their [women's] labor is the property of another. They work under another's will; and what they receive depends not on their labor, but on the power and will of another. (7)

The "sexuo-economic relation" also divided the world into separate spheres of social life— the public and the private. Being relegated to the private sphere of the home, women must suppress and distort their desire for agency by focusing their activities on the personal and the private. For Gilman, the home is the major institution that corrupts the character and life of women. Consequently, women's emancipation is predicated on a transformation of the home and privatized, domestic labor—a project to which she devotes a significant amount of attention. Gilman views privatized domestic labor as a "preindustrial relic," given its inefficiency and lack of specialization as compared with work outside the home. She details various ways in which child care and housework could be carried out to make the home a site for the empowerment of *all* of its members. Her transformed world of the home entails a more collective/communal lifestyle through which child care, food services, laundry, and household cleaning are handled by professional, enlightened, and well-paid workers (Lengermann and Niebrugge-Brantley 1998: 129).

Gilman discussed these transformations of women's work and the home in a number of her writings, such as *Concerning Children* (1900), *The Home* (1903), *Human Work* (1904), *The Man-Made World; or, Our Androcentric Culture* (1911), *His Religion and Hers* (1923), and her utopian novel *Herland* (1915). However, her most widely read work is *The Yellow Wallpaper* [1892] (1995). This feminist novella highlights what Betty Friedan (1963) would later call "**the problem that has no name**"—the depression and phobias that some women experience when they are relegated to work in the home and are allowed few outlets to realize themselves in other forms of labor.

The major character in *The Yellow Wallpaper* is an upper-class woman—notably without a name—who desires to be a writer. Her efforts to write are obstructed by her husband, who is a doctor, and by the medical establishment of her era. This novella critiques not only the paucity of options open for women's work but also medical practices of the late nineteenth century, when doctors prescribed a "rest cure" for women with nervous disorders or "hysteria" (a word derived from the Latin word for womb). Under this rest cure, women were forbidden from doing any productive labor, a cure that Gilman thought only made women's depression worse. Instead of being allowed to write, the main character is required to rest. She is relegated not just to the home, but to a room with barred windows that once was a nursery. For Gilman, the nursery is symbolic of the way the husband in the story treats his wife like a child. The title of the story comes from the intricate, interwoven designs of the hideous wallpaper in the nursery, which to the wife appear as a maze that imprisons women's desire for freedom:

> I really have discovered something at last. Through watching [the wallpaper] so much at night, when it changes so, I have finally found out. The front pattern does move—and no wonder! The woman behind it shakes it. Sometimes I think there are a great many women behind [the wallpaper]. (Gilman [1892] 1995: 52)

Here the decorative wallpaper—which usually makes a home more attractive—becomes a metaphor for how the home and decorative femininity stifle women's labor and creativity. Because Gilman experienced the constraints of the rest cure when she was married, *The Yellow Wallpaper* is, in part, autobiography written as fiction.

A number of twentieth-century authors would repeat this theme of "the problem that has no name" in fictional forms, such as Doris Lessing's short story "To Room Nineteen" (1963) or Helen Simpson's collection *Getting a Life* (2001).[5] Yet such works (including Gilman's) that focus primarily on the negative implications of woman qua housewife have been criticized for ignoring differences between women and considering only the lives of white, heterosexual, and class-privileged women who had the luxury of being homemakers and stay-at-home moms (hooks 1984; Lorde 1984; Lengermann and Niebrugge-Brantley 1998: 129). By contrast, more orthodox Marxist, socialist, and anarchist feminists of the first wave were more careful to highlight class differences between women, their lives, and their types of work.

Class Differences in Women's Lives and Work

Many first wave Marxist, socialist, and anarchist feminists were labor organizers who focused attention on the plight of working-class and poor women, such as Mary Harris "Mother" Jones and Alexandra Kollontai. "Girl Slaves of the Milwaukee Breweries" (1910) was written by Jones, a founder of the major U.S. anarchist labor organization of this era, the Industrial Workers of the World (IWW). "Working Woman and Mother" (1914) was written by Alexandra Kollontai, a Marxist feminist and a key figure in the Russian Revolution and its establishment of the first socialist country in the world, the Union of Soviet Socialist Republics (USSR). While both of these works are more descriptive than theoretical, they poignantly highlight significant class differences that existed between women in the early twentieth century.

Mother Jones calls the women brewery workers in Milwaukee "wage slaves," a term used to stress how wage workers were forced to work in order to eat. Jones describes their long hours, their vulnerability to diseases and other workplace hazards, and the indecent language and treatment they had to endure. Kollantai juxtaposes the lives of different pregnant women to illuminate the stark contrasts. She compares the life of an upper-class, **bourgeois** woman married to an industrial capitalist and the life of a working-class or **proletarian** woman who works as a laundress. The factory owner's wife gets told to rest, not to lift anything heavy, and to eat healthy foods, including such luxuries of the era as fruit and caviar. The laundress works long hours and gets no relief despite her swollen legs and the difficulty she has carrying heavy baskets of wet linen. The factory owner's house is the scene of a "flurry of doctors, midwives and nurses," while the laundress gives birth unattended. The upper-class child grows up "under the eye of various nannies," while the working-class woman leaves her infant with the child next door and worries about her baby all day while she is at work (Kollontai [1914] 2005: 128). Kollantai discusses various policies designed to assist working-class women, such as protective labor legislation for pregnant women, maternity insurance, and state-subsidized child care. Such demands for protective labor legislation for women

BOX 4.1

"Bread and Roses"

As we come marching, marching,
Unnumbered women dead
Go crying through our singing
Their ancient song of Bread;
Small art and love and beauty
Their drudging spirits knew—
Yes, it is bread we fight for,
But we fight for roses, too.

As we come marching, marching,
We bring the greater days;
The rising of the women
Means the rising of us all.
No more the drudge and idler,
Ten that toil where one reposes,
But a sharing of life's glories,
Bread and Roses, Bread and Roses.

From *The American Magazine*, December 1911

placed Marxist, socialist and anarchist feminists in conflict with liberal feminists of this era who called for formal, legal equality between men and women.

Literary works written by women in the late nineteenth and early twentieth centuries often depicted the harsh realities of working-class women's lives. A fine example is Rebecca Harding Davis's pioneering work *Life in the Iron-Mills* (1861), regarded by many critics as marking the transition from romanticism to realism in American literature. In turn, some of the most famous icons of the U.S. women's movement are based on the struggles of working-class women during the first wave. **International Women's Day**, which falls annually on March 8, was established in 1910 to commemorate major strikes by women workers. It was proposed by the German socialist feminist Clara Zetkin, who was well-known in Europe for championing women's rights. The anthem of the women's movement, **"Bread and Roses,"** commemorates a strike of women textile workers in Lawrence, Massachusetts, in 1912 called the Bread and Roses strike. A copy of this famous anthem appears in Box 4.1.

Love, Marriage, and Sexual Practices

It is difficult to realize today how radical it was in the nineteenth and early twentieth centuries to demand that people should have the right to marry and to have sex with people they loved. At that time, marriage was more of an economic arrangement, and women who were not married often lived in dire economic straits. Even unmarried women from privileged class backgrounds often suffered, as George Gissing's *The Odd Women* (1893) and Edith Wharton's *The House of Mirth* (1905) suggest. Marriage law under the **doctrine of coverture** gave husbands control over their wives' incomes and bodies. While most liberal feminists of the first wave called for **voluntary motherhood**—the right to abstain from having sex with their husbands—few went as far as Marxist, socialist, and anarchist feminists to demand rights to birth control and abortion.

Margaret Sanger was a socialist feminist who worked as a nurse with poor and working-class women. She saw firsthand how maternal deaths from childbirth as well as uncontrolled fertility seriously impacted the lives of these women and their families. In this era, it was illegal even for married couples to use birth control except in emergencies. Because birth control information was viewed as pornography, it was illegal to distribute it. Nevertheless, in 1914 Sanger published the *Woman Rebel*, a magazine that provided birth control information. In 1916 she opened a birth control clinic in Brooklyn, New York, that provided women with medical checkups and birth control pamphlets printed in English, Yiddish, and Italian. Despite the fact that hundreds of women used this clinic, the authorities shut it down. When women demonstrated against the clinic closing, Sanger was arrested. In her later years, Sanger founded the organization that later became Planned Parenthood, and she lived long enough to witness the development of the birth control pill. Her major writings on women and birth control can be found in *Woman and the New Race* (1920).

Marxist, socialist, and anarchist feminists also called for "**sex love**" or "**free-love**." In this era, free love did not refer to indiscriminate sex, as it often does today, but rather to the right to marry for love, to have sex with someone you loved, and for women to have the same sexual rights as men. To illustrate this distinction, excerpts from Clara Zetkin's interview with V. I. Lenin, Marxist leader of the Russian Revolution, are presented in Box 4.2. In the interview, Lenin distinguishes between sex love and sexual promiscuity. He describes sexual promiscuity as a bourgeois or upper-class phenomenon and is concerned that young people mistakenly view Marxists and socialists as supporting the view that sex should be as easy as "drinking a glass of water."

BOX 4.2

Lenin on "Sex-Love"

A revolution in sex and marriage is approaching, corresponding to the proletarian revolution. . . . The changed attitude of the young people to questions of sexual life is of course based on a "principle" and a theory. Many of them call their attitude "revolutionary" and "communist." And they honestly believe that it is so. That does not impress us old people. Although I am nothing but a gloomy ascetic, the so-called "new sexual life" of the youth—and sometimes of the old—often seems to me to be purely bourgeois, an extension of bourgeois brothels. That has nothing whatever in common with freedom of love as we communists understand it. You must be aware of the famous theory that in communist society the satisfaction of sexual desires, of love, will be as simple and unimportant as drinking a glass of water. . . .

I think this glass of water theory is completely un-Marxist, and, moreover, anti-social. . . . Of course, thirst must be satisfied. But will the normal person in normal circumstances lie down in the gutter and drink out of a puddle or out of a glass with a rim greasy from many lips? But the social aspect is most important of all. Drinking water is, of course, an individual affair. But in love two lives are concerned, and a third, a new life, arises, it is that which gives it its social interest, which gives rise to a duty towards the community.

As a communist I have not the least sympathy for the glass of water theory, although it bears the fine title "satisfaction of love" . . . in my opinion the present widespread hypertrophy in sexual matters does not give joy and force to life, but takes it away. In the age of revolution that is bad, very bad. . . . The revolution demands concentration. . . . It cannot tolerate orgiastic conditions, such as are normal for the decadent heroes and heroines of D'Annunzio. Dissoluteness in sexual life is bourgeois, is a phenomenon of decay. . . . Self-control, self-discipline is not slavery, not even in love. But forgive me, Clara, I have wandered far from the starting point of our conversation. Why didn't you call me to order? My tongue has run away with me. I am deeply concerned about the future of our youth. It is a part of the revolution. And if harmful tendencies are appearing, creeping over from bourgeois society into the world of revolution—as the roots of many weeds spread—it is better to combat them early. Such questions are part of the woman question.

From "Lenin on the Woman Question," by Clara Zetkin. 1920. Marxists.org; www.marxists.org/archive/zetkin/1920/lenin/zetkin1.htm. A slightly different translation can be found on pp. 103–108 in *The Emancipation of Women: From the Writings of V. I. Lenin*. (New York: International Publishers, 1995).

As a means of highlighting the inequalities embedded in marriage law at that time, Marxist, socialist, and anarchist feminists often referred to conventional marriage as prostitution. They argued that because women had few opportunities for economic independence they were in essence forced to marry for financial security. In this sense, marriage was no different from a form of prostitution. Emma Goldman's "The Traffic in Women," from *Anarchism and Other Essays* (1910), is one of the most famous first wave writings to make this point. Goldman likens conventional marriage to prostitution and views all forms of prostitution as exploitative of women. Because she sees prostitution as caused by poverty and/or lack of employment options for women, she links gender oppression to class oppression. Goldman was critical of liberal feminism, which she called "bourgeois feminism." She criticized how their demands for formal equality undermined protective labor legislation for women as well as how their rejection of birth control and abortion ignored the needs of working-class women. While her views on these topics were shared by many Marxist and socialist feminists of the era, Goldman did not agree on the necessity of a socialist state.

By contrast, Marxist feminists thought that socialism and a socialist state would solve the problems of women's emancipation. Once a socialist government was in power it could pass laws that gave women rights to abortion and birth control and that established the collective kitchens and child care centers that would free women from domestic work. Consequently, they argued that feminists should direct their efforts toward allying with working-class men in the more important class struggle. Any attempt to put feminist issues before class concerns was viewed as pitting working-class men against working-class women and thus divisive of the class struggle. It is this priority given to class over gender, as well as the failure to address how working-class men also oppressed women, that led to a break between Marxist feminists and socialist feminists.

The distinction between Marxist feminism and socialist feminism was not introduced until the second wave. However, Crystal Eastman's first wave writings closely mirror what would later be described as a socialist feminist perspective. Eastman was a labor lawyer, socialist, suffragist, and one of four authors of the Equal Rights Amendment (ERA) when it was first introduced in the 1920s. In *On Women and Revolution* ([1919] 2005: 130–131) she writes that

> the true feminist, no matter how far to the left she may be in the revolutionary movement, sees the woman's battle as distinct in it objects and different in its methods from the worker's battle for industrial freedom . . . as a feminist she also knows that the whole of woman's slavery is not summed up in the profit system, nor her complete emancipation assured by the downfall of capitalism.

Eastman points to the sexism among working-class men that would not necessarily disappear with a socialist revolution as well as to other dimensions of social life that needed to be transformed. These included equalizing the socialization and education of boys and girls, having men engage equally in housework and child care, and providing wages for those who chose housework and child care as their occupation. Overall, socialist feminists thought women's liberation entailed more than a socialist revolution and questioned Marxist feminists' prioritization of class oppression over gender oppression. They demanded that *equal* consideration be given to both gender and class.

Precursors to Ecofeminism in Early Modernity

Because many Marxist, socialist, and anarchist feminists were directly involved in labor organizing, they were among some of the earliest activists to focus attention on hazards in the workplace.[6] By the late nineteenth century, the United States had one of the highest industrial accidents rates in the world. From 1880 to 1900, 35,000 workers died and another 500,000 were injured annually (Taylor 2002: 12). The most serious industrial accident of this era involving women was the 1911 Triangle Factory fire in New York City, during which 146 women garment workers were killed. When environmental historian Robert Gottlieb discussed the pioneering efforts of women activists around these workplace issues he highlighted the role of a number of socialist women, including Rose Schneiderman, Crystal

Eastman, and Florence Kelley (also a member of Hull House) (Gottlieb 2005: 289 and 352).

Rose Schneiderman spoke at the memorial for the women killed in the Triangle Factory Fire.[7] She then helped organize the International Ladies Garment Workers Union and led its 1913 strike. Crystal Eastman was the author of New York's first workman's [*sic*] compensation law in 1907, which became a model for other state laws across the United States. Florence Kelley is best known for working tirelessly for both an eight-hour workday and child labor laws. She also founded the National Consumers League that struggled against sweatshop labor and helped establish the National Association for the Advancement of Colored People (NAACP). She translated Friedrich Engels's *The Condition of the English Working Class* into English and attempted to write a similar book on American labor. When her efforts were thwarted by the absence of adequate labor statistics, she campaigned for the formation of bureaus of labor statistics at the state and national levels.

Left-wing women also employed the concept of nature to promote their labor organizing efforts. In her journal *Mother Earth* first published in 1907, Emma Goldman forged the metaphorical figure of Mother Earth as one who "cares not for the bourgeois household, but for the people en mass" (quoted in Alaimo 2000: 89). Goldman used this image in vivid attacks against the capitalist system:

> Mother Earth, with the sources of vast wealth hidden within the folds of her ample bosom, extended her inviting and hospitable arms to all those who came to her from arbitrary and despotic lands—Mother Earth ready to give herself alike to all her children. But soon she was seized by the few, stripped of her freedom, fenced in, a prey to those who were endowed with cunning and unscrupulous shrewdness. (90)

As noted in chapter 2, there were quite diverse environmental issues in the nineteenth and early twentieth centuries, including air and water pollution, garbage and sanitation issues, safe food, and industrial health and safety. While these problems affected the entire population, they most seriously affected poor and working-class people who lived near industrial factories and in overcrowded, urban areas (Merchant 2007: 120). Because the municipal housekeeping activities of Marxist and socialist feminists focused on the concerns of poor people, these radicals were referred to derogatorily as sewer socialists and became victims of red-baiting during the Red Scare of 1919–1920.

This first Red Scare took place at a time of heightened labor activism. By 1919, hundreds of strikes were taking place every month nationwide, strikes that the conservative press called "conspiracies against the government" and "plots to establish communism" instigated by "foreign agitators" (Levin 1971: 31). The timing of the Red Scare also coincided with the victory of the Russian Revolution and the establishment of the first socialist society—the Union of Soviet Socialist Republics (USSR)—The success of this revolution only increased the antiradical hysteria and provoked mounting fears of a similar socialist revolution taking place in the United States (29).

For many left-wing political activists, the Red Scare meant increased police surveillance, arrests, and the deportation of immigrants suspected of being radicals. Like the post– World War II McCarthy era, the Red Scare of 1919–1920 had a crippling effect on the American Left. It is estimated, for example, that membership in the U.S. Communist Party was reduced by some 80 percent (Schweikart and Allen 2004). Crystal Eastman and Emma Goldman came under surveillance from the newly formed Federal Bureau of Investigation (FBI). Eastman's radical journal *The Liberator* was banned, and she was blacklisted. Emma Goldman, along with more than two hundred other foreign-born radicals, was arrested and deported to the Soviet Union in 1919. Even the Hull House women were victims of red-baiting despite the fact that most of them did not embrace socialism.[8]

MARXIST, SOCIALIST, AND ANARCHIST FEMINISMS BETWEEN THE WAVES

From the 1930s through the 1950s, Marxist, socialist, and anarchist feminists turned their attention to the immense problems bequeathed by the Great Depression, the rise of fascism, and World War II. After the war, they had to contend with the Cold War and McCarthyism. As historian Barbara Deckard ([1979] 1983: 316) explains:

> The radicalism of the 1930s concentrated on unemployment and, in the late 1930s, on the threat of fascism to the practical exclusion of all other issues. The postwar 1946–1960 period was a time of U.S. economic expansion and world dominance, of the cold war and superpatriotism ensured by the witch-hunting of McCarthyism. All radical and liberal groups suffered repression; and possible women's liberation causes—such as child care—were smothered with the rest.

There is no doubt that, between the waves, members of radical political groups were blacklisted, often arrested, and the subjects of heavy surveillance by the state. Women's political concerns clearly took a back seat to the domestic and geopolitical crises of the era. However, contrary to Deckard's statement on child care, government-sponsored day care was provided during the 1930s and 1940s (Steinfels 1973, Kerr 1973). Federally funded day care centers first appeared as a result of New Deal policies and the Works Progress Administration (WPA) during the depression. The WPA nurseries, set up to provide employment for unemployed teachers, were lauded for their fine educational, health, and nutritional care (Kerr 1973: 162). Although the federal government began to dismantle these child care centers as the economy recovered, the entry of thousands of women into the workforce during World War II caused them to be revived. Under the Lanham Act of 1941, day nurseries were established in forty-seven states and serviced approximately 1.5 million children (Steinfels 1973: 67). Although the Lanham Act day care centers were criticized for discriminating against black children and for providing day care to only a small percentage of eligible children, these centers marked the most extensive state-supported day care program ever seen in the history of the

United States (Mann 1986). They were dismantled after the war in a concerted effort by the U.S. government to get women back into the home so that returning soldiers would have jobs.

Despite the crises faced by the Old Left between the waves, new approaches to socialist feminism developed in Europe that eventually would impact feminist thought in the United States. French feminist Simone de Beauvoir developed her existential feminism in *The Second Sex*, first published in French in 1949 and in English in 1952, became a classic of Western feminism. A new approach to Marxism, called Neo-Marxist critical theory, arose in the 1920s. It called for more emphasis on human freedom (including sexual freedom) and rejected all forms of authoritarianism. Another form of socialist politics—social democracy—also developed in the early decades of the twentieth century. It called for a democratic rather than a revolutionary path to socialism and included many public policies that enhanced the well-being of women and their families.

Feminist Social Democracy

Social democracy or democratic socialism arose in the early twentieth century out of a split within the socialist movement between revolutionary socialists and reform-oriented socialists. The first effect of this split was the establishment of the Second International, an organization of socialist and labor parties from twenty countries. Formed in Paris in 1889, the Second International was active until 1916. Its most memorable actions include its declaration in 1889 of May 1 as International Workers' Day and in 1910 of March 8 as International Women's Day. The Second International is remembered also for initiating an international campaign for establishment of the eight-hour workday. It dissolved in 1916 after delegates could not maintain a unified front against World War I. Patriotism trumped international working-class solidarity as many delegates supported their respective nation's role in the war. After the demise of the Second International, revolutionary socialists formed communist parties while reform-oriented socialists joined existing labor parties and/or established social democratic parties. Perhaps the most famous theorist associated with democratic socialism in the early decades of the twentieth century was German theoretician Eduard Bernstein. Bernstein supported women's emancipation and was one of the earliest socialists to demand overturning laws and removing stigmas that penalized homosexuals.[9]

Like welfare liberals (see chapter 2), social democrats favor democracy and a strong activist government that protects women and minorities through civil rights legislation. They also advocate working within the system using legitimate electoral, judicial, and legislative processes. However, there are major differences between these two perspectives. One of the more insightful analyses of these differences can be found in Gøsta Esping-Andersen's *The Three Worlds of Welfare Capitalism* (1990). His analysis of welfare regimes centers on the Marxist-inspired concepts of commodification and decommodification. Following Marx, Esping-Andersen highlights how most people in modern societies become market-dependent; both their labor power and the goods they use in everyday life become commodities that are bought and sold. Thus, individuals are dependent on labor markets for their wages or salaries and on commodity markets to purchase most of the goods they use in everyday life. By contrast, **decommodification** refers to the development of circumstances in which the individual is no longer dependent on the market to sustain a decent living. Rather, the state recognizes that "a service is rendered as a matter of right and a person can maintain a livelihood without reliance on the market" (22). Social services such as health care and paid maternity/paternity leaves are considered rights of all citizens and are ensured through government policies and public funds.

It is on the issue of decommodification that welfare liberals and social democrats differ. In **liberal welfare regimes** the state sector is obliged to interfere only after markets fail. Strict, means-tested support is applied as a way of ensuring that welfare from the state is reserved only for those who are unable to participate in the market (43). For example, U.S. unemployment insurance and direct welfare payments are both limited in duration, and welfare is available only to those whose incomes fall below a government-determined, poverty line. Such forms of government welfare alleviate the worst effects of external forces on the poor, but they also entail social stigma for those who receive benefits and act as a form of labor control. If benefits are meager and associated with social stigma, it is assumed that all but the most desperate will participate in the market (22). Here the notion of social rights is restricted and welfare does not significantly reduce stratification or inequality within society.

The overall benefits of these different welfare regimes to different classes also are strikingly different. Except in times of deep recession or depression, the U.S. welfare system caters primarily to the poor and to lower echelons of the working-class. Other classes must rely on private forms of insurance and occupational fringe benefits. Hence, extensions of welfare and higher taxes are often resisted by these other classes. For example, the 1978 People's Initiative to Limit Property Taxation (better known as California's Proposition 13) that cut property taxes by 30 percent and capped the rate of future tax increases is illustrative of this resistance. This antitax earthquake reverberated throughout the nation, and numerous states followed suit, straitjacketing public officials' tax-raising capabilities (Moore 1998).

By contrast, the **social democratic welfare regime** revolves around the principles of universalism and decommodification. It is universal in the sense that social services and public insurance systems extend to the *entire* population, even if they are graduated in accordance with taxed incomes. The Scandinavian countries exemplify this type of welfare, and their social democratic political parties were the dominant forces behind these social reforms. Rather than tolerate a dualism between state and market or between working-class and middle-class workers, the social democrats pursued a welfare state that would promote services and benefits that were upgraded to middle-class standards rather than just meeting minimum needs. All citizens can potentially benefit from these services, and no stigma is attached to them. Because such services are universal, it is presumed that all citizens will feel obliged to pay for these services, and they do so through much higher taxation rates than those found in liberal welfare systems. Interestingly, Esping-Andersen (1990: 33) found that from 1980–1990 antiwelfare sentiments were weakest in social democratic welfare regimes where taxes were the highest.

Of particular relevance to feminism, social democratic welfare regimes more adequately address family issues. Along with unemployment, health care, and pension funds, the state takes responsibility for caring for children, the aged, and the helpless. This is done to service family needs and to allow women to choose full-time employment outside of the home (28). Thus, quality child and elderly care, as well as *paid* maternity/paternity and sick leave, are integral parts of this system. Because only prolonged leaves require documentation, there is significantly less surveillance and control by the state than in liberal welfare systems.

Box 4.3 provides a graph of benefits that women and families receive in the Scandinavian countries as contrasted with the United States. As this graph suggests, the realm of social rights is more restricted in liberal welfare regimes. By contrast, the social democratic welfare regimes in Scandinavia extend the list of social rights granted to citizens to include many more family-friendly policies that help reduce individuals' dependence on markets and privatized social services.

BOX 4.3

A Comparison of Family-Friendly Public Policies in the United States and Scandinavia

Policy Supports by Welfare Regime Type

	SUPPORT FOR TIME TO CARE		SUPPORT FOR GENDER EQUALITY IN PAID AND UNPAID WORK	
	FAMILY LEAVEPOLICY (FREES TIME FOR MOTHERS OF YOUNG CHILDREN)	**WORKING TIME POLICY** (FREES TIME FOR BOTH PARENTS)	**FAMILY LEAVEPOLICY** (SUPPORTS FATHERS' CAREGIVING)	**EARLY CHILDHOOD EDUCATION AND CARE POLICY** (SUPPORTS MOTHERS' EMPLOYMENT)
Denmark, Finland, Norway, Sweden	high	high/medium	high	high/medium
United States	Low	low	low	low

Source: Table 1 from "Welfare Regimes in Relation to Paid Work and Care," by Janet C. Gornick and Marcia K. Meyers. Pp. 45–68 in *Changing LifePatterns in Western Industrial Societies*, edited by Janet Zollinger Giele and Elke Holst (Amsterdam: Elsevier, 2004).

Among the most influential analyses of poverty, welfare, and poor people's social movements during the second wave were the works of Francis Fox Piven. She served on the Feminist Commission of the Democratic Socialists of America, and two of her most widely read books (coauthored with Richard A. Cloward) include *Regulating the Poor: The Functions of Social Welfare* (1971; updated in 1993) and *Poor People's Movements: Why They Succeed, How They Fail* (1977).

Existential Socialist Feminism

While most liberal U.S. feminists cite Betty Friedan's *The Feminine Mystique* (1963) as the book that launched the second wave, left-wing feminists often view Simone de Beauvoir as the "mother" of the second wave (Henry 2004: 69). de Beauvoir's *The Second Sex*, first published in French in 1949 and in English in 1952, not only predates Friedan's work but also has a more radical analysis of women's oppression. One of de Beauvoir's oft-quoted observations can be found at the beginning of her chapter on "Childhood" ([1952] 1970: 249):

> One is not born, but rather becomes, a woman. No biological, psychological, or economic fate determines the figure that the human female presents in society; it is civilization as a whole that produces this creature, intermediate between male and eunuch, which is described as feminine.

Other famous passages are found in the introduction, where de Beauvoir describes woman as "Other." Here she discusses how woman "is defined and differentiated with reference to man and not he with reference to her; she is the incidental, the inessential as opposed to the essential. He is the Subject, he is the Absolute—she is the *Other*." She then goes on to discuss how "*Otherness* is a fundamental category of human thought"(xvi). While this quote sounds postmodern, Beauvoir does not locate **otherness** in language and discourse but, rather, employs a materialist analysis. She states that the reason for women's "*otherness*" is that "women lack concrete means for organizing themselves into a unit which can stand face to face with the correlative unit. They have no past, no history, no religion of their own; and they have no such solidarity of work and interest as that of the proletariat" (xix). *The Second Sex* develops that history as well as major bases for women's solidarity.

de Beauvoir embraced an existential Marxism that was most fully articulated by the philosopher Jean-Paul Sartre, with whom she had a long and intimate relationship. In the immediate, post–War World War II era, Sartre was the most celebrated philosopher in France for both his intellectual acumen and his role in the Resistance against the Nazi occupation of the country. Together their influential works placed them among the most famous left-wing couples of that era.

Existentialism is a philosophy that focuses on the human subject—not merely as a thinking subject but also as an acting, feeling individual. A basic assumption of Sartre's existentialism is that humans are defined by what they do and by how they act. Life consists, at all junctures, of concrete choices. People make decisions, and these decisions constitute their nature: reality and existence are expressed by action and engagement. As one scholar put it, "We are *condemned* to freedom and to responsibility without any recourse to attenuating alibis. Human beings, therefore, are ongoing projects perpetually engaged in reinventing their humanity" (Cavallaro 2003: 12; her emphasis).

Given de Beauvoir's social constructionist view of gender, she posited that women are transformed into specifically gendered entities as a result of patriarchal institutions. Not only are they categorized as deficient beings, but the gendered world of the home also cripples their ability to act on and to engage in the world. Below are some quotes from her chapter on "The Married Woman" ([1952] 1970) that illustrate the existential repercussions of housework. Like many Marxist and socialist feminists, de Beauvoir focuses on features of women's work in the home that distinguish it from work outside the home. However, she also highlights what this work means for women's consciousness and sense of self:

> Few tasks are more like the torture of Sisyphus than housework with its endless repetition: the clean becomes soiled and the soiled is made clean, over and over, day after day. The housewife wears herself out . . . she makes nothing; simply perpetuates the present. . . . Eating, sleeping, cleaning—the years no longer rise up toward heaven, they lie spread out ahead, gray and identical. The battle against dust and dirt is never won . . . (425).
>
> Woman is tempted—and the more so the greater pain she takes—to regard her work as an end in itself. She sighs as she contemplates the perfect cake just out of the oven: "It's a shame to eat it!" It is really too bad to have husband and children tramping with their muddy feet all over her waxed hardwood floors! . . . For her to acquiesce without regret, these minor holocausts must at least be reflected in someone's joy or pleasure. But since the housekeeper's labor is expended to maintain the *status quo*, the husband, coming into the house, may notice disorder or negligence, but it seems to him that order and neatness come of their own accord. (428–429)

In the above quotes, de Beauvoir points to the *cyclical, repetitive, and invisible* nature of housework. Her prose captures not only the rhythms of this work but also the existential frustrations and monotony experienced by housewives in their day-to-day lives.

de Beauvoir also highlights class differences between women. She notes how rich women may find ways to express their individuality and creativity by decorating their homes with beautiful objects. However, "under impoverished conditions no satisfaction is possible . . . the hovel remains a hovel in spite of woman's sweat and tears" (425). In this mammoth text of more than six hundred pages, de Beauvoir traces women's lives from childhood to old age and addresses their various roles as housewife, mother, and lover. A striking feature of *The Second Sex* is how it articulates the embodied and situated nature of human consciousness and subjectivity "whereby experience and perception are never wholly detachable from the flesh and blood in which human agency is embroiled, nor indeed from the material contexts in which they occur" (Cavallaro 2003: 15).

Neo-Marxist Critical Theorists' Psychoanalytical Approach

Because Marx's and Engels's writings on sexual practices were sparse, Marxists in the early twentieth century often interwove the work of other theorists to develop their analyses of sexual practices in capitalist societies. In the first half of the century, Freud's work was considered more radical than it is today, and many Marxists integrated Freudian concepts and ideas into their theoretical frameworks. Among the more famous Marx–Freud syntheses were those developed by neo-Marxist critical theorists associated with the Frankfurt School. Critical theory arose in Germany in the 1920s as a critique of the authoritarianism of both Stalinism in the Soviet Union and fascism in Europe. Because of their political views, these theorists had to escape from Nazi Germany, and many immigrated to the United States, where their writings later had wide appeal among the New Left. Among the more famous Marx–Freud syntheses developed by theorists associated with the Frankfurt School were the works of Wilhelm Reich, Eric Fromm, and Herbert Marcuse. Concerned with domination in many spheres of social life, these critical theorists addressed many topics that were underdeveloped in orthodox Marxism, such as sexual repression, racism, and anti-Semitism, as well as mass culture and consumerism.

Given their contempt for authoritarian political regimes—whether left wing or right wing—their work focused on why these regimes could garner mass-based support as occurred when Hitler's Nazi party was elected to power in Germany in 1933. When they studied sexual practices, they were most concerned with how sexual repression fostered a docile population. For Freud, sexual repression is a normal part of human development, and such things as Freudian slips or erotic dreams illustrate the ways in which deep-seated, secret desires are repressed within our unconscious. Freud also introduced the notion of sublimation, which referred to how people channel their sexual energies into work or creative activities in so-called normal or well-adjusted ways. For Freud, early childhood socialization and the psychosocial dynamics of parents and children play a major role in whether or not people become sexually well-adjusted. The neo-Marxist critical theorists developed new theories and concepts, such as surplus repression, to highlight how sexual repression was used to discipline people—especially the working class—in advanced, capitalist societies. Referred to today as the repressive hypothesis, it was a subject critiqued by Michel Foucault in his *History of Sexuality* (1976).[10]

The neo-Marxist critical theorists focused on the contradictory ways that sex is used in mass culture and mass consumer societies, such as the proliferation of risqué sexual images in advertising while more puritanical views of sex are prescribed as the normative ways that people should behave in their everyday lives. To resist these forms of repression, they advocated more open and extensive experiences of sexuality through sensuality, fantasy, and the arts (Marcuse 1955, 1964).

As early advocates of the sexual revolution, the neo-Marxist critical theorists enjoyed much popularity among the student New Left in the 1960s and 1970s.

MARXIST, SOCIALIST, AND ANARCHIST FEMINISMS IN LATE MODERNITY

Women's Work in Late Modernity

Marx's conceptual framework for understanding modern capitalism and its particular form of exploitation had a major impact on second wave Marxist and socialist feminists. His view that *the never ending search for capitalist profits was the driving force of the dramatic changes in social conditions heralded by industrialization and modernization* was a key theme. His analysis of profits was rooted in his concept of exploitation or the appropriation of the surplus labor of one group by another. Marx used the term "surplus value" to refer to how capitalists appropriated the difference between the amount of value produced by workers in capitalist production and their wages. Because wageworkers viewed their work as paid by the hour, they rarely realized how much more value they added in the actual production process. Consequently, exploitation was less visible in capitalism than in earlier modes of production, such as when feudal lords appropriated rent from serfs or slave owners appropriated the wealth produced by slave labor. Just as Marx highlighted the hidden nature of the exploitation of the working class under capitalism, Marxist-inspired feminists would reveal the hidden nature of the exploitation of women's labor—both inside and outside the home.

Marxist and socialist feminist analyses of women's work outside of the home are so many and diverse it is difficult to give them adequate coverage here. They provided detailed historical data on gendered inequalities in the workplace and developed the theoretical underpinnings for such feminist demands as **equal pay** for work of equal value and **comparable worth**.[11] Excellent summaries of their research on women's work can be found in Natalie Sokoloff's *Between Money and Love* (1980); Paula England's *Comparable Worth* (1992), and Alice Kemp's *Women's Work* (1994). Marxist and socialist feminists also were prominent in discussing women's work on a global scale. Using neo-Marxist world systems and dependency theories, such authors as Kathryn Ward (1984 and 1990), Maria Patricia Fernandez-Kelley (1983), and Annette Fuentes and Barbara Ehrenreich (1983) focused on the harsh working conditions of women employed in various global locations (see chapter 9).

Because Marxist and socialist feminists viewed women's labor *within* the home as a major obstacle to their emancipation, they also devoted much attention to analyzing women's work that was "hidden in the household" (Fox 1980). The debates that ensued over how to analyze women's work in the home came to be known as the "domestic labor debates" and drew contributors from many different countries. Some of the more influential U.S. contributions include works by Lise Vogel (1973, 1981, 1995), Zillah Eisenstein (1979), and Heidi Hartmann (1981). From abroad, important contributions were made by Mariarosa Dalla Costa from Italy (with Selma James) (1975); Sheila Rowbotham (1975, 1978) and Ann Oakley (1974a, 1974b) from Great Britain; and Margaret Benston (1969), Wally Seccombe (1973), and Bonnie Fox (1980) in Canada. Two of these works that illustrate well the differences between Marxist feminism and socialist feminism are examined below.

Representing a classic second wave Marxist feminist approach is Margaret Benston's "The Political Economy of Women's Liberation," which was published in the *New Left Review* in 1969. This journal was a highly respected, English-language Marxist journal and seldom published writings by women. Indeed, the very publication of Benston's work was testimony to its merits and to its creative use of Marxist concepts to compare and contrast women's work inside and outside of the home.

According to Benston, because women have been historically relegated to primary responsibility for housework and child care (whether or not women work outside the home), *women and men have a "different relationship to the means of production."* This difference centers around the distinction Marx made between production for use and production for exchange. Work outside of the home is **production for exchange** because this labor produces commodities and garners direct income in the form of wages. By contrast, housework and child care (when not done by paid servants) are forms of **production for use**—labor directed toward immediate use or consumption rather than sale. Benston sees this distinction as the structural basis of women's inequality in modern societies because *production for use is unpaid labor and provides no basis for women's economic independence.* Hence, as housewives, women are dependent on the male breadwinner for their economic well-being. Even for employed women, having major responsibility for housework and child care inhibits, interrupts, and reduces the attention and time they can give to their jobs outside the home, thus placing them on an unequal playing field relative to men in terms of earning power.

Benston echoes Charlotte Perkins Gilman when she argues that production for use is a preindustrial form of labor in contrast to work outside of the home. She discusses how housework is organized inefficiently because each household owns its own "means of production" or machinery, such as stoves or washing machines. In factories, machines are centralized in one place and wageworkers work together using a highly specialized and efficient division of labor. By contrast, housewives labor in relative isolation, which makes them more difficult to organize politically. In turn, the division of labor in the home is overlapping and unspecialized whereby a woman is expected to be a Jill of all trades—but a recognized expert at none. Housewives may cook and sew, but they cannot claim to be chefs or tailors if they want to use their past work experience outside of the home. There are no set hours for housework and child care, rather woman qua housewife is expected to be on call at any hour—day or night—for sick family members or hungry infants. Benston also points to the cyclical nature of housework where there are no finished products: clothes, dishes and floors get washed, dirtied, and washed again. In short, *women's work is never done*—a slogan oft repeated during the second wave.

Benston's analysis is clearly reminiscent of passages from *The Second Sex.* Yet while her Marxist concepts provide greater theoretical and analytical precision, they do not have the power of de Beauvoir's prose to evoke how women think and feel while doing this labor. Many feminists turned to literature to capture the existential dimensions of women's work. Socialist feminist Tillie Olsen's portrayals of women's lives and work in her short stories "Tell Me a Riddle" (1961) and "I Stand Here Ironing" (1961) were favorites among feminists of the second wave.[12] Olsen's fiction explored not only the "fraying seams of blue collar life" but also the silencing of those on the margins, and she played an important role in highlighting the *politics of voice* at this time (Holley 2007).

What distinguishes Benston's piece as a Marxist feminist analysis is the way she describes *unpaid domestic labor as primarily serving the capitalist class.* That is, rather than highlighting how it serves men, she emphasizes how it serves the capitalist system in the following ways. First, housewives provide what Marx called a "reserve labor force" of unemployed workers who could always be called upon in times of labor shortages or wars. Second, housewives are less likely to be supportive of labor struggles, such as strikes, because their world of the home is predicated on the income of employed breadwinners. Third, the capitalist system can keep wages low because housework and child care are essentially free. If everyone had to purchase the labor that went into cooking, cleaning, and child care there would be a demand for higher wages. In her solutions, Benston follows the orthodox Marxist path of calling for more collective forms of child care and housekeeping and for feminists to join the class struggle against what she sees as the major beneficiary of privatized domestic labor—the capitalist class.

Socialist feminist Heidi Hartmann criticizes this type of Marxist feminist analysis in her famous article "The Unhappy Marriage of Marxism and Feminism" (1981). Playing on the notion of the doctrine of coverture, Hartmann argues that wedding Marxist theory and feminist theory together only ends up in an "unhappy marriage," since Marxism (like the husband in a traditional marriage) ends up dominating feminism (the wife). To put it another way, synthesizing these two theories left gender subordinate to social class. Like Eastman before her, Hartmann argues that capitalists are not the only beneficiaries of women's relegation to domestic labor but rather that *all* men are beneficiaries—including working-class men. For Marxists to ignore this is to be "gender-blind."

What distinguishes Hartmann's work as a socialist feminist approach is that her theory of **capitalist-patriarchy** gives gender and class *equal* importance. This theory requires that two spheres of social life be examined: the sphere of production (the basis of capitalist domination) and the sphere of the reproduction (the basis of patriarchal domination). Hartmann's term the **"social reproduction of labor power"** also has two dimensions. First, it refers to the day-to-day labor involved in housework or child care that enables adults and children to replenish their labor power or their ability to work, play, or go to school each day. Second, it refers to the intergenerational reproduction of labor power through childbirth and child rearing which provides society with new members. Every society requires these dimensions of social life in order to function adequately. While Marx had examined the sphere of production at great length, socialist feminists demanded that both spheres be examined in their concrete, historical specificity to reveal the integral relationship between capitalism and patriarchy.

Hartmann uses a number of examples to illustrate the links between capitalism and patriarchy, including the rise of a family wage. A **family wage** refers to a wage adequate for one breadwinner (usually the male) to support an entire family. Hartmann argues that over historical time and by way of much conflict (in the form of strikes for greater pay and shorter hours) working-class men and capitalist employers finally agreed on the family wage as an acceptable compromise. Working-class men gained a sufficient wage to hold dominion over the women and children in their households, while capitalists received a more stable and less demanding male workforce. Thus the family wage was a victory for capitalist patriarchy and a defeat for women in that it reinforced their relegation to unpaid work in the home. For a fine overview of feminist responses to Hartmann's socialist feminist theory see *Women and Revolution*, edited by Lydia Sargent (1981).

Overall, a common thread in Marxist and socialist feminisms was their focus on women's role in the social reproduction of labor power through childbearing, child rearing, and housework. They also did a far better job than most radical feminists of analytically distinguishing between child rearing and childbearing. Although childbearing is biologically possible only by women, they highlighted how child rearing could be done by either males or females. Accordingly, they placed more emphasis on men taking responsibility for child care and domestic labor. While theorists like Benston viewed women's labor as *production for use*, other Marxist and socialist feminists saw women's role in the reproduction of labor power as *producing and reproducing the commodity labor power*—the most valuable commodity under capitalism because it produces surplus value (Dalla Costa and James 1975, Seccombe 1973, Blumenfeld and Mann 1980).

Along with the differences in the relative weight given to class and gender discussed above, Marxist feminists, such as Lise Vogel and Martha Gimenez (2007), continue to argue for the power of Marxist categories to understand women's oppression, whereas socialist feminists, such as Zillah Eisenstein (1979) and Heidi Hartmann (1981), integrated premises of Marxist feminism with those of radical feminism to highlight the importance of both class and gender. Overviews of these debates can be found in Bonnie Fox's *Hidden in the Household* (1980) and in Lise Vogel's "Marxism and Socialist–Feminist Theory: A Decade of Debate" (1981). Overall, these political economies of women's work were major contributions of second wave Marxist and socialist feminists.

Feminist Existential Phenomenology

Political philosopher Iris Marion Young provided an early critique of Heidi Hartmann's work as well as an alternative socialist feminist analysis in "Beyond the Unhappy Marriage: A Critique of Dual Systems Theory" (1981). However, far more influential in U.S. feminism were her writings inspired by the existentialist approach of Simone de Beauvoir—especially Young's piece "Throwing Like a Girl: A Phenomenology of Feminine Body Comportment, Motility, and Spaciality" (1977). While de Beauvoir drew from Sartre's philosophical approach, Young draws heavily from the phenomenological insights of Maurice Merleau-Ponty, who centered his work on how human consciousness is situated in the lived body. Here, the "lived body" is understood as always layered with social and historical meaning; it is not simply biological or natural matter (Young [1977] 2005: 7). Young describes how existential phenomenology was the major branch of philosophy in the United States that made embodiment central and thematic in their approach, and she undertook the important task of developing a feminist existential phenomenology (3–4).

In "Throwing Like a Girl," Young follows de Beauvoir in discussing how the constraints of gender and femininity define woman as Other—as the inessential correlate to man, as mere object. As such, woman is denied the subjectivity, autonomy, and creativity that are definitive of being human beings. However, Young focuses far more than de Beauvoir on how feminine bodily comportment and women's actual bodily movements exhibit the tensions between "transcendence" and "immanence"—between being an active, creative subject and being a mere object to others (29). She explains how the body itself (as a natural material) is immanence or object; the human as active subject uses his or her capacities to move out into the world—to act upon it. The transcendence of the lived body, as Merleu-Ponty describes it, is pure fluid action, the continuous calling forth of human capacities that are applied to the world; in doing so, the self is realized and constituted (336).

Young uses the description of "throwing like a girl" as just one example of many physical activities that reflect the constraints of feminine comportment and bodily movement. She writes: "Not only is there a typical style of throwing like a girl, but there is a more or less typical style of running like a girl, climbing like a girl, swinging like a girl, hitting like a girl" (33). Many examples of women's bodily comportment are presented in her work, such as how women tend to restrict their use of space, such as when they sit with their legs together and their arms across their body—constricting and shielding themselves. However, her major point is to show what these feminine bodily modalities have in common, namely, an *ambiguous transcendence*, an *inhibited intentionality* and a *discontinuous unity* with its surroundings (35). For example, feminine bodily movements (like throwing a ball or lifting a heavy weight) often do not engage the entire body in fluid and directed motion; that is, women rarely bring as many of their physical capacities to bear on a task as do men. Similarly, Young observes how the "timidity, immobility, and uncertainty that frequently characterize feminine movements project a limited space for the feminine 'I can'" (40). In short, women lack trust in their bodies to accomplish tasks (43). Women also restrict their use of space more than do men, often experiencing themselves as positioned in space—waiting and reacting rather than going forth to act (39–41). All of these cases illustrate the ambiguous, inhibited, and discontinuous features of feminine action.

Young makes clear that the source of these "modalities of feminine bodily comportment, motility and spatiality" is in neither physical anatomy nor some mysterious feminine essence. "Rather, they have their source in the particular situation of women as conditioned by their sexist oppression in contemporary society" (42).[13] She argues: "*Women in sexist society are physically handicapped*" (42; emphasis added). Young does not view these feminine bodily modalities merely as deprivations or the result of lack of practice, though she admits this may be "an important element" (43). She sees them instead as a "specific positive style of feminine bodily comportment" that is learned as the girl comes to understand she is a girl. Girls may even strive for and practice these feminine comportments to receive status and approval. "The more a girl assumes her status as feminine, the more she takes herself to be fragile and immobile and the more she actively enacts her own bodily inhibition" (44). In her later works, Young likens this learned femininity to a form of gender *habitus*,[14] using Pierre Bourdieu's concept that refers to learned, embodied dispositions or habits that are taken-for-granted features of everyday life.[15]

For Young, the "root" of these feminine modalities "is the fact that the woman lives her body as *object* as well as subject" (44; her emphasis). She describes, for example, how the threat of objectification that a woman lives under includes the threat of bodily invasion—an extreme case being rape. More generally, however, she argues that woman is objectified by the "threat of being seen" (44–45):

> An essential part of the situation of being a woman is that of living the ever-present possibility that one will be gazed upon as a mere body, as a shape and flesh that presents itself as the potential object of another subject's intentions and manipulations, rather than as a living manifestation of action and intention.

"Throwing Like a Girl" introduces a number of themes that will permeate later feminist analyses. Young alludes to what other feminists will call the "bifurcated consciousness" that accompanies woman's existence (Smith 1987), yet she provides a unique existential phenomenological underpinning to this dual consciousness. She also hints at what later feminist theorists, inspired by Foucault's poststructuralism, will call the "panoptical male connoisseur" that resides within each woman, compelling her to police herself in regard to normative standards of feminine beauty and comportment (Bartky 1990; see chapter 6). Overall, "Throwing Like a Girl" is a pioneering work in the scholarly literature on gendering the body that would proliferate in later decades by such writers as Susan Bordo (1993), Judith Butler (1990, 1993), Elizabeth Grosz (1994); Toril Moi (1985); Luce Irigaray (1985); and Julia Kristeva (1980, 1982).

Young does not explicitly address class differences in women's response to this objectification. However, other scholars have discussed how poor and working-class women experience injuries to their self-esteem when they are compared to wealthier women who can afford fashionable clothes and expensive bodily care. These injuries to one's self esteem have been called one of the many **hidden injuries of social class** (Sennett and Cobb 1972; Bettie 2003). Box 4.4 provides an early second wave description of these hidden injuries or class-based feelings of inadequacy.

BOX 4.4

"To My White Working-Class Sisters"

We are the invisible women, the faceless women, the nameless women . . . the female half of the silent majority, the female half of the ugly Americans, the smallest part of the "little people." No one photographs us, not one writes about us, no one puts us on TV. No one says we are beautiful, no one says we are important, very few like to recognize that we are *here*. We are the poor and working-class white women of American, and we are cruelly and systematically ignored. . . .

I read all the middle-class fashion and glamour magazines and tried to look like people who were able to look that way because of a life-style that included a closet full of clothes I couldn't afford and a leisurely existence that allowed them to look cool and unruffled all the time. And there was I working in a luncheonette so shabby I never mentioned it to anyone for a lousy six dollars a Saturday that I immediately spent in vain efforts to make myself "acceptable"-looking. . . .

What can we do about all this? As poor and working-class women, we can *start* asking what is wrong with America and *stop* asking what is wrong with ourselves. . . . We must begin to see ourselves as beautiful in our ability to work, to endure, in our plain, honest lives, and we must stop aspiring to a false-eyelash existence that is not and never has been for us. . . . We are the women who have dealt all our lives with the truths and tragedies of real life. . . . We are the people who have no maids or therapists to dump our troubles on. We know what it is to work hard and we are not guilty of wearing silks while others wear rags. We should never admire the women in *Vogue*, because there is something undeniably ugly about women who wear minks while others can't afford shoes—and no amount of $20-an-ounce makeup can hide that brand of ugliness.

Excerpted from Debbie D'Amico, "To My White Working-Class Sisters," pp. 178–181 of *Writings from the Women's Liberation Movement: Liberation Now!* edited by Deborah Babcox and Madeline Belkin (New York: Dell, 1971); emphases in the original.

Psychoanalytic Approaches of the Feminist New Left

Like the neo-Marxist critical theorists who preceded them, many Marxist and socialist feminists wed the works of Marx and Freud. They also fostered a pro-sex agenda through which sexual freedom was viewed as liberating. Like other feminists, they criticized how Freud rationalized female subordination through such concepts as penis envy. Yet they also recognized how psychoanalytic theory had few parallels as a description of how patriarchal, phallic culture domesticates women.

Juliet Mitchell's *Women's Estate* (1971) was among the most widely read socialist feminist synthesis of Freud and Marx . To the socialist feminists' focus on the spheres of production and reproduction, Mitchell adds the Freudian spheres of sexuality and childhood socialization. For Mitchell, all four of these dimensions of social life were of key relevance to women's emancipation. Mitchell also frequently pointed out contradictions in how capitalist societies dealt with sex and love:

> There is a formal contradiction between the voluntary contractual character of "marriage" and the spontaneous uncontrollable character of "love"—the passion that is celebrated precisely for its involuntary force. The notion that it occurs only once in every life and can therefore be integrated into a voluntary contract, becomes decreasingly plausible in the light of everyday experience—once sexual repression as a psycho-ideological system becomes at all relaxed. (Mitchell 1971: 80)

Mitchell viewed the increase in premarital sex during the 1960s as a major challenge to the disciplinary and puritanical vestiges of the past. She wrote that premarital sex is "now virtually legitimized in contemporary society" and that puritanical views of sex are "on the way out . . . more and more becoming a dead letter"(83). She saw the implications of premarital sex as "explosive for undermining the ideological conception of marriage that dominates capitalist society." (84) Hence, she argued that the "current wave of sexual liberalization" could become "conducive to the greater general freedom of women." (85)

Another second wave feminist advocate of the sexual revolution was the Australian feminist Germaine Greer, who described her perspective rather confusingly as "anarchist-Marxist." She also added to this theoretical mix some of Freud's concepts. Greer argues that women have become separated from their libido—from their faculty of desire and from their sexuality. She titled her book *The Female Eunuch* (1971) because she likens women to castrated beasts who serve their master's aims and are made docile. She sees young girls as "feminized" from childhood by rules that subjugate them and cripple their capacity for action. For Greer, "creating the feminine" maims the female personality. When women embrace the stereotype of adult femininity, they develop a sense of shame about their own bodies and lose their natural and political autonomy.[16] This results in powerlessness, isolation, a diminished sexuality, and a lack of joy. Greer advocated a pro-sex approach and viewed the free expression of sensuality and sexuality as necessary for women's emancipation.

One of the most influential second wave feminist psychoanalytic approaches that appeared in the late 1970s was Nancy Chodorow's *The Reproduction of Mothering* (1978). Chodorow's theory is a synthetic work that builds on a number of earlier theorists and approaches. She grounds her work in Gayle Rubin's analyses of the sex/gender system (see chapter 3) as well as in the links socialist feminists' made between the spheres of social production and social reproduction. The psychoanalytic features of her approach build on Melanie Klein's object relations theory to argue that deep-seated, gendered psychosocial orientations are created in the process of an infant's/child's separation from their primary object of affection—the mother. These psychosocial orientations are then linked to sex role theory in which masculine, **instrumental roles** provide the basis for capitalist production, while feminine **expressive roles** provide the basis for the social reproduction of labor power. By connecting these psychosocial orientations to the demands of the capitalist system, Chodorow introduces a radical critique of capitalist patriarchy that is missing in the liberal and left-liberal feminist psychoanalytic approaches discussed in chapter 2.

Chodorow begins *The Reproduction of Mothering* with the claim that "mothering is one of the few universal and enduring elements of the sexual division of labor" ([1978] 1999: 3). It is women who primarily rear children and who provide them with "affective bonds and a diffuse, multifaceted, ongoing personal relationship" that helps them form their "core gender identity" and "sense of self." While all infants and toddlers must separate from their primary caregivers in order to begin the process of becoming separate selves, girls and boys experience this separation differently. Because boys have to separate from their mothers and take on adult male gender roles, they break the ties between affect (emotion) and sex role learning. This break enables them to be independent and autonomous social actors who engage in the impersonal, instrumental, or task-oriented social action required by capitalist production. In contrast, because girls, like their mothers, enact adult female gender roles, the tie between affect and role learning is maintained. Rather than defining themselves as autonomous beings, girls/women see themselves primarily in relation to others. Their social actions are more personal, expressive, or people-oriented as opposed to impersonal, instrumental, or task-oriented. Through these psycho-social processes, people create family structures that produce and reproduce these unequal sex roles.

According to Chodorow, the most significant difference between girls and boys is the degree to which they see themselves as related to or connected with others. "The basic feminine sense of self is connected to the world the basic masculine sense of self is separate" (3). Thus women develop a more relational personality, while men develop personalities preoccupied with the denial of relation (178). Sex role socialization builds upon and reinforces this "largely unconscious development" (51). Such gendered personalities are the psychosocial counterpart of the adult roles women and men are expected to play: "Women in our society are primarily defined as wives and mothers, thus in particularistic relation to someone else, whereas men are defined primarily in universalistic occupational terms" (178). For Chodorow, the family creates the psychological foundations of acquiescence to different types of work and work skills. In particular, she argues that nuclear families in modern societies prepare men for participation in a male-dominated family and society. This family form orients males toward lesser emotional participation in family life and greater task-oriented participation in the capitalist world of work, where social relations are organized on a rational and impersonal basis (180–181). She explains how these psychosocial orientations relate to domination as follows:

> The boy comes to define his self more in opposition. . . . He becomes the self and experiences his mother as other. The process also extends to his trying to dominate the other in order to ensure his sense of self. Such domination begins with mother as the object, extends to women, and is then generalized to include the experience of all others as objects rather than subjects. (93)

While Chodorow is a sociologist, a similar feminist psychoanalytic analysis can be found in *The Mermaid and the Minotaur: Sexual Arrangements and Human Malaise* (1977) by psychologist Dorothy Dinnerstein. Dinnerstein paints a darker picture of gender relations in that she portray the "child" as feeling more powerless and more preoccupied with the image of an omnipotent and capricious mother who must be controlled by domination or rejection. Chodorow's analysis does not contain the same level of rage and vindictiveness in the "child within" each adult but, rather, highlights men's and women's unconscious need to reproduce in adulthood their infantile experiences of "separation from" or "unity with" the mother (Tong (1998: 147).

Despite the grounding of Chodorow's theory in more radical thought, her political solutions are reform-oriented. She does not call for a qualitative change in the political and economic system but, rather, for reforms that would make it possible for men and women to mother, such as establishing paid maternity and paternity leaves, providing family-friendly policies in the workplace, and ensuring that day care centers and other forms of early childhood education are undertaken by both men and women. Thus, her political solutions appear closer to a form of feminist social democracy.

NEW DIRECTIONS IN FEMINIST THOUGHT INSPIRED BY THE OLD AND NEW LEFT

Many of the Marxist, socialist and anarchist frameworks discussed above were designed to provide comprehensive understandings of women's oppression that followed along the lines of the grand narratives of the Old and New Left. Beginning in the 1980s, a movement away from such comprehensive notions of theory construction to a more complex understanding of situated and perspectival knowledges became visible as an important component of the new directions taken in these feminisms inspired by the old and new left.

Socialist Feminist Standpoint Epistemologies

The intellectual roots of feminist standpoint epistemologies are often traced to G. W. F. Hegel's master/slave dialectic and his reflections on how the vantage point of the slave informed this relationship of servitude. Marx, Engels, and the neo-Marxist critical theorist Georg Lukács later used these insights to discuss the standpoint of the proletariat. It was only a short leap in logic for feminists to apply these insights to women.[17] Some of the most influential contributions to socialist feminist standpoint approaches have been the works of Nancy Hartsock (1983), Dorothy Smith (1987), and Donna Haraway (1991).[18] Although it is more accurate to view their approaches as *methods of inquiry or epistemologies*, the term *standpoint theory* is employed below because of its widespread usage in contemporary feminism.

All of these authors follow Marx in embracing a materialist method that focuses on the *sensuous, practical activities of people* (Hartsock [1983] 2004: 37;

Smith 1987: 126; 1990: 24–25). Like Marx, they also break with conventional, positivist empiricism in a number of ways. They reject the notion that science is neutral or value free as well as its corollary that scientists are detached observers of the social and natural world. Instead, they offer alternative ways of knowing that are critical of and oppositional to dominant ideas and ideologies. As noted in chapter 1, feminist standpoint epistemologies view all knowledge as socially situated and socially constructed. This social constructionist view of knowledge argues that people not only create or construct knowledge but that they do so from situated positions within different social locations, such as different race, gender, and class positions that influence how people view the world. On the one hand, a specific location potentially enables people to see social realities that are less visible to those in other locations. On the other hand, because no one can view the world from all of the various and diverse social locations, each vantage point or perspective is partial or limited.

Standpoint epistemologies also embrace **reflexivity** where researchers acknowledge how their own social locations influence their studies and how the results of their studies can impact other people. They also highlight the differential privilege given to certain people or groups in knowledge production. For example, Dorothy Smith tells the story of riding on a train and seeing through the window an Indian family watching the passing train. Smith realizes that she could describe this incident as she saw it, but to the Indians, this same incident may appear very different. She acknowledges that her account is the one that most likely would be accepted as "knowledge" because as an academic she is privileged to speak and write in contexts that are not accessible to these Indians. In *The Conceptual Practices of Power* (1990: 25) she writes:

> There are and must be different experiences of the world and different bases of experience. We must not do away with them by taking advantage of our privileged speaking to construct a sociological version that we then impose upon them as their reality. We may not rewrite the other's world or impose upon it a conceptual framework that extracts from it what fits with ours.

Standpoint theorists advocate starting social inquiry from the *lived practices of marginalized people who have been traditionally outside of the institutions in which knowledge about social life is generated and classified.* Women, like other subjugated peoples, historically have been excluded from knowledge production because their experiences and knowledges have been viewed as inferior. Thus, the standpoint of women is just one of many social locations that offer critical insights for research problems and agendas.

The Liberatory Potential of the "Feminist Standpoint"

Of the three standpoint theorists discussed in this section, Nancy Hartsock's "The Feminist Standpoint: Developing the Ground for a Specifically Feminist Historical Materialism" (1983) provides the most detailed account of how her feminist standpoint is derived from Marx's theory. A reiteration of her detailed account is not practical here, but suffice it to say that Hartsock ([1983] 2004: 35) describes her project as developing "on the methodological base provided by Marxian theory, an important epistemological tool for understanding and opposing all forms of domination—a feminist standpoint." Like the standpoint of the proletariat in Marxist theory, Hartsock argues that women's lives offer a particular vantage point that can provide a powerful critique of patriarchal institutions and ideology.

Hartsock views the sexual division of labor as the basis for such a standpoint because (whether or not all women do this) women are institutionally responsible for domestic labor and child rearing. Like other Marxist and socialist feminists, she discusses many features of women's work, such as the repetitive nature of housework, how it deals with immediate, concrete processes, like cleaning, that connect it directly with the natural world, and how women who work outside of the home often work longer hours than men because of their double day or second shift. Hartsock also introduces sex role theory to further distinguish how work outside the home is instrumental and task-oriented, while work inside the home is people-oriented, expressive, and relational:

> One does not (cannot) produce another human being in anything like the way one produces an object such as a chair. . . . The activity involved is far more complex than the instrumental working with others to transform objects . . . [it] requires and depends on relational and interpersonal skills learned by being mothered by someone of the same sex. (43)

Hartsock uses a psychoanalytic approach similar to Nancy Chodorow's analysis to explain these gendered orientations to social life. She argues that the girl child, reared by a mother of the same sex, develops a relational view of the world that fosters connections with others and viewing oneself as existing within a web of social relations. In contrast, the boy child has to distance himself from the primary child rearer (the mother) and develops what Hartsock calls "abstract masculinity"—a form of consciousness developed in opposition both to the concrete world of everyday life and to affect/emotions or relatedness. The male thus sees himself not only as more autonomous but also as always in opposition to others even though he must construct social relations in order to survive (45). Because of this more oppositional consciousness, as Hartsock writes, "the [male] desire for fusion can take the form of domination of the other" (46).

For Hartsock, the standpoint derived from female experiences in childhood and in adult life not only "inverts" that of the male but also provides a basis on which to expose abstract masculinity as "both partial and fundamentally perverse." For her, abstract masculinity is "partial" because it is not the only vantage point on reality; it is "perverse" because it reverses the proper valuation of human activity, by making relational, affective ties appear as lesser (46). For women to recognize this inversion and perversion is "an achievement" rather than a given. Such critical insights derived from women's concrete experiences and standpoints must be struggled for and accomplished; they do not just naturally arise. Hartsock calls this a "feminist standpoint" to highlight its "achieved character" and its "liberatory potential" (40). As will be shown below, Dorothy Smith also grounds her notion of standpoint in a gendered division of labor and the concrete, everyday practices of women. However, she calls this the "standpoint of women" and dispenses with any psychoanalytic theory.

Institutional Ethnography and the "Standpoint of Women"

A unique feature of Dorothy Smith's work is how she interweaves Marxism, feminism, and ethnomethodology. A primary concern of ethnomethodologists is to examine *everyday* social practices and to uncover the taken-for-granted features of social life that are prior to discursive positing (Garfinkel 1967). In most social theories, the world of *everyday life* is typically the *backdrop* rather than the *topic* of theoretical inquiries even though it is the grounding of all social life (Ritzer 2011). In *The Everyday World as Problematic* (1987), Smith examines how the social reproduction of labor power is a centerpiece of the world of everyday life. By doing so, she exposes this taken-for-granted world as well as the invisible roles women play in the "reproduction of the everyday/everynight world" (86).

Smith's ethnomethodological approach emphasizes how beginning research from the standpoint and practices of everyday life marks a departure from the concepts and procedures of more conventional social science or what she refers to as "objectified forms of knowledge" (Mann and Kelley 1997). She highlights how the knowledge people have by virtue of their concrete, everyday experiences is for the most part "tacit knowledge"—a knowing of what we do, how we go about things, and what we get done. As examples of this "tacit knowledge" she mentions knowing how and where to go shopping, how to catch a bus, how to wash dishes, or how to sweep floors. She argues that such knowledge is not often discursively appropriated because it is seen as uninteresting, unimportant, or routine (Smith 2004: 265–266).

Smith analytically distinguishes between the "extralocal" world and the world of "everyday life" even though she sees them as integrally tied together in a nexus of sequential activities and social relations. She takes the position of women as her starting point because the dichotomy between the extralocal and everyday life, as well as the **bifurcated consciousness** generated by this dichotomy, is organized primarily on the basis of gender. While women do not inhabit only the domestic world, since many women work outside the home, for the vast majority of women it is the primary ground of their lives, shaping the course of their lives and their relationships with others. *The everyday/everynight world is thus subordinate, suppressed, and ignored despite the fact that it is the social grounding—the taken-for-granted social context—for its superior.* Women who enter the extralocal world and confront its objectivized forms of knowledge experience bifurcation precisely because these forms of knowledge collide with women's concrete experiences in the world of everyday/everynight life.

Smith argues that if we start from women's everyday lives we can see how they are assigned the work of caring for the bodies of men, children, the elderly, and the sick as well as their own bodies. They are assigned responsibility also for the local places—namely, the home—where these activities take place. This kind of women's work not only frees men from these tasks, but *the more successful women are at this concrete work, the more invisible it becomes to men as distinctively social labor* (Smith 1990: 19). Hence, it is not surprising that conventional science and objectivized forms of knowledge produced by men fail to understand women's standpoint as well as the world of everyday life. By contrast, starting from women's lives can generate questions about why it is that women are assigned these tasks and what the consequences are for families, the economy, and the state. Like other Marxist-inspired works, Smith envisions the reproduction of labor power as including women's domestic labor and child rearing as well as the institutions of health, education, and welfare that also play key roles in the reproduction of labor power in modern societies (Dickinson and Russell 1986).

She also discusses "analogous" forms of labor in the extralocal sphere, such as the work of janitors or food service workers, who reproduce the world of everyday life in institutional settings—work that is often done by women or minority men. For Smith (1987: 87), all of these forms of labor are the invisible backdrop of our lives and achievements:

> If we heard in the things that we make use of—typewriter, paper, chair, table, walls—the voices of those who made them, we would hear the multitudinous voices of a whole society and beyond. Were it not for the time lapse involved, our own voices would be part of them.

For Smith, social locations and social practices are what hold the key to a greater understanding of the relations of ruling and not the fact that the knowledge producer is a woman. She is explicit that the standpoint of women "does not imply a common viewpoint among women" (78). She also clarifies throughout her writings that it is not the subjective views of women per se but, rather, their *social locations* and *practices* that generate critical questions about the way the world is organized. Smith (1996: 54) argues that if we simply use "subjectivist interpretations of experience" we can "never escape the circles of our own heads". It is the "standpoint" that arises from examining the social practices of everyday life that distinctively opens up for exploration the conceptual practices of the extralocal relations of ruling and the problematic of everyday life and of women's oppression (Smith 1990: 65). Smith's use of the term "problematic" refers to both the gendered problems revealed as well as the complex of concerns, issues, and questions that arise for possible investigation (Grahame 1998).

Smith characterizes her work as **institutional ethnography** because it examines how the scenes of everyday life are knitted into broader forms of social organization—forms that cannot be fully grasped within everyday life itself. Extralocal forms of organization penetrate the local, but they are not easily grasped in everyday experience (Smith 1987: 152–155). Rather, social relations are linked with activities and work processes in diverse sites and thus reach beyond local settings to involve individuals often unknown to one another in extended sequences of social action. This anatomy of social practices is the subject of institutional ethnography. In one of the more accessible discussions of this approach, "Ethnography, Institutions, and the Problematic of the Everyday World" (1998), Peter Grahame explains how the principle tasks of institutional ethnography include describing the coordination of activities in the everyday world, discovering how ideological accounts define those activities in relation to institutional imperatives, and examining the broader social relations of ruling in which local sites of activity are embedded. It is for this reason that other Smith-inspired researchers portray institutional ethnography as an investigation of the nexus of coordinated activities that progresses through levels and layers, moving from everyday social practices in households to those in local neighborhoods and classrooms to those in institutional bureaucracies and the state (McCall 1996; Grahame 1998).

This broader context is evident in *Mothering for Schooling* (2004), where Smith teams up with her colleague Alison Griffith to illuminate the intricate consequences of mothering practices for the classroom. Mothering for schooling practices include a broad range of competencies, such as their ability to help children with homework or to monitor whether their children use correct grammar. They also include whether mothers can assist their children with the tools used in classrooms, such as facility with pencils, paintbrushes, or computers. The social relations and practices examined in this study also extend to the professional discourses which supply the conceptual framework for institutional and bureaucratic processes.

Smith's method of inquiry shares some similarities with feminist perspectives that have taken the postmodern turn in that she focuses on the relationship between knowledge and power as well as on the socially situated nature of knowledge. However, Smith rejects the judgmental relativism inherent in the postmodernists view that one cannot adjudicate between different vantage points on reality because they are all limited, partial, and relative to one's social location. She argues that feminists *must be able to adjudicate or judge between competing knowledge claims in order for theory to guide political practice*. Smith (1987: 122) writes that "it is essential to the most modest possibilities of knowing how things work" that within the multiplicity of social realities that "accounts can be called into question." If knowledge is to have an impact on politics "there must exist the practical possibility that one account can invalidate another."

> Inquiry does not make sense unless we suppose that there is something to be found and that that something can be spoken of to another, as we might say: "Well this is the way it is. This is how it works." It would not be enough to say: "This is how it looks to me. . . . " If we want to offer something like a map or diagram of the swarming relations in which our lives are enmeshed so that we can find out ways better among them, then we want to be able to claim that what we are describing is actual in the same way as our everyday worlds are actual. (121–122)

"How things work" is the focus of institutional ethnography and its investigation of how the local organization of everyday life is integrally connected with relations of ruling (157–161).

In "Telling the Truth after Postmodernism" (1996) and "High Noon in Textland" (1993a), Smith uses humor and sarcasm to mock the political impotency of postmodern relativism. She likens postmodernism's effect on undermining political practice, with the role of the McCarthy era in undermining political activism:

> In the contemporary context, postmodernism has written the constitution that eliminates from the phenomenal domain of social and cultural thinking, the bases of oppression that Marxism had brought into view, replacing it with a self-reflexive critique of discourse within discourse. Feminist postmodernism is feminism's own variant of the post-McCarthy redesigning of sociological discourse that stripped social science of its relation to political activism beyond the academy. (Smith 1996: 54)

Situated Knowledges and Partial Perspectives

In "Situated Knowledges: The Science Question in Feminism and the Privilege of Partial Perspectives," from her book *Simians, Cyborgs, and Women* (1991), Donna Haraway provides the clearest statement of her standpoint approach. While Haraway shares with both Harstock and Smith the view that all knowledge is socially situated and socially constructed, she uses her article to highlight the importance for feminism of adjudicating between knowledge claims. In a satirical voice Haraway ([1991] 2004: 81) argues that feminists have been "trapped by two poles of a tempting dichotomy on the question of scientific objectivity." The "two poles" to which she refers are: the radical social constructionist claims made by postmodernists that knowledge claims are power moves not moves toward truth, where all claims are viewed as equal and relative; and the view taken by many standpoint theorists that subjugated or marginalized social locations create more critical insights.[19] This latter perspective is often referred to as **privileging the knowledge of the oppressed** (see chapter 5).

In response to postmodern relativism, Haraway argues that the postmodern "equality' of positioning is a denial of responsibility and critical enquiry" (89). It leaves feminists with no basis to judge science from pseudoscience and no basis for accountability: "We would like to think our appeals to real worlds are more than an act of faith like any other cult's" (83). For her, postmodern relativism is the "twin" of the arrogant, positivist notion of scientific objectivity in that both employ the "god-trick" of ostensibly seeing from everywhere and nowhere (see chapter 1).

In response to privileging the knowledge of the oppressed, Haraway highlights the "serious danger" of romanticizing and appropriating the vision of the less powerful and claiming to see from their positions. "The positionings of the subjugated are not exempt from critical re-examination, decoding, deconstruction, and interpretation." These views "from below" are "neither innocent nor "unproblematic" (88). Rather they are partial and limited because no one can simultaneously see from all of the subjugated positions structured by gender, race, class, and nation (which she notes is simply a "short list" of critical locations) (90).

In short, Haraway considers both poles of this "tempting dichotomy" inadequate and calls for a "strong tool" to adjudicate truth claims:

> Feminists must insist on a better account of the world . . . a more adequate, richer, better account of a world, in order to live in it well and in critical, reflexive relation to our own as well as others' practices of domination. (84–85)

For Haraway, the strong tool required for critical feminist science projects is simply the recognition of "situated knowledges" (86). This means reflexively acknowledging the limited and partial features of knowledge claims. She states that we are all answerable or accountable for what we learn how to see and calls for a commitment to a politics of "mobile positioning" where "partiality and not universality is the condition of being heard to make rational knowledge claims" (90 and 92). Such mobile positioning suggests the ability to pivot from the knowledges of one group to the knowledges of others to provide a more complete understanding. Haraway describes this politics of positioning as always interpretive and critical—sensitive to power relations but making assessments—not simply a pluralist conversation or dialogue. In sum, for Haraway, "the science question in feminism is objectivity as positioned rationality"—of "views from somewhere"—that recognize how we as social actors construct knowledge but do so in limited, partial, and situated ways (93 and 95).

Contributions of Socialist Feminist Standpoint Epistemologies

The major goal of the socialist feminist standpoint epistemologies discussed above is to *reveal the relations of power hidden in conventional knowledge production processes.* Standpoint feminisms argue that when greater attention is paid to the social location of knowledge producers, a more transparent rendering of the relations of ruling can be obtained. If there is one characteristic that standpoint feminisms share it is this notion of the social construction of knowledge and its partial and situated nature. Even critics of standpoint epistemologies have acknowledged their important contributions. One of the more famous feminist debates over the merits of standpoint versus postmodern epistemologies took place in 1997 on the pages of *Signs: Journal of Women in Culture and Society.* Here postmodernist Susan Hekman criticized the standpoint approaches of Nancy Hartsock, Dorothy Smith, Sandra Harding, and Patricia Hill Collins, each of whom responded in turn (see chapter 6). Despite Hekman's preference for a postmodern epistemology, she ([1997] 2004: 234) views standpoint theories as part of a larger epistemological "paradigm shift" that entails "a movement away from an absolutist, subject-centered conception of truth to a conception of truth as situated and perspectival." She applauds feminist standpoint epistemologies for being at the forefront of this paradigm shift.

Materialist Feminisms

In the feminist lexicon today, the term *materialist feminism* has virtually supplanted Marxist and socialist feminisms. Major works of materialist feminism include Michèle Barrett's *Women's Oppression Today* (1980), Donna Landry and Gerald MacLean's *Materialist Feminisms* (1993), and Christine Delphy's French deconstructionist-inspired "For a Materialist Feminism" (1981). In turn, some of the most interesting and complex global analyses undertaken by contemporary postcolonial and transnational feminists also merge materialist and deconstructive approaches as will be shown in Chapter 10.

One might expect that this shift in terminology from Marxist and socialist feminisms to materialist feminisms followed the end of the cold war and the balkanization of the once powerful Soviet Union.[20] However, this shift actually occurred almost a decade before the fall of the iron curtain and has more to do with *battles within Western feminism* than with the end of the cold war. In part, the rise of materialist feminisms was a response to the growing popularity of both ecocentric ecofeminisms and intersectional analysis with its focus on the interlocking oppressions of race, gender, class, and sexual orientation (see chapter 5). For example, when the question is raised whether the term *materialist feminist* is simply an alias for Marxist feminism in a postcommunist world, the authors of *Materialist Feminisms* answer "no." Landry and MacLean (1993: 229) argue that materialist feminism is a new approach that focuses on the multiple oppressions of gender, class, race, sexuality, and colonialism and that rejects the anthropocentrism of Marxist ecofeminist approaches.

Materialist feminisms also arose to address the increasing popularity of feminisms that had taken the linguistic turn, such as postmodernism, poststructuralism, and queer theory (see chapter 6). One of the key debates between supporters of these postperspectives and materialist feminists has been over how to conceptualize gender oppression as well as possibilities for social change (McNay 2000: 172). As Lois McNay points out, feminists who embrace these postperspectives tend to use such terms as "discourse," "difference," and "resistance" to highlight how they view social reality as created through discourses and social resistance as outlaw performances that disrupt and subvert dominant discourses. In contrast, for materialist feminists the reduction of society and social relations to issues of language and norms does not sufficiently address structural or institutional power arrangements. They see feminists who have taken the linguistic turn as underestimating *the intractability of systemic forms of oppression* and overestimating changes that can be brought about by individual, as opposed to collective or group actions or practices. Thus, they tend to be more cautious and skeptical about easy routes to social change.

Materialist feminists view social change as difficult, complex and capable of creating unexpected new forms of subordination and dependency. As McNay (2000: 174) writes: "transformations in the gender division of labor and the access it gives to material resources are regarded as more crucial determinants of emancipation or subordination than shifts within gender ideologies and norms." Hence, the emphasis of materialist feminists is on the entrenched regularity of unequal material resources. Their analyses of the reproduction of gender relations, while located in ongoing and repeated actions or practices, draws attention to the material conditions that can block or foster conditions for change. They focus on how people make history "but not as they please," as Marx once put it (quoted in Tucker 1972: 437).[21]

Historical specificity also plays a major role in materialist feminists' analyses. On the one hand, rather than focusing on the ahistorical properties of language and the inherent indeterminancy of meanings that postmodernists favor, materialist feminists focus on concrete, historically specific, human practices. On the other hand, to avoid the dangers that postmodernists associate with grand theories in which metatheorizing takes on a life of its own, materialist feminists seek answers to questions in historically specific studies and avoid master narratives or **totalizing theories** that make broad, sweeping generalizations about social change and its consequences.

Materialist feminists also reject simplistic views of the economic base determining other features of social life and embrace a more complex analysis of the relationship between consciousness, culture, and social structure. One of the theorists most often referred to as the inspiration for these new directions in materialist feminism is the neo-Marxist Raymond Williams, who laid the foundations for the field of cultural studies and for a cultural materialist approach. Williams (1998: 80) argues for the "indissoluble connections between material production, political and cultural institutions and activity, and consciousness" and draws attention to the importance of theorizing lived, everyday social experiences. He also highlights the hermeneutic or interpretative role played by social agents and sees signs, signifying systems, ideology, and discourses as material activities with material effects. As Landry and MacLean (1993: 61) point out, this is "a far cry from older Marxist arguments that the economic base determines everything in culture and society in specific and locatable ways."

Queer Anticapitalism

While second wave Marxist and socialist feminists endorsed the sexual revolution of the 1960s and 1970s, most focused their attention on heterosexual sex and elided the issue of homosexuality. Conversely, even though many second wave lesbian feminists embraced forms of socialism, they were more attracted to other feminist frameworks, such as radical feminism and intersectionality theory (see chapters 3 and 5). Lesbians' distrust of Marxist and socialist feminisms likely reflected the tarnished record many existing socialist societies had for treating homosexuals as decadent and/or pathological.

Yet there were many U.S. second wave socialist feminists who embraced diverse sexual practices and who used a social constructionist approach in analyzing them. For example, Ann Ferguson's "The Sex Debate within the Women's Movement: A Socialist Feminist View" (1984) argued that there is no one universal "function" for human sexuality whether conceived as emotional intimacy or physical pleasure. Rather "sexuality is a bodily energy whose objects, meaning and social values are historically constructed" (12). She distinguishes different analytical approaches *within* radical feminism as well as *between* radical feminists and socialist feminists. One of her major critiques of radical feminism—in all its various forms—is that it fails to appreciate historical specificity. Because she highlights the importance of the social and historical construction of sexual practices, her analysis shares some common ground with poststructuralist and queer theory (see chapter 6).

Appearing in the January 2005 special issue of *Science & Society* on "Marxist-Feminist Thought Today," Alan Sears's article "Queer Anti-Capitalism: What's Left of Lesbian and Gay Liberation?" highlights major differences between a queer Marxist feminism and other forms of queer theory.[22] The title of Sears's piece asserts his anticapitalist stance while the subtitle captures his main argument that what is "left" of lesbian and gay politics today is not a left-wing, radical politics that substantially transforms social relations. Sears counters his "queer Marxist feminism" both to queer theory and to modern gay and lesbian identity politics. He discusses advances in gay and lesbian rights in recent years, such as in Canada where gays and lesbians enjoy various civil rights, including the right to marry. However, Sears argues that once these civil rights are attained, gays and lesbians too often become immersed in consumerism and gay/lesbian entrepreneurial ventures that take advantage of new openings or niches in the gay marketplace (such as the boom in gay tourism in recent decades). What is often forgotten, Sears argues, are the class differences *within* the homosexual community that leave poor gays and lesbians—especially people of color—marginalized and excluded. He writes:

> Clearly, the commodified queer existence is very much captured inside capitalist social relations. Thus, our communities exist largely in the form of exclusionary market spaces; our real diversity is obscured by the dominance of homogenous images; our politics our largely confined to claiming our place in existing social relations through reform ("get me to the church on time!") or transgression detached from transformation ("we're here, we're queer, get used to it!") (2005: 108–109).

Sears argues that a queer Marxist feminist perspective can provide new ways of envisioning a queer anticapitalism that "takes activism back to the best of the liberationist politics that emerged after Stonewall: the militancy, the breadth of vision, and the transformative commitments" (109). While Sears highlights important differences between a radical and an assimilationist queer politics, a number of queer theorists anticipated and addressed similar critiques, as will be shown in chapter 6.

Nevertheless, other anticapitalist scholars echo Sear's criticisms of how queer theory fails to adequately challenge capitalism. Rosemary Hennessy (2000: 108–109) argues that while the "more open, fluid, ambivalent sexual identities" discussed by queer theorists "may disrupt norms and challenge state practices that are indeed oppressive, they do not necessarily challenge neoliberalism or disrupt capitalism." Lois McNay (2000: 173) views the focus of postmodernism, poststructuralism, and queer theory on marginalized sexualities as too often "caught within a privatized and individualistic conception of activity whose radical political status is open to question in so far as it is complicit with, rather than disruptive of capitalism." McNay (1992: 31) further contends that, despite queer theory's rejection of binary thinking, it is often framed in simplistic and amorphous dualisms, such as "domination and resistance," the "normal and the abject," or the "central and the marginal." She suggests that these problems arise from the focus of the postperspectives and queer theory on language and ideas rather than on material conditions.

MARXIST, SOCIALIST, AND ANARCHIST ECOFEMINISMS

As noted earlier in this text, **ecofeminism** describes both the diverse range of women's efforts to save the earth as well as transformations in feminist thought derived from new conceptualizations of the interrelationships between women and nature (Diamond and Orenstein 1990: ix). The major assumptions of ecofeminist approaches with theoretical roots in Marxism and anarchism are explored below. First the major differences between Marxist ecofeminisms and socialist ecofeminisms are highlighted, followed by a comparison of socialist ecofeminisms and anarchist-ecofeminism. The latter is often called social ecofeminism or anarcha-ecofeminism (Merchant 1999). The term *anarcha-ecofeminism* will be used here in order to avoid the confusion of trying to distinguish between such similar sounding terms as *social ecofeminism* and *socialist ecofeminism.*

Distinguishing Marxist and Socialist Ecofeminisms

Marxist and socialist ecofeminists see environmental problems as rooted in a specific mode of production—capitalism. They view *capitalism's insatiable drive for private profits as the major source of environmental degradation.* This does not mean that there were no ancient or preindustrial forms of environmental despoliation. However, these premodern environmental problems pale beside the massive destruction of the environment that has occurred since the birth of industrial capitalism. Marxist and socialist ecofeminists also view women's relegation to housework and child care as providing a special vantage point for perceiving and understanding environmental problems. *Because of their responsibilities for domestic labor and child rearing, women more quickly perceive how environmental hazards affect their reproductive systems, their children's health, and their own households or backyards.* This analysis goes some way toward explaining why women are overrepresented in the antitoxics movement—as both participants and leaders—a finding documented by researchers from a variety of theoretical perspectives (Krauss 1994, Taylor 1997).

Marxist and socialist ecofeminisms diverge on two major ecological issues. First, *their views on science and technology differ.* Socialist ecofeminists view the rise of the science, technology, and instrumental rationality as fostering not only the rise of industrial capitalism but also industrial-growth models that result in "environmental disaster" (Merchant 1999: 9). In contrast, Marxist ecofeminists take a more technocratic or science-can-fix-it approach to solving environmental problems. They embrace instrumental rationality and view science and technology simply as tools that can be used for either progress or destruction. Their concern centers around who controls science or technology and for whose benefit. They reject what they call a Luddite position wherein technology itself is seen as evil.

Second, Marxist and socialist ecofeminist have *divergent views on the relationship between human and nonhuman nature*. The former embrace an **anthropocentric** view through which humans are seen as being superior to or more important than nonhumans. For Marxist feminists the transformation of nature is the essence of human labor and control over nature is important for human progress. Socialist ecofeminists take an **ecocentric** approach in which humans and nonhuman nature are treated as interdependent partners. They are less willing for nature to be placed as totally subservient to human needs (Merchant 1995: 15)

In feminism today, socialist ecofeminisms have a much stronger influence than Marxist ecofeminisms. One branch of socialist ecofeminism has its theoretical roots in the work of neo-Marxist critical theorists. Critical theorists, such as Max Horkheimer and Theodor Adorno, were among the first to identify the Enlightenment's embrace of instrumental rationality as spelling disaster for the environment. Their book *Dialectic of Enlightenment* (1944) begins: "The fully enlightened earth radiates disaster triumphant" ([1944] 1972: 3). One of the most prolific socialist ecofeminists inspired by their approach is environmental historian Carolyn Merchant. Her many books, such as *The Death of Nature* (1981), *Ecological Revolutions* (1989), *Earthcare* (1995), *Ecology* (1999), and *American Environmental History* (2007) are key texts in introducing and mapping the history and diversity of ecofeminist thought.

Merchant's own description of socialist ecofeminism reflects the more democratic and ecocentric approach to social life embraced by critical theorists. She explains that while socialist ecofeminists certainly work in reform-oriented environmental movements, they view reform activities as short-term objectives. Their long-term goals are to direct social change toward an environmentally sustainable and egalitarian socialist state, in addition to re-socializing men and women into nonsexist, nonracist, and anti-imperialist forms of life. Socialism is still a major part of their future vision, though they reject authoritarian forms of socialism. They look to new forms of ecosocialism brought about by green social movements and green political parties with commitments to democracy and to internationalism (Merchant 1995:15–18 and 1999: 8–9).

Another influential branch of socialist ecofeminism was inspired by the work of Rosa Luxemburg, who in the early twentieth century broke with orthodox Marxism on a number of issues (see chapter 8). Among the best-known Luxemburgian-inspired socialist ecofeminists are Vandana Shiva and Maria Mies, whose works are discussed at length in chapter 9. Like Merchant, Shiva and Mies reject the view that the domination of nature is the basis for social progress. Rather than heralding progress, they conclude that progress is a "myth"—that technocratic means too often objectify human and nonhuman life in order to control and dominate them in ways that destroy nature and dehumanize social life. Many socialist ecofeminists follow in their footsteps by refusing to view nature as simply an object for human conquest; rather, humans and nature are life forces that are symbiotically intertwined and interdependent.

Distinguishing Socialist and Anarchist Ecofeminisms

In contrast to socialist ecofeminists, anarcha-ecofeminists argue that socialism is dead as a revolutionary idea. They view socialist societies as just as guilty of environmental degradation as capitalist ones—pointing to ecological disasters like the nuclear fallout at Chernoble or the heavily polluted Baltic Sea. Anarcha-ecofeminists embrace an ecocentric approach to environmental issues and reject technocratic modes of thinking. They typically support small, decentralized, democratic social organizations centered on local and community politics and consider large, centralized, bureaucratic forms to be antithetical to their goals (Merchant 1995: 13–14). Anarcha-ecofeminists have a particular affinity for grassroots movements and local, populist causes that challenge big corporations and centralized national governments whether capitalist or socialist. Such slogans as SMALL IS BEAUTIFUL or SIMPLE LIVING resonate strongly with them (Merchant 1999).

Socialist ecofeminists counter this anarchist preference for the small and local by arguing that the vast majority of economic, social, and ecological problems cannot be adequately addressed at the local level. In an increasingly globalized world—economically, technologically and culturally—environmental issues need to be addressed by macrolevel social organizations, be they regional, national, or global. For example, James O'Connor, one of the foremost socialist ecologists writing today, points to the industrial and agricultural pollution that spills over local, regional, and national boundaries. He argues that problems like acid rain, ozone depletion, nuclear disasters, and global warming are simply beyond the scope of small-scale, local solutions (O'Connor 1997).

Notably, the first ecofeminist course in the United States was taught by Ynestra King at the Center for Social Ecology in Vermont founded by the anarchist theorist Murray Bookchin. A number of anarcha-ecofeminists, such as Janet Biehl and King, built on Bookchin's writings to argue that hierarchy and domination in all forms were antithetical to their goals:

> Social [Anarcha-] Ecofeminism accepts the basic tenet of social ecology that the idea of dominating nature stems from the domination of human by human. Only by ending all systems of domination makes possible an ecological society, in which no states or capitalist economies attempt to subjugate nature, in which all aspects of human nature—including sexuality and the passions as well as rationality—are freed. (Biehl 1991:100)

Another distinguishing feature of anarcha-ecofeminists is their call for transcending the binary or dualistic thinking that underlies many earlier ecofeminist approaches where false separations are constructed between culture/nature, mind/body, male/female, and rational/emotional. For example, anarcha-ecofeminists Val Plumwood and King both highlight how they reject the hidden hierarchies entailed in these binary models in which culture is privileged over nature, mind over body, male over female, rational over emotional, and secular over spiritual (King 1990; Plumwood 1992).

In "Healing the Wounds: Feminism, Ecology, and the Nature/Culture Dualism" (1990), King discusses how such dualisms are reinforced and replicated in debates *between* ecofeminists. Rather than engage in these internecine battles, her approach is more inclusive. She calls for ecofeminists to garner insights from the materialist approach of socialist ecofeminists as well as from the cultural and spiritual ecofeminisms rooted in radical feminism (see chapter 3). King argues that while women are as rational as men, as socialist ecofeminists claim, they should not lose sight of their emotional and caring sides, as highlighted by cultural and spiritual ecofeminists. She calls for a merger of these perspectives, which she terms a "rational reenchantment":

> To fulfill its liberatory potential, ecofeminism needs to pose a rational reenchantment that brings together spiritual and material, being and knowing. This is the promise of ecological feminism. (Quoted in Merchant 1999: 202)

In contrast to King's call for a harmonious merger of spiritual and materialist ecofeminisms, socialist feminist Donna Haraway launches a scathing critique of spiritual ecofeminists' mythology in "A Cyborg Manifesto: Science, Technology, and Socialist-Feminism in the Late Twentieth Century" ([1985] 2005). Haraway dismisses spiritual ecofeminisms and their references to goddesses and the Gaia myth as reactionary (see chapter 3). Her provocative article charts the recent effects of science and technology on social relations and calls for an updated socialist feminism that can analyze the shift from modern, industrial societies to the new postindustrial, information-based societies wrought by the new electronic technologies. As some commentators have argued, Haraway was responding to the rather dark cloud that hung over feminism in the 1980s due to defeat of the ERA and the success of the Moral Majority's antifeminist, family-values campaign. Watching segments of the women's movement embracing goddesses and other "irrational" concerns was especially galling to Haraway in the face of these threats to feminism from the New Religious Right (Landry and MacLean 1993: 37).

Haraway's term "cyborg" refers to a mythic creature that is part human/part machine. The cyborg serves as a metaphor for technocratic approaches which argue that science can fix environmental problems. She counter poses this technocratic approach to the spiritual ecofeminist mythology of women saving the planet through embracing goddess worship and rejecting science, technology, and industry. Haraway views both paths as dangerous for women and the environment. However, in one of her more provocative statements, she ([1985] 2005: 394) writes: "Though both are bound in the spiral dance, I would rather be a cyborg than a goddess." If forced to choose, she finds the irrational, antiscience, spiritual ecofeminist path more politically reactionary. Socialist feminist Haraway was not alone in such scathing attacks on spiritual ecofeminism. The anarcha-ecofeminist Janet Biehl repudiated ecofeminism altogether after she witnessed substantial segments of the women's movement embracing spiritual ecofeminism (Merchant 1995: 14).

CONCLUSION

This chapter focused on a vast array of feminist perspectives that bear the imprint of the Old Left theories of Marxism and anarchism. Attention centered on how Marxist, socialist, and anarchist feminists addressed the issues of gender and social class during the first and second waves of the U.S. women's movement. How different class locations impacted women's lives—not only their income and labor but also their well-being as mothers, wives, and lovers—was examined, as were the conceptual tools provided by the Old and New Left that have been valuable for understanding women's oppression, its historical origins as well as the various ways in which women's labor has been appropriated in modern societies by capitalism and patriarchy. In addition, how the Old and New Left fostered new directions in feminist thought, ranging from queering Marxist feminism to developing standpoint epistemologies to conceiving of entirely new ways of looking at the relationship between women and nature, also was examined, as was the rise in recent decades of materialist feminisms to better address the issues raised by intersectionality theorists, ecofeminists, and feminists who had taken the postmodern turn.

The major thrust of the next chapter is an examination of how U.S. women of color developed a feminist perspective that not only bridged the racial divide that characterized the second wave but also initiated a paradigm shift in feminist thought that bridged the modern and the postmodern. This discussion will focus on many second wave women of color who were self-identified socialists. For example, all members of the Combahee River Collective who founded the feminist approach now called intersectional theory were socialists.[23] Similarly, Angela Davis, who received much media attention in the early 1970s because of her association with the Black Panther Party, was a student of neo-Marxist critical theorist Herbert Marcuse and a longtime member of the U.S. Communist Party. Her book *Women, Race, and Class* (1981) was an early exemplar of intersectional analysis that kept its gaze on how capitalism benefited from race, gender, and class divisions. A discussion of her writings on reproductive issues can be found in the following chapter. As will become clear in that chapter, these U.S. women of color pioneered a new understanding of the intersections of race, gender, and class that is distinct from Marxist and socialist feminist approaches.

Although second wave Marxist and socialist feminists have been criticized for their inadequate analysis of race, the U.S. Communist Party and many U.S. socialists took quite a progressive position on race throughout the twentieth century. In the early decades of the twentieth century, the U.S. Communist Party called for a united front of black and white workers and took an active role in struggles against lynching, Jim Crow, and the disenfranchisement of African-Americans through poll taxes, literacy requirements for voting, and sheer terror. Luminaries in U.S. racial politics and theory during the first wave, such as W. E. B. DuBois, were members of the U.S. Communist Party. In the second half of the twentieth century, Marxist and socialist theorists were at the forefront of analyzing race relations from both internal colonialist and critical race theory perspectives (see chapters 5 and 9).

Nonetheless, omitting the writings of a longtime member of the Communist Party, such as Davis, from this chapter risks fostering the inaccurate portrayal of second wave Marxist and socialist feminists as invariably white and oblivious to race. To counter this portrayal some scholars have taken the tack of documenting how many white feminists did address race in their writings, such as Lise Vogel's article "Telling Tales: Historians of Our Own Lives (1991).[24] Other scholars have focused on the quality, rather than the quantity, of white feminists' analyses of race. Wini Breines (2002: 1112), for example, argues that an "abstract" antiracism characterized the work of many white, second wave feminists. She contrasts this abstract antiracism with a more in-depth understanding of how racism affects the everyday lives of people of color, an appreciation that can be garnered only from interpersonal interactions and socially lived knowledge. Still other scholars, such as socialist feminist Ruth Frankenberg (1993), attribute this "abstract anti-racism" to how the "social construction of whiteness" blinded white feminists to the significance of race in their own lives. Because a whitewashed portrayal of the U.S. second wave is widespread and appears repeatedly in the work of younger feminists of the third wave (Henry 2004), it too is addressed in the following chapter.

Additional writings by Marxist, socialist, and anarchist feminists on global issues can be found in chapters 8 and 9.

CRITICISMS OF MARXIST, SOCIALIST, AND ANARCHIST FEMINISMS

1. That anarchist politics can work on only small scale or local levels. They are unable to deal with large scale, macrolevel, or global social problems because of their disdain for the hierarchy entailed in formal organizations and leadership. To put it simply, critics argue that anarchists confuse leadership and authority with domination (O'Connor 1997).

2. That Marxist and socialist feminists prioritize class and gender oppression and do not give adequate attention to oppressions based on race or sexual orientation. They fail to see the simultaneous and interlocking nature of multiple oppressions where the influence of one type of oppression cannot be separately determined (Smith 1983).

3. That Marxist, socialist, and anarchist feminists do not give sufficient attention to the cultural, symbolic and discursive features of power and oppression. Their materialist focus on political economy treats these spheres of social life as derivative and, hence, fails to see how power manifests itself through discourse (Foucault [1976]1980).

4. That Marxist, socialist, and anarchist feminists fail to see how all ideologies—even those directed toward emancipatory goals—can be disciplinary and silence others. They are not adequately reflexive in regard to how the power of their own ideologies can dominate others (Foucault [1976] 1980).

NOTES

1 *The Ethnological Notebooks* were some of Marx's last writings. He wrote them between 1880 and 1882 before his death in 1883. The importance of these writings has been discussed at some length by Jacqueline Solway in her book *The Politics of Egalitarianism* (2006).

2 Bebel's book was originally titled *Woman in the Past, Present, and Future* (1879) to avoid German antisocialist laws.

3 Marx distinguishes between personal property and income-producing property. For example, the car I drive is property that I use for my own personal use. If I owned a fleet of cars or taxis that people I hired drove and that produced income for me in the form of profits, these cars would be income-producing property. For Marxists, ownership of the important means of production in a society, such as industrial factories and machinery was the key to wealth.

4 Eleanor Leacock also was given the honor of writing the introduction to the 1972 English edition of Engels's *Origin of the Family, Private Property and the State.*

5 The idea that women's domestic roles make women mad (in the sense of both angry and mentally unhinged) pervades literature by women. One book that examines the theme of madness in women's literature from a feminist vantage point cleverly captures this theme in its title *The Mad Woman in the Attic*—from the ostensibly insane wife in the novel *Jane Eyre* (Gilbert and Gubar 1979).

6 Parts of this section first appeared in "Pioneers of Ecofeminism and Environmental Justice," *Feminist Formations* 23, no. 2 (2011): 1–25. Copyright © 2011 Feminist Formations. Reprinted with permission by The Johns Hopkins University Press.

7 Speaking at this memorial Schneiderman said, "I would be a traitor to these poor burned bodies if I came here to talk good fellowship. . . . Every year thousands of us are maimed. The life of men and women is so cheap and property is so sacred. . . . I can't talk fellowship to you who are gathered here. Too much blood has been spilled. I know from my experience it is up to the working people to save themselves" (quoted in Stein 1962: 144–145).

8 For example, Jane Addams was placed under police surveillance even though she was not a socialist. Rather, she favored decentralized, neighborhood organizations and reform rather than revolution and the socialization of property. See wisconsinhistory.org/turningpoints/tp-043 and chapter 2.

9 Bernstein's analysis of homosexuality, titled "The Judgment of Abnormal Sexual Intercourse," was published in *Die Neue Zeit* in May 1895. A translation by Angela Clifford can be found at www.marxists.org/reference/archive/bernstein/works/1895/wilde/homoseual.htm (last accessed on December 2, 2009).

10 A section of Foucault's *The History of Sexuality, Volume I* is devoted to a critique of the "repressive hypothesis." He documents how the children of the upper classes were the most heavily disciplined and restricted in terms of their sexual behavior, a finding that actually supports Engels's more orthodox Marxist thesis that sexual restrictions were designed to protect privileged classes and their private property.

11 Comparable worth refers to the demand that jobs requiring comparable skills, ability, and educational requirements receive similar wages or salaries. This is particularly relevant to sex-segregated occupations in which jobs traditionally held by women (such as elementary school teachers) receive less pay than jobs traditionally held by men (such as plumbers) despite the differences in skill and education required.

12 In the 1930s, Tillie Lerner Olsen was a member of the Young Communist League and was jailed a number of times for her role in labor organizing.

13 Young is explicit that she is referring only to notions of feminine comportment in advanced, postindustrial societies.

14 Bourdieu used the Latin term *habitus* to refer to "a habitual or typical condition, state or appearance, particularly of the body" (Jenkins 1992: 74). Habitus refers to one's embodied dispositions as well as one's worldview that result from social interactions within others. Although these habits are learned, they become taken-for-granted features of everyday life. "To speak of habitus is to assert that the individual, and even the personal, the subjective, is social, collective. Habitus is a 'socialized subjectivity' (Bourdieu and Wacquant 1992: 126). Bourdieu focused primarily on how habitus

derived from class-specific (rather than gender-specific) experiences of socialization in family and peer groups. (Swartz 1997: 102).

15 However, she is careful to point out that her notion is less rigid and more historically specific than Bourdieu's concept (Young 2005: 26).

16 Greer's analysis of how femininity "maims" girls' bodies and actions is a precursor to Iris Marion Young's *Female Body Experience* (2005).

17 Smith (2004: 265) argues that one does not have to seek the roots of feminist standpoint approaches in previous theories. Rather, "such epistemologies and methods came out of and were dialogically implicated in a women's movement that offered a profound challenge to established discourses." Hence, she points to women's concrete experiences in the women's movement as the bases for their development.

18 See also the work of Alison Jaggar (1983).

19 Haraway places in this camp not only Hartsock's piece but also the works of Gloria Anzaldúa and Chela Sandoval, which are discussed in chapter 5.

20 Postmodernists often refer to these developments as the "death of the communist metanarrative" (Landry and MacLean 1993: 10).

21 Marx wrote: "Men [*sic*] make their own history, but they do not make it as they please; they do not make it under circumstances of their own choosing, but under circumstances existing already, given and transmitted from the past. The tradition of all dead generations weighs like a nightmare on the brains of the living" (quoted in Tucker 1972: 437).

22 This special issue of *Science & Society* was edited by two of the more stalwart supporters Marxist feminism, Lise Vogel and Martha Gimenez.

23 The Combahee River Collective's Black Feminist Statement ([1977] 2005: 313) states: "We are socialists because we believe the work must be organized for the collective benefit of those who do the work and create the products, and not for the profits of the bosses. Material resources must be equally distributed among those who create those resources."

24 It may be more accurate to say that less theoretical attention was given to race than to gender and class. For example, in "The Unhappy Marriage of Marxism and Feminism," Heidi Hartmann devotes only a few paragraphs of her article to race while giving class and gender far more coverage.

CHAPTER 5

Intersectionality Theories

> A theory in the flesh means one where the physical realities of our lives—our skin color, the land or concrete we grew up on, our sexual longings—all fuse to create a politics born out of necessity. Here, we attempt to bridge the contradictions in our experience:
>
> We are the colored in a white feminist movement.
> We are the feminists among the people of our culture.
> We are often the lesbians among the straight.
> We do this bridging by naming our selves and by telling our stories in our own words.
>
> —Cherríe Moraga and Gloria Anzaldúa

INTRODUCTION

This chapter focuses on a feminist perspective described as "one of the most important contributions that women's studies has made so far" (McCall 2005: 1771). It was developed by women of color within the United States who felt their concerns were not being adequately addressed by existing feminisms. Born of necessity and neglect, it was based on the profound realization that no one but themselves would adequately address their concerns. Angry and exasperated by continuing to find women of color on the lowest rungs of the social stratification ladder in the United States and repeatedly being asked to bridge the gulf between their own lives and those of their oppressors and their political allies, they often referred to their political work as this "bridge called my back." One of their signal works bore this title. Edited by Cherríe Moraga and Gloria Anzaldúa, *This Bridge Called My Back: Writings by Radical Women of Color* first published in 1981 and reprinted in 1983 by Kitchen Table Press—a small independent press established to publish the works of womanists of color because in the early years of the second wave their works were rarely acquired by large commercial presses (Messer-Davidow 2002: 195–196).

The uniqueness of their contributions may explain why they were the first U.S. feminists to use the term *third wave* to refer to their ideas and political strategies and did so long before a new generation of younger feminists claimed this term as their own (Springer 2002: 1063). Although rarely referred to as the third wave today, their theoretical approach has been known by a number of different names. In the 1970s it was often referred to as the women of color perspective; in the 1980s, as U.S. third world feminism. The term *intersectionality* was coined by legal theorist Kimberlé Williams Crenshaw in 1989, and intersectionality theory is the term most frequently used today. However, all of these names refer to a particular *theoretical perspective.* Women of color have embraced many and diverse feminisms throughout the history of the U.S. women's movement as evident in earlier chapters. *It is a particular theoretical perspective that is examined in this chapter not simply the writings by women of color.*

The 1960s and 1970s witnessed the rise of a number of new social movements that focused on racial/ethnic issues. The Native–American movement, the Chicano movement, the Asian–American movement, and the Puerto Rican movement followed closely on the heels of the civil rights movement. These multiracial struggles against white supremacy for black, brown, red, and yellow power emerged both practically and symbolically as a new common front of "Third World peoples" *inside* the United States (Gosse 2005: 134). As discussed in previous chapters, second wave feminists of color often cut their political teeth in these social movements before organizing on their own behalf. They preferred not to use feminist because of the term's association with white, class-privileged feminists' concerns. African–American feminists referred to themselves as womanists (Walker 1983), while Latinas preferred Chicana feminists, hispanas, and/or xicanistas (Maatita 2005). As members of the two largest minority groups in the United States, their writings have achieved the broadest distribution to date. Yet because all of their voices too often fell on deaf ears, second wave women of color referred to themselves as "sister/outsiders" (Lorde 1984)

While these sister/outsiders eventually succeeded in moving their ideas from the margins to the center of the U.S. women's movement, they were not the first to address differences between women, multiple oppressions, or the importance of different vantage points on social reality. Rather, these ideas in more rudimentary forms were evident in the works of African–American women writers in the nineteenth and early twentieth centuries. As Rachel E. Luft and Jane Ward point out in their award-winning article "Toward an Intersectionality Just Out of Reach: Confronting the Challenges of Intersectional Practice" (2009: 13), to claim intersectionality as the product of women's studies alone without also situating it in the lived experience of black feminist race theorists is a "failure of intersectional historiography." Although feminism has been one of the most receptive and fertile grounds for intersectional work, losing sight of the "racial habitus" that produced this theoretical innovation risks losing the critical imperative for social justice that underlies this theory as a political practice (13). In short, intersectional practice is first and foremost "an activity aimed at intersectional, sustainable social justice outcomes" (11).[1]

PRECURSORS TO INTERSECTIONAL ANALYSES IN EARLY MODERNITY BY JANE WARD AND SUSAN MANN

The integral relationship between race and gender has been evident since the beginning of the U.S. women's movement, and the significant role that racial issues played in triggering the first wave often has been noted. As discussed in chapter 2, many nineteenth-century women learned important political and organizing skills through their abolitionist activism, but they also learned how their rights as women were circumscribed and restricted. Women abolitionists were angry and insulted when they were treated as second-class citizens by male abolitionist leaders, such as when they were segregated in balconies during political gatherings or not allowed to speak publicly. While these political awakenings triggered these women to organize in their own interests, women of color—whether free or enslaved—saw enormous differences between their rights and those of white suffragists, particularly when they compared their social positions to those of the white, middle-class women who became leaders of the major suffrage organizations.

Many of the concerns taken up by white, middle-class feminists in the nineteenth century—access to the public sphere, freedom of employment, the right to control property, and an end to restrictive beliefs about female frailty or weakness—reflected these feminists' own racial and socioeconomic privileges. The nineteenth-century logic of separate spheres suggested that white, middle-class women required protection from the heartless, male-dominated, and sexually volatile public realm, yet women slaves, as well as poor and working-class women of all races, were not included in the narrow category of woman upon which such logic relied. Women slaves, as well as women agricultural and factory workers (across various racial and ethnic groups), engaged in backbreaking work as difficult as any manual labor undertaken by men. Women slaves and prostitutes were frequently subjected to the most brutal forms of sexual violence and torture. These abuses reflected a contradiction in Victorian gender ideology, one that would carry forward into the current era. White and middle-class women were imbued with chastity, purity, and great maternal importance while women of color and all poor women were regularly subjected to demeaning forms of sexual violence and social control.

Such were the contradictions that led ex-slave Sojourner Truth to declare "Ain't I a Woman?" in her famous 1851 speech by that name. This extemporaneous speech took place at a conference on women's rights where white women speakers were heckled by males in the audience who claimed that women had no reasons to complain given how they were put on a pedestal by men. Truth rose to the podium, gave her famous speech, and even exposed her breast to reinforce her claim "Ain't I a woman?" One can imagine how quickly the heckling was hushed as she began:

> That man over there says that women need to be helped into carriages, and lifted over ditches, and to have the best place everywhere. Nobody ever helps me into

> carriages, or over mud-puddles, or gives me any best place! And ain't I a woman? Look at me! Look at my arm! I have ploughed and planted, and gathered into barns, and no man could head me! And, ain't I a woman? . . . I have born thirteen children, and seen them most all sold off to slavery, and when I cried out with my mother's grief, none but Jesus heard me! And, ain't I a woman? (Truth [1851] 2005: 79)

Truth and other black women activists were at the forefront of exposing the racial and class construction of femininity. Their insights laid the groundwork for later feminist theorizing that would expose the impossibility of the feminine ideal—not only for women of color but also for poor women, working-class women, and lesbians of all races and classes.

Race and sexuality were strongly linked in the Victorian imagination as well as in the laws and customs that governed sexuality in daily life. Within European and U.S. culture, African women were portrayed as oversexed by comparison with white women or as possessing excessively sexual bodies and "uncivilized" ideas about sex. Throughout the nineteenth century, African women—such as the slave Saartjie Baartman, who was "exhibited" throughout Europe as a sideshow attraction—were depicted in U.S. and European newspapers and medical literature as having unusually large breasts, hips, buttocks, and labia. Such images, along with racist and sexist ideology about black women's sexual availability, were used by whites to justify the enslavement and sexual assault of Black women. A powerful example of nineteenth-century black feminist literature addressing white sexual violence against black women can be found in *Incidents in the Life of a Slave Girl*, published in 1861 by Harriet Ann Jacobs under the pseudonym Linda Brent. Here Jacobs details the incessant sexual threats made by her lecherous white slave master, his removal of her children to force her into sexual submission, the furious jealousy and blame she endured from his wife, and the years she spent in hiding in a small attic to escape his sexual abuse. Of her slave master and mistress, Jacobs ([1861] 2001: 27–28) wrote:

> He peopled my young mind with unclean images, such as only a vile monster could think of. I turned from him with disgust and hatred. But he was my master, I was compelled to live under the same roof with him—where I saw a man forty years my senior daily violating the most sacred commandments of nature. He told me I was his property; that I must be subject to his will in all things. . . . But where could I turn for protection? . . . The mistress, who ought to protect the helpless victim, has no other feelings towards her but those of jealousy and rage. Even the little child, who is accustomed to wait on her mistress and her children, will learn, before she is twelve years old, why it is that her mistress hates such and such a one among the slaves. . . . If God has bestowed beauty upon her, it will prove her greatest curse. That which commands admiration in the white woman only hastens the degradation of the female slave."

Jacobs's narrative offered not only a rare and significant historical account of women's experiences of slavery but, also, insights into the complex and triangulated relations of power, control, and violence between white men, white mistresses, and black slaves.

In the decades following the abolition of slavery in 1865, black women continued to be excluded from the white image of feminine refinement and chastity. It stands to reason, then, that middle-class black feminists in the Victorian period, such as Anna Julia Cooper, Ida B. Wells-Barnett, and Mary Church Terrell, steered clear of direct discussion of their sexuality and instead emphasized the "intellectual progress" and social respectability of black women. In the Victorian Era, black women in the public spotlight had little choice but to follow in the reformist tradition of emphasizing their virtuous contributions to both black society and American culture in general. Racist and sexist myths held over from slave era ideology (and used to justify slavery), such as the myth of the black rapist or the black Jezebel suggested that people of color were sexually promiscuous, hypersexual, and ruled by their embodied desires rather than intellectual or religious pursuits. In 1898, Terrell, the first president of the National Association of Colored Women, presented the opposite representation of black women in her lecture "The Progress of Colored Women" ([1898] 1995: 64–65):

> Even the white people who think they know all about colored people and are perfectly just in their estimate of them are surprised [by] . . . the rapidity with which a large number of colored women have advanced. . . . To women of the race may be attributed in large measure the refinement and purity of the colored home. . . . Statistics compiled by men not inclined to falsify in favor of my race show that immorality among the colored women of the United States is not so great as among women with similar environment and temptations in Italy, Germany, Sweden, and France. Scandals in the best colored society are exceedingly rare, while the progressive game of divorce and remarriage is practically unknown.

Writing at the same time that white feminists such as Victoria Woodhull and Emma Goldman were calling for the end of marriage and speaking publicly about female sexual arousal, Terrell's emphasis on marriage, domesticity, and the avoidance of scandal was informed by a different history from that of white women. For Terrell and other black feminists, whose parents had been slaves, legal marriage and sexual privacy were rights not to be taken for granted.

Historian Evelyn Brooks Higgenbotham (1993) coined the term the **politics of respectability** to describe the efforts of women of color during the Progressive Era to promote temperance, cleanliness of person and property, thrift, etiquette, and sexual morality. These efforts were part of the "uplift politics" undertaken by the black women's clubs discussed in chapter 2. The politics of respectability bridged the personal and the political. On the one hand, it encouraged African-Americans as individuals to redefine themselves outside of prevailing stereotypes. On the other hand, it was a strategy of resistance designed to undermine the racial stereotypes held by the dominant group. As such, the politics of respectability was directed at both black and white audiences. Some of the negative consequences of this strategy of resistance are discussed later in this chapter.

As noted in chapter 3, while wealthy white women were beginning to have access to colleges in the 1800s, women of color (slaves or free) and poor white women were more likely to attempt to pass as men in order to gain some degree of access to the public sphere. One well-documented account is the case of Mary Fields, a black woman who was born a slave in Tennessee and later earned a good living as a male stagecoach driver. Cora Anderson, an indigenous woman living in the late nineteenth century, became Ralph Kerwinieo, found employment, and married. Yet her description of her motivation for becoming male does not resemble a contemporary transgender narrative or even a narrative about sexuality but, rather, a narrative about survival as a woman in a man's world:

> The world is made by man—for man alone. In future centuries it is probable that woman will be the owner of her own body and the custodian of her own soul. But until that time you can expect that the statutes concerning women will be all wrong. The well-cared for woman is a parasite, and the woman who must work is a slave. Do you blame me for wanting to be a man—free to live as a man in a man-made world? Do you blame me for hating to again resume a woman's clothes? (quoted in Faderman 1991: 86)

Two of the more famous black feminist writers of the late nineteenth and early twentieth centuries—Anna Julia Cooper and Ida B. Wells-Barnett—were able to get an advanced education in the small window of opportunity that opened up during the Reconstruction Era. Cooper and Wells-Barnett were born to former slave women but grew up after Emancipation, attended freedmen schools, and went to college. Cooper even went on to receive a doctorate from the Sorbonne in 1925. Both women focused their attention on how white people, including white feminists, were blind to the plight of African-Americans, and they discussed at length the intersections of race, class, and gender (Lengermann and Niebrugge-Brantley 1998: 176).

In *A Voice from the South: By a Black Woman of the South* ([1892] 1988: 143), Cooper discusses the many contributions of black women and highlights a theme that can be found in many of her writings: "no woman can possibly put herself or her sex outside of any interests that affect *humanity*" (emphasis added). Cooper's awareness of the multiplicity of oppressions that affect people by race, class, gender, and nation, along with her demand that the women's movement address the concerns of *all oppressed peoples*, is clear in the following quote from her speech at the 1892 World's Fair in Chicago (first published in 1893). This speech was even more piercing since women of color were excluded from participating in this World's Columbian Exposition until they mounted a successful protest:

> Let woman's claim be as broad in the concrete as in the abstract: We take our stand on the solidarity of humanity, the oneness of life, and the unnaturalness and injustice of all special favoritisms, whether of sex, race, country, or condition. If one link of the chain be broken, the chain is broken. A bridge is not stronger than its weakest part, and a cause is not worthier than its weakest element. . . . We want, then as toilers for the universal triumph of justice and human rights, to go

> to our homes from this Congress, demanding an entrance not through a gateway for ourselves, our race, our sex, or our sect, but a grand highway for humanity. ([1893] 1998: 204–205)

Cooper's support for the rights of Native–Americans and for people abroad who were fighting against colonialism is discussed in chapter 8. Indeed, she is one of the earliest U.S. feminists to address the issues of internal and external colonialism.

A Voice from the South also contains rudiments of a standpoint epistemology that recognizes both the critical insights of people on the margins as well as the dangers of making "sweeping generalizations of a race" particularly on the "meager and superficial information" provided by white eyes ([1892] 1988: 203). This is evident when Cooper critiques the various ways in which American literature had portrayed blacks as ignorant brutes, submissive "menials," and "bootblacks and hotel waiters, grinning from ear to ear and bowing and curtseying for the extra tips" (206):

> What I hope to see before I die is a black man honestly and appreciatively portraying both the Negro as he is, and the white man, occasionally seen from the Negro's standpoint. There is an old proverb: "The devil is always painted *black*—by white painters." And, what is needed perhaps, to reverse the picture of the lordly man slaying the lion, is for the lion to turn painter. (225; her emphasis)

Cooper also differentiated the standpoint of black men from that of black women, thus highlighting the importance of "incorporating an explicit analysis of patriarchy in any effort to address racial domination" (Crenshaw 1989: 160). Indeed, Cooper often criticized black leaders for claiming to speak for the race but failing to speak for black women. To Martin Delaney's claims that where he was allowed to enter, the race entered with him, Cooper countered: "Only the Black Woman can say, when and where I enter . . . then and there the whole Negro race enters with me" (quoted in Crenshaw 1989: 160).[2]

In *A Voice from the South* ([1892] 1988: 178), Cooper discusses how the exclusion of blacks from access to reading and writing meant that "no artist for many generations" and "no Shakespeare arose" from those who were "imported merely to be hewers of wood and drawers of water." She refers to this exclusion as the "silent factor" in American literature (179). Here Cooper's ideas presage by almost four decades Virginia Woolf's famous discussion of "Shakespeare's Sister" (in *A Room of One's Own* [1929]), which highlighted the distortions entailed in androcentric literature as well as how women had been denied artistic and educational opportunities.

Cooper's contemporary, Ida B. Wells-Barnett, also refused to be silenced and was nationally and internationally renowned for her campaigns against lynching as well as for her activism on behalf of women's rights. Her most famous books, *Southern Horrors: Lynch Law in All Its Phases* (1892) and *The Red Record* (1895), provide detailed documentation of lynchings that occurred in nineteenth-century America. Because the rape of white women was often used as the reason for lynching, white women too often tempered their condemnation of lynching. Barnett demonstrates the falsity of this assumption with her detailed data. In this way she exposes the "myth of the black rapist"—an issue taken up again in late modernity by such second wave black feminists as bell hooks (1984). Wells-Barnett ([1901] 2005: 117) also points out the irony of the so-called "desperate effort of the Southern People to protect their women from Black monsters" given how women of color—particularly slave women—had been raped and brutalized by white man with impunity—reiterating one of the major themes highlighted in Jacobs's earlier work on rape and violence.

The violence perpetrated against black men and women became a central issue in the debates over the Fifteenth Amendment to the U.S. Constitution. As noted in chapter 2, this amendment—which gave black men but not any women the right to vote—divided the U.S. women's movement along racial lines with few exceptions. Many white suffragists were enraged that exslaves would get the vote before them, and their racism erupted during the heated debates over this amendment. White suffragists, such as Elizabeth Cady Stanton (1886: 181) argued for literacy requirements for voters or educated suffrage, thus enhancing the position of literate women and undermining the position of ex-slaves, many immigrants, and poor people in general:

> In view of the fact that the Freedmen of the South and the millions of foreigners now crowding our shores, most of whom represent neither property, education, nor civilization, are all in the progress of events to be enfranchised, the best interests of the nation demand that we outweigh this incoming pauperism, ignorance and degradation, with the wealth, education, and refinement of the women of the republic.

Stanton even argued that giving black men the vote was a license to rape. She writes: "The Republican cry of 'Manhood Suffrage' creates an antagonism between black men and all women that will culminate in fearful outrages on womanhood, especially in the southern states" (1886: 181). "Fearful outrages" and "outrageous assaults" were frequently used by women of this era to refer to rape, as Wells-Barnett ([1901] 2005: 118–119) pointed out.

Some black feminists rejected the Fifteenth Amendment, among them Sojourner Truth ([1867] 2005), who feared it would make black men masters over black women. However, most African-American males and females supported this amendment. One of the most compelling reasons for this consensus was the violence perpetrated by whites against blacks. Consider the words of the abolitionist leader and women's rights activist Frederick Douglass in one of his speeches in support of the Fifteenth Amendment:

> When women, because they are women, are hunted down through the cities of New York and New Orleans, when they are dragged from their houses and hung upon lamp posts; when their children are torn from their arms, and their brains dashed upon the pavement; when they are objects of insult and outrage at every turn; when they are in danger of having their homes burnt down over their heads; when their children are not allowed to enter schools; then they will have an urgency to obtain the ballot equal to our own. (Quoted in Giddings 1984: 67)

Asked if his descriptions were not true for black women as well as for black men, Douglass replied: "Yes, yes, yes. . . . It is true for Black women but not because she is a woman, but because she is Black!" (67).

In sum, nineteenth- and early-twentieth-century women of color addressed a number of important feminist issues using what we would refer to today as rudimentary intersectional analysis. They pointed to differences between women by race and class and criticized homogenized and universalized notions of woman. They highlighted the interlocking nature of the oppressions they faced and called on women's rights activists to take up the concerns of marginalized and subjugated peoples. Anna Julia Cooper provided the most developed epistemology of the socially situated nature of diverse vantage points in this era. However, the works of other women of color, such as Harriet Ann Jacobs and Sojourner Truth, exemplified these diverse vantage points and their voices testified to the value of socially lived knowledge for future feminist theorizing. A more detailed discussion of how these first wave women of color responded to U.S. internal and overseas colonialism can be found in chapter 8.

PRECURSORS TO INTERSECTIONAL ANALYSES BETWEEN THE WAVES

The Harlem Renaissance

The **Harlem Renaissance** was a cultural movement that roughly spanned the decade between the 1920s and the 1930s. Initially it was known as the New Negro Movement because one of its key themes was how African-Americans could challenge racism and transform pervasive racial stereotypes through intellect and the production of art, music, and literature.[3] The literary achievements of black artists during the Harlem Renaissance are legendary. While poet and author Langston Hughes is often viewed as the centerpiece of this renaissance in black culture, many women writers made their mark. The Harlem Renaissance encouraged the appreciation of folk culture and this was exemplified in the writings of anthropologist and novelist Zora Neale Hurston. Her most famous novels, *Jonah's Gourd Vine* (1934) and *Their Eyes Were Watching God* (1937) highlighted the intersections of race, class, and gender in the everyday lives of poor African-Americans. Along with Hurston's works, the writings of other novelists, poets, and playwrights from the Harlem Renaissance became part of the canon of American women's literature, such as those of Nella Larsen, Alice Dunbar-Nelson, and Georgia Douglas Johnson. Their works foreshadowed some of the major intersectional themes found in the literary writings of such contemporary black feminist authors such as Toni Morrison, Alice Walker, and Maya Angelou.[4] Scholar Mary Helen Washington (1989) has noted several major themes that characterized the work of black feminist writers during the twentieth century. These included reconciling the past, present, and future given the history of racism and discrimination faced by black women; conflicts with white women; the various ways white beauty ideals affected women of color; conflicts with black men, including violence against women *within* the black community; and how strong relationships between black women were so vital to their lives.

Music and art also thrived during this vibrant era. As jazz, blues, and the Harlem stride style of piano playing flourished, Count Basie, Duke Ellington, Jelly Roll Morton, and other black musicians and bandleaders became nationally renowned (Huggins 1973). Harlem also was known for famous music/dance venues, such as the Cotton Club, the Apollo Theater, and the Savoy Ballroom, where the careers of Billie Holiday, Ella Fitzgerald, and Sarah Vaughan were launched (Wintz 1996). Some scholars have noted how black women's blues were distinctive—taking on themes that were banished from popular music in this era—such as extramarital affairs, domestic violence, and the short-lived nature of intimate heterosexual relations as well as the theme of women loving women (Collins 2004a: 110; Russell 2008). One of the more memorable songs of this era was Billie Holliday's "Strange Fruit" first recorded in 1939 and inducted into the Grammy Hall of Fame in 1978 (Margolick 2001). This song describes a "pastoral scene of the gallant south" where the "strange fruit" swinging in the Southern breeze was the "bitter crop" of "bulging eyes and twisted mouth" reiterating the anti-lynching theme of earlier black feminists (Stone 2004).[5]

The Harlem Renaissance was based largely on African–American involvement and received much of its support from black patrons as well as black-owned businesses and publications. Nevertheless, there were some white patrons as well as white participants. For example, often mentioned among the leading intellectuals of this movement was Mary White Ovington, a white suffragist, socialist, and cofounder of the National Association for the Advancement of Colored People (NAACP) (Hutchinson 1995). However, the Harlem Renaissance was first and foremost a renaissance of African-American culture. It enabled many black intellectuals and artists to enter the mainstream of American culture and greatly expanded their contacts nationally and internationally.

Although the Great Depression ended this flourishing period of black culture, it has been argued that the achievements of the Harlem Renaissance redefined how both Americans and the world viewed African–Americans. For many, this image changed from one that evoked rural, undereducated former slaves and sharecroppers to one of urban, cosmopolitan sophistication (Wintz 1996). The Harlem Renaissance served as an important point of reference from which African–Americans gained a spirit of self determination and a foundation of black pride that would be manifest in the civil rights movement and in a simmering black radicalism, and militancy.

The Long Civil Rights Era

The title of this section refers to the radical period of struggle over the place of black Americans in national life that spanned the 1930s to the 1970s. Many second wave womanists of color who later developed intersectionality theory were influenced by these radical politics that focused on racial justice—especially their critique of liberalism and their focus on African–Americans as a colonized people *within* the United States. While there is an impressive literature on this topic,[6] the section below draws from Robert Self's article "The Black Panther Party and the Long Civil Rights Era" (2006), which provides a cogent overview of this era that specifically highlights its *anti-liberal* and *anti-colonialist features*.

Self discusses how the conventional narrative of the civil right movement begins in the mid-1950s with the U.S. Supreme Court's decision in *Brown v. Board of Education* (1954) and focuses on the emergence of a liberal, reform-oriented civil rights movement under the leadership of Dr. Martin Luther King Jr. The civil rights movement took aim at ending the racial segregation, terror, and second-class political status of blacks under the American apartheid system, better known as Jim Crow. It employed a compelling mix of Christian fellowship, Enlightenment ideals of freedom and equality as enshrined in the icons of American democracy (if not in its actual practice), and an activism based on nonviolent, civil disobedience learned from Mohandas Gandhi's success in fighting British colonialism in India. Relying heavily on African–American churches for their organizational and grassroots base, civil rights activists forged a coalition composed of black Americans and white liberal Americans. This coalition found some political support in the Democratic Party during the Kennedy/Johnson administrations, although this support was uneven.[7] Among the civil rights movement's most notable successes were the dismantling of Jim Crow and the passage of the Civil Rights Act of 1964 and the Voting Rights Act of 1965.

Yet the portrayal of the civil rights movement as neatly "shoehorned" between the mid-1950s and the mid-1960s has been criticized for "minimizing, if not silencing" the movement's longer association with black radicalism and these radicals' critiques of liberal solutions to American racism (Self 2006: 17–18). By isolating the movement in its most overtly liberal phase, Self argues that the history of two forms of radicalism were silenced and discredited: first, the radicalism of the communist Left and the Popular Front (the united front of black and white workers and political radicals) of the 1930s and 1940s; and second, the black radicalism that in the late 1960s and early 1970s embraced an anticolonialist, internationalist stance.

Self argues that black radicalism was primarily, though not entirely, an urban phenomenon.[8] This radicalism accelerated as a result of the dislocations that accompanied the transformation and mechanization of southern agriculture[9] in the decades following the Great Depression. Sometimes referred to as the "Southern enclosure," in this period approximately eight million people—mainly poor sharecroppers and tenant farmers—were forced off the land (Kirby 1987: 276; Mann 1990a). The exodus of blacks from the rural south to urban areas has been described as "one of the greatest movements of people in history to occur within a single generation" (Fite 1984: 209), far surpassing in magnitude the Great Migration that took place in the early decades of the twentieth century (see chapter 2). Yet, like the Great Migration, it exacerbated the social pressures wrought by racism and segregation in urban ghettoes that later would explode in race riots across the country in cities as diverse as Los Angeles, Detroit, and Philadelphia. Black radicals viewed cities as the sites and sources of black liberation and *saw federal government policies as their enemy, not their ally, in these struggles* (Self 2006: 18–19). Black militants stressed discipline, self-determination, and the necessity of armed resistance to "the brutal force used against us daily" (40). While liberal civil rights leaders, such as Martin Luther King Jr., were harassed by the FBI, black militants experienced much heavier state repression (45). However, both liberal civil rights activists and black radicals faced terror from their attempts to foster social justice. As Fannie Lou Hamer, a Mississippi Freedom Democratic Party leader, stated when her Party was refused seating at the Democratic National Convention in 1964:

> Is this America? The land of the free and the home of the brave? Where we have to sleep with our telephones off the hook, because our lives be threatened daily? (Quoted in Gosse 2005: 1)

Both the antiliberal and anticolonialist stance of black radicals emerged as a response to the rise of the U.S. "welfare–warfare" state in the context of both economic crises at home and geopolitical crises abroad (Self 2006: 18). At home, the welfare state was the New Deal's response to the Great Depression, and it greatly expanded the scope and power of the federal government. The midcentury U.S. welfare state combined social subsidies for specific groups (such as Social Security for the aged, the G.I bill for veterans, and direct welfare payments to poor mothers) with equally important subsidies to middle- and upper-class Americans in the form of federal mortgage programs, highway construction, and urban renewal. These federal policies fostered massive suburban migration, or white flight, from cities, which in turn devastated the tax base and economic well-being of the urban landscape. It is for these reasons that black radicals saw the federal government as the "critical handmaiden to the private market's creation of white suburbs and black urban ghettoes" (19–20).

Because postwar black radicalism evolved in the context of anticolonial struggles in Africa, Asia, and Latin America where various peoples of color struggled to free themselves from Western colonial rule, radicals at home could hardly avoid confronting the question of black Americans' relationship to colonialism (28). Given the role of the United States as the major Western superpower, the reality that the U.S. government, military, and intelligence agencies could decisively affect the outcomes of these struggles also was apparent. As Self points out, the anticolonialist, internationalist stance of black radicals would link color lines in the United States with color lines internationally to form what author Richard Wright called the "color curtain" (quoted in Self 2006: 21).[10]

Despite the important roles played by many second wave womanists of color in the civil rights movement and/or in radical black politics, such as Fannie Lou Hamer, Frances Beal, Toni Cade Bambara, Assata Shakur, Angela Davis, and Elaine Brown (a former chairperson of the Black Panther Party), they also experienced sexism within these movements. Blatant examples include Stokely Carmichael's remark: "The only position for women in SNCC [Student Non-Violent Coordinating Movement] is prone" or Malcolm X's emphasis on women having subordinate roles as well as behaving modestly and morally while he was involved in the Nation of Islam.[11] Disenchanted with this sexism, as well as with the racism in the white, women's movement, a number of second wave womanists of color developed their own political organizations and theoretical analyses.

In 1968, women in SNCC formed the Black Women's Liberation Committee. Within months they expanded to include other women of color and became an independent organization called the Third World Women's Alliance (TWWA) led by Francis Beal. The explicitly anticapitalist and anti-imperialist TWWA also confronted the sexism of black men. The examination of this sexism was heightened when in 1970 poet Toni Cade Bambara published *The Black Woman*, which included a range of perspectives on black women's oppression by black men. In May 1973, the National Black Feminist Organization (NBFO) was formed in New York City, and without money or staff, it held a major conference, issued a manifesto, and by the end of that year had formed dozens of local chapters (Gosse 2005: 168). One group of black feminists who viewed the NBFO's politics as too moderate, formed the Combahee River Collective in 1974. As will be shown below, this collective is credited with developing one of the second wave's major statements of intersectionality theory.

INTERSECTIONALITY THEORIES THAT BRIDGED LATE MODERNITY AND POSTMODERNITY

This Bridge Called My Back

Just as the nineteenth- and early-twentieth-century precursors to intersectionality theory highlighted *differences between women*, so too did the scholarship and politics of many womanists of color during the second wave. One of the most influential pieces to first articulate these differences during the second wave was the Combahee River Collective's "Black Feminist Statement" published in 1977. This collective of black, socialist, and lesbian feminists used the term "horizontal oppressions" to refer to the differences that divided women on the bases of gender, race, class, and/or sexual orientation. They also pointed to the interlocking nature of multiple oppressions, such as their own experiences as black lesbians. A focus on these simultaneous and multiple oppressions would come to form the crux of intersectional theory.

The political stance of the Combahee River Collective is "embodied in the concept of **identity politics**" which they saw as the "most profound and potentially the most radical politics" ([1977] 2005: 313). Identity politics root a person's politics in group identities based on their social locations. The idea here is that identity is taken as a political point of departure, as the motivation for action, and as the basis for delineating political concerns. The links that foster collective action between many and diverse identity-based groups are coalitions, while overlapping oppressions provide the grounds for coalition-building. In contrast to feminists who tried to build a unitary, collective social movement by highlighting the similarities between women, these feminists focused on building a movement based on difference. While this political stance suggests their optimism that women of color can be their own agents of liberation, it also suggests their profound pessimism that white feminists could not be counted on to fight for the rights of the marginalized. They write :"We realize that the only people who care enough about us to work consistently for our liberation is us" (313).

As noted earlier, often women of color were asked to "explain their oppressions to others" and to "stretch out and bridge the gap" between the actualities of their own lives and the consciousness of their oppressors, as well as of their political allies. As poet and activist Audre Lorde points out in *Sister/Outsider* (1984: 114–115):

> Whenever the need for some pretense of communication arises, those who profit from our oppression call upon us to share our knowledge with them. In other words, it is the responsibility of the oppressed to teach the oppressors their mistakes.... The oppressors maintain their position and evade responsibility for their actions. There is a constant drain of energy which might be better used in redefining ourselves and devising realistic scenarios for altering the present and constructing the future.

Similarly, Mitsuye Yamada ([1981] 2005: 365–366) reveals her frustration at frequently hearing white feminists voice stereotypes of Asian–American women because of their ignorance of Asian–American women's histories and struggles:

> No matter what I say or do, the stereotype still hangs on. I am weary of starting from scratch each time I speak or write, as if there were no history behind us, of hearing that among women of color, Asian women are the least political, the least oppressed, or the most polite.

A famous poem written by Donna Kate Rushin about the exasperation with such bridge work felt by women of color is presented in Box 5.1.

BOX 5.1

"The Bridge Poem"

I've had enough
I'm sick of seeing and touching
Both sides of things
Sick of being the damn bridge for everybody
Nobody
Can talk to anybody
Without me
Right?

I explain my mother to my father
my father to my little sister
My little sister to my brother
my brother to the white feminists
The white feminists to the Black church folks
the Black church folks to the ex-hippies
the ex-hippies to the Black separatists
the Black separatists to the artists
the artists to my friends' parents . . .

Then
I've got to explain myself
To everybody

I do more translating
Than the Gawdamn U.N.

Forget it
I'm sick of it.

I'm sick of filling in your gaps
Sick of being your insurance against
the isolation of your self-imposed limitations

Sick of being the crazy at your holiday dinners

Sick of being the odd one at your Sunday Brunches

Sick of being the sole Black friend to 34 individual white people

Find another connection to the rest of the world
Find something else to make you legitimate
Find some other way to be political and hip

I will not be the bridge to your womanhood
Your manhood
Your humanness

I'm sick of reminding you not to
Close off too tight for too long

I'm sick of mediating with your worst self
On behalf of your better selves

I am sick
Of having to remind you
To breathe
Before you suffocate
Your own fool self

Forget it
Stretch or drown
Evolve or die

The bridge I must be
Is the bridge to my own power
I must translate
My own fears
Mediate
My own weaknesses

I must be the bridge to nowhere
But my true self
And then
I will be useful

"The Bridge Poem," by Donna Kate Rushin. 1981. Pp. xxi–xxii of *This Bridge Called My Back: Writings by Radical Women of Color*, edited by Cherríe Moraga and Gloria Anzaldúa (New York: Kitchen Table—Women of Color Press, 1983).

Deconstructing Essentialism

The neglect of women on the margins was highlighted in another major feature of intersectionality theory—its critique of the "essentialist woman" or "sisterhood" of the second wave (Spelman 1988). As has been noted, **essentialism** refers to the belief in innate, intrinsic, or indispensable properties that define the core features of a given entity or group. These properties are used not only to distinguish one group from others (such as women from men) but also to bind members of the group together in collective political practice. Second wave feminist approaches often invoked the notion of sisterhood in order to mobilize women politically and to illuminate women's common concerns. Yet, regardless of whether women's shared traits were theorized as biological, psychological, or social, essentialism downplayed differences in their experiences. In one of the most influential books on this topic—*The Inessential Woman*—author Elizabeth Spelman (1988: x) called essentialism the "Trojan horse of feminist ethnocentrism" for being such a painful source of divisions *within* the women's movement.

In *Sister/Outsider* (1984), Audre Lorde points to numerous cases in which white feminists ignored differences between women. She criticizes Virginia Woolf's famous discussion of "a room of one's own" for its class bias: "A room of one's own may be a necessity for writing prose, but so are reams of paper, a typewriter, and plenty of time. . . . When we speak of a broadly based women's culture, we need to be aware of the effect of class and economic differences on the supplies available for producing art" (116). She also raises issues of race and class when she addresses her more privileged, feminist peers with the following example: "You fear your children will grow up to join the patriarchy and testify against you, we fear our children will be dragged from a car and shot down in the street, and you turn your backs upon the reasons they are dying" (119). Her criticisms are summarized in the following quote:

> There is a pretense to homogeneity of experience covered by the word sisterhood that does not in fact exist. . . . Certainly there are very real differences between us of race, age, and sex. But it is not those differences between us that are separating us. It is rather our refusal to recognize those differences. (115)

Lorde also highlights how we all have internalized patterns of oppression that must be altered if we are to build a successful movement based on difference and warns how "the master's tools will never dismantle the master's house" (110). Illustrating these internalized patterns of oppressions is the poem "When I Was Growing Up" (1981) by Nellie Wong. Reproduced in Box 5.2, this poem reveals how people in marginalized groups internalize or learn to privilege dominant group values, beliefs, and ideologies and how this undermines their own self-esteem and sense of empowerment.

BOX 5.2

"When I Was Growing Up"

I know now that once I longed to be white.
How? You ask.
Let me tell you the ways.

when I was growing up, people told me
I was dark and I believed my own darkness
in the mirror, in my soul, my own narrow vision

when I was growing up, my sisters
with fair skin got praised
for their beauty, and in the dark
I fell further, crushed between high walls

when I was growing up, I read magazines
and saw movies, blonde movie stars, white skin,
sensuous lips and to be elevated, to become
a woman, a desirable woman, I began to wear
imaginary pale skin

when I was growing up, I was proud
of my English, my grammar, my spelling
fitting into the group of smart children
smart Chinese children, fitting in,
belonging, getting in line

when I was growing up and went to high school,
I discovered the rich white girls, a few yellow girls,
their imported cotton dresses, their cashmere sweaters,

their curly hair and I thought that I too should have
what these lucky girls had

when I was growing up, I hungered
for American food, American styles,
coded: white and even to me, a child
born of Chinese parents, being Chinese
was feeling foreign, was limiting,
was un-American

when I was growing up and a white man wanted
to take me out, I thought I was special,
an exotic gardenia, anxious to fit
the stereotype of an oriental chick

when I was growing up, I felt ashamed
of some yellow men, their small bones,
their frail bodies, their spitting
on the streets, their coughing,
their lying in sunless rooms,
Shooting themselves in the arms

when I was growing up, people would ask
if I were Filipino, Polynesian, Portuguese.
They named all colors except white, the shell
of my soul, but not my dark, rough skin

when I was growing up, I felt
Dirty. I thought that god
made white people clean
and no matter how much I bathed
I could not Change, I could not shed
My skin in the gray water

When I was growing up, I swore
I would run away to purple mountains,
houses by the sea with nothing over
my head, my space to breathe,
uncongested with yellow people in an area
called Chinatown, in an area I later learned
was a ghetto, one of many hearts
Of Asian America

I know now that once I longed to be white
How many more ways? You ask.
Haven't I told you enough?

"When I Was Growing Up," by Nellie Wong. 1981. Pp. 7–8 of *This Bridge Called My Back: Writings by Radical Women of Color*, edited by Cherríe Moraga and Gloria Anzaldúa (New York–Kitchen Table—Women of Color Press, 1983.

Simultaneous and Multiple Oppressions

Barbara Smith, editor of the black feminist anthology *Home Girls* (1983) and a founding member of both the Combahee River Collective and the Kitchen Table Press, described what she viewed as the major contribution of black feminist thought:

> The concept of the simultaneity of oppressions is still the crux of a Black feminist understanding of political reality and, I believe, one the most significant ideological contributions of Black feminist thought. (xxxii)

By the simultaneity of multiple oppressions, Smith meant that different forms of oppression, such as race, class, or gender cannot be torn apart from their interactive impact on people's lives. Rather than viewing separate oppressions as distinct categories, "intersectionality describes a more fluid, mutually constructive process" whereby every social act is imbricated by gender, race, class, and sexuality (Luft and Ward 2009: 14). Moreover, because of their simultaneity, intersectionality theorists do not rank oppressions by arguing that one is more important or fundamental than the other. As Smith (1983: xxxii) writes: "We examined our own lives and found that everything out there was kicking our behinds—race, class, sex, and homophobia."

These two features of simultaneous and multiple oppressions are discussed at some length in Deborah King's "Multiple Jeopardy: The Context of Black Feminist Ideology" ([1988] 1993). King compares the notion of simultaneous, multiple oppressions to the various ways in which feminists had dealt with multiple oppressions in the past. Two tendencies were typical. She refers to the first tendency as a "**pop bead approach,**" where multiple oppressions are treated as separate and distinct. Here oppressions are added together, and people are simply described as doubly or triply oppressed. The second and more common tendency was to rank or to **hierarchicalize oppressions**, meaning to treat one form of oppression as more fundamental than another. For example, radical feminists argued that gender oppression was the earliest and most fundamental form of oppression (see chapter 3), whereas Marxist feminists privileged class oppression and treated race and gender oppressions as less important derivatives (see chapter 4).

King argues that oppressions cannot simply be added together such that one could say that a black woman is doubly oppressed as compared to a white woman or that a poor, black woman is triply oppressed as compared to a rich, white woman. Neither can the social impact of such multiple oppressions realistically be singled out in social theory or in research methods, such as in multivariate regression analysis. Rather, they form an integral whole such that each is always imbued with the other. Fully comprehending the interwoven nature of multiple oppressions requires a *radical break with conventional ways of theoretically and methodologically understanding oppression* (Brewer 1999).

Another signal piece that highlighted the importance of recognizing simultaneous and multiple oppressions was Kimberlé Crenshaw's "Demarginalizing the Intersection of Race and Sex: A Black Feminist Critique of Antidiscrimination Doctrine, Feminist Theory, and Antiracist Politics" (1989). Crenshaw focuses on how "single-axis" theoretical frameworks obscure the multidimensionality of women of color's experiences. Her point of departure was the title of one of the most influential anthologies by women of color in this era—*All the Women Are White, All the Men Are Black, but Some of Us Are Brave* (1981) edited by Gloria T. Hull, Patricia Bell Scott, and Barbara Smith. Crenshaw (1989: 140) argues that because intersectional analysis is "greater than the sum of racism and sexism," any analysis that does not take intersectionality into account cannot sufficiently address many of the ways in which women of color are oppressed.

A legal scholar, Crenshaw presented a number of cases to make her point. For example, in 1976 five black women filed a suit against General Motors alleging that the employer's seniority system perpetuated the effects of past discrimination against black women. General Motors did not hire black women prior to 1964, and all of the black women hired after 1970 lost their jobs in a seniority-based layoff. However, because this company had previously hired both "women" (white women) and "Blacks" (black men), the court dismissed the case on the grounds that General Motors had not discriminated on the basis of either gender or race. Crenshaw argued that the scope of antidiscrimination law was limited because sex and race discrimination have come to be defined along a single-axis in terms of the "experiences of those who are privileged *but for* their racial or sexual characteristics" (151). Put another way, "the paradigm of sex discrimination tends to be based on the experiences of white women; the model of race discrimination tends to be based on the experiences of the most privileged Blacks . . . none of which include discrimination against Black women" (151). In short, women of color are erased when intersectionality is not taken into account. How Crenshaw and other intersectionality theorists level this critique against white feminists' analyses of reproductive freedom and violence against women will be shown later in this chapter.

While the term "intersectionality" was coined by Crenshaw in the 1989 article discussed above, other theorists have since introduced a number of new concepts to elaborate on it. One such concept—the **matrix of domination**—was developed by Patricia Hill Collins in her award-winning book *Black Feminist Thought* (1990). Collins describes how, within this matrix, people have a social location and an identity in terms of such important structural forms of oppression as race, ethnicity, social class, gender, and/or sexual orientation. She also describes how people can simultaneously be both oppressed and oppressors because they could occupy social locations of both penalty and privilege. Wealthy, black males, for example, have privilege by their class and gender positions but are penalized by their racial location.

Intersectionality theorists' focus on simultaneous and multiple oppressions also broadened the notion of feminism to include a struggle against *all* forms of oppression. They criticized those who accused women of color of not being "feminist enough" because of their unwillingness to separate the struggle against gender subordination from struggles against other oppressions, such as racism and classism. Consider the words of Enriqueta Longauex y Vasquez and Maria Varela, both activists in the Chicano movement in the early 1970s:

> When a family is involved in a human rights movement, as is the Mexican American family, there is little room for a woman's liberation movement alone. . . . La Raza[12] movement is based on brother- and sisterhood. We must look at each other as one large family. (Longauex y Vasquez 1971: 204).
>
> When your race is fighting for survival—to eat, to be clothed, to be housed, to be left in peace—as a woman, you know who you are . . . For the Chicano woman battling for her people, the family—the big family is a fortress against the genocidal forces in the outside world. It is the source of strength for a people whose identity is constantly being whittled away. (Varela 1971: 198)

Both quotes highlight the importance of racial solidarity in their struggles as well as how the family is an agent of resistance to the forces of internal colonialism within the United States. This view of the family is strikingly different from the perspectives of many feminists discussed earlier in the text, such as the radical feminists and Marxist feminists who cited the family as a major locus of women's oppression (see chapters 3 and 4).

Epistemological Contributions of Intersectionality Theories

Recognizing how science had historically been used against women of color, such as in the nineteenth century when various "sciences" deemed people of color inferior, primitive, or more animal-like, intersectionality theorists were more suspicious than many other modern second wave feminists of science and the way it fostered the interests and ideologies of dominant groups. While intersectionality theorists use scientific analyses in their scholarly work, they approach science more critically and incorporate alternative ways of knowing. They do not dismiss science but, rather, decenter it as *the* major means of adjudicating knowledge claims by making way for alternative ways of knowing. Some of these alternative ways of knowing, such as personal narratives, riddles, proverbs, and poetry, are discussed in chapter 1 (Christian 1988; Lorde 1984). Intersectionality theorists especially highlight the importance of socially lived knowledge or knowledge acquired through everyday life experiences as opposed to knowledge gained from formal education, academic theories, and/or science. Consider, for example, the following quote by an elderly black woman who distinguishes between conventional views of knowledge and the **socially lived knowledge** she calls "wisdom":

> Blacks are quick to ridicule educated fools . . . they have "book learning," but no "mother wit", knowledge but not wisdom. . . . African-American women need wisdom to deal with the "educated fools" who would take a shotgun to a roach. (Quoted in Collins 1990: 208)

Similarly, one of the reasons Barbara Smith titled her anthology *Home Girls* (1983: xxii) was to emphasize the socially lived knowledge she gained from her own home and community:

> I learned about Black feminism from the women in my family—not just from their strengths, but from their failings, from witnessing daily how they were humiliated and crushed because they had made the "mistake" of being born Black and female in a white man's country. I inherited fear and shame from them as well as hope. . . . It is this conflict, my constantly " . . . seeing and touching/both sides of things" that makes my commitment real.

Along with such quotes that highlight "seeing and touching/both sides of things," the materialist approach to theory construction embraced by intersectionality theorists is evident in their call for a "theory of the flesh" ([1981] 1983: 23). Cherríe Moraga's and Gloria Anzaldúa's description of this approach can be found in Box 5.3.

BOX 5.3

"Theory in the Flesh"

A theory in the flesh means one where the physical realities of our lives—our own skin color, the land or concrete we grew up on, our sexual longings—all fuse to create a politic born out of necessity. Here, we attempt to bridge the contradictions in our experience:

> We are the colored in a white feminist movement.
> We are the feminists among the people of our culture.
> We are the lesbians among the straight.
> We do this bridging by naming ourselves and telling our stories in our own words.

The theme echoing throughout most of these stories is our refusal of the *easy* explanation to the conditions we live in. There is nothing *easy* about a collective cultural history of what Mitsuye Yamada calls "unnatural disasters": the forced encampment of Indigenous people on government reservations, the forced encampment of Japanese American people during World War II, the forced encampment of our mothers as laborers in factories/in fields/in our own and other people's homes as paid or unpaid slaves.

Closer to home, we are still trying to separate the fibers of experience we have had as daughters of a struggling people. Daily, we feel the pull-and-tug of having to choose between which parts of our mothers' heritages we want to claim and wear and which parts have served to cloak us from knowledge of ourselves. "My mother and I work to unravel the knot" (Levins Morales).

This is how our theory develops. We are interested in pursuing a society that uses flesh and blood experiences to concretize a vision that can begin to heal our "wounded knee" (Chrystos).

"Theory in the Flesh" by Cherríe Moraga and Gloria Anzaldúa. 1981. P. 23 in *This Bridge Called by Back*, edited by Cherríe Moraga and Gloria Anzaldúa. New York: Kitchen Table—Women of Color Press, 1983. The references mentioned in this quote to Yamada [1981] 1983; Morales [1981] (1983); and Chrystos [1981]1983 have been placed in the reference section of this text.

Another hallmark of intersectionality theory is its *social constructionist view of knowledge* and the *standpoint epistemology* it embraces. In *Black Feminist Thought* (1990) Collins uses the matrix of domination to explain this epistemological stance. She argues not only that people construct knowledge but that they do so from situated positions within different social locations in the matrix of domination and that these positions shape and influence how people view the world. On the one hand, a specific social location potentially enables people to see realities that are less visible to those in other locations. On the other hand, because no one can view the world from all of the various and diverse social locations, each vantage point or perspective is partial or limited. She also discusses **subjugated knowledges** or the knowledges of subordinate groups that have been ignored, silenced, or deemed less credible by dominant groups:

> The overarching matrix of domination houses multiple groups, each with varying experiences with penalty and privilege that produce corresponding partial perspectives, situated knowledges, and, for clearly identifiable subordinate groups, subjugated knowledges.... No one group has a clear angle of vision. No one group possesses the theory or methodology that allows it to discover the absolute "truth" or, worse yet, proclaim its theories and methodologies as the universal norm evaluating other groups' experiences. (234)

Because all vantage points are partial, Collins suggests that a more developed understanding of the world can be generated by "pivoting" from the interpretations and knowledge of one group to those of another group (234). Thus, social knowledge is constructed in a quilt-like fashion where the social realities of diverse vantage points are interwoven to form a more complete fabric of the whole. To form this more complete picture of the whole intersectionality theorists call for **polyvocality** or the inclusion of many voices and vantage points as well as the excavation or retrieval of subjugated knowledges as forms of resistance to dominant knowledges and discourses.

Such excavations are exemplified by the work of feminist historians, such as Gerda Lerner (1979), Paula Giddings (1984), Jacqueline Jones (1985), Deborah Gray White (1985), and Rosalyn Terborg-Penn (1998a). In turn, the first Center for Research on Women that focused on women of color and intersectional analyses was founded in Memphis in 1982 by sociologists Bonnie Thornton Dill, Elizabeth Higgenbotham, and Lynn Weber. This center not only fostered research on race, class, and gender but also developed intersectional pedagogical approaches. Weber's *Understanding Race, Class, Gender and Sexuality* (2010) illustrates well the advances made in this pedagogical work. As a result of such scholarly undertakings, the lives of women of color no longer remained hidden from history but gained representation in the academy.

Readers will recall how many of the feminist standpoint theorists discussed in chapters 1 and 4 also highlighted how knowledge was socially constructed and socially situated. However, these analyses tended to focus on *gendered standpoints*, such as Nancy Hartsock's "feminist standpoint" (1983) or Dorothy Smith's "standpoint of women" (1987). In contrast, *intersectionality theorists often speak in terms of margins and centers to better capture their focus on simultaneous, multiple oppressions where gender is just one of a multiplicity of oppressions that affect peoples' vantage points on reality.* This subtle shift is often ignored even though it has a number of important implications.

From Margin to Center

In *Feminist Theory* (1984) bell hooks discusses two assumptions that characterize the work of many intersectionality theorists: first, marginal social locations generate critical vantage points for understanding social life; and, second, feminist theory would be enhanced by moving the voices of subordinate groups from the margin to the center of feminist discourse. To illustrate these points, hooks uses the example of how life in her racially segregated, Kentucky town required that blacks cross railroad tracks into the world of whites in order to work or to simply carry out their everyday lives. She discusses how blacks' survival depended on an ongoing awareness of the laws and informal rules that ensured their racial subordination. This ongoing awareness of the separation of margin and center became an integral part of their lives. While blacks crossed these social borders frequently, whites seldom entered the margins and knew far less about the lives of blacks. Moreover, frequently crossing these social borders made blacks more aware of how they were a necessary and vital part of the whole, despite their subordination. From this concrete example, hooks moves to a discussion of feminist theory. She argues that such awareness of margins and centers is lacking in existing feminist theory precisely because most theory has been written by privileged women who live at the center and concludes that feminist theory would be enhanced by ideas and analyses that encompass a wider array of experiences. As she writes in the preface: "At its most visionary, it (feminist theory) will emerge from individuals who have knowledge of both margin and center."

These points are central to hooks's critique of Betty Friedan's *The Feminine Mystique* (1963). As discussed in chapter 2, the major problem that Friedan highlighted was "the problem that had no name"—the lack of fulfillment many middle-class women experienced in their roles as housewives and mothers. In one of the more scathing critiques leveled against *The Feminist Mystique*, hooks (1984: 1–2) writes that Friedan

> did not speak of the needs of women without men, without children, without homes. She ignored the existence of all non-white women and poor white women. She did not tell readers whether it was more fulfilling to be a maid, a babysitter, a factory worker, a clerk, a prostitute, than to be a leisure class housewife. She made her plight and the plight of white women like herself synonymous with a condition affecting all American women.

hooks concludes that earlier feminists' emphasis on women's "common oppression" was less a strategy for politicization than an appropriation by privileged women of a radical political vocabulary that masked the extent to which they shaped the movement and promoted their own interests (6). According to hooks, white, middle-class, liberal feminism serves as a dominant discourse that works only in certain women's interests. For example, the "Platform Issues of the Million Woman March"—a political demonstration by women of color first held in Philadelphia in 1997—illustrate well the different concerns held by African-American women. This platform included concerns for prisoners, the homeless, and the gentrification of neighborhoods—concerns rarely found in the political platforms of predominantly white feminist groups.[13]

Drawing on their own socially lived knowledges, Latina intersectionality theorists often used such terms as "world-travelling" or "border crossings" as their metaphors for moving from margin to center (Lugones 1997; Anzaldúa 1987). In *Borderlands/La Frontera* (1987), Gloria Anzaldúa highlights the particular dilemmas faced by people of mixed heritage. Although the text is written in English, Anzaldúa interweaves Spanish and Aztec words so that the very form of the prose reflects the experiences of the mestiza, a woman of mixed heritage. She also focuses on internal forms of oppression that result from such border crossings:

> Because I, a mestiza, continually walk out of one culture and into another, because I am in all cultures at the same time the ambivalence from the clash of voices results in mental and emotional states of perplexity.... Cradled in one culture, sandwiched between two cultures, straddling all three cultures and their value systems, la mestiza undergoes a struggle of the flesh, a struggle of borders, an inner war. (77–78)

Anzaldúa uses the Aztec term **nepantilism** to describe being torn in multiple directions by the diverse cultures the mestiza embodies—the inner war of straddling different cultures. Similarly, in "Playfulness, 'World'-Travelling, and Loving Perception" (1997), María Lugones describes this inner war as almost "schizophrenic." She notes how even when traveling is done "unwillfully to hostile White/Anglo worlds," critical insights and the "flexibility" necessary to move between worlds is accomplished in the process (148–149 and 152).

Anzaldúa raises the dilemma over identity when she asks to which collectivity the person of mixed heritage should listen. Her answer is that the mestiza has to develop a tolerance for contradictions and ambiguities. She has to learn not only how to deal with and sustain contradictions but, also, how to turn these contradictions into something empowering—a **new mestiza consciousness**. Anzaldúa describes this new consciousness as a massive uprooting of dualistic thinking in the individual and collective consciousness that entails a rupture with oppressive traditions in all cultures. No longer should we think in the binary terms that have formed the bases of multiple oppressions, such as white/black, male/female, or heterosexual/homosexual. Rather, one deconstructs these binary discourses and transcends them by learning to prize the contradictions of multiple identities as sites of greater freedom and understanding.

Reflecting on her own social location as a lesbian mestiza, Anzaldúa argues that homosexuals of color are the "supreme crossers" of all cultures and thus have strong bonds with other peoples of mixed heritage and with those who face multiple oppressions:

> Colored homosexuals *have more knowledge* of other cultures; have always been at the forefront (although sometimes in the closet) of all liberation struggles in this country; have suffered more injustices and have survived them despite all odds. . . . People, listen to what your joteria is saying. (Anzaldúa 1987: 85; emphasis added)

The above quote reveals not only how Anzaldúa views marginal social locations as generating critical insights into social life but, also, how she privileges the knowledge of the oppressed. This epistemological **privileging of the knowledge of oppressed** groups has characterized much radical literature and is not unique to intersectional theory (Bat-Ami Bar On 1993; see chapter 4).

In *Black Feminist Thought* (1990), Collins introduces the "outsider-within stance"[14] to exemplify the vantage point of marginalized others. Here African–American women's long-standing employment in white households is used to provide an archetypal story of the movement of black women between the margin and center—between the intimate worlds of whites and their own black families and communities. This angle of vision was unavailable to those who exclusively occupied only the white world. By contrast, black maids had "insider knowledge" of white households and their contradictions even though they were forever "outsiders" and never able to become full-fledged members of this white world. Moreover, while these maids may have been highly respected members of their own communities, they remained "other" and "lesser" in the eyes of whites whose purview and experiences did not include these black communities. As such, the "outsider-within stance" entailed particular insights that could potentially provide important bases for oppositional consciousness and resistance.

However, unlike Anzaldúa and hooks, Collins is careful to point out that these critical insights are only *potentials*. She does not automatically privilege the knowledge of oppressed groups. Rather, in the last section of *Black Feminist Thought* (1990: 207), titled "Black Feminism and Epistemology," she writes:

> Although it is tempting to claim that Black women are more oppressed than anyone else and, therefore, have the best standpoint from which to understand the mechanisms, processes, and effects of oppression, this simply may not be the case.

Collins views the perspectives of the subjugated as neither innocent nor exempt from critical reexamination.[15] She recognizes that the very costs of oppression can limit access to important experiences or opportunities that allow people to expand their awareness of the social world, such as good schools or good health. For Collins, the vantage points of the oppressed represent only partial perspectives among many others.[16] Thus, there are subtle differences in the epistemological frameworks used by different intersectionality theorists. Some of these theorists privilege the knowledge of the oppressed, whereas others do not. These two positions are represented in an exchange between Alice Walker and her mother in which Walker represents the view that all standpoints are partial while her mother privileges the knowledge of the oppressed:

> WALKER: "I believe that the truth about any subject only comes when all sides of the story are put together, and all their different meanings make one new one. Each writer writes the missing parts to the other writer's story. And the whole story is what I'm after."
>
> HER MOTHER: "Well, I doubt if you'll ever get the true missing parts from the white folks—they've sat on the truth so long they've mashed the life out of it." (Quoted in Collins 1990: 17)

Bridging Modern and Postmodern Thought

The description of the standpoint epistemology of intersectionality theorists described above almost sounds postmodern given their critique of modern science, their focus on alternative ways of knowing, and especially Collins's discussion of the partiality of perspectives whereby no one perspective is privileged.[13] As will be shown in chapter 6, the concept of margins and centers frequently appears in postmodernist, poststructuralist, and queer theories and adds to this confusion. However, these epistemologies are distinct. While intersectionality theories bridge modern and postmodern thought, they maintain a firm foothold in modernism. Drawing from the works of Collins and Crenshaw, four differences between standpoint and postmodern epistemologies are highlighted below.

A first difference is that the standpoint epistemology of intersectionality theory *focuses on vantage points as group phenomena as opposed to the individual focus of postmodernists*:

> The notion of a standpoint refers to historically shared, *group*-based experiences. Groups have a degree of permanence over time such that group realities transcend individual experiences. . . . I stress this difference between the individual and the group as units of analysis because using these two constructs as if they were interchangeable clouds understanding of a host of topics. . . . By omitting a discussion of group-based realities grounded in an equally central notion of group-based oppression, we move into the sterile ground of a discussion of how effectively standpoint theory serves as an epistemology of truth. (Collins 2004b: 247–249; her emphasis)

By contrast, for postmodernists, all group categories are essentialist; they have "no single voice or vision of reality" but, rather, are made up of people with heterogeneous experiences (Grant 1993: 94). Differences are infinite, and each individual is potentially unique. For these reasons, postmodernists reject the group concepts used by intersectionality theorists, such as Anzaldúa's "homosexuals of color."[18] (See chapter 6.) Kimberlé Crenshaw explains how intersectionality theorists do not share this postmodern critique of essentialism—which she calls a "vulgarized social constructionism" because it denies how group identities based on the way power is exercised can be sites of resistance for subordinated groups. She argues: "At this point in history, a strong case can be made that the most critical resistance strategy for disempowered groups is to occupy and defend a politics of social location" rather than to vacate, destroy, and deconstruct it ([1997] 2005: 539). The "vulgar constructionism" of postmodernism "distorts the possibility of meaningful identity politics" because it focuses only on group categories as forms of linguistic representation rather than as forms of social oppression (539).

A second difference is that, for intersectionality theorists, *not all differences represent axes of social structural oppression*. Collins argues that feminists must distinguish between structural inequalities and differences or between social stratification and social differentiation.[19] The notion of standpoint refers to groups who have shared histories because of their shared location in *unequal relations of power*. They are neither groups based on identities chosen by individuals nor groups created by bureaucrats or scholars, such as groups distinguished in demographic statistics. For Collins (2004b: 248 and 252–253), to erase hierarchical, structural, and group-based inequalities in the name of critiquing essentialism is simply to move to a "language game of politics." The major goal of the standpoint epistemology of intersectionality theorists is to foster social justice by revealing how relations of power are hidden in knowledge claims.

Although both intersectionality theorists and postmodernists speak of "margins and centers" and "marginalized people," the former anchor the concept of marginality in hierarchically structured, group based-inequalities. In contrast, when postmodernists, poststructuralists, and queer theorists refer to "marginalized people" they mean a number of different things. Often, they are referring to people whose behaviors lie outside of or transgress social norms (see chapter 6). This conception of margins includes a much broader swath of people, where the normative structure, rather than structural social relations of oppression, is determinate. As some critics have argued, unless anchored in the history of structurally oppressed groups, the concept of marginalized people could include a range of people who transgress social norms, from white punk rockers to white militia groups (Pels 2004). Yet clearly such groups are not the marginalized, subjugated peoples to whom bell hooks and Gloria Anzaldúa are referring. This is why Collins (1998: 129) argues that when scholars took the postmodern turn "conceptions of power shifted—talk of tops and bottoms, long associated with hierarchy, were recast as flattened geographies of centers and margins." This is also why she concludes that postmodern conceptions of power "rob the term oppression of its critical and oppositional importance" (136).

A third difference that Collins discusses is how *the deconstruction of macro structures in favor of a micro politics of power leads postmodernists to focus on the local as the most effective terrain of struggle*. In her view such a focus on the local "flies in the face of actual historical successes" and is dangerous for marginalized people because it ignores the structural bases of oppressions that require macrolevel, collective action. By "overemphasizing" local politics, postmodernism provides a seductive mix of appearing to challenge oppression while "secretly believing that such efforts are doomed" (135). For Collins, postmodern epistemological assumptions "erase structural power" and "undercut" political activism (148–149).

A fourth difference, per Collins, is how *postmodern deconstructions of collective or group-based categories as essentialist "undermine the group authority" that is derived from shared standpoints and shared histories.* For her, the value of feminist deconstruction was that it decentered a predominantly privileged, white male tradition. That deconstruction was later used by postmodernists to undermine the authority of marginalized *groups* was the "ultimate postmodern irony"—especially since this new language of postmodernism began to gain hegemony just when the voices of marginalized peoples were finally beginning to move to the center (142–143). In *Fighting Words* (1998), Collins likens postmodernist scholars to "**colonizers who refused**"—a concept first developed by postcolonial theorist Albert Memmi ([1957] 1991). It refers to colonists who sided with anticolonialist struggles but benefited from the power and privilege that their status in the colonial system conferred on them They typically acted as power brokers who represented the interests of the colonized natives to the colonial powers. However, when the colonized natives actually gained voice and power themselves, the colonizers who refused had no place. Collins argues that postmodernists are like colonizers who refused in that they oppose oppression in the abstract but continue to enjoy its material benefits. They cannot withstand the colonized themselves actually coming to voice and politically representing themselves (see Box 5.4).

BOX 5-4

"Colonizers Who Refused"

European decolonization and racial desegregation in the United States share important similarities. In both cases the movement of people of color into formerly all white spaces shattered the illusion of insider security maintained by keeping a safe distance from derogated outsiders. As Albert Memmi observes, "It is not easy to escape mentally from a concrete situation, to refuse its ideology while continuing to live with its actual relationships" (Memmi 1965: 20). In a sense, since there is no place to hide, intellectuals privileged by systems of race, class, and gender oppression must find new ways to "refuse" in proximity to those whose interests they formerly championed and who now inconveniently aim to "come to voice" and speak for themselves. Thus, the problem that confronted colonizers who refused in classic colonialism foreshadows that facing contemporary leftist academics. Under a system of colonialism in which the natives were safely tucked away at a distance, colonizers who refused could claim solidarity with the marginalized and be praised for their efforts. However, what happens when the natives gain entry to the center? . . . Postmodern treatments of power relations suggested by the rubric of decentering may provide some relief to intellectuals who wish to resist oppression in the abstract without decentering their own material privileges. . . . Groups already privileged under hierarchical power relations suffer little from embracing the language of decentering denuded of any actions to decenter actual hierarchical power relations in academia and elsewhere. Ironically, their privilege may actually increase.

Excerpt from pp. 131–137 of Patricia Hill Collins, *Fighting Words: Black Women and the Search for Justice* (Minneapolis: University of Minnesota Press, 1998).

Overall, intersectionality theorists share a standpoint epistemology that highlights the socially constructed and situated nature of different standpoints on social reality. This standpoint epistemology breaks with the epistemology underlying modern science as well as with other feminist epistemological stances. Unlike feminist standpoint approaches that focused on the importance of gendered standpoints, the standpoint epistemology of intersectionality theory recognizes how simultaneous and multiple oppressions give rise to standpoints that represent hybridity, multilocationality, and differences *between* women. Unlike postmodern epistemologies that also focus on difference and marginality, the standpoint epistemology of intersectionality theory remains anchored in hierarchical and structural power relations that reflect group rather than individual standpoints.

Decentering and Difference

The following sections examine intersectional analyses of reproductive justice and violence against women. These analyses illustrate not only how the social justice concerns of intersectionality theorists are different from the concerns highlighted in many white feminist analyses but, also, how decentering white feminist concerns has important implications for political policies and practice.

Reproductive Justice

As discussed in chapter 2, reproductive freedom in the form of access to birth control, sex education, and abortion have been extremely contentious issues in the United States over the past half century. These reproductive freedoms were key targets of conservative, antifeminist efforts to defeat the ERA, and they continue to be volatile issues within the pro-life and pro-natalist politics of the religious right today. Yet, *within* the U.S. women's movement, white second wave feminists often noted a lack of enthusiasm among women of color for reproductive freedom issues.

Womanists of color repeatedly pointed out how their key concerns were for **reproductive justice**—not the freedom to control birth but, rather, the freedom to give birth, to keep their children and not to have contraception forced upon them, something white women in privileged class positions had long enjoyed.[20] Just as Mary Terrell and Linda Brent had done during the first wave, Frances Beal (1971) and Angela Davis (1981) linked second wave women of color's less than enthusiastic response to reproductive freedom to the history of slavery that negated black slaves' rights to keep their own children. They also pointed to the twentieth-century practices of forced sterilization that disproportionately impacted poor women, women of color, and the disabled.[21] Along with other activists, their efforts to expose the class, race, and able-bodied biases in sterilization practices in the United States led to more stringent informed consent laws for sterilization in the early 1970s. Nevertheless, statistics on the sterilization of Puerto Rican women and Native-American women continued to be inordinately high into the 1990s (Davis [1991] 2005: 513).

In "Outcast Mothers and Surrogates: Racism and Reproductive Politics in the Nineties" (1991), Davis again discussed reproductive justice but in the context of new reproductive issues that were in the national spotlight in the late 1980s. Surrogate mothering and the new reproductive technologies developed for infertile couples sparked heated debates about child bearing and mothering in the national media as well as between feminists. One of the most famous cases to make headlines across the country was the 1987 "Baby M" case. Here the surrogate mother, Mary Beth Whitehead (a working-class married woman with children), contracted with an upper-middle class couple, Dr. and Mr. Sterns (a pediatrician and chemist, respectively) to carry a fetus to term. To complicate matters, through artificial insemination Whitehead's egg had been fertilized with Sterns's sperm. After Baby M was born, Whitehead changed her mind, broke the contract, and went into hiding with the infant. In the end, the Sterns were given custody of Baby M and Whitehead received visitation rights. This case and others like it forced state governments to create laws on surrogacy and the new reproductive technologies, but consensus on these issues was rare. Some states criminalized surrogacy as a form of baby selling or slavery, others recognized surrogacy contracts as legal contracts, and some took the more ambiguous position of deeming surrogacy legal but not honoring contracts in the case of disputes.

In the debates over surrogacy class issues have been prominent. Surrogacy, as well as many of the new reproductive technologies that service infertile couples, are very expensive.[22] This means that wealthy women are more likely to make use of these technologies while poor women are more likely to be surrogates. Many feminists saw the commoditization of these services as their most insidious feature. Did we really want to make the creation of human life part of the cash nexus in contemporary societies? The second wave split over these issues. Liberal feminists often supported the legality of contracts, thus indirectly siding with the affluent, infertile couples. Marxist, socialist, and radical feminists took a number of diverse positions on these issues, as Nancy Lublin points out in *Pandora's Box* (1998).[23]

Surrogate mothering and the new reproductive technologies ushered in a host of other controversial issues that divided feminists as well as the general public. For many conservative and fundamentalist right-wing activists the answer is simple: abortion, birth control, and the new reproductive technologies should be banned for interfering with god's plans. For more secular people, these issues are not at all simple because the question of what constitutes motherhood is at stake. Is gestation primary in determining motherhood or is the most salient issue biology or whose egg was involved? Should a social definition of mothering—who would better raise the child—trump either biology or gestation, and how should that be determined—by love or by the parents' standard of living? Should contract law take precedence over these birthing and mothering issues? In short, the meaning of mothering was subjected to new and radical deconstructions.

Davis points out how concerns about the deconstruction of mothering are not something new. The meaning of mothering has long been deconstructed on the bases of race and class. The U.S. slave economy effectively denied many aspects of motherhood to vast numbers of African-American women. These women were valued as *surrogate* breeders but, given the vagaries of the slave market, not as nurturers of their own children. "Many slave states passed laws to the effect that children of slave women no more belonged to their mothers than the young of animals belonged to the females that bore them" (Davis [1991] 2005: 511). Women of color also were viewed as adequate *surrogate* nurturers of other peoples' children given that they often served as nannies to the children of more privileged classes—a practice that continues up to the present day (511; see chapter 9). In turn, working-class women of all races were "cast like their male counterparts, into the industrial proletariat," where the demands of their jobs often conflicted with their ability to mother (509; see also the discussion of Kollantai's work in chapter 4). These examples suggest that surrogacy and the deconstruction of motherhood for profit had many historical precedents.

For Davis, these issues only became salient for white feminists when they directly impacted more privileged women. Indeed, the feminist debates generated by the new reproductive technologies focus on the reproductive issues of affluent, older, infertile women, whereas the reproductive issues most frequently associated with poor, women of color revolve around the fertility of young, single women. Davis describes how "motherhood among Black and Latina teens is constructed as a moral and social evil" even though they are denied accessible and affordable abortions through restrictions on Medicaid funding of abortions (513). By contrast, the federal government willingly funds their sterilization. For Davis, these are just some of the ways that the bodies of women of color "bear the evidence of colonization" (513).

More recent books, such as *Killing the Black Body* (1998) by Dorothy Roberts and *Policing the National Body* (2002), edited by Jael Silliman and Anannya Bhattacharjee, expand on the above points. These authors discuss how pregnancy among poor, women of color is taken has a sign of lack of discipline, promiscuity, and immorality that exposes them to punitive state policies. Roberts cites a long list of violations against women of color where they are denied reproductive choice and offered Norplant, Depo-Provera, and similar forms of birth control that encourage them to choose sterilization. For example, when a judge imposes birth control as a condition of probation or gives a defendant the choice between Norplant and jail, women face steep penalties for their choice to remain fertile. Rather than looking at lack of sex education, poverty, sexual assault, and other factors that catalyze high rates of pregnancy among young women of color, researchers and policy makers often blame the women themselves and assume they are incapable of making their own decisions (Collins 2004a: 104–105).

Today, immigrant women—particularly Latinas—are facing new challenges to reproductive justice given recent demands to deny citizenship to children born in the United States to illegal immigrants (often referred to disparagingly as anchor babies). The proposed legislation, H.R. 1868, the Birthright Citizenship Act, presents a direct challenge to the Fourteenth Amendment. Opposition to birthright citizenship is often linked to fears regarding demographic projections that whites will become a minority in the United States over the next several decades. Conservatives who support this act have found a home in the Tea Party movement that realized significant political gains in U.S. congressional elections in November of 2010 (Burghart and Zeskind 2010).[24]

Underlying such denials of reproductive justice is the assumption that people of color are promiscuous or hypersexual. In *Black Sexual Politics* (2004a), Patricia Hill Collins argues that this assumption is integrally intertwined with nineteenth-century claims that people of color were more animalistic and uncivilized than whites. Such discourses not only excused white males from being convicted of rape when they sexually assaulted black women, but they also provided a rationale for lynching black males as rapists. Data from later years suggest that these discourses operated well into the twentieth century. Between 1930 and 1964, 90 percent of the men executed in the United States for rape were African-Americans, and black-on-white rape continued to evoke the most public outrage even though it was one of the least common forms of sexual assault (D'Emilio and Freedman [1988] 1997: 297). These discourses also continue to be operative in the stigmas attached to teen pregnancy.

As noted earlier, the assumption of promiscuity placed inordinate pressures on women of color to embrace a "politics of respectability." Although initially deployed as a form of resistance, the politics of respectability has had negative effects on African-American scholarship and political practice. On the one hand, *adherence to what was deemed socially "respectable" resulted in a scholarship of omission that tended to highlight the most heroic and successful features of African-American history* (Harris 2003). This was visible, for example, when black scholars criticized womanists of color, such as Zora Neal Hurston and Alice Walker, whose novels depicted incest and rape *within* the African-American community (Appiah and Gates 1993; Wagner-Martin and Davidson 1995: 100; Sartisky 2006).[25]

On the other hand, *the politics of respectability also constituted a concession to mainstream values that seriously inhibited African-American political activism by making it culturally defensive, patriarchal, and heterosexist* (Harris 2003):

> Women, lesbian, gay, bisexual and transgendered people, children, people living with HIV, drug addicts, prostitutes, and others deemed to be an embarrassment to the broader African American community or a drain upon its progress . . . became targets of silencing, persecution, and or abuse. (Collins 2004a: 91)

Given the central role that African-American churches have played in black activism, their continued condemnation of what they deem loose and immoral behavior by homosexuals and unwed mothers has been particularly salient.

Less well known is how leading activists in the civil rights movement criticized and covered up homosexual practices *within* the black community to make their movement look respectable (Collins 2004a). In "The Color of Discipline: Civil Rights and Black Sexuality" (2008), Thaddeus Russell argues that, prior to the civil rights movement, African–American, working-class culture was quite open to homosexuality and other forms of nonheteronormative behavior (such as drag). Not only was Harlem a "homosexual mecca" in the 1920s, but from the 1930s through the 1950s African–American drag balls and drag cabarets drew large audiences in a number of American cities (Russell 2008: 103 and 106). Russell also documents how prominent civil rights leaders, such as Adam Clayton Powell Sr. and Martin Luther King Jr., spoke out against homosexual behavior and sexual "deviancy" within the black community.

Above, we have seen how the denial of reproductive justice has uniquely marked the history of women of color in America. Given this history, it is not surprising that the voices of women of color have been more muted in debates over reproductive freedom and sexual politics. Even members of the third wave of U.S. feminism have commented on this (Henry 2004: 97). For example, Barbara McCaskill and Layli Phillips (1996: 116) discuss how "African-American women have been virtual, conspicuous absentees at worst and passive observers at best" in both the second wave's sex wars and the third wave's debates over power feminism versus victim feminism (see chapters 3 and 7). Like womanists of color before them, they point to the luxury of defining liberation in terms of sexual and reproductive freedom as historically the province of white, class-privileged women. The remarks of these third wave feminists suggest that for almost two centuries women of color's voices in pursuit of *reproductive justice* have been anything but mute. The failure of white feminists to hear these voices is the failure of members of a dominant group to understand and to take seriously the differences between reproductive freedom and reproductive justice.

Violence against Women by Rachel E. Luft

In the groundbreaking article in which she coins the term "intersectionality," Kimberlé Williams Crenshaw (1989: 160) uses the issue of rape to characterize "the paradigmatic political and theoretical dilemma created by the intersection of race and gender." In an even more often cited article on intersectionality published in 1995, she critically analyzes the battered women's movement. It is no coincidence that the subject of violence has been the exemplary site for the articulation of intersectionality. Since sex, violence, and sexualized violence have so often occurred at the nexus of gendered, racialized, and class-based ideology and practice in the United States, violence against women has been one of the primary arenas in which intersectional theorists have developed and applied their theory and intersectional activists have created a critical movement.

Violence against women played a central role in the mainstream second wave women's movement. In consciousness raising groups women shared what they believed to be personal and unusual stories of victimization only to discover in a "click" of recognition that the assaults were all too common (O'Reilly 1972). Radical feminists developed an analysis of "rape culture" in which they linked the structural disempowerment of women to the social construction of gender in what amounted, they argued, to a social recipe for victimization (Brownmiller 1975). In addition to decrying violence, second wave theorists also leveled important critiques against sexual violence law on the grounds that "the objective of rape statutes traditionally has not been to protect women from coercive intimacy but to protect and maintain a property-like interest in female chastity" (Crenshaw 1989:157). The early second wave antiviolence struggle was thus multipronged: to end "rape culture" but also to change violence laws to create more protections for women as full subjects and not merely as sexual objects or property.

While radical feminists of the second wave understood rape culture to be structural and systemic, the white antiviolence movement increasingly directed its energies at the microlevel and single-issue symptoms of this social problem: interpersonal gendered violence. It also prioritized criminal justice system solutions in an effort to eradicate the "second rape" that so many women experienced when turning to law enforcement and the courts. By the 1980s, antiviolence campaigns were moving from *social movements* to institutionalized *social movement organizations*. Rape crisis centers and battered women's shelters were staffed less often by volunteer activists and more often by professional women with credentials in women's studies, counseling, social work, or law (Messer-Davidow 2002: 163). They also were increasingly funded by grants and reliant upon state support, more likely to be working with state agencies instead of against them. Some of the victories highlighted by white second wave feminists included special domestic violence training for police and mandatory arrest legislation under which police responding to domestic violence calls were required to make an arrest. This orientation to criminal justice solutions trend continued, with Congress passing the Violence against Women Act in 1994.

While feminists of color were part of the second wave antiviolence movement, they increasingly challenged its assumptions and orientation, especially as it began to work more closely with the police and the state. In the late 1980s and early 1990s, black feminist scholars like Angela Davis and Kimberlé Williams Crenshaw critiqued the antiviolence movement, arguing that its problems were rooted in a single-issue approach—gender—to violence against women. They noted that single-issue orientations are not only exclusive but also mask privilege, for they tend to highlight the "experiences of those who are privileged *but for* their racial or sexual characteristics . . . [a framework] reflected in the belief that sexism or racism can be meaningfully discussed without paying attention to the lives of those other than the race-, gender- or class-privileged" (Crenshaw 1989: 151, 152; emphasis in the original). An emphasis on interpersonal sexual assault was a focus on the kind of gendered violence that white, middle-class women predominantly face, the experience of "otherwise-privileged members of the group" (140). In fact, writes Crenshaw, *both* sexual assault *and* the state's response, as they have been conceptualized by the mainstream antiviolence movement, constitute "*white* male regulation of *white* female sexuality" (157; emphasis in the original). Women of color and black women in particular experience at least three *additional* kinds of violent social control, which, as Crenshaw emphasizes, are "often shaped by other dimensions of their identities, such as race and class" (357).

First, the violence that poor women of color experience also happens when gender vulnerability is exacerbated by race and class inequality. These structural forces converge to produced patterned conditions such as discriminatory employment and housing practices, lack of financial assets, lack of vehicles, child care responsibilities, surveillance by child welfare services, and social networks that are less likely to include surplus resources, such as money, a car, or an extra room. These effects of racism and poverty are themselves a kind of violence and they interact with gender to increase susceptibility to interpersonal violence, such as by making the ability to avoid or leave it more difficult. As Crenshaw (1995: 359) explains, "intersectional subordination need not be intentionally produced; in fact, it is frequently the consequence of the imposition of one burden interacting with preexisting vulnerabilities to create yet another dimension of disempowerment."

Second, women of color also disproportionately experience violence perpetrated by the very law enforcement and state officials tasked with public safety and order. Perceived to be highly sexual and in need of disciplining, as well as being outside the bounds of full state protections, women of color have been disproportionately sexually assaulted by law enforcement officials who presume and frequently experience impunity. As Andrea Ritchie (2006: 149) explains, "Rape, sexual assault, and sexual harassment by on-duty law enforcement officers are foremost among gender-specific forms of police brutality directed at Black women. Sex workers in particular report endemic extortion of sexual favors by police officers in exchange for leniency or to avoid routine police violence against them, as well as frequent rapes and sexual assault" (149).Their more frequent interactions with law enforcement and state officials as a result of race and poverty—for example, through extreme neighborhood surveillance and frequent interaction with state services—produce situations in which poor

> women and girls, and particularly women of color, are sexually assaulted, raped, brutally strip-searched, beaten, shot, and killed by law enforcement agents with alarming frequency, experiencing many of the same forms of law enforcement violence as men of color, as well as gender- and race-specific forms of police misconduct and abuse. (139)

Because law enforcement agent assaults are facilitated by state policies which disproportionately regulate communities of color, and are perpetrated by individuals in their official capacity as representatives of the state, women of color antiviolence activists call these attacks the manifestation of state violence. Gendered **state violence** refers to policies that heighten the regulation and social control of populations due to their race, class, and/or national status, all of which interact with gender and enable violent outcomes. These include the war on drugs, the war on terror, welfare reform policy, child welfare policy, immigration policy, reproductive policy, zero tolerance policies, and quality-of-life policies (Ritchie 2006). As with the other vehicles of racism and class-based oppression identified above, these policies do not only facilitate interpersonal violence, they are themselves experienced as forms of violence.

Finally, as Crenshaw (1989: 158) notes, women of color have been "placed . . . outside the law's protection." Since sexual violence legislation is rooted in the preservation and control of white women's purity and motherhood, "sexist expectations of chastity and racist assumptions of sexual promiscuity combined to create a distinct set of issues confronting Black women" (159). Antiviolence laws, for the most part, have not been written to protect women of color. Stereotypes about women of color's extreme sexuality and, in the case of black women, aggression, have made it difficult for white law enforcement officials, social service workers, and even white antiviolence activists and organizational staff to recognize their victimization. "Community assumptions about . . . black womanhood," explains Tracie West (1999: 58), "can form a barrier that disqualifies [them] from the right to community empathy," making it more difficult for women of color to get the support they need. In addition, it has meant that they are disproportionately blamed for their assaults, more likely to be themselves arrested under mandatory arrest laws, and awarded stiffer penalties for self-defense. Ritchie (2006: 143, 147) describes how

> women framed as "masculine"—including African American women, who are routinely "masculinized" though systemic racial stereotypes—are consistently treated by police as potentially violent, predatory, or noncompliant regardless of their actual conduct or circumstances, no matter how old, young, disabled, small, or ill. . . . Use of force against women of color is also uniquely informed by racialized and gendered stereotypes—officials often appear to be acting based on perceptions of Black women as "animalistic" women possessing superhuman force, Latina women as "hot-tempered mamas," Asian women as "devious," knife-wielding martial arts experts, and so on.

Because the experiences shared by these women "undermine the women's movement's purported success in increasing women's safety by exposing violence in the 'private sphere' of the home and sensitizing law enforcement officers to take domestic violence seriously," they dissolve the distinction between state and private violence, as well as the notion that the state's primary role is protection (151). The mainstream antiviolence movement's emphasis on interpersonal sexual violence and battery has meant that many of the mechanisms of violence in the lives of women of color are neither recognized nor addressed by antiviolence efforts.

Building on this intersectional analysis, intersectional scholar activists of color made a historic contribution to the struggle against violence in 2000. That year, a conference called "The Color of Violence: Violence against Women of Color" was held at the University of California Santa Cruz. The primary goals of this conference were

> to develop analyses and strategies around ending violence that place women of color at the center; to address violence against women of color in all its forms,

> including attacks on immigrants' rights and Indian treaty rights, the proliferation of prisons, militarism, attacks on the reproductive rights of women of color, medical experimentation on communities of color, homophobia/heterosexism and hate crimes against lesbians of color, economic neo-colonialism, and institutional racism; and to encourage the antiviolence movement to reinsert political organizing into its response to violence. (Smith et al. 2006: 2)

Out of this conference was born Incite! Women of Color against Violence, a national organization "of radical feminists of color advancing a movement to end violence against women of color and our communities through direct action, critical dialogue, and grassroots organizing" (Incite Mission Statement, available at www.incite-national.org). In 2006, Incite! published *Color of Violence: The Incite! Anthology*, which contains short essays by scholars and activists that address the intersectional ways in which gender and race come together with other social forces, such as poverty, national identity, and sexual identity, to produce violence against women of color.

Also included in *Color of Violence* is an essay titled "Gender Violence and the Prison-Industrial Complex," a statement co-produced by Incite! and Critical Resistance, a national prison abolition movement cofounded by Angela Davis. The essay identifies tensions between the women's antiviolence movement, which has emphasized tough-on-crime solutions to interpersonal violence, and the prison abolition movement, which seeks alternatives to incarceration. While the antiviolence movement has primarily looked through the single lens of gender, the prison abolition movement has prioritized race, emphasizing the experience of men of color as disproportionately targeted by law enforcement. "Gender Violence and the Prison Industrial Complex" identifies the limitations of these single issue approaches, noting that they: reproduce the idea that all women are white (interpersonal violence victims) and all people of color are men (prison victims); neglect the particular experiences of women of color who are both victims of violence and also heavily targeted by the criminal justice system; downplay the impact on women of the collective cost of mass incarceration; disregard the reasons women of color frequently do not seek criminal justice solutions to violence; and minimize the ways in which alternatives to the prison system, such as mediation, may not meet the needs of victims of sexual and gender violence.

U.S. Third World Feminism

During the 1980s, the phrase "U.S. third world feminism" was often used to link the plight of U.S. women of color to colonized people across the globe and to argue that white feminist thought was a hegemonic feminism that played the same role as a colonialist ideology. One of the most widely read pieces that made this claim was "U.S. Third-World Feminism: The Theory and Method of Oppositional Consciousness in the Postmodern World," in which Chela Sandoval ([1991] 2003: 75) asserts that

> U.S. third-world feminism provides access to a different way of conceptualizing not only U.S. feminist consciousness but oppositional activity in gender; it

> comprises a formulation capable of aligning such movements for social justice with what have been identified as world-wide movements of decolonization

At first glance the term "U.S. third world feminism" sounds like an oxymoron.[26] How can citizens of a major first world country such as the United States be "third world feminists?" What this term highlights is how U.S. women of color are both victims of and critics of a particular form of colonialism—internal colonialism (see chapter 9).

In the United States, **internal colonialism** (sometimes referred to as settler colonialism) initially took the form of white settlers pushing indigenous peoples off their land (often onto more barren or stipulated lands such as reservations) and/or exterminating them in order to inhabit the lands themselves (McMichael 1996: 17).[27] When mercantile traders from the seventeenth through the nineteenth century brought (legally and illegally) slaves from other parts of the globe to the United States, African–Americans became yet another colonized people. A third internal colony was established when sections of Mexico were annexed after the Mexican–American War (1846–1848). U.S. settler colonialism finally gained hegemony across the North American continent when the western frontier was consolidated after the Massacre at Wounded Knee, often considered the last of the major Indian Wars in 1890.[28] Native-American poet Chrystos, a contributor to *This Bridge Called My Back*, powerfully captures the pain of internal colonialism in "I Walk in the History of My People" ([1981] 1983). This poem decries how the infection in her "wounded knee" has been festering "for 300 years," how her "sacred beliefs have been made pencils, names of cities, gas stations" and how "anger" is the "crutch" that keeps her "still walking" (57).

Racism is an integral feature of both internal and external colonization. As postcolonial theorist Albert Memmi ([1957] 1991: 73–74) points out,

> the racist accusation directed at the colonized cannot be anything but collective, and every one of the colonized must be held guilty without exception.... Theoretically at least, a worker can leave his class and change his status, but within the framework of colonization, nothing can ever save the colonized. He can never move into the privileged clan; even if he should earn more money than they, if he should win all titles, if he should enormously increase his power.... All the efforts of the colonialist are directed toward maintaining this social immobility, and racism is the surest weapon for this aim.... *Racism appears then, not as an incidental detail, but as a consubstantial part of colonialism.* (Emphasis added)

Early in the twentieth century, theories of internal colonialism were articulated by a number of Marxist and postcolonial theorists, such as V. I. Lenin, Antonio Gramsci, Kwame Nkrumah, and Frantz Fanon. In late modernity, this theory was developed specifically for the American context by black radicals, such as in Stokely Carmichael and Charles Hamilton's *Black Power* (1967). A few years later, neo-Marxist Robert Blauner's *Racial Oppression in America* (1972) extended the theory of internal colonialism to other colonized groups in the United States. His theory focused on how people of color in the United States have been subjected to a number of colonizing processes perpetrated by the dominant white population. These include: first, how people of color entered the "host" country involuntarily and/or by force, such as through the slave trade or the military conquest of Mexican- and Native-American lands; second, how their native cultures were destroyed and they had to assimilate to the language and culture of the dominant population; third, how they were relegated to "subordinate labor markets," meaning low-paying, menial jobs that the dominant white population did not want to do, such as harvesting crops, canal and railroad construction, or domestic service; and fourth, how white-dominated state bureaucracies imposed restrictions on people of color that were not imposed on the dominant population, such as the Jim Crow segregation laws or definitions of citizenship that excluded them. In these ways, the twin processes of internal colonalism and racism simultaneously enriched the white colonizers and maintained the dependency of the colonized. The integration of analyses of internal colonialism into intersectionality frameworks has been particularly useful in discussing local/global links (see chapter 9) as well as in struggles for environmental justice.

THE ENVIRONMENTAL JUSTICE MOVEMENT

Women of various classes and races have struggled for environmental justice throughout U.S. history. Yet the major environmental organizations of the nineteenth and twentieth centuries were supported primarily by white, middle- and upper-class men and women (Merchant 2007). Despite the important role played by late-nineteenth- and early-twentieth-century black women's clubs in "municipal housekeeping," their environmental struggles often were not acknowledged by other environmentalists (Mann 2011; see chapter 2). Even the more radical environmental and ecofeminist groups of late modernity were rarely successful in attracting members from different races or social classes (Taylor 2002). It was not until the late 1980s that a radical, multiracial, multiclass, grassroots, environmental movement—the **environmental justice movement**—arose. The application of intersectionality theory to environmental issues is most visible in this movement.

Environmental justice activists highlight how the United States is divided into separate and unequal communities segregated by race and class. They document how working-class and poor people of color have less access to clean air and water as well as experience greater exposure to environmental hazards both at home and on the job. They challenge not only the perpetrators of environmental degradation but also the indifference of mainstream environmental groups to their environmental concerns. Thus, they campaign for environmental justice both within society and within the environmental movement. Drawing insights from the civil rights and the environmental movements, supporters of environmental justice tend to use grassroots organizing and direct-action strategies similar to those used in the civil rights movement. They have organized primarily around issues that plague their particular communities, such as waste facility sites, lead contamination, pesticides, water and air pollution, and workplace safety.

While the overlap of race and social class confounds these issues, numerous studies have shown that people of color face elevated toxic exposure levels even when social class variables, such as income, education, and occupational status, are held constant. Indeed, race has been found to be an independent variable, not reducible to social class, in predicting the distribution of air pollution in our society; the location of municipal landfills, incinerators, and abandoned toxic waste dumps; contaminated fish consumption; and lead poisoning in children (Bryant and Mohai 1992; Bullard 1993 and 1994; Merchant 1999). It is for these reasons that the environmental justice movement highlights the issue of **environmental racism**.

Women of color have been at the forefront of the environmental justice movement and its struggle to bring attention to the environmental problems that harm their communities. Dorceta Taylor's work "Women of Color, Environmental Justice, and Ecofeminism" (1997), Andrea Smith's article "Ecofeminism through an Anticolonial Framework" (1997) and book *Conquest* (2005), as well as, Winona LaDuke's "Mothers of Our Nations: Indigenous Women Address the World" ([1995] 2005) are drawn from in discussing these environmental issues below. While Taylor writes from an African-American womanist perspective, Smith and LaDuke voice the concerns of Native–American women. As Taylor points out in her article, compared with other sectors of the environmental movement, the environmental justice movement boasts a higher percentage of women as leaders and activists. It also boasts significantly more success in recruiting working-class and poor people of color.

These authors discuss how the successful mobilization of people of color requires a *redefinition of which issues are considered environmental.* Mainstream environmental organizations spend most of their resources on wildlife protection, forest and park management, and land stewardship. They are less likely to work on issues of greater concern to people of color, such as occupational safety, hazardous wastes, or incinerators and landfills (Taylor 1997: 50). Although ecofeminists have been heavily involved in the antitoxics movement, the environmental justice movement has found some of their activities problematic. For example, the Not in My Backyard (NIMBY) movement has been criticized for rarely questioning in whose backyard the problem is eventually dumped.

Moreover, environmental activists (including ecofeminists) are often insensitive to the vantage points and experiences of women of color.[29] For example, population control is cited as a major environmental issue by many environmental activists, including ecofeminists. Yet, as discussed earlier, women of color have experienced a long history of abuse by population control policies, such as sterilization without informed consent. They also argue that ecofeminists often ignore how white women oppress people of color, both male and female. They *call for a more complex and multidirectional view of oppressions where males and females are recognized as both oppressed and oppressors.*

For Smith and LaDuke, the failure of mainstream environmental organizations and ecofeminists to embrace an anticolonial framework has led to their failure to understand the origins of environmental problems and patriarchy. They discuss how prior to U.S. settler colonialism indigenous tribes and nations were neither male-dominated nor ecologically debilitated. It was the conquest and colonization of Indian lands by white settlers that led to the domination of both women and nature (see chapter 9). LaDuke ([1995] 2005: 526) highlights how the lands and resources of indigenous peoples have generally been used "for someone else's development program and amassing of wealth." Even with the small amount of land now left to indigenous peoples in the United States, more than two-thirds of uranium resources and one-third of all low-sulfur coal resources are on indigenous lands. Not only has uranium mining left tons of nuclear wastes on these lands, but indigenous people's lands have also served as major sites for the testing of atomic weapons. By the mid-1990s, 650 atomic weapons had been detonated on the Western Shoshone Nation alone (526). The environmental and health impacts of such dumping and testing are of grave concern to these authors.

Overall, these authors provide numerous examples of how the twin practices of internal colonialism and institutional racism left people of color to bear the brunt of past and present injustices in the distribution of environmental risks and hazards. Being placed in low-paying, subordinate labor markets where environmental regulations are absent or weak and being treated as second-class citizens without the rights to safe environments enjoyed by the dominant white group were major battle grounds in their struggles for environmental justice. Given past experiences of indifference to their plight, environmental justice activists are less trusting that environmental agencies and white environmental activists will have concern for their recompense and equity in the future. Consequently, many women activists in the environmental justice movement reject the label of ecofeminist and do not seek to be part of an ecofeminist movement. Instead, they continue the work they are doing and build coalitions with other social movements when it is strategically important. For them, assimilation is not the answer. Rather, unity occurs through building a movement based on difference. In all of these ways, the theory and practice of women of color involved in the environmental justice movements echo the theory and practice of intersectionality theorists.

THE SOCIAL CONSTRUCTION OF WHITENESS

Because women of color historically had different vantage points and experiences in regard to a wide range of feminist issues, they often criticized white feminists' blindness to their concerns. Even when white feminists made concerted efforts to discuss race in their writings and/or engaged in antiracist work, they often did not fully understand the criticisms leveled by women of color. In short, these criticisms just did not register.

One of the more path breaking efforts to explain this white blindness was Ruth Frankenberg's research in *White Women, Race Matters: The Social Construction of Whiteness* (1993). Her work exemplifies one branch of critical studies of dominance (such as whiteness or masculinity studies) that arose in the 1980s. As a socialist feminist in the early 1970s, Frankenberg describes how criticisms by women of color generated "a need to know more" (3). She saw how white feminists who viewed themselves as antiracists had a "limited repertoire of responses" to these criticisms that often included guilt, dismissal, anger, and confusion as well as stasis or withdrawal from multiracial work (2). Frankenberg captured the feelings of many white second wave feminists when she wrote that

> as a white feminist, I knew that I had not previously known I was "being racist" and that I had never set out to "be racist." I also knew that these desires and intentions had had little effect on outcomes. I, as a coauthor, in however a modest way of feminist agendas and discourse, was at best failing to challenge racism and, at worse, aiding and abetting it. How had feminism, a movement that, to my knowledge, intended to support and benefit all women, turned out not to be doing so? (3)

She set out to answer these questions and, by doing so, paved the way for the development of critical whiteness studies. Frankenberg views "whiteness" as having three major dimensions: "a structural location of race privilege; a standpoint from which white people view themselves and others; and a set of cultural practices that often are unmarked and unnamed (1). To speak of the "social construction of whiteness" is to assert that there are locations, discourses, and material relations to which the term "whiteness" applies. While she foregrounds race and gender, Frankenberg is careful to note how class, region, generation, ethnicity, and sexuality further subdivide the terrain of lived experiences of whiteness (236).

She explains how the issues involved here were not only how white women's experiences differed from those of women of color but, also, how white women missed their "racialness" when describing their own experiences; that is, they lacked awareness of how their own positions in society were constructed by race (90). They viewed race as something that affected other people but not themselves. Consequently, their visions of "difference" remained *abstract* (10). In addition, for white feminists—even those who viewed themselves as antiracist activists—the cultural practices associated with whiteness had become so "normal" and taken-for-granted that they were virtually invisible. Often the white women Frankenberg interviewed said that they "did not have a culture" (192). They viewed whiteness as generic, normative, or as an empty cultural space. For example, one of her respondents remarked:

> To be a Heinz 57 American, a white, class-confused American, land of the Kleenex type American, is so formless in and of itself. It only takes shape in relation to other people. (191)

Frankenberg's goal was to demystify these empty conceptions of whiteness so that white complicity with racism could be understood and challenged within the multifaceted fields in which it operated (242 and 243).

She also found it useful to employ certain insights from postcolonial theory to illuminate her points. As discussed in chapter 10, postcolonial theory focuses on the social implications of the *mutually constitutive processes between the colonizer and the colonized* (Said 1978). Frankenberg (1993: 17) observed how the white women she interviewed too often missed this mutually constitutive process; when they discussed race, they failed to consider how their own "white selves" were mutually marked and constituted in their analysis of the racialized other. Frankenberg also discussed a number of similarities between the discourses of whiteness and the discourses of Westerness. Both "White" and "Western" subjects distinguish themselves, in part, by being "not Other." They also tended to view racialized others as representatives of backward or less modern cultural forms (193). By making connections between whiteness and Westerness, Frankenberg's study of the social construction of whiteness linked the local to the global.

Her analysis has implications not only for feminist theory but also for multicultural and diversity programs. Many of these programs in academic institutions, such as Africana or Chicana studies, do not simultaneously reconceptualize the status, content, and formation of whiteness (243). Even in women's studies, references to women of color but not to white women as "racial-ethnic women" implicitly suggest that race does not shape white identities or experience (243). Frankenberg argues that to provide more adequate antiracist education, these mutually constitutive processes have to be incorporated and addressed.

Other feminists interested in the social construction of whiteness developed additional ways of exposing **white solipsism**[30] or the distorted vision that results from viewing the world only through the experiences of a white person in a racist society. Mab Segrest's *Memoir of a Race Traitor* (1994) uses poetic and passionate personal narratives to expose the racism that surrounded her life as a white woman growing up and doing activist work in the American South. Peggy McIntosh's "White Privilege: Unpacking the Invisible Knapsack" (2004: 89) is considered a classic by antiracist educators and has been used in classrooms across the country. McIntosh opens white eyes to both serious and mundane examples of the effects of white privilege in everyday life. The examples she pulls from the "invisible" knapsack of white privilege range from whites not worrying about discrimination on the basis of skin color when they are renting or purchasing a home to using "flesh" colored crayons or bandages without reflecting on whose "flesh" is being mirrored (89). By doing so, she reveals many "unearned advantages" in the life experiences of whites that perpetuate racism and concludes as follows:

> One factor seems clear about all of the interlocking oppressions. They take both active forms which we can see and embedded forms which as a member of the dominant group one is taught not to see. In my class and place, I did not see myself as a racist because I was taught to recognize racism only in individual acts of meanness by members of my group, never in invisible systems conferring

> unsought racial dominance on my group from birth. . . . Disapproving of systems won't be enough to change them. I was taught to think that racism could end if White individuals changed their attitudes; . . . A "white" skin in the United States opens many doors for Whites whether or not we approve of the way dominance has been conferred on us. Individual acts can palliate, but cannot end, these problems.To redesign social systems we need first to acknowledge their colossal unseen dimensions (92–93).

INTEGRATING DISABILITY STUDIES INTO INTERSECTIONALITY THEORY

Like other new social movements that arose in the United States during the second half of the twentieth century, the disability rights movement was inspired by both the civil rights movement and the women's movement. After engaging in various forms of protest, such as sit-ins and demonstrations, this movement's first major success was passage of the Americans with Disabilities Act (ADA) in May of 1990 (Volion 2010). The ADA protects the disabled from discrimination in employment, public accommodations, transportation, government services, and telecommunications. The interdisciplinary field of disability studies was created in 1993 to focus on the contributions, experiences, history, and culture of people with disabilities as well as to formulate their political demands (Society for Disability Studies n.d.).

One of the major scholars to apply intersectionality theory to disabilities studies is Rosemarie Garland-Thomson, author of *Freakery* (1998) and *Extraordinary Bodies* (1997). In "Integrating Disability, Transforming Feminist Theory" she points to how disability studies is sorely lacking in feminist analyses, just as feminist studies often is discussed without reference to disabilities (Garland-Thomas [2001] 2005: 575). She lauds intersectionality theory for being one of the few feminist approaches that has taken into account disability, alongside its focus on gender, race, class, and sexuality.

Garland-Thomson points to various similarities between gendered and disabled social locations. She notes how Western thought historically associated femaleness with disability highlighting how male scholars from Aristotle to Freud defined women as "multilated males" (378–379). Claims that women were less rational, less intelligent, and more hysterical than men also fostered the view that women were the debilitated "other." She points to how feminist theorists, such as Simone de Beauvoir and Iris Marion Young, countered these attacks by exposing how femininity and enforced feminine comportment were sources of women's disabilities (see chapter 4). Garland-Thomson also discusses how the twin ideologies of beauty and normalcy posit female and disabled bodies not only as spectacles to be looked at but also as pliable bodies to be shaped into conformity with these cultural standards (see also Kessinger 2008).

Her work echoes intersectionality theorists when she argues that integrating disability into an intersectional framework is not meant as an additive endeavor.

Rather, such integration entails a "conceptual shift that strengthens our understanding of how these multiple oppressions, intertwine, redefine and mutually constitute each other" (Garland-Thomson [2001] 2005: 577). This conceptual shift casts disability as an issue of continuing, determinative importance in the lives of all people rather than simply as a "minoritizing view" (577). It also broadens the notion of disability to be understood as a "pervasive cultural system" that stigmatizes certain kinds of bodily variations (577).

Garland-Thomson states that, like femaleness, disability is "not a natural state of corporeal inferiority, inadequacy or a stroke of misfortune" (577). Rather it is a socially constructed narrative of the body similar to what we understand as the fictions of race and gender. The disability/ability system produces subjects by differentiating and marking bodies. In doing so it legitimates the unequal distribution of resources, status, and power within a biased social and architectural environment that is not fashioned for the disabled (577).[31] Thus the disability/ability system functions to preserve and to validate privileged designations, such as beautiful, healthy, fit, competent, intelligent—all of which provide material and cultural capital to those who can claim such statuses. As in the case of other subjugated peoples, a plethora of stereotypes are associated with disability—such as crippled, mad, abnormal, dumb, and asexual. She argues that bodies subjugated by race, class, gender, sexuality, and disability all share histories of being depicted as "deficient or profligate" (579).

Precisely because these subjugated bodies have been viewed as inadequate and/or unrestrained, she highlights how they have been targeted for control or elimination by various historical and cultural practices. They have been the objects of infanticide, forced sterilization, segregation, hate crimes, coercive rehabilitation, and normalizing surgical procedures. Overall, Garland-Thomson delivers a complex and compelling argument that integrating disability into intersectionality theory enhances our understanding of how all systems of oppression intersect and mutually constitute each other (579).

CONCLUSION

In summary, major features of intersectionality theory include a critique of feminist essentialism and a focus on differences between women; an analysis of multiple and simultaneous oppressions and their mutually constitutive features; and a standpoint epistemological approach that highlights how socially situated knowledge results in a multiplicity of vantage points on social reality. Intersectionality theorists also call for moving the voices of subjugated peoples from the margins to the center of feminist theorizing. By highlighting how these subjugated social locations are products of U.S. internal colonialism, they link their plight to that of colonized women across the globe.

Intersectionality theorists have made significant headway in bridging the racial divide that had long characterized feminist theory and the U.S. women's movement. They pioneered advances in feminist thought from rudimentary theoretical insights in the nineteenth century to the more fully developed intersectionality theories of today. It took the socially lived experiences of colonized and subordinated peoples on the margins to reveal the simultaneous and interlocking nature of multiple oppressions that affect and mutually constitute us all. Their critical, oppositional gaze led to significant epistemological breaks with both modern science and the dominant white feminisms they encountered. Their insights fostered other scholars to take more seriously particular forms of privilege, such as whiteness or able-bodiedness, that often were ignored in other feminist frameworks.

To date, U.S. feminist thought has been dramatically informed and transformed by the critical insights of intersectionality theorists. These scholar/activists have contributed to new directions in feminist theory that bridged modern and postmodern thought and that decentered the modern, white feminisms of the second wave. However, whether these transformations in feminist thought will result in the social justice outcomes that are the ultimate aim of this feminist theorizing is yet to be determined.

Additional writings by intersectionality theorists on global issues can be found in chapters 8 and 9.

CRITICISMS OF INTERSECTIONALITY THEORIES

1. That intersectionality theorists are guilty of essentialism despite their claims to be critics of essentialism. Critics claim that intersectionality theorists' group concepts ignore how individuals within a group do not have a single vision of reality but rather have heterogeneous experiences and concerns (Grant, 1993). The question of who can speak for or express the standpoint of an entire group of people is also problematic (Pels 2004).

2. That many intersectionality theorists' embrace a politics of identity that restricts freedom and diversity. Critics argue that identities are simply socially constructed fictions that regulate, and discipline people to act and think in terms of these fictional categories. As such, identity politics preclude alternative ways of being. Critics call for resistance to identity to better assert difference (Foucault [1976] 1980, Butler 1993, Seidman, 2000).

3. That the identity politics embraced by many intersectionality theorists divide and fragment social movements. Critics argue that identity politics undermine the formation of mass-based movements that could foster more unified collective action and more effective social change (Agger 1998, Touraine 1998).

4. That at times U.S. intersectionality theorists ignore their own privileged positions as citizens of a first-world nation and a global superpower. Critics claim that opposition by Americans to racism, classism, sexism, and homophobia has never guaranteed opposition to U.S. global hegemony. First-worldness, even when experienced from the bottom, entails certain privileges that must be acknowledged in discussions of local/global links (Shohat [1998] 2001: 37–38; Spivak 1990: 139).

NOTES

1 A special thanks to Rachel E. Luft for her valuable insights and suggestions for improving this chapter.
2 Second wave womanist of color Paula Giddings derived the title of her book on black women's history, *When and Where I Enter* (1984), from this famous quote by Cooper.
3 This movement was centered in the Harlem neighborhood of New York City that had been an exclusive, white, middle- and upper-class suburb until it was abandoned by whites following the influx of immigrants in the late nineteenth century. In 1910, a large block of this neighborhood was purchased by African–American realtors, and it soon became a favorite destination for blacks who left the south during the Great Migration of the early twentieth century (see chapter 2).
4 For example, in Johnson's play "Safe" a mother kills her newborn son so that he will not have to endure racist terror and subjugation, a theme that reappears in Toni Morrison's novel *Beloved.*
5 The music and lyrics were written by Abel Meeropol. For the complete lyrics and analyses of this song as an historical document see Stone 2004.
6 See, for example, Singh 2004, Kelley 1990 , Payne 1995, and Robinson 1983.
7 The support of the Kennedy/Johnson administrations was uneven. For example, community organizers in Mississippi pleaded for the Kennedy administration to intervene in the state-sponsored terror to no avail. The Johnson administration's failure to seat the Mississippi Freedom Democratic Party at the Democratic National Convention in 1964 marked an end to the civil rights liberal approach and the rise of black Power for many activists.
8 Charles Payne (1995) and others have documented how rural-based black militants, such as the Deacons of Defense, also played a critical role in the civil rights movement.
9 A number of factors coalesced as incentives for the mechanization of southern agriculture in this era, such as the impact of New Deal acreage controls, World War II labor shortages, and the loss of foreign markets during the war (Mann 1990a).
10 As racist domination at home came to be seen as part of the more general history of Western imperialism and colonialism, the politics of the color curtain became linked to the politics of the iron curtain as theories of internal colonialism rooted in Marxist–Leninist theory and/or the writings of postcolonial writers, such as Franz Fanon, were used to analyze the plight of people of color in the United States.
11 A few years before his assassination, Malcolm X changed his views on women and also took a more explicit internationalist and anti-imperialist stance.
12 La Raza literally means "the race" and refers to people in the United States who are descended from peoples who were indigenous to the Americas and Spanish colonies.
13 See www.afn.org/~iguana/archives/1998_01/19980108.html (last accessed on March 4, 2011).
14 While initially it appeared that Collins used this stance to describe individuals who found themselves in marginal locations between groups of varying power, she later clarified that her focus is on social locations occupied by groups with unequal power (2004c).
15 Collins's view here is shared by Sandra Harding and Dorothy Smith, as discussed in chapters 1 and 4, respectively (Harding 1991: 191; Smith 1987: 92).
16 The works of Harding and Smith also highlight the *social locations* of marginalized people, rather than their subjective *perspectives,* as the starting point of their inquiries. These differences have significant implications for their theories as discussed in chapters 1 and 4.
17 In the first edition of *Black Feminist Thought* Collins references the work of Michel Foucault (1990: 234). This reference is missing in later editions of this book, which was revised before its second printing.
18 Queer theorist Steven Seidman (2000: 441) speaks directly to these issues when he discusses how even "the assertion of a black, middle-class, American, lesbian identity silences differences in this social category that relate to religion, regional location . . . to feminism, age or education."
19 A fine discussion of the difference between social stratification and social differentiation can be found in Pease, Form, and Rytina 1970.
20 These critical insights are also relevant to the population-control polices advocated by both the U.S. government and many U.S. feminists for poor women abroad (see chapter 9).
21 Forced sterilization had been ignored by most white feminists despite its long history. For example, the sterilization policies of the state of Virginia actually served as a model for Nazi Germany's notorious forced sterilizations in the 1930s and early 1940s.

22 Surrogacy contracts in the late 1980s generally cost around twenty thousand dollars with half of that fee often paid for legal and medical bills. Similarly, a procedure frequently used for infertile couples that implanted an already fertilized embryo into the women's fallopian tubes cost a similar amount in the 1980s.

23 See also Corea 1985 and Purdy 1996.

24 In a recent count, 39 out of 51 members of the Tea Party Caucus in the U.S. House of Representatives are cosponsors of the Birthright Citizenship Act (Burghart and Zeskind 2010: 73).

25 Joshua Sartisky's 2009 paper on Hurston's work first alerted me to these criticisms. As noted in Harris 2003, in recent decades black scholars such as Farah Jasmine Griffin, Mary Frances Berry, and Elijah Anderson have begun to challenge the narrow constructs of respectability by focusing their research on the lives of people of color who are deemed "unrespectable" and who were silenced in previous eras.

26 In popular parlance, we tend to use the term *oxymoron* as a contradiction. But the Greek word means something that is surprisingly true despite its appearance—a paradox.

27 Other settler colonial states include the United States, Australia, Argentina, Canada, and Israel—all of which continue to experience racial/ethnic conflicts that reflect their internal colonialist histories.

28 The last medal of honor for the American–Indian Wars was actually given in 1898 after the Battle of Sugar Point in Minnesota, though smaller skirmishes occurred at later dates.

29 Spiritual ecofeminists are especially criticized by Taylor and Smith. Taylor discusses how African-Americans have worked in close partnership with churches in their civil rights and environmental justice campaigns. Thus, spiritual ecofeminists' lack of tolerance for traditional, god-based religions is often offensive. Smith criticizes spiritual feminists for appropriating Native spiritual traditions in an "imperialist" manner. In her view, they take Native traditions, use them out of context for their own personal advancement, and give nothing back to Native communities.

30 Solipsism refers to the philosophical theory that the self is the only thing knowable to a subject. The term *white solipsism* refers to the distorted views that arise from seeing the world only through the eyes and experiences of a white person in a racist society.

31 See Kessinger 2008 for a discussion of how ergonomics was directed toward designing the socially constructed environment (especially homes and workplaces) for the "normal body."

SECTION II

Feminist Thought after Taking the Postmodern Turn

CHAPTER 6

Postmodernism, Poststructuralism, Queer, and Transgender Theories

BY JANE WARD AND SUSAN MANN

> There is no gender identity behind the expressions of gender . . . identity is performatively constituted by the very "expressions" that are said to be its results.
>
> —JUDITH BUTLER

> Queer is a word that can't be sanitized.
>
> —EVE SEDGWICK

INTRODUCTION

Postmodernism and poststructuralism were developed in France during the1960s and 1970s by writers like Jacques Lacan, Jean-François Lyotard, Jacques Derrida, and Michel Foucault. Unlike other perspectives that contributed to new directions in feminist thought, these French postmodernists and poststructuralists did not always directly engage in theoretical debates with feminism. However, the general issues they addressed paralleled and challenged ongoing concerns in feminist thought. While references to Lacan, Derrida, and Foucault can be found in U.S. feminist writings before 1975, postmodernism and poststructuralism did not significantly influence U.S. feminism until the late 1970s and 1980s (Messer-Davidow 2002: 208). Queer theory arose almost a decade later in the United States, where *queer* came to denote both a new grassroots political movement and a new theoretical framework. Queer theorists were heavily influenced by Foucault's poststructuralism. Yet unlike Foucault's work, from its inception queer theory was engaged in dialogues with feminism over the issues of sex and sexuality. Thus, in many ways queer theory is the transnational offspring of French poststructuralism and U.S. feminism. Also included here will be a brief discussion of transgender theory. While transgender studies constitutes its own distinct field, it has been heavily influenced by queer and feminist theories and, in turn, has transformed the way many scholars today address gender. Throughout this chapter, analyses of the writings of postmodernists, poststructuralists, queer, and transgender theorists will be interwoven to reveal both their common ground and their crossroads. The discussion begins with a brief historical background to the rise of postmodernism and poststructuralism. For purposes of manageability, they will be referred to below as the postperspectives.

HISTORICALLY GROUNDING POSTMODERNISM AND POSTSTRUCTURALISM

Just as social movements of the 1960s exposed inequalities and conflicts that tore at the fabric of American society, similar movements and social divisions existed in France. In both cases, these social cleavages fostered the rise of New Left theories and politics. This was evident in the United States with the rise of the anti–Vietnam war movement, the civil rights movement, the women's liberation movement, the gay and lesbian rights movement, and the environmental movement. Europe witnessed similar **New Left** social movements, and postmodernism and poststructuralism represented some of the more influential New Left positions in France.

Supporters of these new postperspectives rejected many features of the Old Left despite its more prominent political position in postwar France than in the United States. A number of global events contributed to their estrangement. They rejected the authoritarian forms of Marxism associated with Stalinism in the USSR and Maoism in the People's Republic of China. In turn, many had abandoned the French Communist Party after the Soviet invasion of Hungary in 1956 or after the Prague Spring was forcefully brought to an end in 1968. Moreover, just as the Vietnam War caused serious divisions in American society, the Algerian Revolution sharply divided French society and galvanized the Left in France. Algeria's battle for independence from France (1954–1962) was one of the most violent, anticolonialist struggles of that era. Like the Vietnam War, the Algerian Revolution was characterized by guerrilla warfare, terrorism, and the use of torture by both sides. It is important to recall that these bloody histories were intertwined, since the United States did not enter the conflict in Vietnam until after the French surrendered at Dien Bien Phu in 1954, the battle that effectively ended the French colonial presence there.

However events *internal* to France in 1968 also were central to the estrangement of radical intellectuals from the politics of the Old Left. In May 1968 France was the site of an insurrection that came closer to a revolutionary situation than anything that occurred in any other highly industrialized Western society during that era. The events of May 1968 began as student protests against the French government for its tight bureaucratic control of higher education. A number of national and global issues were embedded in these student protests, such as inequality and discrimination in French society and students' rights to demonstrate against the Vietnam War and to side with the North Vietnamese (which highlighted and critiqued the French government's role in creating the conditions that led to this anticolonialist conflict). When the government put a ban on demonstrations, the protests escalated, as thousands of people from diverse social groups and movements joined in. Within the span of a few weeks, strikes and mass demonstrations were occurring daily. By the end of May, ten million workers had responded to the call for a general strike, and the government was forced to dissolve. Military troops were stationed outside of Paris in readiness for a state of emergency. In this power vacuum, many expected the Old Left to take power. However, after winning some concessions, the major leftist trade union federation and the French Communist Party urged strikers back to work. When the strikes ended, the revolutionary situation evaporated almost as quickly as it had developed. The same government that was forced to dissolve in May emerged victorious in new elections held in June. The failure of the Old Left to take leadership was a turning point for many of the French intellectuals who developed postmodernism and poststructuralism.

In their new theoretical approaches, these French intellectuals rejected both the focus of the Old Left on class politics and its view of the working class as the revolutionary agent of social change. Instead, they looked to the transformative potentials of the new social movements. They also developed new analyses of power that centered on language and discourse. They rejected universalistic or **totalizing theories**, such as Marxism, that attempted to encompass and make sense of every aspect of human history. They viewed these theories—even when they were directed toward such emancipatory goals as calling for more equality—as having dominating tendencies that stifled critical thought. To highlight their power, they referred to them in derogatory terms, as master narratives (Lyotard 1984: xxiii–xxvi). They thought such theories had become so rigid and reified over time that they were incapable of dealing with the dramatic changes in social life that characterized the second half of the twentieth century.

Many of these French intellectuals turned their attention to these seismic changes in social life that were beginning to become apparent. As discussed in chapter 1, these changes included the increasing pace and scope of globalization, the rise of information/symbolic industries predicated on the new electronic and computer technologies, the impact of simulations and virtual realities created by these technologies, and the increasing role of mass culture and consumerism in everyday life. For many of these theorists, such dramatic transformations of social life represented a qualitative break with modern industrial societies and ushered in a new era—postmodernity—that required equally seismic transformations of social thought.

These new theories of postmodernity entailed powerful critiques of the fundamental assumptions of modern social thought from the Enlightenment to the present. Modern views of a single reality or truth were held up to critical scrutiny and replaced with the notion of multiple realities and multiple truths (see chapter 1). Modern linear conceptions of social change and progress were called into question, as was the view that science and technology could improve societies. Under the critical lens of these postperspectives, greater knowledge through science did not necessarily mean more freedom. Rather, it also could usher in more regulation and control over social life. By calling into question these hallmarks of modernity, postmodernism and poststructuralism shook the foundations of modern social thought and, in so doing, seriously challenged existing feminist theories and practices.

MAJOR ASSUMPTIONS OF FEMINIST POSTMODERNISMS AND POSTSTRUCTURALISMS

Postmodernism and poststructuralism are somewhat difficult to define because they are umbrella terms for an array of disparate and, at times, competing perspectives (Featherstone 1991, Rosenau 1992). There are dangers entailed in lumping together these various social theories under the rubric of more general perspectives or "isms"—as is being done in this text—because the particularities and nuances of these different theories become less visible in the process.[1] However, arguably there are common assumptions underlying these modes of thinking that enable them to be discussed together with some coherence (Featherstone 1991, Rosenau 1992, Ritzer 2011). Highlighted below are some of the shared assumptions of postmodernism and poststructuralism that challenge the foundations of modern thought underlying most feminisms of the first and second waves. These shared assumptions include their deconstruction of group categories and their postmodern epistemological assumptions.

The Deconstruction of Essentialist Group Categories

As has been noted, **essentialism** refers to the assumption that a group or collectivity has certain intrinsic traits that bind them together in both theory and practice. Feminist postmodernists and poststructuralists have leveled attacks against the essentialism of modern thought. For them, *all group categories can and should be deconstructed as essentialist;* as Judith Grant (1993: 94) argues: "groups are not cut out of whole cloth"; they have "no single voice or vision of reality" but, rather, are made up of people with heterogenous experiences. This argument has critical implications for many earlier feminist approaches. For example, as discussed in chapter 5, intersectionality theorists called into question the essentialist category of "women" as ignoring differences between women by race, ethnicity, social class, and sexual orientation. However, a similar critique could be leveled against their own group concepts, such, such as womanists of color or homosexuals of color (Walker 1983; Anzaldúa 1987). Queer theorist Steven Seidman (2000: 441) uses the example of how even "the assertion of a black, middle-class, American, lesbian identity silences differences in this category that relate to religion, regional location . . . to feminism, age or education." In his view, identity constructions always entail the silencing or exclusion of some differences.

In "Contingent Foundations" (1992), Judith Butler discusses various misinterpretations of what is meant by the deconstruction of the group category "women."

In particular, she discusses how the deconstruction of group categories does not imply their negation—a fear often voiced by opponents of the postperspectives:

> Within feminism, it seems as if there is some political necessity to speak as and for women, and I would not contest that necessity. Surely, that is the way in which representational politics operates, and in this country, lobbying efforts are virtually impossible without recourse to identity politics. So we agree that demonstrations and legislative efforts and radical movements need to make claims in the name of women. (15)

This position is referred to as **strategic essentialism**—the method of using essentialist identity categories for political purposes while simultaneously recognizing the flaws entailed in essentialism (Spivak 1987). However, Butler (1992: 15) goes on to say that "the minute that the category women is invoked as describing the constituency for which feminism speaks, an internal debate invariably begins over what the descriptive content of that term will be." She points to how, in the 1980s, "the feminist 'we' rightly came under attack by women of color who claimed that the 'we' was invariably white, and how the 'we' that was meant to solidify the movement was the very source of a painful factionalization" (15). In short, to take the construction of identities and the construction of the subject as a political problematic is not the same as doing away with identities or with the subject. She writes: "To deconstruct is not to negate or dismiss, but to call into question and, perhaps, most importantly, to open up a term, like the subject, to reusage or redeployment that previously has not been authorized" (15).

Postmodernists, poststructuralists, and queer theorists reject the notion that there are core features that distinguish any groups or collectivities, just as they reject the notion that there are core identities. Rather, group concepts and identities are simply social constructs—social fictions—that serve to regulate behavior and exclude others. Their goal is to deconstruct or dismantle these fictions and, thereby, to undermine hegemonic regimes of discourse. This is why Foucault saw freedom as "living in the happy limbo of non-identity" (quoted in Grant 1993: 131). However, as Butler points out, *resistance to identity categories is not simply negative or destructive, but also creative and dynamic—as opening new spaces for the assertion of difference*. She argues that the rifts and resistance to group identities ought to be "safeguarded and prized" as emancipation from restrictive ontologies and as sites of "permanent openness" to multiple significations of difference (Butler 1992: 16).

A central idea here is that *identity is a construct of language, discourse, and cultural practices*. For example, one of the first questions asked when a baby is born is whether it is a boy or a girl. The answer to this question has significant implications for the life of the child from that day forward. What if our language only had the possibility of replying that the baby was a child? How different might children's lives be if sex distinctions were not part of their social reality? It is in this sense that Lacan and Derrida argue that categories of identity are part of a larger symbolic order—signs and symbols—that construct our notion of social reality through language. For a person to function adequately within any society, they must submit to certain linguistic rules that they learn as children in their acquisition of language. Emphasizing our unconscious acceptance and internalization of language, these theorists argue that we cease to see language as external to us—as a system that antedates us. We also cease to realize how much the *categories of language govern our sense of what is "real," "normal," or "natural."*

These theorists also highlight how *language governs our sense of difference* by the categories it uses. For example, the language of the Inuit can distinguish more than twenty different types of snow, while English is much more limited in this regard. Consequently, people who only learn English may have no sense of the reality of twenty varieties of snow. It is in this sense that these intellectuals argue that reality is discourse dependent. *Words do not represent or mirror reality; rather, they create and order our sense of reality.* For these theorists, whether there is a reality outside of language is in many ways a moot question because if reality eludes language, we cannot think, speak, or act upon it. However, we do have the possibility of deconstucting these social fictions and of creating counter discourses and practices that can challenge prevailing assumptions and open up new spaces for difference.

For Derrida, all meaning is relative and fleeting for it slides incessantly through the mechanism of *différance*, a linguistic principle combining "difference" and "deferral," which assumes that words only mean something by virtue of their difference from other words and that when one tries to establish the meaning of a sign, one is inevitably led to more and more signs (Derrida 1976: 1981). What Derrida's work offers to feminism is the understanding that the values attached to genders and sexualities can never be definitively fixed. The meanings associated with gender difference and the relations of power based upon it are floating signifiers for language's efforts to moor reality, which by definition are bound to fail. Gender difference is a matter of constant deferral; it is impossible to place it so unquestionably that it will be universally applicable to all cultures, places, times, and peoples (Cavallaro 2003: 28).

These understandings of discourse dependency have led feminists today to critically examine one of the more problematic assumptions of Western thought—its tendency to use binary or dualistic thought in categorizing people and things. Examples include the division of the sexes into male/female or of sexualities into heterosexual/homosexual. While these categories are used to define and distinguish one from the other, they are not just different; they are unequal; they entail hidden hierarchies where one side is privileged and the other is viewed as abject or lesser. There is also a sinister tendency to link up the lesser side of the binary with other demeaning or demonizing terms. For example, male/female is often linked to rational/irrational, culture/nature, order/chaos, and so forth. The method of deconstruction is a critical tool that dismantles this binary thinking by exposing its arbitrary, socially constructed nature.

These socially constructed category schemes also limit the possibilities for being; they preclude us from recognizing alternatives, such as the possibility of fluid sexualities that change over time or the multiple sexes discussed in chapter 1 (Fausto-Sterling 1998). It is for such reasons that theorists who embrace the post-perspectives often criticize identity politics. While some reject identity politics outright, others simply want to render identities as permanently open and contestable as to their meaning and political role (Seidman 2000: 441). Rather than viewing the affirmation of identities as politically liberating, these theorists view identities as merely reproducing and sustaining dominant discourses and regulatory power. Steven Seidman explains this well in his critique of the modern gay and lesbian movement and its politics. Because this movement uses affirmative identity politics (pro-gay and pro-lesbian identity politics) to fight for their civil rights, he argues that they actually reinforce rather than undermine the hegemonic discourse of binary thinking. They fall into the trap of legitimating the social fiction of treating heterosexuality and homosexuality as stable categories of identity. In contrast, Seidman (2000: 440) argues that to break out of these dualistic structures and to subvert them is to actually assert difference:

> I take as central to queer theory its challenge to what has been the dominant foundational concept of both homophobic and affirmative homosexual theory; the assumption of a homosexual subject or identity.

In feminist theory and practice these theoretical differences have created two opposing camps. On the one side are those feminists who embrace the postperspectives and their deconstruction of all group categories. On the other side are those feminists, such as radical feminists who use their group identity as women to motivate their politics and intersectionality theorists who believe that "the most profound and potentially the most radical politics come directly out of our own identities" (Combahee Collective [1977] 2005: 312–313). Feminists who embrace identity politics want to move from margin to center, while the post-perspectives critically position themselves politically on the margins as acts of resistance. As Butler (1992: 15) puts it:

> The point is not to stay marginal, but to participate in whatever network of marginal zones is spawned from other disciplinary centers and which, together, constitute a multiple displacement of those authorities.

Linda Alcoff refers to the divisions within feminism over identity politics as "The Identity Crisis in Contemporary Feminism" (1998). She discusses how the major underlying issue in this debate is how feminists can retain collective categories and avoid essentialism. In academic circles, postfeminism did not refer to the smug media claims of the 1980s that feminism was passé (see chapter 7) but, rather, to a series of debates about whether feminism could withstand the deconstructive critiques mounted by postmodernists and poststructuralists that virtually annihilated the group concept of "women" (Siegel 1997a: 53).

Epistemological Assumptions

As noted in chapter 1, a social constructionist approach is central to the assumptions of the postmodern epistemology that underlies both postmodernism and poststructuralism. Following in the philosophical tradition of such theorists as Friedrich Nietzche, they accept the view that if "the epistemological subject is necessarily situated, his [*sic*] knowledge is finite and thus no one perspective can exhaust the richness of reality" (quoted in Granier 1985: 190–191). Thus, a focus on situated knowledges, partial knowledges and their implications for multiple realities are lynchpins of this epistemological approach. Similar to the standpoint epistemologies discussed in chapters 4 and 5, these postperspectives share the view that knowledge is constructed by people situated in diverse social locations and that these social locations influence and limit their vantage points. Consequently, all perspectives are situated and partial.

However, the similarities stop here. In "Truth and Method: Feminist Standpoint Theory Revisited" (2004), Susan Hekman points out how in a postmodern epistemology no view is inherently superior to another. Any claim to having a clearer view of the truth is simply a master narrative—a partial perspective that assumes dominance and privilege. This leads to a position of **judgmental relativism** that contrasts sharply with most modern epistemological assumptions. Most modernists accept the notion of a material reality existing outside of an individual's subjectivity and a knowing, acting subject that seeks to better understand this reality. They believe in true or, at least, less false accounts of the world. In contrast, the postperspectives argue that the very notion of truth must be reevaluated and discarded. For them, reality is multiple and discourse-dependent. Discourse is the foundation of our notions of reality, and what can be known is known only through the subjectivities, interpretations, and narratives of diverse social actors. If all viewpoints are partial and limited, no one viewpoint can be given epistemic privilege over another. *Relativism and uncertainty prevail, resulting in a pluralism of vantage points and views* (Rosenau 1992: 22).

This world of plural constructions and diverse realities calls into question the entire edifice of conventional, modern science (Cheal 1991, 153–153). The most skeptical and nihilistic postmodernists argue that we can never know anything. For such skeptics, myth and magic are on the same footing as theory and empirical science—a position Pauline Rosenau (1992: 117–119) refers to as an "anything goes" methodology. However, there are less nihilistic postmodernists, whom Rosenau refers to as "affirmative postmodernists," who gravitate toward *local or mininarratives based on subjects' everyday life experiences or socially lived knowledge*. This preference for the personal and the local led feminist postmodernists and poststructuralists to be wary of theory as overly universalistic, totalistic, and stifling of difference (Grant 1993: 147).

In summary, the assumptions of a postmodern epistemology challenge fundamental features of modern thought. Their emphasis on socially lived knowledge and alternative ways of knowing not only provides an important critique of expert knowledge and dominant discourses, but it also empowers and gives voice to the subjugated knowledges of many who otherwise might remain silent. Yet some of the epistemological assumptions of these postperspectives have been very controversial for feminism. Some excellent books that address this topic include *Feminism/Postmodernism* edited by Linda Nicholson (1990), *Foucault and Feminism* by Lois McNay (1992) and *Up Against Foucault* (1993) edited by Caroline Ramazanoglu. Because poststructuralism has had the most significant impact on contemporary feminist thought of any of the postperspectives, some tensions between Foucault and feminism are examined below.

TENSIONS BETWEEN FOUCAULT AND FEMINISM

Although Foucault supported feminism as a political activist, his actual engagement with feminism in his theoretical writings was marginal. The glaring omission of any in-depth discussions of women in his voluminous writings—especially those on sexuality—have led some feminist critics to argue that such theoretical detachment veiled a male-centered outlook wherein feminist concerns were of little interest (Soper 1993). Other feminists argue that we cannot afford to ignore Foucault because so many features of his work parallel and challenge feminist concerns (Ramazanoglu 1993). The following sections examine how his treatment of knowledge and truth, power and identities, as well as his radical constructionist views on sex, sexuality, and bodies, have been particularly fertile grounds for new directions in feminist thought.

Knowledge and Truth

Ramazanoglu cites how Foucault's work is especially useful in pointing out how theories—even theories of emancipation—are blind to their own dominating tendencies. For example, Foucault's definition of discourse highlights how different ways of specifying knowledge and truth can both restrict and enable writing, speaking, thinking and acting. Thus, he highlights how *discourses and theories can both empower and constrain*. No doubt, theorists before Foucault discussed how the power of discourses is exercised by elites or officials through institutions, such as Marx's notion of ruling class ideologies. However, Foucault also shows how power lies *within* these discourses and the "truths" they claim. It is for this reason that Foucault ([1976] 1980: 93) asserts: "we cannot exercise power except through the production of truths." He offers a more politically laden view of theory, science, and truth in which "truth" becomes multiple and suspect:

> Truth isn't outside power. . . . Every society has its regime of truth, its general politics of truth: that is, the types of discourse which it accepts and makes function as "truth." (Quoted in Rainbow 1984: 73)

Clearly "truth was in trouble" after taking the postmodern turn, for under the assumptions of both postmodernism and poststructuralism there is no single truth, but many different truths situated in different discourses, some of which are more dominant than others (Gergen 1991).

In contrast, for most modern feminist theories, science and knowledge are important bases for determining the greater "truth" of different knowledge claims. Many feminists use theory and science to adjudicate between competing knowledge claims and to guide their political practice. Scientific knowledge is used to document patriarchal oppression and to empirically challenge claims that women are inferior to or less capable than men. Similarly, modern feminist theorists view knowledge as empowering and as providing the basis for reforming or transforming society in the interests of greater freedom and equality. For them knowledge means more freedom rather than more control (see chapter 1).

For postmodernists and poststructuralists this is a naive view of the relationship between knowledge and power. Feminists who embrace a modern, empiricist approach to science do not recognize that notions of what is "real" and what is "true" are not innocent but, rather, powerful discourses that silence or exclude alternative views (Flax 1992). Foucault's poststructuralist approach intentionally disturbs and upsets these naive and taken-for-granted assumptions. He teaches us to analyze discourses strategically, not in terms of what they say, but in terms of what they do and how they work (Halperin 1995: 30). This does not mean that we treat the content of discourses as irrelevant or uninteresting. After all one has to understand what discourses say in order to analyze what they do and how they work. It means that discourses and the "truths" they claim have to be fought for—not as issues of "truth" but as issues of political strategy:

> Establishing or adjudicating truth claims will not help us achieve a central feminist objective: to destroy all gender-based relations of domination. Claims about domination are claims about injustice and cannot be given extra force or justification by reference to Truth. Claims about injustice belong on the terrain of politics and in the realm of persuasive speech, action and (sometimes) violence. (Flax 1992: 459)

Similarly, Foucault argues that the truth or falsity of particular propositions should not distract us from the power effects they may produce or the manner in which they are deployed within social life. For example, discourses that foster the subordination of certain groups, such as racist or homophobic discourses, operate as part of more general and systematic strategies of delegitimation. Although many of the individual propositions that constitute them may be falsifiable, such discourses cannot be refuted simply on the basis of rational argument or empirical validity. Rather, because they constitute more general strategies of delegitimation, they must be resisted strategically—by fighting strategy with strategy (Halperin 1995: 31).

As one of these strategies, Foucault calls for the resuscitation of discourses that have been silenced or marginalized. He ([1976] 1980: 81–82) uses the term "**subjugated knowledges**" to refer to "whole sets of knowledges" that have been "buried," "disqualified," and/or taken less seriously by existing regimes of power. He also refers to them as "naive knowledges" not because he considers them naive, but because they have been treated as naive by dominant discourses. They have been located lower on the hierarchy of knowledges, beneath the levels of scientific cognition required by dominant forms. For Foucault, the *resuscitation of these subjugated knowledges* is a critical act: "It is through the reappearance of this knowledge, these local popular knowledges, these disqualified knowledges, that criticism performs its work" (81–82).

To their credit, U.S. feminists have been quite active in excavating and retrieving works by women writers that were previously buried or hidden from history. As noted in chapter 1, the modern women's movement transformed the canons of many disciplines. Many of "those damn scribbling women" that Nathaniel Hawthorne referred to with such contempt in the nineteenth century have now been recognized for their contributions. Although feminist thought historically has suffered the fate of being a subjugated discourse, it too has excluded and silenced the voices of others. To further understand Foucault's views on the complex and contradictory roles of discourse, the discussion now turns to a closer examination his analysis of power and discourse.

Power and Discourse

Modern theories of power and inequality tend to conceptualize power as something which an individual or a group either does or does not have—such as material, political, and institutional resources (Gatens 1992). Despite their variations and nuances, modern feminisms, such as liberal feminism, Marxist feminism, socialist feminism, and radical feminism, all hold these hierarchical, binary and top-down views of power. In contrast, the postperspectives call for the demise of binary and dualistic thinking. They do not accept that power operates only in binary, top-down and repressive ways. Rather power is viewed as dispersed and multidirectional. For example, although Foucault ([1976]1980: 100) alerted feminists to the power of discourses, he warned that "we must not imagine a world of discourse divided between accepted discourse and excluded discourse or between dominant discourse and the dominated one." Rather he envisions a more complex and decentralized scenario in which discourses produce and reinforce power but also undermine and expose it, rendering it fragile and capable of being thwarted. For Foucault (93), "power is everywhere" and can "even come from below."

Foucault's *movement away from top-down, hierarchical, and binary conceptions of power and oppression* has been especially difficult for many feminists to deal with because in most feminist frameworks patriarchy is conceptualized in a hierarchical, binary fashion as institutionalized male domination over women. Yet in volume 1 of *The History of Sexuality*, Foucault ([1976] 1980: 94) writes that

> there is no binary and all-encompassing opposition between rulers and ruled at the root of power relations and serving as a general matrix—no such duality extending from the top down and reacting on more and more limited groups to the very depths of the social body.

He further dereifies power by arguing that it is not something acquired, seized, or shared; nor is it a structure or an institution. Rather power is "exercised," and for Foucault, the question theorists should be asking is: *How*, that is, *by what means*, is power exercised? (Tremain 2005: 4). In turn, power is not only a repressive force but also a creative force; "*power also produces*" (Foucault [1976] 1980: 93). In particular, he discusses how the production of subjects and identities are developments fostered by the rise of the modern discourses of social science and medicine.

Foucault's work is primarily an investigation of modernity or "archaeology of modernity" that calls into question the Enlightenment version of history as progress toward ever greater human freedom (Foucault [1975] 1979). One of his major contributions was to show how the rise of democratic republics in the modern era was accompanied by the development of more subtle forms of power, control, and discipline than those used in premodern societies that were based on visible, absolute forms of power. He terms the latter "spectacle societies" because the power of absolute monarchs was manifest in their might and awe—their power over life and death. Of particular interest to feminism is the way Foucault wove an analysis of "bodies" into these discussions of power relations. For example, in *Discipline and Punish* ([1975] 1979), Foucault depicts how torture and harsh punishments in the premodern era reflected a public display of power on the bodies of subjects. Not only were hangings or death by the guillotine public spectacles attended by the masses, but these forms of punishment literally inscribed power onto bodies. As Foucault writes: torture "must mark the victim; it is intended either by the scar it leaves on the body or by the spectacle that accompanies it, to brand the victim with infamy. It traces around or rather on the very body of the condemned man signs that cannot be effaced" (179).

By contrast, in modernity such public executions and torture are largely replaced by more effective forms of socialization and self-inscription where discipline produces "subjected and practiced bodies" or what he often calls 'docile bodies'" (182). Foucault refers to modern, democratic societies as "disciplinary" or "surveillance" societies because they entail subtle forms of control that are directed toward the management of life processes—of bodies as a biological organisms and populations as living, social bodies. This new management of life processes is described by Foucault ([1976] 1980: 140) as **biopower**, which refers to the practice of modern states and their regulation of subjects through an "explosion of numerous and diverse techniques" for achieving the control of bodies and populations. These subtle techniques of control were fostered by the rise of the new scientific discourses about human beings, such as the social sciences and modern medicine that specified, for example, which bodies were normal or abnormal, natural or unnatural, sane or insane. These discourses also scientifically categorized and delineated the differences between bodies—such as the differences between the sexes, the races, or the able-bodied and the disabled. These differences then became the bases by which people came to identify themselves and to distinguish themselves from others.

One of the major goals of both *Discipline and Punish* (1975) and the first volume of *The History of Sexuality* (1976) was to "create a history of the different modes by which, in our culture, human beings are made subjects" (Foucault quoted in Arney and Bergen 1984: 4). Yet, in Foucault's analysis, when human beings are "made subjects" they are also *subjected*, that is, constructed as objects of power (Miller 2008: 252; his emphasis). One of the hallmarks of modernity is how people become of interest to the new sciences and their lives became the object of observations, documentation, and control. These new discourses of the human sciences used the technique of surveillance (hierarchical empirical observation) to provide ever more detailed documentation of people's lives (such as births, deaths, and marriages as well as conduct and morals). They also compared and judged each individual against some scientific standard of normalcy (253). Often in the guise of care and reform, people were observed, tested, and measured, such as through the use of medical or educational tests, to determine normalcy. In this process, identities were created—we were male or female, black or white, heterosexual or homosexual, above or below average intelligence, and so forth. In our everyday lives we monitored ourselves and each other on the bases of these identities. Normal and above normal people tend to receive social approbation while the abnormal often are targets for exclusion, improvement, or correction (Foucault [1975] 1979:191).

These new discourses "cast a net of surveillance and control over the whole population in the name of science" (Miller 2008: 254). This invisible net of a more fluid form of power—power as discourse—flowed in many directions and came from many sources appearing from everywhere and nowhere. What these discourses produced were docile bodies—calculable, manageable, self-monitoring bodies. This is what Foucault meant by saying that we must cease to describe the effects of power in negative terms as simply repressive or restrictive (Foucault [1975] 1979: 194). Foucault also called for a broader notion of government that would be understood to refer to *any form of activity that aims to shape, guide, or affect the conduct of people*. Thus, government includes not only state-generated prohibitions and punishments and global networks of social, economic, and political stratification but also normalizing technologies that facilitate the systematic objectification of some subjects as abnormal as well as the techniques of self-improvements, such as psychotherapy, rehabilitation, and fitness (or beauty) regimes designed to make the abnormal normal (Tremain 2005: 8).

Because power produces the regimes of truth, difference, and normalcy by which we construct our identities, it is not surprising that Foucault rejects identity politics and any notion of identities as the modus operandi for emancipatory politics. For him, identities reduce freedom rather than liberate. For example, if people define themselves as heterosexuals, there are a whole range of sexual practices that they cannot engage in without violating this category of identity. Moreover, the identities created by modern scientific discourses induce people to discipline themselves—to engage in forms of self-policing that regulate their behavior in keeping with the normative guidelines of these discourses. Whether we are fully aware of it or not, we police ourselves in a multitude of interactions we have with others. Rather than the binary and hierarchical views of power that characterize most earlier theoretical analyses, Foucault focuses on these diffuse and microlevel powers that operate in everyday life. While he recognizes macrolevel forms of power, he alerts us to micro powers that also "come from below" (Foucault [1976] 1980: 94).

Riki Wilchins's "A Certain Kind of Freedom: Power and the Truth of Bodies" in *Genderqueer: Voices from Beyond the Sexual Binary* (Nestle, Howell and Wilchins 2002) provides a number of excellent examples of Foucault's view that power comes from everywhere and even from below. Wilchins interweaves Foucault's theoretical insights into her own personal narrative of living as a male-to-female (mtf) trans person. She describes being rebuffed not only by the general public but also by feminists—both gay and straight. These experiences made her especially aware of the narrowness and inflexibility of existing feminist discourses on women's bodies. She discusses how the power of discourses on bodies, sex, and gender was ubiquitous in her everyday life interactions. It was present in the ways people looked at her and responded to her even while she was doing simple and innocuous tasks, such as purchasing a newspaper or sitting on a bus. Wilchins (2002: 51) enables us to understand that the words and meanings given to our bodies, sex, and gender are not simply semantical issues but, rather, "powerful tools for making us experience the world in very specific ways." She describes the power of discourse as—the kind of "small power exercised in hundreds of everyday transactions" (51):

> As good progressives, when we think of Power, we imagine something above us, overwhelming, and harsh that we need laws to rein in. This works well with big, institutional power, like the police powers of arrest, the power of courts, and the government's power to spy on us or restrict our speech. But that kind of power doesn't go very far in explaining . . . (reactions to) my body. After all, there was no central registry tracking me, no government agency compelling my experiences. For that kind of power, we need another model: discourse.

Wilchins also critiques the tendencies of modern Western thought to use binary thinking and to demand a single truth—tendencies that act as "a kind of intellectual fascism that squeezes out individual truths" and "stamp out difference" (39 and 41). Instead she calls for the recognition of multiple truths about bodies, sex, gender, and desire as well as the need to uproot the tyranny of binary thinking that molds people into narrow, fictional, and outdated categories. In place of these outdated categories she offers the notion of "genderqueerness" to challenge the constraints of normative views of sex, gender, sexual practices, and sexuality.

Modern Techniques of Power

A number of feminist scholars have found Foucault's discussion of various techniques of power quite useful. One technique Foucault highlights is the **confessional**, a metaphor for the way in which modern societies use various types of self-confession to elicit information and to keep people within normative guidelines. It can take many forms, such as interrogations, interviews, or consultations. Examples of this include doctor/patient relations, psychological therapies, and teacher/student relations, where the authority figure interprets the confessed information to judge, punish, forgive, console, or rehabilitate the other. While these social relations often appear as innocent or directed toward the care of others, for Foucault they are rituals that always unfold within power relations. Some feminists have used this notion of the confessional to examine how feminism itself entails discourses of power and control over women (Dent 1995; see chapter 7).

The terms **panopticon** or *gaze* are used by Foucault to describe another modern technique of normative discursive power. To illustrate this technique, he describes Jeremy Bentham's architectural design for the Panopticon—a model nineteenth-century prison where security was efficiently maintained. Here a few guards, located within a circular structure at the center of the prison, high above the view of the prisoners, could gaze down upon the inmates and their activities. Whether or not guards were present, the effect was to "induce in the prisoners a state of conscious and permanent visibility that assured the automatic functioning of power." In *Discipline and Punish* ([1975] 1979: 201) Foucault describes how "each becomes to himself his own jailer."

The structure and effects of the panopticon resonate throughout modern society in schools, factories, prisons, and asylums. For example, Foucault discusses how in modern schools students are spatially located so that teachers or professors (usually located higher up at the front behind a podium) can view the entire classroom in one glance. Similarly, factory workers are centralized in large factories where managers can oversee many workers at once. These modern techniques of power and surveillance discipline the body to be both productive and docile. They also are forms of social control that require less direct force or violence:

> There is no need for arms, physical violence, material constraints, just a gaze. An inspecting gaze, a gaze which each individual under its weight will end up interiorising to the point that he is his own overseer, each individual exercising this surveillance over, and against himself. (Foucault ([1975] 1979: 155)

It is important to note here that, in contrast to postmodernists, for Foucault discourse is not foundational. Rather, it is one of many interrelated modes by which power is manifest. Equally important for him are "the institutional and everyday practices by which our experience of the body is organized," including "the spatial and temporal organizing of schools and prisons, the confessional mode between physicians and patients . . . and so forth" (Bordo 1993: 292). Foucault gave sustained attention to the themes of institutional power in his early works and in some of his works that postdate *The History of Sexuality*. As other writers have noted, his view that "power was everywhere" was a discussion of the power of discourses found in liberal, democratic regimes and should not be "decontextualized" or have the specific "historical context minimized" (Collins 1998: 135; Halperin 1995: 18).

In "Foucault, Femininity and the Modernization of Patriarchal Power," Sandra Lee Bartky (1997) uses Foucault's notion of the "panopticon" to explore how women have internalized standards of femininity and beauty. Bartky argues that by adhering to disciplinary practices, such as dieting, body sculpting exercises, and/or using cosmetics and cosmetic surgery, women not only police themselves but also collude in their own subordination. She describes the Foucaultian "gaze" as follows: "A panoptical male connoisseur resides within the consciousness of most women: They stand perpetually before his gaze and under his judgment"

(101). Like Foucault, Bartky does not treat patriarchal power as a binary form of oppression but, rather, as a more diffuse and ubiquitous set of decentralized forces. When she asks who the disciplinarians of femininity and beauty ideals are, her reply echoes Foucault:

> The disciplinary power that inscribes femininity on the female body is everywhere and it is nowhere; the disciplinarian is everyone and yet no one in particular. (103)

Indeed, the sources of disciplinary power in regard to femininity and beauty ideals are many and diverse. They include magazines, billboards, films, and television—indeed virtually every media outlet. We also learn femininity and beauty ideals from our parents, friends, lovers, and even strangers. The disciplinarians are ubiquitous and diffuse—everywhere and nowhere in particular (103).

Despite Bartky's poststructuralist analysis of power and its techniques, she sounds more like a modernist when she writes: "We are born male or female, but not masculine or feminine." Here she treats sex as a biological given and femininity as a cultural artifice or "an achievement" (95). This distinction between sex and gender was typical of modern feminist thought in the 1960s and 1970s. By contrast, poststructuralism goes further to argue that both sex and gender are social constructs, as shall be shown below.

Sex, Sexuality, and Deconstructing the "Natural"

For Foucault, notions of *sex and sexuality are historically specific constructions.* People are not naturally anything nor do they have any essential features in this regard. Rather we are socially constructed selves that also are historically variable. Foucault's investigations into sexual practices in antiquity were particularly insightful in demonstrating how sexual practices had very different meanings and interpretations from those of today. For example, when he discusses the sexual practices of free, male citizens in Greece in the fourth century B.C., one is struck by the relative absence of official (legal, moral, or juridical) controls on sexual behavior. People conducted themselves properly in sexual matters neither because the law enjoined them to do so, nor because of deep-seated conceptions of sin or evil (McHoul and Grace 1993). Good living and good sexual conduct were more a question of the everyday care and mastery of the self. For example, Foucault discusses how masturbation was not viewed as sinful, evil, or against any law. Rather it was viewed as a waste, a lack of moderation. In sexual practices, moderation not only suggested mastery of one's self, but it also enhanced the pleasure of the act. That is, too much—even of a good thing—lessened the quality of the experience.

One of the major purposes of Foucault's historical investigations was to overturn the conception that sexuality was a human constant so as to liberate analyses of sexuality from the notion of the "ahistorical desiring man" (Foucault [1976] 1980: 5). Through these investigations, he also invites the reader to define life as "aesthetics" or "life as a work of art":

> What strikes me is the fact that in our society, art has become something which is related only to objects, not to individuals or to life. . . . But couldn't everyone's

> life become a work of art? . . . From the idea that the self is not given to us, I think there is only one practical consequence: we have to create ourselves as a work of art. (Quoted in Rainbow 1984: 350)

For Foucault, viewing life in this manner also suggests *new ways of defining sexual practices—not as acts conceived in scientific or reproductive terms—but more as forms of eroticism or bodily acts that give rise to pleasures.* Here the focus is on the erotic; these bodily pleasures can be many and can vary from individual to individual—providing a more open and creative notion of sexuality. Such insights are supportive not only of those who by choice resist or violate normative sexual practices but, also, of those who by necessity must creatively address their sexual practices. For example, studies of the sexual practices of the severely disabled have shown how they engage in erotic sexual practices that differ from the normative association of sexual practices with the genitalia (Wilkerson 2002, Shuttleworth 2004, Siebers 2008, Volion 2010). As Shelley Tremain's anthology *Foucault and the Government of Disability* (2005) reveals, scholars in disability studies have found Foucault's poststructuralist approach to bodies fruitful for articulating a wide range of issues that concern the disabled, including the very notions of what is meant by bodily impairments and disability (see Box 6.1).

BOX 6-1

Foucault and the Government of Disability

Foucault was the first (or, the most persuasive at least) to describe how, through a supposed knowledge of the "normal case" differences among people became targets of power. . . . The idea of perversion was one of the first ideas to surface from the medicalization of sexuality in the nineteenth century. . . . Sexual perversions are not medical discoveries about human nature, but are rather artifacts implanted among us by the experts who "know." A version of this claim has been made for so-called impairments, which, it is argued, are constructed or artifactual (Tremain 2005). The argument that impairment is implanted undercuts the assumption that impairment is a physiological condition distinct from (yet somehow underlying) disability. From the World Health Organization (1980), to Disabled Peoples' International (1982), to the Americans with Disabilities Act (1990), an impairment is understood as an individual's deviation from a biomedical norm. . . .

Impairment, like perversion (and disability), is not something missing, not a lack or absence; it is something added, an unasked-for supplement, contributed by disciplinary knowledge and power. It is as impossible for a person to be "impaired" without reference to a statistically constructed "normal case" as for a person to be criminal except by reference to the law. A discourse about bio-medical norms, scientific though it may be, is not more true to nature, or physically true, than a discourse about criminals. Any norm is an artifact of the discipline that measures it, and has no physical being or reality apart from that practice.

Impairment is real (as real as crimes or money), though not a naturally given abnormality, but rather an artifact of the knowledge that measures the deviation from the norm. Norms and normal cases are like statutory laws and criminals. They exist, they are real, that is, effective, but only because people agree to take them seriously as objects of knowledge. . . . Impairment has no reality apart from the social mathematics of normalizing judgment. A hearing child who grows up on an island of the deaf would not notice its people's difference "from the human norm." In a world arranged to accommodate differences, it is not an impairment.

Excerpt from "Foucault's Nominalism," by Barry Allen. From pp. 93–95 of *Foucault and the Government of Disability*, edited by Shelley Tremain (Ann Arbor: University of Michigan Press, 2005).

Such examples illustrate how Foucault's excursions into antiquity and his archaeology of modernity are very much part of his "ontology of the present" because they bear on the conditions under which we operate today and might yet operate in the future as social beings. His insistence on debunking many of our most cherished assumptions about the social world—especially those that expose seemingly natural categories as social constructs—is widely recognized as one of his greatest overall contributions (Jones and Porter 1994: 5; McWhorter 1999: 36). In turn, his hostility to the "truths" of the human sciences that attempt to construct our identities and to label what is normal or natural not only alerts us to the damage done by privileged discourses, but it also helps foster a healthy skepticism that the social world can be otherwise. Indeed, Foucault has been referred to as the "philosopher of the otherwise" precisely because he makes us realize how variable and diverse social constructions of what is "natural" have been historically (McHoul and Grace 1993: 125). Thinking otherwise or the critical act of considering alternative possibilities by thinking against the grain of normalizing practices is central to Foucault's view of philosophy:

> What is philosophy today—philosophical activity, I mean—if it is not the critical work that thought brings to bear on itself? In what does it consist, if not in the endeavor to know how and to what extent it might be possible to think differently, instead of legitimating what is already known? (Foucault 1986: 8–9)

Is the Subject "Dead"?

Critics argue that that poststructuralism and postmodernism lead to the "death of the subject" and to a nihilistic approach to politics. Whereas modern thought posits a subject who confronts, resists, shapes, or transforms institutional or political fields, the postperspectives argue that power already exists at the level at which the subject and its agency are constructed and made possible. For example, feminist poststructuralist Judith Butler (1990) rejects the notion that gender is a role that expresses an interior "self." Rather gender is a performance:

> One is not simply a body, but, in some very key sense, one does one's body and, indeed, one does one's body differently from one's contemporaries and from one's embodied predecessors and successors as well. (272)

In *Feminism after Postmodernism?* (2000), Marysia Zalewski provides some useful metaphors that may help readers to distinguish between the modern and postmodern views of the self. She suggests that modern notions of the self are similar to an apple that has a solid core. In contrast, postmodern views of the self are more like an onion, which after peeling back all of the layers reveals no core—no doer behind the deed. In the same way that an onion is stripped of its layers, individuals' identities can be deconstructed down to a number of discourses or scripts that when performed construct the individual. For theorists who have taken the postmodern turn, *there is no core self, identity, or subject who acts to express herself or himself, but, rather, performances or actions create the interior self.*

Critics argue that if subjects are themselves constituted by matrices of power and discourses, there is no human agency upon which to base politics and resistance to power (O'Neill 1995). For scholars drawing on Foucault's work, the question of agency—of the actor's autonomy or freedom to resist, to refuse, or to change the way he/she is constructed through dominant discourses was a concern. Here again the question arose: without a core self how can a subject act?[2] This question was raised most urgently by feminist scholars who felt the oppressive weight of "policing," especially over their bodies and sexualities (Miller 2008: 257). Whereas some feminist scholars scorned Foucault for the death of the subject (Moi 1985), others recognized how his critique resonated with their own silenced lives. Those who embraced his writings pointed out how he always insisted that whenever power was exercised, resistance also was present (Foucault [1976] 1980: 12). Moreover, dominant discourses and knowledges maintain their power by means of an ongoing struggle—not a fait accompli. Foucault's notion of "subjugated" or "naive" knowledges suggests that other ways of knowing and speaking—the voices of subordinate groups—were not absent but, rather, pushed to the margins (Foucault 83). As noted earlier, the excavation and retrieval of these subjugated knowledges is itself a form of resistance:

> This interpretation [of resistance] fragmented the earlier, totalizing sense of discourse attributed to Foucault and produced a picture of "truth" as the product of ongoing contestation between dominant discourses and marginalized ones. In all, it turned the earlier reading of Foucault on its head, and for some scholars amounted to a call to empower the silenced voice of the underdog. (Miller 2008: 258)

Feminist scholars have used such ideas of resistance to pioneer new directions in feminist thought. The deconstruction of dominant and essentialist discourses as well as the resuscitation of subjugated knowledges has proliferated among feminists scholars. Despite criticisms that the postperspectives lead to the death of the subject, there appears to be ample room in these approaches for social agency and resistance. As Butler (1992: 15) points out, to take the construction of the subject as a political problematic does not mean to negate or dismiss the subject. It means to call into question and to open up this term to expose its multiplicity (15). Rather than the death of the subject, the deconstruction of the subject is designed to foster more freedom.

L'ÉCRITURE FÉMININE AND WRITING THE BODY BY DIMITRA CUPO

The French academic tradition of the 1960s produced the writings of Jacques Lacan, Jacques Derrida, and Michel Foucault and a new theoretical lens through which social thought made a monumental shift toward an emphasis on the inter-workings of power, discourse, and language. Among the most influential French feminist thinkers to come out of this theoretical and historical juncture were Luce Irigaray, Julia Kristeva, and Hélène Cixous. While there are important differences between them, each writer took up the task of explaining what this paradigm shift might mean for women when examined through a feminist lens. While coming to terms with a differently situated "subject," that is, a subject constituted by power, discourse, and language, these "French Feminists" looked at the effects of masculinist, phallocentric discourse on women's lives, bodies, and desires.

We might say that, as a group, the French Feminists found that the whole of culture, philosophy, literature, and language was built on the exclusion of women, specifically, the suppression of women's speech and the negation of women's sexuality and desire. For these writers, psychoanalysis offered the most promising space from which to reclaim a positive femininity because it offers a theory on the prelinguistic development of self and desire. They felt there is a possibility before women learn language (developed by men) and before women learn the allowable forms of desire (conceived by men) that an authentic female experience of self and desire can exist. The entirety of the problem that women face according to the French Feminists is with language, symbolic systems, and even philosophy itself (Moi 1991, Cavallaro 2003). The solution therefore involves bringing women's experience to writing, encouraging women to use the flawed and male-biased language system to speak about their own lives and bodies. This practice of women writing for themselves, or **écriture féminine**, is fundamental to uncovering a pre-patriarchal femininity.

The roots of the French Feminists' theoretical lens lay with Jacques Lacan, who, while writing a critique of Freudian psychoanalysis, articulated a philosophy built around one's emergence into language and, by extension, the social world. He emphasized the role of language in the formation of the unconscious (Phoca and Wright 1999) and the structuring of what we are allowed to say and therefore what we may think or dream or desire. Emphasizing that language is the most fundamental of all social institutions (Evans 1996), he believed that our coming to language is what makes us "subjects" or social actors. As a psychoanalyst, Lacan focused on the special significance that mother–infant relationships have in the development of the "self." Initially, there is no real distinction for the baby between self and mother (Hill 2009); since this is a time before visual acuity and verbal skills, other people (and therefore language) are unnecessary. This initial phase must soon be replaced by the young child's entrance into the world beyond the mother, as he or she must learn the rules of the social universe and thus become a part of the larger symbolic order. In order to do this, individuals must master the network that connects each to the other; that is, we must accept and learn to work within language.

The poststructuralist emphasis on language was shaped also by Ferdinand de Saussure's notion of language as a closed network of deferred meaning (Lemert 2004). Saussure's theory posits that words are not really descriptive in that they do not report on the empirical world. Rather, language is a system that sets up differences whereby meaning is conferred through conceptual contrast. We know what "blue" is only from knowing that it is not quite green or purple. Thus, we can say that language does not actually have positive terms (Salih 2002: 31). Concepts are defined negatively; they can be precise only in being what other concepts are not (Saussure in Lemert 2004:156).

Building on this idea, Jacques Derrida wrote about the "politics" of well-known and often used dualities or "binaries." A binary is a twofold concept, each part relying on the other for its own definition (good/evil for example). Derrida found that binaries are inherently hierarchical and that certain terms are denigrated in order to privilege their counterparts (Grosz 1994). He found that binaries do not innocently describe two things in relation to each other, as in objectively comparing and contrasting two phenomena. Rather, when a binary describes *one* thing, it does so by expelling and subordinating that which it is not and in so doing establishes a border and privileges one term (Grosz 1994). For example, "chaos" must exist around "order" to understand the very concept of "order"—that "order" is fundamentally the absence of "chaos." In another example, "passion" must be held in the mind in order to fully understand what is meant by "reason"—reason is defined as the positive counterpart to the excesses and negativity that exist in the notion of "passion." Similarly, thought the French Feminists, "woman" as a concept exists as the denigrated counterpart to "man." Building on these theoretical precursors, the French Feminists found that law itself, even the idea of "order," was built on the radical denigration, suppression, and ultimate exclusion of women's bodies, desires, and experiences.

In *Speculum of the Other Woman* (1974) and *This Sex Which Is Not One* (1977), Luce Irigaray makes the case that women's sexuality is not understandable within the phallic symbolic economy that we live within and speak through. For her, a woman's very anatomy challenges the phallocentric notion that there is one sexual organ and that sexual activity has a beginning and an end. Instead, women's genitals consist of two lips that are continuously in contact, always actively caressing each other such that women do not distinguish activity from passivity or one from two (Irigaray 1977). A woman's erogenous zones exist along her entire body and resist the phallic definition of sex that it is the penis that begins and ends a sexual act. Instead, women's sexuality is far more rich and complex than this linear notion can capture. Since women's sexual organs are not one, they are mistakenly counted as none, a hole, or a lack, as they cannot be defined or represented within this signifying system (Irigaray 1977). She also notes that women's anatomy is much more compatible to the concepts of nearness, multiplicity, and unity—notions which are in stark contrast to the familiar phallic notions of separation, division, and possession—concepts which pervade our laws, our economy, even the understanding of our own bodies. Because our ideology and social structure were founded on the exclusion of women, women cannot be represented by this masculinist way of thinking.

According to Irigaray, phallocentric discourse has reduced the differences between the sexes into only one sex, the masculine and its necessary negative counterpart—the feminine. Therefore, our signifying system does not represent two sexes; instead, it silences and reduces the feminine into the masculine. The feminine has been "constructed and defined by the laws, logic, orders, institutions, and language designed by men for men's use" ([1977] 1985: 86). Indeed, she finds a masculine bias and phallocentrism in the entire literary tradition of the Western canon. She concludes that all literature, law, social structure, and language rest upon the curious absence of a positive maternal force or, more sinisterly, the purposeful death of the feminine force. Take for example, the Judeo-Christian "God the Father" and his only "Son," with a "holy spirit" completing the well-known trinity. Noticeably absent here is an equally powerful maternal or feminine force. According to Irigaray, in order for the maternal force to reclaim its rightful position in what is an overwhelmingly patriarchal world, we must go back to a place not only before monotheistic religions but also before language and even logic.

Similarly, Julia Kristeva finds that our logical and ordered world is skewed toward male-centered explanations that erase many of women's experiences. In *Desire in Language* (1977) and *Powers of Horror* (1980), she rejects the patriarchal ideas of division and exclusion required by current formulations of logic. For example, she replaces the familiar phrase of "one *or* the other" with the unifying and simultaneity of "one *and* the other" (Phoca and Wright 1999). She uses this phrase to capture uniquely female experiences, such as the time before mother and child are separate, when one pregnant woman is also two people. For her, this is an example of how masculinist discourse has advanced a certain political agenda on the world demanding order, separation, and classification and how a different arrangement of terms (an alternate "logic") is possible when women's experiences are included. She finds that the "logic" of patriarchy, the rule of the father, has been erected against the life, the body, the desires, and even the very acknowledgment of the mother (Kristeva 1977). Upon entering the symbolic order of language, one must repress the experience, knowledge of and intimacy with the mother. This repression later manifests itself in "slippages" or contradictions in meaning or gaps in our explanations. Writing (poetics) is the place for women to challenge these erasures that deny the power of the mother.

Hélène Cixous shares the view that resistance to male domination is possible in language. For Cixous, it is writing as a woman, bringing one's experience as a woman to the writing process, or *l'écriture féminine*, that carries the possibility of asserting a positive femininity. In "The Laugh of the Medusa" (1975), she advocated the exploration of female desire as an act of resistance against what male domination has made of women's bodies and desires. Out of such a transformational reaffirmation of women's pleasure, we may "come" to writing (Gilbert 1986:

xv). She argues for a celebration of unity and multiplicity over and against the division and separation (wrongly and violently) imposed upon women since the "erection" of male-dominated culture. Cixous's notion of "writing the body" makes the case that our bodies are the space from which to argue for what has been silenced and violently erased in how language, "the Word," structures the world and our ability to make sense of it. When women write their lived experience, it is an act of liberation from the oppressive discourse that is all culture and economy and politics (Cixous 1975). As women do this, they necessarily challenge all things that rely on masculine ideology. She argues for a revalidation and valorization of the workings, intricacies, and mysteries of the female body and in doing so has been criticized for relying on outdated notions of essentialism (Moi 1991, Gilbert 1986). To her credit, she affirms that her notion of *l'écriture féminine*, or the act of writing in "white ink," is a political strategy and not a statement of biological essences (Gilbert 1986: xv). Rather, it is a strategic move that is necessary to right the wrongs of male domination and female oppression.

Feminine writing cannot be defined within our phallocentric system because it surpasses our modes of thinking and our current organization of concepts that represent only the masculine. Feminine writing—by women and about women—exists outside of this and necessarily threatens to dismantle it all. Women writing about their sexuality, their desire, and their bodies are most subversive and threatening because a positive female sexuality cannot even be conceptualized by a system and a language and a culture built by men in the service of male desires (Cixous 1975).

In a broad sense, the French Feminists attempted to place women in the subject position within a system of language and discourse that excluded and denied them. They sought to reclaim the idea of a feminine force that was not a patriarchal construct. They felt that women's sexuality needed to be reclaimed and articulated from the point of view of a female "subject." By doing so, the French Feminists emphasized the differences between men and women in their search for what could be a positive feminine space within what language allows us to say and what symbolic systems allow us to think (Moi 1991, Phoca and Wright 1999). For these reasons, one might argue that their woman-centered writings reflect a postmodern version of radical feminism.

THE BASICS OF QUEER THEORY

Queer theory emerged in the early 1990s as an interdisciplinary synthesis of poststructuralism, feminist theory, and gay and lesbian studies. While queer theory built on each of these bodies of thought, it also pushed them in new conceptual directions that would place sexuality, and particularly the origins and consequences of *sexual norms*, at the center of analysis.

Although queer theorists were heavily influenced by poststructuralism and its fluid notions of identity and power, they also recognized that poststructuralists had not analyzed the profound role played by sexuality in the ongoing production of social meaning. Extending poststructuralist concepts, queer scholars revealed that sexuality was, in fact, central to binary systems of thought and the invention of the modern "subject" (Rubin 1984). In contrast with poststructuralism, feminist theory had long been directly engaged with issues of sex and sexuality but primarily through the lens of men's subordination of women and women's resistance to that subordination. Queer scholars noted that this focus, while of vital importance, left little room for attention to gender and sexual fluidity, especially as manifested in nonheterosexual forms. And finally, lesbian and gay studies had taken up the crucial work of documenting lesbian and gay history, politics, and subculture, but it too often assumed a clear and stable line between heterosexuals and homosexuals. This notion of a rigid heterosexual/homosexual binary, still believed by many people (of various sexual identifications) to be a simple matter of biology, is challenged by queer theory's emphasis on the fluidity and historical and social construction of sexualities. According to queer theorists, and as explained later in this chapter, homosexuality and heterosexuality do not refer to "real" aspects of the self or to a quantifiable set of (hetero- or homo-) sexual acts but to the specific *discourses* used to classify and regulate sexual practices in a given time and place.

Queer Theory's Feminist Foremothers

Though queer theory breaks from feminist theory on a few important fronts that are discussed later in this chapter, queer paradigms owe a considerable debt to feminist theory and in many ways have evolved in continuity with feminist thought. Long before the emergence of queer theory, feminist scholars had examined the social construction of gender and had drawn attention to a binary gender system that positioned women as deviant, or "Other," vis-à-vis a male ideal (de Beauvoir 1952). This argument that gender (and sexuality) are socially produced and used as instruments of power is foundational to queer theory. Lesbian feminists also wrote prolifically about the ways that patriarchal culture attempted to foreclose lesbian desire and reproduce heterosexuality in the service of men's control of women, a body of writing that laid the groundwork for queer analyses of **heteronormativity** (Rich 1980). And throughout the 1980s, womanists of color in the United States and postcolonial feminists around the globe contested the existence of universal truths about womanhood, emphasizing instead the ways that women's complex subjectivities are shaped by multiple, fluid, and intersecting forms of consciousness, experience, and oppression (Davis 1981, Anzaldúa 1987, Mohanty 1984, Minh-ha 1989). These intersectional challenges to singular and universal conceptualizations of identity would also become a crucial referent for queer scholars engaged in rethinking the meaning and effects of sexual identities.

Given the strong relationship between many feminist projects and the aims of queer theory, it should come as little surprise, then, that the term "queer theory" was first articulated by feminist film theorist Teresa de Lauretis, whose own path to queer theory was guided by "questions about the ability of women to speak about and otherwise represent themselves . . . in a social and political order that took little account of women" (Turner 2000: 5). Although de Lauretis's scholarship had been focused primarily on issues of feminist representation, she recognized—as did Eve Sedgwick, Gloria Anzaldúa, Judith Butler, Gayle Rubin and other feminists who would shape the field of queer theory—the complex connections between feminist theoretical problems and questions of gender transgression and queer sexualities. Yet, at the same time, queer theory's feminist foremothers also took note of the limitations of the feminist canon. With its focus on *women* and *lesbians*, feminist studies had failed to fully address matters of gender ambiguity, cross-gender identification, gender performativity, the social construction of gendered bodies, and the diversity of nonnormative sexualities not easily classified as lesbian or gay. These subjects would become the focus of the new and feminist-infused field of queer theory.

The Politics and Premises of Queer Theory

Queer theory, like feminist theory, is a deeply political enterprise, one that evolved from the belief that we must acknowledge, celebrate, and preserve sexual difference. Just as feminist theory feeds into, and is inspired by, grassroots feminist activism, queer theory also exists in a dynamic relationship with the on-the-ground political work of lesbian, gay, bisexual, and transgender (LGBT) activists. In the 1970s, gay liberation activists expanded the concept of "the political" by exposing the powerful impact that queer embodiment and performance, such as drag, could have on the broader culture and its taken-for-granted ideas about the "nature" of male and female bodies. Later, in the 1980s and 1990s, queer activists risked violence and arrest to demand that the U.S. government not only respond to the growing AIDS crisis but also inform the public that the exchange of bodily fluids, not homosexuality, was to blame for the spread of HIV. In these examples, many lesbian and gay activists were informed by an emerging body of queer scholarship that had begun to theorize the difference between sexual and gendered practices, identities, and bodies; meanwhile, queer theorists took inspiration from the protest strategies and artistic and subcultural projects in which lesbian, gay, bisexual, and transgendered people were engaged.

Perhaps the most important thing to understand about the term *queer*, as queer theorists articulate it, is that it is not a synonym for LGBT identity or a reference to nonheterosexuality. Instead, **queer** is a critique of all things oppressively *normal*, especially conventional ideas about sex; it also is an embrace of sexual and gender *difference*. By most accounts, queer theory emerged as a body of scholarship in the early 1990s. In the influential anthology *Fear of a Queer Planet*, queer theorist Michael Warner (1993: xxvi) proclaimed that the term queer "rejects . . . simple political interest representation in favor of a more thorough resistance to regimes of the normal" and "defin(es) itself against the normal rather than the heterosexual." Similarly, in her influential essay "Making it Perfectly Queer," queer theorist Lisa Duggan (1992: 15) explained that within queer theory, "the rhetoric of difference replaced the more assimilationist liberal emphasis on similarity to other groups." In other words, queerness is not about taking a stand against heterosexual desire, nor is it about being an average, respectable gay or lesbian citizen who lives just like her or his heterosexual counterparts. Instead, it is about resisting the cultural and institutional forces that attempt to make *all people* conform to normal, or "straight," ways of life, such as "settling down," getting married, having children, and aspiring to be just like everybody else.

In fact, this critique of **normativity**—or "conventional forms of association, belonging, and identification" (Halberstam 2005: 4)—can be understood as the first major premise of queer theory. Queer theorists recognize that the requirements for being normal hinge directly upon rigid ideas about gender and sexuality, including the dictate to organize our lives around monogamous marriage, nuclear family, and a gendered division of labor. Most of us are taught that mature and decent people are those who grow up, enter a monogamous marriage (ideally with a person of the opposite sex), keep their sexuality private, avoid risks, and strive to make as much money as they can so as to buy material objects for their families. As discussed later in this chapter, queer theory refuses the notion that these choices are the most fulfilling and politically responsible ways to connect with other people and instead celebrates alternative ways of life, such as subcultural engagement, nonmonogamy, communal living, and public displays of gender and sexual rebellion. The second major premise of queer theory is that gender and sexual identities—man/woman, heterosexual/homosexual—are artificial and unstable, and, hence, we should be far less invested in these identities than we are. As Judith Butler (1990) has famously argued, although most of us take our gender and sexual identities for granted and presume them to be essential aspects of who we are, it is more accurate to view them as sociohistorical inventions that have long been used to classify, rank, and discipline people. For instance, that gender identities are not inherent but constituted by an ever-changing set of rules and demands explains why we are compelled to work so hard to try to achieve gender ideals (in the current era, perhaps by shaving our legs and wearing makeup, lifting weights, repressing emotions). Rather than taking comfort in the notion that gender differences are automatic and natural, we go to great lengths to make our bodies and personalities adhere to prevailing gender norms.

Similarly, heterosexuality and homosexuality are not universal categories that have existed since the dawn of time; instead, peoples' sexual desires change over the course of their lives, have different names and meanings across time and place, and are profoundly influenced by their religious and cultural beliefs and political–economic conditions. Following from these insights, queer theorists argue that gender and sexual identities are fundamentally "false"; they appear to simply describe who we are, but instead they signify a cultural standard by which we are measured and from which we almost always fall short. Furthermore, because identities are more often than not used to keep us in our place (as women or men, for example) rather than to create more opportunities for social change and the appreciation of difference, queer theorists also urge us to be wary of identity-based activism, such as organizing around our ostensibly common identities as LGBT people, women, people of color, and so forth. Instead, a queer approach views outsiderness, strangeness, and gender and sexual rule breaking as unifying political strategies that are all the more effective when not anchored to any one predictable identity.

The third major premise of queer theory is that, within most cultures, sexual norms constitute a distinct hierarchy that includes, but is not limited to, hierarchies of gender and sexual orientation. In her groundbreaking 1984 essay "Thinking Sex," feminist queer scholar Gayle Rubin illustrated that ideas about normal and ethical sexuality are used to discipline *all* people, including people with considerable gender, racial, and socioeconomic privilege. Consider, for instance, the impeachment in 1998 of President Bill Clinton, who despite his status as a white, heterosexual, male president of the United States, was severely scrutinized and punished for his sexual relationship with a young, white, female White House intern. For Rubin, the regulation of Clinton's sexuality should come as little surprise given that in the United States, "good" sexuality is not only heterosexual but, also, "married, monogamous, procreative, non-commercial, in pairs, in a relationship, no pornography, bodies only (no sex toys or objects), and vanilla (not kinky)." Clinton's affair with Monica Lewinsky broke several of these rules and cast him, despite his enormous power and privilege, as an unreliable political leader of questionable morality. While Clinton's impeachment may have been "politically motivated," the fact that his sex practices (and not his policy decisions) were considered his most unforgivable actions tells us a great deal about the role that sexuality plays in American culture and governance. As Rubin argues, ideas about good and bad sex constitute their own regulatory regimes and frequently take center stage in moral, political, legal, and cultural formations in the United States and globally.

While queer theory recognizes the oppressive effects of various sexual norms (including those seemingly unrelated to homosexuality), it also reveals that prohibitions against same-sex desire are connected to most aspects of sexual regulation. **Heteronormativity**—or the assumption that heterosexuality is natural, normal, and right —is an especially far-reaching component of the sexual hierarchy, one with consequences well beyond discrimination against lesbians and gay men (Warner 1993). Queer theorists argue that heteronormativity is core to the very construction of woman, man, masculinity, femininity, romance, intercourse, adulthood, morality, marriage, childbirth, parenting, and aging. For instance, sociological research indicates that fear of being called a "fag" in high school looms over nearly *all* boys and results in compulsive displays of masculinity, aggression, and violence against girls (Kimmel and Mahler 2003, Pascoe 2007). In other words, even presumably heterosexual boys exert tremendous effort negotiating heteronormativity, and girls (regardless of their sexual identities) suffer the consequences alongside them. The widespread effects of heteronormativity are one reason why queer theory typically focuses more on the concept of heteronormativity than on the related but narrow term **homophobia**, the latter referring to heterosexuals' fear of, and discrimination against, lesbians and gay men. Instead of emphasizing the fluidity and diversity of same-sex desire, attention to homophobia can sometimes have the effect of reinforcing the heterosexual/homosexual binary by characterizing heterosexuals as untouched by homophobia and gays as a fundamentally different type of people in need of tolerance and special protection. In contrast, placing heteronormativity at the center of analysis involves shifting one's focus to the cultural beliefs and institutional practices that require *all* of us to account for our relationship to same-sex desire, thereby making us all vulnerable to homophobic violence.

Being versus Doing: Central Questions in Queer Theory

As stated above, one of the major premises of queer theory is that gender and sexual identities are artificial, unstable, and performative. They appear to describe the truth about who we *are* as individuals (e.g., I'm a woman, I'm a heterosexual, etc.), but from a queer perspective, these identities—and identities in general—tell us more about the symbolic meaning assigned to particular bodies, desires, and practices. French historian and poststructuralist philosopher Michel Foucault is the theorist most commonly credited with laying the historical and conceptual groundwork for this argument. Although Foucault died of an AIDS-related illness in 1984, before the rise of queer theory, Eve Sedgwick, Judith Butler, David Halperin, and other queer scholars elaborated his ideas in ways that profoundly influenced the field.

In volume 1 of *The History of Sexuality*, Foucault (1976) explained that conceptualizing sexuality as private—and viewing sex "talk" as shameful, embarrassing, exciting, arousing, personal, and revealing—is a relatively recent way of relating to sex, one that crystallized in the late 1800s, during the Victorian Era. Many of us take it for granted that sex is more exciting than other bodily functions, such as sleeping or bathing, and that sex is a private, naughty, or transcendent experience. But for Foucault, who was writing just following the sexual revolution of the late 1960s and early 1970s, the question remained: why is sex so culturally and politically meaningful (and not simply a politically inconsequential bodily requirement, like eating or sleeping)? Why can't we stop talking and thinking about sex? And, more importantly, why can't we stop talking about how we *shouldn't* be talking about sex? As a historian, Foucault noted the tremendous effort the Victorians had expended to repress, control, hide, and confess their sexual desires, and he observed how these practices carried forward into late modernity, albeit in different forms.

For Foucault, the answer to these questions about the modern obsession with sex lies in the fact that, during the Industrial Revolution, the regulation of sexuality emerged as a principal means of governing modern society and enlisting the general public in their own bodily self-discipline. Sex became a guiding metaphor for the distinction between good and bad, normal and abnormal. The threat of sexual perverts, disorders, and misdeeds also justified the growing power of modern authorities—such as doctors, psychiatrists, judges, police, and educators—who increasingly participated in the work of identifying and controlling sexual problems. More, the fear of being labeled sexually abnormal or being punished for improper sexuality conditioned people to regulate their own sexual desires and, hence, to feel shame when they violated a sexual norm, even if no one knew they had done so. Christianity-based religions also encouraged people to confess their sexual transgressions to religious leaders, a practice that carried over to the kind of confessional narratives people would be encouraged to tell in psychotherapy and, later, on television talk and "reality" shows.

The Invention of Homosexuality and Heterosexuality

Foucault argued that the invention of the reviled "homosexual" is one of the most significant and enduring legacies of this period in sexual history as well as a classic example of the way in which assorted sexual acts were reconceptualized in the late nineteenth century from fleeting practices to symptoms of permanent disorder and sexual personage. Of course, people have engaged in same-sex sexuality as long as sex itself has existed, and in some regions and time periods homosexual practices have been celebrated while in others they have been stigmatized and even criminalized in ways comparable to other nonprocreative sex acts, such as masturbation or oral sex. Yet nineteenth-century European physicians were the first to suggest that participating in homosexual acts marked one as a fundamentally different type of person, a homosexual (then called an invert), who could be identified, studied, and perhaps even cured with the right forms of medical intervention. Inverts, according to Victorian sexologists, expressed homosexual desire because they suffered from **gender dysphoria**, or the sensation of being a man trapped in a woman's body or a woman trapped in a man's body. This theory, like many theories of sexual orientation today, was widely accepted by the medical establishment, even though it conflated gender with sexual desire and failed to account for bisexuality, changes in sexual desire over the life course, or other forms of sexual fluidity. (It is worth noting here that European physicians also attempted to invent a masturbator personality type in the same way they had invented the homosexual. Imagine if we now believed that everyone fell into one of two sexual identity categories: masturbators and nonmasturbators. Would there be masturbator pride parades? Masturbator bars? What would *your* sexual identity be under such a system?)

The important point here is that contrary to the argument that heterosexuality has always been accepted as the most natural and ethical sexual orientation, Foucault's historical analysis reveals that the concept of sexual orientation and, hence, the categories heterosexual and homosexual, are less than 150 years old. One might wonder, then, why these concepts emerged at all and what was so unique about the Victorian Era that it produced the conditions for this new way of thinking about sex. Queer historians suggest that the link between rapid industrialization in the late nineteenth century and the invention (and sanctioning) of homosexuality is a logical though troubling one given that capitalism required an ever-increasing supply of docile workers who would limit their sexuality to reproductive (heterosexual) activities and focus on self-discipline over personal pleasure (D'Emilio 1983). Furthermore, the rise of the city—including restaurants, bars, parks, and public transportation—enabled the emergence of sexual enclaves and subcultures, as people were no longer restricted to small towns and villages in fulfilling their sexual desires.

In addition to being a gendered and socioeconomic process, the nineteenth-century invention of homosexuality was also a racialized one. In order to make their case about the fundamental difference between heterosexuals and homosexuals, Victorian sexologists borrowed heavily from the terminology and theoretical frameworks associated with the racist sciences of the era, such as craniometry (which divided humans into racial hierarchies based on the size and shape of their skulls) and eugenics (which drew on Darwinian principles to identify "undesirable" human traits—such as dark skin—with the aim of eliminating these traits in future generations). European and American sexologists looked to the prevailing racial hierarchy as a model for dividing people into the ranked and presumably congenital categories of heterosexual and homosexual (Somerville 2000). They sought to identify and eliminate homosexuality by using many of the same methods employed in the name of preserving white racial purity, such as measuring various body parts to diagnose homosexuality and using institutionalization, criminalization, and forced sterilization to "cure" it. And they compared inverts (believed to be neither purely male nor purely female) to mulattos, suggesting that homosexuals and people of mixed race were distinct populations that nonetheless shared a similar form of abnormality and impurity. In sum, white racism—itself infused with whites' beliefs about virtuous and normal sexuality and its primitive and predatory counterparts—functioned as a primary template for naming and disciplining homosexuality.

Rethinking the Closet

The story of the modern invention of the homosexual is, in many ways, the story with which queer theory begins and the place where queer theory departs from the gay and lesbian movement's emphasis on "coming out" as the only means of "being who you really are." Following from Foucault, queer theorists ask: If heterosexuality and homosexuality are historical inventions, produced not to liberate but to control us, then why should we identify as "gay men" or "lesbians" (or "heterosexuals") in the first place? And why place so much emphasis on "coming out"? In her groundbreaking book *Epistemology of the Closet* (1990), Eve Sedgwick argues that the heterosexual/homosexual binary is far too simplistic a way of understanding sexuality, one that arbitrarily makes the gender of our sex partners the most important element of our erotic lives. For lesbians and gay men to use the metaphor of the closet—the symbolic hidden place from which they must come out and reveal their "true" selves—is to collude with very idea that the genders of our sexual partners determines who we *are* rather than simply reflects one aspect of what we sometimes (or often) *do*. In this sense, some queer activists and scholars suggest that to come out as lesbian or gay is to agree that the binary distinction between heterosexuals and homosexuals is a *fact* and a fact of the utmost erotic, social, and political significance (even when we know that most people who identify as heterosexual experience same-sex desire). For Sedgwick, then, the act of announcing one's homosexuality is more a *performance* of what we now call "being gay" than it is a factual report of some preexisting and indisputable truth. She offers this example:

> A T-shirt that ACT UP sells in New York bearing the text "I am out, therefore I am" is meant to do for the wearer, not the constitutive work of reporting that s/he *is* out, but the performative work of coming out in the first place. (4)

For queer theorists such as Sedgwick, it is not that being gay is your "true self" and therefore you are instinctively conditioned to announce your gay identity. Rather, if you engage in acts that signify "gay" in your particular historical and cultural context, it is likely that you will be told that you are gay, you will understand yourself to be gay, and you will announce: "I am gay." In other words, you will be *disciplined* into performing a gay identity.

Performativity Theory

Attention to the disciplinary and performative nature of identities is a key project within queer theory, one most notably undertaken by the queer feminist philosopher Judith Butler. According to performativity theory, gender and sexuality come into being through our repeated performance of signs, norms, and conventions associated with heterosexual maleness and femaleness (Butler 1990, 1993). For Butler, heterosexuality—which relies on the binary categories male and female—is not a fact determined by nature, but a cultural ideal or symbolic goal that we are measured against and held accountable to every day of our lives. As noted above, Butler (1990: 279) rejects the notion that gender is a role which expresses an interior "self" or an inner reality of sex; rather, gender is a **performance**—ritualized acts by an individual that construct the social fiction of a psychological interiority: "My argument is that there need not be a 'doer' behind the deed, rather the 'doer' is variably constructed in and through the deed" (Butler 1990: 181). Butler uses the concept of **performativity** to describe how gender acts are derived from gender discourses that are handed down from generation to generation—preceding the life of any one individual—much as a script survives the particular actors that make use of it. "Like a script" the performance of gender requires individual actors to "actualize and reproduce it as reality once again" (272). The involuntary and repetitive work of displaying that one is a woman or a man, heterosexual or queer, is never complete, and it is through this very ritualized and disciplined process of performing gender and sexuality that our seemingly coherent and natural "self" is formed.

Butler's argument is complex, but it has two main components. First, although gender and sexual orientation are commonly believed to be straightforward and timeless conditions of human existence, they can be more accurately understood as contested, unstable, and marked by countless contradictions. For centuries, people have been born with bodies that are neither male nor female (or both); lived gendered lives inconsistent with the prevailing norms associated with their bodies (e.g., a person with a vagina living as a man); experienced a broad array of sexual intimacies that defy classification as either heterosexual or homosexual;

been severely punished for breaking what now appear to be bizarre and arbitrary gender and sexual norms; and engaged in gendered or sexual practices that were understood in vastly different ways across different regions of world (Fausto-Sterling 2000). Second, despite these complexities and contradictions, people are ultimately subject to the "disciplinary regimes" of their given time and place or the sum total of accepted ideas about which genders, bodies, and sexual desires are possible for people to inhabit or express (Foucault [1976] 1980). In this sense, our performance of gender and desire is not under our own control but, rather, a daily repetition of the cultural norms available to us (Butler 1990). Butler is clear that even when we perform queer or otherwise defiant genders and sexualities, these performances take place "under and through constraint, under and through the force of prohibition and taboo, with the threat of ostracism and even death controlling and compelling the shape of the production, but not . . . determining it fully in advance" (95). Understanding these two main components of Butler's argument helps to illuminate the reasons why she describes gender (and heterosexuality) as a "copy for which there is no original." Gender and sexuality, in Butler's view, are composed of acts of striving to achieve a seemingly natural and universal ideal that has never actually existed in the pure form to which we aspire.

Postcolonial and Critical Race Applications

Although postcolonial theory will be discussed at more length in chapter 10, it is important to note here that the failure to recognize homosexuality and heterosexuality as socially constructed concepts is not simply an intellectual problem, but one with political, cultural, and economic consequences for people around the globe. Queer postcolonial studies trace precisely these consequences, with emphasis on the ways that Western models of gay identity are being imposed on the global south. In many indigenous cultures and global south countries, homosexuality is not a sexual orientation, but a long-observed rite of passage (Herdt 1993), a component of spiritual leadership (Williams 1986), a respected service provided in exchange for money (McLelland 2005), a fluid means of structuring kinship (Wekker 2006), and/or an accepted part of a multigendered, nonbinary social system (Leap and Boellstorff 2004). Whereas Western thinking about homosexuality is based on the premise that anyone who engages in same-sex sexuality is *a homosexual* who should be honest about this fact and "come out," other societies do not think about homosexuality in identitarian or confessional terms, and many cultures attribute less meaning to whether participants are of the same sex than to particular aspects of the sex itself, such as whether money is exchanged or whether participants are penetrative, receptive, or both (Almaguer 1993).

Despite the rich diversity of ways in which homosexuality is enacted and understood cross-culturally, gay and lesbian movements in the global north have actively worked to universalize the gay identity model, packaging it to the global south as a presumably more modern and liberated way of thinking about sexuality. As queer postcolonial theorist Jasbir Puar (2007) has argued, the Western gay identity model can be understood as an imperialist and "homonationalist" project in which "good gay citizens" (gays who are self-proclaiming and proud) are contrasted with those whose sexuality is believed to be "backwards" or bound by religious traditions and cultural hang-ups (embodied by Muslims and Arabs in Puar's analysis). Many researchers have documented the structural effects of **homonationalism**, which include exploitative conditions for "gay" sex workers in the global south (Collins 2004a), the deployment of homophobic and racist violence by the U.S. military, such as in the case of the torture of prisoners at Abu Ghraib (Enloe 2007), and the imposition of Western notions of gay and lesbian identity on same-sex desires around the globe (Leap and Boellstorff 2004, Manalansan and Cruz-Malavé 2002). Moreover, with lesbian and gay activists in the United States often being the loudest voices articulating the meaning of "gay rights" on the global stage, many global south governments have begun to adopt violent policies against the ostensibly "Western" practice of homosexuality (see Box 6.2).

In addition to its oppressive effects in the global south, the hegemony of gay identity also has effects within the United States. Queer critical race theorists point out that central concepts in lesbian and gay political discourse, such as "the closet," "coming out," "lifestyle," and "sexual identity," are rooted in white and middle-class conceptualizations of the relationship between self, sexuality, and community. The gay and lesbian movement's reliance on these concepts works to render the same-sex desires and queer subjectivities of people of color unintelligible or invisible within U.S. queer politics.

BOX 6-2

Homonationalism: A Queer Analysis of Patriotism

There has been a curious and persistent absence of dialogue regarding sexuality in public debates about counterterrorism, despite its crucial presence in American patriotism, warmongering, and empire building . . . Through this binary-reinforcing "you're either with us or against us" normativizing apparatus, the war on terror has rehabilitated some—clearly not all or most—lesbians, gays, and queers to U.S. national citizenship within a spatial-temporal domain I am invoking as "homonationalism," short for homonormative nationalism. Homonormativity has been theorized by Lisa Duggan as a "new neo-liberal sexual politics" that hinges upon "the possibility of a depoliticized gay culture anchored in domesticity and consumption." Building on her critique. . . . I am deploying the term homonationalism to mark arrangements of U.S. sexual exceptionalism explicitly in relation to the nation. . . .

Paralleling an uneasy yet urgent folding in of homosexuality into the "us" of the "us-versus-them" nationalist rhetoric, LGBTIQ[3] constituencies took up the patriotic call in various modalities. Gay conservatives such as Andrew Sullivan came out in favor of bombing Afghanistan and advocated "gender patriotism": butching up and femme-ing down to perform the virility of the American nation, a political posture implying that emasculation is unseemly and unpatriotic. The American flag appeared everywhere in gay spaces, in gay bars and gay gyms, and gay pride parades became loaded with national performatives and symbolism: the pledge of allegiance, the singing of the national anthem, and floats dedicated to national unity. . . . Aspects of homosexuality have come within the purview of normative patriotism, incorporating aspects of queer subjectivity into the body of the normalized nation; on the other hand, terrorists are quarantined through equating them with the bodies and practices of failed heterosexuality, emasculation, and queered others. This dual process of incorporation and quarantining involves the articulation of race within nation. Nation, and its associations with modernity and racial and class hierarchies, becomes the defining factor in disaggregating between upright, domesticatable queernesses that mimic and recenter liberal subjecthood, and out-of-control untetherable queernesses.

Excerpt from "The Sexuality of Terrorism," by Jasbir K. Puar. Pp. 37–78 in *Terrorist Assemblages: Homonationalism in Queer Times* (Durham, N.C.: Duke University Press, 2007).

Theorizing and (Re)Defining Queerness

A vital and ongoing project in queer studies is the work of defining and redefining the meaning of queerness itself. Prior to being reclaimed by activists on the margins of the mainstream gay and lesbian movement, *queer* was long used in the United States as a derogatory term to describe people who expressed some form of gender nonconformity or same-sex desire, conditions commonly believed to be synonymous with disease, shame, and isolation. Understandably, prior to the 1970s, many gay men and lesbians struggled to avoid association with such a stigmatized term, one that carried not only social but often legal and economic consequences (such as job loss, housing discrimination, and violence). However, by the 1990s, some lesbian and gay activists found themselves empowered by the gains of the gay liberation movement, outraged by the U.S. government's slow and homophobic response to HIV/AIDS, and fed up with the assimilationist strategies and gender normativity that had come to characterize the mainstream movement. As these forces converged, they took the new and powerful approach of reclaiming *queer*, embracing the very outsiderness that earlier generations had fought hard to overcome (Gamson 1995). Unlike their predecessors, they asked: why *not* celebrate what is unique about queer culture, including (and especially) what is strange, freaky, and perhaps even *scary* to the masses of "normal" people? They also recognized that queer could be a useful umbrella term to describe the broad range of ways that people defy gender and sexual norms—not simply by being gay, lesbian, bisexual, or transgendered but also by being kinky, promiscuous, polyamorous, and so forth. Furthermore, queerness avoided many of the pitfalls of identity politics by being less an *identity* than a mode of sexual difference and political critique. Distinct from the gender essentialist and identitarian categories of lesbian and gay, *queer* allowed people to mark their sexual outsiderness without requiring them to foreground their own gender or the gender of their sexual partners.

While the emergence of queer critique has had productive and energizing effects on late modern LGBT politics, queer theorists also recognize that its broad focus on nonnormativity also makes it vulnerable to abstraction and cooptation.

In a time when drag queens, flamboyant gay men, and androgynous lesbians appear frequently in mainstream media and advertising, or when the term *queer* has become associated with designer clothing, gourmet foods, and expensive hair products (think *Queer Eye for the Straight Guy*), is it still radical to be queer? When gender-bending, sexual rule breaking, and bisexuality are so frequently the material of popular culture, what does it actually mean to be queer, anyway?

Queer theorists explain that queer subjectivity is not about making trendy aesthetic choices or engaging in particular (homo)sexual practices or individual acts of rebellion—especially when these actions are being marketed to consumers by the corporate media! Instead, if we recall the original use of the term *queer*—to refer to that which is unclassifiably strange and ambiguously sexual—we are reminded that queerness aims to sit outside of the possibility of commodification and mainstream acceptance. In this sense, the content of queerness is ever changing but always characterized by a collective, subcultural resistance to the institutional and state forces that compel us to be normal, especially with regard to gender and sexuality (Eng, Halberstam, and Muñoz 2005). Drawing on Foucault's assertion that "homosexuality threatens people as a 'way of life,' rather than a way of having sex," queer theorist Judith Halberstam has argued that "queer" is not a category defined by homosexual sex but by the experience of living on the margins of domestic safety and sexual respectability. "Queer subjects," according to Halberstam (2005: 10), might be defined as those who

> live (deliberately, accidentally, or of necessity) during the hours when other sleep and in the spaces (physical, metaphysical, and economic) that others have abandoned, . . . [including] "ravers, club kids, HIV-positive barebackers, rent boys, sex workers, homeless people, drug dealers, and the unemployed.

In Halberstam's analysis, queer subjects are those who live their lives according to "queer time" and within "queer spaces." For instance, whereas heteronormative culture encourages young adults to marry, have children, and focus on their nuclear families, queer subculture is often centered around local bars, public performances, art scenes, activist projects, collective sexual exploration, and extended communities. As a result, queer adults often remain engaged in activities that heterosexual adults deem immature, self-indulgent or idealistic (such as performing in drag, playing in a punk band, or organizing street protests)—the very activities that grown-ups are encouraged to leave behind as they become responsible adult citizens. Queer time, then, defies the norms associated with heteronormative adulthood, and queer place includes those sites, like bars, that enable queer subculture to survive. Halberstam (2006) adds that queer subjectivity is also characterized by its undesirability and, hence, unmarketability to heterosexual audiences and consumers (consider, for instance, how few butch dykes—not androgynous dykes like the Shane character on *The L Word*—actually appear in the mainstream media). Many other queer theorists have worked to hone in on the specificity of queerness, especially as a form of opposition to the gay and lesbian movement's narrow focus on assimilationist causes, such as same-sex marriage and access to the

U.S. military (via repeal of the military's Don't Ask, Don't Tell policy). These efforts to gain access to normative institutions exemplify what queer historian Lisa Duggan (2004) has termed the "new **homonormativity**" or the promotion of a gay and lesbian politics organized exclusively around the pursuit of rights granted to white, middle-class heterosexuals, such as privacy, domesticity, consumption, and patriotic citizenship. Duggan argues against the prevailing belief that what lesbians and gay men want most is access to a married and upwardly mobile existence filled with high fashion, stylish home décor, and the possibility of parenthood. Like Halberstam, she argues for the preservation of queer subculture, which she views as the antidote to homonormativity. For Duggan, queerness must be redefined as resistance to homonormativity.

Taking a different but related approach, some queer scholars have drawn on psychoanalytic theory to explore the subversive psychic and emotional characteristics of queerness. Rather than continually characterizing queers as happy, campy, and proud, such scholarship considers what might be gained from exploring the tragic and troubled side of queerness. Through analysis of mainstream political discourse as well as representations of gay men and lesbians in film and literature, a queer psychoanalytic approach reveals that queer figures have long been viewed as dark, ashamed, and melancholic (Love 2007), threatening to children, antifamily, futureless, and surrounded by death (Edelman 2004), and as failures or losers (Halberstam 2006). While queer theorists could deny these associations, they instead point to the ways in which queer people and queer ways of life function as a repository for the full range of human emotions and as a powerful symbol of the possibility of rejecting "success." For instance, Halberstam (2006) argues that in a time when our most successful figures are the people making decisions that carry violent global consequences (she offers President George Bush as an example), perhaps it is better to embrace being failures and losers than to strive for heteronormative success.

Queer Approaches to Sex

Like feminist theory, queer theory recognizes that "the personal is political," a principle of particular relevance to the realms of sex and sexuality. While homosexuality is a term that refers to sex between people of the same gender, **queer sex** refers to a broader range of sexual practices, practices unified by the ways that they challenge gender and heterosexual norms. Sexualities that are kinky (involving fetishes, bondage, sadomasochism, sex toys, etc.), cross-generational, nonmonogamous, non-love-based, "promiscuous," for-pay, "unsafe," and/or homosexual are among those that do not conform to traditional, state-sanctioned ideas about the romantic and heterosexual purpose of human sexuality (Rubin 1984). Queer conceptualizations of sex begin with the premise that, for many people, these sex practices are just as fulfilling as heteronormative reproductive sex practices. But more importantly, queer scholars of sexuality assert that we must be wary of any claims of a single, universal sexual idea. As queer scholar Gayle Rubin ([1984] 1993: 15) explains, it is just as oppressive to suggest that queer or kinky sexual practices should be pleasurable to everyone as it is to suggest that monogamous, reproductive sex is the most meaningful form of sexual expression:

> The notion of a single ideal sexuality characterizes most systems of thought about sex. For religion, the ideal is procreative marriage. For psychology, it's mature heterosexuality. Although its content varies, the format of a single sexual standard is continually reconstituted within other rhetorical frameworks, including feminism and socialism. It is just as objectionable to insist that everyone should be lesbian, nonmonogamous , or kinky, as to believe that everyone should be heterosexual, married, or vanilla—though the latter set of opinions are backed by considerably more coercive power than the former.

Such an approach diverges from earlier lesbian–feminist and gay liberationist discourses, which frequently posited same-sex desire and nonmonogamy as the most liberating forms of sexual interaction.

Queer theorizations of sexuality also depart from the feminist tendency to emphasize equity or mutual empowerment as the most important elements of sexual experience. In contrast, queer scholars view power—including people's conscious engagement with unequal roles—as a vital and malleable force within sexual relationships. Queer scholars have elaborated the complexities of desire by developing a "more precise sexual vocabulary" that allows for a panoply of sexual acts, identities, roles, and power relations—none of which need be determined by the gender presentation or biological sex of the participants (Newton and Waltons [1984] 2000). In an early articulation of this position, Esther Newton and Shirley Waltons (1984) argue that there is no natural link between one's biological sex category (male or female), gender (masculine, feminine, genderqueer), sexual identity (gay, straight, queer), sexual role (initiator/receiver, nurturer/provider, dominant/submissive, both or all of these) and preference for particular sex acts (oral sex, vaginal or anal sex, penetration or no penetration, fantasy play, etc). Although most of us are taught to believe that two people who are attracted to each other and who share the same "sexual orientation" will experience sexual compatibility (e.g., two gay men, or, a heterosexual man and woman), a queer approach considers that there are many other variables that figure into sexuality compatibility. A heterosexual man and woman may be physically attracted to one another, for instance, but if both of them want to feel "dominant" during sex, this may introduce conflict, and they may wonder why their sexual interactions are less than satisfying. This may seem like a somewhat obvious point, but in fact it is obscured by a gender binary that would have us believe that women and men are "opposites," that men always want to be sexually dominant, that women always want to be sexually passive or receptive, and so forth. In other words, within a heteronormative erotic system, sex and gender are presumed to tell us everything we need to know about people's sexual desires.

In contrast, a queer approach to sexuality challenges heteronormative assumptions as well as questions why gay and lesbian models of sexuality place sex and gender at the center of sexual desire. Recognizing that the gender binary constrains sexual expression, transgender activist and author Kate Bornstein has argued for new ways of thinking about sexuality detached from biological sex (see Box 6.3). How, she asks, might we classify our desires if not according to the sex and gender of our sexual partners? In *Gender Outlaw* (1994), Bornstein imagines four models of sexual desire that cannot be reduced to biological sex: the butch/femme model, the top/bottom model, the role-play model, and the sexual behaviors model. In a butch/femme system, people are not specifically attracted to women or men but to masculinity, femininity, or a combination of both. A person who is primarily sexually attracted to femininity, for instance, could be attracted to feminine women as well as feminine men. In other words, while *gender* (masculinity/femininity/genderqueerness) remains relevant in such a system, biological sex (whether one has a penis or a vagina) does not. In a top/bottom system, people would understand sexuality primarily through the lens of power. A person attracted to strong and powerful sex partners could find these qualities enticing in people of all sexes and genders. In a role-play system, the most important aspect of sexual desire would be the specific fantasies people wished to enact (such as having sex in public or "playing doctor" or being seduced with wine and chocolate). Potential sex partners would be selected based on their common interest in these fantasies rather than their particular genitals. And lastly, in a sexual behaviors system, people would desire specific sex acts (for instance, oral sex, anal sex, gentle sex, rough sex), which could be experienced with a broad range of people, regardless of sex or gender.

BOX 6-3

What Is Sexuality without the Gender Binary?

Here's the tangle that I found: sexual orientation/preference is based in this culture solely on the gender of one's partner of choice. . . . This results in minimizing, if not completely dismissing, other dynamic models of a relationship which could be more important than gender and are often more telling about the real nature of someone's desire. There are so many factors on which we *could* base sexual orientation. Examples of alternate dynamic models include [the] Butch/Femme model, however that may be defined by its participants; [the] Top/Bottom model, which can further be sub-classified as dominant/submissive or sadist/masochist. . . . There are plenty of instances in which sexual attraction can have absolutely nothing to do with the gender of one's partner. Sexual preference *could* be based on genital preference. (This is not the same as saying preference for a specific gender, unless you're basing your definition of gender on the presence or absence of some combination of genitals.) Preference could also be based on the kind of sex *acts* one prefers, and, in fact, elaborate systems exist to distinguish just that, and to announce it to the world at large. . . . If we buy into categories of sexual orientation based solely on gender—heterosexual, homosexual, or bisexual—we're cheating ourselves of a searching examination of our real sexual preferences. In the same fashion, by subscribing to the categories of gender based solely on the male/female binary, we cheat ourselves of a searching examination of our real gender identity.

Excerpt from "What Is Sexuality without the Gender Binary?" by Kate Bornstein. Pp. 32–38 of *Gender Outlaw: On Men, Women, and the Rest of Us* (New York: Vintage Books, 1994).

TRANSGENDER THEORY

Although transgender studies is its own distinct field, it is one that has been heavily influenced by queer and feminist theory and has, in turn, changed the face of these fields (Stryker 2008). Like queer studies, transgender studies expands feminist analyses of sexism and patriarchy so as to examine *gender oppression* more broadly, including the varied forms of regulation and violence associated with gender ambiguity and cross-gender identification. A centerpiece of transgender studies is the concept of the **gender binary**, which refers to the idea that humans exist in two essential, biologically determined forms (male and female). The gender binary is sustained by dividing people into gender roles based on their presumed location as male or female, disciplining people into believing in the naturalness of their gender location, and policing any violations to the male/female gender order. From this perspective, women's oppression is a pervasive and enduring outcome of the gender binary, but it is not its only troubling effect. Queers, transgendered people, intersexed people and anyone whose body or gender expression does not adhere to the male/female binary are subject to discipline in a society that believes in only two, opposite genders. In fact, since all of us inevitably fail to live up to the rigid gender ideals of our respective cultures (especially as children, when we are still being introduced to gender norms), the gender binary has oppressive effects for everyone.

While feminist theorists have long viewed *gender* as socially constructed, they have been slow to view *biological sex* as a product of social interaction (Stryker 2008). Until the emergence of queer and transgender theorizing in the 1990s, many feminists understood biological femaleness and maleness as the fixed, material foundation upon which gender roles (femininity and masculinity) were imposed. Scholars of transgenderism and intersexuality challenged this way of thinking by revealing that even the body and its sexed components (such as genitals, gonads, chromosomes, secondary sex characteristics, hormones, and so forth) are given shape and meaning by preexisting beliefs about gender, including the gendered assumptions of medical authorities (Fausto-Sterling 2000). For instance, in the United States, close to two percent of children are born **intersexed,** that is, they possess some combination of the physical features that typically distinguish males and females. Although this is a natural occurrence, the Western belief that people are either exclusively male or female has, for many decades, led doctors in the United States to surgically or otherwise "treat" intersexed children, altering their bodies in order to ensure their conformity to one sex category or another. Another example of the way that ideas about gender actually change our bodies is the ever-shrinking gap in the performance of male and female athletes. While some would argue that female athletes are constrained by their natural physical limitations and therefore destined to perform below their male counterparts, in fact we find that as women are provided greater access to competitive sports (and other physically demanding activities, such as military service, firefighting, etc.) their muscle mass increases, their body fat percentage decreases, their menstruation becomes infrequent or stops altogether, and their embodiment and physical performance more closely resembles that of men (Fausto-Sterling 2000).

Recognizing that "woman" and "man" are evolving, malleable, and contested categories is a key component of transgender theory, which is primarily concerned with the ways that gendered personhood is mapped onto the physical body. Whereas feminist scholarship is generally focused on the *effects* of this mapping (or the violence and misrecognition that occurs once a body is assigned female), transgender studies centers on how and why this sex assignment happens in the first place and what happens when our sex assignment is contested or disavowed. Transgender theory questions the baseline requirements for recognition as male or female: What makes bodies male or female? How have these requirements changed over time? How is biological sex, and not simply gender, socially constructed?

Another centerpiece of transgender studies is what we might call the problem of misrecognition. Our bodies, especially in late modernity, are frequently read as signs of our subjectivity, continually viewed and interpreted by others to determine who we "are" and how we should be understood. Because the sex and gender characteristics of our bodies carry so much meaning (including potentially oppressive meanings), we have all learned to fashion gendered bodies that elicit the most livable circumstances and responses from others. While all of us work at presenting our bodies in gendered ways, transgender theorists and activists call attention to this process, arguing that every person must be able to fashion the kind of body that will elicit the best available form of recognition, especially in such a gender-obsessed world. This includes being transgendered—claiming a gender that does not match one's sex assignment at birth—and being able to alter one's body in order to be recognized according to one's desired gender. This right, though of great importance for trans people, has applications for all people, including non-trans women. For example, while a long-term feminist goal may be for women's breasts to be as politically and economically irrelevant as men's breasts, until that goal has been achieved many women will understandably crave to be able to create larger or smaller breasts, or to remove or hide breasts, in order to be treated like the kind of woman that best matches their subjectivity or that delivers the kind of recognition they long for.

Transgender subjectivities emerge out of multiple kinds of gender misrecognition. Gender dysphoria, the most widely circulated and medicalized narrative about trans identity, has its roots in nineteenth-century theories of homosexuality (then called inversion). Gender dysphoria refers to the experience of feeling "trapped in the wrong body" or feeling essentially male or female despite possessing the physical traits of the "other sex." While many trans people describe their gender identity in these terms (sometimes because they are compelled to do so by physicians and psychologists), many others do not. A second way of thinking about transgenderism is to place the spotlight on mainstream society's response to gender fluidity and diversity. From this vantage point, trans people do not have a medical or psychological condition, or a "wrong body," but rather are responding to a lifetime of being told by others—parents, teachers, peers, psychologists, the media—that their gender expression is out of synch with their biological sex. Many trans people—in fact, almost *all* people—are punished as children for violating the gender binary. For some trans people, societal regulation of their childhood and/or adolescent gender was quite extreme; hence, the desire to transition may arise less from an inherent longing to be the other sex and more from a longing to no longer have one's gender be the subject of confusion, fear, and scrutiny. Yet a third way of thinking about trans identity is to recognize the pleasure that many of us would experience if we were to break free of the constraints of the gender binary. The **genderqueer** movement emphasizes precisely this potential by celebrating those who play with gender, live between genders, and embody both, neither, or multiple genders. From this perspective, to be transgendered is neither a medical condition nor a result of an oppressive society but, rather, a guide or model for how *all* of us could interrogate our own investments in gender normativity and expand our gendered possibilities.

QUEER ECOFEMINISMS

As shown above, both transgender theorists and queer theorists are careful to point out how *all* people are affected by gender normativity and heteronormativity.[4] In "Toward a Queer Ecofeminism" (1997), Greta Gaard continues this line of thought when she discusses how the problem of oppression based on sexuality is much larger than the issue of heterosexism versus homosexuality. Following Foucault, she locates this larger problem in the **erotophobia** of Western culture, a fear of the erotic so strong that only one form of sexuality is overtly allowed and only in the context of certain legal, religious, and social sanctions (such as marriage and procreation). She highlights how the systemic oppression of the erotic entails a view of what is "normal sex" that polices and restricts the erotic activities of all people, regardless of their forms of sexuality. Drawing on the works of queer theorist Eve Sedgwick and anarcha-ecofeminists Karen Warren and Val Plumwood, Gaard uses her discussion of erotophobia to expose shortcomings in existing ecofeminist theories. In particular, Gaard criticizes contemporary ecofeminists for their failure to link the domination imposed by heteronormativity to the domination of nature, despite their claims to address sexism, racism, classism, imperialism, and heterosexism. In her view, they simply add "heterosexism" to their long list of oppressions, acting as if one can just "add queers and stir" (115). The goal of her article is to develop these links and thereby end the "theoretical gap" in analyses of heteronormativity and nature. She states: "I believe it is time for queers to come out of the woods and speak for ourselves" (116).

Gaard elaborates how Western culture's devaluation of the erotic and any non-heterosexual practices parallels its devaluations of women and nature. She focuses on three major issues here. First, she discusses how the discourse that homosexuality is a "crime against nature" ignores the diverse forms of sexuality found in the sexual practices of nonhuman nature, particularly in other animal species, thus distorting the reality of what is "natural." Second, she points to how dominant discourses invariably associate "natural sex" with "procreation," drawing similarities between the restrictions on homosexual sexual practices because they are deemed "unnatural" and restrictions on women's sexuality when it is not directed toward procreation and motherhood. Third, she discusses how a focus on homosexuality as a "crime against nature" distracts attention from the serious crimes against nature committed by dominant groups who exploit nature for social and commercial interests.

Gaard also critiques binary thought and how it has been used to link the domination of women, homosexuals, and nature. She rejects this dualistic thought because it is exclusive rather than inclusive and oppositional rather than complementary. She highlights how binaries involve hidden hierarchies in which superiority is attributed to one side of the dualism and how in each case the subordinate "other"—be it the female other in the male/female binary or the homosexual other in the heterosexual/homosexual binary—is *feminized, animalized, and naturalized.* In Chapter 10, Gaard's work will be revisited in examining the role that erotophobia played in the colonial conquest of the Americas. Suffice it to say here that Gaard's work provides a fine example of how ecofeminism can learn from queer theory and how queer theory can learn from ecofeminism.

CONCLUSION

It is important to reiterate, in closing, that one of the most important lessons to learn about the term *queer* as queer theorists articulate it is that it is a critique of all things oppressively *normal.* Therefore, one last example will be provided in an attempt to cement in readers' minds the recognition that queer theorists address far more than just the issues of sex, gender, sexuality, and bodies. This is illustrated well in Eve Sedgwick's book *Tendencies* (1993), where she explicitly asks the question "What's Queer?" Here Sedgwick focuses on the significant power that is wielded when discourses from a multitude of sources join together to voice the same message. Other writers have used the terms "**model monopolies**" or "**ideological codes**" to refer to normative prescriptions that are replicated and reinforced by discourses from multiple and various sites (Levine 1993, Smith 1993b). These ideological codes can generate similar meanings or messages in widely different settings—be they legislative, social scientific, popular writing, television shows, advertising, and so forth (Smith 1993b: 51–52). They can become so deeply embedded in our consciousness that we are not even aware that we often use them as yardsticks to measure others and their practices as normal or abnormal.

In her discussion of "What's Queer?" Sedgwick provides examples of how heterosexuality and the nuclear family serve as model monopolies for judging alternative sexualities and alternative family forms as deviant, as well as a much more surprising example: how the discourses of Christmas in the United States serve as a model monopoly (see Box 6.4).

Sedgwick refers to the Christmas season as being a time in the United States when all of the major social institutions are "speaking with one voice" (5). Despite the separation of church and state under formal law, the "state talks" in conjunction with the dominant Christian religion by ordaining legal holidays, decorating

BOX 6-4

What's Queer about Christmas?

What's queer? Here's one train of thought about it. The depressing thing about the Christmas season—isn't it?—is that it's the time when all the institutions are speaking with one voice. The Church says what the Church says. But the State says the same thing: maybe not (in some ways it hardly matters) in the language of theology, but in the language the State talks: legal holidays, long school hiatus, special postage stamps, and all. And the language of commerce more than chimes in, as consumer purchasing is organized ever more narrowly around the final weeks of the calendar year, the Dow Jones aquiver over Americans' "holiday mood." The media, in turn, fall in triumphally behind the Christmas phalanx: ad-swollen magazines have oozing turkeys on the cover, while for the news industry every question turns into the Christmas question—Will hostages be free for *Christmas*? What did that flash flood or mass murder (umpty-ump people killed and maimed) do to those families' *Christmas*? And meanwhile, the pairing 'families/Christmas' becomes increasingly tautological, as families more and more constitute themselves according to the schedule, and in the endlessly iterated image, of the holiday itself constituted in the image of 'the' family.

The thing hasn't, finally, so much to do with propaganda for Christianity as with propaganda for Christmas itself. They all—religion, state, capital, ideology, domesticity, the discourses of power and legitimacy—line up with each other so neatly once a year, and the monolith so created is a thing one can come to view with unhappy eyes.

Excerpt from "Queer and Now," by Eve Kosofsky Sedgwick. Pp. 1–22 in *Tendencies* (Durham, N.C.: Duke University Press, 1993); her emphasis.

streets and buildings, and creating special postage stamps. The economy and "the language of commerce" chime into this discourse as consumer society gears up for Christmas spending. The mass media joins the chorus with "ad-swollen magazines oozing turkey on the covers," Christmas music, TV specials, and the "endlessly reiterated image of the holiday itself constituted in the image of 'the' family"—both holy and earthly (5). For marginalized people, these model monopolies created when the discourses of power and legitimacy "line up with each other so neatly once a year" can be quite painful for some people (6). In this particular case, for those who do not share the Christian religion, for those who are alone or without a normative family structure, and/or for those without sufficient funds to spend on this event, Christmas can be a deeply painful and depressing time that can only be viewed with "unhappy eyes" (6).

By calling for the demise of ideological codes and model monopolies, queer theory serves as a voice for those on the margins. Unlike other marginalized voices, "queers" do not seek to move to the center. Rather, they posit themselves permanently on the margins as critics of the status quo. In this way, queer theorists and activists make us ever mindful of the power that discourses can wield in stamping out difference and causing pain to marginalized others.

Additional analyses of feminist postmodernists, poststructuralists, and queer theorists on global issues can be found in chapter 10.

CRITICISMS OF POSTMODERN AND POSTSTRUCTURALIST FEMINISMS

1. That the epistemological assumptions of these postperspectives result in a relativist view of "truth" where there are no criteria for adjudicating between competing knowledge claims. Rather, there are only multiple and competing vantage points that are all partial and limited. For critics, discarding the notion of "truth" and replacing it with uncertainty and relativism opens ups a Pandora's box for any and every viewpoint to claim legitimacy—even those that are harmful to the interests of women or other oppressed groups (Harding 1993, Smith 1993a).

2. That because the postperspectives focus on the micro powers of discourse and resistance to them, power relations increasingly become analyzed not at the level of large-scale social structures, but at the local level of the individual. For these critics, when binary analyses of power are rejected, there is no place for a critique of the pervasive, institutionalized axes of stratification, such as gender, race, and class. Hence, this postmodern turn will result in the loss of the macrostructural analyses that are essential to an effective politics that can transform social structures (Fraser and Nicholson 1997, Collins 1998, Hartsock 1990).

3. That the post-postperspectives' deconstruction of group categories coupled with their tendency to link difference to micro powers of discourse rather than to macrostructural forms of oppression results in the notion of difference becoming trivialized. Consequently, differences emerging from historical and systemic patterns of oppression that affect entire groups of people, such as race, gender, class, and sexual orientation, become submerged within a host of more trivial, individual differences (Collins 1998).

4. That the postperspectives' call for the demise of binary and dualistic thinking leads to flattened hierarchies and diffuse notions of power that undermine macrostructural social change. Hence, concepts of power shift such that hierarchical notions of specific groups that oppress and specific groups that are oppressed are recast as conflated geographies of centers and margins that rob the term of oppression of its critical and oppositional importance (Collins 1998).

CRITICISMS OF QUEER THEORY

1. That the term *queer* is too inclusive—such that anything or anyone can be claimed as queer (recall Judith Halberstam's suggestion that "homeless people, drug dealers, and the unemployed" are queer). If queer becomes too broad a category, critics argue, then it loses its political power and historical specificity, making it difficult to name anyone as lesbian or gay (Gamson 2000).

2. That queer theory is too abstract. It has taken theoretical abstraction to such a level that it is inaccessible to most people or elitist (a common critique of poststructuralist theory more generally) (Stein and Plummer 1996, Zita 1994). Some gay men and lesbians have disavowed queer theory for this reason, calling instead for more attention to the history and daily lives of LGBT people as well as for research and ideas directly aimed at mobilizing and unifying LGBT communities (Edwards 1998).

3. That queer theory places too great a focus on cultural texts and performativity, thereby failing to offer practical solutions that address structural inequalities and assist in the redistribution of material resources. For instance, while queer practices, such a drag, may make many heterosexuals uncomfortable by challenging gender and sexual norms, some critics question the extent to which these challenges will result in greater acceptance of, and increased civil rights for, LGBT people. Some critics also suggest that queer theory's focus on sexual fluidity does not reflect the reality of most people's gender and sexual identities, which generally are more fixed than such accounts would suggest (Edwards 1998).

4. That queer theory downplays the importance of feminist politics and the structural significance of gender, often failing to recognize the interconnections of gender, race, class, and sexuality. For instance, some feminist scholars have expressed concern that queer theory often addresses matters of sex and sexuality without consideration of gender, thereby relegating gender to feminist inquiry and locating the study of sexuality outside of feminism (Jeffreys 1994, Weed 1997). To the extent that queer theory fails to address the material inequities that shape women's lives, it is arguably a less useful body of theory for lesbians than for gay men (Stein 1992). Some critics have suggested that by centering heteronormativity in its analysis, queer theory glosses over other forms of oppression (Zita 1994).

NOTES

1 For example, Judith Butler (1992: 4) rebukes feminists for not recognizing important distinctions between these perspectives: "It may come as a surprise to some purveyors of the Continental scene that Lacanian psychoanalysis in France positions itself officially against poststructuralism, that Kristeva denounces postmodernism, that Foucaultians rarely relate to Derrideans".

2 Foucault's approach is different from the social constructionism that developed in the United States in the 1960s and 1970s, which assumed an active, creative subject who constructed social reality; see, for example, Peter Berger and Thomas Luckmann's *The Social Construction of Reality* (1967). This form of social constructionism characterized various microlevel sociological perspectives, such as symbolic interactionism and ethnomethodology. The postperspectives entail a more radical social constructionism that views the subject as constituted by discourses and practices such that there is no doer behind the deeds (Holstein and Gubrium 2008: 31–33).

3 LGBTIQ refers to lesbian, gay, bisexual, transgendered, intersexed, and queer. This acronym has gotten longer in recent years to include even more sexual practices and/or identities.

4 For a discussion of how queer ecofeminists have criticized identities and identity politics, see Catriona Sandilands's "Mother Earth, the Cyborg, and the Queer: Ecofeminism and (More) Questions of Identity" (1997). Sandilands states in the second paragraph of her article that "ecofeminism must rethink—perhaps even deconstruct—some of its undiscussed assumptions about identity, politics and the relations between the two" (18).

CHAPTER 7

Third Wave Feminisms

> Gently swelling, rising and then crashing, waves evoke images of both beauty and power. As feminists, we could do much worse than be associated with this phenomenon.
>
> —Cathryn Bailey

INTRODUCTION

In the 1990s, the women's movement in the United States witnessed a resurgence of feminist activism and scholarship among a new generation of young feminists that was so large and unexpected that some referred to it as a "genderquake" (Wolf [1993] 1994: 25).[1] While other members of this same generation were criticized for being "the most politically disengaged generation in American history" (Halstead 1999: 33), these young feminists were immensely active. In 1992, they founded Third Wave Direct Action—an organization designed to mobilize young people politically and to foster young women's leadership. Its inaugural project was a voter registration drive that registered more than twenty thousand new voters. By 1996, they had established the Third Wave Foundation—a national organization committed to supporting women from ages fifteen to thirty in activities devoted toward gender, racial, social, and economic justice.

Young feminists also hold conferences, teach-ins and skills-sharing workshops across the nation and have created hundreds of feminist zines, webzines, magazines, and other publications. They are involved in diverse areas of mass culture, particularly popular music, where they influenced a wide range of genres from punk, to rock 'n' roll, to rap and hip hop (Cashen 2002, Morgan, 1999). Indeed, a number of their supporters characterize popular culture and sexual politics as key sites of activism for these younger feminists. These sites were selected not only because they are so influential in the lives of young people but also because a major tactic of these young feminists is "to use desire and pleasure, as well as anger to fuel their struggles for justice" (Heywood and Drake 1997: 4; Orr 1997: 10).

While THIRD WAVE has become the banner under which these younger women identify their new brand of feminism, clearly demarcating exactly who constitutes this new wave is not without difficulty. They have been referred to in myriad ways that tend to focus more on age than on their contributions to feminist theory and activism. For example, some writers use specific dates of birth, such as birth dates between 1963 and 1974, while others use more collective imagery, such as "Generation X," the "twenty-somethings," or the "Jane Generation" (Heywood and Drake 1997, Kamen 1991, Johnson 2002). "Mother–daughter tropes" also are used to describe these younger feminists' relationship to their second wave predecessors, often resulting in themes of generational conflict or rebellion (Quinn 1997, Henry 2004).

Clearly chronological age is problematic for distinguishing a feminist group and their perspective (Bailey 1997, Henry 2004). Not only is the notion of "younger women" a shifting constituency of those who will eventually become "older women," but, also, does it really matter whether a woman is fifty-five or twenty-five if she adheres to a certain brand of feminist theory and activism? (Siegel 1997a: 55). Instead, some writers have suggested using the concept of a **political generation** to designate the third wave. This concept does not refer to chronological age and may include more than one chronological generation (Whittier 1995, Henry 2003). The key to such political generations is that they reflect the life experiences and concerns of a particular historical moment—the moment *when* a person becomes politicized (Schneider, 1988). As the Nancy Whittier, the author of *Feminist Generations* (1995: 15), writes:

> What it means to call oneself "feminist" varies greatly over time, often leading to conflict over movement goals, values, ideology, strategy, or individual behavior. In other words, coming of political age at different times gives people different perspectives.

The following section, "Historically Grounding the Third Wave," discusses how coming of age as a feminist in postmodernity is quite different from doing so in other historical eras.

The primary focus of this chapter is on third wave feminism as a *theoretical perspective*, one that any feminist—young, old, or middle-aged—could embrace. While clearly all third wavers do not share a singular or uniform perspective, their major publications share a number of important theoretical assumptions that enable us to discuss their unique contributions to feminist thought. In particular, it will be argued that *third wave feminism is based on a synthesis of postmodernism, poststructuralism and intersectionality theory* (Mann and Huffman 2005). This view of third wave theory is most explicitly discussed in Deborah Siegel's "The Legacy of the Personal: Generating Theory in Feminism's Third Wave" (1997a), which states that "postmodernist, poststructuralist and multicultural critiques have shaped the form and content of third wave expressions" (46). This chapter expands on Siegel's analysis to suggest a number of ways in which these earlier perspectives inform the third wave's agenda. Calling this theoretical approach a synthetic derivation is not meant to suggest that the third wave agenda lacks originality. Rather, it is the complex ways that the third wave weaves particular threads of these earlier feminisms together that makes the theoretical fabric of third wave feminism both unique and fashionable to young feminists.

Yet untangling these threads is difficult because third wave feminism is the least *explicitly* theoretical of all of the feminist frameworks discussed in this text.

The preferred writing genre of these young feminists—*personal narratives*—is one of the more difficult genres from which to unravel their theoretical assumptions, precisely because these narratives are so individual and subjective. For this reason, a number of critics have argued that third wave writings are without theory. For example, Phil Haslanger's review of Rebecca Walker's signal work of the third wave, *To Be Real: Telling the Truth and Changing the Face of Feminism* (1995), describes this anthology as "not a book of feminist theory" but, rather, "a very personal book filled with anecdotes about individuals' own struggles" (quoted in Siegel 1997a: 67). A harsher critic, Wendy Kaminer, refers to the contributors to *Listen Up: Voices from the Next Feminist Generation* (1995) as "amateur memoirists" who confuse "feeling bad" with oppression and who "believe their lives are intrinsically interesting to strangers" (quoted in Siegel 1997a: 67). Equally harsh is Katha Pollitt's 1999 article titled "The Solipsisters," which highlights the third wave's "self-absorbed writings" that naively assume "personal testimony, impressions and feelings are all you need to make a political argument" (quoted in Baumgardner and Richards 2000: 19–20). Even avid supporters of the third wave call for more concerted efforts to develop theory. Rory Dicker and Alison Piepmeier, editors of *Catching a Wave: Reclaiming Feminism for the 21st Century* (2003), argue that "it is time to move beyond personal accounts to political and collective action" and urge their third wave sisters to use personal experiences "as a bridge to larger political and *theoretical* explorations" (12 and 13; emphasis added).

Although personal narratives still dominate third wave writings, "claims that the third wave is a theory-free movement . . . are epistemologically naïve, historically inaccurate, and, ultimately, misinformed" (Siegel 1997a: 49). There are common threads running through these narratives that weave together the underlying theoretical fabric of third wave feminism. Siegel refers to these common threads as "common tropes, images, motifs, narrative patterns and general issues of concerns" (51). By whatever name, they reveal the common theoretical ground shared by this wave. However, because these theoretical assumptions are less obvious, it is necessary to read between the lines, so to speak, to discover this less explicit theory that some feminists have referred to as "embodied theory" (Bordo 1993: 184–185).

HISTORICALLY GROUNDING THE THIRD WAVE

The world encountered by third wavers when they reached adulthood and/or when they became politicized in the 1980s and 1990s was immensely different from the world encountered by their second wave predecessors in the 1960s and 1970s. Politically, they were confronted with a highly mobilized New Right who had a significant voice in national politics through the Ronald Reagan/George Bush Sr. years. Readers will recall from chapter 2 that, after a long and difficult battle, the Equal Rights Amendment (ERA) was defeated in 1982, a crushing blow to the second wave. During the 1980s, the Moral Majority's so-called family values campaigns captured the national limelight, and conservative Republicans enjoyed a sweep of electoral victories. These victories further transformed the composition of the U.S. Supreme Court and of federal district courts that during the 1970s had been quite friendly to second wave feminist demands. These right-wing successes were due in large part to how Reagan's 1980 presidential campaign and the STOP-ERA movement had so adeptly coalesced fundamentalist Christians with more secular conservatives.

Economically, third wave feminists faced the worst job market since World War II and were the first postwar generation expected to fare worse than their parents (Heywood and Drake 1997). By the time these third wavers reached adulthood, globalization had so restructured the U.S. economy that it had transformed the gender, racial, and ethnic composition of the labor force as well as the nature of job opportunities available to young people. Given the decline in manufacture and the rise of low-paying service jobs, third wave feminist Michelle Sidler (1997: 25) refers to this bleak economic era as "living in McJobdom." She discusses how the high price of college tuition left many of her peers with huge debts and how, even with college degrees, high-paying jobs were few and far between. She fears that her generation faces a future of sustained underemployment. She also notes: "Most women of my generation must work, whether we have families or not, to survive economically" (30). Hence, "leaving domestic roles to pursue a career is no longer a political statement either [as it was for many in the second wave]; it is a necessity that does not constitute activism for twenty-something women" (37). This era of backlash and economic uncertainty contrasts sharply with the progressive social movements and the post–World War II economic prosperity of the1960s and early 1970s.

On a more positive side, the third wave's path had been paved by the earlier struggles of their second wave predecessors who had made great strides in improving many areas of women's lives. These younger women grew up amid these achievements, at times taking them for granted. Frequently found in third wave texts is the idea that "for our generation feminism is like fluoride. We scarcely notice that we have it—it's simply in the water" (Henry 2005: 81; Baumgardner and Richards 2000: 18). Some of the second wave achievements that made the road smoother for third wave feminists are highlighted in "A Day without Feminism," from *Manifesta: Young Women, Feminism, and the Future* (2000), written by third wavers as a tribute to their second wave sisters. Here, authors Jennifer Baumgardner and Amy Richards imagine what life would be like without the accomplishments of the second wave:

> Imagine that for a day it is still 1970 . . . the name of your Whirlpool gas stove is Mrs. America. . . . Women can't study at Dartmouth, Columbia, Harvard . . . a gal can get a legal abortion only if she lives in New York or is rich enough to fly there . . . women make, on average, fifty-two cents to the dollar earned by males . . . a female lawyer looks for work under "Help Wanted Male" . . . twenty states have only five female gynecologists or fewer . . . women workers can be fired or demoted for being pregnant . . . and a woman without make-up and a hairdo is as suspect as a man with them (415).

The rise of the new electronic technologies, such as microchip computers, the Internet, and satellite communications have saturated the lives of third wavers with mass marketing, mass culture, and mass communications on a scale not possible in earlier eras. This media-savvy generation has used these new technologies to expand the venues for their voices (Alfonso and Trigilio 1997, Duncan 2005, Bates and McHugh 2005). The Internet provides a means of interaction where youth can be the initiators and producers of their own social agendas and representations. Cyberspace is "a space where neither the mainstream media nor other institutions have the last word . . . a way of maintaining integrity . . . an underground with no center" (Cashen 2002: 15 and 18). Thus, the new electronic technologies provide entirely new ways for the third wave to spread their ideas and to organize politically as compared with the techniques available to their predecessors.

However, living in an information society also means that women of all ages and walks of life experience a barrage of information from both old media forms as well as new media outlets that were unavailable in previous decades. The sheer volume of information increased exponentially. This included an onslaught of mass media claims that the United States had entered a postfeminist era in which feminism was dead or no longer relevant. Writing on the eve of the third wave's birth, journalist Susan Faludi (1991: ix) referred to this media onslaught as yet another form of "backlash"—an "undeclared war against American women." Family values were heavily intertwined in this media backlash. Feminism was portrayed as the antithesis of a loving and meaningful family life—a sad and lonely frontier—where bitter single and childless women existed alongside superwomen who were exhausted from trying to do it all. Women were told to fear a man shortage and the ticking of their biological clocks if they postponed marriage; poverty and loneliness if they got divorced; and a cold, impersonal world of men and women in suits if they pursued a career. Even Betty Friedan—mother of the U.S. second wave—joined this pro-family chorus. In *The Second Stage*, published in 1981, Friedan argued that feminists' failure "was our blind spot about the family" (quoted in Faludi 1991: 318). Friedan's second-stage solutions encouraged women to "rediscover the family circle" and "the power of the women's sphere" as the bases of their identity (see chapter 2).

Having come to feminism in this conservative political climate, third wavers have described themselves as members of a generation that "have no utopias" and who live in the midst of "backlash" and the "media demonization of 'sisterhood' " (Heywood and Drake 1997: 48–49). Given this absence of "utopias" it is, perhaps, not surprising that there are few statements of the collective aims or goals of the third wave. One such statement can be found in *Manifesta: Young Women, Feminism, and the Future* (2000), where Jennifer Baumgardner and Amy Richards provide a thirteen-point agenda that they call their "Third Wave Manifesta" (see Box 7.1). However, the absence a collective voice and a more individualistic approach to feminism appears to be the modus operandi of most third wavers as will be shown later in this chapter.

BOX 7.1

Third Wave Manifesta: A Thirteen-Point Agenda

1. To out unacknowledged feminists, specifically those who are younger, so that Generation X can become a visible movement and, further, a voting block of eighteen- to forty-year-olds.
2. To safeguard a woman's right to bear or not to bear a child, regardless of circumstances, including women who are younger than eighteen or impoverished. To preserve this right throughout her life and support the choice to be childless.
3. To make explicit that the fight for reproductive rights must include birth control; the right for poor women and lesbians to have children; partner adoption for gay couples; subsidized fertility treatments for all women who choose them; and freedom from sterilization abuse. Furthermore, to support the idea that sex can be—and usually is—for pleasure, not procreation.
4. To bring down the double standard in sex and sexual health, and foster male responsibility and assertiveness in the following areas: achieving freedom from STDs; more fairly dividing the burden of family planning as well as responsibilities such as child care; and eliminating violence against women.
5. To tap into and raise awareness of our revolutionary history, and the fact that almost all movements began as youth movements. To have access to our intellectual feminist legacy and women's history; for the classics of radical feminism, womanism, *mujeristas*, women's liberation, and all our roots to remain in print; and to have women's history taught to men as well as women as a part of all curricula.
6. To support and increase the visibility and power of lesbians and bisexual women in the feminist movement, in high schools, colleges and the workplace; to recognize that queer women have always been at the forefront of the feminist movement, and that there is nothing to be gained—and much to be lost—by downplaying their history, whether inadvertently or actively.
7. To practice "autokeonony" ("self in community"): to see activism not as choice between self and community but as a link between them that creates balance.
8. To have equal access to health care, regardless of income, which includes coverage equivalent to men's and keeping in mind that women use the system more often than do men because of their reproductive capacity.
9. For women who so desire, to participate in all reaches of the military, including combat, and to enjoy all the benefits (loans, health care pensions) offered to its members for as long as we continue to have an active military. The largest expenditure of our national budget goes toward maintaining this welfare system, and feminists have a duty to make sure women have access to every echelon.
10. To liberate adolescents from slut-bashing, listless educators, sexual harassment, and bullying at school, as well as violence in all walks of life, and the

silence that hangs over adolescents' heads, often keeping them isolated, lonely, and indifferent to the world.

11. To make the workplace responsive to an individual's wants, needs, and talents. This includes valuing (monetarily) stay-at-home parents, aiding employees who want to spend more time with family and continue to work, equalizing pay for jobs of comparable worth, enacting a minimum wage that would bring a fulltime worker with two children over the poverty line, and providing employee benefits for free-lance and part-time workers.
12. To acknowledge that, although feminists may have disparate values, we share the same goal of equality, and of supporting one another in our efforts to gain the power to make our own choices.
13. To pass the Equal Rights Amendment so that we can have a constitutional foundation of righteousness and equality upon which future women's right conventions will stand.

"Third Wave Manifesta: A Thirteen-Point Agenda," by Jennifer Baumgardner and Amy Richards. Pp. 278–280 in *Manifesta: Young Women, Feminism, and the Future* (New York: Farrar, Straus, and Giroux, 2000)

POSTFEMINISM AND FEMINISM'S "DISSENTING DAUGHTERS"

The surge of third wave activism in the 1990s was, in part, a response to media claims that the United States had entered a "postfeminist era" (Ellerbe 1990, Hogeland 1994, Shapiro 1994). When Rebecca Walker (1992: 41) asserted on the pages of *Ms.* magazine that "I am not a postfeminist feminist. I *am* the third wave" (her emphasis), it was an act of defiance, a stance of political resistance to popular pronouncements that feminism was dead or no longer relevant (Henry 2004). Walker was responding to obituaries for feminism that had begun as early as 1982, when journalists labeled women in their teens and twenties as the "postfeminist" generation (Bolotin 1982).[2] Even the *New York Times*—usually considered the bastion of liberal journalism—struck up a dirge with a cover story in its weekly magazine that began "The women's movement is over" (quoted in Faludi 1991: 76). Yet as more careful observers noted: "Despite its wide-ranging currency on dust-jackets, on late night talk-shows and in 'serious' feature articles, 'postfeminism' has rarely been defined" (Coppock and Richter 1995: 3–4).

In "The Myth of Postfeminism" (2003), feminists Elaine Hall and Marnie Salupo Rodriguez examined this conceptual ambiguity. Using content analysis, they studied a total of ninety popular and research publications and found that "**postfeminism**" referred to a number of diverse claims. The four most frequently repeated claims were: (1) that overall support for the women's movement had decreased in the years from 1980–1990, (2) that antifeminism had increased among "pockets" of women—young women, women of color, and full-time homemakers, (3) that feminism was irrelevant and no longer needed, and

(4) that women were reluctant to identify as "feminists" even if they supported many women's rights issues. Using public opinion surveys from 1980–1999, Hall and Rodriguez then examined whether these claims were empirically accurate and found them to be largely "myths." Support for the women's movement remained stable or even increased over time. Both young women and women of color were more supportive of the women's movement than were other women. Respondents' views of the relevance of the women's movement did not change, and there was no empirical support for the claim of declining levels of self-identification with either the women's movement or with feminism. The only claim that had some validity was that a substantial number of homemakers believed the women's movement had made family life more difficult(898–899).

Despite their overall finding that postfeminism was a "myth," Hall and Rodriguez voiced concern that if such ideas were repeated often enough from a variety of media outlets that they would gain the "appearance of truth" whether or not they have any validity (898–899). Faludi (1991: 79) sounded a similar warning based on her study of journalistic portrayals of feminism presented in *Backlash: The Undeclared War against American Women*:

> Trend journalism attains authority not through actual reporting but through the power of repetition. Said enough times, anything can be made to seem true. A trend declared in one publication sets off a chain reaction, as the rest of the media scramble to get the story, too. The lightning speed at which these messages spread has less to do with the accuracy of the trend than with journalists' propensity to repeat one another.

Faludi also discussed how countering trend journalism with more responsible information became especially difficult in the 1980s as independent presses "fell into a very few corporate hands" (79). Many of the independent presses associated with the women's movement failed or were eclipsed by large commercial presses in the late 1970s and early 1980s (Messer-Davidow 2002). However, the major point that Faludi, Hall, and Rodriquez are making is that feminists must be aware of how easily myths "that appear as truths" can be socially constructed in the new information society. They fear that such "apparent truths" can have real effects on people's understanding of the world and on the future. This is "the ultimate danger of the postfeminist argument" (Hall and Rodriguez 2003: 899).

Along with this media backlash and its postfeminist claims, the surge in third wave activism came also on the heels of strong criticisms of the second wave by the **"feminist dissenters"** or feminism's "dissenting daughters," such as Katie Roiphe and Rene Denfeld (Bauer-Maglin and Perry 1996, Siegel 1997b, Sorisio, 1997). Both Denfeld and Roiphe were among the first of the younger generation to portray second wave feminism as obsessed with controlling women's sexuality by highlighting the dangers rather than the pleasures of sex. Roiphe's *The Morning After: Rape, Fear, and Feminism on Campus* (1993) claimed that, in their "date rape hysteria," the second wave overstated the prevalence of sex offenses in ways that debilitate young women and foster an environment of fear. In a similar vein, she argued that it is not sexual harassment that creates a "chilly" climate for women on campus but, rather, feminists' surveillance of sexual practices on campuses (referenced in Sorisio 1997: 137). Roiphe referred to the second wave as a "rape crisis feminism" that denied female sexual desires and infantilized women.

Rene Denfeld's *The New Victorians* (1995) has been dubbed "the sequel" to Roiphe's book (Siegel 1997b: 59). Denfeld (1995: 11) portrays the feminism she confronted on reaching adulthood as "remarkably similar to Victorians in significant ways, and not only in their vision of sexuality." She sees feminism as too often embarking on a moral and spiritual crusade that restricts sexual practices and that portrays women as fragile and helpless. For Denfeld: "This is the New Victorianism. And this is why women of my generation are abandoning the women's movement" (11). Both Roiphe and Denfeld use the phrase "taking back feminism" to describe their own approaches, playing on Take Back the Night rallies organized by campus rape crisis centers in the 1980s (many of which continue today). It is precisely these types of events initiated by second wave feminists that Roiphe and Denfeld see as fostering an excessive environment of fear.

Another early contributor to this sexually restrictive view of second wave feminism was Naomi Wolf. Although Wolf sparred with Roiphe for her "ethically irresponsible" term "rape-crisis feminism" and for mocking "Take Back the Night" events, she is credited with coining the term "**victim feminism**" (referenced in Siegel 1997b: 59 and 63). In *Fire with Fire: The New Female Power and How to Use It*, Wolf ([1993] 1994: xvi) argues that "victim feminism is obsolete". In her view, "women's psychology and the conditions of women's lives have been transformed enough" so that "it is no longer possible to present the impulses to dominate, aggress, or sexually exploit others as 'male' urges alone (xviii). Like Denfeld and Roiphe, Wolf portrays the younger generation as "weary of being cast as maidens in distress" (Green 1995). Women are urged to move from victim feminism to **power feminism** and to embrace a worldview that lets them "walk with an open mind, a loving heart, and a very big stick called clout" (Wolf [1993] 1994: 289). Wolf rejects the old feminist model, which she terms the "intimate ideal of political affiliation" that celebrated women's focus on connectiveness and consensus through always listening and "talking things through" (294). For Wolf, this model that "intended to hold women together with the honey of personal love" was "highly 'feminine' " and "far too weak" (294). In contrast, she advocates the "power group," which models itself on the "old boys' network" where "men pool their power" and "pass it to their friends" (297) She writes that powerful men "do not hoard their power, they select a group of men whom they get along with and take every possible opportunity to do them favors" (297). Wolf suggests a similar type of feminist organization in which women meet once a month but do not claim or pretend they are a collective. Rather, each woman tells the group what she is doing, what contacts and resources she has, and what contacts and resources she needs. Anyone can contact anyone else to make a request, propose a project, exchange information, or suggest a deal. "Thus every woman can take what she needs without being compelled to follow the agenda of *the almighty group*" (298–290; emphasis added).

For Wolf, such power groups could ensure that women focus on what is possible and empowering, unlike the second wave's consciousness-raising groups that focused on what is oppressive. She thinks power groups will ease "women's psychological anxieties about seeking power" because members are able to empower themselves at the same time that they contribute to the empowerment of other members of the group in terms of contacts and resources (300). Wolf also envisions power groups as making feminism lucrative. She contrasts her power feminist perspective to Marxist feminists who "scorned capitalism" and suggests instead that women invest in other women's independence, likening this to the extension of microcredit to poor women in the Third World (301).[3] Wolf even suggests that women "make deals to do for each other whatever it is that would get them fired—or terrify them—if they had to do it for themselves" (308). Her guidelines for power feminism also include the more traditional reformist paths taken by liberal feminists, such as women's power to elect government officials, to act as lobbyists, to use their consumer clout to compel marketers and advertisers to address their demands, to give charity, and to create awards for other women. Despite Wolf's claims that her approach is new, critics argue that her guidelines for power feminism are, at most, a thinly veiled version of liberal feminism. Without the label "feminist," Wolf's guidelines could have been written by the Junior League. Critics ask: Is power feminism just a feminist version of trickle-down economics?[4] Do women who lack contacts or resources simply remain recipients of charity from their well-to-do and well-connected sisters? (Sorisio 1997: 139; Senna 1995):

> The power feminism phenomenon represents not a "new school" in feminism, but rather a very old school imbedded in whiteness, privilege, "beauty", and consumerism. . . . They publish article upon article celebrating capitalist-feminism and like true superwomen, have children at home being cared for by West Indian nannies. For the women they employ, power feminism offers few solutions to the problems they face in feeding their children, paying the rent and getting home safely in a dangerous city. (Senna 1995: 17–18)

Danzy Senna's 1995 critique of power feminism echoes intersectionality theorist bell hooks's critique of liberal feminism from a decade earlier (see chapters 2 and 5).

Other power feminists within the third wave explicitly support wielding the weapons previously used against women—especially their sexual power—to enhance women's roles as active, powerful subjects. Take, for example, Elizabeth Wurtzel (1998: 34), who argues:

> These days putting out one's pretty power, one's pussy power, one's sexual energy for popular consumption no longer makes you a bimbo. It makes you smart.

Similarly, Joan Morgan (1999: 218) admiringly quotes Queen Latifah's refusal to criticize female hip hop stars for their sexually explicit lyrics: "I think we need to get over ourselves. . . . The bottom line . . . is that pussy is a powerful thing. And I've come to realize that some women can use it to gain things for themselves because they see it as their greatest strength." Clearly Morgan, Wolf, and Wurzel ignore Audre Lorde's warning (1984: 110) that "the master's tools can never dismantle the master's house."

Overall, the third wave's responses to power feminists and the feminist dissenters have been mixed. Some third wavers distance themselves from these perspectives. Senna (1995: 16–18) describes power feminism as "a cloak for conservatism, consumerism, and even sexism." Leslie Heywood and Jennifer Drake refer to Roiphe, Denfeld, and Wolf as "conservative feminists" and lump them together with those who heralded a postfeminist era. They (1997: 1) write: "Conservative post-feminism is in every way more visible than is the diverse activist work that terms itself "third wave." Deborah Siegel (1997b: 76) says she cannot tolerate the thought of the dissenting daughters purporting to take back feminism as "taking it back from me." Siegel offers a different understanding of what it means to name oneself a victim. For her, as for many second wave feminists, it is not a defeatist confession. Rather, "to name oneself a victim is an articulation of strength, for *to give a name to the injustices that continue to oppress is to adamantly refuse victim status*" (76; emphasis added).[5]

Many third wavers reject pretty power and obsessions with body image. This is illustrated well in the anthology *Adiós, Barbie: Young Women Write about Body Image and Identity* (1998), edited by Ophira Edut. For example, Lisa Jervis's contribution to this anthology, "My Jewish Nose" (62–67), describes how she resisted her mother's suggestions to get cosmetic surgery (rhinoplasty) by arguing that she did not want to erase the ethnicity from her face. However, the contributors to *Adiós Barbie* often discuss these serious issues in a humorous, playful, and engaging style that is exemplified in Box 7.2.

BOX 7.2

Barbie Dolls I'd Like to See

Birkenstock Barbie. Finally, a doll made with horizontal feet and comfortable sandals. Made from recycled materials.

Bisexual Barbie. Comes in a package with Skipper and Ken.

Butch Barbie. Comes with short hair, leather jacket, "Silence + Death" T-Shirt, pink triangle buttons, Doc Martens, pool cue and dental dams. Packaged in cardboard closet with doors flung wide open. Barbie Carpentry Business sold separately.

Harley Barbie. Equipped with motorcycles, helmet shades. Tattoos are non-toxic and can be removed with baby oil.

B-Girl Barbie. Truly fly Barbie in midriff-baring shirt and baggy jeans. Comes with skateboard, hip hop accessories and plenty of attitude. Pull her cord, and she says things like, ""I don't *think* so," "Dang, get outta my face" and "You go, girl." Teaches girls not to take shit from men and condescending white people.

Transgender Barbie. Formerly known as G.I. Joe.

From "Klaus Barbie, and Other Dolls I'd Like to See.," by Susan Jane Gilman. Pp. 20–21 in *Adiós Barbie: Young Women Write about Body Image and Identity*, ed. Ophira Edut (Seattle, Wash.: Seal, 1998).

While it is rare to find the works by Roiphe or Denfeld in third wave anthologies, works by other power feminists are often included. Rebecca Walker's anthology *To Be Real* (1995) has a contribution by Naomi Wolf as well as a piece by power feminist and supermodel Veronica Webb. Hip hop feminist Joan Morgan's *When Chickenheads Come Home to Roost* (1999) is a mainstay of third wave feminism. Other third wavers take a more nuanced approach that appreciates the rebellious desire of power feminists to reclaim what was previously used against them but that also recognizes how this entails inherent political dangers (Baumgardner and Richards 2000: 138). Still others argue that excluding any perspectives from the third wave only makes the third wave as restrictive as they claim their second wave sisters to be (Henry 2004).

Regardless of the position third wavers take on the feminist dissenters or on power feminism, it is fair to say that Denfeld's, Roiphe's and Wolf's accusations of the second wave as a "victim-feminism" magnified the image of this wave as prudish and puritanical (Henry 2004: 100–101). This view of the second wave permeates third wave discourse. As some third wavers put it, the second wave has "more restrictions than green lights when it comes to sexuality" (Alfonso and Trigilio 1997: 12).

THE THIRD WAVE AND POSTSTRUCTURALISM

The influence of poststructuralism on third wave feminism is evident in regard to a number of different topics. In particular, poststructuralism and its stepchild queer theory have strongly influenced the third wave's views on sexual practices, its epistemological stance and its views on identities. These topics are examined in the sections that follow.

Third Wave "Bad Girls" and "Pomosexuals"

In *Not My Mother's Sister* (2004), Astrid Henry provides one of the most informative discussions of third wave views on sex and sexuality. Below I draw from her chapters "Taking Feminism to Bed" and "Neither My Mother nor My Lover," in which she highlights how many third wavers claim sexuality as one of their key sites of struggle. Similarly, Nan Bauer-Maglin and Donna Perry, editors of *"Bad Girls"/"Good Girls"* (1996: xvi), write:

> Sexuality in all its guises, has become the lightning rod for this generation's hopes and discontents (and democratic vision) in the same way that civil rights and Vietnam galvanized [an earlier] generation in the 1960s.

Not only are sexual freedom and bodily pleasure viewed as their particular contributions to feminism, but many third wavers also celebrate their willingness to engage in nonnormative or transgressive sexual practices as part of the new "Jane generation." This generational label was coined by Merri Lisa Johnson in her book *Jane Sexes it Up* (2002). Along with flaunting a sexy, bad girl image, diverse sexual practices have become de rigueur among the third wave. In describing the "women of the New Girl Order," *Bust* coeditor Debbie Stoller (1999: 84) writes:

> In our quest for total sexual satisfaction, we shall leave no sex toy unturned and no sexual avenue unexplored. Women are trying their hands (and other body parts) at everything from phone sex to cybersex, solo sex to group sex, heterosex to homosex. Lusty feminists of the third wave, we're more than ready to drag race down sexual roads less traveled.

These sexually aggressive and bad girl images fostered the rise in the mid-1990s of a new feminist label—the "do me feminists." The term was coined by Tad Friend in a 1994 article in *Esquire* in which he hailed the rise of a "new breed" of feminists who had shifted from a "paradigm of sexual abuse" to a "paradigm of sexual pleasure."[6] While this provocative label received a lot of publicity, it masked how third wavers and their publications (like *Bust* quoted above) discuss serious issues of concern to young women, such as fear of sexually transmitted diseases, problems with body image, and ethnic and racist sexual stereotyping (Karp and Stoller 1999).

Various reasons have been given for why young feminists are attracted to a pro-sex politics that focuses on pleasure. Paula Kamen, author of *Feminist Fatale* (1991), discusses how younger women feel more comfortable with sex than did earlier generations. They live in an era in which many and varied sexual practices are more visible and openly discussed. They also are surrounded by a mass culture that celebrates youth and sexuality. From the teenage soap operas on prime time reality television to the bootie-shaking, midriffs in popular music, the mass media's new breed of sexual woman seems to be ever younger and more sexually active. Their second wave predecessors also left a legacy of greater access to sex education, birth control, and abortion as well as more knowledge about female bodies (Henry 2004). Few third wavers fail to mention how they grew up reading *Our Bodies, Ourselves*, a book first published by the Boston Women's Health Collective in 1971 that focuses on enhancing women's understanding of health issues, sexuality, and their own bodies.[7]

Despite such contributions by second wave feminists to a better understanding of female bodies and sexuality, the view that their older sisters had "few green lights" in regard to sexual practices is shared by many third wavers regardless of their sexual orientations. As Henry points out, many younger lesbians explicitly reject the ideas of such major theorists of second wave lesbian feminism as Adrienne Rich or Charlotte Bunch, who viewed lesbianism as "womyn-oriented," "womyn-born," and a "profoundly female experience." These lesbian theorists also highlighted differences between male and female types of sex, celebrating the nurturing and commitment they associated with female sexual intimacy (Rich 1980, Bunch 1972; see chapter 3). In contrast, third wave lesbians celebrate a sexier and lustful approach to sex and describe their second wave sisters as frumpy, dowdy, and asexual. As Henry (2004: 124) notes, such criticisms targeted second wave lesbians' sexual practices as well as their lifestyles and dress: "the Birkenstock, flannel-wearing, radical separatist lesbian culture" is viewed by third wavers not only as "bad fashion" but, also, as "out of fashion."

Second wave lesbian feminists who embraced this separatist culture also criticized various gendered subjects, such as butch/femme or "trans persons," for emulating traditional heterosexual roles, just as they criticized certain sexual practices, such as sadomasochism (s/m), for fostering male-oriented, power-laden sexual practices. They also rejected political alliances with gay males, pointing to how gay men benefited from many patriarchal privileges and how they too were involved in power-laden sexual practices (see chapter 3). The womyn-oriented, separatist lesbian feminism of the second wave encouraged feminists to remove themselves as much as possible from male-dominated activities and institutions, including those of gay males.

However, the AIDS crisis of the 1980s was pivotal in fostering more joint struggles of lesbians and gay men to fend off the rampant homophobia that accompanied this crisis. Through these joint efforts, many lesbians became intrigued with gay males' "enthusiastic embrace of the sexual" and their focus on eroticism and pleasure—things they viewed as absent from lesbian culture (Ruth Schwartz quoted in Henry 2004: 121). This also meant that many younger lesbians rejected the womyn-oriented assumptions about sexuality fostered during the second wave, preferring queer politics and queer analyses of sexuality that arose in the 1990s. Astrid Henry writes: "Like the 'third wave', the term 'queer' has been used to mark a new formulation of politics and identity" for this new generation of feminists (115).

This rejection of second wave lesbian feminism in favor of queer theory is poignantly lamented in Lillian Faderman's afterword to Dana Heller's *Cross Purposes: Lesbians, Feminists, and the Limits of Alliance* (1997):

> Is the lesbian-feminist of the older generation feeling like the mother—who had been "very advanced" in her youth—whose daughter, having just come of age, rudely rejects all mama's ideas as dated and dowdy though she only half understands them. . . . Does mama, with menopause looming on the horizon, feel betrayed and abandoned and worried sick by the favorite daughter who should now be paying her the tribute of wanting to follow closely in her footsteps instead of running off with strange young men? (221)

"Running off with strange young men" is a reference to how young queer women today have followed the lure of male gay sexual culture, a path often described as "going fag." These young women embrace more lusty and diverse sexual practices, such as nonmonogamy, sadomasochism, constructing daddy/boy or daddy/girl relationships, and frequenting women's sex clubs (Henry 2004: 140). In turn, the dildo is routinely cited as a marker of this shift in lesbian sexual practices. For example, Emma Healey, author of *Lesbian Sex Wars* (1996), writes:

> If in the 1980s the typical dyke about town owned a cat and a bicycle, her 1990s sister seems much more likely to possess a dog and a dildo. The dildo reviled by [second wave] lesbian feminism as a tool of patriarchy, has now become a potent symbol of lesbian sexuality. (Quoted in Henry 2004: 133)

Healy contrasts the "non-sexual bicycle" to the "hedonistic dildo" and celebrates "the new 1990s dildocracy" (133). Moreover, many third wavers view such lusty and transgressive sexual practices not only as "outlaw performances" that challenge and subvert but, also, as promoting a feminism that is more open to a profusion of gendered subjects, like butch, femme, transexuals, and transgendered people (Jeannine DeLombard in Walker 1995; Koyama 2003: 246–247).

The sexual politics of third wave feminists could best be described as "**genderqueer**" (Wilchins 2002; see chapter 6) or as "**pomosexual**." Carol Queen and Lawrence Schimel (1997: 21) explain this latter concept in the following way:

> Pomosexuality lives in the space in which all other non-binary forms of sexual and gender identity reside—a boundary-free zone in which fences are crossed for the fun of it, or simply because some of us can't be fenced it. . . . It acknowledges the pleasure of transgression, as well as the need to transgress limits that do not make room for all of us.

As Queen and Schimel explain, "pomosexual" is similar to **genderqueer** but more explicitly acknowledges its roots in postmodernism and poststructuralism (20). Indeed, the third wave's focus on sex as pleasure is similar to the way poststructuralist Michel Foucault framed sexual practices—not as acts conceived in scientific, reproductive, or moralistic terms but, rather, as erotic and pleasurable bodily acts (see chapter 6). In turn, *poststructuralist and queer theorists* view transgressing norms of sexual behavior as subversive acts that expose the social construction of sex and sexuality (Butler 1990 and 1993). Thus, it is not surprising that many third wave lesbians identify as queer:

> Queerness and postmodernism serve to mark a break with past understandings of gay and lesbian studies, identities, and, frequently, sexual practices. They are also used to signal a new relationship between lesbianism and feminism. (Henry 2004: 138)

Most third wavers seem unaware that many second wave feminists held prosex views (as documented in chapters 3 and 4 herein). Only a few of their more history-conscious peers have criticized the third wave's historical amnesia. In *Not My Mother's Sister* (2004), Astrid Henry discusses the "historical ignorance" of third wavers who fail to realize that the "sex wars" of the 1980s were intragenerational, not intergenerational (88–114). Yet Henry also understands the third wave's desire to present itself as new and different. She uses the term "**disidentification**" to explain why social movement activists often distinguish themselves from their predecessors in order to present themselves as unique (7–8). Deborah Siegel (1997b: 59 and 61) also acknowledges the energy and vitality the third wave gets from viewing itself as new and different. However, she points to the fallacy of "assuming a metonymic view of the second wave, in which a part of second wave activity is substituted for the whole" and warns that if dialogue between feminists of different generations is to move forward, it has to move beyond narrative scripts that construct *any* wave as monolithic or that erase the heterogeneities of feminism at any one moment.

The Third Wave's Epistemological Stance

A number of the third wave's theoretical assumptions suggest the strong influence of a postmodern epistemology and its radical social constructionist view of knowledge. As noted in chapters 1 and 6, social constructionists highlight how people construct knowledge from different vantage points or social locations. Because all vantage points are partial and limited, they embrace polyvocality or the inclusion of many voices and vantage points to construct their sense of social reality. Evidence of this commitment to **polyvocality** can be found in the third wave's explicit awareness of differences between women and in the multiracial and multicultural approach that characterizes most third wave publications. Indeed, the third wave prides itself on being more sensitive to diversity than their second wave sisters.

While the standpoint epistemology of some second wave feminists did highlight differences between women, these differences referred to group phenomena, such as when second wave socialist feminists highlighted how women in different classes experienced the world differently or when intersectionality theorists discussed the situated knowleges that rose from multiple social locations of penalty and privilege on their matrix of domination (Collins 1990 and 2004b; see also chapters 4 and 5). By contrast, third wavers approach differences between women in an *individualistic* fashion that has more in common with postmodernists and poststructuralists who view *all* group categories as **essentialist** (see chapter 6).

The third wave's individualism is reflected in their "penchant for personal narratives" (Springer 2002: 1060) in which multiple authors present their distinct vantage points to form an anthology of readings. Rebecca Walker's *To Be Real* (1995) and Barbara Findlen's *Listen Up: Voices from the Next Feminist Generation* (1995) exemplify this approach to voicing difference. Contributors to these anthologies come from diverse social locations by race, ethnicity, and/or sexual orientation (though their social class locations are seldom mentioned). Their stories are personal stories about the contradictions, uncertainties, and dilemmas that each of these feminists have faced in their everyday lives. Many third wave zines, webzines, magazines, and other publications are personal—much like diaries or journals written to vent anger and frustration (Cashen 2002: 17). Rarely did second wave feminists write in such a personal manner. Rather they argued that analysis should move from an individual, personal response to a collective, political response. Typical was the following statement by Carol Hanisch

(1969:1): "There are no personal solutions at this time. There is only collective action for a collective solution."

A strong strand of individualism is visible also in the third wave's **"do it yourself" (DIY) feminism**. Examples abound in third wave literature of the empowering potential of DIY feminism. **Riot Grrrl**, a significant inspiration to many third wavers, embraced DIY feminism and made a space for women within punk rock by creating their own music and zines, developing their own record labels, and ensuring that mosh pits were safe for women (Klein 1997). Other examples of the DIY approach are presented in Dawn Bates and Maureen McHugh's "Zines: Voices of Third Wave Feminists" (2005) and Barbara Duncan's "Searching for a Home Place: Online in the Third Wave" (2005). These authors describe various ways in which third wavers empowered themselves by producing their own zines and creating home places online to disseminate their political messages. Box 7.3 explains what zines are and the role that Riot Grrrl bands played in promoting zines. It also lists some of the major feminist zine collections in the United States.

BOX 7-3

"Don't You Know—We're Talking about a Revolution? Sounds Like a {Zine}!"

Zines (or minimagazines) have quite an eclectic past. They can be traced as far back as chapbooks or the pamphlets that Thomas Paine used to incite the colonists to fight the Revolutionary War in 1776. The do-it-yourself (DIY) nature of zines encourages people from all classes, races, genders, sexualities, and politics to express themselves freely and without the usual editorial or publishing restrictions of books. Zines—or fanzines as they were called in the 1920s—were created by science fiction readers to develop a community of avid sci-fi fans who could express their admiration for sci-fi authors and ponder what curiosities the future held for humans living in . . . 2011. Just like the zines created in the 1970s punk rock scene and in the late 1990s Riot Grrrl movement, fanzines were shared among sci-fi readers through the mail or in homes to unite a marginalized group in society. As part of the late 1970s punk scene, zines were used to promote the underground music scene and to express the disgust and anger felt by the British working class toward the upper class. At this time, too, zines were revolutionary in nature, as they helped launch the punk rock music phenomenon with a zine titled "Punk."

Later in the early 1990s, a group of women in Olympia, Washington and Washington, D.C., began creating zines that gave a voice to third wave feminism, and the revolution for young women began. The Riot Grrrl zinesters not only created powerful feminist discourse, but they also formed bands with the same names as the titles of their zines, such as Bikini Kill. They made music that electrified their message of empowerment and independence. The zines served many purposes for these women and their readers First, they made the personal political so that writing about taboo subjects, such as menstruating, sexual escapades, and anger, was accepted and encouraged. Second, the third wave Riot Grrrl zines expressed a deep distrust and rejection of mainstream media and its stereotypes of women. The zines were made by hand, but some were created on typewriters and later on computers for very little money. They were photocopied, stapled, and distributed in coffee shops, bookstores, record stores, and music venues. Zines can also be acquired through distributors called distros.

Distros (Distributors) and Where to Find Zines
The following zines are free and easily accessible:
Microcosm: www.microcosmpublishing.com/catalog/zines
Parcell Press: www.parcellpress.com
Sweet Candy Distro: sweetcandydistro.weebly.com

Archives and Libraries
Barnard College Library: www.barnard.edu/library/zines
Nadine Vorhoff Library, Newcomb College Institute: http://tulane.edu/newcomb/vorhoff-biblioblog.cfm
Smith College Library: http://asteria.fivecolleges.edu/findaids/sophiasmith/mnsss356_main.html
Queer Zine Archive Project: www.qzap.org/v6/index.php
ZineLibrary.Info: www.zinelibrary.info/search/node/feminism

"Don't You Know—We're Talking about a Revolution? Sounds Like a {Zine}!" by Beatrice Calvert, gender and women's studies librarian, Newcomb College Center for Research on Women, Tulane University, New Orleans. 2011. (Title inspired by "Talkin' 'bout a Revolution" by Tracy Chapman.) Printed for the first time with permission of Beatrice Calvert.

Some scholars argue that the individualism of the third wave reflects its resistance to using the essentialist, second wave's collective "we" and speaking for other women (Siegel 1997a: 57; Henry 2004: 43). This is a critical stance they learned from the deconstructionist methods of postmodernism and poststructuralism as well as from intersectionality theorists' critique of white, second wave feminists who too often spoke for "all women" and ignored difference. All of these perspectives discuss how people should be accountable for their voices and visions. They do not pretend that knowledge is neutral or objective; they acknowledge how their own social locations influence their knowledge claims and how their knowledge claims can affect other people both positively and negatively. This highly reflexive approach to knowledge melds well with the third wave's preference for personal narratives and DIY zines because such genres are among the most *transparent* ways of acknowledging authorial presence and one's role in the construction of knowledge.

The Third Wave's Poststructuralist Turn on Identities

A major topic on which third wavers embrace poststructuralism but part ways with intersectionality theory is the issue of identities. Many intersectionality theorists, such as the members of the Combahee River Collective, embraced identity politics as their major form of politics (see chapter 5). In contrast, poststructuralists prefer more fluid and shifting notions of identities because they view identity categories as both essentialist and restrictive. Readers will recall from chapter 6 how poststructuralist Michel Foucault saw freedom as "living in the happy limbo of non-identity" (quoted in Grant 1993: 131). Similarly, Judith Butler advocated subversive performance politics as a means of deconstructing and resignifying rigid notions of identity in order to open a space for difference (Butler, 1990).

The third wave clearly follows on this poststructuralist path when it *views identities as disciplinary and restrictive.* Consider Rebecca Walker's words in *To Be Real* (1995: xxxiii):[8]

> We fear that identity will dictate and regulate our lives, instantaneously pitting us against someone, forcing us to choose inflexible and unchanging sides, female against male, black against white, oppressed against oppressor, good against bad.
>
> This way of ordering the world is especially difficult for a generation that has grown up transgender, bisexual, interracial, and knowing and loving people who are racist, sexist, and otherwise afflicted.

In turn, a recurring third wave theme is *using contradictions and performance politics to deconstruct and resist identities or categorization.* For example, Riot Grrrl band members adopted a feminine "girlie" type of dress juxtaposed with combat boots or wrote words like "slut" on their bodies as a critique of the construction of the feminine (Cashen 2002: 13–14). In *Third Wave Agenda* (1997), Leslie Heywood and Jennifer Drake discuss at length how the third wave embraces contradiction, "**feminist hybridity**," and "**lived messiness**" to deconstruct rigid and conventional notions of sex, gender, and race:

> The lived messiness characteristic of the third wave is what defines it: girls who want to be boys, boys who want to be girls, boys and girls who insist they are both . . . people who are white and black, gay and straight, masculine and feminine. (8)

This quote also suggests how third wave feminists reject binary thinking that divides social reality into categories, such as white/black, heterosexual/homosexual, or male/female, because they view these categories as limiting the possibilities of being (Mack-Canty 2005). Thus, for a number of reasons, the third wave takes a poststructuralist turn in its rejection of core identities and binary thought as well as its preference for ambiguous and shifting identities. As one third wave feminist put it, "breaking free of identity politics" gave her "an awareness of the complexity and ambiguity of the world we have inherited" (Senna 1995: 20).

Rejecting a Disciplinary Feminism

Third wave feminists also embrace poststructuralists' warning that theories and discourses—even emancipatory theories and discourses—can serve as moves for power or dominance rather than as attempts at greater clarity (see Chapters 1 and 6). Of all of the feminist frameworks discussed in this text, *the third wave appears to be the most wary that feminism can serve as a dominant and disciplinary discourse.* The term **disciplinary feminism** is used to describe how feminism restricts social practices and authoritatively sits in judgment on women's ideas and practices. Rather ubiquitous in third wave writings are claims that second wave feminism is restrictive not only in terms of sexual practices as discussed above but also in terms of *what it means to be a feminist.* Barbara Findlen, editor of *Listen Up: Voices from the Next Feminist Generation* (1995) describes how many of her peers think that "if something is appealing, fun or popular, it can't be feminist" (xiv). A similar refrain echoes throughout many third wave writings where second wave feminists are referred to as their "serious sisters."

One path taken by some third wavers wanting to break away from their more serious predecessors is **Girlie** feminism, which reclaims the word "girl" to address what these feminists view as the antifeminine, anti-joy features of the second wave. For them, wearing pink, putting on nail polish, and celebrating pretty power makes feminism playful and fun. Critics have labeled such politics as "babe feminism" or "bimbo feminism,"[9] yet many third waver's defend it. Jennifer Baumgardner and Amy Richards (2000: 161) write: "As feminists, *we* love Girlie because it makes feminism relevant and fun and in the moment. . . . A lot of what Girlie radiates is the luxury of self expression that most second wavers *didn't feel they could or should indulge in*" (emphasis added).

Playful forms of performance politics also have captured the imagination of third wavers. *The Vagina Monologues*, an episodic play written by second wave feminist Eve Ensler and first performed in 1996, is regularly produced on college campuses, and the proceeds from these performances are used to raise funds to combat violence against women. Also popular among third wavers are the **Radical Cheerleaders**—a group that leads political chants at various protests and demonstrations—and the **Guerrilla Girls**—a group that addresses the underrepresentation of women artists in museums and throughout visual culture more generally (see Box 7.4). All of these forms of performance politics use humor and sarcasm to deliver serious feminist messages and analyses.

BOX 7-4

Guerrilla Girls

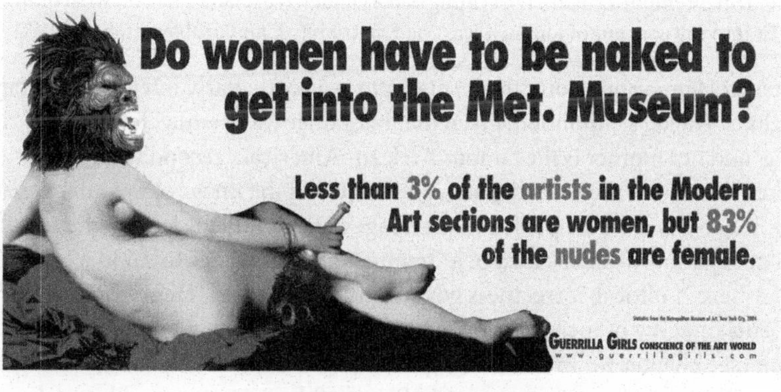

Copyright © by Guerrilla Girls; Courtesy www.guerrillagirls.com

As depicted in the poster above, the Guerrilla Girls wear masks to remain anonymous. Their website describes them as follows:

> The Guerrilla Girls are feminist masked avengers in the tradition of anonymous do-gooders like Robin Hood, Wonder Woman and Batman. We use facts, humor and outrageous visuals to expose sexism, racism and corruption in politics, art, film and pop culture. We undermine the idea of a mainstream narrative in visual culture by revealing the understory, the subtext, the forgotten, the overlooked, the understated and the downright unfair. Our work has been passed around the world by our tireless supporters, who use us as a model for doing their own crazy kind of activism.
>
> In the last few years, the Guerrilla Girls have appeared at over 100 universities and museums around the world. We created a large scale installation for the Venice Biennale, brainstormed with Greenpeace, and participated in Amnesty International's Stop Violence against Women Campaign in the UK. In 2006, we unveiled our latest anti-film industry billboard in Hollywood just in time for the Oscars, appeared at the Tate Modern, London, and created large scale projects for Istanbul and Mexico City. In 2007 we dissed the Museum of Modern Art at its own Feminist Futures Symposium, examined the museums of Washington DC in a full page in the Washington Post, and exhibited large-scale posters and banners in Athens, Rotterdam, Bilbao, Sarajevo, Belgrade and Shanghai. In 2008–9, we did actions at the Broad Contemporary Art Museum at LACMA, Los Angeles, Bronx Museum, New York, Ireland and Montreal.

Excerpt from "Our Story"; www.guerrillagirls.com/press/ourstory.shtml, with permission.

A less playful, more critical view of the second wave as a disciplinary feminism can be found in Rebecca Walker's anthology *To Be Real* (1995: xxix):

> A year before I started this book, my life was like a feminist ghetto. Every decision I made, person I spent time with, word I uttered had to measure up to an image I had in my mind of what was morally and politically right according to my vision of female empowerment. Everything had a gendered explanation, and what didn't fit into my concept of feminist was "bad, patriarchal, and problematic."

As Astrid Henry points out, the term *ghetto* is a particularly interesting metaphor in light of Walker's childhood, given that her father was a white, Jewish, civil rights lawyer and her mother is the famous African-American, second wave author Alice Walker. As used in the United States, ghetto evokes the image of the impoverished, black inner city; in Europe, it evokes images of the walled, Jewish ghettos of the Nazi occupation. Walker's idea of a "feminist ghetto" brings to mind a prison-like place where "political correctness governs its inhabitants" (Henry 2004: 149).[10]

This imagery of incarceration evokes Foucault's discussion of the Panopticon prison (see chapter 6). In this late-eighteenth-century model prison, a few guards stationed in a high circular tower out of view of the prisoners could gaze down on the inmates and monitor their activities. Whether or not guards were present, the effect was to "induce in the prisoners a state of conscious and permanent visibility that assured the automatic functioning of power" (Foucault [1975]1979: 201). The result of this internalized and prescriptive "**panoptical gaze**" was to make the prisoners their own jailers (155). For Foucault, this is a major technique of power used in modern societies in which people internalize prescriptive discourses about what is normal or abnormal, sane or insane, healthy or pathological, and self-policing becomes a major means of social control.

In "Unpacking the Mother/Daughter Baggage: Reassessing Second- and Third-Wave Tensions," Cathryn Bailey (2002: 150) uses Foucaultian imagery to discuss how feminism can be experienced as a repressive form of power and authority:

> Many younger women see themselves as struggling against becoming the kind of feminist subjects they thought that they were supposed to become. As such, they may be offering a kind of resistance that is not immediately directed at actual feminists, but rather to an internalized version of a feminist governor—a "panoptical feminist connoisseur."

By saying this is a problem for "younger women," Bailey implies that the "panoptical" disciplinary feminism is second wave feminism. Rebecca Walker (1995: xxix) is even more explicit that second wave feminism was the "feminist ideal" she was measuring herself against and that appeared to be scrutinizing every decision she made and every word she uttered. By constantly policing her own behaviors to ensure that she met these "ideal" standards, Walker felt incarcerated. Only by "being real" and "telling the truth" about herself and this disciplinary feminism did Walker break free of the chains that constrained her—free to establish a feminism of her own making that resisted moral and political prescriptions.

Another one of Foucault's techniques of discursive power—the **confessional**—has at least a spiritual presence in third waver Gina Dent's analysis of the austere and disciplinary nature of feminism. In "Missionary Position" (1995), Dent uses religious imagery to liken how feminists dictate politically correct behaviors to how missionaries instructed people of other cultures that the "missionary position" was the only proper way to have sex. Dent never mentions Michel Foucault, but more than a decade earlier he had discussed how confessions were used to elicit information and to keep people within normative guidelines in modern societies (see chapter 6). Dent (1995: 69) takes a similar tack when she describes her experience at a feminist conference where one of the panelists, a former sex worker, "confessed" that she had been a prostitute. The panelist then reveals how feminism taught her "to define the harm" and gave her the "missionary zeal" to purge this evil from the lives of other sex workers on their behalf. Dent asked the panelist: "How and when did feminism become a religion? When did we [feminists] begin to proselytize, on the basis of this moral obligation we have, to save?" (69). The organizers of the conference severely chastised Dent for her questions. She was made aware that she had "violated a sacred rite"—what the conference organizers referred to as "the coming to voice" of another woman (66).

Unlike Bailey and Walker, Dent does not see "**missionary feminism**" as simply a second wave problem. Rather, her analysis is more similar to Foucault's in that she sees this missionary stance as a problem that can plague any feminism or any political ideology. Dent asks: "In what moments are we, as feminists, authorized to speak for other women about what we as theorists and activists, interpret as their oppression?" (65).[11] She argues that, once we demand a particular form of feminist practice, confession becomes "not only a dynamic within feminism, but a means of policing its borders" (71). As shown above, many third wavers share Dent's view that feminists "should rethink our positions around sex and woman's pleasure without assuming we can describe and determine a single missionary feminist point of view—the missionary position" (74). Dent concludes:

> I propose, then, that we must begin to think critically about how to take the religion out of feminism, how to break down the illusion that we comprise a community that has agreed upon its rules of existence. (74)

This critique of rules as oppressive and its corollary—*that unruliness is politically subversive*—characterizes third wave feminism and reflects the strong influence of poststructuralism and its stepchild queer theory.

THE THIRD WAVE AND INTERSECTIONALITY THEORY

Earlier chapters of this text noted how racial issues spurred the mobilization of feminist activists throughout the history of the U.S. women's movement. During the first wave, suffragists honed their political and organizing skills in the abolitionist movement, while during the second wave many women activists cut their political teeth in the civil rights movement (see chapters 2 and 5). As Astrid Henry (2004: 161) points out, third wavers often cite the confirmation hearings for Clarence Thomas's nomination to the U.S. Supreme Court in 1991 as sparking their feminist activism. These hearings were racially and politically complex from the start. If confirmed, Thomas would be the second African-American justice on the U.S. Supreme Court. He would replace Thurgood Marshall—a liberal judge renowned for his civil rights activism, whereas Thomas had a conservative record on civil rights. During the hearings, an African-American lawyer—Anita Hill—accused Thomas of sexual harassment ten years earlier when he had been her boss at the Equal Employment Opportunity Commission. Hill's testimony and the condescending responses to Hill by both Thomas and the members of Senate Judiciary Committee infuriated many women—especially women of color.[12] Shortly after the hearing, second wave, intersectionality theorist Beverly Guy-Sheftall (1995: 19) claimed it "sparked the most profound intraracial tensions around sexual politics that the modern African American community had ever experienced." Henry

(2004: 161) describes the Thomas hearing as inspiring a feminist reawakening across the country:

> The Thomas hearing mobilized women of all ages into action; they worked to elect record numbers of women into political office in 1992. The Thomas hearing helped put feminist issues back into the media spotlight after the bleak anti-feminist 1980s.

Race has been of signal importance to third wave activism and theory in other ways. Women of color and biracial women are in key leadership positions of the third wave making it the first wave of U.S. feminism to be led by women of color (163). Many third wavers also describe how *their politics are profoundly shaped by the theoretical writings of second wave women of color—especially the writings of, intersectionality theorists (also known as U.S. Third World Feminists).*[13] Vivien Labaton and Dawn Lundy Martin, editors of *The Fire This Time: Young Activists and the New Feminism* (2004), locate the inspiration for their activism in the writings of bell hooks, Gloria Anzaldúa, and Audre Lorde. Their focus on multiple, interlocking oppressions led activists in the third wave to embrace broader notions of inequality and social justice.[14] In *Third Wave Agenda*, Heywood and Drake (1997: 13) state: "It was U.S. Third World Feminism that modeled a language and a politics of hybridity that can account for our lives at the century's turn." Bushra Rehman and Daisy Hernandez (2002: xxi), editors of *Colonize This! Young Women of Color in Today's Feminism*, describe their anthology as "continuing the conversations" first initiated by second wave intersectionality theorists. In the anthology *Feminist Fatale*, Paula Kamen (1991: 17) acknowledges that the "authors with the most undeniable influence on my generation . . . are women of color." Poignantly, third waver Veronica Chambers (1995: 24) writes:

> When I bought Barbara Smith's *Home Girls: A Black Feminist Anthology*, I carried it like a prayer book. It was in this book that I first read Audre Lorde, Michelle Cliff, June Jordan and Luisah Teish. When I read Michelle Cliff's "If I Could Write This Fire, I Would Write This Fire," the title alone reverberated in my head like a drumbeat.

The third wave also has a deep appreciation for *socially lived knowledge*—another hallmark of intersectionality theory. Third wavers frequently make distinctions between the socially lived knowledge they experience in their everyday lives and the academic knowledge they garnered from women's studies programs:

> Like many young women of all colors and ethnic backgrounds, I had my first feminist awaking at college. Through books and classes and a dynamic women's studies teacher. . . . I found Simone de Beauvoir and Gloria Steinem, Alice Walker and Paula Gunn Allen. My first year, Barbara Smith gave a lecture, and for me, she was like a silver-screen apparition. . . . I come from a family of strong black women, but to my mother, feminism was a four-letter word. . . . To be strong, smart, independent and *unashamed* were necessary elements for survival in the Brooklyn of my youth. The black women I knew growing up embodied these qualities . . . they were, in other words, sisters who didn't take no shit. I knew strength, and I was taught it at birth. (Chambers 1995: 23, her emphasis)

Although Chambers credits women's studies for her first "feminist awakening," her article is titled "Betrayal Feminism" because of the racism she found among white feminist students at her college. She writes: It is . . . invisibility and betrayal that makes many young feminists of color think that the idea of a women's movement may not necessarily serve their best interests. . . . I stand on the shoulders of women like Barbara Smith, Audre Lorde and Luisah Teish, but I suffer as they did from a numbing isolation. I cannot change the mind of every white feminist that I encounter. That is not my interest or my job" (27).

In *When Chickenheads Come Home to Roost* (1999), Joan Morgan also distinguishes between socially lived and academic knowledge. She calls for a feminism that speaks to young black women, the way hip hop does: "One that claims the powerful richness and delicious complexities inherent in being black girls now—sistas of the post-Civil Rights, post-feminist, post soul, hip hop generation" (56–57). Morgan also refers to herself as a "hip hop feminist" instead of a "third wave feminist," much like second wave black feminists substituted "womanist" for "feminist" to state their disassociation from white feminism and to claim their own particular perspective. Although Morgan is grateful that the university curriculum exposed her to intellectuals who were womanists of color,[15] she is critical of academic feminism for having "little to do with her everyday life" (37):[16]

> If feminism is to have any relevance in the lives of the majority of black women, if it intends to move past theory and become functional it has *to rescue itself from the ivory towers of academia.* Like it or not hip hop is not only the dominion of the young, black and male, it is also the world in which young black women live and survive. (76; emphasis added)

Both Chambers and Morgan experience a disconnect between their socially lived knowledge and the feminism they encountered in college. Both are critical of how "academic feminism" is the only knowledge authorized to wear the title of feminism with a capital "F" (Henry 2004: 172). By contrast, intersectionality theorists recognized how *both* socially lived knowledge and academic theory revitalize each other and are necessary for political practice (hooks 1994; see chapter 1).

Deborah Siegel (1997a) suggests that differences between second and third wave views on academic feminism may reflect the historical contexts in which each wave arose. There were few if any women's studies classes to attend when most second wave feminists came of adult age. They had to create the feminism of the academy through their own socially lived knowledge and political action. There also was little feminist theory existing when the second wave women's movement arose in the 1960s. As noted in chapter 2, aside from a few notable exceptions, first wave analyses of women's oppression were descriptive rather than theoretical. Consequently, the second wave had to construct feminist theory as well as the feminist academy. By contrast, many third wavers developed their feminist consciousness through women's studies in the academy (61). They are more likely to experience disconnects between theory and practice precisely because these spheres are more disconnected in their own lives.

Disconnects between feminism and their own everyday lives are also reflected in how many third wave women call for a feminism committed to "keeping it real" (Morgan 1999: 154) In rap and hip hop music, "**being real**" came to signify authenticity—something that could not be faked—such as street or hood credentials. Astrid Henry (2004: 148–180) devotes an entire chapter of *Not My Mother's Sister* to showing how the term "being real" is used in different ways by third wave feminists. For the purposes of this text, only a few examples of the modern and postmodern variations on this theme found in third wave writings will be highlighted. For Rebecca Walker (1995), "being real" refers to feeling free to live one's personal life as one chooses—even if this means transgressing some earlier notion of what it means to be a "feminist." Thus, her notion of "being real" suggests being "authentic" or "true to oneself" and employs modern epistemological assumptions in that it assumes there is a core self (as does the notion of "being real" in rap and hip hop music). In contrast, Danzy Senna (1995) discusses how she spent much of her young life searching for "authenticity" only to find that there was no such thing. Here, Senna takes a postmodern epistemological stance by deconstructing the notion of authenticity and arguing that she can only "be real" within a feminism that encompasses multiple perspectives, complexity, ambiguity, and contradictions. Hip hop feminist Joan Morgan (2004: 56–57) sounds like a modernist when she calls for a feminism that speaks to the average black woman (as if there were such a person), yet her call for a feminism that speaks with "delicious complexities" to the distinct social and cultural realities of her post–civil rights, postfeminist, post-soul, and hip hop generation sounds more postmodern. The following sections examine how other third wavers merged modern with postmodern thought in both promising and problematic ways.

THIRD WAVE THEORY APPLICATIONS

Clearly the third wave has not had as much time as previous waves either to produce feminist theory or to apply their theoretical perspective to diverse topics. To date, there does not appear to be a third wave approach to ecofeminism comparable to those generated by other feminist frameworks examined in this text. Colleen Mack-Canty's article "Third Wave Feminism and Ecofeminism: Reweaving the Nature/Culture Duality" (2005) initially looked promising because she discusses how various "theoretical characteristics" of third wave feminism, such as their interest in "breaking down dualistic constructs" and their focus on the "intersectionality of oppressions," are reflected in third wave activism (195). However, her article was based on interviews with only twenty activists and did not sufficiently spell out what was new or different about third wave ecofeminism.[17] Rather than omit a theory applications section from this chapter, I chose to change the topic and examine how third waver Julie Bettie utilized assumptions of postmodernism, poststructuralism, and intersectionality theory to address social class differences between women.

As discussed in chapter 4, analyses of social class have been underdeveloped in contemporary feminism (Belkhir 1998: 19; Kandal 1995: 143). Even most third wave writings typically pay far more attention to race, gender, and sexuality than to social class. In contrast, Julie Bettie's *Women without Class* (2003) is one of the most impressive works on gender and social class written in recent decades. It won numerous awards, including the American Sociological Association Sex and Gender Section's most prestigious book award for 2004. The title of her book has multiple meanings. On the one hand, it denotes how her study focuses on young women from modest class backgrounds—women without class privilege. On the other hand, it highlights how the vast majority of social scientific studies on social class have been gender-blind, leaving women without adequate class analyses (32–41).

Women without Class: Girls, Race and Identity is based on an ethnographic study of the lives of Mexican–American and anglo girls in a senior high school. As the subtitle suggests, Bettie uses an intersectional analysis to examine how race, gender, and class are interwoven in the construction of these young girls' identities. Following in the path of intersectionality theorists who reject **hierarchicalizing oppressions** where one form of oppression is viewed as more important than another (see chapter 5), Bettie carefully points out how she "foregrounds" but does not privilege class (32). Rather, she views race, gender, and class as interlocking, mutually constitutive, and inseparable features of these girls' lives.

Bettie also draws explicitly from poststructuralism. For example, her conceptual scheme is modeled on the anti-essentialist work of Diana Fuss (1989):

> I do not mean to reassert a modern subject, but rather, in the context of recognizing that identity and experience are always constructed discursively, I wish to emphasize here an 'understanding of identity as self presence' to point to the less theorized, spontaneous understanding of identity and experience of everyday actors. (Bettie 2003: 53)

She also employs the work of Judith Butler to discuss how social class entails both "**performance**" and "**performativity**" and what this means for the relationship between social agency and social structure. In modern approaches, **social agency** refers to an individual's ability to act on and to influence the world in which she or he lives. **Social structure** refers to the way that patterned social relationships become institutionalized and shape or influence individuals' lives. The impact of these patterned social relations, such as racial, class, and gender relations appear as external to the individual—as having a life of their own, so to speak. In Bettie's work performativity refers to the impact that social structure has on people's lives but in a more fluid and less rigid way than most modernists recognize, because she highlights how social structures and institutions are continually reproduced by and owe their very existence to people's *everyday performances or practices* (52). Bettie's notion of performance implies social agency in that people perform class or gender through their actions, but it includes a poststructuralist twist. That is, she views actions as always embedded in discourses that give them meaning and that constitute the subject. Echoing Butler, for Bettie there is no "doer behind the deed"; rather, "the actor is constructed by the performance" (52 and 53).

To this theoretical synthesis of poststructuralism and intersectionality theory Bettie also interweaves the concepts of cultural capital and *habitus* from the work of the modern class theorist Pierre Bourdieu.[18] She emphasizes the cultural dimensions of social class and even refers to social class as a "cultural identity" (42). Bettie discusses how one's experience of class is expressed not only in one's work identity and income but also in many social relations unrelated to employment, such as family and friendship relations.[19] She is particularly interested in how consumption practices are "identity formation material" since women often have been defined as the major shoppers or consumers in modern societies (42). She laments how the positioning of women as consumers has been framed as nonproductive labor, especially by Marxists. For her, "consumer girl culture" is a site of resistance, not simply a site of false consciousness (42):

> If women express the symbolic boundaries of class culture through consumption practices and commodities targeted at women, then the gender-specific "hidden injuries of social class" [the psychological burdens of class anxiety] have to do with these markers. (43)

Thus, one of the more unique contributions of *Women without Class* is its focus on cultural and symbolic markers of class or what she terms an "economy of style" (61).

Another unique contribution is her focus on *social class as performance*. Although much attention has been paid to gender as performance in recent decades (Butler 1990;, West and Zimmerman 1987), little attention has been paid to social class as performance. As Bettie (2003: 51) points out, this type of class analysis has made only "cameo" appearances in feminist literature. To appreciate her contribution here readers must understand that the notion of social class as performance differs significantly from more conventional views of class as a social position or social location. One way to think about this is that when theorists refer to social class as a performance they are thinking of class as a verb; people are "doing class" in their everyday actions and behaviors and becoming class subjects in the process. In contrast, when class is viewed as a social position or location, it is used as a noun or adjective. Whether it is a middle-class, working-class or upper-class social location it is a position that people have rather than practices that they do. Viewing class as a position or location **reifies** it or makes it into a thing.[20] Viewing class as a verb and individuals as always in process of becoming class subjects through their performances places more emphasis on social agency and highlights the dynamic, dialectical relationship between social agency and social structure.[21]

Bettie discusses how different class performances were evident in the various student cliques at the high school she studied. While there were many cliques, a few examples will suffice for our purposes here. The girls from wealthier families most often were white girls in a college preparatory track at the school. They hung out together in a clique called the preps. White students from working-class and poorer families who were in a vocational track hung out in a clique called the smokers. The major clique of Mexican-American girls—las chicas—included girls from working-class families who also were in a vocational track at the high school. Each clique had its own "symbolic economy of style" that differentiated it from the other cliques (61). Differences were reflected in hairstyles, clothing, and even the color of nail polish or lipstick the girls wore. For example, as compared with the preps, las chicas wore more makeup, brighter lipstick and nail polish, and sexier clothes. Such differences in clothing and cosmetics also were perceived as markers of sexual morals, with las chicas being viewed by other students and teachers as the most sexually active girls regardless of whether this was actually the case. Class differences were further evident in the students' study habits, their classroom behavior, and their extracurricular activities.

When Mexican–American girls dressed or acted like the preps they were accused of "acting white" by their Mexican–American peers (83–86). Some theorists have called this a "**strategy of dismissal**"—a strategy used to control and to ostracize the actions of group members that are found threatening (see chapter 10). While Bettie recognizes this, she highlights how these students often confused and conflated racial and class categories. For example, Bettie asked why "acting white" was associated with acting like preps rather than like smokers (since both cliques were white). In response, the Mexican–American students dismissed the smokers as irrelevant. For Bettie, the relative invisibility or unimportance of working-class whites to these students was because the preps or the wealthier students "inflicted the most class injuries" in the school (84). Here she is not referring to direct, physical injuries but, rather, to what some theorists have called "**the hidden injuries of social class**"—the damage done to people's self-esteem—when people feel vulnerable, intimidated, or inadequate due to their lower class positions (Sennett and Cobb 1972; see chapter 4). Overall, the use of terms like "acting white" when class differences were actually being demarcated exaggerated the importance of race and underplayed the importance of class, thus making the role of social class less visible in students' lives. For this reason, Bettie (2003: 45) terms the subcultural styles reflected in different cliques as "class-barely-aware-of-itself."

Like other third wave writers, Bettie is not adverse to or uncomfortable with drawing from modern and postmodern approaches. Rather than seeing these perspectives as contradictory, as would many other social theorists, Bettie feels free to employ what she sees as the strengths of both. Her work demonstrates the recurring theme of embracing contradictions in third wave thought, as well as the richness that can be garnered from such a theoretical synthesis. Nevertheless, some problems that can accompany such couplings will now be examined.

CONCLUSION: THE "UNHAPPY MARRIAGE" OF THE MODERN AND THE POSTMODERN

The term *marriage* for the merging of two different theoretical perspectives has almost become a cliché in contemporary U.S. feminism. Prefacing it with the adjective *unhappy* is meant to conjure up memories of marriage law under the **doctrine**

of coverture whereby the husband held dominion over his wife (see chapter 2). In the early 1980s, Heidi Hartmann referred to the "unhappy marriage of Marxism and feminism" to criticize how in second wave Marxist feminism, Marxism came to dominate over feminism (see chapter 4). In the early 1990s, Cheshire Calhoun discussed the "unhappy marriage of feminist theory and lesbian theory" in her critique of how feminism dominated lesbianism in many second wave radical feminisms (see chapter 3). Perhaps it is only fitting that the third wave arranged its own marriage—this time between the modern and the postmodern, between intersectionality theory and poststructuralism. Below I use the second wave feminist slogan THE PERSONAL IS POLITICAL to illustrate the conflicts engendered by this unhappy marriage and to show how the assumptions of poststructuralism dominate over the assumptions of intersectionality theory.

As noted in chapter 3, THE PERSONAL IS POLITICAL was a slogan embraced by second wave feminists from a wide array of political perspectives. This slogan had both emancipatory and disciplinary features. It was emancipatory in that it empowered women by showing how many gender-related, interpersonal problems should be addressed not at the individual level but, rather, collectively as problems rooted in the social and political institutions. Prior to the modern women's movement, issues like rape, domestic violence, and sexual harassment often were treated as personal problems that should be dealt with privately and individually. By claiming that the personal is political, second wave feminists transformed these so-called personal problems into political issues and demanded that they be addressed collectively by the women's movement. Solutions were sought at the systemic macrostructural or institutional level rather than simply at the micro-interpersonal or individual level.

The disciplinary side of the personal is political called on feminists to live their politics in their everyday lives, in short, to practice what they preached. If they were engaged in personal lifestyle choices that undermined feminist politics, they should make every effort to change their lives so that their personal practices were consistent with their political views. These two dimensions of the personal is political were a powerful duo. They linked the micro and macro levels of society as well as social agency and social structure by requiring a transformation of both the individual and society.

The emancipatory implications of the personal is political are seldom debated among feminists of either the second or the third wave. Rather, it is the disciplinary side of this double-edged sword that third wavers rail against for taking the fun, fashion, and sexiness out of feminism. It is these disciplinary features that Gina Dent (1995: 71) highlighted when she spoke of a "missionary feminism" or when she characterized "the personal is political" as a "mantra" that entailed "self-policing of one's behaviors." It also is this disciplinary side that makes second wavers appear as the third wave's serious, dowdy, and asexual sisters.

It would appear that one possible way to resolve these conflicts would be to make clearer distinctions between lifestyle choices that have important political implications and those that do not. Clearly, not all lifestyle choices have political implications, and even those that do could range from trivial to serious. For example, Girlie feminism represents a rather benign form of breaking away from the more serious feminisms of the second wave. Whether or not individual feminists wear pink or use nail polish does not appear to have very serious implications for feminist theory or practice.

In contrast, viewing the women's movement as an "anything goes" movement has disturbing implications for effective collective action. Consider the words of Marcelle Karp, coeditor of *The Bust Guide to the New Girl Order* (1999: 310–311):

> We've entered an era of DIY feminism—sistah, do-it-yourself—and we have all kinds of names for ourselves: lipstick lesbians, do-me feminists. . . . No matter what the flava is, we're still feminists. Your feminism is what you want it to be and what you make of it. Define your agenda.

A similar view is echoed in the "free to be me" stance in Rebecca Walker's anthology *To Be Real* (1995), where one finds authors who want "to be free" to engage in vigilante violence and to eroticize the violent rape of a child with a baseball bat. Walker refers to such acts as "anti-revolutionary acts" because she knows they would be criticized by most second wavers. Yet, these acts do not cross any ethical boundaries in her third wave feminism; rather she views these authors' "courageous reckoning" with "anti-revolution acts" as liberating: "If feminism is to continue to be radical and alive, it must avoid reordering the world in terms of any polarity, be it female/male, good/evil" (xxxvii and xxxv).

The idea that feminism should avoid making any ethical judgments as to good or evil, right or wrong, belies its role as a politics. What are politics but the practices by which people make decisions that affect other citizens of the polity? Politics entail decisions about what is right and wrong, fair and unfair, equal and unequal and what should be done to resolve, remedy, reform, or transform these situations. Walker's stance that a vibrant feminism must avoid making ethical judgments reflects the influence of postmodern relativism. As discussed in chapter 6, the logic of postmodern relativism proceeds as follows: given the multiplicity and diversity of vantage points where every view is partial and limited, who is to decide which vantage point is correct or correct? If one perspective legislates the politically correct way to live one's life or to practice one's feminism, is that not a power move seeking dominance?

Only a few third wave feminists have criticized the relativism that pervades third wave feminist thought. In *Catching a Wave: Reclaiming Feminism for the 21st Century* (2003), editors Rory Dicker and Alison Piepmeier argue that it is fine for third wavers to challenge a restrictive notion of feminism not of their own making. They also agree with opening up and broadening the notion of feminism to make it appealing to a more diverse array of women. However, in their view, the absence of any boundaries on what feminism means "empties feminism of any core set of values and politics" and results in a "feminist free-for-all" (17). Hence, they oppose such an unbounded meaning of feminism and call for a feminism that can transform both the individual and society (17). What Dicker and Piepmeier call a "feminist free-for-all" reflects not only *ethical* and *judgmental relativism* but, also, the *strong strand of individualism* within the third wave. As Leslie Heywood and Jennifer Drake (1997: 11) write, "Despite our knowing better, despite our knowing its emptiness, the ideology of individualism is still a major motivating force in many third wave lives."

The political implications of this individualism is critically examined in Astrid Henry's "Solitary Sisterhood: Individualism Meets Collectivity in Feminism's Third Wave" (2005: 82):

> Third wave feminists rarely articulate unified political goals nor do they often represent the third wave as sharing a critical perspective on the world. Rather, third wave texts are replete with individual definitions of feminism and individualistic narratives of coming to feminist consciousness.

For Henry, if feminism becomes nothing more than whatever one wants it to be, it loses its "critical political perspective" (84).

Those who consider the third wave's individualism as a "virtue" argue that defining feminisms loosely means that third wave feminism can appeal to more people and be more inclusive than were earlier feminisms (Wolf [1993] 1994: xix). Even critics, such as Henry (2004: 41), admit that "the excessive focus on individualism by many third wavers reveals . . . a means of resisting the group identity implied by the terms 'feminists' and 'women' "—a trait learned from various critiques of second wave essentialism.

Although intersectionality theorists were among the first to challenge many second wavers' essentialist notion of sisterhood, they did not embrace a relativistic feminism. For example, more than two decades ago, intersectionality theorist bell hooks criticized relativism in her book *Feminist Theory* (1984: 23):

> Currently feminism seems to be a term without any clear significance. The "anything goes" approach to the definition has rendered it practically meaningless. . . . such definitions usually focus on the individual's own right to freedom and self-determination.

hooks is especially critical of feminism being viewed as a "lifestyle choice" rather than as a "political commitment" (27). She argues for a feminism defined in "political terms" that stresses collective rather than individual well-being and that calls for social revolution rather than simply personal lifestyle reform (23). Given that hooks was writing in 1984, she was not addressing the third wave but, rather, earlier divisions within the second wave over how feminism should be defined. Yet her words remain relevant today. Dicker and Piepmeier (2003: 17) are among the few third wavers today that have articulated the dangers of postmodern relativism and how this contradicts the intent of intersectionality theory:

> If everything and everyone can fit within the third wave—it doesn't matter what they actually think, do or believe. . . . This is the worst interpretation of bell hooks' edict that "feminism is for everybody": it implies that anybody can be a feminist, regardless of her or his actions.

Joan Morgan (1999: 231–232) also recognizes the importance of hooks' call for "political commitment" in bridging the individualistic versus collectivist threads of the third wave:

> I know that ours has never been an easy relationship. Sistahood ain't sainthood. . . . That being said, know that when it comes to sistahood, I am deadly serious about my commitment to you. . . . As long as inequality and oppression remain constants in our lives, sistahood is critical to our mutual survival. . . . The quest for power is not a solo trip.

Such conflicts over *individualism versus collectivism* and *relativism versus adjudicating political decisions* are at the root of the third wave's unhappy marriage of the postmodern and the modern. If the individualistic and relativistic sides of this debate come to dominate this marriage, the political will become entirely personal—reversing the intent of the second wave's notion that the personal is political. Whether the majority of third wave feminists take the postmodern path of *individualism* and *relativism* to embrace an "anything goes feminism" or whether they choose to develop a body of politics that they can *collectively* share appears to be one of the most important ongoing debates within the third wave. To date, they appear to be living uncomfortably with the "lived messiness" of these contradictory epistemological assumptions. Given these unresolved tensions within third wave feminism, it seems only fitting to end this chapter with a characteristically playful prognosis from Baumgardner and Richards' *Manifesta* (2000: 166):

> "Without a body of politics, the nail polish is really going to waste."

Additional writings by third wave feminists on global issues are examined in chapter 10.

CRITICISMS OF THIRD WAVE FEMINISMS

1. That the strong strand of individualism within the third wave makes their politics into a revolution of self rather than society. Critics argue that this individualism results in a subject-centered ethics that allows individuals free rein to pursue their interests at the expense of others. In contrast, according to these critics mutual well-being and collectivity should be crucial organizing principles of feminism (Pollitt 1999, Piñeros 2002).

2. That many third wave feminists distort the history of the second wave. They fail to acknowledge the many and diverse competing feminisms that actually made up this earlier wave. As such, they "imagine" a restrictive feminism that never existed. While some attribute this to ignorance, others argue that third wave feminists use this distorted portrayal to stress their own uniqueness (Angela Davis in Walker 1995: 281, Henry 2004).

3. That the relativism embodied in many third wave writings empties feminism of any core set of values and belies its ineffectual role as a politics. Relativism results in a "feminist free-for-all" where feminism can mean anything and everything and, thus, becomes meaningless (Dicker and Piepmeier 2003: 17).

4. That the third wave's embrace of queer sexual politics promotes rather than undermines patriarchy. Critics argue that third wave sexual practices, such as queer women "going fag" or taking on a "bad girl" image, are presented as radical and subversive. However, they actually are based on male sexual practices. Hence, the third wave allows male sexual practices to represent the possibility of sexual agency and freedom (Henry 2004, Jeffreys 1994).

NOTES

1 Sections of this chapter first appeared in S. A. Mann and D. J. Huffman, "Decentering Second Wave Feminism and the Rise of the Third Wave," *Science and Society* 69, no. 1 (2005): 56–91. The author thanks Guilford Press/Publications for providing permission to reprint them.

2 The term *postfeminism* was first used in the 1920s, when the dissipation of interest in the women's movement was taken as a sign not of failure, but of completion (Faludi 1991: 50–51).

3 For a critical analysis of microcredit see chapter 10.

4 See the preface to the 1994 paperback edition of *Fire with Fire* for Wolf's response to these criticisms.

5 Siegel (1997b: 76) writes: "In my desire to break through the racist, classist, sexist, heterosexist, ageist ties that continue to bind, I am not a 'victim feminist', I am a feminist activist who actively refuses to be a victim."

6 Astrid Henry (2004: 111) points out how Friend's discussion of "do me feminism" included both second and third wave feminists. Consequently, they were not all a "new breed" of feminists.

7 *Our Bodies, Ourselves* had its origins in a 35-cent booklet titled *Women and Their Bodies* first published in 1970. The Boston Women's Health Collective was part of the second wave's self-help movement and initiatives.

8 As some observers have noted, Walker is "emblematic" of the third wave (Henry 2004: 23). Not only is she credited with coining the term "third wave" and founding the Third Wave Foundation, but as a biracial and bisexual woman her own life reflects the fluid identities so valued by third wavers.

9 See Anna Quindlen quoted in Baumgardner and Richards (2000: 255).

10 In the afterword of *To Be Real*, second wave feminist Angela Davis describes with amazement (and some skepticism) how *most* contributors to the anthology felt that feminism had "incarcerated their individuality—their desires, aims, and sexual practices" (Angela Davis in Walker 1995: 281).

11 A similar question is asked by postcolonial theorist Gayatri Spivak, when she discusses the dangers of speaking for or representing another (see chapter 10).

12 A six-paragraph statement with 1, 603 signatures titled "African American Women in Defense of Ourselves" was published in the *New York Times* a month after the hearings (Henry 2004: 161).

13 Second wave womanists of color were the first to describe their own theoretical perspective as the third wave (Springer 2002: 1063). As noted in chapter 5, this term never caught on, and their theoretical perspective is better known today as intersectionality theory, U.S. Third World feminism, or multicultural feminism.

14 Third wave feminist politics no longer necessarily center on issues specific to women. Rather, they bring their feminist analyses to other sites of activism, such as the environmental movement or the antiglobalization movement (Mack-Canty 2005: 201). In this way, they disperse out into other social movements rather than center their work on bringing activists into the women's movement. In turn, women's issues are more broadly defined: *all efforts directed toward greater social equality or justice are women's issues* (Labaton and Martin 2004: xxxi).

15 Morgan (1999: 36) writes: "Unfortunately this happened far more frequently in African-American studies courses than it did in Women's Studies."

16 Morgan is rare among Third Wave women of color in that she criticizes both white and black feminist theorists. As Astrid Henry (2004: 155) wrote, "Morgan seems to suggest that academia is like a bleaching agent, inevitably whitening those who choose it as a career path. Whiteness and intellectualism both have the same effect: a feminism that is out of touch with young black women."

17 Mack-Canty's discussion of an ecofeminism that breaks down binary thought and addresses multiple oppressions is not a new perspective, since these features are integral to second wave anarchist ecofeminism or social ecofeminism. (See chapter 4.)

18 Bettie includes Bourdieu's concepts even though she considers his class analysis to be too structural or "overdetermined" (Bettie 2003: 44).

19 See also the work of Aihwa Ong (1991), whose global analysis includes a discussion of the cultural dimensions of class (chapter 10).

20 When Bettie discusses students' "class of origin" she reverts back to defining class in a more conventional way by social location (such as income, occupation and educational attainment) rather than by performance. Here students' parents' class locations are used to discuss their class of origin (Bettie 2003: 50). She does not adequately address this shift and its potential inconsistencies for her work.

21 Viewing social class as a social relation (as do many Marxist and socialist feminists) also serves to dereify class and presents an alternative way of analyzing social class that entails both social agency and social structure (see chapter 4).

SECTION III

Theory Applications—Bridging the Local and the Global: Feminist Discourses on Colonialism, Imperialism, and Globalization

> Indeed, conceit, arrogance, and egotism are the essentials of patriotism. . . . Patriotism assumes that our globe is divided into little spots . . . Those who have had the fortune of being born on some particular spot, consider themselves better, nobler, grander, more intelligent than the living beings inhabiting any other spot. It is, therefore, the duty of everyone living on that chosen spot to fight, kill, and die in the attempt to impose his superiority upon all the others.
>
> —Emma Goldman

INTRODUCTION

Global issues appeared to be placed solidly on the feminist agenda when the United Nation's Decade of the Women (1975–1985) was followed a decade later by the United Nation's Fourth World Conference on Women in Beijing, China, and the Forum for Non-Governmental Organizations (NGOs) in Huairou, China. This latter forum drew more than thirty thousand women from across the globe and marked the largest international conference of women for women in world history. These historic events provided feminists with great hope for the future and valuable insights into the ways their own lives locally were intertwined with the lives of women across the globe. However, these insights also pointed to various ways in which globalization and the New Global Order had resulted in the increasing feminization of global labor and global migration—twin processes that often fragmented women's solidarity by pitting women of diverse classes, ethnicities, geographies, and communities against each other.

Such divisions between women across the political and geographical landscape were sorely exacerbated in the following decade by the traumatic events surrounding September 11, 2001, and the military conflicts that the United States and its allies subsequently waged in Afghanistan and Iraq. Despite the increasing focus in recent decades of U.S. feminism on embracing diversity and difference, passage of the U.S. Patriot Act and establishment of the Homeland Security program have led to increased fear and suspicion of the "other." These global conflicts were accompanied by the resurgence of nationalism and religious fundamentalism at home and abroad, both having a long history of weakening women's solidarity and circumscribing women's rights. The teaming up of politics and religious fundamentalism at the center of the world stage forces feminists to seriously address how best to respond to these conflicts engendered by militarism, fundamentalism, and globalization (Suzan Pritchett in Wilson, Sengupta, and Evans 2005: 11–13).

To enhance our ability to address these important global issues today, this section of the text focuses on *how feminists have applied their theoretical perspectives to the topic of imperialism and colonialism from the late nineteenth century to the present.* By holding the topic constant, paradigm shifts in global feminist thought from early modernity to postmodernity should become more visible. Attention is paid to how these transformations of feminist thought are grounded in changing social, economic, and historical conditions and how they affect feminist political practice. Given that a major goal of this text is to enhance critical thought, the strengths and weaknesses of the many and diverse feminist frameworks that have undertaken analyses of imperialism and colonialism will be examined.

Conceptualizing Imperialism and Colonialism

Because concepts change over time to reflect changing social conditions, readers will see throughout this last section of the text how new conceptual schemes arise to address global processes in different historical eras. This section begins with an introduction to some of the major concepts that were used to distinguish forms of imperialism and colonialism in early modernity following the analytical distinctions made by one of the earliest feminist theorists of imperialism, Rosa Luxemburg. Born in Poland in 1871, Luxemburg spent most of her life in Germany, where she served as a leader of the international socialist movement. Her book *The Accumulation of Capital*, first published in 1913, still stands as one of the major theoretical works on imperialism.

Imperialism generally refers to a foreign power's forceful extension of economic, political, and cultural domination over other nations or geopolitical formations. Luxemburg, however, makes a clear distinction between premodern and modern forms of imperialism. Earlier forms of imperialism, such as the imperial conquests of ancient Rome, subjugated indigenous populations and exploited them largely through heavy taxation but generally left their forms and social relations of production in place. By contrast, **modern imperialism** destroys indigenous forms of production by usurping and privatizing land and forcing premodern economies into market economies (Luxemburg [1913] 1951: 416 and [1908] 2004: 110).

Modern imperialism and colonialism also reflect how nations or global locations with more technological development and market-oriented forms of production have the potential to dominate other areas of the globe. Their greater technological development often enhances their military and industrial capabilities while their market-oriented forms of production thrive on the expansion of markets across international boundaries for the circulation of their commodities. The combination of superior technological development and this internal drive to accumulate wealth also enhances their productive capacity, such that the larger volume and cheaper prices of their commodities enable them to compete successfully against premodern, indigenous, and petty/artisan forms of production.[1] Thus modern imperialism undermines and transforms indigenous forms of production (Luxemburg [1908] 2004: 110).

Historically, there have been different forms of modern imperialism that affected people in the geopolitical area now known as the United States. The first form to impact U.S. history was mercantile imperialism where explorers and conquistadors from Europe went abroad in the fifteenth and sixteenth centuries in search of new trade routes. In doing so, they had their first encounters with indigenous tribes in certain areas of the so-called New World. Mercantile imperialism was predicated on the circulation of goods and raw materials through trade and markets and the appropriation of foreign lands, peoples, and resources by military force. Of particular significance to U.S. history, these explorers and conquistadors first staked claim to the land and resources of various indigenous tribes, thereby transforming their lives and culture. The mercantile circulation of commodities for the world market took the form not only of nonhuman commodities but, also, of capturing and enslaving people from other continents to buy and sell in regional slave markets.

Capitalist imperialism differs from mercantile imperialism in that it involves, along with the purchase and sale of commodities, the actual production of commodities using wage labor. Here profits are derived primarily from the difference between the productivity of labor power and the market price of labor. Given the importance of labor productivity to this equation, technological inventions that enhance labor productivity are imperative. Thus, constant technological advances are a hallmark of capitalist production that further fosters its technological superiority. In turn, the importance of labor and other production costs leads capitalist imperialism on a never-ending search for cheaper labor and raw materials as well as new markets. Hence, the internal logic of capitalist accumulation is a driving force that fosters it to spread beyond national borders for both its production and its markets. Military force (or the threat of) often is necessary to safeguard and secure these global ventures, thus integrally involving the nation-state or government in these practices.

Both mercantile imperialism and capitalist imperialism have used colonialism as one of their major mechanisms for spreading globally. **Colonialism** refers to a foreign power holding direct political control over another country or geopolitical region, and it can take different forms. In **colonies of rule**, foreign governments use an oligarchy of colonial administrators to organize the social, cultural, economic, and political life of indigenous peoples in the colonies and to facilitate their home country's economic and political aims. British rule in India exemplifies this type of colonialism. By contrast, in **settler colonialism** the oligarchy of colonial administrators is accompanied by immigrants who settle on the lands of indigenous peoples and wield social, cultural, economic, and political domination over them (McMichael 1996: 17).

Initially, of course, the United States was itself a colony. During the last quarter of the eighteenth century, the colonists united against the British Empire and successfully severed their colonial ties through the Revolutionary War, or, American War of Independence. In today's vernacular this revolution would be called a **national liberation movement** because it established the United States as an independent country, free from colonial rule. This nationalist and anticolonial revolution, based as it was on the Enlightenment ideas of freedom, liberty, and individual rights, gave a "radical" (for that era) ideological basis to the birth of the United States (see chapter 2). This ideology may be one of the reasons that the U.S. government has been able to successfully and seemingly without contradiction mobilize its own people under the banners of freedom and democracy even while engaged in imperialist ventures that obstructed the freedom and self-determination of others.

Socialist feminists, such as Luxemburg, argued that settler colonialism generally leads to **internal colonialism**. As discussed in chapter 5, internal colonies are subjugated groups that share a number of key experiences: their entrée into the host country is often by brute force; they are forced to assimilate the dominant group's language and culture; they are denied the same citizenship rights enjoyed by the dominant group; and they often are relegated to subordinate labor markets or menial areas of work. For example, the first colony *within* the United States was established when white settlers pushed indigenous peoples off their land onto more barren or stipulated lands, such as reservations. Another internal colony was formed when mercantile traders from the seventeenth through the nineteenth century brought thousands of slaves (legally and illegally) to the United States from countries abroad. A third internal colony was established when sections of Mexico were annexed after the Mexican–American War (1846–1848). All of these conquered peoples experienced forced entry into the U.S. and forced assimilation into the dominant English language and culture. For long periods of American history, they also were treated as second-class citizens who faced discrimination and segregation and were denied suffrage and other rights of citizenship. In turn, they were primarily relegated to menial occupations or subordinate labor markets—jobs that the dominant group did not want to do. As discussed in chapter 5, racism was integral to the success of settler and internal colonialism. In summary, U.S. settler colonialism gained hegemony across the North American continent when the western frontier was consolidated after the last of the major Indian Wars in the 1890s.[2] Thus, the United States had developed many of its own *internal colonies* before it expanded abroad to claim overseas colonies in the late nineteenth century.

Despite the long history of various forms of imperialism and colonialism that have impacted the area we now call the United States, *theories of modern imperialism were late-nineteenth and early-twentieth-century inventions.* These theories were Eurocentric or Western in the sense that whether the theorist was a supporter or critic of imperialism, all of these theories were written from the vantage point of European or Western global social locations. Along with Luxemburg's *The Accumulation of Capital*, the major nineteenth- and early-twentieth-century works on modern imperialism included John Hobson's *Imperialism* (1902), Rudolf Hilferding's *Finance Capital* (1910), V. I. Lenin's *Imperialism* (1917), and Joseph Schumpeter's *Imperialism and Social Classes* (1919). This Eurocentric or Western approach to analyses of imperialism would influence U.S. feminist thought for much of the next century.

NOTES

1 It is in this sense that Karl Marx ([1848] 1972: 339) wrote of capitalist imperialism: "The cheaper prices of its [capitalism's] commodities are the heavy artillery with which it batters down all Chinese Walls . . . compelling all nations on pain of extinction to develop the capitalist mode of production."

2 Although other smaller skirmishes occurred at later dates, the last medal of honor for the American–Indian Wars was actually given in 1898 after the Battle of Sugar Point in Minnesota.

CHAPTER 8

Feminism and Imperialism in Early Modernity

Our tribe and others which were matriarchal have become assimilated and have adopted the cultural value of the larger society, and, in doing, we've adopted sexism. We're going forward and backward at the same time. As we see a dilution of the original values, we see more sexism.

—Wilma Mankiller

Militarism is the oldest and has been the most unyielding enemy of woman.

—Carrie Chapman Catt

The cause of freedom is not the cause of a race or a sect, a party or a class—it is the cause of human kind. . . . Why should woman become plantiff in a suit versus the Indian or the Negro or any other race or class who have been crushed under the iron heel of Anglo-Saxon power and selfishness?

—Anna Julia Cooper

INTRODUCTION

Reclaiming our historical past has been a major activity and accomplishment of the women's movement in the United States.[1] This excavation of earlier feminist writings and activism not only serves to legitimize feminism as a serious and ongoing political struggle, but it also unearths the subjugated knowledges of those whose theory and practice had been buried, silenced, or deemed less credible by more androcentric historical narratives. To the credit of those who have excavated and reclaimed our historical past, great efforts have been made to discover the diverse standpoints, visions, and voices of our feminist predecessors. As discussed in early chapters, much has been learned about the relationship between women's oppression and other systemic forms of oppression that affected U.S. women in early modernity, such as racism, classism, and heteronormativity (Rossi 1974, Giddings 1984, Cott 1987, Lerner 1993).

Yet even with this greater emphasis on diversity, U.S. feminists' gaze often has been too inward and U.S.-centered. This inward, nation-centered gaze has deflected attention from the global issues that confronted feminists in the United States during the first wave of the U.S. women's movement, especially the issue of U.S. imperialism. Indeed, it is rare to find references on this topic in any U.S. feminist textbooks, despite the fact that famous leaders of the women's movement during the late nineteenth and early twentieth centuries entered the debates about U.S. westward and overseas expansion (Mann 2008). This omission is surprising given that many feminists of the 1960s and 1970s who began excavating our predecessors' histories cut their political teeth during the anti–Vietnam war movement and had a profound interest in the issues of militarism and imperialism (see chapter 9). While U.S. feminists undertook their own global analyses from the 1970s to the present, rarely did they look back to see what they could learn from our past.

Fortunately, over the past two decades some feminist historians have begun to examine how suffragists addressed the issue of U.S. imperialism.[2] Below I draw from Allison Sneider's *Suffragists in an Imperial Age* (2008) and Kristin Hoganson's "'As Badly Off as the Filipinos': U.S. Woman Suffragists and the Imperial Issue at the Turn of the Twentieth Century" (2001).[3] I also provide an excerpt from Hoganson's *Fighting for American Manhood* (1998), which discusses how issues of masculinity fueled the imperialist impulse. The primary purpose of this chapter is to examine how various leaders of the U.S. women's movement responded to U.S. colonialism and imperialism during the late nineteenth and early twentieth centuries.

WHOSE VOICES, WHOSE VISIONS?

While it is tempting to use the first wave as shorthand for describing the feminist perspectives that developed in early modernity, as noted in chapter 1, wave approaches tend to focus on the hegemonic feminist organizations during each wave that were led by white, middle-class women. This tendency frequently obscures the contributions of more radical feminisms within the movement as well as those feminists who were more marginalized by race, ethnicity, and/or social class (Ruth 1988, Giddings 1984). To better highlight the diversity of feminists' responses to imperialism and colonialism during this era, below the first wave is divided into three camps to reflect the diverse standpoints and political perspectives of feminists on these local/global topics.

Representing the moderate liberal camp are the views of Matilda Joslyn Gage, president of the National Woman Suffrage Association (NWSA) from 1875–1876, as well as the first three presidents of the National American Woman Suffrage Association (NAWSA): Elizabeth Cady Stanton (1890–1892), Susan B. Anthony (1892–1900), and Carrie Chapman Catt (1900–1904). From the left–liberal camp the writings and political practices of Jane Addams and Jeanette Rankin are examined. Representing the perspectives of womanists of color during this era are the writings of Native–Americans Sarah Winnemucca and the La Flesche sisters as well as the African-American feminist writers Anna Julia Cooper and Ida B. Wells-Barnett. Exemplars of first wave Marxist, socialist, and anarchist feminisms include Rosa Luxemburg, Charlotte Perkins Gilman, and Emma Goldman, respectively. All of these women are well-known historical figures, whose original writings are published, and this was a prerequisite to discerning their views on imperialism. These published writings set not only the parameters of this analysis but, also, its limitations, as many women during this era were illiterate or did not have the time or resources to publish their ideas.

Given that the first women's rights convention in the United States—the Seneca Falls Convention—took place in 1848, U.S. feminists were not sufficiently mobilized to call themselves a women's movement when the annexation of Mexican lands and the Mexican-American War took place in the 1840s. Nevertheless, writings by U.S. suffragists on other forms of expansionism provide some indication of how the U.S. annexation of Mexican lands was viewed. In turn, most suffragists during this era did not view slavery and institutional segregation as fostering a form of internal colonialism for African-Americans. Rather, imperialism and colonialism were associated with the U.S. government's annexation of *new lands*.[4] A developed analysis of internal colonialism to deal with the plight of African-Americans arose later in U.S. history, as described in chapter 5. However, the annexation of Native American lands after the Civil War along with U.S. overseas expansion in the following decades raised issues of citizenship and suffrage in these new territories that were of great interest to feminists in the late nineteenth and early twentieth centuries. As Sneider adeptly shows in *Suffragists in an Imperial Age* (2008), both of these forms of territorial expansion helped suffragists keep the woman question alive in national political debates.

U.S. WESTERN EXPANSION AND THE "WOMAN QUESTION"

As Federal troops withdrew from the south beginning in 1877, thereby signaling the end of government-sponsored Reconstruction, the U.S. government increasingly turned its attention westward. As early as 1871, Congress passed legislation declaring that "hereafter no Indian nation or tribe within the territory of the United States shall be acknowledged or recognized as an independent nation, tribe, or power with whom the United States may contract by treaty" (Sneider 2008: 62). Between 1860 and 1880, U.S. citizens migrated west, nearly doubling the population of the western states and territories. Previously, the gold rush of the 1840s had fostered a large western migration of settler colonialists that was consolidated when California became a state in 1850. In the 1860s, the most important trigger for western migration was the Homestead Act of 1862, which gave freehold title to 160 acres of undeveloped land outside of the original thirteen colonies. While powerful southerners had fought against earlier homestead proposals because plantation owners feared that free farmers would threaten the viability of slavery, the secession of the south from the Union in 1861 cleared the way for passage of this act. Hence, southern internal colonialism was deeply interwoven with western settler colonialism.

The conflicts that flared between indigenous peoples and the settler colonialists represented a clash between distinct modes of production and social formations. In this case, as horticulturalists or as hunters and gatherers, many Native–Americans lived within a more communal, subsistence-oriented, and non-commodified social formation that depended on open access to the land and natural resources. By contrast, the way of life of the settler colonialists was predicated on privatized land ownership and commercial production, which meant dividing and fencing in these lands. Petty commodity producers, such as family farmers, as well as the capitalist farmers, ranchers, and railroad companies had vested interests in making commodity forms transcontinental so as to foster and expand markets. When the settler colonialists looked at the west they saw an open frontier for social and economic development. That this so-called frontier was inhabited by Native–Americans whose way of life was predicated on the land remaining open provided the social contradictions that in the late nineteenth century erupted in the Indian wars that raged across the west as settlers and Native–Americans took up arms in Kansas, Nebraska, Texas, Oregon, California, Utah, Colorado, Montana, and Idaho. As increasing numbers of U.S. settlers clashed with indigenous peoples on the western frontier, the project of transforming the western territories into new states replaced Reconstruction on the national political agenda (Sneider 2008: 62). A transcontinental empire became the central goal of the U.S. government and was believed to be the manifest destiny of its citizens.

The extent of what Luxemburg called the "devastation" of premodern societies by modernization and development was visible in the United States. For example, in 1850 Native peoples still had control over approximately one-half of the land mass now called the United States. By 1880, they controlled about one-eighth of this area. Today, the 314 reservations scattered across the continental United States account for just 2 percent of the country's land area. In turn, it is estimated that when the first Europeans arrived in the late fifteenth century the indigenous population numbered in the millions. By the beginning of the twentieth century, their number totaled a mere 250,000 (Macionis 2011: 283; Dobyns 1966; Tyler 1973). The decimation of the indigenous population was the result of a number of factors, including their inability to cope with the new diseases brought by white settlers, the scarcity of wild game that accompanied the expansion of western settlement, and outright **genocide** by the U.S. military.

Although Native–Americans would not obtain U.S. citizenship and suffrage until 1924, as early as the 1870s a number of national legislators increasingly favored giving Native–Americans citizenship in order to "resolve the hostilities." Indeed, this was the major impetus of Republican senator John Ingall's proposed bill in 1877 that sought to turn indigenous peoples across the continent into U.S. citizens (Snieder 2008: 57 and 61). This proposed bill generated intense debates because both settler colonialists and Native–Americans recognized that citizenship was a double-edged sword. Many Native–Americans rejected the idea of citizenship because it would mean their tribal lands would be broken up and privatized and their communal strength weakened. They realized that their tribal sovereignty and independence were at odds with U.S. intentions to assert sovereignty and title over all Native lands and peoples.

A few white, middle-class suffragists took up the Native–Americans' cause in this regard. These suffragists were often women who had grown up in close proximity to indigenous tribes and who, from their early childhood, had closer associations with Native peoples. For example, NWSA president Matilda Joslyn Gage, who was raised in New York near the Iroquois nation, exposed how this proposed "gift of citizenship" was actually the means by which the U.S. government wanted to end tribal sovereignty and break up Native–American lands. In an 1878 article on "Indian Citizenship" published in her woman suffrage paper, *National Citizen and the Ballot Box*, Gage (quoted in Sneider 2008: 65) discussed how giving Native–Americans citizenship "would open wide the door to the grasping avarice of the white man for Indian lands."

> That the Indians have been oppressed—are now, is true, but the United States has treaties with them, recognizing them as distinct political communities, and duty towards them demands not an enforced citizenship but a faithful living up to its obligations on the part of the government. (quoted in Sneider 2008: 57)

Although Gage decried the brutal treatment of indigenous people in her writings and speeches and even was admitted to the Iroquois Council of Matrons, she was angered when the federal government seemed poised to confer citizenship on them and grant suffrage to Native–American males. Like many other white, middle-class suffragists, Gage feared that extending citizenship and voting rights to Native–American men would make it even harder for women to gain the vote. This latter view was the position taken at the NWSA convention of 1877, where the question of Native–American citizenship and suffrage became a topic of movement concern. Signed by the new NWSA president, New York physician Clemence Lozier, as well as by Susan B. Anthony, this convention's announcement declared that "Indian men" as voters would create "an additional peril to the women citizens of the United States and that they were likely to "vote solid against woman suffrage" like "Mexicans, half-breeds, [and other] ignorant, vicious men" (quoted in Sneider 2008: 63).

These suffragists were livid that Indian men might be offered voting rights, while "educated, enlightened and Christian women" had to "beg in vain" for such "crumbs cast contemptuously aside by savages" (Gage quoted in Sneider 2008: 58). However, they did not entirely ignore the plight of Native–American women but stated in their 1877 NWSA announcement, that "Indian men turned their women into beasts of burden" (64). In this way, they could target the vileness of indigenous men but still show sympathy for indigenous women. This also enabled them to portray themselves as rescuing uncivilized women from their uncivilized men—a response that would be characterized by many feminists today as a colonialist stance or feminist missionary framework (Mohanty, 1984; see chapter 10).

No doubt, educated, middle-class suffragists were exposed to a number of competing discourses on Native–Americans during this era that gave their analyses more complexity. They were exposed, for example, to the Romanticists' view of Native–Americans as noble savages, as described in Walt Whitman's *Leaves of Grass* (1855) and James Fenimore Cooper's *Leatherstocking Tales* (1823). The term **noble savage** refers to a human who is unencumbered by civilization, who lives in harmony with nature, and who demonstrates both great moral courage and untutored wisdom derived from harsh life experiences. This romantic, settler colonialist stereotype fostered some appreciation of indigenous peoples and portrayed them as morally worthy, despite their perceived social and economic inferiorities. Like a double-edged sword, this stereotype critiqued imperial excesses, but maintained Native–Americans as "the exotic other."

Many educated suffragists were familiar also with anthropological writings in that era that highlighted how some indigenous tribes had matrilineal patterns of descent which enabled Native–American women to retain greater autonomy within marriage. Indeed, a number of contemporary feminists have documented how anthropological writings on Native–Americans were of particular interest to suffragists in this era (Landsman 1992). For example, Lewis Henry Morgan's *Ancient Society; or, Researches in the Lines of Human Progress from Savagery, through Barbarism to Civilization* (1877) argued that Iroquois women had substantial political rights within tribes that were unavailable to their U.S. sisters. This work was well known to many nineteenth-century U.S. women's rights activists as well as to European feminists.

As discussed in chapter 4, Morgan's book provided the data for Karl Marx's *Ethnological Notebooks* ([1882] 1986) and for Friedrich Engels's *The Origin of the Family, Private Property, and the State* ([1884] 1972), two of the most famous nineteenth-century Marxist works on the origins of women's oppression. However, unlike Marx and Engels, these white, U.S. suffragists did not make the connection that Native–American women's productive labor as the primary gatherers and horticulturalists might be a major reason why they enjoyed political rights and freedoms within their tribes. Instead, suffragists attributed the Iroquois women's greater equality to matrilineal descent and viewed their labor as a tragedy that made them "beasts of burden" (Sneider 2008: 64). The real tragedy for these indigenous women was that when settler colonialists imposed their "civilized views" on indigenous peoples they eroded the greater equality that Native–American women shared with men in some tribes.[5] For example, in tribes where Native–American women were the major cultivators, U.S. government officials encouraged and even legislated that Native–American men take over farming—a process that, as will be shown in Chapter 9, occurred in many other cases of imperialism and colonialism. As contemporary Native–American feminist activist Wilma Mankiller writes:

> Our tribe and others which were matriarchal[6] have become assimilated and have adopted the cultural value of the larger society, and, in doing, we've adopted sexism. We're going forward and backward at the same time. As we see a dilution of the original values, we see more sexism. (Quoted in Mihesuah 2003: 42)[7]

Given the competing discourses on indigenous people during this era, it is not surprising to find a number of contradictions in Matilda Joslyn Gage's writings and activism. Clearly, she was more active than most suffragists in publicizing the unjust treatment of Native-Americans by the U.S. government and in exposing the "avarice" underlying their proposed "gift" of citizenship to indigenous peoples. At the same time, she railed against giving Native-American males the vote before white, educated women like herself. She also showed more appreciation than most suffragists for indigenous cultures and the rights afforded to Native-American women within these cultures. Nevertheless, even for Gage, Native-Americans remained the "exotic other" who should be kept separate and unequal.

Such contradictions are found not only in the writings of white, middle-class women but also in the works of famous indigenous women of this era. We must keep in mind that these indigenous women were well known in this era because they could speak, read, and write in English. They were not representative of Native-American women but, rather, bridged two worlds, which no doubt contributed to their contradictory views and actions. Indeed, theorizing about feminism, colonialism, and indigenous women during this era poses many complex and difficult problems that are carefully detailed in such books as Linda Tuhiwai Smith's *Decolonizing Methodologies* ([1999] 2006) and Devon Abbott Mihesuah's *Indigenous American Women* (2003). An excerpt from Mihesuah's work on some of the problems entailed in discussing and conceptualizing indigenous women is presented in Box 8.1.

BOX 8.1

Conceptualizing Indigenous Women

There was and is no such thing as a monolithic, essential Indigenous woman. Nor has there ever been a unitary "worldview" among tribes, or especially after contact and interaction with non-Natives, even among members of the same group. . . . Traditional Native women were as different from progressive tribeswomen as they were from white women, and often they still are. Even within a single tribe (and sometimes within the same family), females possess a range of degrees of Native blood, of skin and hair color, and of opinions about what it means to be Native. . . . Although it is preferable to refer to the Indigenous people of this country by their specific tribal names, for the sake of space I opt for "Indigenes" or "Natives" instead of "Native Americans" . . . I am well aware of the debates over these terms and am cognizant that many find "Indian" offensive; however my family and most friends and "Indians" I know say "Indians". "First Nation", "Indigenous Peoples" and other terms are fine for scholars, but most Indians' especially older ones, are puzzled hearing them. "Indigenous" most accurately describes the first peoples of this hemisphere.

Excerpts from *Indigenous American Women: Decolonization, Empowerment, Activism*, by Devon Abbott Mihesuah (Lincoln: University of Nebraska Press, 2003), pp. xv and xxi–xxii.

Sarah Winnemucca Hopkins (c. 1844–1891)[8] was one of the most famous indigenous women speakers and writers of that era. Placed at a young age in the household of a Nevada white family in which she was educated, Winnemucca is the first Native-American woman known to secure a copyright and to publish in the English language. Her book, *Life among the Paiutes* (1883), is an autobiographical account of her people during the first forty years of their contact with explorers and settlers. Known by the press in that era as "the Paiute Princess," she lectured to women's groups and to other public gatherings on the injustices perpetrated on indigenous peoples. However, Winnemucca also worked as a translator, scout, and message carrier for the U.S. Army, a role for which she was harshly criticized by many indigenous peoples for being traitor. These contradictions caught up with Winnemucca when her own tribe—the Northern Paiutes—were forced by the army to march to a reservation where they endured great deprivation. Winnemucca lectured on their behalf and even lobbied the secretary of the interior to allow their return. Before she died, she also built a school for Native-American children to promote indigenous lifestyles and languages. This school operated for only a short time, however, before the Dawes Severalty Act of 1877 required Native-American children to attend English-speaking boarding schools (Mihesuah 2003: 46).

As Mihesuha points out in Box 8.1, diverse and contradictory views of indigenous women could even be found within the same family. For example, the four LaFlesche sisters, Rosalie LaFlesche Farley (1861–1900), Susan LaFlesche Picotte (1865–1915), Margueriet LaFlesche Picotte Diddock (1861–1900), and Susette LaFlesche Tibbles (1854–1903), were the daughters of Omaha leader Joseph LaFlesche and Mary Gale, the Métis daughter of a white man and his Omaha wife. Susan, Marguerite, and Susette were educated in white schools. Susan was the first Native-American woman to receive a medical degree and, like her father, was an advocate of the Omaha adopting white ways. Susette lectured extensively to white audiences about broken treaties, tribal cultural deterioration, and the loss of tribal lands, though she too favored assimilation. By contrast, Rosalie pushed for Native-American self-government and self-sufficiency, while Marguerite saw education as a major means of making tribes self-sufficient (46–47).

One of the least contradictory views of feminists in that era was that of black feminist Anna Julia Cooper. In "Women versus the Indian," from her book *A Voice from the South* (1892), Cooper directly responds to papers presented at the National Woman's Council of 1891 by Susan B. Anthony and Anna Shaw that highlighted the "inferiority" of Native-American men to buttress their contempt for the idea of giving these men the vote. Cooper writes:

> Woman should not, even by inference, or for the sake of argument disparage what is weak. For women's cause is the cause of the weak. . . . The cause of freedom is not the cause of race or a sect, a party or a class—it is the cause of human kind. . . . If the Indian has been wronged and cheated by the puissance of this American Government, it is woman's mission to plead with her country to cease to do evil and to pay its honest debts. . . . Let her rest her plea, not on Indian

> inferiority, nor on Negro depravity, but on the obligation of legislators to do for her as they would have others do for them were relations reversed. (Quoted in Lengermann and Niebrugge-Brantley 1998: 188)

Cooper's sensitivity to inequalities by race and class, as well as her call for a feminism that fosters the liberation of humankind, marks her as a major precursor to U.S. Third World feminism—an approach discussed in chapters 5 and 9.

In summary, above we have seen how race, class, gender, and nation were imbricated in a range of feminists' views on the relationship between the woman question and U.S. imperialist and colonial expansion. Allison Sneider's major point in *Suffragists in an Imperial Age* (2008) is that both westward and overseas U.S. expansion kept the suffrage issue on the national political agenda. As new lands were annexed, whether in the American west or overseas, legal and constitutional issues over citizenship and suffrage were reopened. Most suffragists wanted these two issues united so that as "citizens" they would automatically have the right to vote. Yet, in the nineteenth and early twentieth centuries the federal government maintained control over citizenship while state governments controlled voting rights. Debates over these issues remained politically salient so long as new lands were annexed to the United States. In this way, the woman question remained integrally interwoven with U.S. imperialism and colonialism.

THE RISE OF U.S. GLOBAL IMPERIALISM

The Spanish–American War is considered to be a watershed in American history marking the point at which the United States translated its growing industrial might into military and political power on a global scale. From the last decade of the nineteenth century to First World War, the United States took possession of Hawaii, the Philippines, Puerto Rico, Guam, and Samoa. It also established protectorates over Cuba, Panama, and the Dominican Republic and mounted armed interventions in China, Mexico, Haiti, and Nicaragua (Fain 2005). The emergence of the United States as a global imperial power in the Pacific Far East and Latin America was closely related to the spectacular growth of both the American economy and the federal government in the last quarter of the nineteenth century. These changes ushered in not only a modern industrial economy but, also, a centralized nation-state. Between Reconstruction and World War I, the American economy was transformed from one based largely on family-owned and operated businesses and farms to one dominated by large-scale, capitalist enterprises.

In key respects, American overseas expansion was rooted in periodic crises of overproduction generated by the booms and busts in the economic cycles of its highly volatile economy. Industrial leaders, such as Andrew Carnegie and John D. Rockefeller, as well as many farmers and politicians, argued that the health of American industry depended on expansion. They claimed that the failure to establish new foreign markets for the swelling output of U.S. goods would result in industrial slowdowns and economic stagnation at home (Fain 2005). They feared that unemployment resulting from such stagnation would only increase already growing working-class radicalism and militancy. For capital accumulation to proceed, overseas expansion was the logical sequel to the closing of the frontier.

Political and ideological factors also played key roles in U.S. expansionism. Maintaining hemispheric security by keeping the European powers out of the Caribbean and Latin America was a prominent aim of the increasing enforcements and extensions of the Monroe Doctrine during this era. The goal of spreading the values of American Progressivism abroad, as well as the missionary zeal of extending American Protestantism overseas, fostered ideologues from across the political spectrum to join the pro-imperialist chorus. Even gender ideologies concerned with the robust nature of American manhood chimed in during this particular era of U.S. history (see Box 8.2). Hence, a wide range of economic, political, and ideological ambitions came together to fuel the imperialist impulse. The major question addressed in the following section is what role did American feminists of the late nineteenth and early twentieth centuries play in fostering or resisting this expansionist thrust?

BOX 8-2

Fighting for American Manhood

Adding gender to the historical picture helps explain why the United States went to war at the turn of the century by illuminating two important issues: jingoes'[9] [zealous pro-imperialists'] motivations and the methods they used in political debate to build support for their aggressive policies. To start with motives, jingoes looked to martial policies to address their anxieties about manhood. These concerns can be traced, in part, to the urbanization, industrialization, and corporate consolidation of the late 19th century. The middle- and upper-class men who held supposedly soft white-collar jobs and could afford the comforts of modern life were particularly worried about the seeming dangers of 'overcivilization.' They feared that a decline in manly character would impair their ability to maintain not only their class, racial and national privileges, but also their status relative to women, especially when assertive New Women scoffed at submissive ideals of womanhood. The aging of the Civil War generation and the closing of the frontier focused further attention on male character, for it seemed that modern young men, lacking their own epic challenges, would not be able to live up to their forefathers. . . . Jingoes imagined war as the most rigorous challenge possible, the most effective means to develop the characteristics such as courage and physical strength that were sorely lacking in modern men. They also regarded war as the best way to foster fraternalism and a regard for high ideals among men and to highlight distinctions between men and women.

Excerpt from *Fighting for American Manhood: How Gender Politics Provoked the Spanish–American and Philippine–American Wars*, by Kristin L. Hoganson (New Haven, Conn.: Yale University Press, 1998), pp. 200–201.

U.S. OVERSEAS EXPANSION AND THE "WOMAN QUESTION"

In an effort to provide a more powerful, united front in the struggle for woman suffrage, the two major U.S. suffrage organizations combined in 1890 to form the National American Woman Suffrage Association (NAWSA). To feminists today, it might seem obvious that woman suffrage and struggles against colonialism and imperialism rested on the common principle of self-government. As Kristin Hoganson points out, Catherine Waugh McCulloch, president of the Illinois Equal Suffrage Association, recognized these common interests when, at a NAWSA meeting in 1900, she spoke on behalf of those involved in anti-imperialist struggles abroad:

> They too feel the desire for freedom, opportunity, progress; the wish for liberty, a share in the government, emancipation. . . . The practical method by which these aspirations can be realized is through the ballot. The Outlander wants it; so does the Filipino, the Slav, the Cuban; so do women. (Quoted in Hoganson 2001: 18)

Yet the NAWSA did not side with anti-imperialists in this heyday of America's surge to acquire territories in the Far East and Latin America. Rather, it split over this issue.

My immediate thought was that these suffragists did not want to ally with a small group of anti-imperialists and endanger their chance to obtain the vote. But, in point of fact, the opposite was true. The major organization that protested U.S. imperial policies—the **American Anti-Imperialist League**—was a much larger organization than the NAWSA. Established in 1898 during the Spanish–American War, the League had more than one hundred affiliated organizations, approximately thirty thousand members, and over five hundred thousand contributors by the turn of the twentieth century. In contrast, membership in NAWSA was about half that size in the late 1890s, numbering at most fifteen thousand (Deckard [1979] 1983: 277; Beisner 1968: 225).

Hoganson raises the interesting question of why, given how the suffrage movement at this time was chronically short of cash, faced stiff opposition in Congress, and elicited outright hostility from much of the general public, so few suffragists saw the advantage of building a coalition with anti-imperialists to broaden their base of support, much as they had done when they allied with abolitionists in the pre–Civil War era. She discusses a number of reasons why suffragists split on this issue, with race- and class-based notions of citizenship being among the most important factors. The late nineteenth century witnessed the concentration and centralization of economic wealth alongside shrinking political rights for minorities and the poor; thus, classes and races were becoming increasingly polarized. After Reconstruction, black men were largely disenfranchised in the south while poll taxes and literacy tests marginalized white, working-class, and poor men. As Hoganson (2001: 21) writes: "Many white, middle-class suffragists approved of this state of affairs, hoping they could parlay their positions of social privilege into voting rights within a political system that favored whiteness, wealth, and education over manhood."

White, middle-class suffragists used the same arguments against victims of U.S. imperialism that they had used against black males during the heated debates over the Fifteenth Amendment. They claimed that ignorant and illiterate people were incapable of self-government (Giddings 1984, Terborg-Penn 1998b). They also did not hesitate to reveal their fears that people of color were violent and savage. Elizabeth Cady Stanton, for one, wrote: "The great public topic just now is 'expansion', of which I am in favor. . . . I am strongly in favor of this new departure in American foreign policy. What would this continent have been if we had left it to the Indians?" (quoted in Sneider 2008: 102). Indeed, Stanton held paternalistic views of many people, including blacks, immigrants, workers, and Cubans (Griffith 1984: 206 and 259). In a similarly racist and elitist way, Susan B. Anthony claimed it was "nonsense to talk about giving those guerrillas in the Philippines their liberty for that's all they are that are waging this war. If we did, the first thing they would do would be to murder and pillage every white person on the island" (quoted in Hoganson 2001: 13–14). Even in later years, when arguing for women's suffrage in Hawaii, Puerto Rico, and the Philippines, these feminists made it quite clear that they supported suffrage with limits, such as educational and property qualifications for voting (Sneider 2008: 109). Their proposed limits would have meant, for example, that out of the 110,000 inhabitants of Hawaii in 1893, the number of eligible voters would have been around 2,700 (98).

Early presidents of the NAWSA had strategic reasons for supporting imperialism (Hoganson 2001: 14). Support for empire provided a good opportunity for suffragists to demonstrate their political worthiness as citizens by asserting their loyalty and allegiance to their government, much as many pro-imperialist British feminists had done earlier (Burton 1994). Moreover, the Republican Party was more pro-imperialist than the Democratic Party in this era, and NAWSA members believed that continued support for the Republicans would more likely lead to women's suffrage. However, fearing that Filipino men might get the vote before they did under American imperial rule, the NAWSA passed a resolution that Congress should grant Filipinas whatever rights it conferred on Filipino men (Hoganson 2001: 14).

An issue that generated anti-imperialist sentiment among some white, middle-class liberal suffragists during the Spanish–American War was the revival of assertions that women should not vote because they did not render military service. In her address as president of the NAWSA in 1901, Carrie Chapman Catt highlighted this point, arguing that "militarism is the oldest and has been the most unyielding enemy of woman" (quoted in Hoganson 1998: 195). As claims of male privilege based on military service grew stronger, Catt, while visiting Manila for a suffrage meeting of Filipina and U.S. activists, recanted her earlier jingoism and formally endorsed Philippine independence (Hoganson 2001: 26). Notably, Catt maintained her opposition to militarism and joined with more left-wing feminists in 1915 to form the first women's peace organization—the Woman's Peace Party.

Overall, first wave, white, middle-class suffragists were divided over the issue of imperialist wars. There were those like Susan B. Anthony, whose Quaker background fostered her pacifism and whose experience during the Civil War made her recognize how wars distracted attention away from the suffrage movement (Sneider 2008: 88). In regard to the Spanish–American War, Anthony wrote:

> It looks now as if there is no escape from the clash of arms, and of course, when so many families have the men of their households at the front, and are constantly fearing news of their death, it will be exceedingly hard to mobilize them to work for women's enfranchisement. (Quoted in Sneider 2008: 88)

Other suffragists embraced the notion prevalent during that era that women were more peace loving than men. These suffragists used women's ostensible "tenderness" and "higher morality" to argue for their right to suffrage (Sneider 2008: 92). There also were suffragists, like Elizabeth Cady Stanton, who thought it was a mistake to argue for suffrage on any ground other than social justice and who seized opportunities to speak in favor of war as a means of undermining this romanticized view of women (Sneider 2008: 92; Griffith 1984: 109). As Stanton wrote in a letter to her son, "I am sick of all this sentimental nonsense about 'our boys in blue' and 'wringing mother's hearts'" (quoted in Sneider 2008: 92).

Another issue that attracted suffragists to the pro-imperialist cause was the so-called "civilizing mission" of imperialist ventures. For example, suffragists in organizations like the Young Women's Christian Association (YWCA), the Women's Christian Temperance Union (WCTU), and the American Woman's Foreign Mission Movement were sent abroad to spread American values and culture (Tyrrell 1991). These same women were incensed to learn about the U.S. Army's role in regulating prostitution in the Philippines to reduce venereal disease among soldiers.[10] The NAWSA joined with the WCTU in condemning the military inspections of Filipina prostitutes and tried to use this "element of savagery in Army circles" as another reason to give Filipina women the vote (Sneider 2008: 123). Although such "vice" on the part of American soldiers undermined claims of U.S imperialism's "civilizing" mission abroad, these suffragists were not critiquing imperialism in their condemnation of the army; they simply wanted a more "chaste imperialism" (Hoganson 2001: 25).

African–American men and women also were enticed by the pro-imperialist ideologies of fostering a more "robust manhood" and of "civilizing" foreign lands. Because of their particular concern for their ancestral homeland of Africa, many African–Americans (including suffragists) were drawn to the missionary ideology of imperialism (Jacobs 1981). However, in Africa, female missionaries faced sexism from their male counterparts and racism from both white missionaries and imperial officials (Jacobs 1995). The Spanish–American War offered the opportunity for black males as soldiers to "claim U.S. masculinity for themselves" (Sneider 2008: 93–94). Many volunteered for the army even though the sight of black men in uniform often provoked violent responses from white racists. Yet, as the ties between domestic and international racism grew more apparent, they became a major theme used by black feminists who condemned U.S. expansionism during this era.

Along with her critique of U.S. westward expansion and the injustices perpetrated on Native-Americans in *A Voice from the South* (1892), Cooper criticized overseas imperialism in her doctoral dissertation *Slavery and the French Revolutionists: 1788–1805* written in 1925. The subject she addressed (no doubt with some irony) was attitudes in France toward slavery in the French colonies during the French Revolution which heralded the ideals of liberty and equality.[11] Cooper argued that colonial conflicts were the result of internal race and class differences that were aggravated and exacerbated by white colonizers pursuing their own advantage. She concluded that the overall fate of the colonies was not due to their "backwardness" but to the ways in which the colonizing powers exerted their influence and appropriated natural and human resources (Lemert and Bhan 1998: 268–269). Some scholars have likened Cooper's analysis to neo-Marxist dependency and world-systems theories (269; see Chapter 9). However, others argue that her attention to race, gender, class, and geographic locations is more similar to U.S. third world feminism (Lengermann and Niebrugge-Brantley 1998: 172; see chapters 5 and 9).

In contrast to Cooper, Ida B. Wells-Barnett initially saw great opportunities for African–Americans abroad and encouraged them to go to Africa to assist with its development. However, when the link between domestic and international racism became clearer to her, she dropped her support for black involvement in imperialist goals (Hoganson 2001: 20). Overall, the black press and African–American activists were more likely than their white counterparts to take an anti-imperialist stance during this era (Gatewood 1975, Jacobs, 1981). However, it took some time for this stance to develop. Sneider (2008: 94) notes how the initial silence of black suffragists at the start of the Spanish–American War changed over the course of this war as these women came to recognize the links between imperialism abroad and white racism at home.

By the end of the nineteenth century, the number of opponents of U.S. imperialism had grown significantly, and their diversity crossed racial, ethnic, gender, and social class lines. Although the settler colonialist campaign against Native–Americans and the Mexican–American War had generated only mild resistance from most U.S. "citizens" (Foner and Winchester 1984: xix and 3), people from all walks of life expressed apprehension and resistance to the United States establishing formal political control *overseas*. The Anti-Imperialist League garnered a huge following within the span of only a few years. However, the League was not a cohesive group but more of a confederation of local organizations that included very different people: "Their arguments, sometimes noble, idealistic, historical and rooted in the concept of self determination, were, on other occasions, nativist, racist, paternalistic and grounded in narrow self interest" (xix).

The anti-imperialist motives of League members spanned the political spectrum. They included leftists, such as W. E. B. DuBois, who was committed to self-government and equality both domestically and abroad, as well as racists, such as Varina Howell Davis (Jefferson Davis's wife), who said her "most serious objection to making the Philippines an American territory is because three-fourths of the population is made up of Negroes" (235). The vast majority of League members, however, genuinely objected to the antidemocratic nature of U.S. imperialism, emphasizing the irony of a former colony becoming a colonial master. Despite consensus on the principle of self-government, the League never extended its political critique to cover women's disenfranchisement. For most League members, suffrage and self-determination, whether at home or abroad, were the provinces of men (Hoganson 2001).

Even in the face of this sexism, many feminists were active in the Anti-Imperialist League and/or spoke out against U.S. imperialism. For example, Jane Addams, who was active in Chicago's Anti-Imperialist League, spoke adamantly against the brutality of the armed interventions undertaken by the United States. As a member of the women's college of the Chicago School of Sociology, she was part of the "new sociology of race" that focused on the social dimensions of race as opposed to biology and addressed such matters as urbanism, immigration, and imperialism. This link between domestic racism and what they referred to as the racial frontier of imperialism was a laudable feature of the Chicago School's analysis of race. In contrast, its more conservative counterparts in the sociology of that era were committed to a biological model of racial difference that, in its evolutionary view of human development, tended to racialize premodern peoples and treat them as lesser, uncivilized, savages (Winant 2007).

Charlotte Perkins Gilman, though a member of the Anti-Imperialist League, did not write extensively on the issue of imperialism. In *Women and Economics* ([1898] 1966: 329 and 322), she notes how soldiers in the modern industrial era are "ruthlessly exploited to some financial interests" and criticizes how many of her counterparts uncritically and contemptuously use the term "savages" to describe people in premodern societies. Gilman's socialist-inspired, materialist approach to values and ethics pointed to a view of premodern peoples subjected to colonialism and imperialism that was far more enlightened than the racist and ethnocentric views of many of her feminist contemporaries.

The prominent Montana feminist and pacifist Jeannette Rankin also was active in the Anti-Imperialist League. Rankin, who in 1916 became the first woman elected to the U.S. House of Representatives, was one of only fifty representatives who cast their vote against U.S. entry into World War I. This unpopular vote not only resulted in many suffrage groups cancelling her speaking engagements, but it also shortened Rankin's tenure in the House. Indeed, she was not successful in being elected to Congress again until 1940. Shortly after this election, she again earned notoriety by being the only member of the House to cast a vote against U.S. involvement World War II. In her later years, Rankin practiced her principles of nonviolence and self-determination in the civil rights movement and in the anti–Vietnam war movement (Lopach and Luckowski 2005, Woelfe, 2007). She is often remembered for her famous words "You can no more win a war than an earthquake!" (quoted in Gioseffi 1988: 12).

The anarchist–feminist Emma Goldman was among the most vocal U.S. feminists in condemning U.S. expansionism. In "Patriotism, a Menace to Liberty"

(1911), she specifically attacked U.S. policies in the Mexican–American War, in Cuba, and in the Spanish–American War:

> Indeed, conceit, arrogance, and egotism are the essentials of patriotism. . . . Patriotism assumes that our globe is divided into little spots. . . . Those who have had the fortune of being born on some particular spot, consider themselves better, nobler, grander, more intelligent than the living beings inhabiting any other spot. It is, therefore, the duty of everyone living on that chosen spot to fight, kill, and die in the attempt to impose his superiority upon all the others .

Imprisoned many times for her activism, Goldman's longest jail term was the direct result of her organizing efforts against the involuntary conscription of men during World War I. Generally speaking, first wave feminists who held more left-wing political views and who were more attuned to racism and the needs of working-class and poor women were the most active in the anti-imperialist struggles of this era.

Notably, some U.S. feminists kept up the struggle against imperialism throughout World War I and even after the American Anti-Imperialist League disbanded in 1921. For example, the Woman's Peace Party (WPP), founded by Carrie Chapman Catt and Jane Addams in 1915, approved a platform calling for the global extension of suffrage to women and for U.S. women to take part in an international conference to offer continuous mediation as a way of ending war. In that same year, the party sent representatives to the International Women's Congress for Peace and Freedom held at The Hague, where more than a thousand participants from both neutral and belligerent nations adopted the platform of the WPP and established an International Committee of Women for Permanent Peace (ICWPP) with Jane Addams as president.[12] As Addams wrote:

> The great achievement of this congress to my mind is the getting together of these women from all parts of Europe, when their men-folks are shooting each other from opposite trenches . . . it is a supreme effort of heroism to rise to the feeling of internationalism, without losing patriotism. (Quoted in Sklar, Schuler, and Strasser 1998: 204)

Even to attend this meeting was an act of heroism given that the participants faced severe censure for undercutting their nation's war efforts (43 and 205).

In later years the WPP became the U.S. section of the Women's International League for Peace and Freedom (WILPF), the oldest, international women's peace organization in the world (Alonso 1993, Schott 1997, Rupp 1997). It is beyond the scope of this chapter to address the entire history of the women's peace movement, but it should be noted that this internationalist stance on peace was a significant development in the feminist struggle against imperialism. It is also important to remember that women's roles in peace efforts are ancient. The first antiwar poem known to human history was written by the Sumerian priestess Enheduanna circa 2300 B.C. (Gioseffi 1988: 14). An excerpt from her poem "Lament to the Spirit of War" is presented in Box 8.3.

BOX 8.3

The First Antiwar Poem

"Lament to the Spirit of War"

Like a fiery monster you fill the land with poison.
As a rage from the sky,
you growl over the earth,
and trees and bushes collapse before you.
You're like blood rushing down a mountain,
Spirit of hate, greed and anger,
dominator of heaven and earth!
Your fire wafts over our tribe,
mounted on a beast,
with indomitable commands,
you decide all fate.
You triumph over all our rites.
Who can fathom you?"

"Lament to the Spirit of War," by Enheduanna, circa 2300 B.C.. Pp. 199–200 in *Women on War: Essential Voices for the Nuclear Age*, ed. Daniela Gioseffi (New York: Simon & Schuster, 1988).

The following section examines Rosa Luxemburg's analysis of imperialism. Despite the international links forged by many first wave U.S. suffragists, I could find no evidence that any of them were familiar with Luxemburg's work. Granted *The Accumulation of Capital* was not available in English until 1951. In turn, the German delegates at the 1915 Hague peace conference only included representatives from the German liberal women's movement, though members of the International Congress of Socialist Women sent greetings (Sklar, Schuler, and Strasser 1998: 196 and 193). With U.S. entry into World War I, avenues of communication between U.S. feminists and those living in Europe were largely cut off. The most likely candidate to be familiar with Luxemburg's work was the anarchist-feminist Emma Goldman. She was fluent in German and in 1919 was deported to Russia, where Luxemburg's works were well known. Both were deeply committed to an internationalist stance, and both were leading revolutionary figures in the West. It is surprising, therefore, that Goldman never mentions Luxemburg in her writings. One of her biographers suggests that her "bitter rejection of Marxism" may have led her to ignore Luxemburg's contributions (Wexler 1989: 243).

Even more surprising is that U.S. feminists of the 1960s and 1970s who came out of the New Left and the anti–Vietnam War movement did not pay adequate attention to Luxemburg's work. No doubt her Marxism made her less visible in the cold war freeze that affected mainstream social thought for many decades, just as her unorthodox Marxism led her work to be vilified by Stalin and, at best, treated condescendingly by U.S. leftists (Sweezy 1965). Luxemburg clearly had stature as a major leader and theoretician of the international socialist movement during her lifetime. However, her position as a woman and her unique political perspective made her what feminists today would call an "outsider/within" the socialist movement of her era (Collins 1990; see Box 8.4). While many feminists today would share Luxemburg's view that imperialism is a feminist issue, she may have been excluded from the U.S. feminist canon during the second wave because most of her writings did not specifically focus on women's issues.[13]

In contrast, Luxemburg's works have long been praised by feminists abroad.[14] Chapter 9 discusses how contemporary global feminist analyses inspired by her

BOX 8.4

Rosa Luxemburg and Feminism

Born in Poland in 1871, Luxemburg spent most of her life working in Germany as a journalist and teaching in the party school of the German Social Democratic Party (SPD)[15]—the largest socialist workers' party in the world at that time (Hudis and Anderson 2004: 9). She broke with the SPD in 1916 because of their support for World War I and founded the Spartacus League, which later became the German Communist Party (Merrick 1988: 2). She was arrested in 1919 during an uprising against the German government and was killed by soldiers while being transported to prison. Over her brief life span, she produced approximately seven hundred publications, including articles, pamphlets, speeches, and books.

Luxemburg had to fight for her position at the forefront of the international socialist movement, the leadership of which was almost exclusively male (Haug 1992). She angered many male leaders for refusing to assume the stereotypical roles women in political organizations played at that time (Frolich 1972: 56). On joining the SPD, she rejected the suggestion from party leaders that she turn her attention to organizing women, which she knew would sidetrack her from the mainstream of the party's political life (Merrick 1988: 4). "While she understood the importance of organizing women to take part in the revolutionary struggle . . . she steadfastly refused to be forced into any traditional women's role within the party" (Waters 1970: 8). Rather, she encouraged left-wing women to take an independent role in politics and to free themselves from their husband's domination (Howard 1971: 236).

Luxemburg was a close friend of Clara Zetkin, leader of the SPD's section on women, and shared her view that women's emancipation was an integral part of socialist transformation. Luxemburg's writings on women demonstrate how she saw them as an exploited group, along with the working class, minorities, and peasants (Merrick 1988: 4–5). She was critical of liberal feminism (which she termed "bourgeois feminism") and made demands for women that were far more radical than those of the hegemonic liberal feminist organizations of that era (Abraham 1989: 67). However, Luxemburg, like other Marxist feminists, believed that women could achieve their full liberation only with the triumph of a socialist revolution. Consequently, she devoted her energies to addressing the key issues of imperialism, social class, and revolutionary strategies that were being debated by the male leadership of the international socialist movement.

ideas were written by European and East Asian women, read by American feminists, and then incorporated into U.S. feminism. A goal of this chapter is to bypass this circuitous international route by encouraging U.S. feminists to become more familiar with Luxemburg's work.

ROSA LUXEMBURG ON IMPERIALISM

Rosa Luxemburg's major treatise on imperialism, *The Accumulation of Capital*, first published in 1913, focused on the economic factors that compelled capitalist enterprises to expand beyond their national borders. Uncovering the economic roots of imperialism was an urgent task at this time in history, when the scramble for global territories was creating severe tensions between the major European powers—tensions that eventually erupted in the First World War. While other leaders of the German Social Democratic Party (SPD), such as Karl Kautsky and Eduard Bernstein, viewed imperialism as an aberrant form that was not intrinsic to capitalist development, Luxemburg argued that capitalism was driven to expand into noncapitalist areas in order to protect its very existence. These political debates were not simply academic; they had serious implications for whether the SPD and the large German labor movement it represented would support imperialist ventures (Hudis and Anderson 2004).

Unlike those of more orthodox Marxists, Luxemburg's analysis of imperialism was based on an underconsumptionist model of capitalist development. She argued that capitalism was severely restricted and ultimately would be destroyed by its need to accumulate capital by ever expanding the number of goods it produced. Eventually capitalists would run out of effective consumer demand for the growing number of commodities produced for their home markets and would have to rely on people outside of the capitalist system:

> The immediate and vital conditions for capital and its accumulation is the existence of non-capitalist buyers of surplus value . . . the accumulation of capital, as an historical process, depends in every respect upon non-capitalist social strata and forms of social organization. (Luxemburg [1913] 1951: 366)

For Luxemburg, this meant that the capitalist system was locked in an inescapable contradiction. On the one hand, it depended on noncapitalist markets to realize the ever-expanding value it produced. On the other hand, as capitalism penetrated noncapitalist markets it destroyed native handicraft and artisan forms of production that could not compete with the mass-produced commodities of large scale, industrial, capitalist enterprises. As capitalism spread globally it not only created a world in its own image, but it also dug its own grave by annihilating the noncapitalist forms it was dependent on for further expansion:

> Non-capitalist organizations provide a fertile soil for capitalism; more strictly: capital feeds on the ruins of such organizations, and although this non-capitalist milieu is indispensable for accumulation, the latter proceeds at the cost of this medium, nevertheless by eating it up. (416)

Few Marxists of her era ever matched her depth of concern over the Western imperialist destruction of premodern social relations (Hudis and Anderson 2004: 17). Instead of highlighting the backwardness of such formations, she focused on their extraordinary tenacity, elasticity, and adaptability. In particular, Luxemburg emphasized how European imperialism destroyed the world's remaining indigenous communal formations—formations that had "afforded the most productive labor process and the best assurance of its continuity and development for many epochs" (quoted in Hudis and Anderson 2004: 16).

> The intrusion of European civilization was a disaster in every sense for primitive social relations. The European conquerors are the first who are not merely after subjugation and economic exploitation, but the means of production itself, by ripping the land from underneath the feet of the native population. . . . What emerges is something that is worse than all oppression and exploitation, total anarchy and a specifically European phenomenon, the uncertainty of existence. (Luxemburg [1908] 2004: 110)

This theme of the ruination of natural economies pervades Luxemburg's critiques of the impact of French imperialism in Algeria, of British imperialism in India and China, of U.S. imperialism in the Pacific and Latin America, and of various European colonial ventures in Southern Africa (Luxemburg [1913] 1951).

For Luxemburg, the imperialist destruction of natural economies exemplified the process of primitive accumulation that Marx had discussed in *Capital* to explain the origins of capitalism in Western Europe (Marx [1867] 1967: 667–670). For Marx, **primitive accumulation** referred to the use of brute force and violence to turn peasants into proletariat and to plunder riches from the New World, which the merchants and conquistadors of the mercantile era then brought back to Europe in order to stimulate their burgeoning capitalist enterprises. Unlike Marx, Luxemburg ([1913] 1951: 369–371) theorized that primitive accumulation was not just relevant to the origins of capitalism but, rather, was *a recurring process in the imperial drives of capitalism into foreign lands*:

> The accumulation of capital employs force as a permanent weapon, not only at its genesis, but rather right on down to the present day. . . . In fact, it is invariably accompanied by a growing militarism as an integral part of the logic of modern imperialism.

As numerous critics have pointed out, Luxemburg's underconsumptionist argument is flawed for several reasons. First, looking past the production of consumer goods to the production of the means of production shows how capitalist accumulation and realization can take other forms when it is realized through investments in additional machinery or means of production. Second, capitalism does not produce commodities just to meet human needs. Rather it constantly creates new needs and, hence, new possibilities for markets within any given national market. Third, as one critic rather scathingly put it, Luxemburg's analysis "implies the absurdity that backward nations have a surplus in monetary form large enough to accommodate the surplus-value of the capitalistically advanced societies" (Mattick 1978: 4). Fourth, empirical studies of international markets during Luxemburg's era demonstrate that major market activities took place between the developed imperial powers rather than between developed and less developed countries (Hobson [1902] 1971: 71).

Although Luxemburg's theory is flawed, she made a number of important contributions to future analyses of imperialism. First, her writings are notable for highlighting the role that Western imperialism played in the destruction of indigenous, noncapitalist social relations across the globe. Second, by stressing how capitalism depends on state violence to expand globally, her work contains the seeds of a theory of a permanent arms economy that was developed by later neo-Marxists (Magdoff 1969). Third, she predicted the growth of militarism and conflict between capitalist countries that repudiated any notion of the peaceful development of capitalism and foreshadowed the world wars of the twentieth century (Cox 2003: 8). Fourth, her theory has had a significant influence on contemporary global feminist analyses, as will be shown in the following chapter.

CONCLUSION

This chapter focused on how feminists in early modernity addressed the issues of imperialism and colonialism. It showed how feminists from a wide array of theoretical and political perspectives responded to and analyzed the rise of U.S. imperialism in the late nineteenth century. It also showed how race, class, and gender were interwoven into their debates and analyses. Those feminists who were more attuned to race and class oppressions were more likely to take an anti-imperialist stance. Suffragists who took a pro-imperialist stance during this era often did so to foster their own domestic race, class, and gender interests. In short, their own social locations and standpoints were reflected in their discourses on imperialism.

Through this examination, this chapter addressed two shortcomings in U.S. feminists' discussions of feminism and imperialism in early modernity. On the one hand, it focused on the inadequate attention U.S. feminists have paid to how major leaders of the U.S. women's movement responded to both U.S. internal colonialism and to the expansion of U.S. overseas imperialism. On the other hand, it discussed the contributions of Rosa Luxemburg's theoretical analysis of imperialism, which has received scant attention by U.S. feminists. Through this process it retrieved and reclaimed part of our historical past. Perhaps the most important reason for unearthing our past is to learn from it, so as to better chart our future and change the oppressive power relations encoded in the name of gender, race, class, nation, and empire.

Note: Because all of these early modern feminist approaches were critiqued in earlier chapters, these criticisms are not repeated here.

NOTES

1 Large sections of this chapter first appeared in Susan A. Mann, "Feminism & Imperialism, 1890–1920: Our Anti-Imperialist Sisters; Missing in Action from American Feminist Sociology," *Sociological Inquiry* 59, no. 4 (2008): 461–489. The author wishes to thank John Wiley & Sons for permission to reprint them here.

2 See Terborg-Penn 1998b, Dubois 1991 and 1994, Rupp 1994 and 1997, and Mann 2008.

3 Together Hoganson (1998 and 2001) and Sneider (1994 and 2008) provide some of the most important contributions to date for understanding the relationship between U.S. imperialism and the woman question during the first wave. However their works tend to focus on suffragists in the more hegemonic, liberal feminist organizations and ignore the role of more radical feminists during this era (Mann 2008).

4 Henry Brown Blackwell published an article titled "Domestic Imperialism" in the *Woman's Journal* (1902) in which he tried to make the case that disenfranchised women within the United States, much like Puerto Ricans and Filipinos, were internal colonial subjects. However, Allison Sneider (2008: 115–116) notes that because white and black suffragists preferred to view themselves as "civilizers" rather than as colonial subjects this idea did not gain a significant following.

5 Not all indigenous tribes in the area we now call the United States were matrilineal before contact with settler colonialists. For a discussion of differences between tribes see Mihesuah 2003: 49–53.

6 There have been many debates in anthropology over whether the term *matrilineal* is a more accurate description of these tribes than *matriarchal.* While matrilineal refers to lines of descent and inheritance following the mother's side of the family, matriarchal implies domination of men and children by women. Indeed, some anthropologists argue that there never have been any matriarchal societies in human history.

7 Mankiller was the first female in modern history to lead a major Native-American tribe. Her family name, Mankiller, is an old military title that was given to the person in charge of protecting the tribal village. Native-American activist Winona LaDuke echoes Mankiller's views here when she writes: "It is also critical to point out at this time, that the most matrilineal societies, societies in which governance and decision making are largely controlled by women, have been obliterated from the face of the Earth by colonialism and subsequently industrialism" (quoted in Mihesuah 2003: 41).

8 She was referred to as Sarah Winnemucca Hopkins after she married Lewis H. Hopkins an Indian Department employee in 1883.

9 *Jingoism*, coined in 1878, is a British term used to refer to zealous pro-imperialists' extreme patriotism and aggressive stance on foreign policy. It was derived from the lyrics of a song sung in pubs and music halls at that time: "We don't want to fight but *by Jingo* if we do, we've got the ships, we've got the men, we've got the money too."

10 These suffragists were incensed but not surprised to learn about the U.S. Army's regulation of prostitution, since this issue had been raised earlier by British feminists when the British military engaged in similar practices to reduce venereal diseases among soldiers and sailors (Butler [1871] 2005).

11 The French title of Cooper's dissertation is "l'Attitude de la France a l egard de l'esclavage pendent la Revolution" (see Lemert and Bhan 1998: 272).

12 Although these late-nineteenth and early-twentieth-century first wave organizations described themselves as international, they only included representatives from First World countries in Europe and North America (Ferree and Tripp 2006).

13 Luxemburg's work is often absent from U.S. discussions of major women theorists during the first wave even though other European women, such as Harriet Martineau and Marianne Weber, are included (Finlay 2007, Ritzer 2011, Lengermann and Niebrugge-Brantley 1998). Some notable exceptions are Adams and Sydie 2002, Landry and MacLean 1993, and Caulfield 1984.

14 In 2007, more than 20,000 Europeans attended a demonstration in Berlin to honor the anniversary of Luxemburg's death (Grossman 2007).

15 Luxemburg's teaching position at the German SPD School was previously held by Rudolf Hilferding, another major writer on imperialism.

CHAPTER 9

Feminism and Imperialism in Late Modernity

> Central Intelligence Agency interventions overseas, support for "friendly" dictators, the overthrow of the Allende government in Chile, Watergate, the efforts to overthrow the Sandinista regime [in Nicaragua], the nuclear arms buildup—all have served to strengthen the image of the United Sates as an aggressive, ruthless and unethical nation. For Americans to understand Anti-Americanism they must take off their cultural blinders and see their country as others see it.
>
> —MARGARITA CHANT PAPANDREOU

INTRODUCTION

After the Second World War, the globe was literally transformed; new countries came into being and old countries changed their names. As the sun set on the European empires, a large number of former colonies gained their independence, in part, because the European powers could not sustain their colonial rule during and after the devastation wrought by this war. Between 1945 and 1981 more than one hundred new countries joined the United Nations, tripling its ranks from 51 to 156 nations (McMichael 1996: 25). It was expected that, no longer under colonial rule, these countries would modernize and develop of their own accord.

Yet, these newly independent countries emerged within a global framework that was shaped by a Western conception of what development and modernization entailed. Under this framework, development was defined primarily by economic growth. Such growth was expected to follow similar patterns to the West, where science and technology enhanced agricultural productivity and fostered urbanization and industrialization. It was assumed that this economic growth would usher the rest of the world into "modernity" in that it would be accompanied by increasing standards of living and political freedoms as well as the rationalization and secularization of social life. Some writers have referred to this Western model as "the development project" to highlight how it represented "particular *historical and political choices*, rather than an inevitable unfolding of human destiny" (McMichael 1996: 18; his emphasis). Other writers have argued that the very idea of "modernity" was one of the "central tropes" through which the West constructed itself as the center and the rest of the world as its periphery (Mary Louise Pratt quoted in Spurlin 2006: 23).

However, colonial independence did not necessarily transform the uneven and unequal nature of global stratification. Many former colonies did not modernize or industrialize; rather large portions of their populations remained plagued by absolute poverty—lacking the basic necessities of human life, such as food, water, and shelter. Moreover, while national liberation movements had promised greater freedom and democracy in their anticolonialist, revolutionary zeal, they often ended up with small, indigenous elites enjoying great wealth and power amid the poverty of the masses or what Franz Fanon called "the wretched of the earth" (Fanon [1961] 1967). The major reasons for this extremely uneven and unequal global development became the central questions debated by theorists of global development after the Second World War.

These theorists introduced a number of new concepts to describe the postcolonial landscape. Yet because this post–World War II period was also the cold war era, much of this new terminology reflected cold war politics. Indeed, the Iron Curtain divide between capitalism and socialism/communism was used to distinguish between the First, Second, and Third Worlds. The **First World** referred to industrially developed, capitalist countries; the **Second World**, to industrially developed, socialist/communist countries; the **Third World**, to countries that were still largely agrarian, whether capitalist or socialist.[1] As noted in chapter 8, the term **colonialism** refers to a foreign power holding *direct* political, economic, and cultural control over a country or region. Because many former colonies achieved their political independence after World War II, a new term, **neocolonialism**, began to be used to describe the *indirect* political, economic, and cultural control of a politically independent country by a foreign power(s)—a form of control that many Western powers continued to maintain.

Beginning in the 1960s, one of the most visible, new economic developments was the rapid expansion of multinational, labor-intensive industries to the Third World. The term *global restructuring* refers to the emergence of these global factories or multinational corporations in which research and management is controlled by first world countries while assembly line production work is relegated to peoples in less privileged nations within the global economy. These factories found lucrative homes in Third World countries with First World–friendly elites and political regimes, low levels of unionization and regulation, and high unemployment. This new development contrasted sharply with previous eras, when the First World was the center of industrial manufacturing and the Third World largely produced the raw materials for these finished products. This era also witnessed the proliferation of export processing zones (EPZs) and tax free zones (TFZs) where governments offered such concessions as infrastructural subsidies and/or tax breaks in order to attract foreign investment. The first EPZ was established in Ireland in 1958; by the mid-1980s, roughly 1.8 million workers were employed in more than 170 EPZs across the globe (McMichael 1996: 92 and 94).

The post–World War II era also witnessed a significant increase in the role of global **finance capital**. Finance capital makes profits off of lending, investing, and/or manipulating money and currencies. While this shift from the importance of industrial capital to finance capital had been predicted by theorists in the early twentieth century (Hilferding [1910] 2007, Lenin [1917] 1996), its impact on the global landscape became more evident only in later decades. Two major international financial agencies established after World War II later became major players in global development policies. The **World Bank**[2] was established in 1944 primarily to oversee the rebuilding of postwar Europe. Its role shifted dramatically in later decades when it became the world's largest supplier of development capital and advice. The **International Monetary Fund (IMF)**, also established 1944, significantly enlarged its scope of activities over time to include overseeing global exchange rate policies, providing financial assistance to members with balance of payments problems, and giving technical assistance for policies, institutions, and statistical analyses (Symington 2005). The visibility of these financial institutions on the global economic landscape became clearer as their impact became harsher. In the 1980s, the World Bank and the IMF began to impose economic requirements on countries that had accepted loans or aid through policies known as **structural adjustment programs (SAPs)**. As a means of repaying debts, SAP prescriptions included such measures as cutting government expenditures on local health, education, and welfare programs, slashing wages, fostering export commodities and cash crops, and devaluing local currency—all of which had negative effects on the lives of many Third World peoples—especially women, as will be shown below.

Overall, the success of these development projects and their central tenet that living standards in Third World countries would be raised by industrialization were very limited in the first few decades following World War II. The "newly industrializing countries" (NICs) that lent legitimacy to this project were few. Moreover, a number of these NICs held strategic positions in the international order during the Cold War and had received substantial direct and indirect economic assistance from the Western powers that other Third World countries did not receive (McMichael 1996: 83). Consequently, strong geopolitical forces contributed to their growth. Because of this limited success, by the final decades of the twentieth century many people—including feminists—had become far more critical of the development projects proposed in the post–World War II era. The growing strength of the environmental movement fueled these critiques as people became increasingly aware that the earth could not sustain the prospect of all nations following the First World path of industrialization and mass consumption.

Such insights were not readily apparent to many U.S. feminists in the 1970s and early 1980s. Regardless of whether these feminists' theories were reform-oriented or revolutionary, they often embraced development projects that viewed Western forms of development as the political–economic model for the Third

World. In part, U.S. feminists were blinded to the Western/Eurocentric bias of their analyses because global politics in that era were so heavily embroiled in cold war politics. To them, the primary debate was over *which* path to follow—the first world's capitalist path or the second world's socialist path? As such, they rarely questioned the economic growth assumptions underlying *both* of these paths to development.

The Vietnam War was probably the most important event that fostered U.S. second wave feminists' engagement with the issues of imperialism, militarism, and global development. Unlike the more recent wars in Iraq and Afghanistan, fought by a volunteer army, the Vietnam War was based on conscription or compulsory military service. While college deferments were initially allowed, they were later eliminated. This meant that young men of all classes and races were eligible for the draft and required to serve. No doubt, many young men from affluent backgrounds found ways to avoid direct combat, such as serving in the National Guard (which, unlike today, meant that they were unlikely to be sent overseas). However, conscription for all men between eighteen and twenty-five years of age lessened the class bias in military service that had existed in earlier years of the war. Indeed, a common belief about the Vietnam era was that antiwar activism increased as more middle-class soldiers came home in coffins (Fisher 1989). The carnage was severe. For example, approximately two hundred U.S. soldiers were killed *every week* in 1967, and that rate was considerably higher in 1968, the war's peak year (Gosse 2005: 94). By war's end, more than fifty-eight thousand U.S. soldiers had died, more than one hundred and fifty-three thousand were wounded, and at least two million Indochinese had perished (Gosse 2005: 86 and 109).

THE ANTI-VIETNAM WAR MOVEMENT

The Vietnam War directly impacted second wave feminists as their husbands, lovers, brothers, and friends were conscripted into the U.S. armed forces. Such a direct impact made them pay more attention to global issues and to the role of the U.S. military and the Central Intelligence Agency (CIA) in overt and covert ventures abroad. The My Lai Massacre and the secret bombing of Cambodia in the late 1960s, as well as the Iran–Contra scandal in Nicaragua and the CIA's involvement in the overthrow of a democratically elected socialist government in Chile in the early 1970s, all were exposed in the national press. In turn, a number of books written on women's issues abroad, such as Ruth Sidel's *Women and Child Care in China* (1973), Susan George's *How the Other Half Dies: The Real Reasons for World Hunger* (1976), and Margaret Randall's powerful duo, *Cuban Women Now* (1974) and *Sandino's Daughters: Testimonies of Nicaraguan Women in Struggle* (1981), provided U.S. feminists with a better understanding of Third World women's concerns and how U.S. government practices contributed to their problems. Many of these authors spent time living abroad and were sensitive to the rapidly growing anti-Americanism they encountered there.

Using both Old and New Left theories, antiwar activists criticized the U.S. government for bolstering an antidemocratic government in South Vietnam and for intervening in the Vietnamese people's right to self-determination. They viewed the U.S. military as an occupying force and strongly contested their use of torture and chemical weapons, such as napalm and Agent Orange.[3] Over time support for anti–Vietnam war activism grew at home and across the globe. After taking part in a 1974 World Tribunal on the Vietnam War Simone de Beauvoir wrote:

> Our unanimous decision (made by judges from around the world) was that Americans did make use of forbidden weapons, that they did treat prisoners and civilians in an inhuman manner contrary to the laws of war." (Quoted in Gioseffi 1988: 194–195)

Many women who were (or who would become) second wave feminists were engaged in the anti–Vietnam war movement. There they learned important political and organizing skills and were immersed in the theories and political practices of the Old and New Left. Through their antiwar activism, these women also saw how male activists expected them to make coffee, cook, and do other tasks that relegated them to behind-the-scenes activism. Just as first wave activists came to realize their second-class status within the abolitionist movement, many second wave activists came to feminism because of the sexism within the New Left and the Anti–Vietnam War Movement. Radical feminist Robin Morgan (1970: xxiii) describes this sexism below:

> Thinking we were involved in the struggle to build a new society, it was a slowly dawning and depressing realization that we were doing the same work and playing the same roles in the Movement as out of it: typing speeches that men delivered, making coffee but not policy.

Yet through their antiwar activism these feminists gained a profound interest in militarism and imperialism that was to carry over into their global feminist analyses. They also participated in a collective mass movement that inspired their own mass actions on behalf of feminism.

The social movement against the Vietnam War was the largest antiwar and peace movement in U.S. history. Powerful moral suasion was added to the antiwar movement when the Catholic Left as well as Dr. Martin Luther King Jr. lent their support. The role played by the Vietnam Veterans against the War added even more credibility to the claims of antiwar protestors. As historian Van Gosse (2005: 100) wrote: "The sight of radical nuns, priests, soldiers and veterans shocked mainstream Americans profoundly." The antiwar movement reached its peak in 1969 under the Nixon administration when more than two million people participated in Vietnam Memorial protests across the country. In the late spring of 1970, after the U.S. invasion of Cambodia and the campus shootings at Kent State and Jackson State,[4] student strikes shut down more than five hundred colleges and universities across the country and over one hundred thousand antiwar protestors marched on the nation's capital (Anderson 2007: 247). In April and May of the following year, the number of antiwar demonstrators who descended on

Washington, D.C., swelled, with various demonstrations ranging from five hundred thousand to seven hundred and fifty thousand (Gosse 2005: 106). That May, so many protestors were "illegally" arrested (twelve thousand) that they had to be corralled into Robert F. Kennedy Stadium (106). The antiwar movement sharply deepened the ideological divide in a country that already had been sorely ruptured by the civil rights movement. It also indirectly contributed to a number of signal events of that era, such as the release of the Pentagon Papers, the formation of the infamous Plumbers, the Watergate break-in, and, ultimately, the demise of the Nixon administration.[5]

Feminists' antiwar activism would be used against them during their efforts to pass the Equal Rights Amendment. While many controversial issues were employed to mobilize the successful STOP-ERA movement[6] (see chapter 2), one of these issues was the claim that feminists were unpatriotic (Marshall [1989] 1995). Phyllis Schlafly—the STOP-ERA movement's most vocal leader—pointed to feminists' antiwar activism and their support for draft dodgers as evidence of their lack of patriotism. She also made mileage off her claim that the ERA would place women in combat. Not only was this idea alarming to the general public, but it also raised fears that the ERA would undermine the strength of the armed forces. In *The Power of the Positive Woman* (1977), Schlafly writes that feminists "will exercise their freedom of choice to avoid military service" but "are willing to inflict involuntary military duty on all other eighteen-year old girls." (1977: 24).

Overall, participation in the anti–Vietnam War movement politicized second wave feminists about global and military issues. The next section of this chapter examines how some of the earliest second wave "global feminist analyses" (as they were called in the 1970s) were inspired by two major theoretical perspectives that dominated global political analyses in the 1960s and early 1970s. Yet, because feminists of the second wave were far more critical of the military and militarism than all but their most radical first wave predecessors, it is fitting to first illustrate this using the work of one of the most prolific second wave feminists on these topics—Cynthia Enloe. Box 9.1 shows how Enloe, writing in 2007, still used second wave feminist insights, what she calls "feminist curiosity," to critically examine the inner workings of the U.S. military long after the Vietnam War.

BOX 9.1

The Importance of Feminist Curiosity in the Military

Since the mid-1970s, feminist have been introducing new questions to pose and crafting skills to explain when and why organizations become arenas for sexist abuse. One of the great contributions of the work done by what is often referred to as the "Second Wave"...has been to shed light on what breeds sex discrimination and sexual harassment inside organizations otherwise as dissimilar as a factory, a stock brokerage, a legislature, a university, a student movement, and a military....By 2004, this feminist explanatory concept—organizational "climate"—had become so accepted by many analysts that their debt to feminists had been forgotten....

The first lesson: to make sense of any organization, we always must dig deep into the group's dominant presumptions about femininity and masculinity....

It is not as if the potency of ideas about masculinity and femininity had been totally absent from the U.S. military's thinking. Between 1991 and 2004, there had been a string of military scandals that had compelled even those American senior officials who preferred to look the other way to face sexism straight on. The first stemmed from the September 1991 gathering of American navy pilots at a Hilton Hotel in Las Vegas. Male pilots (all officers), fresh from their victory in the first Gulf War, lined a hotel corridor and physically assaulted every woman who stepped off the elevator....Within months, members of Congress and the media were telling the public about "Tailhook"—why it happened and who had tried to cover it up....Close on the heels of the "Tailhook" scandal came the army's Aberdeen training base sexual harassment scandal, followed by other revelations of gay bashing, sexual harassment and rapes by American male military personnel (Enloe, 1993 and 2000).

Then in September 1995, the rape of a local school girl by two American male marines and a sailor in Okinawa sparked public demonstrations, the formation of new Okinawan women's advocacy groups and more congressional investigations in the United States. At the start of the 21st century, American media began to notice the patterns of international trafficking in Eastern European and Filipino women around American bases in South Korea prompting official embarrassment in Washington....And in 2003...four American male soldiers returning from combat missions in Afghanistan murdered their female partners at Fort Bragg, North Carolina; a pattern of sexual harassment and rape by male cadets of female cadets—and superiors' refusal to treat these acts seriously—was revealed at the U.S. Air Force Academy; and at least sixty American women soldiers returning from tours of duty in Kuwait and Iraq testified that they had been sexually assaulted by their male colleagues there....

So it should have come as no surprise to senior uniformed and civilian policymakers...that a culture of sexism had come to permeate many sectors of U.S. military life. If they had thought about what they had all learned...from Tailhook, Aberdeen, Fort Bragg, Okinawa, South Korea, and the U.S. Air Force Academy, they should have put the workings of masculinity and femininity at the top of their investigatory agendas. They should have made feminist curiosity one of their principal tools.

Excerpts from Cynthia Enloe, *Globalization and Militarism: Feminists Make the Link* (New York: Rowman & Littlefield, 2007), pp. 105–108.

MODERNIZATION THEORY AND DEPENDENCY THEORY

In late modernity the major theories used to explain uneven global development reflected the capitalist versus socialist battle grounds of the cold war. Modernization theorists tended to be either conservative or liberal, pro-capitalist theorists who located the problems of Third World countries in *internal factors* that hindered their development, such as overpopulation, illiteracy, lack of resources, and traditional values/cultures. Dependency theorists, conversely, tended to be left-wing, anticolonialist, and/or pro-socialist theorists who argued that the uneven and unequal development of Third World countries was due primarily to *external factors*, namely, exploitation by First World countries that thwarted their development. To them, modernization theorists simply blamed the victims of the First World's own colonialist and neocolonialist practices.

Dependency theorists developed a *relational theory* that viewed First World development as integrally intertwined with Third World underdevelopment. They argued that First World countries had developed by using the twin exploitative processes of colonialism and neocolonialism to provide the necessary capital or wealth for their own industrialization. For example, dependency theorists discussed how the conquest and enslavement of indigenous peoples, such as the Mayans or the Aztecs, by the colonialists and conquistadors of the mercantile era created the wealth that was sent back to Europe to foster the development of First World industrial capitalism. They pointed to how forms of neocolonialism in late modernity, such as the exploitation of cheap, Third World labor by multinational companies, also funneled wealth from the Third to the First World. In short, the external processes that created First World wealth also perpetuated the dependency of Third World countries. Hence, they called themselves dependency theorists and referred to these interrelated processes of First World enrichment and Third World exploitation as the "**development of underdevelopment**" (Frank 1976, Amin 1977).

Dependency theorists' solutions to Third World underdevelopment were often twofold. First, they asserted that Third World peoples should break their colonial ties to the First World through anticolonial, national liberation movements. Following their political independence, these countries should then break or closely restrict their economic ties with the First World. This latter solution took a variety of forms that reflected the different politics of dependency theorists. Moderate theorists called for the strict regulation of foreign trade and investments. Radical theorists called for the appropriation and nationalization of the land and factories owned by foreigners and multinational corporations. Marxist and socialist dependency theorists added to this radical anticolonialist demand a call for socialist revolutions to end the power of wealthy, indigenous ruling classes *within* Third World countries (Frank 1976, Amin 1977).

In contrast, modernization theorists ignored or downplayed the processes of colonialism and neocolonialism. Rather than a relational analysis, they treated global inequality as a more **atomistic**, *individualistic* or country-specific problem. The reasons for a Third World country's lack of development were located internal to that country in its own traditional culture or lack of resources. As such, Third World countries were viewed simply as being at an earlier stage of development than those of the First World. If given sufficient aid, trade, and capital investments, along with the diffusion of advanced, Western technologies, these Third World countries could "take-off" and modernize or develop (Rostow 1960, Parsons 1966). Rather than cut off ties, they argued for more interaction between the First World and the Third World in the form of more aid, trade, and foreign investments to foster development. To deal with the internal problems they saw as obstructing Third World development, such as overpopulation or traditional values, their solutions included birth control and family planning as well as more Western-style education in the methods and techniques of modernization. Teachers and advisors were sent abroad, and student exchanges were employed to foster this modernizing culture and education. Through these mechanisms, the First World could reshape the Third World in its own image. Modernization theory was hegemonic in the United States, and the government tended to embrace this theory regardless of whether Democrats or Republicans were in power.

The theoretical debates between modernization and dependency theorists were not merely academic exercises; they also were used to decide the international aid, trade, and educational policies of governments and world bodies, such as those of the IMF and the World Bank. These theoretical perspectives also were used ideologically to buttress military conflicts that erupted in the 1960s and 1970s, such as when First World governments used their economic, political, and military resources to fight against communist or socialist insurgents in El Salvador, Nicaragua, Chile, and Vietnam. During the second wave, most liberal feminists embraced modernization theory while many revolutionary feminists embraced dependency theory or at least incorporated various assumptions held by dependency theorists into their theories. Despite their differences, one of the most important contributions of *all* of these second wave global feminisms was to show how *gender matters in the outcomes of global modernization and development.* Prior to the work of these second wave feminists, rarely did theories of global development—politically left, right, or center—have any discussion of the differential impact of development on men versus women. Rather, the subjects of their global studies were without gender. As one commentator sarcastically noted: "It is remarkable how intellectual life...was conducted on the tacit assumption that human beings had no genitals" (Eagleton 2003: 3–4).

LIBERAL FEMINISMS INSPIRED BY MODERNIZATION THEORY

One of the earliest and most influential liberal feminist analyses to genderize modernization and development studies was Ester Boserup's *Woman's Role in Economic Development* (1970). Using an impressive array of quantitative and qualitative cross-cultural data, Boserup documented how Third World women were more negatively impacted by modernization and development than were their male counterparts. For example, in discussing how Third World rural women's status declined under European colonial rule, Boserup (1970: 53–54) wrote:

> European settlers, colonial administrators and technical advisers are largely responsible for the deterioration in the status of women in the agricultural sectors of developing countries. It was they who neglected the female agricultural labor force when they helped to introduce modern commercial agriculture to the overseas world and promoted the productivity of male labor.

Boserup discussed various reasons for these rural women's decline in status. For example, she argued that because European colonial administrators assumed men were better farmers than women they neglected to provide instruction to Third World female cultivators when they introduced new agricultural techniques, even in locales where women had historically been the primary farmers. As a result, men were more likely to use modern technologies and to engage in the production of cash crops while women were commonly relegated to more traditional farming methods and subsistence production. As such, men's agricultural productivity and incomes rose relative to those of women (54–55).

To her credit, Boserup was careful to distinguish between women of different classes within rural and urban areas, between women of different ethnicities and races, and between women's roles in different forms of agricultural production (such as labor-extensive versus labor-intensive). For example, she pointed to how some rural women benefited from the exploitation of other men and women—particularly in areas where the existence of a class of poor, wage laborers existed alongside groups that owned land or who had tribal rights to land (67). She even discussed the overlap of race, ethnicity, and class in certain locales, as when the wives of landowning Tutsi chiefs had power over Hutu men and women, who were at the bottom of the social hierarchy because of their ethnicity and their position as wage laborers (67). Contrary to present-day claims that white second wave feminists ignored differences between women, Boserup was quite aware of these differences.

Boserup also was careful not to simply portray Third World women as passive victims of modernization and development. She devoted sections of her book to discussing their various forms of resistance to externally imposed colonization and modernization, such as the famous 1929 anticolonialist revolt in the Abo region of Nigeria by some two thousand rural women who demanded the elimination of all foreign institutions and foreigners (63–64). Boserup also dispelled prevalent Western stereotypes of Third World women as victims of their own culture's traditional practices. She discussed how such practices as polygamy or restricting women to the home were often preferred by rural women in certain locales of Africa. In locales where women were not restricted to the home, more wives meant more sharing of agricultural and domestic labor. In locales where women were restricted to the home, this restriction meant that they did not have to work in the fields. From the standpoints of these women, they were beneficiaries rather than victims of these traditional cultural practices. In contrast, Western colonial administrators could only envision that all women would want to end polygamy and/or restrictions on their movements and were totally baffled when these Third World women responded angrily to colonial policies prohibiting these practices (43).

Overall Boserup's study was a milestone in showing how "gender matters" in terms of the outcomes of modernization and development as well as the importance of women's race, ethnicity, and social class in development policies. Despite these important contributions, she provided no fundamental critique of either colonialism or modernization. Rather, her conclusions suggested that if colonial administrators gained more cross-cultural insights and if Third World women gained more education and opportunities to participate in the modernized sectors of the economy, modernization would lead to progress. In this sense her solutions echoed the solutions of modernization theorists. She also pointed to the need for the wider use of birth control and the mechanization of domestic work in the Third World as important routes to progress. She focused on improving educational and vocational training for women and encouraging them to seek employment in the modernized sectors of their economies (224–225). Thus First World, Western-style capitalist modernization and development were her keys to third world success.

In *Theoretical Perspectives on Gender and Development* (2000), Jane Parpart, Patricia Connelly, and Eudine Barriteau do a fine job of showing how different feminist perspectives influenced different development policies and I will draw from their analyses in discussing the links between feminist theory and political practice throughout this chapter. For example, in the early 1970s, the term women in development (WID) was coined by the Women's Committee of the Washington, D.C., Chapter of the Society for International Development, a network of female development professionals who were influenced by Boserup's work and similar liberal feminist global analyses (Tinker 1976, Maguire 1984). The policies that WID advocated were rapidly adopted by the United States Agency for International Development (USAID) and its Office on Women in Development. The initial focus of these policies was on equity, or, bringing Third World women and men into the development process through access to education, employment, and the marketplace (Parpart, Connelly, and Barriteau 2000). Later approaches emphasized anti-poverty, efficiency, and empowerment strategies mirroring general trends in Third World development policies from basic needs strategies to compensatory measures associated with structural adjustment policies (Moser 1993: 55). These policy solutions also mirrored those of modernization theory, particularly its individualistic and market-oriented approaches to dealing with global and gender issues. Just as modernization theorists focused on individual countries improving their economic growth, the liberal feminist WID approach focused on individual women improving their skills so that they could participate in modern forms of economic growth.

MARXIST AND SOCIALIST FEMINISMS INSPIRED BY DEPENDENCY THEORY

The more revolutionary U.S. feminisms of the 1970s and early 1980s—especially Marxist and socialist global feminisms—were inspired by dependency theory and its relational approach to global stratification. In these approaches, it was not problems internal to individual Third World countries that inhibited their development but, rather, *social relations of exploitation between Third World and First World countries* that took center stage—namely the social relations of colonialism and neocolonialism. Feminist dependency theorists did not focus on women as individuals in the development process but on *gender relations of exploitation* that encompassed various areas of social life, including women's roles in the production of commodities outside of the home as well as in the social reproduction of everyday life through domestic labor, child rearing, and subsistence production.

Because the literature on women and development is so vast, I cannot address all of the different analyses undertaken by feminist dependency theorists. Instead, I will show how U.S. socialist feminists who used dependency theory addressed two important global developments of the post–World War II era—the rise of labor-intensive, global factories and the feminization of migration. The former disproportionately employed Third World women's labor in the production of commodities for the world market while the latter entailed Third World women's labor in the social reproduction of everyday life. These examples illuminate how feminist dependency theorists viewed the lives of First and Third World women as integrally intertwined in global, gendered relations of exploitation.

Global Factories

Beginning in the 1960s, but increasing rapidly in later decades, one of the most visible new economic developments was the rapid expansion of multinational, labor-intensive industries to the Third World. Such global factories found lucrative homes in countries that had established export processing zones (EPZs) and tax free zones (TPZs). Especially significant to feminists was the fact that young, Third World women overwhelmingly constituted the labor force of these global factories. For example, in Mexico by the turn of the twenty-first century approximately eighty-five percent of the EPZ labor force comprised young women. The EPZ incentive for investment in Sonora (one of Mexico's poorest border states) was one hundred percent free taxation for the first ten years and fifty percent taxation for the following decade (McMichael 2008: 92 and 94).

Among the most widely read U.S. feminist works in the early 1980s that exemplified feminist dependency theory were Annette Fuentes and Barbara Ehrenreich's *Women in the Global Factory* (1983), Maria Patricia Fernandez-Kelley's *For We are Sold, I and My People* (1983), and Wendy Chapkis and Cynthia Enloe's *Of Common Cloth: Women in the Global Textile Industry* (1983). Recurring themes in these works are the ways in which the division of labor inside and outside of these multinational factories created competition and conflict between women. Fernandez-Kelley discussed the intense competition between Mexican women for jobs in these global factories or *maquiladoras*. Such jobs were particularly enticing to women with children because they often provided medical benefits. Yet, if women had too many children they were less likely to get hired. Consider this quote from a thirty-year-old mother of six:

> I have been looking for work since my husband left me two months ago. But I haven't had any luck. It must be my age and the fact that I have so many children. Maybe I should lie and say I've only one. But then the rest wouldn't be entitled to medical care once I got the job." (Quoted in Fernandez-Kelley 1983: 282).

As noted in this quote, age also was a significant factor in getting a job. Women over the age of twenty-five were less likely to get hired, as were women without local, personal references. Such personal references served as a means of social control over these women since their employment was tied to their own informal social networks of obligation and trust.

Fernandez-Kelly further highlighted the intense competition between women on the shop floor. She noted how most garment maquiladoras operated through a combination of low wages and piecework. Piecework greatly increased the intensity of work, pitted individual women workers against each other, and seriously endangered the jobs of workers who levels of productivity were not up to speed. This was especially problematic on assembly lines, where seamstresses depended on thread cutters or when sleeves could not be sewn onto shirts without collars and cuffs. Delay at any stage of the assembly line slowed up the entire production process and generated conflict between these women workers.

From her participant observation of these maquiladoras, Fernandez-Kelly documented the sheer volume of work expected of these women workers. Coupling this information with data on their wages, she highlighted the high levels of exploitation involved. She wrote of her experience sewing on sleeves in a garment maquiladora: "As for the production quota, I was expected to complete 162 pairs of sleeves every hour, which is one every 2.7 seconds, more than 1,200 per shift" (Fernandez-Kelley 1983: 281). On weekdays, her shift began at 3:45 p.m. and ended at 11:30 p.m.; on Saturdays, the shift started at 11:30 a.m. and ended at 9:30 p.m. Half-hour breaks were allowed within each shift, and women worked an average of forty-eight hours per week for the equivalent of sixty cents an hour in U.S. dollars.

In "The Globetrotting Sneaker" ([1995] 2004), Cynthia Enloe pointed to similar levels of exploitation of Third World women workers by multinational companies such as Reebok and Nike. She discussed how in the early 1980s these companies decided to manufacture most of their athletic footwear in South Korea and Taiwan, hiring primarily local women. When other multinational sneaker manufacturers followed suit, some Third World countries in the Far East, including South Korea, Taiwan, and Indonesia, became the "sneaker capitals" of the world. Enloe provided a comparative chart of hourly wages in athletic footwear factories that ranged from $7.00–$8.00 in the United States to $2.00–$2.50 in South Korea to about 20 cents per hour in Indonesia ([1995] 2004: 454). She also documented how a pair of Nike shoes that sold for $70.00 in the United States actually cost about $11.00 (U.S.) to produce, with Nike and the retail stores that sold their shoes splitting the remaining profits (455).After women workers in South Korea organized to improve their working conditions their efforts initially paid off. They gained the right to organize their own women's unions and received pay increases. However, it was not long before the sneaker companies began shutting down their South Korean factories and moving to nearby Taiwan and Indonesia where the workforce was not unionized and where wages were substantially lower.

Enloe highlighted how thousands of women across the globe were threatened with plant closures and threats to move abroad if they demanded decent working conditions or higher wages. This not-so-new policy of divide and conquer by the multinational companies affected competition between Third World working-class women as well as between First and Third World working-class women. In this way, Enloe presented a feminist version of dependency theory that not only was sensitive to gender but that also showed how gender and class overlap in these global scenarios. She argued that working-class women had more to gain from global solidarity rather than from viewing themselves as rivals. However, she realized how many factors, including nationalism, racism, and ethnic chauvinism, greatly inhibit such solidarity:

> Big business will step up efforts to pit working women in industrialized countries against much lower-paid women in "developing" countries, perpetuating the misleading notion that they are inevitable rivals in the global job market. (Enloe [1995] 2004: 454)

Enloe was adamant that class differences within the First and Third Worlds be addressed. In *Bananas, Beaches, and Bases: Making Feminist Sense of International Politics* (1989: 199), she noted how the use of Third World as a concept fosters a form of thinking in which "important differences between women in less industrialized countries will be ignored." She continued: "By portraying all women in Third World societies as sewing jeans, not buying jeans, as prostitutes, not as social workers and activists, we again under-estimate the complex relationships it takes to sustain the current international political system" (199). Enloe's work provided another good example of how some U.S. second wave feminists were sensitive to the inadequacies of the homogenizing concepts of "First World" and "Third World" and how differences between women in both of these locales had to be addressed (93).

For Marxist and socialist global feminists, an adequate analysis of the relations between First and Third World women hinged on recognizing class distinctions between them. The rise of labor-intensive global factories in the post–World War II era negatively impacted the lives not only of Third World working-class women but of First World working-class women as well. Such concepts as *runaway plants, deindustrialization, and outsourcing* point to how blue-collar and more recently white-collar workers in the First World suffer as their jobs are moved across the globe to locales with cheaper, nonunionized labor, and fewer environmental regulations. Between 1965 and 1985, U.S. industrial manufacturing employment dropped from 60 percent to 26 percent while employment in service sector jobs rose from 40 percent to 74 percent (Stacey 1991: 18). These new service sectors jobs were lowly paid and lacked the medical and pension benefits associated with blue-collar, unionized labor and so did not compensate for the loss of blue-collar manufacturing jobs. As a consequence of this wage erosion, the demographic profile of the U.S labor force changed significantly as more women, especially women with children, entered the labor force to buttress their household incomes. Whereas only 15 percent of mothers with children under the age of six were employed in the U.S. labor force in the 1950s, by 2002 their number had increased to 65 percent

(Ehrenreich and Hochschild [2002] 2004: 8). It is likely that deindustrialization has had a far greater influence than the women's movement on the entry of U.S. women with children into the labor force.

First World deindustrialization together with the increase of First World women's labor force participation also had significant repercussions on Third World women's work. As First World–based, multinational corporations migrated to Third World countries for cheap labor, so too did Third World people migrate to the First World to fill the growing, low-paid service sectors of these economies. What was new about these global migrations was that women made up an increasingly large percentage of this migratory labor.

The Feminization of Migration

The term **feminization of migration** was coined by Stephen Castles and Mark J. Miller in *The Age of Migration: International Population Movements and the Modern World* (1993). It refers to the increasing number of women migrant workers crossing the globe in search of jobs. After World War II and up until about 1979, men constituted the vast majority of global migrant laborers. That changed beginning in the 1980s, as women became a larger part of the global migrant work force. By the 1990s, women made up 50 percent of Filipino migrants to all countries, 50 percent of Mexican and Korean migrants to all countries, 40 percent of Algerians and Moroccans living in France, and 84 percent of Sri Lankan migrants to the Middle East. By the early twenty-first century, it was believed that more than half of the world's estimated 120 million migrant workers were women (Ehrenreich and Hochschild [2002] 2004: 5–6).

An example of the use of feminist dependency theory to analyze these migrations is *Global Women: Nannies, Maids, and Sex Workers in the New Economy* ([2002] 2004), edited by Barbara Ehrenreich and Arlie Russell Hochschild. *Global Women* documents how the increasing global migration of women has been primarily from poor countries to rich countries where they serve as sex-workers, as nannies and maids in private homes, and as caregivers in institutional settings such as hospitals, hospices, child care centers, and nursing homes.[7] Although the contributors to this volume discuss Third World migrant women's roles in various types of employment, I will focus primarily on their analyses of the global migration of nannies and domestic servants.

It is tempting to simply attribute this new global phenomenon to affluent First World families exploiting Third World women as lowly paid caretakers. However, Ehrenreich and Hochschild place part of the blame on governments, such as that of the United States, that act like deadbeat dads by not providing sufficient family-friendly work policies for employed women. As noted in chapter 4, the U.S. government fares badly in comparison with governments of other highly industrialized societies in terms of providing child care centers, maternity and paternity leaves, and other caregiving policies. The contributors to the volume also blame men from across the globe for failing to take on additional housework in order to make up for the rise in women's labor force participation and for abdicating their child care responsibilities in cases of divorce and abandonment (8–9).

Structural adjustment policies (SAPs) prescribed to governments of indebted Third World countries also fostered the feminization of migration. Consider how U.S. Third World feminist Grace Chang described this process in her chapter "The Global Trade in Filipina Workers," in *Dragon Ladies: Asian-American Feminists Breathe Fire* (1997: 132):

> SAPs strike women in these [Third World] nations the hardest and render them most vulnerable to exploitation both at home and in the global labor market. When wages and food subsidies are cut, wives and mothers must adjust household budgets, often at the expense of their own and their children's nutrition. As public healthcare and education vanishes, women suffer from a lack of prenatal care and become nurses to ill family members at home, while girls are the first to be kept from school to help at home or go to work. When export-oriented agriculture is encouraged... peasant families are evicted from their lands to make room for corporate farms, and women become seasonal workers in the fields or in processing areas.

Chang also discusses how Third World governments receive huge sums of remittances from their overseas workers each year. For example, in 1994 the Central Bank of the Philippines recorded the receipt of 2.9 billion in U.S. dollars from remittances by overseas workers. These remittances are the country's largest source of foreign exchange and provide currency for payments toward their national debt. Hence, Third World governments also recruit men and women to migrate abroad, at times using deceptive advertising.

Ehrenreich and Hochschild argue that even affluent countries, such as the United States and Great Britain, had their own versions of structural adjustment programs in the 1980s and 1990s, when their governments engaged in "welfare reform" and other cutbacks in health care and social services. These measures made the need for privately funded home care even more necessary. These developments also introduced more competition between poor women in the First World and foreign migrant laborers. For example, migrant women have increasingly replaced First World women in menial and caretaking jobs in the First World. Today, Latinas from Mexico and Central America outnumber African-American women in domestic service in the United States; North African women replaced rural French women in France; and Turkish women and women from the former East Germany replaced rural women from the former West Germany in the unified Germany of today (Ehrenreich and Hochschild, [2002] 2004: 6–7). This competition is heightened because Third World women who migrate for jobs as nannies and domestic workers are sometimes better educated than First World peoples who seek similar jobs in domestic service. Female migrants from the Philippines often have high school and even college degrees—yet their home country lacks job opportunities or the jobs that exist are lowly paid (10). Their higher educations are preferred by First World employers, especially when these Third World women serve as caretakers of children or elderly family members.

Just as earlier dependency theorists highlighted their fears of a Third World "brain drain" resulting from international student migrations,[8] feminist versions of dependency theory highlighted how the migration of educated women from the

Third World resulted in both a "brain drain" and a "care drain." Chang (1997: 133) reported that out of the approximately one hundred thousand registered nurses in the Philippines almost none reside in that country. Ehrenreich and Hochschild ([2002] 2004: 17) echoed these concerns:

> As rich nations become richer and poor nations become poorer, this one-way flow of talent and training continuously widens the gap between the two. But in addition to this brain drain, there is now a parallel but more hidden and wrenching trend, as women who normally care for the young, the old, and the sick in poor countries move to care for the young, the old, and the sick in rich countries.... It's a care drain.

Ehrenreich and Hochschild refer to this new "care drain" as a "global heart transplant" and the "dark child's burden" (22 and 27). Today an estimated thirty percent of Filipino children—some eight million of them—live in households where at least one parent has gone overseas. These children have counterparts in Africa, India, Sri Lanka, Latin America, and the former Soviet Bloc countries. Compared to their classmates, the children of migrant workers are more frequently ill, more likely to express anger, confusion and apathy, and more likely to perform particularly poorly in school (22).

Feminist dependency theorists called for more First World responsibility and accountability for Third World problems. They also called for collective political action both locally and globally, such as unionization of workers and demonstrations to protest decisions harmful to working-class and poor people by international bodies, such as the World Bank. They highlighted the need for policies that protect the interests of poorer women globally, such as the policies generated at the official United Nations Fourth World Conference on Women held in Beijing, China, in 1995 or those fomented at the Forum of Non-Governmental Organizations (NGOs) held that same year in Huairou, China (Kirk and Okazawa-Rey [1998] 2001: 264).

In the mid-1970s and 1980s, dependency theory was overshadowed by a different neo-Marxist form of analysis, world-systems theory. This theoretical perspective shares many underlying assumptions of dependency theory's relational approach to global exploitation and underdevelopment. However, a distinguishing feature of world-systems theory is that national boundaries no longer serve as the defining features of the world system. Because the focus is on the rise of a world market and a global division of labor, world-systems theory stands as a precursor to transnational global analyses.

SOCIALIST FEMINIST WORLD-SYSTEMS THEORIES

World-systems theory had its roots in the work of neo-Marxist theorist Immanuel Wallerstein. Volume I of his book *The Modern World System: Capitalist Agriculture and the Origins of the European World-Economy in the Sixteenth Century* (1974) fostered entirely new approaches to studying the global system and became a classic in the field of social change. World-systems theory uses a tripartite division of the world into core, semiperiphery, and peripheral areas, with the core referring to developed areas of the globe that dominate the capitalist world economy, peripheral areas referring to those areas of the globe that produce the raw materials for the core, and the semiperiphery referring to regions somewhere between the other two in terms of their role in the international division of labor. These global areas are linked through the development of the world market, and Wallerstein analyzed their rise and decline over time.

Some outstanding global analyses can be found in the works of U.S. feminists who embraced world-systems theory, such as *Households and the World-Economy* (1984), edited by Joan Smith, Immanuel Wallerstein, and Hans Dieter Evers; *Before European Hegemony: The World System AD 1250–1350* (1989) by Janet Abu-Lughod; and *Women in the World-System: Its Impact on Status and Fertility* (1984) by Kathryn Ward. Below I focus on Ward's later edited volume, *Women Workers and Global Restructuring* (1990), which addresses a significant area of women's work in the global economy often neglected by earlier writers—the informal sector.

In simple terms the **informal economy** refers to unregulated income-producing labor. It is characterized by the absence of a contractual relationship between labor and capital where the conditions of work and pay are not legally regulated or protected (Ward 1990). The informal sector is extremely heterogeneous and comprises various forms of agricultural production, small-scale production and trade, subcontracting to home-based producers, and semilegal or clandestine enterprises, such as sweatshops. This new focus on the informal sector reflects the many ways in which feminist scholars in late modernity not only redefined women's work to include wage and nonwage labor but also analyzed distinctions within these forms, such as formal labor, informal labor, and housework.

Although a number of earlier theorists had examined the informal sector of the global economy (Portes 1985, Portes and Sassen-Koob 1987), they often ignored gender stratification in this sector (Truelove 1987). Yet, as Ward (1990: 2) pointed out, one of the major features of global restructuring was the marked increase of female workers in the informal sector. These women made less money than men working in this sector and seldom had the opportunity to fill management and supervisory roles within this sector that were controlled by men (Truelove 1987). This omission of women and gender stratification from earlier theoretical analyses was significant, since the informal sectors of Latin American and Asia consisted mostly of women while women workers formally employed by multinational corporations (MNCs) constituted a much smaller proportion of the female global workforce (Ward 1990: 4–5; Lim 1985).

Ward argued further that by focusing primarily on women's formal work, researchers had failed to analyze the permeable or overlapping boundaries between women's formal work, informal work, and housework that are quite distinct from the boundaries of men's work. The tensions and contradictions between these various spheres of work go some way to explaining why most women who engaged in informal sector work did so for the survival and maintenance of their families. In contrast, most men who worked in the informal sector used their labor as a means of social mobility (Ward 1990: 7). Using such analyses, feminist world-systems theorists highlighted not only the *blurred boundaries of the global economic system but also the blurred boundaries of women's work within this system.*

World-systems theory's focus on global areas linked by a world market better captured social transformations that had occurred in late modernity than did the more narrow focus of dependency theory on relations between developed and underdeveloped nations. In early modernity, the international division of labor primarily entailed the separation of raw material extraction from industrial manufacture or the production of finished commodities. While the former was primarily located in Third World countries, the latter was located in First World countries. Hence, it made more sense for theories of economic development to focus on the geographic boundaries of nation-states and to discuss relationships between First and Third World nations. After World War II, multinational corporations increasingly migrated across the globe in search of cheap labor, setting up export processing and tax-free zones, thereby dividing the world into core areas, where most capital originated, and peripheral areas, where the highest profits were realized. However, in recent years, the world-systems model has come under criticism for its static formulation. As critics such as transnational feminist Aihwa Ong have noted, this model can no longer deal with contemporary "flexible" global capitalism where corporations tap into different labor pools located anywhere in the world where optimal production, infrastructural, marketing, and political conditions exist; and where the division of labor in the production of a single commodity has become transnational (Ong 1991: 281–282; see chapter 10).

In summary, while many U.S. global feminist analyses in the 1970s and early 1980s were inspired by dependency and world-systems theory, throughout this era the liberal feminists' WID approach, derived from modernization theory, remained the dominant approach of First World governments, international relief and development agencies, and bilateral donor agencies. The anticapitalist features of feminist dependency and world-systems theories thwarted their ability to have as much influence on international agencies. As will be shown later in this chapter, feminist dependency and world-systems theorists joined forces with Third World feminists in the 1980s to develop an approach that in the following decades would become more hegemonic in activist and NGO global feminist arenas (Parpart, Connelly, and Barriteau 2000: 91). It is generally acknowledged that the work of these feminists moved the liberal feminist WID agencies in the 1980s to focus more on the concerns of poor women and antipoverty initiatives (Parpart, Connelly, and Barriteau 2000: 61; Moser 1993). Yet before these particular developments are discussed, it is necessary to review another U.S. second wave feminist approach that had a significant impact on global analyses radical feminism. In contrast to the global feminist analyses examined above, which focused on political economy, radical feminists focused on patriarchal cultural practices as the major problem facing women globally.

RADICAL FEMINIST GLOBAL ANALYSES

Beginning in the early 1970s, radical feminists took a leading role in highlighting how patriarchal cultural practices placed obstacles in the path of women's liberation globally.[9] As noted in chapter 3, two features that distinguished radical feminism from other second wave feminisms were its heavier focus on culture and its claim that patriarchy is the most fundamental form of oppression. Because criticisms of patriarchal culture formed the centerpiece of their global analyses, other forms of oppression, such as those based on class, race, or nation, took a back seat to an analysis of gender and patriarchy in their writings.

Many radical feminist global analyses entailed essentialist assumptions. As noted earlier in this text, **essentialism** refers to the belief in innate, intrinsic, or indispensable properties that define the core features of a given entity or group (see chapters 3 and 5). Although some radical feminists opposed this essentialism, I shall first focus on those who viewed women across the globe as sharing common oppressions due to their victimization by patriarchal cultures. For example, Lori Heise's article "The Global War against Women" ([1977] 1993) often appeared in U.S. feminist theory anthologies to represent a radical feminist global analysis.[10] Heise began her article by stating that despite the many serious problems facing Third World women, such as poverty or the lack of medical care, their major concern was male violence against women. In this way, Heise prioritized patriarchy as the most fundamental form of oppression faced by these women. She highlighted how violence against women was "pandemic" and pointed to a number of Third World practices, such as female circumcision, dowry deaths, female infanticide, and widow immolation to illustrate her points.

Mary Daly's book *Gyn/Ecology: The Metaethics of Radical Feminism* (1978) provided one of the most fully developed radical feminist analyses of these global, patriarchal cultural practices. It had chapters on Indian suttee or widow self-immolation (*sati*), Chinese foot binding, and African female genital mutilation as archetypes of Third World "sado-rituals" against women. Daly also included historical examples of U.S. violence against women, such as witch burning to show the pandemic nature of this violence. Andrea Dworkin's earlier book *Woman Hating* (1974) included a similar discussion of global cultural practices, such as Chinese foot binding, alongside U.S. "gynocidal cultural practices." Both of these authors emphasized what Daly ([1978] 1990: 112) called the *"universal sameness of phallaocratic morality"* (emphasis added). In the "Prelude" to *Gyn-Ecology*, Daly states that she will "analyze a number of barbaric rituals" to seek out the "basic patterns they have in common" that constitute a patriarchal "Sado-Ritual Syndrome" (111):

> Those who claim to see racism and/or imperialism in my indictment of these atrocities can do so only by blinding themselves to the fact that the oppression of women knows no ethnic, national, or religious bounds. There are variations on the theme of oppression, but the phenomenon is planetary. (112)

The goal of radical feminists was to get women across the globe to recognize their common oppression. This focus on similarities between women is reflected in the title of Robin Morgan's path-breaking book *Sisterhood Is Global* (1984). Conceived in 1969, Morgan's book took fifteen years to compile and involved an extraordinary degree of international networking and research. It included moving essays as well as detailed statistical information on the status of women in more than eighty countries. When it was published in 1984 it was described by Western reviewers as "an international feminist encyclopedia" and as "the definitive text on the international women's movement" (Morgan [1984] 1996: vii). The activist legacy of this book was visible in the establishment of the **Sisterhood is Global Institute** in 1984, the first international feminist think tank to organize actions on behalf of women's rights globally. Some of the projects fostered by this institute included female literacy, women prisoners' rights, the first Urgent Action Alerts regarding women's rights, the first global campaign to make visible women's unpaid labor in censuses, and human rights manuals (in twelve languages) specifically designed for women in Muslim societies (www.sigig.org).

Radical feminists' global politics differed significantly from the liberal feminist WID approach in that they enjoined women to create alternative social institutions, separate from men, where women could organize in their own interests. During the 1970s, this approach influenced the thinking and practice of activists primarily in nonprofit or nongovernmental organizations who called for women's projects that were completely autonomous from those of men. As Parpart, Connelly, and Barriteau (2000) point out, this was referred to as the Women and Development (WAD) approach and stressed the distinctiveness of women's knowledge, women's work, and women's goals and responsibilities. Organizing efforts were oriented toward strengthening bonds among women through active, autonomous, local groups and networks. WAD activists argued that mainstream organizations carried the risks of domination by patriarchal interests, the marginalization of women, and inadequate funding of women's concerns. WAD offered a corrective to what radical feminists deemed as WID's naive assumption that simply having a women's bureau in male-dominated national or international organizations would adequately alter gender inequities (Parpart, Connelly, and Barriteau 2000: 60). By the time Morgan's book was published, WID-oriented women's bureaus were already experiencing problems of marginalization and inadequate funding in their day-to-day political operations.

Together, the WID and WAD initiatives were instrumental in the U.N.'s adoption in 1979 of the **Convention on the Elimination of All Forms of Discrimination against Women (CEDAW)**, which called on member states to transform customs, attitudes, and practices that discriminated against women. Because CEDAW does not impose any penalties on governments for failure to comply, it is difficult to enforce. However, it does require members to periodically report to an international committee on the status of CEDAW implementation. It has been used with limited success by women's groups to help put international pressure on their localities for change (www.wedo.org/files/CEDAW). Women in Colombia, for example, used CEDAW to make domestic violence a crime and to require legal protection for its victims. Women in Thailand and the Philippines used CEDAW to pass laws to stop sexual trafficking of women and girls. By the end of the first decade of the new millennium, one hundred eighty countries had ratified CEDAW. Yet, despite claims to be a leader in human rights legislation *the United States remained the only industrialized country in the world that had not ratified it.*[11] Although WAD was a major modernist approach that focused on similarities between women, it would soon be challenged by the oppositional gaze of Third World feminism that focused on differences between women.

THIRD WORLD FEMINISMS

Responding to considerable pressure from women across the globe, the United Nations declared 1975 as International Women's Year. That year, the first United Nations–sponsored World Conference on Women opened in Mexico City. Amid much fanfare and optimism, participants came together to celebrate and strengthen global sisterhood. However, this conference revealed some important cleavages between First and Third World women. By the mid-1970s, Third World feminist scholars and activists increasingly voiced their concern that global research agendas and analyses were being dominated by First World women. Drawing on Third World women's own indigenous experiences and scholarship, along with writings by U.S. intersectionality theorists, as well as feminist dependency and world-systems theorists, a new Third World feminism began to emerge (Parpart, Connelly, and Barriteau 2000: 91). It distinguished itself from the First World–conceived WID and WAD approaches by its Third World vantage point and its focus on problems specific to Third World women—in particular, the impacts of racism, colonialism, and global inequalities (Arizpe and Aranda 1981, Kishwar and Vanita 1984). Despite differences among these Third World feminists, they generally agreed on the need to focus on Third World poverty, on the importance of global economic inequalities, and on grounding solutions to women's problems in the experiences of poor, Third World women. *This was the beginning of a decentering of First World feminist hegemony in the global women's movement* that would become further consolidated at later world conferences on women, such as those in Nairobi in 1985 and in Bejing in the 1995 (see Box 9.2). The Bejing conference coupled with the NGO forum that accompanied it marked the largest meetings of women in world history (Kirk and Okazawa-Rey [1998] 2001: 264).

BOX 9.2

"Taking on the Global Economy"

The rain was with us every day, washing us, a metaphor for the tears of women from across the planet who came to share the pains and victories of their peoples. The earth turned to bog, wheelchairs became stranded and events were canceled.

For some, the inconvenience of incessant rain symbolized the expected relegation of women to substandard facilities. For others, we felt the monsoon working on us, softening the definitions of land and boundaries of peoples, preparing the ground for the new seed that women carried here to share.

The distributed seeds held the kernels of analysis that women first brought to trial at the 1985 world women's conference in Nairobi. There, women from countries of the south were raising their analysis of the social disinvestment that was making women poorer in their countries. The disinvestment they experienced in '85 was a result of their countries overdue foreign debts. The financial institutions that could help them out were dictating structural adjustment policies which compelled them to restructure their economies along free market principles to help exact the debt payments. Things like food, health, and other social infrastructure subsidies were jettisoned to meet these alignments. In 1985, this was new to women from the United States, where, by the way, the financial institutions enforcing these policies were located.

At the Beijing conference in 1995, women from around the world, and particularly women of color, carried a further-developed version of this analysis. Structural adjustment policies were only one component of what women could now more specifically name as the detrimental aspects of the globalization of the economy. They brought criticism of the destructive nature of a world economic system that is driven by consumption and western industrial values. By 1995, women were much more unified in their understanding of the global deregulation that allows market capitalism to run more freely in its pursuit of "maximizing profits." From country after country, women reported disinvestment in social support programs, privatization, increasing domination by western media, and the "westernizing-down" of cultural integrity because of these influences. It was this discussion, about the effects of globalization on communities around the world that marked a defining change in the world women's movements. World economic issues were now women's issues.

Excerpt from Kalima Rose, "Taking on the Global Economy," *Crossroads*, March 1996. Rose attended the NGO Forum of the United Nations Fourth World Conference on Women in 1995. She is a senior director of the Oakland, Calfornia-based PolicyLink.

Recognition of differences between women was the centerpiece of Third World feminism. For example, when Western feminists followed radical feminists in initiating campaigns against genital mutilation or dowry deaths at international conferences, they often met with resistance from Third World feminists who accused them of being ethnocentric or of viewing their own culture as superior to others. U.S. radical feminists' mantra that "sisterhood is global" became the metaphorical punching bag of Third World feminist critics both for its essentialist use of the term "sisterhood" that ignored differences between women and for its assumption of universality to the problems shared by women globally. The same year that Robin Morgan's *Sisterhood is Global* (1984) was published, postcolonial theorist Chandra Talpade Mohanty published her influential article "Under Western Eyes: Feminist Scholarship and Colonial Discourses" (1984) which critiqued the homogenizing and universalizing features of both Morgan's and Daly's work. Mohanty's writings are examined at length in chapter 10. Suffice it to say here that her goal was to deconstruct and dismantle these Western feminists' tendency to ignore important differences between Third World women.

Third World feminism was buttressed by the rise of a number of institutions for feminist research and activism during the late 1970s and 1980s, which gave it more equal footing in global policy arenas. The Center for the Development of Brazilian Women was founded in 1975; The Association of African Women for Research and Development (AAWORD) was established in 1977; and the The Gender and Development Unit of the Asian and Pacific Development Center, the Pacific and Asian Women's Forum and the Asian Women's Research Action Network were developed in the 1970s. Indian feminism, in particular, has had a tremendous influence on U.S. feminist thought. It flowered in the 1980s inspiring the creation of such organizations as Economists Interested in Women's Issues Group, the Centre for Women's Development Studies, and Development Alternatives with Women for a New Era (DAWN). The latter began as a small Third World women's organization in Bangalore, India and developed into an international forum for Third World women concerned with development strategies, policies, theories, and research, with a particular focus on poor women (Parpart, Connelly, and Barriteau 2000: 92).

From the grassroots organizational experiences and scholarly writings of Third World feminists, the Gender and Development (GAD) approach emerged as an alternative to WID and WAD. This approach was most clearly articulated by DAWN and was launched at the 1985 Nairobi International NGO Forum—an event attended by fifteen thousand women activists and held parallel to the official World Conference on Women. GAD adopted a two-pronged approach to the study of gender and development that investigates both women's material and cultural lives. It takes a social constructionist approach that views women as agents, rather than simply victims (WAD) or recipients of development (WID). The GAD approach highlights how women experience oppression differently according to their race, class, colonial history, culture, and position in the international economic order (Moser 1993; Sen and Grown 1987). Hence it is a form of global intersectionality theory that particularly focuses on the needs of poor women. Its policies recognize and address both women's short-term practical needs, such as food and shelter, as well as more long term strategic interests such as gender equality (Molyneux 1985).

A classic work of Third World feminism was *Development, Crises, and Alternative Visions* (1987) by Gita Sen and Caren Grown. This book was the result of a collective effort on the part of DAWN and synthesized three decades of economic, political and cultural policies towards Third World women. These authors documented how the socio-economic status of the vast majority of Third World women had worsened considerably over the United Nation's Decade for the Advancement of Women (1975–1985), pointing to the failure of Western "development projects" (16). Their focus on decentering dominant groups and dominant feminisms was evident in their call for an "alternative vision" that began from "the perspective of poor Third World women." For these authors this vantage point provided both a "much needed reorientation to development analysis" and a means of "empowering" these women in the global context (18). Their focus on differences between women was emphasized when they "strongly supported" the notion that feminism *cannot* be monolithic in its issues, goals, and strategies, but rather must highlight the diversity of women and the diversity of feminisms that characterize different regions, classes, nationalities, and ethnic backgrounds. They further emphasized how the different needs and concerns of different women should be "defined by them for themselves"—placing poor, Third World women and their socially-lived knowledge at the center of their analyses (19). They also called for a broadening of the notion of feminism to include a struggle against *all* forms of oppression and criticized those who accused women of not being "truly feminist" because of their unwillingness to separate the struggle against gender subordination from struggles against other oppressions, such as racism, classism, and/or imperialism (19).

This latter issue was the focus of another classic of Third World Feminism, Kumari Jayawardena's *Feminism and Nationalism in the Third World* (1986). Her book examined the rise of feminist movements and women's participation in political struggles within eleven Asian countries that had been directly subjected to domination by imperialist powers or "indirectly manipulated" into serving the interests of imperialism. One of her major goals was to show how *feminism was not imposed on or imported to Third World countries by the West but, rather, arose out of these women's indigenous experiences.* Jayawardena expanded the notion of feminism to include forms of women's activism in different types of struggles from national liberation movements to local acts of resistance against racism, classism, and imperialism. In this way, her work shows how feminist movements and feminist activism had developed in non-Western countries during the nineteenth and twentieth centuries even though this activism previously had been "hidden from history" (3). Such work also reminds us that while gender is always imbricated in the matrix of power, exploitation and resistance that characterizes imperialism and colonialism, it is not always the predominant factor in people's consciousness nor is it always the most effective rallying point for social change (Lewis and Mills 2003: 20).

Along with more documentation of women's social, economic, and political positions within Third World countries, Third World feminism also fostered more scholarship on Western women's roles in imperialism. For example, Nupur Chaudhuri and Margaret Strobel's edited book, *Western Women and Imperialism* (1992), focuses on the role women colonialists played in imperialist ventures. By examining these Western women's roles from a Third World vantage point, quite a different picture arises from how these Western women viewed their own endeavors. By juxtaposing the roles of feminists and social reformers of various political stripes with those of pro-imperialist women, the essays in this book provide important insights into the workings of gender, class, race, and empire in geographical locales that range from India to Africa. The 1990s witnessed a surge of studies by both Third World feminists and postcolonial feminists that integrated women's studies and colonial history to unravel the complex and sometimes contradictory effects Western women had on imperialism and colonialism (Lewis and Mills 2003:10–11).

U.S. Third World Feminisms: Intersectionality Theory Applied to Global Issues

Chapter 5 discussed how intersectionality theorists referred to themselves as U.S. Third World feminists in the 1980s. The political implications of this nomenclature were twofold: on the one hand, it better highlighted how internal colonialism *within* the United States affected many women of color; on the other hand, it linked their subjugated status to that of colonized women across the globe (see chapter 5). For these reasons the writings of U.S. Third World feminists are given a prominent place in contemporary postcolonial anthologies, such as Reina Lewis and Sara Mills's *Feminist Postcolonial Theory* (2003: 4). Some postcolonial theorists even refer to them as "postcolonial subjects" (see Box 9.3). In this chapter, I use the phrase *U.S. Third World feminism* to represent the application of intersectionality theory to global issues.

BOX 9.3

African-American Women as Postcolonial Subjects

Let me propose what may at first seem odd: in the struggle against *internal* colonization, it is the African-American who is the *post*colonial in the United States.... Postcoloniality is the achievement of an independence that removes the legal subject-status of a people as the result of struggle, armed or otherwise. In terms of internal colonization, the Emancipation, Reconstruction and civil rights were just such an achievement....Postcoloniality is not a signal for an end to struggle but rather a shifting of the struggle to the persistent register of decolonization. Here, too, the situation of the African-American struggle offers a parallel....I am claiming postcolonialist for the African-American, then, not because I want to interfere with her self-representation but because I want to correct the self-representation of the new immigrant academic as the postcolonial, indeed as the source of postcolonial theory [in the United States].

Excerpt from Gayatri Chakravorty Spivak, "Teaching for the Times." Pp. 478–479 in *Dangerous Liasons: Gender, Nation, and Postcolonial Perspectives* (1997), edited by Anne McClintock, Aamir Mufti, and Ella Shohat (Spivak's emphasis).[12]

That U.S. Third World feminists linked the problems perpetrated by internal colonialism at home to imperialism and colonialism abroad is visible in one of their earliest statements, the Combahee River Collectives' "A Black Feminist Statement" published in 1977:

> We realize that the liberation of all oppressed peoples necessitates the destruction of the political-economic systems of capitalism and imperialism as well as patriarchy...([1977] 2005: 313–314).

Moreover, like feminist postcolonial theorists, U.S. Third World feminists also were critical of the homogenizing tendencies of radical feminist global approaches and their failure to recognize difference. Audre Lorde's "Letter to Mary Daly" published in 1984, criticized Daly's refusal to adequately acknowledge the "herstory" of non-white and non-Western women:

> it was obvious that you were dealing with non-European women, but only as victims and preyers upon each other. I began to feel my history and my mythic background distorted by the absence of any images of my foremothers in power. Your inclusion of African genital mutilation was an important and necessary piece in any consideration of female ecology.... To imply, however, that all women suffer the same oppression simply because they are women is to lose sight of the many varied tools of patriarchy (Lorde 1984: 67 and 69).

Lorde's letter to Daly has been characterized as one of the "paradigmatic examples of challenges to white feminist theory by feminists of color in the 1980s" (Katherine 2000: 267). Such criticisms by intersectionality theorists, postcolonial colonial theorists, and Third World feminists across the globe marked a turning point in U.S. feminist global analyses.

It is in the context of these criticisms that radical feminist Adrienne Rich wrote her influential and self-reflexive piece, "Notes Toward a Politics of Location" in 1984:

> A few years ago I would have spoken of the common oppression of women, the gathering movement of women around the globe...the failure of all previous politics to recognize the universal shadow of patriarchy, the belief that women...may join across all national and cultural boundaries to create a society free of domination. (Rich [1984] 2003: 29).

Instead, Rich writes that this is *not* what she is going to say. Rather, she highlights the blinders created by her own "white", "Western eyes" and her social location in "the center" (30 and 34). She concludes that "there is no collective movement that speaks for each of us all the way through" and that as feminists we must always question "Who is *we*?" (37 and 41; her emphasis). Rich's focus on differences between women, as well as her reflexive deconstruction and decentering of her own Western feminist ideas exemplifies the type of transformation in social thought that many U.S. feminists would share as Third World feminism gained greater hegemony both globally and locally.

U.S. Third World feminists also critiqued how white, class privileged, Western eyes often were unable to understand the vantage point of Third World women. For example, Angela Davis' critical insights on reproductive justice discussed in chapter 5 are applicable to the population control policies advocated for the Third World and by the U.S. government and many U.S. feminists. To class privileged citizens of the First World it might appear irrational that poor, Third World women have high birth rates and/or reject birth control or abortion even when it is freely provided. Yet for women faced with high infant and child mortality rates, who need child labor to contribute to family subsistence and who lack pensions in their later years, having many children is an entirely rational decision (George 1976). In this sense, they too were concerned with reproductive justice or the freedom to give birth and not to have contraception forced upon them. Consequently, just as Davis pointed out how any campaign that spoke on behalf of *all* women was likely to be premised on a disregard for differences between women by race and social class (Davis 1981), the population policies fostered abroad were not always in the best interests of all Third World women.

A number of chapters in *Policing the National Body* (2002), edited by Jael Sillman and Anannya Bhattacharjee, speak to this issue. This anthology is a project of the Committee on Women, Population and the Environment (CWPE)—a multiracial alliance of feminist community activists, scholars and health practitioners who promote the social and economic empowerment of women in a global context. Betsy Hartmann's contribution "The Changing Faces of Population Control" (2002: 259) discusses how the United Nation's population conference Cairo+5 in 1999 transformed the language of their documents to emphasize women's empowerment rather than population *control* but did not actually transform its underlying assumption that "overpopulation is a major, if not the major, cause of poverty, environmental degradation and political instability." According to Hartmann, this belief serves as "powerful glue" that binds liberal feminists and many ecofeminists to political solutions that overlook global inequalities and that blame the fertility of poor women for their own poverty, as well as for ecological destruction (159).

Since the mid-1960s, the U.S. government has been a major player in funding, designing, and organizing population control efforts in the Third World. The goal of family planning programs has been to reduce birth rates as quickly and cheaply as possible through the mass provision of abortion, sterilization and contraceptives. In recent years, it has taken the form of more long-lasting contraceptive methods such as Depo-Provera, Norplant and the IUD (269). Hartmann argues that, while these methods are effective, they are also risky. They leave more power in the hands of the providers since women cannot remove these devices at will. Incentives, such as payments to recipients, to recruiters and/or to communities who achieve family planning targets, still remain in many places. In turn, the neglect of safer barrier methods is especially problematic given the prevalence of HIV/AIDS and other STDs.

Although Hartmann credits the Cairo+5 conference for rhetorically opening up space for reform of international family planning by adopting a more voluntary approach that reduces the former emphases on using sterilization and fixed target goals, she remains concerned that the role played by income inequalities in women's reproductive health has been ignored. She documents how over half of the funding still goes to family planning rather than to basic reproductive health and issues such as safe water and sanitation that lead to high maternal death rates and infant mortality. Moreover, the Cario+ 5 conference did not adequately address the impact of structural adjustment policies (SAPs) imposed by the World Bank and the IMF that have undermined public health services by imposing user fees on previously free services, increasing pharmaceutical prices and contributing to the overall deterioration of living standards for poor women (264–265):

> Building a reproductive health program on top of a nonexistent or deteriorating health system—and in many countries in the context of a rapidly escalating AIDS epidemic—is like building a house on a foundation of sand.

Just as U.S. Third World feminists witnessed U.S. women's organizations—such as battered women's shelters or rape crises centers—become deradicalized by their reliance on grants and professional staff (see chapter 5), Hartmann raises similar concerns for global feminist NGO's. She states that "ultimately, they face the question of accountability." Are they most accountable to governments and international funders or to the constituencies of women they are supposed to represent? (272).

U.S. Third World feminists also have been ardent critics of U.S. imperialist wars. Angela Davis and Assata Shakur were early and vocal critics of the Vietnam War. These women were hounded by the FBI for their radical activism. Audre Lorde was another strident critic of U.S. imperialism who decried how the U.S. military and intelligence forces propped up dictatorships across the globe and undermined democratic, populist, and socialist movements that organized against these dictatorships. One of her most compelling anti-imperialist statements can be found in her critique of the U.S. invasion of Grenada (1984). Similarly, many Asian-American feminists interwove their narratives of navigating racism at home with the impact on their families of imperialism. More than half of the contributors to the anthology *Dragon Ladies: Asian American Feminists Breathe Fire* (1997) discuss the role U.S. imperialism played their lives. Not only has U.S. imperialism in the Philippines, in the Pacific Islands and in many countries of the Far East had a long history, but also the Korean War and the Vietnam War were conflicts that directly impacted the lives of these women and their families:

> The reasons to talk about Asian American women as a single group is because we all share the same rung on the racial hierarchy and on the gender hierarchy. It is not that our lives are so similar in substance, but that our lives are all monumentally shaped by three major driving forces in U.S. society: racism and patriarchy most immediately, and *ultimately, imperial aggression against Asia* as well (Shah 1997: xiii; emphasis added).

By linking racism and internal colonialism at home with imperialism abroad, U.S. Third World feminists served as important critics of imperialism in late modernity.

Nevertheless, some postcolonial and transnational feminists have criticized U.S. Third World feminists for not being sufficiently reflexive regarding their own privilege as citizens of such a powerful First World country as the United States. In *Talking Visions: Multicultural Feminism in a Transnational Age* ([1998] 2001), Ella Shohat, who describes her perspective as "post-multicultural, transnational feminism," levels the following criticism:

> "First Worldness," even when experienced from the bottom, brings certain privileges that must be considered as we reconceptualize a multicultural, transnational, cross-regional feminism. Living in the U.S...can generate certain advantages, such as a powerful currency and an open-sesame passport (37–38).

Shohat also notes how "opposition to racism, sexism and homophobia in the United States has never guaranteed opposition to U.S. global hegemony" (38). She points to how First World people of color consume products at lower prices due to cheap Third World labor and how imperial militaries often serve as paths to upward mobility for Americans of color:

> Many people of color have fought as soldiers on the U.S.'s behalf in the last decade—in the Middle East, in Panama, in Somalia, in Haiti—occasionally alongside soldiers whose origins are in these countries.... The interwovenness of geopolitics and global economy suggests that our "hands are not clean" (38).

An important book that tries to bridge the differences between Third World feminism and postcolonial theory is *Feminist Futures: Re-imagining Women, Culture, and Development* (2003) edited by Kum-Kum Bhavnani, John Foran, and Priya Kurian. They propose a Women, Culture and Development approach (WCD) that gives a greater role to the significance of culture in women's lives. They argue that both development and Third World studies have "reached an impasse" in their assessment of future prospects for the Third World due to "their failure to see the significance of culture" (7). These authors identify with the "new cultural studies" where culture is treated more as "lived experience." As Bhavnani writes: "In drawing on culture as lived experience, a WCD lens brings women's agency into the foreground (side by side with and within the cultural social, political and economic domains) as a means of understanding how inequalities are challenged and reproduced" (8). The WCD approach also pays more attention to ecological sustainability and to fundamental flaws in development projects that focus primarily on economic growth. Indeed, the concept of "maldevelopment" is central to the WCD approach. This concept was introduced by European and East Asian writers who drew their inspiration from Rosa Luxemburg's theory of imperialism as will be shown below.

GLOBAL FEMINIST ANALYSES INSPIRED BY LUXEMBURG'S WORK

Given that Rosa Luxemburg's collected works were first available in the German Democratic Republic, it is not surprising that German feminists led the way in using Luxemburg's theory to discuss contemporary global feminist issues. Maria Mies's *Patriarchy and Accumulation on a World Scale*(1986) and *Women: The Last Colony* (1988), coauthored with Veronika Bennholdt-Thomsen, and Claudia Von

Werlhof were signal works in this regard. These authors argue that embedded in Luxemburg's theory of imperialism is an analysis of women's work that was not even visible to her. As Von Werlhof, writes: "Paradoxically, Rosa Luxemburg was unaware that she had written about the women's question in *The Accumulation of Capital*..." (14).

One of the major arguments of *Women: The Last Colony* is that *women's labor is the archetype of global nonwage labor*. The authors use Luxemburg's analysis of capitalism's dependence on nonwage labor to highlight how much of women's work across the globe is nonwage labor. They discuss how women in the First, Second, and Third Worlds are primarily responsible for unpaid (nonwage) housework and childcare whether or not these women work outside of the home. They also point, as Luxemburg did, to how many Third World workers (whether male or female) are engaged in nonwage forms of production, like subsistence agriculture or petty commodity production that is based on family labor rather than wage labor. These feminists conclude that, if nonwage labor is so important to understanding capitalism's imperialist expansion, than the so-called woman question is integral to an analysis of imperialism:

> But who are these "non"-capitalist producers...? They are the majority; housewives throughout the world, peasants of both sexes, mainly in the Third World producing for their own subsistence, and the army of males and females so-called "marginalized" people, most of whom also live in the Third World .
>
> The situation of Third World rural and urban subsistence producers, the "marginal mass", most closely resembles that of women. It is not women who have a colonial status, but the colonies that have a woman's status. (Werlhof in Mies, Bennholdt-Thomsen, and Von Werlhof 1988: 14–15 and 25)

The last chapter of *Women: The Last Colony* describes Third World men and women as the "world housewives" whereby "the relation between husband and wife is repeated in the relation between the First and the Third World" (177). In this way, these authors make a direct link between First and Third World women's labor and between patriarchy and imperialism. They also highlight how "gender matters" in the outcomes of capitalist development. Maria Mies describes the impact of capitalism on women in India as follows:

> Although we need a much broader and deeper study of the present processes affecting rural subsistence-producers, the above analysis of available data permits the formulation of a thesis: namely, *that capitalist penetration leads to the pauperization and marginalization of large masses of subsistence producers; and secondly, that women are more affected by these processes than men*, who may still be partly absorbed into the actual wage labour force.... There is a growing inequality and polarization between the sexes. The capitalist penetration [of noncapitalist forms abroad], far from bringing about more equality between men and women...has, in fact introduced new elements of patriarchalism and sexism. (40 and 41; her emphasis)

Mies describes how this process leads to the feminization of poverty in the Third World and an increase in violence against women as their position deteriorates relative to men. She also discusses the dissolution or break-up of families as pauperized men migrate to the cities for wage labor while wives and daughters stay in the local villages doing subsistence farming or turning to prostitution to make ends meet (Mies, Bennholdt-Thomsen, and Von Werlhof 1988: 42–43). As will be shown throughout this chapter, the thesis that Third World women are more negatively affected than their male counterparts by modernization and development is well-documented in feminist analyses today. However, the claim that women's nonwage labor is the archetype for examining labor in the Third World has been less influential. It may be more logical to argue the reverse that certain nonwage forms of production are the archetype for women's labor (Mann 1990a: 131–135).

Another theoretical contribution inspired by Luxemburg's work is the concept of **maldevelopment** (Shiva 1989: 1; Kirk and Okazawa-Rey 2001: 269). Published only a year after *Women: The Last Colony* (1988), Indian feminist Vandana Shiva's *Staying Alive: Women, Ecology, and Development* (1989) used Luxemburg's analysis of the impact of capitalist development on natural economies to discuss "maldevelopment":

> Yet, as Rosa Luxemburg has pointed out...colonization is a constant, necessary condition for capitalist growth: without colonies, capitalist accumulation would grind to a halt....Development thus became a continuation of the colonization process; it became an extension of the project of wealth creation in modern, Western patriarchy's economic vision (1)

By arguing that contemporary forms of modernization and development are simply a "continuation of colonization," Shiva begins *a critical interrogation of what is meant by "development" and thereby marks a paradigm shift in global feminist political analysis.* Previous analyses of development, whether politically left, right or center, primarily used economic growth as their major indicator of development. These theories argued that in order to increase production and alleviate Third World poverty, wage labor and industrialization has to replace less efficient, precapitalist, nonwage forms of production. This view was held by pro-capitalist modernization theories (Rostow 1960, Parsons 1966) as well by as pro-socialist dependency and world-systems theories (Frank 1976, Amin 1977, Wallerstein 1979). In short, wage labor and industrialization were common threads in both capitalist and socialist paths to development. Shiva (1989: 13) rejects these paths to development:

> The old assumption that with the development process the availability of goods and services will automatically be increased and poverty will be removed is now under serious challenge from women's ecology movements in the Third World, even while it continues to guide development thinking in the centers of patriarchal power.

Shiva claims that prior to colonization and imperialism Third World peoples were not in need of "development." She highlights how they lived in systems based on subsistence agriculture that were organically connected to nature and where women lived in an interdependent and complementary division of labor with men. She focuses on how the violation of these organic and interdependent systems signaled both the "death of nature" and the "death of the feminine principle." By the "death of nature", she means the beginnings of Third World environmental despoilment and pollution. By the "death of the feminine principle", she is referring to the demise of a holistic world view where belief in the life force of mother earth or "Prakriti" (as it is called in India) is interwoven with women's socioeconomic roles as food providers and as mothers. Shiva documents these two forms of destruction by showing how the replacement of subsistence agriculture with modern cash crops in India resulted in a scarcity of water, food, fodder, and fuel that had a negative effect on women's work.

If global feminist theorists such as Shiva reject both capitalist and socialist visions of the future, what do they support? Shiva's vision for the future is most clearly articulated in *Ecofeminism* (1993), in which she teams up with Maria Mies. Because Shiva is from India and Mies is from Germany their book merges different global vantage points. Their "new vision" for the future is designed to address the concerns of Third World people who "cannot ever expect to reap the fruits of 'development,'" as well as First World peoples who are "disenchanted and despairing about the end-results of modernization" (Mies and Shiva 1993: 297). Indeed, there are good social reasons to consider even highly modernized Western societies such as the United States as maldeveloped. This idea was satirically suggested by Mohandas Gandhi, the leader of India's anti-colonialist struggle against the British, when he was asked what he thought of Western civilization and replied: "I think it would be a very good idea."[13] Box 9.4 below provides some statistics that buttress Gandhi's response.

BOX 9-4

"Imagine a Country—2009"

Imagine a country where one out of four children is born into poverty, and wealth is being distributed upward....The top 1 percent has more wealth than the bottom 90 percent of households combined.

It is not Jamaica...."

Imagine a country where the infant death rate for children in the nation's capital is higher than for children in Kerala, India....Imagine a country where the typical white household has six times the net worth of the typical household of color....

It is not South Africa...."

Imagine a country that ranks first in the world in wealth and military power, and just 40th in child mortality (under age five), tied with United Arab Emirates, Slovakia, Serbia, and Lithuania, and behind countries such as Cuba, Thailand, Portugal, and Singapore. If the government were a parent, it would be guilty of child abuse. Thousands of children die preventable deaths....

It is not Brazil...."

Imagine a country that's ranked just 69th—right behind Uzbekistan—when it comes to the percentage of women in national legislative bodies.

It is not Russia."

"IT'S THE UNITED STATES."

Excerpt from Holly Sklar, "Imagine a Country—2009." Pp. 307, 311, 313, and 314–315 in *Race, Class, and Gender in the United States*, 8th ed. (2010), edited by Paula S. Rothenberg. New York: Worth.

Mies and Shiva use the terms "*subsistence perspective*" and "*survival perspective*" interchangeably to refer to their alternative vision. A major feature of this subsistence perspective is changing the aim of economic activity from producing an ever-expanding "mountain of commodities" to satisfying fundamental human needs. Other features include replacing money or commodity relationships for principles of reciprocity, mutuality, solidarity, sharing, and caring. Reliance on barter and social bonds of community replace the market and financial institutions, while natural resources such as water, soil and oil, are neither privatized nor commercialized but treated as community responsibilities (Mies and Shiva 1993: 319–321). Their preference is for the small and local. They typically support small, decentralized, democratic social organizations centered in local and community politics and slogans like "simple living" resonate strongly with them. They have a particular affinity for grassroots movements and local populist causes that challenge big corporations and centralized national governments, whether the latter are capitalist or socialist. This type of populist solution is very popular in global feminist and ecofeminist circles today and is embraced by feminists of various political persuasions including anarcha-feminists, radical and cultural ecofeminists and many younger feminists of the third wave (Merchant 1995: 3–26; Reger 2005: 207–208).

Mies and Shiva root their theoretical perspective in the work of Rosa Luxemburg because she appreciated the tenacity and stability of premodern, indigenous, communal formations. Yet Luxemburg never romanticized these premodern forms nor did she hold them up as a model for Third World development. As a Marxist feminist, she advocated industrial socialism as the best road for both First and Third World peoples. Her position is most clearly articulated in a section of the *The Junius Pamphlet* titled "Socialism or Barbarism?" ([1915] 2004). In turn, in various political settings she also allied with socialist leaders who rejected the populism of her era (Nettl 1969: 28 and 42).[14]

Despite these rather serious political differences, contemporary feminists who were inspired by Luxemburg's theory of imperialism made a number of important contributions. First, they retrieved Luxemburg's work and used her theory to develop their own unique global analyses. Second, they highlighted the importance of nonwage labor to the contemporary global landscape and in doing so connected a major form of women's labor to this framework. Third, they critically interrogated Western notions of development through their concept of maldevelopment. Fourth, they seriously discussed how the earth cannot ecologically sustain the prospect of every Third World country following the highly industrialized paths of the West. Fifth, they provided an alternative vision for the future that is neither capitalist nor socialist, but is predicated on simple, sustainable living and rooted in localized, grassroots, populist social movements.

CONCLUSION

Overall, late modernist global feminist theories heightened our awareness of how *gender matters in global development*. All of these feminist perspectives showed how modernization and development had different impacts on women as opposed to men. They also shared certain strengths and weaknesses. Feminist modernization theory shared with feminist dependency theory a focus on nation-states as their major units of analyses. By contrast, feminist world-systems theory focused on global areas linked by a world market where national boundaries became more fluid. This focus better captured global transformations in late modernity.

The global feminist perspectives inspired by dependency theory, world-systems theory, Luxemburg's theory, and Third World feminism differ from liberal feminist modernization theory in that they all focused on structural relations of exploitation. They pointed to how development and underdevelopment were mutually constitutive moments whereby the rich got richer, while the poor got poorer. The Luxemburgian-inspired feminist approaches went the farthest in critically interrogating Western models of development and in recognizing the negative ecological implications entailed in these models. Radical feminism focused most heavily on the way cultural practices impacted women globally. With a few notable exceptions, such as the work of Adrienne Rich, radical feminists were the most blind to differences between women by race, class and nation. By contrast, Third World feminists were the most astute at highlighting a politics of difference. Recent writings from this perspective also better incorporate ecologically sustainable development and culture as lived experience into their analyses.

The next chapter examines the contributions of postcolonial and transnational feminisms. These theoretical perspectives retain many of the strengths, but discard many of the weaknesses of the late modern frameworks discussed in this chapter. They highlight the fluidity of national borders, interrogate the assumptions of Western models of development and focus on difference, decentering and the mutually constitutive features of colonialism. They also chart important new directions in feminist thought.

Note: Because these late modern feminist approaches were critiqued in previous chapters, these criticisms are not repeated here.

NOTES

1 Third World is the English translation of *le tiers monde*, a term that emerged in France in the 1950s alongside the heightened anticolonial consciousness that accompanied the newly independent nations in Africa and Asia (Parpart, Rai, and Staudt. 2002: 28).

2 The formal name is the International Bank for Reconstruction and Development.

3 Agent Orange was the nickname given to an herbicide/defoliant used by the U.S. armed forces in Vietnam, so-called because of the color of the orange-striped barrels in which it was shipped. It is estimated that nineteen million gallons of Agent Orange were deployed in Vietnam. Not only did this chemical ruin crops, but it also caused a number of health problems for those exposed to it during the War. Vietnam veterans sought damages for the maladies that they and their children suffered; however, no Vietnamese victims ever received compensation.

4 In May of 1970, four unarmed students were killed at Kent State in Ohio, and later that same month, two more were killed at Jackson State in Mississippi (Anderson 2007: 249).

5 The anti–Vietnam War movement fostered former Pentagon aide Daniel Ellsberg to release the Pentagon Papers, which helped undermine President Nixon's authority in Congress and among the larger American public. This unauthorized release of the Pentagon Papers led to the formation the Plumbers, a covert investigated unit funded by the White House, the members of which were later convicted for their role in the Watergate scandal that eventually brought Nixon's presidency to an end (Barringer 1998).

6 STOP-ERA was an acronym for Stop Taking Our Privileges—Extra Responsibilities Amendment and was used to criticize feminists for encouraging women to work outside of the home, thus adding "extra responsibilities" to housework and child care. The so-called privileges these antifeminist women were referring to were the privileges of being a stay-at-home mom who was financially supported by a husband/breadwinner. Other key issues that mobilized antifeminists at this time were feminists' pro-choice stance on abortion and more general claims that feminists were not supportive of family values (Schlafly 1977: 104; Marshall [1989] 1995: 554).

7 Of the four major streams of global female migration today, one goes from Southeast Asia to the Middle East and Far East; one flows from the former Soviet Bloc to Western Europe; and two others move upstream from south to north in the Americas and from Africa to different parts of Western Europe (Ehrenreich and Hochschild [2002] 2004: 6).

8 A major problem for Third World countries is that their highly educated workers, whether schooled at home or abroad, often migrate to First World countries to take advantage of highly paid jobs. From a Third World vantage point, even international student exchanges were problematic because they could result in a "brain drain" as Fidel Castro has argued (Castro 2007).

9 Radical feminists share feminist dependency and world-systems theorists' concern with the political and economic exploitation of Third World peoples. They also critique U.S. global practices as imperialist.

10 For example, Heise's article appeared repeatedly in *Feminist Frameworks: Alternative Theoretical Accounts of the Relations between Women and Men*—a feminist theory anthology edited by Alison Jaggar and Paula Rothenberg ([1978] 1993) that could boast numerous editions published from the late 1970s to the early1990s.

11 For reasons why the United States has not ratified this treaty see www.wedo.org/files/CEDAW and www.cwalac.org.

12 For Spivak's explanation as to why she does not include Native–Americans and Mexican–Americans in her discussion of postcoloniality see Spivak in McClintock, Mufti and Shohat 1997: 479.

13 This quote, along with other famous quotes by Mohandas Gandhi can be found at www.Brainyquote.com/Mohandasgandhi.

14 A subsistence-based, populist alternative was not unheard of in Luxemburg's era. Populists and Marxists debated the relative merits of capitalist, socialist and populist paths to development especially in late-nineteenth-century Russia, where this debate was known as the "Agrarian Question." Luxemburg never allied with the populists but, rather, joined forces with such famous Russian leaders as Plekhanov and Lenin, who favored the socialist road to development (Nettl 1969: 28 and 42; Mann 1990a: 22).

CHAPTER 10

Feminism and Imperialism in Postmodernity

> The West is painfully made to realize the existence of the Third World in the First World, and vice versa. The Master is bound to recognize that His Culture is not as homogeneous, as monolithic as He believes it to be. He discovers with much reluctance, He is just an other among others.
>
> —TRINH T. MINH-HA

INTRODUCTION

In late modernity, the cold war was at the center of the global political stage. The conflicts and ideological struggles of this era were primarily over the type of political-economic systems that would prevail across the globe. Theories of imperialism and colonialism—whether left, right or center—focused on existing structural configurations of nation states and their political, economic and military forces as the motor forces of global power. In postmodernity the operation of global forces have blurred, dispersed and unsettled economic and geopolitical boundaries such that theorists now speak more fluidly of scapes, circuits, and networks as opposed to the modern notions of more rigid, stable, hierarchical national and international social relationships.

Theoretical analyses also shifted from a focus on imperialism to a focus on globalization. Globalization not only sounds less politically charged than the concept of imperialism, but also it refers to a much broader array of developments that include, but extend beyond political and economic concerns. For example, global theorists such as Arun Appadurai (1996) discuss a number of "scapes" that constitute the process of globalization. Alongside economic and finance scapes that straddle the globe, Appadurai discusses ethnoscapes that result from the significant increase in global travel, migrations and diasporas today. He also discusses the global technoscapes, mediascapes, and ideoscapes made possible by the new technologies such as the internet, and satellite communications which enable mass media, mass communications, and mass culture to transcend national boundaries.

The blurring of boundaries is evident in the new conceptual schemes that replaced the nation-focused and cold war–inspired concepts of First World, Second

World, and Third World countries. By the 1990s (after the decline of the Soviet Union as a superpower) the concepts of "**global North**" and "**global South**" came to be used more frequently by feminist writers to distinguish high income/high consumption areas of the globe from those characterized by low income/low consumption. Here the "North" and "South" do not designate specific geographic locations, but rather *locations of inequality*. Other concepts used by contemporary feminists, such as the "**One-Third versus the Two-Thirds World**," highlight not only the stark inequalities between the developed and maldeveloped areas of the world, but also the volumes of people that suffer from maldevelopment. While the nation state was still visible when one spoke of a First World or Third World country, it becomes less visible when one refers to the global "North" and "South" or the "One-Third" and the "Two-Thirds World". Box 10.1 below provides an excerpt from a poster used at the Earth Summit in Rio de Janeiro Brazil in June of 1992 that depicts the inequalities and population imbalances of the "One Third and the Two-Thirds World."

Just as the term *globalization* has replaced the term *imperialism*, the concept of **transnational** has replaced *international*. While the latter refers to relations *between nations*, the former refers to social forms that *fail to correspond to or transcend the boundaries of the nation state*. These new transnational forms have confounded earlier conceptual schemes and have "challenged theory to catch up

BOX 10.1

Who Lives in the "Global Village"?

If the world were a village of 1, 000 people, it would include:

584 Asians
124 Africans
95 East and West Europeans
84 Latin Americans
55 Soviets (now former Soviets)
52 North Americans
6 Australian and New Zealanders

One-third of these people would be children and only half of them would be immunized against infectious diseases like measles and polio. Just under half of the women have access to and use modern contraceptives. Two hundred people in this village receive 75% of the income; another 200 receive only 2% of the income. About one half of the people have access to clean, safe drinking water and only half of the adults are literate.

---

with lived realities" (Ong 1991: 279). There is a growing sense among theorists of postmodernity that an adequate understanding of social life can no longer be derived from an analysis that is conceptually limited to the geopolitical order of the nation-state (Smart 1993: 135). Rather, the ways in which economic, political, cultural, and technological features of social life transcend specific geographical locations is now the focal point of social thought. Some writers have highlighted how the concept "transnational" makes us aware of the "artificiality of the idea of nation" (Mendoza 2002: 299–300); others treat the nation as an "imagined community" (Franco [1989] 1997). Transnational theorists also depict global processes more as flows, linkages, and scapes rather than as rigid and well-defined binary and vertical hierarchical relations (Grewal and Kaplan [1994] 2006).

The term transnational also became more popular in economic parlance as global companies began to rethink their strategies, shifting from the vertical-integration model of the multinational corporation (MNC) to the horizontal dispersion of the transnational corporation (TNC). Transnational corporations appear more dispersed for a number of reasons. On the local level, they often subcontract out parts of the production process to much smaller, local, indigenous entrepreneurs to reduce risk and to avoid dealing directly with local problems and issues. As some observers noted: "**Subcontracting** means that the so-called manufacturer [transnational corporation] need not employ any production workers, run the risk of unionization or wage pressures, or be concerned with layoffs resulting from changes in product demand" (Appelbaum and Gereffi 1994: 44). Rather, local subcontractors face the conflicts and risks that arise around these issues. Subcontracting has increased rapidly and appears to be one of the major features of the New Global Order. Hence, on the level of appearances, capitalist production appears more dispersed and decentralized today even though its power and wealth is more concentrated.

Yet even the more powerful sectors of the global capitalist class appear more fluid and difficult to locate today using either national terms or terms such as "core" or "First World." For example, the five hundred, largest, transnational corporations that dominate and structure the global economy are headquartered across the globe—rather than in the United States and Europe. The actual ownership of shares in these corporations reveals even more fluidity. As transnational feminist theorists Inderpal Grewal and Caren Kaplan ([1994] 2006: 10–11) point out, it is difficult to maintain national distinctions in the conventional sense if the Japanese-headquartered, corporation SONY owns a Hollywood studio or if a Saudi Arabian investor owns the U.S. news organization UPI. Add to these transformations in global capital the rise of economic units such as the **European Union (EU)** and the **North American Free Trade Agreement (NAFTA)** that transcend the nation state. NAFTA includes the countries of the United States, Mexico and Canada, while the European Union includes more than two dozen countries and even has its own currency. These are relatively new transnational forms that were developed to enhance the movement of commodities and capital across international borders and to compete more successfully on the world market. All of these developments illustrate the blurred boundaries and dispersal of power that characterize the transnational features of global social relations today, which Grewal and Kaplan refer to as the "scattered hegemonies" of the New Global Order .

Flexible capitalism is another name given to these economic developments because of the way corporations move and adapt to existing circumstances. Unlike earlier multinational corporations where research, design and corporate control were located in the most economically developed countries, today *transnational corporations tap into different labor pools (skilled or unskilled, blue collar or white collar, foreign or domestic) regardless of where they are located.* As such, mixed production systems are anywhere in the world where optimal production, infrastructural, marketing, and political conditions exist (Harvey 1989, Ong 1991: 281–282). This resulted in another distinctive feature of the new global landscape where *the division of labor in the production of a single commodity has become transnational* with different parts of a commodity being produced and assembled in different geographical locals (see Box 10.2).

Many of these developments could not have taken place in earlier eras when geographic distances placed obstacles to the time and cost of such endeavors. Today the new technologies have sufficiently compressed time and space to facilitate the freer movement of labor, capital, commodities, and information across the globe. The demise and balkanization of the former Soviet Union also reduced many previous political obstacles to the global spread of free enterprise even opening up much of the Second World to global capitalism. Consequently, theorists of postmodernity argue that such dispersal strategies have become the *modus operandi* of flexible capitalism today.

Chapter 9 discussed how direct foreign investments by U.S. corporations increased tenfold between 1960 and 1980 as many companies flocked across international borders to reap higher profits from cheap labor abroad (Thurow 1996: 42). Also discussed was the significant increase in the role of finance capital

BOX 10.2

"Transnational Barbie"

Most Barbies sold in the United States through the 1990s were made in China, Malaysia and Indonesia, with plastics made in Taiwan, from oil bought from Saudi Arabia, hair from Japan, and packaging from the United States. Making Barbie is extremely labor-intensive work, requiring at least fifteen separate paint stations and an enormous supply of cheap labor. Labor costs were about 35 cents for a Barbie costing about $10 (out of which $8 went to shipping, marketing, and wholesale and retail profits; Mattel made about $1 of this amount). Using the services of Asian women paid low wages for assembly line work, Barbie's production was as gendered as its consumption and circulation.

Excerpt from "Transnational Barbie," by Inderpal Grewal. Pp.80–120 in *Transnational America: Feminisms, Diasporas, Neoliberalisms*.

in the post-World War II era and how, by the 1980s, the World Bank and the International Monetary Fund (IMF) had begun imposing structural adjustment programs (SAPs) on indebted countries. These harsh measures were fostered by **neoliberalism**—an economic ideology that arose in response to the economic downturn and international debt crises of the late 1970s and 1980s. Neoliberalism is based on a belief in free markets, promoting competitive capitalism, private ownership, free trade, export-led growth, strict controls on balances of payments and deficits, and drastic reductions in government social spending. This laissez-faire economic philosophy fostered the deregulation of economic practices both at home and abroad. Though capital was decentered in the sense of being relocated globally, it was not weakened, but became more powerful and anarchic as regulations over economic behavior weakened (Touraine 1998).

The debt crises of the 1980s fostered a new direction in the world capitalist order often referred to as the "globalization project"—an alternative way of organizing economic growth corresponding to the growing scale and power of transnational banks and corporations (McMichael 2008: 189–190). The increasing volume of economic exchanges and the enhanced mobility of money and firms required forms of organization beyond the nation state, but also embedded within the system of nation states. The globalization project assigns communities, regions and nation-states new niches or specialized roles in the global economy—as exemplified by regional free trade agreements. It also established new forms of authority, discipline and regulation that bridged the local, national and global. The establishment of the **World Trade Organization** (WTO) in 1995 as a new addition to the dynamic duo of the World Bank and the IMF exemplifies these developments. The WTO was established to oversee trade agreements and negotiate disputes that emerged from the General Agreement on Tariffs and Trade (GATT). It has been described as the "institutional face of globalization" and is one of the most wide-reaching of all international players today (Symington 2005: 36). Together this powerful trio—the World Bank, the IMF and the WTO—have been referred to as the driving forces of globalization policies in the contemporary era.

In the face of continued and increasing global inequality and poverty, the policies of these global financial institutions were reformulated in the 1990s as "globalization with a human face" starting with the Heavily Indebted Poor Countries Initiative of 1996 to provide exceptional assistance to countries with unsustainable debt burdens. While still committed to debt repayments, these new neoliberal polices were repackaged in more participatory rhetoric and they incorporated **nongovernmental organizations** (NGO's) or nonprofit organizations, as well as other local institutions, into helping to author and oversee these financial and development plans. These plans known as the Poverty Reduction Strategy Papers (PRSPs) were a form of "crisis management" in the face of deepening global inequality (McMichael 2008: 188–189).

One of the more widely publicized techniques employed in this new crisis management was the extension of **microcredit to poor women**, often using NGO's as intermediaries. While microfinance initiatives in the Third World were initiated as early as the 1970s, later decades were to witness a significant increase in these developments—especially in the form of microloans to poor women. The extension of microcredit has been trumpeted as a major means of empowering poor women in recent years. At a time when "development" was under attack because neoliberal economic policies appeared to have largely failed, these positive evaluations gave international financial institutions a much-needed legitimacy. This legitimacy was further evidenced when economist Muhammad Yunus—the principal architect of microfinance and founder of the successful Grameen Bank in Bangladesh—was awarded the 2006 Nobel Prize for Peace.

There are both benefits and costs associated with microcredit (see Box 10.3). Evidence suggests that microcredit has improved the income levels of poor women and their families. However, women's work loads have increased as they have taken on more economic activities, as well as more responsibility for social services abdicated by governments under the SAPs (Lairap-Fonderson 2002: 184 and 185). Recipients of microloans also have been subject to new forms of discipline and to new forms of cooptation that, while stabilizing the informal world of the poor, have done so at the price of depoliticalization (McMichael 2008:189; Lairap-Fonderson 2002).

BOX 10.3

The Extension of Microcredit to Poor Women: One Step Forward, Two Steps Backward?

In recent years, microcredit has been heralded as a major means for empowering poor women in the Third World/South (Khandker 1998). Microcredit refers to the extension of small loans—often ranging from a few to a couple hundred dollars—to the poor for investment in income-generating activities. The loans come from private donors and from semiformal or formal financial institutions. These loans are not handouts. Rather, they must be repaid with interest in a timely manner. Conditions for receiving loans generally require training sessions in saving, repayment and investment, as well as the demonstration by potential recipients of their ability to save before they obtain eligibility. Loans are often given to small groups rather than to individuals, making all members of the group responsible for loan payments. After a year of good payment records, an individual or group can graduate to larger loans given over a longer time frame.

The success of microfinance has destroyed some commonly held myths. It has shown not only that the poor are credit worthy, but also that poor women prove to be better credit risks than poor men. For example, all three of the major microcredit programs in Bangladesh target poor women, with women making up 94 percent of Grameen Bank participants. These women had loan default rates of only 3 percent as compared with a 10 percent default rate for men (Khandker 1998: 149–150). A similar pattern has been found in other countries (Lairap-Fonderson 2002: 192). Women recipients tend to invest in activities that require little separation of household and industry, such as poultry production, beer brewing, hairdressing, crafts, and selling processed or unprocessed foods in local markets (192). Hence, these activities mesh more easily with domestic chores and childrearing.

By 2008 thousands of microfinance institutions in more than one hundred countries were serving about 25 million people (McMichael 2008: 189). They had expanded rapidly to deal with the increasing global inequality that was exacerbated by the harsh impact of structural adjustment programs (SAPS) (Lairap-Fonderson 2002: 191). Microcredit became a major weapon in the crisis management arsenal of neoliberal economic policies. It fit well with these policies not only because it required recipients to pull themselves up by their own bootstraps, but also because it integrated the poor into market activities using a relatively low cost solution, given that loans had to be repaid.

The successes of microcredit schemes have been documented in reduced absolute poverty and increased household nutrition. For many poor families, it has meant the difference between three meals a day, rather than one. Women recipients have been able to send more of their children to school and have reported less dependence on their husbands or male partners (Khandker 1998: 149–150). However, recent research has uncovered a number of the limitations to microcredit solutions. Critics argue that the economic gains have been marginal. Many women micro-entrepreneurs seldom net an income above the minimum daily wage. Their workloads have increased dramatically from their entrepreneurial activities as well as from their responsibility for social services abdicated by governments under the SAPs (Lairap-Fonderson 2002: 184–185). Findings also are inconsistent as to whether women micro-entrepreneurs enjoy more power within their households. Some critics argue that as women take on more of the bread-winning role, men's roles have shifted to merely "heading" the household and doing less work (Sithole-Fundire, et al. 1995: 60). Others have described husbands as more resentful, sullen and even violent because of their wives' greater control of income (Lairap-Fonderson 2002: 185). While increased women's income has enabled more children to attend school, daughters are more likely than sons to be removed from school when their micro-entrepreneurial mothers need help. Thus girls may suffer more in the long term than boys from these developments.

The extension of microcredit also has transformed the roles of many local NGOs and women's organizations. As donor organizations increasingly directed their funds to local, grassroots groups, governments and international organizations began actively encouraging the formation of women's associations and/or NGOs in order to attract foreign aid. In Kenya, for example, the number of women's groups grew from 152 to 802 between 1980 and 1984, while membership in these organizations increased almost eight-fold from 528 to 4,232 over the same time period (Lairup-Fonderson 2002: 190). However, a number of problems arise when activist women's groups and NGOs serve as intermediaries for national or international institutions. Some critics argue that they become co-opted within the dominant political structures and institutions that foster these loans and/or no longer have sufficient time to address other political issues (Lairap-Fonderson 2002: 183; Karl 1995; Gordon 1996; Snyder and Tadesse 1995). They risk becoming "gender experts" and/or "subcontractors" as well as more regulatory- and surveillance-oriented than advocacy groups (Alverez 1999; Naples 2002; Lairap-Fonderson 2002).1 These critiques suggest that various costs both to individuals and to social movements may accompany the benefits of microfinance.

Along with the transnational development of finance, military clashes also are transnational today. While communism was a transnational ideology, U.S. military clashes with communist insurgents during the cold war era usually took the form of nations fighting nations, such as in the Vietnam War or the Korean War. Though funding or military aid may have come from other countries, the actual participants in these wars represented particular countries or areas within countries.[2] In contrast,global clashes today often involve transnational cultural/ethnic/religious communities that garner volunteer armies from multiple countries but do not claim to represent any particular country, such as Al-Qaeda. Their Western opponents still rely on traditional international forms of organization, such as the North Atlantic Treaty Organization (NATO), though they do not share as strong a consensus on global issues today as they did during the cold war.

The new electronic technologies have aided and abetted transnational military clashes. For example, combatants in less technologically developed areas of the globe have long used guerrilla warfare to fight technologically superior foes. One of the strengths of guerilla warfare is that it enables combatants to scatter and disappear into the indigenous population. However, this scattering also requires combatants to operate in a more decentralized fashion and makes them less able to publicize their successes and demands to a global population. By contrast, today scattered combatants can have their demands and actions visible globally within seconds through cell phones, the internet and satellite TV. These new technologies not only enable them to appear more centralized and unified, but also facilitate their military and organizing efforts. It is one of the ironies of postmodernity that technologies like the internet and satellite communications, which were initially developed to enhance the power of First World militaries, now are being used against these militaries with some success. Moreover, agencies that deal with the social and environmental problems generated by militarism and war also have taken transnational forms today, such as Amnesty International, Green Peace, the Red Cross/Red Crescent, or Doctor's without Borders.

POSTCOLONIAL AND TRANSNATIONAL FEMINISMS

The rise of postcolonial and transnational feminist perspectives sparked the most significant paradigm shifts in global feminist analyses. Many feminists today prefer to characterize their perspectives as **transnational** rather than following the conceptual paths of earlier, modernist global feminist analyses with their First World/Third World and core/periphery frameworks for a number of reasons. First, these earlier theoretical frameworks contain the remnants of Eurocentrism or of a "Euro-North American-centric" worldview where global power brokers at the core are presented as the movers and shakers of world history, while the complex class divisions at the local level are ignored (Grewal and Kaplan [1994] 2006: 12). Transnational feminists argue that, without the cooperation and logistical backing of local mediators and agents, transnational firms would not be able to exercise their power (Grewal and Kaplan [1994] 2006: 12; Ong 1999).

Second, in the earlier First World/Third World or core/periphery frameworks the direction of influence was too often viewed as only one way—as emanating from the highly developed Western countries. Transnational feminists argue that local subjects are not passive receptacles of transnational powers and that social, economic and cultural forces operate in multiple directions representing more of a process of hybridization than of simple, unidirectional, homogenization.They also challenge and break with the "inadequate and inaccurate binary divisions" embedded in these earlier frameworks (Grewal and Kaplan [1994] 2006: 13).

Third, the term "transnational" is used to problematize a purely locational politics of global-local or core-periphery in favor of viewing the lines cutting across these locations (13). As discussed later in this chapter, Chandra Talpade Mohanty calls for new forms of cross-national solidarity between women who share similar, specific social locations in the global division of labor. Given how transnational corporations draw from diverse labor pools across the globe, these locations could be inhabited by Third World women, as well as by women in the First World. Similarly, Aihwa Ong (1999: 4) stresses the importance of focusing on the horizontal and relational nature of the economic, social, and cultural processes that stream across global spaces:

> *Trans* denotes both moving through space or across lines, as well as changing the nature of something. Besides suggesting new relations between nation-states and capital, transnationality also alludes to the *trans*versal, the *trans*actional, the *trans*lational, and the *trans*gressive aspect of contemporary behavior and imagination that are incited, enabled, and regulated by the changing logics of states and globalization.

The term **postcolonial** is sometimes misconstrued as a temporal concept meaning the time after colonialism ceased or when a colony broke free asserting its national independence. In the context of postcolonial theorizing, it is a more critical concept that refers to *engaging with and contesting the legacy of colonialism's discourses, power structures and social hierarchies.* With the rise of postcolonial and transnational analyses there is a heavier focus on cultural and discursive manifestations of globalization. This is not to say that postcolonial and transnational analyses ignore political economy, but rather that political/economic concerns are so interwoven with cultural and discursive analyses that the old modernist dividing lines between materialist and idealist theories become more fluid and ambiguous (as also was evident in the new directions taken by materialist feminists discussed in chapter 4).

Both postcolonial and transnational feminisms reject linear views of history and development that depict the social world as moving from traditional to modern or from less developed to developed. In these new conceptual schemes, time is neither accumulated vertically (such that some social formations are more advanced than others) nor horizontally (in terms of a one-directional view of social change). Rather than employ these hierarchical and linear narratives that characterize most modernist approaches, time is "scrambled and **palimpsestic**" with the premodern, the modern and the postmodern coexisting globally (Shohat [1998] 2001: 20; Alexander 2005: 190). A palimpsest is a parchment that has been inscribed and re-inscribed with the previous text being imperfectly erased and remaining partly visible. Using this metaphor, *social change and sociohistorical time are viewed as imperfect erasures, with the visibility of the past always in the present.* As M. Jacqui Alexander (2005: 190) writes: "A palimpsestic approach rescrambles the here and now with the there and then." Examples of this approach will be provided later in this chapter. Suffice it to say here that postcolonial and transnational feminists urge pedagogical and analytic frameworks to become more palimpsestic by recognizing the mutually constitutive processes at work in the past and present.

Edward Said's *Orientalism* (1978) is one of the most famous founding works of postcolonial theory. Said was a Palestinian writer concerned with the persistent Western prejudice again Arabo-Islamic and Asian peoples/cultures which he referred to as "**Orientalism**." Using a blend of poststructuralism and Marxist theory, he described the way in which "the Orient" was in many ways a fantasy or myth—a material-discursive construct of "the West" that was then projected onto and inscribed upon the lands and peoples of the colonized East. This process entailed an "othering" of "the Orient" that, in turn, helped to define and solidify the "West." For Said, the object of postcolonial theory was to a*nalyze the social implications of the mutually-constitutive processes between the colonizer and the colonized.*[3]

Despite postcolonial theory's criticisms of Eurocentric and Western thought, it draws heavily from Western and Eurocentric theoretical perspectives.[4] Some forms of postcolonial theory follow Said in closely blending Foucaultian poststructuralism with Marxism, while in other forms Foucault's work is clearly dominant. Although Marx frequently addressed imperialism and colonialism in his writings, he has been faulted by postcolonial writers for his Eurocentric development-oriented approach. In contrast, Foucault has been faulted for largely ignoring the imperial context of Europe in his genealogies of modernity (Spivak 1988). As postcolonial theorist Ann Stoler (1995: 19) writes: "An inducement for students to work out Foucault's genealogies on a broader imperial map should be spurred simply by their glaring absence." Notably, Stoler undertakes this ambitious task in her book *Race and the Education of Desire: Foucault's History of Sexuality and the Colonial Order of Things* (1995).

Despite Foucault's elision of the question of empire, his analysis of knowledge and power is central to postcolonial theory. The strong influence of poststructualism on feminist postcolonial theory is articulated well by Reina Lewis and Sara Mills in their introduction to *Feminist Postcolonial Theory* (2003: 1–2):

> As Michel Foucault has shown, the establishment of knowledges and disciplines is never innocent: knowledges are also formations of power which not only delineate specific inclusions but enforce overt and covert exclusions. It is the marginalization and exclusion of a separate trajectory of feminist thought about race, power, culture, and empire that this collection seeks to address.

It is precisely the power of knowledges that feminist postcolonial theorists address in one of their major themes—the *decolonization Western feminist thought.* The object here is to show how knowledges of the world generated by both colonizers and the colonized are produced under specific power relations that complicate and texture our understanding of social reality. Particular emphasis is given to interrogating First World global feminist discourses to reveal their privilege and ethnocentrism, as well as their essentialist approach to understanding Third World peoples. Employing Foucault's work on resistance, these theorists also examine the creative forms of resistance that colonized peoples have employed. Some of the major efforts undertaken by feminist postcolonial writers to decolonize feminist thought are examined below.

Decolonizing Feminist Thought

Chandra Talpade Mohanty's "Under Western Eyes: Feminist Scholarship and Colonial Discourses" ([1984] 2005) was a signal piece in transforming the global frameworks of many U.S. feminists. Mohanty's aim was to deconstruct and dismantle the privilege and ethnocentrism of many First World, global feminist discourses. She was especially critical of the essentialist notions of Third World women that pervaded Western feminist analyses:

> What I wish to analyze is specifically the production of the 'third world woman' as a singular monolithic subject in some recent (Western) feminist texts. The definition of colonization I wish to invoke here is a predominantly *discursive* one, focusing on a certain mode of appropriation and codification of "scholarship" and "knowledge" about women in the third world by particular analytic categories employed in specific writings on the subject which take as their referent feminist interests as they have been articulated in the United States and Western Europe. (372; her emphasis)

Mohanty criticizes how Western feminists too often ignore differences between women by constructing a singular, composite notion of "third world women" as a coherent group with identical interests and desires, regardless of their actual class, ethnic or racial locations. She argues that this homogenous construction of "third world women" frequently implies that they are poor, ignorant, tradition-bound, and victimized. Unspoken, but assumed here, is that First World women by contrast are educated, modern, have control over their own bodies and sexualities, and are free to make their own decisions (374). This type of binary discourse not only entails a "paternalistic attitude towards women in the third world," but also reduces Third World women to victimized objects, "robbing them of their historical and political agency." In contrast, First World women appear as active, creative subjects of their lives (377–378).

In place of such essentialism, Mohanty calls for historically specific and local analyses that take into account differences between Third World women, as well as the concrete realities of their lives. She writes: "These arguments are not against generalization as much as they are for careful, historically specific generalizations responsive to complex realities" (377). Mohanty provides various examples to illustrate how historically specific approaches better illuminate the complexity of Third World women's lives, particularly in regard to indigenous practices that are viewed as universally oppressive "under Western eyes." For example, she shows how the meanings women attach to veiling vary widely in different social and historical contexts by comparing the politically regressive veiling of women in Iran under Islamic law, to the progressive use of veils during the revolution of 1979 when Iranian middle-class women voluntarily veiled themselves to show solidarity with their working-class sisters.

Uma Narayan's writings also have played a major role in unveiling Western feminist eyes to the complexities of women's interpretations of traditional cultural practices in the context of colonialism and neocolonialism. In *Dislocating Cultures: Identities, Traditions, and Third World Feminism* (1997) Narayan discusses how many Western feminist understandings of Third World traditions are evident in their call for universalistic, human rights-based interventions into certain "cultural practices" affecting Third World women, such as *sati* and dowry-murder. *Sati* refers to the practice of widow immolation that took place in particular castes and regions of India where wives threw themselves on the funeral pyres of their dead husbands. This practice was legally banned in 1829 although it still occurs today in rare instances. Dowry-murder or bride-burning, which is more prevalent today, refers to husbands killing their wives when dowries are not paid, often making these deaths appear as the result of kitchen fires. Such cultural practices have served as archetypes for Western feminists' discussions of patriarchal violence against women in Third World countries (Daly, 1978).

Dislocating Cultures explores representations of "third world traditions" that replicate what Narayan calls a "colonialist stance" toward Third World peoples and cultures (43). She uses U.S. radical feminist Mary Daly's work as her example of how Western feminists too often take a **colonialist stance**. In explaining what she means by a colonialist stance, Narayan makes clear that she does not think all western feminist criticisms of Third World cultural practices are inherently colonialist or imperialist. She also does not think that taking a colonialist stance necessarily entails ethnocentrism (58–59). She argues that taking a colonialist stance entails representations that employ a **missionary framework** where Third World women are viewed as victims that must be rescued from their own cultural traditions. Colonialist stances erase the historical and contextual framework in which cultural traditions arose and developed whereby these traditions are treated as if they are unchanging and "perennially in place." As such, Third World women are viewed as without agency, as unable to represent themselves. Third world countries appear as "places with no history" and no indigenous forms of resistance (48–49). Rather they are depicted as stagnant, backward and in need of change from without.

Western feminist portrayals of dowry murders are used to illustrate her points. Narayan discusses how dowries in some areas of India were instituted as a way for women to inherit wealth from their fathers and, hence, had different political implications in different social and historical contexts. She also discusses how dowry murder in India is a contemporary phenomenon not one historically associated with dowries. While such practices should be criticized by feminists, they should not be used in a way that portrays Third World countries as if they are transhistorically and uniformly in the grip of traditional practices that insulate these contexts from the effects of historical change. It is this portrayal that wrong-headedly replicates the binary notion of the West as modern and progressive and the East as shackled and paralyzed by tradition. It is this portrayal that constitutes a colonialist stance by implicitly characterizing Third World people as victims in need of Western assistance, as too backward to represent themselves.

Narayan also deconstructs and unravels the meanings given to terms such as "westernization." She discusses how the term "westernized" is often used as a "**strategy of dismissal**" where Third World feminists who advocate for women's rights are categorized as Westernized "betrayers" of their nation or "traitors to their communities" to undermine their feminist demands and actions. She points to how her opponents selectively choose what is deemed "Westernized." They drive cars or use computers and do not consider these actions as "Westernized betrayals." She calls for more critical debate about what terms like "Westernization" mean so as to deconstruct the uses and abuses of this term. She writes: "All national contexts need to promote the abilities of their various members to think critically about the elements that should be preserved and those that need to be challenged" (31). Like Kumari Jayawardena's work discussed in chapter 9, Narayan highlights how feminism is not simply a Western import. Rather the coming to feminist consciousness of many Indian women was based on their own socially-lived knowledge as Indian women.

Because Narayan lived for over a decade in the United States before her book was published, she frequently moves between Indian and U.S. cultural contexts to show how her critique is useful in both cultures. She points to how a "strategy of dismissal" has been used against African-American womanists *within* their own communities to dismiss their feminism as espousing a "white" political agenda. Similarly, she criticizes those U.S. feminists who readily point to Third World women as victims of cultural practices but who are oblivious to any analyses of "death or injury by their own culture." As Narayan points out, U.S. women have been victimized by the "distinctively American cultural phenomenon of wide-spread, gun-related, domestic violence." (117). Overall, there are important lessons to learn from her notion of dislocating cultures:

> We need to move away from a picture of national and cultural contexts as sealed rooms, impervious to change, with a homogenous space 'inside' of them, inhabited by 'authentic insiders' who all share a uniform and consistent account of their institutions and values. Third-World national and cultural contexts are pervaded by plurality, dissension and change, just as are their 'Western' counterparts. (33).

Diasporas and the Gender Politics of Postcolonial Space

Whereas modern global feminist writers focused on labor migrations which flowed from one country to another, postcolonial feminists highlight the more fluid sense of global population movements captured in the term **diaspora**. Diaspora derives from the Greek *dia* "through" and *speirein* "to scatter." It embodies the notion of a locus or "home" from where the dispersion or scattering of peoples occurs. One of the most insightful works on this topic is Avtar Brah's *Cartographies of Diaspora* (1996). Brah documents not only how migrations across the globe rapidly increased since the 1980s but also how by 1992 some estimates put the total number of migrants at 100 million, of whom 20 million were refugees and asylum seekers ([1996] 2003: 613):

> The notion of "economic migrant" as referring primarily to labour migrants was always problematic. . . . These new migrations call this construct even more seriously into question, as global events increasingly render untenable such distinctions as those held between the so called "political" and "economic" refugees. (613).

Explicitly using the work of Foucault, Brah discusses how the concept of diaspora offers a critique of modern discourses of fixed geopolitical identities/locations. It also better captures the complexities of geopolitical identity/location that is a confluence of economic, political, cultural, and psychic processes. She highlights how diasporas are not only about who travels, but when, how, and under what circumstances. For example, she asks what socio-economic, political, and cultural conditions mark the trajectories of these journeys? What regimes of power inscribe the formation of a specific diaspora? And what do the subjects of these diasporas view as their home or their geopolitical identity?

Modern thought was much more fixed and nation-oriented, such as the concept of Mexican–American that highlights the country of origin and the country of arrival. For Brah the concept of "diaspora" is a more complex concept that signals *the processes of multilocationality across geographical, cultural and psychic boundaries* (625). Even when the term "diaspora" was used by modern writers, it was often presented in binary forms, such as Jew/Gentile, Arab/Jew, Irish/English. Brah points to the fallacies of such binary thinking by highlighting how there are multiple social locations embedded within and across these binary analyses, such as those signifying gender, class, race, religion, or generation. She argues, for example, that when Jewish people fled persecution in Europe or Russia to come to the United States, wealthy Jews had different diasporic experiences from poor Jews, just as darker-skinned Sephardic Jews had different disaporic experiences from lighter-skinned Ashkenazis. Orthodox Jews remained more segregated as a subjugated minority in their new locations then did non-Orthodox Jews. Some Jews who fled fascist persecution abroad became settler colonialists and displaced other peoples as the dislocation of Palestians from their homeland suggests. Thus, diasporas result in diverse and contradictory experiences or what Brah calls "*locationality in contradiction*."

Rather than simply portraying global migrants as victims of diasporas, Brah also points to how these people constantly challenge the peripheralizing impulses of the cultures of dominance. In this way she shows how dominant cultures also change in the process. She uses the example of how Britishness has been disassembled and reconstituted since World War II as a result of the vast immigration to Great Britain by people from its former colonies and the demands for self-government by the Welsh, Scots, and Irish. Thus even the most powerful colonial power of the nineteenth century has been disassembled today to include multiple ethnicities, including African-Carribbeanness, East Asianess, Irishness, and so on. In this process Englishness becomes just another ethnicity among many (632–633).

This idea is captured well by Trinh T. Minh-ha in *Women, Native, Other: Writing Postcoloniality and Feminism* (1989: 99–100):

> The West is painfully made to realize the existence of the Third World in the First World, and vice versa. The Master is bound to recognize that His Culture is not as homogeneous, as monolithic as He believes it to be. He discovers with much reluctance, He is just an other among others.

Like other postcolonial writers, Brah and Minh-ha focus on these contradictions of culture and identity formation to undermine the notion of "authentic insiders" to any culture and to highlight the multi-locationality of identities in postmodernity. For them, every cultural formation is a hybrid. By contrast, "the dominant Western attitude toward hybridity is that it is always elsewhere or it is infiltrating an identity or location that is assumed to be, to always have been, pure and unchanging" (Grewal and Kaplan [1994] 2006: 8). Correcting this assumption is a goal of "decolonizing" Western thought.

The writings discussed above provide excellent examples of the cultural and discursive focus of many postcolonial and transnational feminist theorists. Yet even supporters of these approaches fear that there remain gaps in postcolonial and transnational analyses that derive from an "undertheorization" political economic issues (Mendoza 2002: 303; Gupta 2006: 25). These gaps can lead to an entrapment in cultural and discursive debates that elide the issues of economic exploitation and the role capitalism plays in the structuring of global social relations.

MATERIALIST–DECONSTRUCTIVE POSTCOLONIAL AND TRANSNATIONAL APPROACHES

Recent decades have seen the rise of transnational and postcolonial feminisms that more closely blend materialist approaches with poststructuralism. These writings bring together feminist postcolonial cultural and discourse analyses with political economic concerns. Below, I examine works by Gayatri Spivak, Chandra Talpade Mohanty, Aihwa Ong, Inderpal Grewal, and Caren Kaplan as exemplars of this materialist-deconstructive approach. All of these works are attentive to the micropolitics of context, subjectivity, social agency, and local struggles, but they view them as embedded in a macropolitics of global economic and political processes. They also pay close attention to how issues of gender, race, class, and nation are imbricated in their global analyses. By doing so they recuperate the centrality of capitalism to the New Global Order that earlier feminist postcolonial analyses left undertheorized (Mendoza 2002: 304).

Can the Subaltern Speak?

Gayatri Chakravorty Spivak is one of the most theoretically sophisticated postcolonial scholars writing today. A signal feature of her work is her ongoing attempt to find a critical vocabulary that is appropriate to describe the experiences and histories of individuals and social groups who have been historically dispossessed and exploited by Western colonialism. Spivak challenges the assumption held by many feminists today that clear, transparent language is the best way to represent issues of oppression (Collins 1998: 142; Christian 1988: 71; Di Stefano 1990). Rather she argues that transparent forms of writing often make readers feel more comfortable, but they mask the complexity of social life (see chapter 1). For her, adhering to the linear conventions of Western thought makes it difficult to employ a palimpsestic approach that links disparate histories, places, and methodologies. Because her writings are difficult, students may benefit from first reading Stephen Morton's *Gayatri Chakravorty Spivak* (2003), which I draw from below. Morton studied with Spivak and he provides a clear and accessible introduction to her major ideas.

One of Spivak's most controversial essays "Can the Subaltern Speak?" (1985) addresses the issues of "**radical alterity**." As readers will recall from earlier chapters, there are certain people or groups who are defined as "Other" or "lesser" and relegated to marginalized places in society. In Western thought, women, blacks, homosexuals, and Third World peoples often have been placed in this role of "other." For Spivak, it is by defining oneself in relation to the "other" that the two concepts—self and other—are mutually constituted (Morton 2003: 37). She also frequently uses the term **subaltern** in her writings. While this term initially referred to a low rank in the British military, the critical theoretical roots of this concept lie in the work of the Italian Marxist theorist Antonio Gramsci. As a political prisoner in fascist Italy, Gramsci used the term "subaltern" in his famous *Prison Notebooks* (1932) to refer to subordinate groups and more specifically to the peasantry who were undertheorized in Marx's writings. This term later was used and extended by the Indian-based Subaltern Studies Collective to refer to "the general attribute of subordination in South Asian society, whether this is expressed in terms of class, caste, age, gender, or any other way" (Morton 2003: 48). Although Spivak embraces the historical analyses of the Subaltern Studies Collective, she argues that both Gramsci and this collective privileged the male subaltern as the primary subject in their works. She proposes an alternative definition of subaltern, informed by feminism and deconstruction, which takes women's lives and histories into account. She finds the term "subaltern" particularly useful because it accommodates the contradictory social and class locations of people (like many women) who do not fall easily into the categories of orthodox Marxist class analysis (45).

So how does her notion of the "subaltern" fit into her analysis of colonialism and imperialism? For Spivak, the imposition of imperial codes and practices upon the colonized fractures all indigenous sign-systems of the colonized—a process Spivak terms "**epistemic violence**." The cultural effects of this violent rupture are complex, but they include the effect of silencing authentic native cultures. When the native is forced to speak, that is when the native can speak and be understood, it is most likely to be in the language of the imperialist. This project assures that "the other" will speak only in the alien language and will not to be able to "answer back" in any native language uncomplicated by imperial contact. This epistemic violence also constitutes the native as an "informant"—as a potential source of information about the local culture, hence, as knowledge and power for the imperialist, such that the colonizer and the colonialist become mutually constitutive of each other.

In "Teaching for the Times" ([1992]1997), Spivak quotes from Assia Djebar's novel *Fantasia: An Algerian Cavalcade* (1985) the voice of an Algerian-Muslim woman who experienced this epistemic violence:

> The overlay of my oral culture is wearing dangerously thin. . . . Writing of the most anodyne of childhood memories leads back to a body bereft of voice. To attempt an autobiography in French words alone is to show more than its skin under the slow scalpel of a live autopsy. Its flesh peels off and with it, seemingly, the speaking of childhood which can longer be written is torn to shreds. Wounds are reopened, veins weep, the blood of the self flows and that of others, a blood which has never dried. (Djebar quoted in Spivak [1992] 1997: 485).

The concept of epistemic violence relates to Spivak's view that colonialism and imperialism are not hegemonic and homogenizing forces that mold the "colonized other" entirely into the pattern of the West. Rather they create hybridity—a term used by Spivak and her compatriot Homi Bhabha to distinguish their own positions from such homogenizing views of imperialism. **Hybridity** is the culturally specific effect of colonialism that has within it the potentiality (but not the necessity) of resistance:

> If the effect of colonial power is seen to be the production of hybridization rather than the hegemonic command of colonialist authority or the silent repression of native traditions, then an important change of perspective occurs. It . . . enables a form of subversion . . . that turns the discursive conditions of dominance into the grounds of intervention. (Bhabha 1994: 97).

This focus on how hybridity can embody cultural and political resistance rather than simply abject capitulation to imperial domination has a number of implications. For example, rather than a nostalgia for lost traditions as we have seen in the works of Vandana Shiva and others who romanticize the premodern or precolonial subaltern, the project of postcolonial criticism consists of analyzing the workings of ideology in the complex material-discourse that make up the scenes of colonial and decolonized space. For Spivak, those who are truly "subaltern"—the most marginalized—cannot "speak." If the subaltern could speak, he or she would no longer occupy the place of the subaltern.

Some writers have interpreted this position as a dismissal or silencing of the native as an historical subject and combatant (Parry 1987: 34). However, Spivak means something very different from this. For her, anti-imperialist writers and activists are clearly not "outside" the field of imperialism as a discursive field since they address it directly. Those positioned to engage in a critique of colonial discourse or to provide political alternatives to imperial ones, can hardly themselves occupy the place of the subaltern (Morton 2003: 66–67). Their own privilege and hybridity needs to be recognized and acknowledged (Landry and Maclean, 1993: 200).

This position differs from the position of U.S. Third World feminists, who discuss the "other" in terms of "moving from margin to center" or "crossing borderlands," such as bell hooks (1984) and Gloria Anzaldúa (1987). Both hooks and Anzaldúa argue that the voices and visions of the subaltern entail the most critical vantage points (see chapter 5). In contrast, Spivak (1989: 86) views such a project as "in the long run deeply insulting." She argues that it can only be under the guise of "representing" the subaltern that these writers make such claims. For Spivak, the problem of "othering" or "radical alterity" is not simply one of "essentialism" of ignoring differences or homogenizing the other, but of claiming uncritically to "represent" the other. She uses Marx's writings in *The Eighteenth Brumaire of Louis Bonaparte* ([1852] 1978) to distinguish between two meanings of "represent." One meaning is "Vertretung" or stepping into someone's place as an elected government representative might do when he/she legitimately votes or acts for a certain constituency; the other is "Darstellung" which means providing a proxy or portrait of the other as when he/she characterizes their constituency as "working class" or as "the black minority" and themselves as their spokesperson:

> The debate between essentialism and anti-essentialism is really not the crucial debate. It is not possible to be non-essentialist [in terms of using group categories]. . . . The real debate is between these two ways of representing. (Spivak 1990: 109).

If one was to pretend to actually represent the other without acknowledging the imaginative displacement or "portraiture" involved, then *one would be complicit in a new form of domination even if it is constructed on radical or liberationary practice.* Feminist standpoint theories exemplify this problem. Even though many standpoint theorists claim to privilege the critical knowledges rooted in the standpoint of marginalized people—it is the feminist intellectual who *interprets* and *speaks for* the standpoint of the marginalized. In this way feminist intellectuals align their critical claims with a broader historical force and a more oppressed (and compelling) social reality than their own. They foreground the standpoint of the marginalized, but actually hide in the background by not acknowledging either their interpretative role or the displacement involved when they speak for and interpret the standpoint of subjugated peoples (Pels 2004).

While Spivak applauds the writings by U.S. womanists of color for their important role in awakening U.S. white feminists to the politics of difference and locationality, she also separates her own theoretical position on radical alterity from them in other ways. She argues that "radical alterity" or the problematic of "the Other" in a global context has produced many contested positions. Among these contested positions are the tendencies to *gloss over differences between anti-racist and anti-imperialist theories and praxis.* Spivak argues that if challenging both imperialism and imperial feminisms are to remain useful political strategies then distinctions between movements for anti-racism and anti-imperialism need to be maintained. For her, citizens of the empire however divided amongst themselves by class, race, ethnicity, gender, and/or sexual orientation, still share, however unequally, in certain imperial privileges:

> Anti-racism is yearly brought to crisis by anti-imperialism when we begin to see that even the most disenfranchised U.S. black person can get a U.S. passport, which is an incomparably superior thing to, say, an Indian passport (Spivak 1990: 139).

Spivak's work is valuable in the way it makes such analytical distinctions while at the same time insisting on forging connections between women—often of a difficult global kind. By doing so, she urges feminists to acknowledge that *all feminist thinking whether written by western whites, Western womanists of color and/or by postcolonial peoples has to be interrogated and deconstructed for possible imperial logic in its analyses and prescriptions on behalf of other women.*

Spivak also introduces the notion of **strategic essentialism**. Though this concept acknowledges that essentialist categories of human identity should be criticized, it emphasizes that one cannot avoid using collective categories in order to make sense of the social and political world. She argues that, for subordinate groups in particular, the use of essentialism as a short-term strategy to affirm political identity can be effective so long as this identity does not become fixed. For example, the affirmation of gay and lesbian identities as a positive term of identification during Gay Pride marches may serve as an effective political strategy in certain contexts. For Spivak, strategic essentialism is a context-specific strategy, not a theory nor a long term political solution to ending oppression and exploitation (Morton 2003: 75).

While much of Spivak's work is directed toward decolonizing feminist thought, she centers her discursive and cultural critiques within a capitalist world economy. She is careful to characterize global capitalism in terms of its various historical stages and different forms. She makes distinctions between the colonial era and the neocolonial era, as well as between industrial and finance capital. In these different eras and under these different forms "epistemic violence" also differs. She argues that the processes of subject formation through colonial education, legal codification and training in [proper Western-style] consumerism that produced the old colonial subject are quite different from the production of the transnational, neocolonial subject today (Spivak 1987: 223; Sanders 2006: 85–86). Such "elaborate" measures taken to colonize subjects are no longer needed for the disempowered, neocolonial women in the export-processing zones (EPZ's) who experience "superexploitation" today (Spivak 1987: 167):

> This elaborate constitution of the [colonial] subject is not necessary under international subcontracting in post-modern or electronic capitalism. No legal structure need be laid down for the army of 'permanent casuals', only the circumventing of rudimentary labor and safety regulations is on the agenda. No consistent training into consumerism is any longer needed. The industries can move on. The markets are elsewhere. (224).

Spivak also endeavors to make privileged women of the North realize how their positions depend upon the disempowered women in the South. This dependence is not just predicated on the cheaper commodities people of the North can buy when they are produced by the neocolonial global subaltern—points made by earlier feminist theorists. Spivak highlights, for example, how the universities in which we teach and learn have "dubious investments" abroad, just as the hotels that host academic conferences "use third-world female labor in a most oppressive way," bringing home the complicities of metropolitan feminists in the inequities of the global division of labor (291 and 44). In such ways, she calls on feminists to critically examine the relationship between rapidly changing forms of capitalism today and their own lives. She teaches us to critically "read the world" and to "unlearn one's privilege" as an ethical and political responsibility (Sanders 2006: 93; Spivak 1990: 30 and 42).

Feminism without Borders

Earlier in this chapter I discussed how Chandra Talpade Mohanty's article "Under Western Eyes: Feminist Scholarship and Colonial Discourses" (1984) was a signal piece that ushered in calls for the decolonization of Western feminist thought. This was her first "feminist studies" publication and marked her presence in the international feminist community (Mohanty [2003] 2006: 221). *Feminism without Borders: Decolonizing Theory, Practicing Solidarity* ([2003] 2006), published almost two decades later, discusses how her concerns shifted over time. She notes how a number of transformations in the political and economic landscapes of the New Global Order fostered this shift in focus. These transformations include the rising significance of transnational institutions and religious fundamentalisms, the increasing militarization of the globe and the "profoundly unequal" but powerful influence of the "information highway" created by the new electronic technologies and satellite communications (Mohanty [2003] 2006: 228–229).

Her major focus is no longer on the colonizing effects of Western feminist thought, not because these problems no longer exist, but rather because other feminist scholars have taken up this task (237). She now views "the politics and economics of capitalism as a far more urgent locus of struggle" (230). Mohanty is careful to point out that it is her focus rather than her analytic framework that has changed over time. She is still attentive to the micro-politics of everyday life, as well as to the macro-politics of global economic and political processes, just as she still sees the link between political economy and culture as crucial. She explains her change in focus as follows:

> It is just that global economic and political processes have become more brutal, exacerbating economic, racial, and gender inequalities, and thus they need to be demystified, reexamined, and theorized (230).

Mohanty describes her methodology as akin to "historical materialism" and discusses how it entails both a "materialist" and a "realist" approach that is antithetical to postmodernist relativism. (231)[5]

Another shift in her focus is visible in her discussion of the implications of her theoretical approach for political practice. Whereas "Under Western Eyes" focused on the distinctions between "Western" and "Third World" feminist vantage points downplaying their commonalities, in *Feminism without Borders* her focus is more "on the possibilities, indeed on the necessities, of anticapitalist, transnational feminist solidarity and organizing against capitalism" (230). She argues that it is especially on "the bodies and lives of women and girls from the Third World/ South—the Two-Thirds World—that global capitalism writes its script" (234–235). Even in the twenty-first century, women and girls still make up 70 percent of the world's poor, own less that one-hundredth of the world's property, and receive one tenth of the world's income. Women are hit hardest by the effects of war, the degradation of environmental conditions, and the privatization and/or elimination of social services under the structural adjustment policies (SAPS). They make up 80 percent of displaced persons and the majority of the world's refugees. It is by paying attention to and theorizing the experiences of these communities of women and girls that she hopes to reveal capitalism as a system of debilitating sexism, racism, and neocolonialism. Her goal is "to better see the processes of corporate globalization and how and why they recolonize women's bodies and labor" (237). For her, any analysis of the effects of globalization must address the experiences and struggles of these particular communities of women and girls.

Mohanty began this practice earlier in *Feminist Genealogies, Colonial Legacies, Democratic Futures* (1997), coedited with M. Jacqui Alexander, where she examined how women's labor is exploited transnationally by comparing the cases of lace-makers in India, computer industry line workers in California, and migrant women workers in Great Britain. In all three contexts she observed how women's work is constructed through existing hierarchies and ideologies, such as class, ethnicity and gender, as well as cultural norms governing family relations and femininity. Gender identity structured the ways these women workers were permitted or excluded from activities in their societies, while norms of gender, race, and other social/cultural hierarchies were made to seem "natural" because they were propagated through the work women do. She argues that the structural and ideological commonalities among these forms of exploitative labor transnationally make possible a theory of these women's concrete (rather than abstract) common interests, grounded in similar critical social conditions despite their diverse geographical locations (Mohanty [2003] 2006). It is these concrete, common interests that are the potential bases of "cross-national solidarity" (381).

Mohanty is referring to women employed by transnational corporations who "have a potential identity in common, an identity as *workers* in a particular division of labor at this historical moment" (382; her emphasis). Because transnational corporations draw from diverse labor pools across the globe, women who share similar, specific social locations in the international division of labor could be Third World women, as well as immigrant and/or poor women in the United States and Western Europe. Consequently, this notion of transnational organizing "makes possible a way of reading the operation of capital from a location . . . which, while forming the bedrock of a certain kind of global exploitation of labor, remains somewhat invisible and undertheorized" (382–383). This practice of trying to make visible that which is hidden, ignored or mystified suggests important similarities and continuities over time in her work. Just as "Under Western Eyes" sought to make the operations of discursive power visible—her later works seek to "draw attention to what is unseen, undertheorized, and left out in the production of knowledge" today—how capitalism "depends on and exacerbates racist, patriarchal, and heterosexist relations of rule" (230–231).

Scattered Hegemonies and Transnational America

Like Mohanty, Inderpal Grewal and Caren Kaplan discuss the importance of theorizing the seismic changes that have taken place in the era of postmodernity in *Scattered Hegemonies* ([1994] 2006: 21):

> recognizing the structure and dynamics of postmodernity is a necessity rather than a luxury or a simple choice. For world cultural, economic, and political conditions have become such that we must devise ways in which feminist practices can work against ever-changing, patriarchal collaborations all over the globe. However, many feminists who see the value of postmodern philosophies also forget the economic and material changes in this postindustrial era that have an impact on the movement of cultural flows.

Along with discussing the development of transnational economic forms and the inadequacy of earlier modern theoretical frames for addressing these new features of postmodernity, these writers also focus on the challenges created by the growth of transnational forms of militarism and religious fundamentalism in the post-9/11 era. Rather than viewing these transnational global clashes simply as "culture wars," Grewal and Kaplan call for a materialist-deconstructive approach that examines the political and economic roots of the intensification of religious fundamentalisms today (19). Before their approach is examined, a discussion of what is meant by the term "culture wars" is needed.

The portrayal of global clashes today as *culture wars* has become hegemonic in the U.S. mass media. For example, Christiane Amanpour's lauded CNN special "God's Warriors" (2007), which highlighted the culture wars waged by Christian, Jewish and Moslem fundamentalists against secular, modern culture is illustrative of this trend. Amanpour portrayed the major reasons for these culture wars *within the United States and abroad* as a clash between fundamentalist religious morals and what fundamentalists perceive as a morally bankrupt, modern secular culture that fosters sexual promiscuity, drug and alcohol abuse, and consumerism. Amanpour's analysis should be applauded for examining fundamentalisms in a number of different global religions and social locations including Christian fundamentalism within the United States. However, in her global morality play, the West becomes associated with either its Judeo-Christian traditions or its modern, secular culture—both of which are portrayed as enemies of transnational, radical Islam.

Some contemporary social theorists also depict contemporary global clashes primarily as culture wars. They view these clashes not as religious or moral battles, but rather as local ethnic groups trying to maintain their diverse cultures, traditions, and ethnohistories against the homogenization and disenchantment of the world that modern, secular, rational cultures and techniques entail. These clashes are framed as a "homogenization versus diversity" debates (Ritzer 2008: 574 and 598). In a similar vein, global theorists who center their sites on the discursive level point to the decline of the **Western narrative** or the **Euro-American Master**

Narrative. As discussed in chapter 9, these terms refer to modern discourses which began with the Enlightenment and continue up unto the present day where modernization and development are seen the key to economic growth, increased standards of living and political freedoms, as well as to the rationalization and secularization of social life. Thus, such Western ideals as democracy, the separation of church and state, freedom of speech, and individualism are viewed as rooted in and engendered by the modernization process (Smart 1993; Appadurai 1996: 300). Here *global clashes are portrayed as backlashes by traditional cultural communities to the discursive frameworks fostered by modernity.* Some concrete examples of culture wars inside and outside of the United States can be found in Box 10.4.

BOX 10.4

Culture Wars at Home and Abroad

"Display of Controversial 'Chocolate Jesus' Sculpture Cancelled"

New York—An angry crowd of outraged Catholics, including Cardinal Edward Egan, forced the cancellation Friday of a planned Holy Week exhibition featuring a nude, anatomically correct chocolate sculpture of Jesus Christ. The hotel that houses the Lab Gallery announced the shutdown of the "My Sweet Lord" show after it was inundated with complaints regarding the six-foot confectionary Christ. . . . The chocolate creation of artist Cosimo Cavallaro . . . fashioned from more than 200 pounds of milk chocolate, presented Christ with his arms outstretched as though nailed to an invisible cross. The Cavallaro creation, in contrast with typical religious portrayals of Christ, did not include a loincloth. Word of the milk chocolate Christ infuriated Catholics, including Egan, who described it as "a sickening display." Bill Donohue, head of the watchdog Catholic League, said it was "one of the worst assaults on Christian sensibilities ever."

Associated Press, March 30, 2007 (Friday); Fox News.com.

Jyllands-Posten Muhammad Cartoons Controversy

Denmark—The *Jyllands-Posten* Muhammad cartoons controversy began after twelve editorial cartoons, most of which depicted the Islamic prophet Muhammad, were published in the Danish newspaper, *Jyllands-Posten* on 30 September 2005. In Islam, the mere depiction of the prophet is considered blasphemous. Danish Muslim organizations responded by holding public protests. The controversy deepened when further examples of the cartoons were reprinted in newspapers in more than fifty other countries. This led to protests across the Muslim world, some of which escalated into violence with police firing on the crowds (resulting in more than 100 deaths). Some critics of the cartoons described them as Islamophobic or racist, and pointed out how they are blasphemous to people of the Muslim faith. Supporters have said that their publication is a legitimate exercise of the right of free speech. Danish Prime Minister Anders Fogh Rasmussen described the controversy as Denmark's worst international crisis since World War II.

http://europenews.dk/en/node/7143
(retrieved November 11, 2011)

The examples above illustrate culture clashes between traditional religious values and the modern, secular right to freedom of speech. However, students also may want to consider whether it matters if contested material provokes a majority population as when the U.S. artist provoked a dominant Christian U.S. population or if contested material provokes a minority population as in the Danish cartoon case. In the latter case, some critics viewed the cartoons as intentionally published to provoke ethnic/racial hostility against the minority Moslem population in Denmark. If so, this might be considered a hate crime, rather than simply an issue of freedom of speech especially since it occurred in the already tense, post-911 global context.

In contrast to the discursive focus on culture wars discussed above, Grewal and Kaplan argue that, if we view global culture wars and the widespread nature of anti-Western sentiments abroad as fomented by the earlier *political-economic impacts of colonialist and neocolonialist policies,* we can better see how the hegemonic Western powers are, in part accountable for creating a world of their own making. For example, in their imperial heyday, the British led the Western powers in literally carving up the globe and creating some of the world's contemporary political hotspots as in the 1920s when they mishandled their Mandate of Palestine or when they created the country of Iraq (Anti-Defamation League 1999, Simon and Tejirian 2005). Similarly, the United States created its own hotspots when the CIA helped foster the coup that brought Mohammad Reza Pahlavi, shah of Iran, to power in 1953. It was his autocratic rule that was eventually overthrown in 1979 by right-wing forces who established an Islamic Republic (Gasiorowski and Byrne 2004). The U.S. government also gave military and financial support to the Taliban in the 1980s when it was fighting the Soviets in Afghanistan. Then, less than two decades later, the United States was at war with the Taliban, and President George W. Bush tried to woo American women's support for this war against the Taliban.[6]

No doubt the fundamentalist ideology and practices of the Taliban are antithetical to feminism, but Grewal and Kaplan call for a more complex analysis where the West takes some responsibility for its actions in earlier eras that showed little regard for the indigenous inhabitants of the lands that Western powers carved up and the autocratic governments they bolstered (see chapter 9). In short, Western feminists cannot allow historical amnesia to blind us to the West's role in and accountability for global clashes today. They call for a more sophisticated understanding of these global clashes where U.S. feminists recognize the past in the present and fight against such militarist and imperialist actions on their home ground rather than abstractly condemning radical Islam as the only center of aggression. In turn, rather than simply focusing on the patriarchal nature of fundamentalist Islam, they urge U.S. feminists to examine how Christian fundamentalism within the Republican Party has affected the lives of millions of women worldwide through funding and development practices that restrict reproductive and contraceptive choices. In this way, they discuss how the concept of *multiple locations* can link U.S. domestic politics with its foreign policies (Grewal and Kaplan [1994] 2006: 20).

In *Transnational America* (2005), Inderpal Grewal employs a common trope used by various theorists to describe a major feature of societies today—the "new risk society" (Beck 1992, Giddens 1990). These theorists do not mean that social life is inherently more risky than it was in earlier eras; indeed for most people this is not the case. Rather, they argue that risk becomes fundamental to the way both lay actors and technical specialists organize the social world (Giddens 1990: 124–125). Some scholars highlight new risks, such as environmental devastation or nuclear war that were unknown or unanticipated by theorists in earlier eras (Giddens 1990, Bronner 1995). Others use "risk" as a synonym for chance or random accidents that pervade the lives of even the most privileged citizens today and that have expanded the role of social institutions like insurance. In *Transnational America* (2005: 201–203), Grewal uses the idea of "risk" to discuss mechanisms that manage "danger" and "security" in the post-9/11 world:

> If we examine one mode of addressing risk not through insurance but through incarceration, then the synonym for risk is not chance or randomness but 'danger' and 'terror',[7] and the means for securing the population from this danger is the incarceration of other populations judged by various modes of expertise as dangerous. From the 'criminal' at one level of risk for violence to the 'terrorist' at a higher level of representing a risk to the nation, we can see the progressively higher levels of risk associated with particular bodies within specific locations.

By understanding risk in this way, we can see how the identification of populations at risk are allied to the idea that racial and gendered (and often sexual) minorities are a danger to themselves and to others and must be subject to forms of state and community regulation. Here Grewal makes an important distinction between criminals and terrorists. Criminals have some recourse to legal rights and to health care. Persons designated as "terrorists" have little recourse to legal rights and are viewed as totally "beyond redemption" (201).

Grewal also wants us to see how race and gender as systems of classification are changing historical constructions. For example, African–American males have been incarcerated in ever larger numbers in the United States through the twentieth century because they are seen by dominant groups as ostensibly presenting a "high risk" for inflicting violence on the population. Today the "Muslim" as "terrorist" and the person who "looks like a Muslim" are the new racial figures of terror. They have become part of the visual history within a culture of managing and disciplining those who are believed to pose the highest risk to the nation. These "terrorists" are depicted as fanatical, dangerous, and barbaric to differentiate them from the "civilized" Westerner (202 and 207).

Grewal discusses how, within racial hierarchies in the United States, another racial formation was created post-911 that produced a "new Other" (albeit from an old history of Orientalism). She argues that this "racial profiling" meant that large numbers of U.S. citizens and immigrants from countries as diverse as Pakistan, India, Saudi Arabia, Kuwait, Iran, Jordan, and Yemen began to be suspect. Many of these people were not even Muslims, much less supporters of radical Islam, but they "looked Muslim" (212). As Grewal writes, "flying while brown" became a problem for many who had thought such pathologies were only directed toward African Americans or Latinos in the United States. Hundreds of incidents of racism by the public and by airlines, coupled with the widespread approval of racial profiling suggest the "limits of U.S. multiculturalism" (214). Grewal also points to the extraordinary technologies of power and surveillance, as well as the suspension of civil rights, that have been exercised within and outside of the United States with the passage of the Patriot Act, the acts of rendition, the creation of secret prisons broad, and the treatment of prisoners in the U.S. military prison at Guantanamo Bay, Cuba.

Grewal's analysis of terrorism evokes the provocative thesis of the Italian theorist Georgio Agamben who claims that "states of exception" are increasingly used in democratic societies and, may even become the norm, rather than the exception (Agamben 2005). The **state of exception** refers to the suspension of normal laws to deal with national emergencies or national security. It is that "paradoxical domain in which law has been suspended in the name of preserving law" (Foster 2011). Not only are normal legal processes suspended for citizens, but the feared "other" is subject to extra-judicial violence or violence not restrained by normal rules—such as when the U.S. government refused to follow the Geneva Convention's rules governing treatment of prisoners in the case of suspected terrorists and transnational combatants.

Agamben uses the term *homo sacer* to refer to those people who have been defined as lying outside political boundaries.[8] Because *homo sacer* is outside of those limits, many things can be done to this person that cannot be done to other humans. They can be killed, tortured or reduced to utter bare life by the traumatic use of political power. Moreover, whoever commits such acts cannot be convicted of a crime because *homo sacer* is outside of the law and the polity. For Agamben, the Nazi extermination of the Jews was a "flagrant case of homo sacer" and the concentration camp itself exemplified a topological zone—a "space without law" (2005: 51). Others have pointed to the hooded prisoner in the infamous photograph from Abu Ghraib as the iconic figure of *homo sacer* today (Foster 2011: 31). Given how global terrorism is likely to be a long lasting feature of the contemporary global landscape, for Agamben there is increasingly little difference between democratic and totalitarian states (Ritzer 2011: 627). Building his theory on Foucault's notion of biopolitics and the administration of human life (see chapter 6), Agamben argues that the concentration camp is the "new biopolitical nomos of the planet" (quoted in Foster 2011: 31:

> Faced with the unstoppable progression of what has been called a "global civil war," the state of exception tends increasingly to appear as the dominant paradigm of government in contemporary politics (Agamben 2005: 2).

In summary, despite claims by some transnational theorists that the rise of transnational social forms signals the demise of the nation state, the writings of

Grewal and Agamben suggest the opposite. By focusing on the heightened role of the U.S. government and its military both at home and abroad these types of analysis put the political back into political economy. As shown below, the work of Aihwa Ong provides further ammunition for the important role of the state today, given how she points to export processing zones as yet another case of state-sponsored zones of exception that have been increasing in recent decades.

The Cultural Logics of Transnationality

In *Flexible Citizenship: The Cultural Logics of Transnationality*, first published in 1999, Ong rejects the idea that the role of the nation-state is shrinking in postmodernity. Rather, she argues that the nation-state's role is both changing and enlarging in the face of transnational developments:

> Contrary to the popular view that sees the state in retreat everywhere before globalization, I consider state power as a positive generative force that has responded eagerly and even creatively to the challenges of global capital. (Ong [1999] 2006: 22).

Ong introduces a number of new concepts, as well as some compelling examples to buttress her argument. She discusses how the horizontal dispersal of transnational corporations (TNCs) entailed the creation of "zones of variegated sovereignty" such as export processing zones (EPZs) and tax free zones (TFZs) *in which different rules and regulations applied from those that exist within the rest of the nation state*. She writes: "These zones, which do not correspond to political borders, often contain ethnically marked class groupings, which in practice are subjected to rights and obligations that are different from those in other zones" (7).[9] The state "has to will" a piece of territory to be placed outside the normal juridical order as in the case of setting aside specific zones for foreign capital and global factories (239). Similarly, the state has to agree to allow guest migrant labor across its borders or illegal migrant labor to be hired by its own domestic industries. That these are hotly contested issues in contemporary politics is certainly visible in the battles over immigration in the United States today.

Like Agamben, Ong uses Foucault's notion of governmentality to argue that the social terms, codes, and norms that constitute these "exceptional zones" whereby subject populations are included or excluded under different forms of "flexible sovereignty" are important aspects of the relations between politics and the more "flexible capitalism" of the current era. These are just some examples of how the state accommodates flexible capitalism that are less evident than the more visible role of the state in military or policing ventures at home or abroad. Ong argues that the state deployment of both disciplinary and pastoral forms of biopower (in the Foucaultian sense) has "enlarged" rather than reduced the space of the political in the era of transnationality. (239).

Ong's work provides other interesting contrasts in that she refuses to follow the path of many postcolonial theorists in viewing the world as a mutually constructed contest between "the West and the rest." She argues that we are "restrained" by the postcolonial critique that attributes modes of domination to Western colonialism,

Western capitalism and Western cultural imperialism without also paying close attention to historical and emergent forms of power and oppression *in other regions* of the globe (22). She focuses on how the Asian tiger economies and the new narratives of Asian modernity spun from the self-confidence of these vibrant economies are not simply a pale imitation of some Western form of development. Rather, ascendant regions of the world such as the Asia Pacific region are articulating their own modernities as distinctive formations that both borrow from the Western Enlightenment's notion of rationalization and progress, but also contest and resist certain features of Western modernity.

Indeed, the fastest growing economies today—China, India and Indonesia—are all emerging economies in the developing—not the highly developed—world (McMichael 2008). During the great recession of recent years, the United States and Europe witnessed the worst economic downturn since the 1930s. By contrast, these emerging economies just kept growing, although more slowly. Unburdened by serious financial crises due to their highly regulated banks, China and India are now generating their own growth instead of relying on exports to the developed Western societies. Their emerging middle classes are generating this internal demand. Ong's analysis alerts us to the importance of recognizing the role of these vibrant economies in the new world order and how their development is decentering the West.

Ong also argues against the tendency of postcolonial and transnational theorists to depict diasporas and transnational migrations of people as narratives of sacrifice and exploitation, whereby these new transnational victims of global capitalism are vested with the agency and hopes formerly sought by leftists in the working class or the subaltern subject. She writes: "The unified moralism attached to subaltern subjects now also clings to diasporan ones, who are invariably assumed to be members of oppressed classes and therefore constitutionally opposed to capitalism and state power" ([1999] 2006:13). In *Spirits of Resistance and Capitalist Discipline* (1987), Ong provides an ethnography of some of these exploited postcolonial subalterns. However, in *Flexible Citizenship* ([1999] 2006), she focuses on the experiences of wealthy, diasporan, Chinese merchants and entrepreneurs who by the 1970s had "come to play nodal and pivotal roles in the emergence of the new, flexible capitalism of the Asia Pacific region" (17). These wealthy diasporic subjects respond more fluidly and opportunistically to changing political and economic conditions and host governments provide them with more "flexible citizenship" options.

Analyses of the role of gender and family relations are ever present throughout Ong's work. She discusses, for example, how wealthy, male Chinese "cosmopolitans" hold multiple passports and inhabit multiple global residences, often maintaining separate families in different locations. They have been likened to astronauts shuttling across borders, their extended families strung across oceans, their "parachute kids" getting dropped off in one or another country in the midst of these transnational business commutes (20). She also discusses how "new regimes of sexual exploitation"—keeping mistresses, pornographic culture, prostitution—proliferate alongside these translocal business networks (21). By illuminating the practices of elite transnationalism and diasporas, Ong shows the complex ways in which any notion of ethnic absolutism is subverted and how the process of othering takes place with diverse consequences in different class, gender, and ethnic locations. For example, she discusses how affluent Chinese businessmen and their families invoke fear in the West of being invaded materially and symbolically by Asian corporate power (21).

In her article "The Gender and Labor Politics of Postmodernity" (1991: 279), Ong discusses how the feminization of labor in the new global factories exposes the fallacy of treating culture and political economy as two separate and autonomous spheres of social life. She documents the role of ethnicity and culture in disciplining labor and in forms of labor resistance. She discusses, for example, how in Hong Kong and Taiwan, the filial claims of many Chinese families on their members' labor—especially the view that daughters' labor should repay parents for the cost of bringing up a "useless daughter"—enforced female workers' compliance with the demands of industrial employment and diminished class-based solidarity. At some industrial sites, factory women were so overwhelmed by the needs and demands of their families that this restrained their ability to participate in sustained political action. Forms of resistance directed against their domination by family, industry and societal/cultural norms, did not always take the form of class consciousness or class agency predicted by earlier theories, but rather entailed more nuanced forms of *cultural resistance*. As Ong writes, by insisting on measures of class agency "we risk diluting the political significance of cultural resistances to encounters with capitalism" (295).[10]

Overall, Ong's work is a fine example of how recent paradigm shifts in feminist thought entail a notion of social agency that bridges the earlier modern divide between macro- and microlevel analyses. In particular, she rejects what she calls "top down models" whereby the global is macro-political economic and the local is culturally creative and resistant. Her theory of practice does not view political economic forces as external to everyday meanings and actions, but rather sees the latter as the means by which political economic forces are constituted and reproduced. Her challenge is to consider the reciprocal construction of gender, ethnicity, race, class, and nation in processes of capital accumulation ([1999] 2006: 5). Because her ethnographies *view gender, class, race, ethnicity, and nation as something people do, rather than as something people have, these ethnographies deconstruct macrostructures into everyday social practices of ruling and being ruled.* She refers to her ethnographies of the everyday effects of transnationality, the agency of displaced subjects, and the attempts by the state to regulate the activities and identities of these transnational subjects as an exploration of the "new cultural logics of transnationality" (23).

In summary, all of the theorists discussed above embrace a materialist-deconstructive approach that is attentive to discursive and cultural issues, as well as to the micropolitics of everyday life. Yet their works also point to how discourse, culture and everyday life practices are embedded in macroglobal economic and political practices that inherently require an analysis of contemporary capitalism.

Having examined some of the debates and contrasting views within postcolonial and transnational feminist theorizing, let us now examine how these theories and the new global conditions they analyze have impacted feminist political practice.

TRANSNATIONAL FEMINIST ORGANIZING

By the 1990s, global feminist organizing had adopted new forms and operated through different sites that reflect the rise of transnational global politics. Not only had the United Nations and its myriad conferences become the focal point for political work, but many groups had refashioned themselves as nongovernmental organizations (NGOs) using the more fluid forms of organizing provided by the new electronic technologies (Wilson, Sengupta, and Evans 2005). Myra Marx Ferree and Aili Mari Tripp's edited book, *Global Feminism: Transnational Women's Activism, Organizing and Human Rights* (2006), discusses various forms of transnational organizing by feminists—both historical and contemporary. They point to global efforts undertaken by the first wave, such as the establishment of the first transnational women's organization the Association Internationale des Femmes in 1868, the International Congress of Women in 1888 and The International Women's Suffrage Association in 1904. As Ferree explains, these early organizations were "inter-national" where members usually were sent as "national" representatives. By contrast, in today's world characterized by internet linkages, cheaper airfares, global phone service, organizations are more fluid and are made up of people from many parts of the world who interact routinely and who do not represent a particular nation to be participants (Ferre in Ferree and Tripp 2006: 12).

Not only the form of organizing, but also the political constituencies and political concerns of global feminist organizations changed. As discussed in chapter 8, the late-nineteenth- and early-twentieth-century international organizations included representatives primarily from Europe and North America who dominated the design and content of international feminist agendas. With the rise of nationalist and anti-colonialist movements after World War II, women across the globe became far more active in international women's organizations and resistance to First World feminists' hegemony increased.[11] According to Tripp, by the mid-1980s the challenges posed by women from the "global South" to the ideological dominance of the "global North" in framing the international women's agenda had become sufficiently concerted to be effective. The UN Conference of Women in Nairobi in 1985 and the formation of Third World–based international networks like DAWN or Women in Law and Development in Africa (WiLDAF) marked the beginning of this decentering or shift in the center of gravity in global women's mobilization dynamics (Tripp in Ferree and Tripp 2006: 60–61). The blending together of two strands of transnational women's organizing- human rights issues and sustainable development concerns—in the 1990s portended an even greater role to the concerns of women from the global South. The merger of these two strands of transnational women's organizing was consolidated during the 1995 conferences in Beijing and Huairou.

Along with the increase in transnational forms of political organizing, many feminists began to argue for **transversal politics** as an alternative both to the universalizing tendencies of the "sisterhood is global" politics and to the balkanizing tendencies of the identity politics of earlier feminisms. For transnational feminists, both of these earlier types of politics included essentialist notions of women (or subgroups of women) that often hardened the lines of conflict between women. In contrast, transversal politics are more dialogical and reflexive. Transversal politics aim to soften the conflicts between women by dialogue that crosses borders both horizontally (such as shared experiences by race, class and sexuality) and vertically (such as different positions of power and privilege between women).[12] In this process, while one may "root" ones arguments in one's own experience and social location, one must also "shift" to encompass the views of others. In turn, a person cannot view themselves as "representatives" of others, unless they are democratically elected and accountable for their actions. For example, an African-American woman cannot speak for all African–American women just because of her standpoint or location. In turn, advocates do not have to be members of the constituency for whom they advocate as is the case with identity politics. Rather in transversal politics it is the message not the messenger that is important. All of these knowledges are viewed as partial or "unfinished." Using the principles of encompassment and polyvocality, the goal is to find more common ground for political solutions to controversial issues (Yuval-Davis 1994, 1997, and 2006; Cockburn 1998; Eschle 2001).

Inspired by postcolonial and transnational feminisms a new approach to global policies was developed—the *Women, Environment and Alternative Development* (WED) approach. WED challenges the Western/Eurocentric features of previous development projects and repudiates its rationalized and economistic forms of knowledge and policy that presume universal application. They view these knowledges/policies as abstracted from the concrete, everyday realities of non-Western peoples' lives and imposed upon them in ways that resemble a colonial stance of rescuing Third World peoples from the wretchedness of their own lives and cultures. WED stresses that development is relative; that women's roles in economic, cultural and ecological relations are complex, place specific, and incapable of being reduced to universal formulas. Hence, political concerns should refer to specific local circumstances, not to abstract ideas.

The WED approach rejects linear views of history and development in favor of a more palimpsestic approach that highlights the ways social and historical processes are interrelated and mutually constitutive. Hence, it does not privilege certain forms of development as more advanced than others or automatically devalue or seek to displace local practices and cultures. It views power as dispersed throughout the global polity rather than centralized in the nation state and the economy. It also views feminist struggles not as based on a definable political group with a common essence and identity—like women—but rather as a struggle against multiples forms in which the category of 'women' is constructed in subordination (Naples 2002: 278; Otto 1996). Like the WCD approach discussed earlier,

WED also pays more attention to ecological sustainability and views culture and political economy as integral rather than autonomous spheres of social live.

The Women's Action Agenda 21 that came out of a women's tribunal held in 1991 in Miami exemplifies this approach. It combined women's voices across the divides of North/South, race, ethnicity, and class in a common vision of alternative development practice to Western models (McMichael 2008: 228–230). For a more detailed discussion of these political issues, Nancy Naples and Manisha Desai's *Women's Activism and Globalization* (2002) provides a useful analysis of the strengths and weaknesses of various transnational organizing strategies and techniques. Examined below are different feminist analyses of transnational sex trafficking to illustrate shifts that have taken place in global feminist political strategies.

Transnational Sexual Trafficking

Prostitution is often referred to as the world's "oldest profession" and even transnational sexual trafficking has quite a long history (Guy 1990, Gibson 1986, Bernstein 1995). Although it is impossible to get accurate comparative historical data on such practices that were often outlawed or underground, it appears that the global restructuring of the world economy in recent decades and its negative affects on women, together with the rise of new technologies that compressed the time and distance entailed in world travel and communication, have had a profound impact on the globalization of the sex industry and the increase in sexual tourism.

The most orthodox version of a modern, radical feminist approach is illustrated by work of the Coalition against Trafficking in Women which is an NGO formed in the United States in 1991 under the direction of Kathleen Barry. Barry earned her reputation as a major spokesperson on prostitution and sexual trafficking in the 1970s with the publication of *Female Sexual Slavery* (1979). Her later book, *The Prostitution of Sexuality* (1995), includes a more extensive discussion of her strategy for framing these issues in human rights discourse. Barry and the coalitions with which she has worked proposed a new Convention against Sexual Exploitation that calls for the abolition of the international prostitution industry. The demands of this Convention have been proposed unsuccessfully at a number of international conferences.[13] Barry defines prostitution as the use of women's bodies as commodities to be bought, sold, or exchanged (whether or not for money) and she includes prostitution in brothels, military prostitution, pornography, sex tourism, and mail-order-bride markets (Barry 1995: 306). She uses human rights discourse to argue that women as a group should be free from all of these forms of sexual exploitation because they abrogate a person's human rights to dignity, equality, autonomy, and physical/mental well being.[14]

Building on the work of other U.S. radical feminists, such as Andrea Dworkin (1974) and Catharine MacKinnon (1988), Barry views all prostitution—whether consensual or not—as a coercive violation of human rights. Hence, any migration of sex workers becomes trafficking in this perspective. Barry justifies this view as follows: "When the human being is reduced to a body, objectified to sexually service another, whether of not there is consent, violation of the human being has taken place" (Barry 1995: 23). In contrast, a more moderate position is exemplified by the Global Alliance against Traffic in Women which opposes only "forced" prostitution and thereby defines "trafficking" as forced labor where people are lured or deceived into forms of contemporary slavery. This more moderate position recognizes not only a difference between forced and consensual prostitution, but also that "traffic in persons" is not only for the purposes of prostitution, but also for a range of other activities as well, such as domestic service. Here the element that defines "trafficking" is force and not the nature of the labor performed (Murray 2003: 415).

The challenge to these perspectives does not seek the abolition of prostitution, but rather focuses on sex workers' rights and places more emphases on local as opposed to global contexts. While there are differences in the ways various feminist theorists advance this position (Truong 1990, Chapkis 1997, Murray 2003), I will draw from Kamala Kempadoo's analysis in her introduction to *Global Sex Workers: Rights, Resistance, and Redefinition* (Kempadoo and Doezema 1998) to point out some of the major features of this perspective. One of its hallmarks is that, rather than depicting women as *victims* of prostitution and sexual trafficking, this perspective focuses on sex workers' social agency. Here sex workers are positioned as actors in the global arena—as persons making choices and decisions—not simply as victims that are harmed, exploited and/or enslaved by others (9). The use of the term "sex worker" as opposed to prostitute is meant to highlight sex work as a form of income-generating labor—like other forms of labor—all of which involve specific parts of the body and particular types of energy and skills. Kempadoo argues that situating prostitution as "work" allows for the recognition of what postcolonial theorists like Chandra Talpade Mohanty see as "common concrete interests" and shared locations that enable the "potential bases of cross-national solidarity" between women (8).

Racism and colonialism also play a more significant role in Kempadoo's approach. She discusses how images of "the exotic" are intertwined with ideologies of racial and ethnic difference such that the racist "exoticization of the Third World 'other'" is as equally important as economic factors in positioning women in global sex work. Yet while such racist ideologies fuel sex tourism, she points to how "whiteness" continues to represent the hegemonic ideal of physical and sexual attractiveness with white labor still reigning as the most valued in the global sex industry (10–11). Kempadoo highlights the neocolonialist stance of writers like Barry who evoke the notion of rescuing Third World women sexworkers who are portrayed as too poor, too ignorant, and too victimized to be capable of self-determination.

Kempadoo argues that this neocolonialist stance further entails a particular view of sex that is Western, moralistic, and dismissive of local subaltern understandings and sexual practices, such as those found in the Caribbean where "one can speak of a continuum of sexual relations from monogamy to multiple partners and where sex may be considered as a valuable asset for a woman to trade with."

(12). Thus, in Kempadoo's approach different cultures and contexts are taken into account whereby diversity and difference are addressed. By contrast, in Barry's approach there is one solution for all sex workers and this universal solution is decided from a particular Western vantage point. In Kempadoo's approach there is also a shift from a focus on women to a focus on gender in that she pays attention both to women sex workers as well as to the "renta-dreads" and beach boys who dominate the sex tourism industry of some islands (6). In contrast, Barry rejects such a shift from "women" to "gender" arguing that it makes women—who are the vast majority of "victims of prostitution"—less visible.[15] In short, Kempadoo criticizes the univeralizing and totalizing effect of unnuanced Western, feminist theorizing on prostitution and trafficking.

Rather than abolishing prostitution, Kempadoo calls for the decriminalization of prostitution, applying occupational health and safety standards to workplaces, and working to eradicate restrictive immigration policies that contribute to the exploitation of migrant sex workers. This perspective was advocated, for example, by The Network of Sex Work Projects (NWSP) which provided a sex worker presence to counter the anti-prostitution/anti-trafficking perspective at the UN Conference on Women/NGO Forum in Beijing in 1995. Proponents argue that the most egregious situations which anti-traffickers rail against are a result of economic, political, racial, and gender inequalities and it is those inequalities that should be the focus of feminist activism. To buttress their position, these theorists are more likely to use studies based on the concerns of sex workers themselves to show not only how the choice of sex work is in many cases voluntary, but that there are many myths as to why and how people come to choose sex work as their occupation. They see the prohibition of prostitution and restrictions on travel as what attracts organized crime, as well as prostitutes' need for protection and assistance. In sum, they argue that the vast range of sex industries and contexts require an understanding of diversity/difference and a realization that prohibition and unitary 'moral values' are part of the problem, not the solution (Murray 2003: 425).

QUEERING GLOBAL ANALYSES

It took the AIDS crises of the 1980s to make lesbian, gay, bisexual, and transgender (LGBT) people more visible to global development agencies. Beginning in the mid-1980s funding for LGBT organizations was provided by development agencies to address issues of HIV/AIDS among gay men and other populations considered at risk. Yet, because of the focus on AIDS, gay men's organizing efforts received far more attention and funding than their female counterparts, resulting in male organizations having significantly more power (Lind and Share 2003: 56 and 67). Another irony here was that, while sexuality had rarely been discussed by international agencies other than in terms of women's reproductive rights and health, the AIDS epidemic contributed to an explosion of public debates on sexuality, especially on homosexuality, and this began the process by which the traditional silence on homosexuality slowly unraveled (65).

However, stereotypes persist in terms of claims that homosexuality is a form of decadence derived from the West. Third World LGBT and queer activists often are viewed as traitors to nationalist movements and confront similar "strategies of dismissal" to those Third World feminist activists faced when "feminism" was decried as a Western import. On the other hand, as noted in chapter 6, postcolonial queer theorists have been wary of the imposition of Western notions of gay and lesbian "health" and "discrimination" issues on nonprofit organizations abroad. To reiterate, postcolonial queer theorists argue that the Western gay identity model can also be understood as a colonialist and "homonationalist" project in which the "good gay citizens" of the West are viewed as modern, self-proclaiming, and proud, whereas those in other global locations are viewed as "backward," bound by religious traditions or cultural hang-ups, and in need of saving by the West (Puar 2007).

Such critiques have fostered both LGBT and queer theorists to be more sensitive to the issue of imposing Western notions of sexuality onto Third World peoples. For example, some theorists have pointed to the difficulties of using Western terms for same-sex desires, like "lesbian" to describe desires and relationships in Third World indigenous contexts (Spurlin 2006: 10). They also have discussed how, within these indigenous contexts, debates have flourished over how to define oneself in terms of sexuality and gender. Some Third World people have embraced the "American" way of being gay while others reject it; some have chosen to reclaim historically pejorative indigenous terms such as "maricon" in Latin America or "moffies" in South Africa to describe themselves or their LGBT friends, much like the term "queer" is used in the United States (Lind and Share 2003: 60; Spurlin 2006: 26). Yet, while both LGBT and queer theorists are increasingly sensitive to imposing Western categories on the sexual practices of Third World peoples, a major difference between these approaches is that LGBT theorists see as their goal "the hope that institutionalized heterosexuality will one day be seen as but one sexual/gender identity among many others" (Lind and Share 2003: 70). Postcolonial queer theorists do not seek this assimilationist solution. They seek a much broader goal—ending erotophobia and freeing up of desire. Following Foucault they view sexuality, not as an issue of identities, but as an issue of erotic bodily practices. Hence, their goal of ending **erotophobia** refers to ending the governing of a wide range of sexual practices—from gender roles, to same-sex behaviors to heterosexual practices (Gaard 1997: 129).

As William Spurlin points out in *Imperialism within the Margins* (2006: 7), *postcolonial queer theorists undertake the two-pronged task of decolonizing the Western biases of queer theory and queering the heterosexist bias of postcolonial theory.*[16] For example, using their palimpsestic view of time, postcolonial queer theorists have begun to rectify the heterosexual bias in the literature on colonialism and imperialism. Greta Gaard and M. Jacqui Alexander use data from a number of historical works to illustrate how the early history of European colonialism in North America, Latin America and Asia entailed the imposition of European regimes of gender and sexuality on a variety of heterosexual and nonheterosexual erotic practices of indigenous peoples. From the colonialists' standpoint, the "aberrant" sexual behaviors of indigenous peoples were used as proof of their heathen and uncivilized nature and, thereby, provided justification for their colonization. Gaard uses examples from Jonathan Ned Katz's *Gay American History* (1976), Will Roscoe's *The Zuni Man-Woman* (1991) and Ramón Gutiérrez's *When Jesus Came, the Corn Mothers Went Away: Marriage, Sexuality, and Power in New Mexico, 1500–1846* (1991) to document early explorers' and missionaries' responses to native sexual practices. Gaard describes how one explorer wrote: "The people of this nation (the Choctaw) are generally of a brutal and coarse nature. They are morally quite perverted and most of them are addicted to sodomy. These corrupt men . . . have long hair and wear skirts like women" (quoted in Gaard 1997: 126–127). The conquerors sought to eliminate indigenous forms of Indian homosexuality as part of their attempt to destroy Native cultures and, in some cases, used them as an excuse for exterminating natives. M. Jacqui Alexander (2005: 196) relays the grisly story of how the conquistador Vasco Núñez de Balboa killed forty Panamanian male Indians he "found dressed in women's apparel" and fed them to his dogs.

The role of the *nadleeh* or transgendered persons particularly offended Western European sensibilities. A Franciscan missionary reported with shock that "almost every village" in what is now Southern California had two or three transgendered persons, but prayed that "these accursed people will disappear with the growth of missions" (quoted in Gaard 1997: 127). Similarly, reports dating back to the sixteenth-century mention the "sinfulness" of native sexual behavior—the lack of inhibition, the prevalence of sodomy, and the tolerance or even respect for transgendered persons—all of which buttressed the Spanish explorers' argument for the colonization of native peoples and their lands in the name of Christianity.

Heterosexual practices devoid of the restrictions imposed by Christianity were objectionable also to European colonizers. For example, missionaries objected to the heterosexual practices of the Pueblo Indians, calling them "bestial" because "like animals, the female placed herself publicly on all fours" (129). These same missionaries viewed the "muher supra virum" (woman above the man) as "absolutely contrary to the order of nature" (129). Many people today joke about how the "missionary position" has governed Western ideas of sexual practices, but few are aware of the horrors that befell indigenous peoples when European conquistadors and colonialists enforced their sexual regimes.

By excavating this history, postcolonial queer theorists show how the discourse and practices of colonialism contained specific conceptions not only of race and gender, but also of sex and sexuality that authorized their colonial and imperialist ventures. Colonization can therefore be seen as an act of nationalist self-assertion of identity and definition over and against the other, "whereby the queer erotic of non-westernized peoples, as well as their culture and their land is subdued into the missionary position—with the conqueror 'on top'" (Gaard 1997: 131). M. Jacqui Alexander (2005: 198) writes:

> In this somewhat classic struggle between (heterosexual) civilization and (sodomitic) savagery, indigenous heterosexual interests needed to be rescued from

> themselves. Only an outside power could perform that act of rescue and invest in the heterosexual the presumed power of restoring order out of chaos, of sexually cleansing the newly conquered body politic from its own internal infection. The spectacle of war and the spectacle of sexual cleansing meet on territorial grounds so that territorial claims around the body politic might be secured.

These "sexual cleansings" not only affected indigenous peoples in the colonies, they also *mutually constructed* notions of race, gender, sexuality, and nation for the colonialists. In *Imperial Leather: Race, Gender, and Sexuality in the Colonial Contest* (1995), Anne McClintock draws on novels, advertising, diaries, poetry, and oral histories to illustrate how these mutual constructions affected the British during the heyday of their imperial power. In *Carnal Knowledge and Imperial Power* (2002), Ann Laura Stoler documents the impact of these mutual constructions on Dutch colonialists in the East Indies. In *Race and the Education of Desire* (1995: 8), Stoler discusses more generally the relation between the policing of sex and sexuality in Europe and its imperial conquests in the mid-nineteenth century as follows:

> Within the lexicon of bourgeois civility, self-control, self-discipline and self-determination were defining features of bourgeois selves in the colonies. These features, affirmed in the ideal family milieu, were often transgressed by sexual, moral and racial contaminations in those same European colonial homes. Repression was clearly part of this story, but . . . it was subsumed by something more. These discourses on self-mastery were productive of racial distinctions, of clarified notions of 'whiteness" and what it meant to be truly European. These discourses provided the working categories in which an imperial division of labor was clarified, legitimated, and—when under threat—restored.

Stoler shows how European discourses on sexuality in the eighteenth and nineteenth centuries were "refracted through the discourses of empire and its exigencies" and how race and racism were entangled in these discourses (7). Overall, *Race and the Education of Desire* is an impressive work that undertakes the task of working out Foucault's genealogies of sexuality onto a broader imperial map.

In *Pedagogies of Crossing* (2005), M. Jacqui Alexander uses a palimpsestic approach to interweave the past with the present. After discussing the sixteenth-century sexual cleansings by the conquistadors of the New World, she moves to late-twentieth-century imperial militarization in the United States and asks the following:

> What kind of sexuality befits responsible soldiering? In what sexual garb does the white manly citizen soldier wish to be clothed as an invading army brings sovereign nation-states within an imperial ambit? . . . These questions posed in terms of one geography will now be revisited in another. (199)

In this way she moves to discuss the "Public Debate over Homosexuals in the Military" that took place in the 1990s just after the U.S. army's involvement in the first Gulf War. She writes that, while the report by the Military Working Group on this topic appeared both sanitized and dehistorized, "the mode of address, the narrative solipsisms and rhetorical sleights of hand all helped to fashion a particular regime of truth that can most accurately be understood as quintessentially Balboan" (200).

The analyses of postcolonial queer theorists travel not only across time, but also across borders using the theme of gay diasporas. In Cindy Patton and Benigno Sánchez-Eppler's edited volume *Queer Diasporas* (2000) contributors explore how sexuality and sexual identities change when individuals and discourses/ideologies move across literal and figurative borders. Other writers highlight how the persecution of nonheterosexual practices has resulted in various types of queer diasporas that have crisscrossed the globe from third to first worlds and vice versa. Persecution in the West drove a number of Europeans and Americans to make Third World locations their homes or their respites from this persecution. For example, the establishment of Tangiers as an international zone by Western interests in the years 1923–1956 provided a tax-free zone for economic interests, as well as a free zone for sexual permissiveness:

> The special attraction of Tangiers can be put in one word: exemption—exemption from interference, legal or otherwise. Your private life is your own, to act exactly as you please. . . . It is a sanctuary of non-interference. (Burroughs 1989: 59)

In foregrounding the imperial, postcolonial queer theorists have not shied away from noting how the intersection of these "gay sanctuaries" with the historical and economic factors of Western colonialism allowed for a level of colonial privilege and sexual exploitation (Boone [1995] 2003: 481). While modern social theorists tend to treat sexual exploitation in a more simplistic "exploiter versus victim frame," postcolonial queer theorists treat this topic with a complexity that affirms the social agency on both sides of these social relationships. For example, postcolonial queer theorists point out how such "collisions" between Western sexual categories (the homosexual, the pederast) and the equally stereotypical colonialist tropes (the beautiful brown boy, the virile, sexually well-endowed, exotic other) generated ambiguity and contradiction rather than simply Western domination over an Eastern object of desire (478). They note how the Western enclaves abroad sometimes allowed for the emergence of desires and practices resistance to dominant Western sexual regimes. They also discuss the contradictions between Western gays' rebellion against the sexual orthodoxy that had victimized them in their homelands and their simultaneous tendency to "objectify" their Eastern partners as "valuable additions to their collections" (478). The role that Eastern subjects played in these sexual relations is also treated as complex and ambiguous. Families were often complicit in passing their sons over to these men, and, at times, Eastern men and boys fulfilled their own sexual desires and yearnings through these liaisons. Rather than simply being "objects" or "victims" of sexual desire, they too had their own complex social interpretations and social agency.

In *Pedagogies of Crossing*, Alexander brings these issues into the present era with her critique and expose of the "erotic consumptive patterns" of First World gay tourism. Alexander argues that contemporary gay tourism follows some of the same privileged and colonialist trajectories as those of heterosexual tourism

(58). She documents how the rise of First World gay tourism in recent decades has become a lucrative area of growth for both gay and straight businesses and how various "guides" to gay and lesbian tourism entail some of the same colonial discourses (such as "friendly natives" or "exotic tropical beauty" as a trope for Blackness) that prevail in heterosexual travel guides. Alexander shows little hesitation in discussing colonial and neocolonial forms of sexual consumption that reify and fetishize the bodies of colonized others in ways that do not provide fertile ground for constructing "critical communities" or a "loving freedom" (88).

In summary, while some theorists have leveled scathing critiques against both LGBT and postcolonial queer theorists for their focus on sex and sexuality when other global issues seem far more pressing,[17] this section has shown how the queering of global analyses reveals important insights into how colonialism and imperialism are and always have been inflected by race, gender, class, nation, and sexuality.

THIRD WAVE FEMINISM ON GLOBAL ISSUES

To date, U.S. third wave writings have focused heavily on how young women navigate their lives in the United States and rarely address women's lives abroad. Given their sensitivity to difference and their claims that their Third Wave agenda is more global than their second wave predecessors' (Mack-McCanty 2005: 196; Labaton and Martin, 2004: xxviii–xxix), critics have been quick to pick up on this contradiction. For example, in her article "Global Feminisms, Transnational Political Economies, and Third World Cultural Production" (2003: 1), Winnie Woodhull points to this neglect not only in major publications by Third Wave feminists but also on their websites:[18]

> If anything can be said with certainty about third wave feminism, it is that it is mainly a first world phenomenon generated by women who . . . have limited interest in women's struggles elsewhere on the planet.

In "Postcolonial Theory and the Third Wave Agenda," Filipina feminist Angeli Diaz (2003: 11) notes a similar neglect: "The omission of any references to the global political, economic, and cultural scenarios in the writings of Third Wave feminists predisposes their celebration of diversity and inclusiveness to be paradoxically an exclusive one." Diaz locates this problem in the third wave's individualistic focus or what she calls their "focus on Me." Diaz argues that "in re-fashioning what it means to be a woman, third wave feminists deliberately turn their gaze inward to the Self and focus on ways by which the Self is produced and reproduced via lived experiences within a particular milieu"—that particular milieu being their homelands in the First World (11). It is this that Diaz finds "alienating" as a Filipina woman and a student of postcolonial theory. She writes:

> But while my consciousness is pervaded by my place in the global hierarchy due to my colonial and postcolonial experiences, I sense no such reciprocal awareness of my presence in Third Wave feminist writings." (10)

My own analyses of U.S. third wave writings arrived at more nuanced conclusions. Clearly a major theme of U.S. third wave feminists is how they negotiate their lives and identities *within* First World contexts. Yet because of the diversity of third wave voices, especially in terms of race and ethnicity, often these authors or their families have experienced U.S. internal colonialism and/or migrations from other areas of the globe. There also are a number of critical insights within some third wave publications that echo the assumptions of postcolonial critiques of Western feminism. For example, in the "Introduction" to *Colonize This!* (2002), editors Daisy Hernandez and Bushra Rehman explicitly take an anticolonialist stance by stating how they are deeply critical of the "us-and-them mentality" of U.S. political discourse that too often depicts "we" the "liberated Americans" as saving "them" the oppressed women of Third World countries. While this statement is meant as a general critique of U.S. political stances, the authors were specifically referring to the news of the U.S. invasion of Afghanistan that enabled Afghan women to "throw off their veils." Hernandez and Rehman (2002: xvii) write: "What kind of feminist victory is it when we liberate women by killing their men and any woman or child who happens to be where a bomb hits." Susan Muaddi Darraj, a contributor to this volume, voices a similar critique of the patronizing nature of Western feminism when she writes: "The tone of white Western feminism—with its books about 'lifting the veil on Arab women' and Arab women 'lifting the veil of silence'—was that Arab feminism was nothing greater than an amusing oxymoron" (Darraj 2002: 298). Such criticisms of the "colonialist stance" in Western feminist thought are noteworthy features of this book.

Third wave texts that focus on activism are the most fruitful in showing the younger generation's engagement in global issues. As Colleen Mack-Canty points out in the anthology *Different Wavelengths: Studies of the Contemporary Women's Movement* (2005), third wavers have been very engaged in global ecofeminist concerns. They have been a mainstay of antiglobalization struggles, such as those in Seattle in 1999 and in Cancún in 2003, protesting policies of the World Trade Organization (Symington 2005: 40).[19] *The Fire This Time: Young Activists and the New Feminism* (2004) edited by activists from the Third Wave Foundation, Vivien Labaton and Dawn Lundy Martin, includes numerous analyses of the local/global links made in these third waver's activism. Examples include third wave involvement in organizing immigrant Asian women working in the United States and protests against the U.S. military occupation of Vieques, Puerto Rico. One fine example of local/global links is Kathryn Temple's "Exporting Violence: The School of the America's, U.S. Intervention in Latin America, and Resistance." Temple has been involved in demonstrations against the U.S.-based School of the Americas (SOA) located in Fort Benning, Georgia which trains foreign military forces. She links this training to violence against women abroad in the form of torture, rape and the warfare that ensued when these U.S.-trained, foreign military forces buttressed autocratic regimes abroad.[20]

In 2005, the "first international collection by young feminists," *Defending our Dreams: Global Feminist Voices for a New Generation*, was published (Wilson,

Sengupta, and Evans 2005). This book was, in part, the product of DAWN's (Development Alternatives with Women for a New Era) Training Institute in Feminist Advocacy for young women (ages twenty-five to thirty-five). It evolved out of conversations between participants at a 1998 conference of the Association for Women's Rights in Development (AWID)[21] in Cape Town, South Africa and was written by young feminists from more than eleven countries representing all populated continents. *Defending our Dreams* not only documents how young women represent a significant constituency within various organizations and movements for global justice, but it also highlights some of the new issues and concerns of young women today, such as the HIV/AIDS crises globally, the role of financial institutions like the World Trade Organization, and the role of the new technologies, such as nanotechnology and genetically modified organisms and seeds—issues that were not existent (or at least not very visible) during the second wave in the 1960s and 1970s (Wilson, Sengupta, and Evans 2005). While many of the authors combine personal introspection with their analyses of global issues, there is much more focus on structural analysis and the material lives of women abroad than is found in most U.S. third wave writings. One of the major contributions of the authors of *Defending our Dreams* is their adeptness at relating personal experiences to structural analyses or what they refer to as the practice of **conscientization** (Antrobus 2005: xiv).

Indigo Williams Willing's work on transnational adoptions in *Defending our Dreams* (2005) provides a fine example of conscientization. Born in Vietnam and adopted by Australian parents, she discusses the costs and the benefits of her experiences as an adopted child whose racial and cultural background was different from her parents. Willing then moves from her personal experiences to analyzing various structural features of international adoptions. For example, she links them to global militarism and war by pointing out how international adoptions became more common when thousands of war orphans were flown from Korea in the 1950s to be adopted into families living in Australia, Europe and North America. This pattern was repeated two decades later because of the Vietnam War. She also identifies the AIDS epidemic as another huge source of orphans as it left an estimated 1.8 million orphans living in the global South and South-East Asia by 2003 (97). These particular events, along with the more general issue of global inequalities have fostered the rise in transnational adoptions which today involve more than thirty thousand children a year moving between more than one hundred countries. Most transnational adoptions involve orphans from poorer communities in Asia, Africa, the post-Communist nations, the Caribbean, and the Pacific Islands moving to comparatively wealthier ones in the North. Willing thus expands her analysis from the micro-politics of growing up and negotiating her own mixed identity in a First World location, to the macro-level issues of militarism, imperialism and global inequalities that foster and enable the global migration of children.

In summary, U.S. third wave feminist writings to date speak to the multilocationality and diversity of women within First World locations, but are in need of more analyses of local/global links. By contrast, their political activism has been more substantially directed toward global issues. Recent writings by third wave feminists from other countries show more integration of theory and practice on global issues and more promise in relating their own personal experiences to global structural analyses.

CONCLUSION

The purpose of the theory applications section of the text was to illuminate paradigm shifts in the conceptual frameworks of global feminist thought from modernity to postmodernity. These conceptual shifts include movement away from feminisms that use First World/Third World or core/periphery frameworks to new transnational and postcolonial feminisms that highlight a world of scattered hegemonies that are articulated using concepts like transnational, diaspora, hybridity, and multiple-locationality to describe the global landscape. These new approaches center their critical gaze on how earlier Western feminist frameworks too often viewed the world through "Western eyes" and wittingly or unwittingly took a "colonialist stance" in their analyses.

Postcolonial feminist theorists most heavily criticized U.S. radical feminists for taking a colonialist stance in their global analyses, especially in their analyses of violence against women. Yet, this colonialist stance also was evident in the writings of liberal feminist modernization theorists who called for more interaction between the first and third worlds in terms of introducing Western-style technologies, methods of education and family planning to the Third world. Feminist modernization theories were criticized not only for operating within a framework that ignores the exploitative dimensions of modernization and development, but also for implying that the modern, technologically developed First World would rescue the Third World from the paralysis of its social, economic, and cultural traditions. To postcolonial feminists, such Western feminist approaches were just another version of the "missionary stance" or the "white man's burden," though this time modern men *and women* of the First World would be the ones to save the backward peoples of the Third World from their arrested development.

Even the focus on global stratification and exploitation in feminist dependency theories, world-systems theories, and Luxemburgian-inspired global theories did not save them from the critical gaze of postcolonial feminists. These critics pointed to how First World/Third World and core/periphery frameworks were difficult to maintain in a world structured by transnational flows of capital, commodities, culture, and people. They also criticized these feminist frameworks for continuing to center the First World or the West as the source of significant social change—the mover and shaker of world social relations—again treating the Third World as areas plagued by never-changing traditions. In contrast, postcolonial feminisms call for a decentering of the West and a critical interrogation of Western essentialist views in order to highlight difference and hybridity.

Postcolonial feminisms also reveal how complex and textured the colonial projects of imperial powers were in problematizing the relations between Western women and post-colonial women. Many Western feminist global approaches were shown to entail a colonialist stance that was repetitively circulated in global political discourse and which served hegemonic interests despite their radical or emancipatory goals. While these interrogations of the impact of various colonial projects often pointed to the complicity of Western feminists' involvement in empire both symbolically and materially, the ultimate goal of the new postcolonial feminisms is to develop politically effective and critical feminisms that transcend the artificially constructed boundaries of geographic location and global space.

Both supporters and critics agree that postcolonial and transnational thought are expressive not only of a real crisis in the ideology of linear progress and development, but also of a crisis in the modes of comprehending and conceptualizing the world today (Dirlik 1997: 502). Thus, when contrasted with earlier modernist frameworks, postcolonial and transnational thought resonates well with the recent transformations in global social relations in postmodernity. These transformations, such as the rise of transnational social forms, the diasporic movement of populations across national boundaries, and the unprecedented mobility and dispersal of capitalism and mass culture enabled by the new electronic technologies' compression of time and space, all serve to blur previous global boundaries. Whether in its queer or non-queer guises, postcolonial and transnational theories address the challenges of developing analyses of gender, class, race, and nation in an era where geographic boundaries, locations and identities became more blurred amid the fast and flexible capitalism that now inhabits post-colonial space. Thus, a major contribution of these paradigm shifts in global feminist thought from late modernity to postmodernity is that they "answered the conceptual needs of the social, political and cultural problems thrown up by this New World Order" (502). Whether these conceptual tools will serve to adequately address these problems remain the subject of theoretical debates in feminism today.

CRITICISMS OF TRANSNATIONAL AND POSTCOLONIAL FEMINISMS

1. That the modern fixing of social locations rejected by transnational feminist theorists at least permitted the identification of the perpetrators of exploitation, whereas the more scattered, fluid, and ephemeral hegemonies of transnational analyses leave centers of power more ambiguous and difficult to target. By highlighting the dispersal rather than the concentration of corporate power, these theorists have mystified the ways in which totalizing structures persist in the midst of apparent fluidity (Prakash 1997).

2. That postcolonial theorists do not undertake what they constantly demand of others—to historicise the conditions of their own emergence as authoritative voices—conditions that cannot be described without reference to class relations.

Not only do these theorists fail to acknowledge their own class privilege, but postcolonial theory itself elides the issue of social class by focusing on empire and ethnicity (Appiah 1997, Eagleton 2003).

3. That postcolonial theorists miss the fact that without capitalism as the foundation of European power and the motive force of its globalization, Eurocentrism would have been just another ethnocentrism. By "throwing the cover of culture and discourse over material relations" (Dirlik 1997: 515–516), postcolonial theory substituted the task of critiquing Eurocentric ideology for critiquing capitalism.

4. Because of its antiessentialist logic, postcolonial theory supports little beyond local struggles. It rejects collective categories that in the past were used to mobilize political action (such as among Third World women) evoked by structural commonalities, such as shared histories of colonialism, neocolonialism, and racism. These commonalities enabled people to form alliances that could provide the bases for more than just local struggles (Shohat 1992: 111; Dirlik 1997: 515).

Note: Criticisms 2, 3 and 4 are not relevant to those postcolonial theorists who embrace a materialist–deconstructive approach.

NOTES

1 This also happened in the United States to grassroots, activist, rape crises, and battered women's shelters of the 1970s, when they began depending more on grants in the financial crises of 1980s. Grant funds—whether private or public—were more easily obtained by credentialed women. Thus the staff of formerly activist, grassroots organizations became more professionalized and institutionalized.

2 There are a few examples of transnational combatants earlier in the twentieth century, such as the Spanish Civil War (1936–1939), during which leftist militias from many different countries fought against the Fascist Nationalists. However, these leftist transnational ventures were so rare that they became celebrated icons of the communist and anarchist left.

3 Some genealogists of postcolonial theory trace its origins back to other classic works on colonialism, such as Albert Memmi's *The Colonizer and the Colonized* (1957) or Franz Fanon's *The Wretched of the Earth* (1961) and *Black Skins, White Masks* (1967).

4 These Eurocentric theoretical roots have been used to critique postcolonial theory. For example, critic Arif Dirlik (1997: 512) writes that, although postcolonial theorists repudiate Eurocentric analyses, the language of postcolonial discourse is the language of Eurocentric poststructuralism—a point they concede, but do not adequately address.

5 Jyotsna Gupta (2006: 25) claims that Mohanty's shift toward a greater focus on political economy was inspired by the works of Maria Mies and Vandana Shiva, thus indirectly pointing to the influence of Rosa Luxemburg on Mohanty.

6 Natasha Walter wrote in the October 12, 2004, edition of *The Guardian*: "Bush has frequently used his policy in Afghanistan as evidence of his commitment to women's rights and as an attempt to woo women voters. Recently, Laura Bush spoke at an election rally at which women in the audience held placards saying, 'W stands for women.'" According to Walter's report, however, this is not how women in Afghanistan saw it. Rather, Afghani women told Walter they believed that power was still being parceled out to brutal regional commanders who made their situations more dangerous and insecure than before the U.S. invasion. Hence, the title of Walter's article, "The Winners Are Warlords, Not Women."

7 Grewal's analysis here would be sharpened by realizing that it is the appearance of "random and chance" danger and violence that underpins both "fear of crime" and "fear of terrorism". This enables those who foster a "culture of fear" to mobilize people across race, ethnicity, gender, and class lines to support incarceration, even when actual crime rates are declining.

8 In the Roman social order, *homo sacer* referred to the lowest of the low (Foster 2011: 31).

9 Using Agamben's concepts, one could argue that those who work in export processing zones represent a form of *homo sacer* although to a less traumatic degree.

10 This conclusion regarding the inaccuracy of using earlier, leftist notions of "class struggle" is echoed in Chandra Talpade Mohanty's analysis of transnational women workers and the forms of ideological domination they face in the New Global Order (Mohanty [2003] 2006: 393).

11 The membership of the International Council of Women (ICW) jumped from having 78 percent of its affiliate councils based in Europe and the United States in 1938 to having only 47 percent of its membership from these countries by 1963. Tripp traces the initial challenges to Western dominance in framing the issues of international conferences to the UN World Conference of Women in Mexico in 1975 (Tripp in Ferree and Tripp 2006: 59 and 64).

12 According to Yuval-Davis (2006: 280), transversal politics was a form of autonomous left politics first used in Italy in the 1970s.

13 The Convention against Sexual Exploitation has been proposed without success at a number of international venues, including the Conference on Human Rights in Vienna in 1993 and the UN Conference on Women/NGO Forum in Beijing in 1995. The 1994 version of this Convention can be found in the appendix of Barry's book (1995: 323–344).

14 Although Barry also includes child prostitution in her analysis, the UN has a Convention on the Rights of the Child that opposes child sexual exploitation and abuse (Barry 1995: 325).

15 A similar debate over whether to call their programs women's studies or gender studies took place among U.S. feminists in universities across the country.

16 South Africa has become a significant location for queer studies today, given that it is among only a few countries in the world to include in its postapartheid constitution a clause that expressly protects sexual orientation.

17 For example, Terry Eagleton (2003: 6) levels the following criticism against queer theory: "Not all students of culture are blind to the Western narcissism involved in working on the history of pubic hair while half the world's population lacks adequate sanitation and survives on less than two dollars a day."

18 Woodhull (2003: 1) argues that major works like *Third Wave Agenda* (1997) and *Manifesta* (2000) "exhibit little concern with the politics of gender and sexuality outside of the West." She also says that third wave websites that claim to be global are often focused more on First -World locations. She cites, for example, "Digital Eve," which characterizes itself as a global organization but that has chapters only in the United States, Canada, the United Kingdom, and Japan.

19 Alison Symington (2005) also has a fine discussion of why young feminists need to understand the roles of the World Trade Organization, the World Bank and the International Monetary Fund in global politics.

20 It is notable that, in *The Fire This Time*, Rebecca Walker, founder of the Third Wave Foundation, takes a stand against "global hypercapitalism" and also reflects on the "privileged" stance of many third wave feminists who, like herself, are educated women raised in the United States (Walker in Labaton and Martin 2004: xviii and xx).

21 The Association for Women's Rights in Development (AWID) is an international membership organization headquartered in Toronto; it has over 6, 000 members from more than one hundred countries (Wilson, Sengupta, and Evans 2005).

Conclusion

Paradigm Shifts in Feminist Thought

> In the past twenty years, the founding principles of contemporary western feminism have been dramatically challenged, with previous shared assumptions and unquestioned orthodoxies relegated almost to history. These changes have been of the order of a "paradigm shift", in which assumptions rather than conclusions are radically overturned.
>
> —Michèle Barrett and Anne Phillips

INTRODUCTION

One of the major goals of this text has been to illuminate paradigm shifts in feminist thought from the American Revolution to the present. As the chapters moved through chronological time and addressed different feminist perspectives we witnessed how certain foundational assumptions that guided first and second wave feminisms have been seriously challenged by feminist perspectives that became more prominent in postmodernity. While there were many and diverse feminisms that characterized the early modern and late modern waves of the U.S. women's movement, they shared certain underlying assumptions that have characterized modern social thought since the Enlightenment. Although the conflicts and debates between the various feminisms of the first and second waves often hid their shared assumptions, in recent decades their common ground has become more visible by challenges to this modernist terrain. The aim of this concluding chapter is to highlight these transformations in feminist thought.

As noted in chapter 1, the notion of paradigm shifts in feminist thought is not unique to this text. One of the more insightful discussions of these paradigm shifts can be found in Michèle Barrett and Anne Phillips's *Destablizing Theory* (1992). Unlike this text, these authors limited their focus to the "gulf" between "1970s and 1990s Western feminisms" where they noted a "sharp contrast" between their "shared assumptions" and "unquestioned orthodoxies" (2). By contrast, this text observed paradigm shifts over a much broader historical context. Nevertheless, I share with Barnett and Phillips the view that the crux of this shift is a transformation from the "modernist impulse" that characterized the feminisms of early and late modernity to the "postmodern impulse" that characterizes the hegemonic Western feminisms of today (2). While some of these feminisms still straddle the modern–postmodern divide, they nonetheless question fundamental assumptions that have undergirded modernist thought since the Enlightenment.

These paradigm shifts followed closely on the heels of a vast new scholarship of difference that depicted the experiences of women and men from diverse classes, races, ethnicities, sexualities, and nations. Globally, this diversification of studies has been linked to the collapse of Europe's hold on it colonial empires in the post–World War II era, as well as to the social conflicts within European and American societies in the 1960s (Lemert 2004). The rise of postcolonial feminisms called into question the essentialist and ethnocentric assumptions of Western feminisms and unveiled Western eyes to the colonialist stance embedded within many Western theoretical perspectives. They also taught us how both the colonizers and the colonized were mutually constituted in this process. Within the United States these new feminisms were spawned by the rise of new social movements in the 1960s and 1970s, such as the movements of peoples of color for civil rights and social justice as well as the anti–Vietnam War movement and the gay and lesbian rights movement. Together these new social movements highlighted the conflict, inequality, and diversity that characterized U.S. society. They also gave voice to a multiplicity of vantage points previously ignored, silenced, or hidden from history. By doing so, they fostered a new scholarship and politics of difference that, like its postcolonial counterparts, eschewed universalistic and essentialist theoretical approaches.

In their search for nonuniversalistic and nonessentialist perspectives, many U.S. feminists turned to standpoint epistemologies, a focus on historical specificity and/or to ethnomethodologically driven feminisms that focused on the concrete social practices of everyday life. Many found a new home in a branch of feminist thought that bridged the modern and the postmodern—intersectionality theory. Others found new homes in the various postmodern, poststructuralist, postcolonial, and queer projects that became more prominent in the 1980s and 1990s. The younger generation of U.S. feminists who arose in the 1990s under the banner of the third wave was profoundly influenced by these feminisms and incorporated their underlying assumptions into their own third wave agenda. For the sake of manageability, these particular feminist frameworks are referred to below as the *new feminisms of postmodernity* even though more rudimentary forms of these ideas were voiced by theorists in early and late modernity. While earlier chapters of this text highlighted the distinctions and contested terrain between these feminist perspectives, in this concluding chapter attention focuses on their common ground. *The crux of this common ground is a shared focus on difference, deconstruction and decentering.*

DECENTERING THEORY AND SCIENCE

One of the signal features of recent paradigm shifts in feminist thought is a *transformation in how both theory and science are viewed.* In modern feminist approaches, theories—whether deductive or inductive—were viewed as tested and modified by scientific evidence in the pursuit of ever greater truth or accuracy. Much attention was focused on understanding the origins or causes of women's oppression so as to link solutions to women's oppression to these causes. The goal was to develop an overarching theory that could explain the social world with ever greater veracity and guide political practice with ever greater success. As such, modern theory construction was directed toward building a single universalizing perspective that could more adequately explain social life than its predecessors.

In recent decades these particular ways of theorizing have come under intense scrutiny. In place of the privilege given to reigning theoretical paradigms and empirical validation in the modern world, the new feminisms of postmodernity present a world of plural constructions and diverse realities that call into question the notion of a single, universal truth or reality. Science comes to be viewed as a more humble enterprise as truth gives way to tentativeness and contingency. Facts are no longer treated as subversive ammunition in the struggle for freedom and emancipation, but rather as "compact faiths"[1] that often hide political agendas. The new feminisms also are more radically *reflexive* in nature—designed to expose or to make conscious the power relations by which objectified forms of knowledge are created. No knowledge is viewed as value free, neutral or objective; rather *all* knowledge is constructed by people who are situated differently in the social world, who have distinctive understandings of the world and who have access to different levels of privilege in regard to disseminating their knowledge. For these reasons, modern theories and science are criticized for creating an appearance of neutrality and impersonality that conceal class, gender, and racial subtexts. The new feminisms call for more critical and reflexive approaches where researchers acknowledge their own roles in the social construction of knowledge, as well as the differential privilege given to certain people or groups in knowledge production.

The new feminisms of postmodernity also elevate other forms of knowing—especially *socially lived knowledge*. This emphasis on everyday life experiences is central to a critique of privileged, objectified forms of knowledge. If theories are only socially constructed knowledges by privileged "experts" or formally educated peoples, then if and when these theories guide social research, the lives of the subjects of social inquiry are more likely to be molded into certain preconceived theoretical or conceptual assumptions. However, if the subjects' everyday lives are the starting point of research, knowledge emerges from lived actualities and is less likely to be shaped or constrained by the preconceived notions of privileged groups. Thus the new feminisms give more legitimacy to alternative knowledge claims and to *local and everyday experiences*. They call for *polyvocality*—the inclusion of many voices—as well as the *retrieval of subjugated knowledges* as critical acts that empower marginalized groups who previously had been silenced or deemed lesser. Modern pretensions to producing universal theories give way to theoretical inquiries characterized by a focus on *reflexivity, diversity and localism*.

One can trace these transformations in feminist thought by closely examining earlier feminist theory textbooks. For example, *Feminist Frameworks: Alternative*

Theoretical Accounts of the Relations between Women and Men, edited by Alison Jaggar and Paula Rothenberg, was a widely used feminist theory anthology that survived multiple editions from the late 1970s to the early 1990s. In their 1978 and 1984 editions, the editors view the "main tasks of feminist theory" as "accurately" describing and explaining the social realities of women's subordination and as "offering recommendations" to guide the transformation of those realities in the interests of women's emancipation. By contrast, their 1993 edition reveals a "skepticism that any single framework will be adequate for all situations" (xv–xvi). In that same year, the editors introduce the metaphor of "lenses" to reflect the partiality and multiplicity of theoretical perspectives, noting how "this metaphor signals something of a *change* in our conception of feminist frameworks" (xv; emphasis added):

> People typically employ different lenses depending on what they are studying and *their location* with respect to the object of study. . . . The metaphor of lenses also suggests the flexibility of feminist conceptual tools and the *openness and contingency of our theoretical choices*." (xii; emphasis added)

In the new feminisms of postmodernity, theory also is viewed in a more dynamic fashion—as a form of power that can both give voice and silence. While the more critical modern perspectives highlighted how the ideas and knowledges of privileged groups could dominate others, they rarely highlighted how *all* discourses and theories—even those designed to promote emancipatory ideals such as feminist theory—could simultaneously constrain and empower. Unlike their predecessors, the new feminisms have a more profound wariness of theory that is deeply wedded to their focus on difference. Postmodern and poststructuralist feminisms explicitly make this point, as do third wave feminists who frequently criticize what they call "disciplinary" or "missionary feminisms." Postcolonial theorists address this problem by decolonizing Western feminist thought, while intersectionality theorists highlight how dominant, white, class privileged feminisms silence their concerns. Standpoint feminists from a number of perspectives point to this problem when they critique "objectified forms of knowledge" (Smith 1987) or discuss how theories can be viewed as potential "power moves to dominate others through discourse" and stifle difference (Haraway 1991: 181). Hence, the overarching, universalizing theories that were the goal of earlier, modern feminists are now viewed as myopic in their failure to recognize difference and cyclopic in their pursuit of power. In contrast, the new feminisms of postmodernity are more sensitive to the *dynamic* nature of theories and to the *integral relationship between knowledge and power*.

DECONSTRUCTING SEX AND GENDER

Historically most feminist perspectives have been constructionist on some level as few accepted that existing gender arrangements were either natural or unchangeable. Feminists in both the first and second waves of the U.S. women's movement recognized gender as socially constructed, historically and culturally variable, and subject to change or reconstruction through conscious social and political action (Marshall 2008: 687). In modern feminisms it was common to distinguish between "sex" as a biological phenomenon and "gender" as a socially learned or cultural product. In contrast, the new feminisms embrace increasingly more radical forms of social constructionism. We now find feminisms that depict *both sex and gender as socially constructed* (Butler 1990, Marshall 2008, Crawley and Broad 2008). Feminist scholars today also highlight how biology is much less fixed than we once presumed and how bodies themselves are inscribed by meaning and discourses (Fausto-Sterling 1998 and 2000). While poststructuralists and queer theorists point to the fictional and unstable nature of gender identities, transgender feminists go the farthest in discussing sexual practices that lie outside the gender binary (Bornstein 1994). This strong constructionism of recent decades rejects stable sex and gender categories unlike the weaker constructionism that characterized the feminisms of early and late modernity (Connell 1987, Marshall 2008).

Critics fear that under the gaze of the new feminisms the category of "women" is "in danger of being deconstructed out of existence" (Richardson 1996: 146). No doubt the postmodern attack on essentialist categories shifted analysis away from sites of oppression that women share to a full-scale critique of group or collective categories. While much has been gained from critiquing overly homogenous constructions of the category "woman" that fail to take into account differences between them (Lorde 1984, Mohanty 1984), there also have been losses. A key concern has been the loss of the collective "we" in political mobilization (Marshall 2008: 692). Because few feminist theorists are willing to accept the wholesale deconstruction of the category woman, terms like *strategic essentialism* or *necessary fictions* are used in contemporary scholarship to rescue feminism from this political impasse (Spivak [1985] 1988).

DECONSTRUCTING SOCIAL STRUCTURE

Another important effect of the deconstruction practices that characterize the new feminisms of postmodernity is that social structure has been dereified—it is no longer viewed as a thing, but as a social process. In late modernity, race, class and gender often were treated as structural phenomena that were objective and external to individuals. The various ways that people produced and reproduced these structures in *everyday life* was virtually ignored with the notable exception of works by ethnomethodologists (West and Zimmerman 1987, Smith 1987). With the rise of the new feminisms, the focus shifted to *the linkages between human agency and structure—to how people create, re-create, or resist social structures through their everyday practices.* Now gender is frequently viewed as a *practice* rather than as a category or thing. Indeed, many contemporary feminist scholars—both modern and postmodern—talk today of doing gender, performing gender or accomplishing gender. Similar shifts have transformed analyses of race and class, as well (Bettie 2003). Consequently, in the holy trinity of the scholarship of difference—race, class and gender—are now viewed as something people do, rather than something people have. This shift to a focus on social agency and its role in the reproduction of social structures is not unique to feminism but is part of a more general trend in contemporary social thought (Ritzer 2008). Some observers claim that a theoretical perspective's ability to link social agency and social structure has become the "acid test" of its merits in contemporary theory (Archer 1988: x; Dawe 1978: 379).

Moreover, when modern feminists discussed social structure they often maintained a sharp divide between the material and the ideal spheres of social life whereby the material/economic and the discursive/cultural were treated as autonomous, independent spheres. In recent decades feminist thought has shifted toward integrating these spheres of social life. We have witnessed an extensive "turn to culture" in feminism and an increasing recognition of the links between culture, power and domination (Barrett 1999: 2–4). In turn, cultural forms of resistance are now given more attention and salience in the new feminisms (Bettie 2003, Ong [1999] 2006). Some scholars also have noted a shift "from things to words" (Barrett 1999: 18). No longer is language treated merely as a vehicle of expression that mirrors social reality. Rather it is viewed as having the power to construct rather than to simply convey meaning.[2] These developments have led critics to worry that social structural analyses is being replaced by discourse analyses and that political-economic struggles get subordinated to cultural struggles (Fraser and Naples 2004: 1111).

However, some of the most exciting developments in feminist theory today reflect moves to merge culture and materialism within a constructionist feminist framework. Not only do the new materialist feminists interweave culture as "lived experience" into their analyses, but also some of the most complex feminist analyses today are by postcolonial and transnational feminists who embrace materialist-deconstructive approaches (Spivak 1989, Mohanty [2003] 2006, Ong [1999] 2006). Such a rapprochement between the cultural and the material is achieved by pursuing a more sociological rather than simply a linguistic form of constructionism that is concerned not only with meaning-making and discourse, but also with the more sedimented aspects of social structures of power and inequality that constrain and/or enable various ways of making meaning (Marshall 2008: 697).

PARADIGM SHIFTS IN ANALYSES OF POWER AND DIFFERENCE

The modern theories that characterized early and late modern feminisms tended to conceptualize power as something which an individual or a group either does or does not have—such as material, political, and institutional resources (Gatens 1992). Despite their variations and nuances, modern feminisms, such as liberal feminism, Marxist feminism, socialist feminism and radical feminism, all hold these hierarchical, binary, and top-down views of power. In contrast, the new feminisms of postmodernity call for the demise of binary and dualistic thinking. They do not accept that power operates only in binary, top-down, and repressive ways. Rather power is viewed as dispersed and multidirectional: as both creative and repressive. Power is also dereified; it is viewed as exercised or practiced. Consequently, it too becomes a verb rather than a thing.

Even intersectionality theorists, who maintain a foothold in the modern camp with their structural views of inequality that continue to reflect the divide between the haves and the have nots, talk of matrices of domination that are more complicated than the old binary models of oppression because they entail multiple sites of simultaneous, interlocking oppressions. They also speak more broadly of *margins and centers* because each axis of oppression—such as race, class and gender—is no longer treated as separate and autonomous. Transnational and postcolonial theorists go even further to show how margins and centers are mutually constitutive. They emphasize *hybridity*—a concept that captures how power is never one way or absolute but has within it the potentiality of resistance or subversion. They also highlight how hegemonies are dispersed and scattered today, requiring transversal forms of organization and resistance across global space. All of these *multilocational conceptual schemes* call for *historically specific analyses* in contrast to many of the universalistic theories that characterized modern thought.

The matrices of domination conceptualized by intersectionality theorists maintain a hierarchical view of power relations as do the postcolonial and transnational theorists who employ deconstructive–materialist approaches. By contrast, some of the postperspectives flatten out these hierarchies with their focus on power as everywhere and their emphases on micropowers. These divergent paths among the new feminisms also reflect how *difference* is conceptualized in conflicting and competing ways (Barrett 1999). For intersectionality theorists difference is rooted in *hierarchical, structural inequalities* that affect *groups* with shared histories of oppression. For postmodernists, poststructuralists and queer theorists, *linguistic, discursive and normative prescriptions create and construct difference.* Given their heavy emphases on the deconstruction of group categories, the latter also present a more *individualistic notion of difference.* These distinctions reflect how the new feminisms continue to straddle the modern–postmodern divide in ways that result in competing and conflicting claims (33).

DECENTERING DOMINANT FEMINISMS

Hegemonic modern feminisms of the first and second waves too often expressed the vantage point of women who were privileged by their social class locations as well as by their Western, white lineages. While class differences were addressed by the more critical (and nonhegemonic) Marxist, socialist, and anarchist feminists, other forms of oppression, such as race, took a back seat to gender and class in these feminist analyses. In turn, even when these more critical modern feminisms critiqued imperialism and colonialism, they were still wedded to the notion that social progress was predicated on modernization and industrialization.

Indeed, since its inception the United States has been a modernist project but one requiring brute force to consolidate its hegemony. After the victory of the

American Revolution against British colonialism, this modernist project later consolidated its dominance through a number of other wars. During the Civil War, the modern, industrial north defeated the rural, slave south while the conquest of Mexican and Native-American lands was achieved on their respective Western battlefields. In every instance of this consolidation, people of color were subordinated. While African-Americans experienced a brief window of opportunity immediately after the Civil War, as soon as the Union troops left the south, both former slaves and free people of color lived under a system of American apartheid that kept them subordinated. As such, many people of color in the United States lived under a system of marginalization and subordination wrought by the history of internal colonialism.

It was not until these marginalized peoples gained political ground after the "long civil rights movement" that their theoretical insights began to gain hegemony in U.S. feminist thought. By articulating a framework based on multiple, interlocking oppressions and developing an epistemological stance that recognized diverse standpoints, they demonstrated how any universalistic feminist approach that claimed to speak for all women was speaking on behalf of particular interests and ignoring important differences between women. As their intersectional analyses rose to hegemony in the 1980s, it decentered the race and class-privileged feminisms of the first and the second waves.

Such decentering also took place on the global stage. During the late nineteenth and early twentieth centuries, international organizations included representatives primarily from Europe and North America, who dominated the design and content of international feminist agendas. With the success of nationalist and anticolonialist movements, after World War II women across the globe became far more active in international women's organizations, and First World feminists' hegemony began to be criticized.[3] By the mid-1980s the challenges posed by women from the "global South" to the ideological dominance of the "global North" in framing the international women's agenda had become sufficiently concerted to be effective (Tripp in Ferree and Tripp 2006: 60–61). This global shift in the center of gravity from the high-income North to the low-income South, or from the West to the rest, occurred around the same time that U.S. white, class-privileged feminisms were being decentered locally.

FEMINIST POLITICS AMID THE RADICAL INSECURITY OF POSTMODERNITY

Another major goal of this text was to historically ground paradigm shifts in feminist thought in the social transformations wrought by postmodernity. This historical grounding showed how the new feminisms that became more prominent in the 1980s and 1990s "better answered the conceptual needs of the social, economic, political and cultural problems thrown up by the New World Order" (Dirlik 1997: 502). They better captured how globalization has blurred, dispersed, and unsettled geopolitical boundaries as well as how the deindustrialization of the First World and the industrialization of the Third World have transformed the gendered and racial compositions of labor forces at home and abroad. While capital is less regulated and more anarchic than in the past, it also is more flexible and powerful despite its dispersed appearance. Accordingly, feminist scholars became more astute at analyzing the multilocationality of power relations in a world of scattered hegemonies. They also honed their skills in decoding the signs and symbols of the new information societies where the lines between artifice and reality are often blurred and where ingenious new electronic technologies have increased the speed and spread of mass culture, mass communications, mass production, and mass consumption. These seismic changes in social conditions transformed not only the gendered nature of social life but also the various ways that we think and understand this new world order.

The unruly features of flexible capitalism are mirrored in social thought by increasing skepticism regarding the rules governing scientific inquiry and what is deemed as credible knowledge. The deconstruction of science by the standpoint and postmodern epistemologies of the new feminisms not only revealed the hidden fingerprints of power underlying scientific inquiries; it also led to a radical uncertainty in regard to what constitutes "truth." The multiplicity of vantage points on social reality belied the notion of any one single truth and led many postmodern feminists to embrace an "anything goes" judgmental relativism. Radical uncertainty was exacerbated by increasing attacks on the modernist assumption that the rationalization of social life through science and technology would lead to social progress. Today, this fundamental assumption that anchored modernist thought since the Enlightenment is depicted as just another masternarrative—one that placed the modernized West at the center of human history. Rather than heralding progress, the new feminisms see more clearly how postmodernity is plagued by serious new risks, some of which threaten planetary survival. They no longer turn uncritically to science and technology to fix these problems; they are more wary of how rational means can lead to irrational ends.

The turbulent social processes that have affected our political landscape in the new millennium also contributed to the present conditions of radical uncertainty and insecurity. While 9/11 was the most dramatic event that ruptured our sense of security in the United States, it was not alone in creating these conditions. Since the turn of the new century, the United States has witnessed a heavily disputed presidential election, massive deception as the justification for the Iraq War, secret renditions to equally secret prison camps; the not-so-secret states of exception represented by Abu Ghraib, Quantanamo Bay, and the Patriot Act; government incompetence in the face of national disasters, such as Hurricane Katrina; and a great recession sparked by the toppling of finance capital's house of cards, which has since led to widespread unemployment, debt, and mortgage crises (Foster 2011: 32).

Today, within the United States, the most politically organized response to these insecurities have come not from the left, but rather from a right-wing backlash in the form of the Tea Party and its allies. Already these right-wing politics have succeeded in dismantling many government services that affect the lives of women and children—especially the lives of poor and marginalized women and children. The budget cuts to Medicaid and to social programs, such as the Women, Infant and Child (WIC) nutrition program,[4] along with recent battles over federal funding of Planned Parenthood, are illustrative here. Although the Tea Party is an umbrella term for a diverse array of political groups, many of these groups represent not only a backlash to advances in gender politics, but also to advances made by people of color over the last half century. These groups include whites who fear they are losing their hegemony in U.S. society and who view government services as disproportionately serving people of color.[5] Such racist overtones are evident in their strong anti-immigrant stance and their clamoring for President Barack Obama to produce his birth certificate (Burghart and Zeskind 2011).

On the one hand, the very existence of a backlash is testament to the advances made by the new scholarship and politics of difference. On the other hand, these unstable and threatening conditions place even greater urgency on the new feminisms of postmodernity to be as successful in gaining and maintaining their hegemony in political practice as they have been in the realm of theory. This text has stressed how feminist thought cannot be detached from its political implications—that the raison d'etre of doing feminist theory is political. While postmodernity has given rise to a number of new, exciting, and more complex feminisms that focus on deconstruction, difference, and decentering to better understand the vanishing present, it remains to be seen whether their critical theoretical insights can be translated into political practices capable of dealing with the serious conflicts, inequalities, and insecurities presented by this new world order.

NOTES

1 These are words of the Australian poet Les Murray (quoted in O'Rourke 2011).

2 Seyla Benhabib views these transformations as shifts from consciousness to language, from the denotative to the performative and from the proposition to the speech act (Benhabib in Barrett 1999: 22).

3 The membership of the International Council of Women (ICW) jumped from having 78 percent of its affiliate councils based in Europe and the United States in 1938 to having only 47 percent of its membership from these countries by 1963. Tripp traces the initial challenges to Western dominance in framing the issues of international conferences to the UN World Conference of Women in Mexico in 1975 (Tripp in Ferree and Tripp 2006: 59 and 64).

4 WIC provides federal grants to states for supplemental food, health care referrals, and nutrition education programs geared to low-income, pregnant and postpartum women and to infants and children up to the age of five who are found to be nutritionally at risk.

5 See, for example, Devin Burghart and Leonard Zeskind, "Tea Party Nationalism (2011)." This ninety-four-page report by the Institute for Research and Education on Human Rights can be found at www.teapartynationalism.com.

Glossary

By Kristin Schwartz, Laura Dean Shapiro, Dimitra Cupo, Kristin Lewis, and Susan Mann

achieved status. A social position attained on the basis of individual merit.

affirmative action. Under this legislation, designed to make up for past injustices, racial minorities and women receive preferential hiring or selection if they are qualified candidates.

American Anti-Imperialist League. Founded in 1898 to oppose U.S. acquisition of colonies and territories abroad, by the turn of the twentieth century it comprised more than one hundred affiliated organizations, approximately thirty thousand members, and over five hundred thousand contributors.

androcentric. A perspective structured around men and a male point of view.

androgyny. Where people display such a melding of masculine and feminine characteristics that the performance of distinct gender roles is no longer visible or necessary.

anthropocentric (also homocentric). An approach to the environment that places the value of human beings above other forms of nature and where nature is viewed as an object that exists to provide for the needs of human beings.

ascribed status. A social position acquired at birth, such as one's race, gender, or the social class. Ascribed statuses can heavily impact life chances, and they affect groups rather than simply individuals.

atomistic approach. Holds the individual or an individual social form (such as a nation) as primarily responsible for its achievements or failures. This approach downplays the significance of social relationships *between* individuals or *between* social forms for these outcomes.

being real. A concept Rebecca Walker borrowed from rap and hip-hop music to denote how third wave feminists should stay true to themselves rather than be driven by feminist ideas not of their own making. It is used in her critique of second wave feminism as being too disciplinary and restrictive.

bifurcated consciousness. A term developed by Dorothy Smith to highlight how the standpoint of women leads to critical insights due to the contrast between the labor involved in the social reproduction of everyday life and work outside the home. Because these two worlds operate differently, this standpoint reveals the contradictions that arise when the demands of these worlds collide.

binary thought. A Western philosophical tradition that orders social reality in dualisms whereby the first term is defined in relation to a second term, which is treated as its negation and as lesser. Examples of commonly used binaries include male/female, mind/body, culture/nature.

biopower. Michel Foucault's term for how modern states regulate their subjects through a number of subtle techniques to achieve control over bodies and populations. He focused especially on the role played by medical and social scientific discourses in creating a discourse of normality that categorized people's bodies and social practices as normal or abnormal.

blue stockings. Name deriving from the Blue Stocking Society, Elizabeth Montagu's famous eighteenth-century salon. Blue stockings later became a pejorative term for educated women. *See also* **salon culture**.

bourgeoisie. Marxist term for the capitalist class, the members of which own businesses or capital assets and hire wage labor. Marx divided this class further into financial, industrial, and mercantile capitalists.

Bread and Roses Anthem. The first anthem of the international women's movement and a commemoration of a famous strike of women workers in Lawrenceville, Massachusetts, in 1912.

capitalist-patriarchy. A concept used by socialist feminist Heidi Hartmann to argue that feminist theory must examine two realms of society—social production and social reproduction—in order for class oppression and gender oppression to be given equal importance.

Chipko movement. A grassroots, women-initiated movement to save forests from commercial felling in India. In the Hindi language, *Chipko* means to "embrace," and these women literally hugged trees to keep lumberjacks from cutting them down.

colonialism. Refers to direct social, economic, political, and cultural control of a region or country by a foreign power. In *colonies of rule*, an oligarchy of colonial administrators organizes the life of indigenous people in the colonies to facilitate the home country's economic and political aims. In *settler colonialism* the colonial administrators are accompanied by immigrants who settle on the lands of indigenous peoples. *See also* **internal colonialism**.

colonialist stance (or missionary stance). Used in postcolonial theory to criticize Western feminists when they portray Third World women as victims of stagnant, backward, cultural traditions who are unable to politically act on their own behalf and who need to be rescued by modern, enlightened feminists from the West.

colonies of rule. *See* **colonialism**.

colonizers who refused. Albert Memmi's term referring to colonists who sided with the anticolonial struggles and who often represented the interests of colonized peoples to the colonial rulers. Although they side with anticolonialist struggles, they also benefit from the class and race privilege of being colonists and lose their role once the colonized gain political ground and represent themselves.

comparable worth. The demand that jobs which require comparable skills, ability, and educational requirements should receive similar wages or salaries. This is especially relevant to sex-segregated areas of the workforce where jobs traditionally held by women often are paid less than jobs traditionally held by men that require less skill or education.

comprador intelligentsia. A term coined by theorist Kwame Anthony Appiah to highlight how many postcolonial theorists come from privileged class positions in their native Third World countries and hold prestigious academic positions at First World universities. Appiah suggests that, while postcolonial theorists may oppose neocolonialism in the abstract, they reap material rewards by teaching and publishing about it.

compulsory heterosexuality. Adrienne Rich's concept challenging the so-called naturalness of heterosexuality. It refers to how heterosexuality has been rigidly enforced by patriarchal institutions to maintain women's subservience through emotional and erotic loyalty to men. Rich asks: if heterosexuality is natural, why do societies need to employ such violent strictures to enforce it?

concept. An abstraction used to name and to organize concrete perceptions of reality in intelligible ways.

confessional. Michel Foucault's metaphor for the way modern societies use various types of self-confession to elicit information and to control people's practices so as to keep them within normative guidelines. Examples include interrogations, interviews, therapies, or exams.

conscientization. A term used by third wave feminists to refer to the practice of relating personal experiences to social structural analyses.

Convention on the Elimination of All Forms of Discrimination against Women (CEDAW). Adopted by the United Nations in 1979, this legislation called on all U.N. member-states to eliminate attitudes and practices that discriminated against women. To date, 180 countries have signed this legislation.

cult of domesticity (or cult of true womanhood). A set of ideals stemming from the doctrine of separate spheres that romanticized women's place in the home as loving wife, nurturing mother, and moral servant.

decommodification. When certain social needs, such as basic food, shelter or health care, are citizen rights in a society rather than goods or services that must be purchased. This term has been used to describe social services in social democratic welfare states.

deep ecology. A radical environmentalist perspective that calls for an ecocentric approach to the environment and that places preserving and restoring wilderness and wildlife above human need.

deindustrialization. The process that results when corporations move manufacturing abroad so that the manufacturing share of total employment in the home country drops significantly and is replaced by lower paying service jobs.

development of underdevelopment. A term dependency theorists use to highlight the interrelated processes that foster First World enrichment through the exploitation of Third World countries that blocks the latter's development.

diaspora. A term used to capture the notion of a dispersal or scattering of peoples from their homelands to multiple locations as a consequence of global labor migrations.

disciplinary feminism. A term highlighting how feminism as a discourse and practice can be restrictive, punitive, and controlling when it exercises authority and judgment over women's ideas or practices when those practices differ from or challenge feminist ideals.

discourse. Refers to historically specific structures of concepts, ideas, statements, and categories that enable one to speak, think, and act.

disidentification. A term used by Astrid Henry to describe the tendency of emerging social movements to exaggerate their claims to uniqueness in order to emphasize how they are distinct from earlier social movements.

doctrine of coverture. Common law doctrine holding that once a man and woman are married, they become one under the law. This *one* was the man, who controlled the property and income of the household and who had the right to chastise or punish his wife and children.

doctrine of separate spheres. A nineteenth-century ideology that relegated women's roles to the private sphere of the home and men's roles to the public sphere outside of the home.

do-it-yourself (DIY) feminism. Used by third wave feminists as a call to action emphasizing the ability of young feminists to undertake activities without relying on outside help or guidance. It also implies a more individualist approach whereby feminism can be anything an individual wants it to be and that holds that women should not be restricted by political ideals not of their own making.

dowry-deaths (or bride-burning). The practice of husbands killing their wives when dowries are not paid. These killings are often made to look like they resulted from kitchen fires.

ecocentric approach (or biocentric approach). An approach to the environment whereby humans are viewed as just one of many parts of the natural world and interdependent with it. Humans are not viewed as morally or ethically superior to nonhuman forms of nature.

ecofeminism. A term used to describe a diverse range of women's efforts to save the earth and transformations in feminist thought that have resulted in new conceptualizations of the relationship between the domination of women and the domination of nature.

Écritire féminine. A concept used by French feminists that called upon women to write and speak about their own lives, bodies, and experiences to transcend male-biased language, symbolic systems, and philosophies.

empirical. Evidence observable through one's sense of sight, sound, smell, taste, or touch and verifiable by others.

environmental justice movement. A multiracial, multiclass grassroots movement which emerged in the 1980s and organized around environmental issues that disproportionately affect communities of color, such as pollution, toxic hazards, and the location of waste facilities.

environmental racism. Refers to how race is an independent variable, not reducible to social class, in predicting the distribution of environmental hazards and pollution in societies.

epistemic privilege. When one knowledge claim is judged as more valid or superior to another.

epistemic violence. A term coined by postcolonial feminist Gayatri Chakravorty Spivak to refer to the destruction of indigenous languages, culture, and thought that accompanies colonial conquest.

epistemology. Refers to the study of who can be a knowledge producer, how knowledge is produced, and what constitutes privileged knowledge.

equal pay. Equal pay for work of equal value has long been a feminist demand. The Equal Pay Act was passed in 1963, and although women's earnings vis-à-vis those of men have risen, they still stand at about 80 percent of men's earnings for similar work.

erotophobia. A fear of the erotic that legitimizes only certain sexual practices and allows them only in the context of legal, religious, and social sanctions (such as marriage and procreation).

essentialism. An approach that attributes certain qualities, traits, or behaviors to all members of a group.

ethnocentrism. Viewing one's own cultural practices as superior to other cultural practices.

Euro-American master narrative. *See* **Western narrative.**

Eurocentric (or Euro-American centric). Privileging European or Western locations and vantage points with an implicit or explicit assumption of superiority.

European Union (EU). An agreement between European nations to remove restrictions on the movement of commodities, services, capital, and labor with the goal of competing more successfully on the world market. Established in 1993, it now includes more than two dozen nations.

expressive roles. In sex role theory, these are emotional, people-oriented, caretaking roles assigned to women that are contrasted to the impersonal, instrumental roles assigned to men.

family wage. A wage adequate for one (usually the male) breadwinner of a family to financially support a spouse or partner and children.

feminine mystique. Concept introduced by Betty Friedan in her book of the same name published in 1963; it refers to how learned "femininity" undermined gender equality. Friedan lamented how young women were taught to pity "unfeminine" career women and how they eschewed the opportunities for higher education, political rights, and financial independence that the first wave had struggled to achieve.

feminism's dissenting daughters. A term used to describe certain third wave feminists writing in the early 1990s who were highly critical of what they saw as the sexually repressive and victim-oriented stance of their second wave predecessors.

feminist hybridity. A phrase emphasizing how third wave feminists embrace contradictions and subversive performances that deconstruct conventional notions of gender, race, and sexuality.

feminist mystique. A term coined by Betty Friedan in 1981 to argue that 1980s' career women were no less oppressed than 1960s' stay-at-home moms. Friedan reversed her earlier call for women to gain power, financial independence, and self-fulfillment through work outside the home when she saw how her daughter's generation ran themselves ragged in the name of feminism trying to be both fulltime career women and homemakers/mothers. Her new emphasis was placed on the well-being of family and social relationships.

feminization of global migration. A phenomenon witnessed in the 1980s when women made up an increasing proportion of people who migrated from poor to rich countries in search of jobs.

finance capital. Enterprises that generate profits from lending money, making investments, and/or manipulating currencies (such as banks or insurance companies) in contrast to industrial capitalist enterprises that generate profit from the actual production of commodities.

first wave. The surge of U.S. women's rights activism beginning in the 1830s and culminating around the campaign for woman suffrage that ended or at least went into abeyance in 1920 with passage of the Nineteenth Amendment to the U.S. Constitution.

First World. A concept developed during the cold war to refer to highly developed, industrial, capitalist countries.

flexible capitalism. A term used to reflect how transnational corporations adapt to changing political and economic conditions and tap into different labor pools (skilled or unskilled, blue collar or white collar, foreign or domestic) regardless of where they are located so long as optimal production, infrastructural, marketing, and political conditions exist.

gender binary. Refers to the idea that humans exist in two essential, biologically determined forms (male and female). This binary is sustained by dividing people into gender roles based on their presumed location as male or female, disciplining people into believing in the naturalness of their gender location, and policing any violations to the male/female gender order.

gender dysphoria. Refers to a person's sensation of being trapped in a body of the "wrong" sex.

genderqueer movement. This movement celebrates and works in the political interests of those who break free of the constraints of the gender binary by subversively playing with gender norms, living in between genders, and embodying both, neither, or multiple genders.

genocide. The deliberate, systematic killing of a racial, cultural, or religious group.

girlies. Third wave feminists who reclaimed the word "girl" from its diminutive connotations and address what they see as the antifeminine, anti-joy features of the second wave. Girlies often wear pink and celebrate "pretty power" to make feminism more fun and attractive.

global North. A term used by contemporary theorists to refer to high-income, high-consumption societies.

global South. A term used by contemporary theorists to refer to low-income, low-consumption societies.

god trick. A critical term used to refer to scientists' claims that they can view the world in a detached, impartial, objective, and value-free manner.

Guerrilla Girls. Groups of anonymous women who dress up in gorilla masks and protest the underrepresentation of women in visual culture. The first group was formed in the United States in the mid-1980s. Since then, their numbers have increased, and they engage in various forms of performance politics at museums and visual culture venues across the county and abroad.

Harlem Renaissance. A cultural movement that spanned the period roughly between the 1920s and the 1930s and that enabled African–Americans to challenge racism and transform negative racial stereotypes through their intellect and the production of art, music, and literature.

heteronormativity. The assumption that heterosexuality is natural, normal, and socially appropriate. It becomes the standard by which other sexual practices are deemed deviant.

hidden injuries of social class. A term used to describe the damage done to people's self-esteem when they are made to feel inadequate because of their lower class position.

hierarchicalizing oppressions. Treating one form of oppression as more fundamental and important than another.

historical specificity. A term used by feminists who call for concrete analyses of a specific time and place to avoid the dangers of making broad, sweeping generalizations that often ignore differences between women and differences in how various social phenomena affect women.

historicism. This approach places social theorists and their works within their historical context and social locations (such as gender, race, and class) to reveal the socially situated nature of knowledge. The focus is not on the truth or falsity of knowledge claims but, rather, on revealing the hidden power relations behind the construction of theories and knowledge.

homonationalism. A term developed by queer theorists to critique the incorporation of normative gay men and lesbians into a pro-U.S. nationalist rhetoric that distinguishes morally upright patriots (both heterosexual and homosexual) from perversely sexualized terrorist enemies.

homonormativity. A term developed by queer theorists to critique gay and lesbian politics (such as the LGBT political agenda) that are organized exclusively around the pursuit of equal rights and the rights granted to white, middle-class heterosexuals, such as privacy, domesticity, consumption, and patriotic citizenship.

homophobia. Heterosexuals' fear of and discrimination against lesbians and gay men.

homo sacer. A term used by Georgio Agamben to refer to people who have been defined as lying outside political and juridical boundaries. Because they lie outside of these boundaries, things can be done to these people that cannot be done to other humans. They can be killed, tortured or reduced to utter bare life by the traumatic use of political power.

hybridity. In postcolonial theory, a term used to contest the notion that colonialism remakes indigenous peoples and cultures in its own image. Rather than abject capitulation, colonial domination is always imperfect because the colonizer and the colonized are mutually constructed. This leaves space for resistance and subversion by the colonized.

identity politics. Where people's politics are rooted in group identities, such as their race, gender, or sexual orientation. Identity is the motivation for political action and the basis for delineating political concerns, such as the lesbian and gay rights movement.

imperialism. A foreign power's forceful economic, political, and cultural domination over another nation or geopolitical formation. As contrasted to premodern forms of imperialism, modern imperialism destroys indigenous forms of production by usurping and privatizing land and by forcing premodern economies into market economies.

informal economy. Refers to unregulated labor characterized by the absence of a contractual relationship and conditions of work and pay that are not legally regulated or protected.

institutional ethnography. A term used by Dorothy Smith to describe her research, which examines how the social practices of everyday life affect, are affected by, and are linked to the social practices undertaken in social institutions and organizations. It makes visible how social practices are the anatomy of social life and how they can reproduce or resist the status quo.

instrumental rationality (or technocratic approach). The belief that rational means, such as science and technology, can solve social and environmental problems. Critics argue that this approach ignores how rational means can produce these problems and, thus, how rational means can have irrational ends.

instrumental roles. In sex role theory, these are the impersonal and task-oriented roles assigned to men that are contrasted to the expressive, emotional roles played by women.

internal colonialism (or settler colonialism). Refers to colonies existing *within* a country where subordinate groups (often of a different race) are relegated to menial and low-paying jobs, denied the citizenship rights held by the dominant group, and forced to assimilate the language and culture of the dominant group. The peoples and lands that constitute these internal colonies were historically established by force, such as through slavery or military conquest.

International Monetary Fund (IMF). An agency established at the end of World War II to oversee the international monetary system to ensure the stability of currency and to stimulate trade. Its efforts later expanded to regulate repayments of loans made to indebted countries.

International Women's Day. Celebrated each year on March 8 to honor the social, political, and cultural achievements of women. It was established by the Second International in 1910 to commemorate major strikes by women workers.

intersexed. Refers to persons born with some combination of the physical characteristics that typically distinguish males from females.

judgmental relativism. The postmodern epistemological stance that, because all knowledge is socially situated and socially constructed, no one knowledge claim or vantage point can be judged as superior or more valid than any other.

lavender menace. A term used to describe the fears of some feminists that lesbians were undermining and discrediting the women's movement. It arose in the late 1960s after Betty Friedan called lesbian issues the "lavender herring" of the women's movement.

lesbian continuum. A concept used by Adrienne Rich to highlight the importance of a wide range of women-centered experiences, such as mother–daughter relationships, sister-to-sister relations, and friendships as well as well as sexual intimacy between women. This continuum was used not only to describe lesbianism as more than simply a sexual issue but also to foster common ground for unifying lesbian and straight women.

Liberal welfare regimes. A form of government welfare that alleviates the worst effects of poverty but where welfare is available only to households whose incomes fall below a certain government-determined poverty line. It serves as a form of labor control; if benefits are meager and stigmatized, it is assumed that most people will choose employment over welfare.

life as aesthetics (or life as a work of art). Based on the assumption that the self is constructed, Michel Foucault uses this concept to suggest that individuals live their lives as if they were constructing a work of art; hence, continually aiming to enhance them.

lived messiness. A phrase used to describe how third wave feminists embrace contradictions and deconstruct rigid notions of gender, race, and sexuality through subversive practices.

Luddite position. A contemporary term used for people who view technology as the cause of social problems. The Luddites were British textile workers in the nineteenth century who destroyed machinery to protest the working conditions that accompanied the industrial revolution.

maldevelopment. A term introduced by Vandana Shiva to critically interrogate what is meant by "development" by highlighting the negative impacts of the modernization of premodern indigenous societies.

masternarrative. A partial view or particular vantage point that claims privilege or superiority. *See* also **totalizing theories.**

matrix of domination. A concept developed by Patricia Hill Collins to describe multiple axes of privilege and oppression. Within this matrix, people have a social location in terms of structural forms of oppression as race, ethnicity, social class, gender, and/or sexual orientation. Thus people can simultaneously be both oppressed and oppressors because they could occupy social locations of penalty and privilege. Wealthy black males, for example, have privilege by their class and gender positions but are penalized by their racial location.

microcredits to poor women. A policy to reduce poverty in developing countries through small loans from financial institutions or private donors to poor women for use in income-generating activities.

missionary feminism. *See* **disciplinary feminism.**

missionary framework. *See* **colonialist stance.**

model monopolies (or ideological codes). Refers to normative prescriptions that are replicated and reinforced by discourses from multiple and various sites. Because similar messages appear from diverse sites, the message appears to have greater truth value or validity.

modern imperialism. *See* **imperialism.**

modernity. A term used to describe the social patterns set in motion by the Industrial Revolution that began in Western Europe in the mideighteenth century. Modernization refers to the process of industrialization and the political, social, and cultural changes that accompanied it, such as urbanization, the increasing use of science and technology, the rationalization and secularization of social life, the rise of the nation-state, and an increasing focus on the individual.

Ms. magazine. Established in 1971, *Ms.* was the first mass-produced, commercially successful, U.S. women's magazine to feature prominent women demanding the repeal of laws that criminalized abortion, to advocate for passage of the Equal Rights Amendment, to rate presidential candidates on women's issues, to commission a national study on rape, and to put domestic violence and sexual harassment on the cover of a women's magazine.

municipal housekeeping. A term used for women's environmental activism in the nineteenth and early twentieth centuries. In an era when political activism by women was viewed as improper, framing their concerns over municipal sanitation and clean air, water and food, as extensions of domestic roles within the home gave their environmental activism more legitimacy.

National American Woman Suffrage Association (NAWSA). Formed in 1890 through a merger of the National Women's Suffrage Association and the American Women's Suffrage Association, NAWSA was the largest suffrage organization during the feminist first wave.

National Association of Colored Women (NACW). In 1896, the three largest federations of black women's clubs unified to form the NACW. This organization boasted more than one hundred local women's clubs and predated the founding of the National Association for the Advancement of Colored People (NAACP).

national liberation movement. A social movement to free a country or region of colonial rule.

National Organization for Women (NOW). Founded by liberal feminists in 1966, NOW has been the largest feminist organization in the United States over the past half century.

National Woman's Party (NWP). Formed by Alice Paul in 1916 to work exclusively for a federal woman suffrage amendment using a wider array of tactics that Paul had learned from her contact with militant British suffragists. Members of the NWP picketed the White House, organized parades and demonstrations, went on hunger strikes, and some were imprisoned for their activism.

neocolonialism. A term developed to describe the indirect economic, political, and cultural control of a formally independent country by a foreign power.

neoliberalism. An economic ideology that arose in the late 1970s based on open, unrestricted markets and free trade. It promotes competitive capitalism, deregulation, and reductions in government size and government spending in favor of privatization.

nepantilism. A term used by Gloria Anzaldúa to describe how people of mixed heritage feel as if they straddle different cultures and are torn in multiple directions by the contrasts between the diverse cultures that constitute their identity.

New Left. Refers to the new social movements of late modernity, such as the civil rights movement, the women's movement, the gay and lesbian rights movement, and the anti–Vietnam war movement. Along with focusing on social class, the New Left addressed the conflicts and cleavages generated by inequalities of race, gender, sexuality, and global location.

new mestiza consciousness. A term developed by Gloria Anzaldúa to express how people of mixed heritage can empower themselves by recognizing the richness of the contradictions and ambiguities entailed in their hybridity. This new consciousness is a powerful critique of binary thought because it treasures diversity and the fluidity of identities.

NIMBY (not in my backyard). A grassroots movement by residents who oppose environmental and toxic wastes being dumped in their neighborhoods or backyards.

noble savage. A settler-colonial stereotype that romanticizes indigenous peoples as unencumbered by civilization, living in harmony with nature, and as having courage and untutored wisdom as a result of their harsh life experiences.

nongovernmental organizations (NGOs). Nonprofit organizations that operate globally but are not officially representing a particular government or government agency.

normativity. A term used by queer theorists to refer to conventional forms of association, belonging, and identification that are prescribed as socially appropriate at a given time and place. Critiquing normativity is a major premise of queer theory.

North American Free Trade Agreement (NAFTA). Signed into law in 1993, an agreement between Canada, the United States, and Mexico that reduced barriers to trade and investment between the signatory countries.

Old Left. Term referring to the political perspectives of Marxism and anarchism that arose in the nineteenth-century with the goal of establishing societies free of oppression. While the Old Left struggled against many forms of oppression, their political movements focused on class oppression and championed the working class as the primary agent of revolutionary social change.

one-third versus the two-thirds world. A phrase used to highlight the stark inequalities between the developed and maldeveloped areas of the world as well as the disproportionate number of people who suffer from maldevelopment globally. *See also* **maldevelopment**.

Orientalism. A term developed by Edward Said to highlight the socially constructed and mythic notion of the "Orient" imposed upon the land and peoples of the colonized East that served to "other" this region and to mutually construct the concept of the West as superior.

outsourcing. Where certain aspects of a production process are transferred to foreign countries where labor is cheaper and/or working conditions are less regulated and more profitable.

palimpsestic. A palimpsest is a parchment that has been inscribed and re-inscribed with the previous text being imperfectly erased and partly visible. Postcolonial theorists use this concept as a metaphor for their view of social change and sociohistorical time as imperfect erasures whereby the past is always visible in the present.

panopticon (or panoptical gaze). Michel Foucault's term to describe the powerful effects on individuals when institutional and normative surveillance is internalized. This modern technique of power leads people to police their own behaviors and practices in order to avoid stigma or punishment and, thereby, reduces the need to use direct force in controlling deviance.

paradigm shift. A fundamental change in the theoretical assumptions underlying an entire school of thought or worldview. As conceptualized by Thomas Kuhn (1962), a paradigm shift results not simply in different scientific conclusions but, also, in a transformation of the entire conceptual framework of social thought prevailing in a given discipline or area of study.

patriarchy. Institutionalized male dominion over women and children.

performance. Ritualized acts or practices by an individual that construct the social fiction of a psychological interiority to identities, such as race, gender, or social class.

performance politics. The performance of contradictory or stigmatized practices to expose the unnatural, artificial, and socially constructed nature of identities.

performativity. A concept developed by Judith Butler to discuss and to dereify the impact of social structure on people's lives. It highlights how social structures and institutional norms are continually reinforced and reproduced through peoples' performances or actions.

personal is political. Second wave slogan asserting that gender-related problems treated as personal problems should be addressed politically, as problems rooted in social institutions. It also enjoined feminists to live their politics in their everyday lives, thus motivating transformations at the level of both the individual and society.

political generation. Refers to the life experiences and political concerns of an historical era when one becomes a political activist; it may include more than one chronological generation, such as when one speaks of becoming politicized in the cold war era or the post-911 era.

politics of respectability. A term coined by historian Evelyn Brooks Higginbotham to describe the efforts of African–American women during the Progressive Era to promote temperance, cleanliness of person and property, thrift, etiquette, and sexual morality.

polymorphously perverse. A Freudian term used to describe innate, undifferentiated sexual impulses of very young children that encompass a wide range of pleasure-objects and that require humans to be taught socially acceptable or normative sexual practices.

polyvocality. A term highlighting the value of including many diverse voices or multiple vantage points in the creation of knowledge.

pomosexuals. Individuals who celebrate unconventional sexual practices that lie beyond the gender binary and who explicitly acknowledge how their approach to gender is rooted in postmodern or poststructuralist epistemological assumptions. *See also* **genderqueer**.

pop bead approach. A term used by Deborah King to highlight the inadequacies of treating multiple oppressions as separate and distinct rather than as simultaneous and interlocking.

postcolonial. A critical concept that refers to engaging with and challenging colonial discourses as well as the social, economic, political, and cultural legacies of colonialism.

postfeminism. Refers to a number of diverse media claims in the 1980s that support for the women's movement had decreased; that feminism was no longer relevant; that antifeminism had increased among young women, women of color, and homemakers; and that even women who supported women's rights were reluctant to identify as feminists.

postmodernity. refers to the new social, economic, political, and cultural conditions that arose over the past half century. These include how globalization has blurred, dispersed, and unsettled geopolitical boundaries; how the new electronic technologies have increased the speed and spread of mass culture, mass communications, mass production, and mass consumption; and how the deindustrialization of the First World and the industrialization of the Third World have transformed the gendered and racial compositions of labor forces at home and abroad.

power feminism. A term coined by Naomi Wolf to promote a new, more aggressive direction in feminist activism that did not dwell on the victimization of women but modeled itself on the "old boys' network" through which men pooled their power and shared it with their friends and political allies.

primitive accumulation. Karl Marx's term for how the origins of capitalism entailed brute force and violence to transform premodern economies into industrial capitalism. Rosa Luxemburg argued that it was also a recurring process in the imperial drive of capitalism into foreign lands.

privileged discourse. A knowledge claim or a way of knowing that is given more status, credibility, and power than other forms of knowledge.

privileging the knowledge of the oppressed. An epistemological stance taken by many standpoint theorists who argue that the social locations of marginalized or subordinated people provide superior vantage points for critically understanding power relations.

problem that has no name. Betty Friedan's term for the persistent depression found among housewives of her era, which she attributed to traditional gender roles that provided few avenues for individual self-fulfillment for these women.

production for exchange. A Marxist phrase that describes labor that produces commodities (goods for sale) or that garners an income. It is used by Marxist and socialist feminists to analytically distinguish different types of work done by women.

production for use. A Marxist phrase that refers to unpaid labor performed for immediate use or consumption. It is used by Marxist and socialist feminists to highlight how the unpaid labor done by homemakers (such as cooking, cleaning, and child care) places women in a dependent position financially in market economies.

proletariat. A Marxist term for wage laborers or the working class in a capitalist system. In Marx's era, wage laborers were primarily blue-collar workers.

queer. A critique of all things oppressively normal, especially conventional ideas about sex. As such, it embraces sexual and gender difference.

queer sex. Refers to a broad range of sexual practices that are unified by the ways they challenge gender and heterosexual norms. Sexualities that are kinky (involving fetishes, BDSM, or sex toys), cross-generational, nonmonogamous, non–love based, promiscuous, for-pay, unsafe, and/or homosexual exemplify sexual practices that do not conform to traditional, state-sanctioned ideas about the romantic, procreative, and heterosexual purposes of human sexuality.

radical alterity. A concept postcolonial theorists use to highlight ways in which the "other" is not an arbitrary or autonomous category but, rather, necessary to establish the notion of the "self." Thus, the "self" "and the "other" are mutually constituted. *See also* **othering.**

Radical Cheerleaders. Performance artists and political activists who dress up in mock cheerleader uniforms and lead protest chants at political demonstrations and other political events.

Redstockings. A radical feminist organization that reclaimed the pejorative label "bluestockings," used for educated women in the nineteenth century, by combining it with the color red to signify their radical politics. Their 1969 Redstockings Manifesto was one of the earliest statements of the assumptions and goals of radical feminism.

reflexivity. The recognition that one's ideas and behaviors are influenced by one's own social location and how one's ideas and behaviors affect other people. A reflexive approach to research methods requires that researchers acknowledge their roles in knowledge production and how their social locations might influence the results of their studies. It also requires that they consider how their research and findings may impact others.

reification. To treat people, social processes, or social relationships as if they were things; to objectify human relations or human beings.

reproductive justice. A term used by women of color to emphasize their concerns about having the freedom to give birth, to keep their children, and to not have contraception or sterilization forced upon them.

Riot Grrrls. Feminists who made space for women within punk rock by creating their own music and zines, developing their own record labels, and ensuring that mosh pits were safe for women. They inspired many third wave feminists to engage in political activism.

runaway plants. Enterprises that move to foreign countries in search of cheap labor and/or more profitable and less regulated working conditions.

salon culture. Gathering places where intellectual, social, political, and cultural elites exchange ideas. Before higher education was open to women, salons enabled them to share their work, engage in critical analyses, and be introduced to the ideas of other intellectuals.

sati. The practice of widow immolation (wives throwing themselves on the funeral pyre of their late husbands) in certain castes and regions of India. It was legally banned in 1829.

second wave. The resurgence of U.S. feminist activism in the 1960s; this wave ends or at least suffers major setbacks with the defeat of the Equal Rights Amendment (ERA) in 1982.

Second World. A cold war–era concept referring to industrially developed socialist and/or communist countries.

Seneca Falls Declaration of Sentiments. A document listing the political demands approved by attendees of the first women's rights convention held in the United States, in Seneca Falls, New York, in 1848. Modeled on the Declaration of Independence, the Declaration enumerated the various ways women were denied civil rights in that era.

separatism. Women's conscious and willful separation from various aspects of patriarchal control. In its purest form it would mean not living with or having anything to do with adult males.

settler colonialism. *See* **colonialism** and **internal colonialism**.

sex-love (or free-love). Term first wave feminists used to refer to the right to marry for love, to have sex with someone you loved, and for women to have the same sexual rights as men.

sex role theory. An approach to understanding gender that highlights the role of the normative structure of society by focusing on how individuals learn and perform socially prescribed and socially appropriate gender roles.

sex-segregated occupations. This refers to how some occupations traditionally have been gender specific, whereby women dominate in certain areas of work such as nurses and elementary school teachers , while men dominate in other areas of work such as plumbers or electricians. (See the term "comparable worth" above for the negative implications of sex-segregated occupations).

sexual reformism. A thread of feminist theorizing beginning in the late eighteenth century that emphasized a woman's right to make sexual choices based on rationality, dignity, and autonomy.

Shakespeare's sister. A fictional character developed by Virginia Woolf to lament how women voices were missing from literature because they were denied opportunities for education and writing. Woolf calls on women to take up the pen and write their way into history.

Sisterhood Is Global Institute. Established in 1984, this organization was the first U.S. feminist think tank to do research and develop policies on behalf of women globally.

situated knowledges. A phrase used to highlight how all knowledge is constructed from and influenced by one's social location (such as race, gender, and class).

social agency. An individual's ability to act on and influence the world. It emphasizes how people construct the social world in which they live through their ideas and practices.

social democratic welfare regimes. A form of welfare based on the principles of universalism and decommodification. Government services and public insurance systems extend to the entire population, and basic necessities (such as food, shelter, and health care) are viewed as citizen rights that are funded through graduated taxation.

social reproduction of labor power. A term used by second wave Marxist and socialist feminists to refer to the day-to-day reproduction of labor power through domestic labor, such as how cooking, cleaning, and caretaking enable people to go back to work each day refueled and rejuvenated. It also includes the intergenerational reproduction of labor power through childbirth and childrearing.

social structure. Refers to how patterned social relations of privilege and inequality, as well as norms governing socially appropriate behavior, become institutionalized in societies such that they shape and influence people's ideas and practices. The coercive effects of social structures are evident in the penalties people face when they violate, resist, or try to change institutional norms and social arrangements, such as stigma, shunning, arrest, and/or corporal punishment.

socially lived knowledge. Refers to knowledge gained from everyday life experiences in contrast to knowledge garnered from formal education or training.

state of exception. A concept introduced by Georgio Agamben to refer to the paradox of suspending laws in the name of preserving law. Examples include the suspension of normal laws and judicial processes to deal with national emergencies or national security.

state violence. A term used by women of color to highlight how law enforcement policies often entail heightened surveillance, regulation, and social control over populations due to their race, class, and/or national status. They contrast this with white, class-privileged feminists' interests in working with law enforcement agencies to deal with violence against women.

Stonewall riots. Riots that took place at a gay bar in New York City in 1969 that are cited as the defining event marking the beginning of the U.S. lesbian and gay rights movement.

STOP-ERA movement. An antifeminist movement led by Phyllis Schlafly in the 1970s and early 1980s to stop passage of the Equal Rights Amendment to the U.S. Constitution.

strategic essentialism. A concept introduced by Gayatri Chakravorty Spivak that refers to using collective or group identity categories for practical political purposes while simultaneously recognizing how such group categories erase differences between individuals within the group.

strategy of dismissal. Ostracizing the ideas or actions of group members that are found to be threatening to group cohesion or control.

structural adjustment programs (SAPs). Methods of repayment imposed by the IMF and the World Bank on heavily indebted countries to ensure that loans do not go into default. These measures include reducing government funds spent on social programs (such as health care, education, and welfare) and focusing economic activity on export production.

subaltern. A concept that Antonio Gramsci used for subordinate groups in general and especially for groups (such as peasants) that did not fit easily into Marxist class categories. Feminist postcolonial theorist Gayatri Chakravorty Spivak extended the utility of this term to include women and other postcolonial subjects.

subcontracting. A practice used by multinational and transnational corporations that involves hiring local entrepreneurs for certain parts of the production process to reduce costs and risks.

subjugated knowledges. Refers to knowledges (often of subordinate groups and marginalized people) that dominant groups have ignored, silenced, or deemed to be less credible.

Take Back the Night marches. First held in Pittsburgh in 1977, the purpose of these marches is to dramatize women's right to enjoy public spaces in safety without fear of rape. These marches continue to be held today in many cities across the United States.

technocratic approach. *See* **instrumental rationality**.

theories. Developed discourses that offer a general account of how a range of phenomena are interconnected by placing individual items within a larger context to understand both the whole and the parts constituting that whole. Feminism is incipiently theoretical in that it understands the plights of individual women as connected with each other, as instances of *systemic subordination* rather than as the results of individual, accidental, or coincidental misfortune.

third wave. The resurgence of U.S. feminist activism in the 1990s, especially by younger feminists who came of adult age after the second wave.

Third World. A concept referring to all countries in the post–World War II era (whether capitalist or socialist) that were not industrialized but where large proportions of the population were still engaged in direct agricultural production.

totalizing theories. Also referred to as grand theories or master narratives, totalizing theories attempt to make sense of human history by offering comprehensive, universalistic explanations of social phenomena. Feminist totalizing theories attempt to explain all of the various features of women's oppression by using one overarching theoretical framework and assuming that there is only one correct theory that can be generalized to all situations or cases.

transnational. A term that highlights how new social forms transcend or fail to correspond to the boundaries of the national state. This term is used to highlight the multidirectionality of global influences, the multilocationality of many people's lives, and the social relations that cut across global locations.

transversal politics. An approach to transnational feminist politics aimed at enhancing polyvocality and reducing conflicts between women by dialogue that crosses borders both horizontally (such as shared experiences by race, class, and sexuality) and vertically (such as different positions of power and privilege). A person cannot speak for others unless democratically elected to do so, and advocates do not have to be members of the constituency for whom they advocate, as in the case of identity politics. It is the message, not the messenger, that is important, and all views are recognized as partial.

victim feminism. A term coined by third wave feminist Naomi Wolf to criticize the second wave for overemphasizing how women were oppressed and victimized. She calls for feminists to place more emphasis on women's power and social agency.

voluntary motherhood. A nineteenth-century feminist demand that women have the right to abstain from having sexual relations with their husbands. It was a position taken by first wave feminists who did not support birth control or abortion but who wanted some control over reproduction.

Western narrative (also Euro-American master narrative). Refers to modern theories and discourses which began with the Enlightenment and that view modernization and economic growth as key to social progress. This narrative also assumes that economic growth is accompanied by the rationalization and secularization of social life as well as increasing standards of living and political freedoms.

white solipsism. A distorted vision resulting from viewing the world only through the experiences and vantage point of white people in a racist society.

woman-identified-woman. A term coined by radical feminist Charlotte Bunch to describe women who are committed to meeting each other's political, economic, and emotional needs rather than giving their primary commitments to men.

womanist. A term coined by Alice Walker and embraced by many African–American women to highlight how their concerns are different from those of privileged, white, feminists.

World Bank. Established in 1944 as the International Bank for Reconstruction and Development to oversee the rebuilding of Europe after World War II, the World Bank has since become the largest dispenser of development capital to Third World countries.

World Trade Organization (WTO). Established in 1995 to oversee and regulate international trade agreements. Along with the World Bank and the International Monetary Fund, the WTO is one of the major political institutions affecting global economic practices today.

Box Credits

1.1. "What Is Feminism?" Excerpt from pp.158–161 of *The Feminist Dictionary*, edited by Cheris Kramarae and Paula A. Treichler. Boston: Pandora, 1985. With appreciation to Cheris Kramarae.

1.2. "Minimalist Definitions of Feminism." Excerpt from pp. 27–28 of Chris Beasley, *What Is Feminism? An Introduction to Feminist Theory*. Thousand Oaks, Calif.: Sage, 1999.

1.3. "The Unforgivable Transgression of Being Caster Semenya," blog post by Tavia Nyong'o, September 8, 2009; http://bullybloggers.wordpress.com/tag/caster-semenya. With appreciation to bullybloggers.com.

1.4. "Poetry Is Not a Luxury," by Audre Lorde. From pp. 37–38 of *Sister/Outsider*. Trumansburg, N.Y.: Crossing, 1984.

2.1. "Selected Letters from the Adams Family Correspondence," by Abigail Adams and John Adams, 1776. From pp. 10–11 of *The Feminist Papers: From Adams to de Beauvoir*, edited by Alice S. Rossi. New York: Bantam, 1974.

2.3. "1968—National Organization for Women (NOW) Bill of Rights." From pp. 439–440 of Judith Hole and Ellen Levine, *Rebirth of Feminism*. New York: Quadrangle, 1975.

3.1. "Sappho's Reply," by Rita Mae Brown. From *Poems*. Freedom, Calif: Crossing, 1971.

3.2. "The Bitch Manifesto," by Joreen [Jo Freeman]. 1968. Reprinted on pp. 213–217 of *Feminist Theory: A Reader*, 2nd ed., edited by Wendy K. Kolmar and Frances Bartkowski. Boston: McGraw Hill, 2005. Copyright by Jo Freeman, www.jofreeman.com.

3.3. "Redstockings Manifesto." Issued as a mimeographed flyer in New York City on July 7, 1969, the manifesto was designed for distribution at women's liberation events. Further information about the Manifesto and other source materials from the rebirth years of feminism in the 1960s are available from Redstockings Women's Liberation Archives for Action at www.redstockings.org; or at P.O. Box 14017 Gainesville, Florida 32604.

3.4. "Use," by Susan Griffin. 1987/1989. From pp. 52–54 of *Woman & Nature: The Roaring inside Her*. New York: Harper Colophon, 1980.

4.1. "Bread and Roses Anthem." *American Magazine*, December 1911.

4.2. "Lenin on the Woman Question," by Clara Zetkin. 1920. Marxists.org; http://www.marxists.org/archive/zetkin/1920/lenin/zetkin1.htm. Reprinted on pp. 103–108 of *The Emancipation of Women; From the Writings of V. I. Lenin*. New York: International, 1995.

4.3. Table 1 from "Welfare Regimes in Relation to Paid Work and Care," by Janet C. Gornick and Marcia K. Meyers. Pp. 45–68 in *Changing Life Patterns in Western Industrial Societies*, edited by Janet Zollinger Giele and Elke Holst. Amsterdam: Elsevier, 2004. Copyright 2004 by Elsevier.

4.4. "To My White Working-Class Sisters," by Debbie D'Amico. Pp. 178–181 in *Writings from the Women's Liberation Movement: Liberation Now!* edited by Deborah Babcox and Madeline Belkin. New York: Dell, 1971.

5.1. "The Bridge Poem," by Donna Kate Rushin. 1981. Pp. xxi–xxii of *This Bridge Called My Back: Writings by Radical Women of Color*, edited by Cherríe Moraga and Gloria Anzaldúa. New York: Kitchen Table—Women of Color Press, 1983.

5.2. "When I was Growing Up," by Nellie Wong. 1981. Pp. 7–8 in *This Bridge Called My Back: Writings by Radical Women of Color*, edited by Cherríe Moraga and Gloria Anzaldúa. New York: Kitchen Table—Women of Color Press, 1983.

5.3. "Theory in the Flesh" by Cherríe Moraga and Gloria Anzaldúa. P. 23 in *This Bridge Called My Back: Writings by Radical Women of Color*, edited by Cherríe Moraga and Gloria Anzaldúa. New York: Kitchen Table—Women of Color Press, 1983.

5.4. Excerpt from "Colonizers Who Refused," by Patricia Hill Collins. From pp. 131–137 of *Fighting Words: Black Women and the Search for Justice*. Minneapolis: University of Minnesota Press, 1998.

6.1. Excerpt from "Foucault's Nominalism," by Barry Allen. From pp. 93–95 of *Foucault and the Government of Disability*, edited by Shelley Tremain. Ann Arbor: University of Michigan Press, 2005.

6.2. Excerpt from "The Sexuality of Terrorism," by Jasbir K. Puar. Pp. 37–38 in *Terrorist Assemblages* (Durham, N.C.: Duke University Press, 2007). Copyright 2007 by Duke University Press. All rights reserved. Reprinted by permission of the publisher.

6.3. Excerpt from "What Is Sexuality without the Gender Binary?" by Kate Bornstein. Pp. 32–38 in *Gender Outlaw: On Men, Women, and the Rest of Us*. New York: Vintage, 1994.

6.4. Excerpt from "Queer and Now," by Eve Kosofsky Sedgwick. Pp. 1–22 in *Tendencies*. Durham, N.C.: Duke University Press, 1993. Copyright 1993 by Duke University Press. All rights reserved. Reprinted by permission of the publisher.

7.1. "Third Wave Manifesta: A Thirteen-Point Agenda," by Jennifer Baumgardner and Amy Richards. Pp. 278–280 in *Manifesta: Young Women, Feminism, and the Future*. New York: Farrar, Straus and Giroux, 2000.

7.2. From "Klaus Barbie, and Other Dolls I'd Like to See," by Susan Jane Gilman. Pp. 20–21 in *Adiós Barbie: Young Women Write about Body Image and Identity*, edited by Ophira Edut. Seattle, Wash.: Seal, 1998.

7.3. "Don't You Know—We're Talking about a Revolution? Sounds Like a {Zine}!" by Beatrice Calvert. (Title inspired by "Talkin' 'bout a Revolution" by Tracy Chapman.) Printed for the first time with permission of Beatrice Calvert. Copyright 2011 by Beatrice Calvert.

7.4. Excerpt from "Our Story," Guerrilla Girls; www.guerrillagirls.com/press/ourstory/shtml, with permission. Copyright 2011 by Guerrilla Girls.

8.1. Excerpts from *Indigenous American Women: Decolonization, Empowerment, Activism*, by Devon Abbott Mihesuah. Pp. xv and xxi–xxii. Lincoln: University of Nebraska Press, 2003.

8.2. Excerpt from *Fighting for American Manhood: How Gender Politics Provoked the Spanish–American and Philippine–American Wars*, by Kristin L. Hoganson. Pp. 200–201. New Haven, Conn.: Yale University Press, 1998.

8.3. "Lament to the Spirit of War," by Enheduanna, circa 2300 B.C. Pp. 199–200 in *Women on War: Essential Voices for the Nuclear Age*, edited by Daniela Gioseffi. New York: Simon & Schuster, 1988.

9.1. Excerpts from pp. 105–108 in Cynthia Enloe, *Globalization and Militarism: Feminists Make the Link*. New York: Rowman & Littlefield, 2007.

9.2. "Taking on the Global Economy," by Kalima Rose. 1996. *Crossroads*, March. With appreciation to Kalima Rose who is a senior director of the Oakland, California-based PolicyLink.

9.3. Excerpt from "Teaching for the Times," by Gayatri Chakravorty Spivak. Pp. 177–202 in *The Decolonization of Imagination*, ed. Jan Nederveen Pieterse and Bikhu Parekh. London: Zed, 1995; http://zedbooks.co.uk/. Reprinted with permission of Zed Books.

9.4. Excerpts from "Imagine a Country—2009," by Holly Sklar. Pp. 307–316 in *Race, Class, and Gender in the United States*, 8th ed., edited by Paula S. Rothenberg. New York: Worth, 2010.

10.1. Excerpts from "Who Lives in the 'Global Village'?" by Donella Meadows. 1992. Copyright Sustainability Institute. This article from The Donella Meadows Archive is available for use in research, teaching, and private study. For other uses, please contact the Sustainability Institute at 3 Linden Road, Hartland, Vt. 05048; or call (802) 436–1277.

10.2. "Transnational Barbie," by Inderpal Grewal. Pp.80–120 in *Transnational America: Feminisms, Diasporas, Neoliberalisms*. Copyright 2005 by Duke University Press. All rights reserved. Reprinted by permission of the publisher.

10.4. Associated Press. "Display of Controversial 'Chocolate Jesus' Sculpture Cancelled." Fox News.com, March 20, 2007 (Friday).

"*Jyllands-Posten* Muhammad Cartoons Controversy." n.d.; http://europenews.dk/en/node/7143 (retrieved November 11, 2011).

References

Abelove, Henry, Michèle Aina Barale, and David M. Halperin, eds. 1993. *The Lesbian and Gay Studies Reader*. New York: Routledge.

Abraham, Richard. 1989. *Rosa Luxemburg: A Life in the International*. Oxford: Berg.

Abu-Lughod, Janet. 1989. *Before European Hegemony: The World System, AD 1250–1350*. New York: Oxford University Press.

Acker, Joan. 2006. *Class Questions: Feminist Answers*. New York: Rowman & Littlefield.

_____. 1992. "Gendered Institutions: From Sex Roles to Gendered Institutions." *Contemporary Sociology* 21(September): 565–568.

Adams, Bert, and R. A. Sydie. *Classical Sociological Theory*. Thousand Oaks, Calif.: Pine Forge.

Addams, Jane. 1916. *The Long Road of Women's Memory*. New York: Macmillan.

Agamben, Giorgio. 2005. *State of Exception*. Chicago: University of Chicago Press.

Agger, Ben. 1998. *Critical Social Theories: An Introduction*. Boulder, Colo. Westview.

Alaimo, Stacy. 1994. "Cyborg and Ecofeminist Interventions: Challenges for an Environmental Feminism." *Feminist Studies* 20(1): 133–152.

_____. 2000. *Undomesticated Ground: Recasting Nature as Feminist Space*. Ithaca, N.Y.: Cornell University Press.

Alcoff, Linda. 1997. "The Politics of Postmodern Feminism Revisited." *Cultural Critique* 36: 5–27.

_____. [1998] 2005. "'Cultural Feminism versus Post-Structuralism: The Identity Crisis in Feminist Theory.'" Pp. 426–436 in *Feminist Theory: A Reader*, 2nd ed., ed. Wendy K. Kolmar and Frances Bartkowski. Boston: McGraw-Hill.

Alexander, M. Jacqui. 2005. *Pedagogies of Crossing: Meditations on Feminism, Sexual Politics, Memory, and the Sacred*. Durham, N.C.: Duke University Press.

Alexander, M. Jacqui, and Chandra Talpade Mohanty. 1997. *Feminist Genealogies, Colonial Legacies, Democratic Futures*. New York: Routledge.

Alfonso, Rita, and Jo Trigilio. 1997. "Surfing the Third Wave: A Dialogue between Two Third Wave Feminists." *Hypatia: A Journal of Feminist Philosophy* 12(3): 8–16.

Allen, Barry. 2005. "Foucault's Nominalism." Pp. 93–95 in *Foucault and the Government of Disability*, ed. Shelley Tremain. Ann Arbor: University of Michigan Press.

Almaguer, Tomás. 1993. "Chicano Men: A Cartography of Homosexual Identity and Behavior." Pp. 255–273 in *The Lesbian and Gay Studies Reader*, ed. Henry Abelove, Michèle Aina Barale, and David M. Halperin. New York: Routledge.

Alonso, Harriet Hyman. 1993. *Peace as a Woman's Issue: A History of the U.S. Movement for World Peace and Women's Rights*. Syracuse, N.Y.: Syracuse University Press.

Alvarez, Sonia E. 1999. "Advocating Feminism: The Latin American Feminist NGO 'Boom.'" *International Feminist Journal of Politics* 1(2): 181–209.

Amanpour, Christiane. 2007. CNN Special, "God's Warriors." August 21–23.

Amin, Samir. 1977. *Unequal Development: An Essay on the Social Formations of Peripheral Capitalism*. New York: Monthly Review.

Anderson, Margaret, and Patricia Hill Collins, eds. 1994. *Race, Class, and Gender: An Anthology*. New York: Wadsworth.

Anderson, Terry H. 2007. "Vietnam is Here: The Anti-War Movement." Pp. 245–264 in *The War that Never Ends: New Perspectives on the Vietnam War*. Ed. David Anderson and John Ernst. Lexington, K.Y.: University of Kentucky Press.

Anonymous Queers. [1990] 1997. "Queers Read This." In *We Are Everywhere: A Historical Sourcebook of Gay and Lesbian Politics*, ed. Mark Blasius and Shane Phelan. New York: Routledge.

Anthony, Susan B. [1872] 2005. "Speech after Arrest for Illegal Voting." Pp. 91–95 in *Feminist Theory: A Reader*, 2nd ed., ed. Wendy K. Kolmar and Frances Bartkowski. Boston: McGraw-Hill.

Anti-Defamation League. 1999. "The Creation of the State of Israel"; www.ad.org/Israel/Record/creation.asp (retrieved Jan. 6, 2010).

Antrobus, Peggy. 2005. "Forward." Pp. xii–xvi in *Defending Our Dreams: Global Feminist Voices for a New Generation*. Eds. Shamillah Wilson, Anasuya Sengupta and Christy Evans. London: Zed.

Anzaldúa, Gloria. 1987. *Borderlands/LaFrontera: The New Mestiza*. San Francisco: Aunt Lute Books.

_____. [1987] 2005. "'La Conciencia de la Mestiza: Towards a New Consciousness' from *Borderlands/La Frontera: The New Mestiza*." Pp. 420–425 in *Feminist Theory: A Reader*, 2nd ed., ed. Wendy K. Kolmar and Frances Bartkowski. Boston: McGraw-Hill.

Appadurai, Arjun. 1996. *Modernity at Large: Cultural Dimensions of Globalization*. Minneapolis: University of Minnesota Press.

Appiah, Kwame Anthony. 1997. "Is the 'Post-' in 'Postcolonial' the 'Post-' in 'Postmodern'?" Pp. 420–444 in *Dangerous Liaisons: Gender, Nation, and Postcolonial Perspectives*, ed. Anne McClintock, Aamir Mufti, and Ella Shohat. Minneapolis: University of Minnesota Press.

Appiah, Kwame Anthony, and Henry Louis Gates. 1993. *Identities*. Cambridge, Mass.: Harvard University Press.

Aptheker, Bettina. 1989. *Tapestries of Life: Women's Work, Women's Consciousness, and the Meaning of Daily Experience*. Amherst: University of Massachusetts Press.

Archer, Margaret. 1988. *Culture and Agency: The Place of Culture in Social Theory*. Cambridge: Cambridge University Press.

Ariès, Philippe. 1962. *Centuries of Childhood: A Social History of Family Life*. New York: Vintage.

Arizpe, Lourdes, and Josefina Aranda. 1981. "The 'Comparative Advantages' of Women's Disadvantages: Women Workers in the Strawberry Export Agribusiness in Mexico." *Signs: Journal of Women in Culture and Society* 7(2): 453–473.

Arney, William, and Bernard Bergen. 1984. *Medicine and the Management of Living: Taming the Last Great Beast*. Chicago: University of Chicago Press.

Astin, Helen, Allison Parelman, and Anne Fisher. 1975. *Sex Roles: A Research Bibliography*. Washington, D.C.: Department of Health, Education, and Welfare.

Babox, Deborah, and Madeline Belkin, eds. 1971. *Writings from the Women's Liberation Movement: Liberation Now!* New York: Dell.

Baca Zinn, Maxine, and Stanley Eitzen. 1993. *Diversity in Families*. New York: Longman.

Bailey, Cathryn. 1997. "Making Waves and Drawing Lines: The Politics of Defining the Vicissitudes of Feminism." *Hypatia: A Journal of Feminist Philosophy* 12(3): 17–28.

_____. 2002. "Unpacking the Mother/Daughter Baggage: Reassessing Second- and Third-Wave Tensions." *Women's Studies Quarterly* 30(3–4): 138–154.

Bakunin, Mikhail. [1876] 1991. *Statism and Anarchy*. Cambridge: Cambridge University Press.

Balbus, Isaac D. 1982. *Marxism and Domination: A Neo-Hegelian, Feminist, Psychoanalytic Theory of Sexual, Political, and Technological Liberation*. Princeton, N.J.: Princeton University Press.

Bambara, Toni Cade, ed. 1970. *The Black Woman: An Anthology*. New York: Signet.

Bar On, Bat-Ami. 1993. "Marginality and Epistemic Privilege." Pp. 83–100 in *Feminist Epistemologies*, ed. Linda Alcoff and Elizabeth Potter. New York: Routledge.

Barrett, Michele. 1980. *Women's Oppression Today: Problems in Marxist Feminist Analyses*. London: Verso.

_____. 1999. *Imagination in Theory: Culture, Writing, Words, and Things*. New York: New York University Press.

Barrett, Michele, and Anne Phillips, eds. 1992. *Destabilizing Theory: Contemporary Feminist Debates*. Stanford, Calif.: Stanford University Press.

Barringer, Mark. 1998. "The Anti-War Movement in the United States"; www.english.illinois.edu/maps/vietnam/antiwar.html (retrieved Feb. 2, 2007).

Barry, Kathleen. 1979. *Female Sexual Slavery*. New York: New York University Press.

_____. 1995. *The Prostitution of Sexuality*. New York: New York University Press.

Bartky, Sandra. 1990. *Femininity and Domination: Studies in the Phenomenology of Oppression*. New York: Routledge.

_____. 1997. "Foucault, Femininity, and the Modernization of Patriarchal Power. Pp. 92–111 in *Feminist Social Thought: A Reader*, ed. Diana Tietjens Meyers. New York: Routledge.

Bates, Dawn, and Maureen C. McHugh. 2005. "Zines: Voices of Third Wave Feminists." Pp. 179–194 in *Different Wavelengths: Studies of the Contemporary Women's Movement*, ed. Jo Reger. New York: Routledge.

Baudrillard, Jean. 1983. *Simulations*. New York: Semiotext(e).

Bauer-Maglin, Nan, and Donna Perry, eds. 1996. *"Bad Girls"/"Good Girls": Women, Sex, and Power in the Nineties*. New Brunswick, N.J.: Rutgers University Press.

Baumgardner, Jennifer, and Amy Richards. 2000. *Manifesta: Young Women, Feminism, and the Future*. New York: Farrar, Straus and Giroux.

Beal, Frances. [1971] 1995. "Double Jeopardy: To Be Black and Female." Pp. 146–155 in *Words of Fire: An Anthology of African American Feminist Thought*, ed. Beverly Guy-Sheftall. New York: New Press.

Beasley, Chris. 1999. *What Is Feminism? An Introduction to Feminist Theory*. Thousand Oaks, Calif.: Sage.

Bebel, August. 1904. *Women under Socialism*. New York: Labor News.

Beck, Ulrich. 1992. *Risk Society: Towards a New Modernity*. London: Sage.

Beisner, Robert L. 1968. *Twelve against Empire: The Anti-Imperialists, 1898–1900*. New York: McGraw-Hill.

Belkhir, Jean. 1998. "Race, Gender, Class, and Marxism." Paper presented at the annual meeting of the American Sociological Association, Aug. 21–25, San Francisco.

Benston, Margaret. [1969] 1971. "The Political Economy of Women's Liberation." Pp. 139–144 in *Writings from the Women's Liberation Movement: Liberation Now!* ed. Deborah Babcox and Madeline Belkin. New York: Dell.

Berger, Peter. 1967. *The Social Construction of Reality*. Garden City, NY: Anchor.

_____. 1977. *Facing Up to Modernity: Excursions in Society, Politics, and Religion*. New York: Vintage.

Berger, Ronald J., Patricia Searles, and Charles E. Cottle. 1991. *Feminism and Pornography*. Westport, Conn.: Praeger.

Bernstein, Eduard. 1895. "The Judgment of Abnormal Sexual Intercourse." Translated by Angela Clifford. Marxist Internet Archive; www.marxists.org/reference/archive/bernstein/works/1895/wilde/homosexual.htm (retrieved Dec. 2, 2009).

Bernstein, Laurie. 1995. *Sonia's Daughters: Prostitutes and Their Regulation in Imperial Russia*. Berkeley, CA: University of California Press.

Best, Steven, and Douglas Kellner. 2001. *The Postmodern Adventure: Science, Technology, and Cultural Studies at the Third Millenium*. New York: Guilford.

Bettie, Julie. 2003. *Women without Class: Girls, Race, and Identity*. Berkeley: University of California Press.

Bhabha, Homi. 1994. *The Location of Culture*. London: Routledge.

Bhavnani, Kum-Kum. 2004. "Tracing the Contours: Feminist Research and Feminist Objectivity." Pp. 65–77 in *Feminist Perspectives on Social Research*, ed. Sharlene Nage Hesse-Biber and Michelle Yaiser. New York: Oxford University Press.

Bhavnani, Kum-Kum, John Foran, and Priya Kurian, eds. 2003. *Feminist Futures: Re-imagining Women, Culture, and Development*. New York: Zed.

Biehl, Janet. 1991. *Finding Our Way: Rethinking Ecofeminist Politics*. Montreal: Black Rose.

Blackwell, Henry Brown. 1902. "Domestic Imperialism." *Women's Journal*, 15 (November).

Blauner, Robert. 1972. *Racial Oppression in America*. New York: Harper & Row.

Blumberg, Rae Lesser. 1978. *Stratification: Socioeconomic and Sexual Inequality*. Dubuque, Iowa: Wm. C. Brown.

Blumenfeld, Emily, and Susan Mann. 1980. "Domestic Labour and the Reproduction of Labour Power: Towards an Analysis of Women, the Family, and Class." Pp. 277–283 in *Hidden in the Household: Women's Domestic Labour under Capitalism*, ed. Bonnie Fox. Toronto: Women's Press.

Bodek, Evelyn Gordon. 1976. "Salonières and the Bluestockings: Educated Obsolescence and Germinating Feminism." *Feminist Studies* 3(3–4): 185–189.

Bolotin, Susan. 1982. "Views from the Postfeminist Generation." *New York Times Magazine*, Oct. 17.

Bonacich, Edna, Lucie Cheng, Norma Chinchilla, Norma Hamilton, and Paul Ong, eds. 1994. *Global Production: The Apparel Industry in the Pacific Rim*. Philadelphia: Temple University Press.

Bookchin, Murray. 1986. *The Modern Crisis*. Philadelphia: New Society.

_____. 1990. *Remaking Society: Pathways to a Green Future*. Cambridge, Mass.: South End.

_____. 1995. *The Philosophy of Social Ecology: Essays on Dialectical Naturalism*. Montreal: Black Rose.

Boone, Joseph. [1995] 2003. "Vacation Cruises or the Homoerotics of Orientalism." Pp.460–486 in *Feminist Postcolonial Theory: A Reader*, ed. Reina Lewis and Sara Mills. New York: Routledge.

Bordo, Susan. 1990. "Feminism, Postmodernism, and Gender-Scepticism." Pp. 133–156 in *Feminism/Postmodernism*, ed. Linda J. Nicholson. New York: Routledge.

_____. 1993. *Unbearable Weight: Feminism, Western Culture, and the Body*. Berkeley: University of California Press.

Bornstein, Kate. 1994. *Gender Outlaw: On Men, Women, and the Rest of Us*. New York: Vintage.
Boserup, Esther. 1970. *Women's Role in Economic Development*. London: Allen & Unwin.
Boston Women's Health Book Collective. 1973. *Our Bodies, Ourselves: A Book by and for Women*. New York: Simon & Schuster.
Bourdieu, Pierre, and Loïc J. D. Wacquant. 1992. *An Invitation to Reflexive Sociology*. Chicago: University of Chicago Press.
Bouvier, Virginia M. 2001. *Who's America? The War of 1898 and the Battles to Define the Nation*. Westport, Conn.: Praeger.
Brah, Avtar. 1996. *Cartographies of Diaspora: Contesting Identities*. New York: Routledge.
_____. 2003. "Diaspora, Border, and Transnational Identities." Pp. 613–634 in *Feminist Postcolonial Theory: A Reader*, ed. Reina Lewis and Sara Mills. New York: Routledge.
Bread and Roses Anthem. 1911. *American Magazine*, December.
Breines, Wini. 2002. "What's Love Got to Do with It? White Women, Black Women, and Feminism in the Movement Years." *Signs: Journal of Women in Culture and Society* 4(27): 1095–1133.
Brewer, Rose. 1999. "Sociology and Transformation." In *Race, Gender, & Class: Towards an Inclusive Curriculum*, ed. Jean Belkhir. Washington, D.C.: American Sociological Association.
Briggs, Laura. 2002. *Reproducing Empire: Race, Sex, Science and U.S. Imperialism in Puerto Rico*. Berkeley: University of California Press.
Bronner, Stephen Eric. 1995. "Ecology, Politics, and Risk: The Social Theory of Ulrich Beck." *Capital, Nature and Socialism* 6: 67–86.
Brooks, Ann. 1997. *Postfeminisms, Feminisms, Cultural Theory, and Cultural Forms*. London: Routledge.
Brown, Rita Mae. 1971. *Poems*. Freedom, Calif.: Crossing.
Brownmiller, Susan. 1975. *Against Our Will: Men, Women and Rape*. New York: Simon & Schuster.
Bruns, Cindy M., and Collen Trimble. 2001. "Rising Tide: Taking Our Place as Young Feminist Psychologists." Pp. 19–36 in *The Newest Generation: Third Wave Psychotherapy*, ed. Ellen Kaschak. Binghamton, N.Y.: Haworth.
Bryant, Bunyan, and Paul Mohai, eds. 1992. *Race and the Incidence of Environmental Hazards: A Time for Discourse*. Boulder, CO: Westview Press.
Buchwald, Emile, Pamela Fletcher, and Martha Roth, eds. 1993. *Transforming a Rape Culture*. Minneapolis, Minn.: Milkweed.
Bullard, Robert, ed. 1993. *Confronting Environmental Racism: Voices from the Grassroots*. Boston: South End Press.
_____. 1994. *Unequal Protection: Environmental Justice and Communities of Color*. San Francisco, CA: Sierra Club.
Bunch, Charlotte. [1972] 1993. "Lesbians in Revolt." Pp. 144–148 in *Feminist Frameworks: Alternative Theoretical Accounts of the Relations between Men and Women*, 3rd ed., ed. Alison M. Jaggar and Paula S. Rothenberg. Boston: McGraw-Hill.
_____. [1979] 2005. "'Not by Degrees: Feminist Theory and Education.'" Pp. 12–15 in *Feminist Theory: A Reader*, 2nd ed., ed. Wendy K. Kolmar and Frances Bartkowski. Boston: McGraw-Hill.
_____, and Niamh Reilly. 1994. *Demanding Accountability: The Global Campaign and Vienna Tribunal on Women's Human Rights*. New Brunswick, N.J.: Rutgers University Press.
Burghart, Devon, and Leonard Zeskind. 2010. "Tea Party Nationalism." Institute for Research & Education on Human Rights; www.teapartynationalism.com (retrieved Jan. 7, 2010).
Burroughs, William. 1989. *Interzone*. New York: Viking.
Burton, Antoinette. 1994. *Burdens of History: British Feminists, Indian Women, and Imperial Culture, 1865–1915*. Chapel Hill, N.C.: University of North Carolina Press.
Butler, Josephine. [1871] 2005. "'Letter to My Countrywomen, Dwelling in the Farmsteads and Cottages of England.'" Pp. 86–90 in *Feminist Theory: A Reader*, 2nd ed., ed. Wendy K. Kolmar and Frances Bartkowski. Boston: McGraw-Hill.
Butler, Judith. 1990. *Gender Trouble: Feminism and the Subversion of Identity*. New York: Routledge.
_____. 1992 "Contingent Foundations: Feminism and the Question of Postmodernism." Pp. 3–21 in *Feminists Theorize the Political*, ed. Judith Butler and Ann W. Scott. New York: Routledge.
_____. 1993. *Bodies That Matter: On the Discursive Limits of Sex*. New York: Routledge.
Butterfield, L. H., Marc Friedlaender, and Mary-Jo Kline. 1975. *The Book of Abigail and John: Selected Letters of the Adams Family, 1762–1784*. Cambridge, Mass.: Harvard University Press.
Calhoun, Cheshire. 2003. "Separating Lesbian Theory from Feminist Theory." Pp. 334–352 in *Feminist Theory Reader: Local and Global Perspectices*, ed. Carole McCann and Seung-Kyung Kim. New York: Routledge.
Cameron, Deborah. 1992. "Review of Deborah Tannen's *You Just Don't Understand*." *Feminism and Psychology* 2: 465–468.
Carmichael, Stokely, and Charles Hamilton. [1967] 1992. *Black Power: The Politics of Liberation*. New York: Vintage.

Carpenter, Cari M., ed. 2010. *Selected Writings of Victoria Woodhull: Suffrage, Free Love, and Eugenics.* Lincoln: University of Nebraska Press.

Carson, Rachel. 1962. *Silent Spring.* Boston: Houghton Mifflin.

Cashen, Jeanne. 2002. "The Revolution Is Mine: Grrrl Resistance in a Commodity Culture." Unpublished manuscript, University of New Orleans.

Castillo, Anna. 1994. *Massacre of the Dreamers: Essays on Xicansma.* New York: Plume.

Castles, Stephen, and Mark J. Miller. [1993] 1998. *The Age of Migration: International Population Movements in the Modern World.* 2nd ed. Basingstoke, U.K.: Macmillan.

Castro, Fidel. 2007. "Reflections of President Fidel Castro: The Brain Drain." International Movement for a Just World. Posted Aug. 2; www.just-international.org.

Caulfield, Mina Davis. 1984. "Imperialism, the Family, and Cultures of Resistance." Pp. 374–379 in *Feminist Frameworks: Alternative Theoretical Accounts of the Relations Between Women and Men,* 2nd ed., ed. Alison M. Jaggar and Paula S. Rothenberg. Boston: McGraw-Hill.

Cavallaro, Dani. 2003. *Beyond the Big Three: French Feminist Theory Today.* New York: Continuum.

_____. 2006. *French Feminist Theory: An Introduction.* New York: Continuum.

Cayleff, Susan. 1995. *Babe Didrikson: The Greatest All-Sport Athlete of All Times.* Champaign, IL: University of Illinois Press.

Chambers, Veronica. 1995. "Betrayal Feminism." Pp. 21–28 in *Listen Up: Voices of the Next Feminist Generation,* ed. Barbara Findlen. Seattle: Seal.

Chang, Grace. 1997. "The Global Trade in Filipina Workers." Pp. 132–152 in *Dragon Ladies: Asian American Feminists Breath Fire,* ed. Sonia Shah. Cambridge, Mass.: South End.

Chapkis, Wendy. 1997. *Live Sex Acts: Women Performing Erotic Labor.* New York: Routledge.

Chapkis, Wendy, and Cynthia Enloe. 1983. *Of Common Cloth: Women in the Global Textile Industry.* Washington, D.C.: Institute for Policy Studies.

Chaudhuri, Nupur, and Margaret Strobel. 1992. *Western Women and Imperialism: Complicity and Resistance.* Bloomington: Indiana University Press.

Chavetz, Janet Saltman. 1990. "Some Thoughts by an Unrepentant 'Positivist' Who Considers Herself a Feminist Nonetheless." Paper presented at the annual meeting of the American Sociological Association, Aug. 14, Washington D.C.

Cheal, David. 1991: *Family and the State of Theory.* Toronto: University of Toronto Press.

Chodorow, Nancy. [1978] 1999. *The Reproduction of Mothering: Psychoanalysis and the Sociology of Gender.* Berkeley: University of California Press.

Christ, Carol P. 1999. "Why Women Need the Goddess." Pp. 309–321 in *Ecology: Key Concepts in Critical Theory,* ed. Carolyn Merchant. New York: Humanity.

Christian, Barbara. 1988. "The Race for Theory." *Feminist Studies* 14(1): 67–79.

Chrystos. [1981] 1983. "I Walk in the History of My People." P. 57 in *This Bridge Called My Back: Writings by Radical Women of Color.* ed. Cherríe Moraga and Gloria Anzaldúa, New York: Kitchen Table—Women of Color Press.

Cixous, Hélène. [1975] 1976. "The Laugh of the Medusa." Translated by Keith Cohen and Paula Cohen. *Signs: Journal of Women in Culture and Society* 1(4): 875–893.

Cixous, Hélène, and Catherine Clement. [1975] 1986. *The Newly Born Woman.* Translated by Betsy Wing. Minneapolis: University of Minnesota Press.

Clark, Lorenne, and Lynda Lange. 1979. *The Sexism of Social and Political Theory.* Toronto: University of Toronto Press.

Cockburn, Cynthia. 1998. *The Space between Us.* London: Zed.

Collins, Patricia Hill. 1990. *Black Feminist Thought: Knowledge, Consciousness, and Empowerment.* Boston: Unwin Hyman.

_____. 1998. *Fighting Words: Black Women and the Search for Justice.* Minneapolis: University of Minnesota Press.

_____. 2004a. *Black Sexual Politics: African-Americans, Gender, and the New Racism.* New York: Routledge.

_____. 2004b. "Comment on Heckman's 'Truth and Method: Feminist Standpoint Theory Revisited': Where's the Power?" Pp. 247–253 in *The Feminist Standpoint Reader: Intellectual and Political Controversies,* ed. Sandra G. Harding. New York: Routledge.

_____. 2004c. "Some Group Matters: Intersectionality, Situated Standpoints, and Black Feminist Thought." Pp. 66–84 in *Feminist Frontiers,* ed. Laurel Richardson, Verta Taylor, and Nancy Whittier. Boston: McGraw-Hill.

Combahee River Collective. [1977] 2005. "'A Black Feminist Statement.'" Pp. 311–316 in *Feminist Theory: A Reader,* 2nd ed., ed. Wendy K. Kolmar and Frances Bartkowski. Boston: McGraw-Hill.

Connell, Raewyn. 1987. *Gender and Power: Society, the Person, and Sexual Politics.* Stanford, Calilf.: Stanford University Press.

Coontz, Stephanie. 2000. *The Way We Never Were: American Families and the Nostalgia Trap.* New York: Basic.

Cooper, Anna Julia. [1892] 1988. *A Voice from the South*. New York: Oxford University Press.
______. [1892] 1997. "Excerpt from 'Woman versus the Indian.'" Pp. 184–189 in *The Women Founders: Sociology and Social Theory, 1830–1930*, ed. Patricia Madoo Lengermann and Jill Niebrugge-Brantley. Boston: McGraw-Hill.
______. [1893] 1998. "The Intellectual Progress of the Colored Women in the United States since the Emancipation Proclamation." Pp. 201–205 in *The Voice of Anna Julia Cooper*, ed. Charles Lemert and Esme Bhan. Lanham, Md.: Rowman & Littlefield.
______. [1925] 1988. *Slavery and the French Revolutionists: 1788–1805*. Trans. Frances Richardson Keller. Lewiston, NY: Mellon Press.
______. [1925] 1998. "The Social Conditions of the French-American Colonies: The Class Structure." Pp. 272–279 in *The Voice of Anna Julia Cooper*, ed. Charles Lemert and Esme Bhan. Lanham, Md.: Rowman & Littlefield.
Cooper, James Fenimore. [1823] 1984. *The Leatherstocking Tales*. New York: Library of America.
Coppock, Deena Haydon, and Ingrid Richter. 1995. *The Illusions of "Post-Feminism": New Women, Old Myths*. London: Taylor & Francis.
Corber, Robert, and Stephen Valocchi. 2003. "Introduction." Pp. 1–20 in *Queer Students: An Interdisciplinary Reader*, ed. Robert J. Corber and Stephen Valocchi. New York: Blackwell.
Corea, Gena. 1985. *The Mother Machine*. London: Women's Press.
Cott, Nancy. 1987. *The Grounding of Modern Feminism*. New Haven, Conn.: Yale University Press.
Cox, Judy. 2003. "Can Capitalism Go On Forever? A Review of Rosa Luxemburg's *The Accumulation of Capital*." *International Socialism Journal* 100: 8–9.
Crawford, Mary. 1995. *Talking Difference: On Gender and Language*. Thousand Oaks, Calif.: Sage.
Crawley, Sara L. 2002. "Narrating and Negotiating Butch and Femme: Storying Lesbian Selves in a Heteronormative World." Ph.D. diss., University of Florida.
Crawley, Sara L., and Kendal L. Broad. 2008. "The Construction of Sex and Sexualities." Pp. 545–566 in *Handbook of Constructionist Research*, ed. James Holstein and Jaber Gubrium. New York: Guilford.
Crawley, Sara L., Lara J. Foley, and Constance L. Shehan. 2008. *Gendering Bodies*. Lanham, MD: Rowman & Littlefield.
Crenshaw, Kimberlé Williams. 1989. "Demarginalizing the Intersection of Race and Sex: A Black Feminist Critique of Antidiscrimination Doctrine, Feminist Theory and Antiracist Politics." *University of Chicago Legal Forum* 1989: 139–167.
______. 1995. "Mapping the Margins: Intersectionality, Identity Politics, and Violence against Women of Color." Pp. 357–383 in *Critical Race Theory: The Key Writings That Formed the Movement*, ed. Kimberlé Williams Crenshaw, Neil Gotanda, Gary Peller, and Kendall Thomas. New York: New Press.
______. [1997] 2005. "'Intersectionality and Identity Politics: Learning from Violence against Women of Color.'" Pp. 533–541 in *Feminist Theory: A Reader*, 2nd ed., ed. Wendy K. Kolmar and Frances Bartkowski. Boston: McGraw-Hill.
Dalla Costa, Mariarosa, and Selma James. 1975. *The Power of Women and the Subversion of the Community*. Bristol, U.K.: Falling Wall.
Daly, Mary. [1978] 1990. *Gyn/Ecology: Metaethics of Radical Feminism*. Boston: Beacon.
D'Amico, Debbie. 1971. "To My White Working-Class Sisters." Pp. 178–181 in *Writings from the Women's Liberation Movement: Liberation Now!* ed. Deborah Babcox and Madeline Belkin. New York: Dell.
Darraj, Susan Muaddi. 2002. "It's Not an Oxymoron: The Search for an Arab Feminism." Pp. 295–311 in *Colonize This! Young Women of Color on Today's Feminism*, ed. Daisy Hernández and Bushra Rehman. New York: Seal.
Davis, Angela. 1981. *Women, Race, and Class*. New York: Vintage.
______. [1991] 2005. "'Outcast Mothers and Surrogates: Racism and Reproductive Politics in the Nineties.'" Pp. 509–514 in *Feminist Theory: A Reader*, 2nd ed., ed. Wendy K. Kolmar and Frances Bartkowski. Boston: McGraw-Hill.
Davis, Rebecca Harding. [1861] 1995. *Life in the Iron-Mills*. Pp. 197–228 in *The Oxford Book of Women's Writing in the United States*, ed. Linda Wagner-Martin and Cathy N. Davidson. New York: Oxford University Press.
Dawe, Alan. 1978. "Theories of Social Action." Pp. 362–417 in *A History of Sociological Analysis*, ed. Tom Bottomore and Robert Nisbet. New York: Basic.
de Beauvoir, Simone. [1952] 1970. *The Second Sex*. New York: Knopf.
______. 2004. "Reports from the World Tribunal on Vietnam." Pp. 193–195 in *Women on War: Essential Voices for the Nuclear Age*, ed. Daniela Gioseffi. New York: Simon & Schuster.
Deckard, Barbara Sinclair. [1979] 1983. *The Women's Movement: Political, Socioeconomic, and Psychological Issues*. New York: Harper & Row.

Delmar, Rosalyn. 1986. "What Is Feminism?" Pp. 8–33 in *What Is Feminism?* ed. Juliet Mitchell and Ann Oakley. Oxford: Blackwell.

DeLombard, Jeannine. 1995. "Femmenism." Pp. 21–34 in *To Be Real: Telling the Truth and Changing the Face of Feminism*, ed. Rebecca Walker. New York: Anchor.

Delphy, Christine. 1981. "For a Materialist Feminism." *Feminist Issues* 1(2): 69–76.

D'Emilio, John. 1983. "Capitalism and Gay Identity." Pp. 100–113 in *Powers of Desire: The Politics of Sexuality*, ed. Ann Snitow. New York: Monthly Review.

D'Emilio, John, and Estelle B. Freedman. [1988] 1997. *Intimate Matters: A History of Sexuality in America*. 2nd ed. Chicago: University of Chicago Press.

Denfeld, Rene. 1995. *The New Victorians: A Young Woman's Challenge to the Old Feminist Order*. New York: Warner.

Dent, Gina. 1995. "Missionary Position." Pp. 61–76 in *To Be Real: Telling the Truth and Changing the Face of Feminism*, ed. Rebecca Walker. New York: Anchor.

Derrida, Jacques. 1976. *Of Grammatology*. Baltimore, Md.: Johns Hopkins University Press.

_____. 1981. *Positions*. London: Athlone/Continuum.

Diamond, Irene, and Gloria Feman Orenstein. 1990. *Reweaving the World: The Emergence of Ecofeminism*. San Francisco: Sierra Club.

Diaz, Angeli R. 2003. "Postcolonial Theory and the Third Wave Agenda." *Women and Language* 26(1): 10–18.

Dicker, Rory, and Alison Piepmeier, eds. 2003. *Catching a Wave: Reclaiming Feminism for the 21st Century*. Boston: Northeastern University Press.

Dickinson, James, and Bob Russell, eds. 1986. *Family, Economy, and State: The Social Reproduction Process under Capitalism*. London: Croom Helm.

Dinnerstein, Dorothy. 1977. *The Mermaid and the Minotaur: Sexual Arrangements and Human Malaise*. New York: Harper Colophon.

Dirlik, Arif. 1997. "The Postcolonial Aura: Third World Criticism in the Age of Global Capitalism." Pp. 501–528 in *Dangerous Liaisons: Gender, Nation, and Postcolonial Perspectives*, ed. Anne McClintock, Aamir Mufti, and Ella Shohat. Minneapolis: University of Minnesota Press.

"Display of Controversial 'Chocolate Jesus' Sculpture Cancelled." 2007. Fox News.com, March 20.

Di Stephano, Christine. 1990. "Dilemmas of Difference: Feminism, Modernity, and Postmodernism." Pp. 63–82 in *Feminism/Postmodernism*, ed. Linda J. Nicholson. New York: Routledge.

Djebar, Assia. 1985. *Fantasia: An Algerian Cavalcade*. London: Quartet.

Dobyns, Henry. 1966. "An Appraisal of Techniques with a New Hemispheric Estimate." *Current Anthropology* 7(4): 395–446.

DuBois, Ellen Carol. 1991. "Woman Suffrage and the Left: An International Socialist-Feminist Perspective." *New Left Review* 18(6): 20–45.

_____. 1994. "Woman Suffrage around the World: Three Phases of Suffragist Internationalism." Pg. 252–274 in *Suffrage and Beyond: International Feminist Perspectives*, ed. Caroline Daley and Melanie Nolan. New York: New York University Press.

Duggan, Lisa. 1992. "Making it Perfectly Queer." *Socialist Review* 22(1): 11–31.

_____. 2004. *The Twilight of Equality? Neoliberalism, Cultural Politics, and the Attack on Democracy*. Boston: Beacon.

Duggan, Lisa, Nan Hunter, and Carole Vance. 1985. "False Promises: Feminist Antipornography Legislation in the U.S." Pp. 130–151 in *Women against Censorship*. ed. Varda Burstyn. Vancouver, Canada: Douglas & McIntyre.

Duncan, Barbara. 2005. "Searching for a Home Place: Online in the Third Wave." Pp. 161–178 in *Different Wavelengths: Studies of the Contemporary Women's Movement*, ed. Jo Reger. New York: Routledge.

Durkheim, *Émile*. [1893] 1964. *The Division of Labor in Society*. New York: Free Press.

Dworkin, Andrea. 1974. *Woman Hating: A Radical Look at Sexuality*. New York: E. P. Dutton.

_____. 1976. *Our Blood: Prophesies and Discourses on Sexual Politics*. New York: Harper & Row.

_____. 1981. *Pornography: Men Possessing Women*. New York: Plume.

_____. 1987. *Intercourse*. New York: Free Press.

Eagleton, Terry. 2003. *After Theory*. New York: Basic.

Eastman, Crystal. [1919] 1978. *On Women and Revolution*. New York: Oxford University Press.

_____. [1919] 2005. "'Now We Can Begin' from *On Women and Revolution*." Pp. 130–133 in *Feminist Theory: A Reader*, 2nd ed., ed. Wendy K. Kolmar and Frances Bartkowski. Boston: McGraw-Hill.

Edelman, Lee. 2004. *No Future: Queer Theory and the Death Drive*. Durham, N.C.: Duke University Press.

Edut, Ophira, ed. 1998. *Adiós Barbie: Young Women Write about Body Image and Identity*. Seattle: Seal.

Edwards, Tim. 1998. "Queer Fears: Against the Cultural Turn." *Sexualities* 1(4): 471–484.

Ehrenreich, Barbara, and Deirdre English. 1973. *Witches, Midwives, and Nurses: A History of Women Healers*. Old Westbury, N.Y.: Feminist Press.

_____. 1978. *For Her Own Good: 150 Year of the Experts' Advice to Women*. Garden City, N.Y.: Anchor.

Ehrenreich, Barbara, and Arlie Russell Hochschild. [2002] 2004. *Global Woman: Nannies, Maids, and Sex Workers in the New Economy*. New York: Metropolitan.

Eisenstein, Zillah, ed. 1979. *Capitalist Patriarchy and the Case for Socialist Feminism*. New York: Monthly Review.

_____. 1986. *The Radical Future of Liberal Feminism*. Boston: Northeastern University Press.

Ellerbe, Linda. 1990. "The Feminist Mistake." *Seventeen*, March.

Ellis, Havelock. [1905] 1906. *Studies in the Psychology of Sex*. Philadelphia: F. A Davis.

Elshtain, Jean Bethke. 1981. *Public Man, Private Woman: Women in Social and Political Thought*. Princeton, N.J.: Princeton University Press.

_____. 2002. *Jane Addams and the Dream of American Democracy: A Life*. New York: Basic.

Eng, David L., Judith Halberstam, and José Esteban Muñoz. 2005. "Introduction: What's Queer about Queer Studies Now?" *Social Text* 23(3–4):1–18.

Engels, Friedrich. [1884] 1972. *The Origin of the Family, Private Property, and the State*. New York: International.

England, Paula. 1992. *Comparable Worth: Theories and Evidence*. New York: Aldine de Gruyter.

English, Deirdre, Amber Hollibaugh, and Gayle Rubin. 1981. "Talking Sex: A Conversation on Sexuality and Feminism." *Socialist Review* 11(4): 50–62.

Enheduanna. 2004. "Lament to the Spirit of War." Pp. 199–200 in *Women on War: Essential Voices for the Nuclear Age*, ed. Daniela Gioseffi. New York: Simon & Schuster.

Enloe, Cynthia. 1989. *Bananas, Beaches, & Bases: Making Feminist Sense of International Politics*. Berkeley: University of California Press.

_____. [1995] 2004. "The Globetrotting Sneaker." Pp. 453–457 in *Feminist Frontiers*, ed. Laural Richardson, Verta Taylor, and Nancy Whittier. Boston: McGraw-Hill.

_____. 2007. "Wielding Masculinity inside Abu Ghraib and Guantanamo: The Globalized Dynamics." Pp. 93–115 in *Globalizaiton and Militarism: Feminists Make the Link*. New York: Rowman & Littlefield.

Ensler, Eve. 2001. *The Vagina Monologues*. London: Virgo.

Eschle, Catherine. 2001. *Global Democracy, Social Movements, and Feminism*. Boulder, Colo.: Westview.

Esping-Andersen, Gosta. 1990. *The Three Worlds of Welfare Capitalism*. Princeton, N.J.: Princeton University Press.

Evans, Dylan. 1996. *An Introductory Dictionary of Lacanian Psychoanalysis*. New York: Routledge.

Faderman, Lillian. 1981. *Surpassing the Love of Men: Romantic Friendship and Love between Women from the Renaissance to the Present*. New York: William Morrow.

_____. 1991. *Odd Girls and Twilight Lovers: A History of Lesbian Life in Twentieth-Century America*. New York: Columbia University Press.

_____. 1997. "Afterword." Pp. 221–229 in *Cross Purposes: Lesbians, Feminists, and the Limits of Alliance*, ed. Dana Heller. Bloomington: Indiana University Press.

Faderman, Lillian, and Stuart Timmons. 2006. *Gay LA: A History of Sexual Outlaws, Power Politics, and Lipstick Lesbians*. New York: Basic.

Fain, W. Taylor. 2005. "Neighborhoods and Markets: The United States in Latin America and Asia, 1890–1917." Virginia Center for Digital History; www.vcdh.virginia.edu/solguide/VUS09/essay09a.html (retrieved Sept. 5, 2008).

Faludi, Susan. 1991. *Backlash: The Undeclared War against American Women*. New York: Crown.

Fanon, Frantz. [1961] 1967. *The Wretched of the Earth*. New York: Penguin.

_____. 1967. *Black Skins, While Masks*. New York: Grove.

Fausto-Sterling, Anne. [1985] 1992. *Myths of Gender: Biological Theories about Women and Men*. Revised Ed. New York: Basic Books.

_____. 1998. "The Five Sexes: Why Male and Female Are Not Enough." Pp. 42–47 in *Women's Lives: Multicultural Perspectives*, ed. Gwyn Kirk and Margo Okazawa-Rey. 1st ed. Mountain View, Calif.: Mayfield.

_____. 2000. *Sexing the Body: Gender Politics and the Construction of Sexuality*. New York: Basic.

Featherstone, Mike. 1989. "Postmodernism, Cultural Change, and Social Practice." Pp. 117–138 in *Postmodernism, Jameson, Critique*, ed. Douglas Kellner. Washington, D.C.: Maisonneuve.

_____. 1991. *Consumer Culture and Postmodernism*. London: Sage.

Feinberg, Leslie. [1993] 2003. *Stone Butch Blues: A Novel*. Boston: Alyson.

Ferguson, Ann. 1984. "Patriarchy, Sexual Identity, and the Sexual Revolution." *Signs: Journal of women in Culture and Society* 7(1): 158–172.

Ferguson, Roderick. 2004. *Aberrations in Black: Toward a Queer Color Critique*. Minneapolis: University of Minnesota Press.

Fernandez-Kelley, Maria Patricia. 1983. *For We Are Sold, I and My People: Women and Industry in Mexico's Frontier*. Albany: State University of New York Press.

Ferree, Myra Marx, and Aili Mari Tripp, eds. 2006. *Global Feminism: Transnational Women's Activism, Organizing, and Human Rights*. New York: New York University Press.

Ferree, Myra Marx, Judith Lorber, and Beth Hess. 2000. *Revisioning Gender*. Walnut Creek, CA: Alta Mira Press.

Findlen, Barbara, ed. 1995. *Listen Up: Voices from the Next Feminist Generation*. Seattle: Seal.

Finlay, Barbara. 2007. *Before the Second Wave: Gender in the Sociological Tradition*. Upper Saddle River, N.J.: Prentice Hall.

Firestone, Shulamith. [1970] 1971. *The Dialectic of Sex: The Case for Feminist Revolution*. New York: Bantam.

Fisher, James Terence. 1989. *The Catholic Counterculture in America: 1933–1962*. Chapel Hill: University of North Carolina Press.

Fiske, Shanyn. 2008. "Piecing the Patchwork Self: A Reading of *The Color Purple*." *The Explicator* 66: 150–153.

Fite, Gilbert. 1984. *Cotton Fields No More: Southern Agriculture, 1865–1980*. Lexington: University of Kentucky Press.

Flax, Jane. 1992. "The End of Innocence." Pp. 445–463 in *Feminists Theorize the Political*, ed. Judith Butler and Joan W. Scott. New York: Routledge.

Foner, Philip, and Richard Winchester, eds. 1984. *The Anti-Imperialist Reader: A Documentary History of Anti-Imperialism in the United States*, vol. 1, *From the Mexican War to the Election of 1900*. New York: Holmes & Meier.

Foster, Hal. 2011. "I am the Decider." *London Review of Books*, March 17.

Foucault, Michel. [1975] 1979. *Discipline and Punish: The Birth of the Prison*. New York: Vintage.

_____. [1976] 1980. *History of Sexuality, Volume 1: An Introduction*. London: Penguin.

_____. 1986. *History of Sexuality, Volume II: The Use of Pleasure*. London: Viking.

Fox, Bonnie, ed. 1980. *Hidden in the Household: Women's Domestic Labour under Capitalism*. Toronto: Women's Press.

Franco, Jean. [1989] 1997. "The Nation as Imagined Community." Pp. 130–137 in *Dangerous Liaisons: Gender, Nation, and Postcolonial Perspectives*, ed. Anne McClintock, Aamir Mufti, and Ella Shohat. Minneapolis: University of Minnesota Press.

Frank, Andre Gunder. 1976. *On Capitalist Underdevelopment*. New York: Oxford University Press.

Frankenberg, Ruth. 1993. *The Social Construction of Whiteness: White Women, Race Matters*. Minneapolis: University of Minnesota Press.

Fraser, Nancy, and Linda Nicholson. 1997. "Social Criticism without Philosophy: An Encounter between Feminism and Postmodernism." Pp 131–146 in *Feminist Social Thought: A Reader*, ed. Diana Tietjens Meyers. New York: Routledge.

Fraser, Nancy, and Nancy Naples. 2004. "To Interpret the World and to Change It: An Interview with Nancy Fraser." *Signs: Journal of Women in Culture and Society* 29(4): 1103–1124.

Freed, Alice F. 1992. "We Understand Perfectly: A Critique of Deborah Tannen's View of Cross-Sex Communication." Paper presented at the Second Berkeley Women and Language Conference, April 4 and 5, Berkeley, California.

Freeman, Jo [Joreen]. [1968] 2005. "'The BITCH Manifesto.'" Pp. 213–217 in *Feminist Theory: A Reader*, 2nd ed., ed. Wendy K. Kolmar and Frances Bartkowski. Boston: McGraw-Hill.

_____. 1979. "The Women's Liberation Movement: Its Origins, Organizations, Activities, and Ideas." Pp. 557–574 in *Women: A Feminist Perspective*, 2nd ed., ed. Jo Freeman. Palo Alto, Calif.: Mayfield.

_____. 1989. "From Suffrage to Women's Liberation: Feminism in Twentieth Century America." Pp. 567–580 in *Women: A Feminist Perspective*, 4th ed., ed. Jo Freeman. Palo Alto, Calif.: Mayfield.

Freud, Sigmund. [1905] 2000. *Three Essays on the Theory of Sexuality*. Translated by James Strachey. New York: Basic.

Friedan, Betty. [1963] 1983. *The Feminine Mystique*. New York: Laurel.

_____. [1963] 2005. "'The Problem That Has No Name' from *The Feminine Mystique*." Pp. 198–202 in *Feminist Theory: A Reader*, 2nd ed., ed. Wendy K. Kolmar and Frances Bartkowski. Boston: McGraw-Hill.

_____. [1981] 1988. *The Second Stage*. Cambridge, Mass.: Harvard University Press.

Friend, Tad. 1994. "Yes." *Esquire*, February.

Frisken, Amanda. 2004. *Victoria Woodhull's Sexual Revolution: Political Theater and the Popular Press in the Nineteenth Century*. Philadelphia: University of Pennsylvania Press.

Frolich, Paul. 1972. *Rosa Luxemburg: Her Life and Work*. New York: Monthly Review.

Frost-Knappman, Elizabeth, and Kathryn Cullen-Dupont. 2005. *Women's Suffrage in America: Eyewitness History*. New York: Facts on File.

Frye, Marilyn. [1978] 1997. "Some Reflections on Separatism and Power." Pp. 406–414 in *Feminist Social Thought: A Reader*, ed. Diana Tietjens Meyers. New York: W. W. Norton.

Fuentes, Annette, and Barbara Ehrenreich. 1983. *Women in the Global Factory*. Cambridge, Mass.: South End.
Fuss, Diana. 1989. *Essentially Speaking: Feminism, Nature, and Difference*. New York: Routledge.
Gaard, Greta. 1997. "Toward a Queer Ecofeminism." *Hypatia: A Journal of Feminist Philosophy* 12(1): 114–137.
Gaard, Greta, and Patrick D. Murphy, eds. 1998. *Ecofeminist Literary Criticism: Theory, Interpretation Pedagogy*. Urbana: University of Illinois Press.
Gamson, Joshua. 1995. "Must Identity Movements Self Destruct?" *Social Problems* 42(3): 390–407.
_____. 2000. "Sexualities, Queer Theory, and Qualitative Research." Pp. 347–365 in *Handbook of Qualitative Research*, 2nd ed., ed. Norman K. Denzin and Yvonna S. Lincoln. Thousand Oaks, Calif.: Sage.
Garfinkel, Harold. 1967. *Studies in Ethnomethodology*. Englewood Cliffs, N.J.: Prentice Hall.
Garland-Thomson, Rosemarie. 1997. *Extraordinary Bodies: Figuring Physical Disability in American Culture and Literature*. New York: Columbia University Press.
_____. 1998. *Freakery: Cultural Spectacles of the Extraordinary Body*. New York: Columbia University Press.
_____. [2001] 2005. "'Integrating Disability, Transforming Feminist Theory.'" Pp. 575–586 in *Feminist Theory: A Reader*, 2nd ed., ed. Wendy K. Kolmar and Frances Bartkowski. Boston: McGraw-Hill.
Gasiorowski, Mark, and Malcolm Byrne, eds. 2004. *Mohammed Mosaddeq and the 1953 Coup in Iran*. Boulder, Colo.: Westview.
Gatens, Moira. 1992. "Power, Bodies, and Difference." Pp. 120–137 in *Destabilizing Theory: Contemporary Feminist Debates*, ed. Michele Barrett and Anne Phillips. Stanford, Calif.: Stanford University Press.
Gatewood, Willard. 1975. *Black Americans and the White Man's Burden, 1898–1903*. Urbana: University of Illinois Press.
George, Susan. 1976. *How the Other Half Dies: The Real Reasons for World Hunger*. Montclair, N.J.: Allanheld.
Gergen, Kenneth J. 1991. *The Saturated Self*. New York: Basic.
Gibson, Mary. 1986. Prostitution and the State in Italy 1860–1915. New Brunswick, NJ: Rutgers University Press.
Giddens, Anthony. 1990. *The Consequences of Modernity*. Stanford, Calif.: Stanford University Press.
Giddings, Paula. 1984. *When and Where I Enter: The Impact of Black Women on Race and Sex in America*. New York: Bantam.
Gilbert, Sandra M. 1986. "Introduction: A Tarantella of Theory." In *The Newly Born Woman*. Minneapolis: University of Minnesota Press.
Gilbert, Sandra M., and Susan Gubar. 1979. *The Madwoman in the Attic: The Woman Writer and the Nineteenth-Century Literary Imagination*. New Haven, Conn.: Yale University Press.
Gilligan, Carol. 1982. *In a Different Voice: Psychological Theory and Women's Development*. Cambridge, Mass.: Harvard University Press.
Gilman, Charlotte Perkins. [1892] 1995. "The Yellow Wallpaper." Pp. 41–55 in *The Oxford Book of Women's Writing in the United States*, ed. Linda Wagner-Martin and Cathy N. Davidson. New York: Oxford University Press.
_____. [1898] 1966. *Women and Economics*. New York: Harper & Row.
_____. 1900. *Concerning Children*. Boston: Small, Maynard.
_____. 1903. *The Home: Its Work and Influence*. New York: Macmillan.
_____. 1904. *Human Work*. New York: McClure, Phillips.
_____. 1911. *The Man-Made World; or, Our Androcentric Culture*. New York: Charlton.
_____. [1915] 1979. *Herland*. New York: Pantheon.
_____. 1923. *His Religion and Hers:* A Study of the Faith of Our Fathers and the Work of Our Mothers. New York: Charlton.
Gilman, Susan Jane. 1998. "Klaus Barbie, and Other Dolls I'd Like to See." Pp. 20–21 in *Adiós Barbie: Young Women Write about Body Image and Identity*, ed. Ophira Edut. Seattle: Seal.
Gimenez, Martha E. 2001. "Marxism and Class, Gender and Race: Rethinking the Trilogy." *Race, Gender, and Class* 8(2): 23–33.
Gimenez, Martha, and Lise Vogel. 2005. "Marxist-Feminist Thought Today: Introduction." *Science & Society* (special issue: *Marxist–Feminist Thought Today*) 69(1): 5–10.
Gioseffi, Daniela, ed. 1988. *Women on War: Essential Voices for the Nuclear Age*. New York: Simon & Schuster.
Gissing, George. [1893] 1977. *The Odd Women*. New York: W. W. Norton.
Goldman, Emma. 1910. *Anarchism and Other Essays*. New York: Mother Earth.

_____. [1910] 2005. "'The Traffic in Women' from *Anarchism and Other Essays*." Pp. 120–123 in *Feminist Theory: A Reader*, 2nd ed., ed. Wendy K. Kolmar and Frances Bartkowski. Boston: McGraw-Hill.

_____. 1911. "Patriotism: A Menace to Liberty." Marxist.org; www.marxist.org/reference/archive/goldman/works/1911/patriotism.html (retrieved July 10, 2009).

_____. 1912. BrainyQuote.com; www.brainyquote.com/quotes/authors/e/emma_goldman.html (retrieved Aug. 20, 2011).

Goldsmith, Barbara. 1998. "The Woman Who Set American on Its Ear." *Parade Magazine*, 8 March.

Goodman, Dena. 1994. *The Republic of Letters: A Cultural History of the French Enlightenment*. Ithaca, N.Y.: Cornell University Press.

Gordon, April. 1996. *Transforming Capitalism and Patriarchy: Gender and Development in Africa*. Boulder, Colo.: Lynne Reinner.

Gordon, Linda. 1995. "Black and White Visions of Welfare: Women's Welfare Activism, 1890–1945." Pp. 449–485 in *We Specialize in the Wholly Impossible: A Reader in Black Women's History*, ed. Darlene Clark Hine, Wilma King, and Linda Reed. Brooklyn: Carlson.

Gornick, Janet C., and Marcia K. Meyers. 2004. Table 1 from "Welfare Regimes in Relation to Paid Work and Care." Pp. 45–68 in *Changing Life Patterns in Western Industrial Societies*, ed. Janet Sollinger Giele and Elke Holst. The Netherlands: Elsevier.

Gosse, Van.. 2005. *Rethinking the New Left: An Interpretative History*. New York: Palgrave Macmillan.

Gottlieb, Robert. 2005. *Forcing the Spring: The Transformation of the American Environmental Movement*. Washington, D.C.: Island.

Gough, Kathleen. 1961. *Matrilineal Kinship*. Berkeley: University of California Press.

Gould, Stephen Jay. 1980. *The Panda's Thumb*. New York: W. W. Norton.

Grahame, Peter R. 1998. "Ethnography, Institutions, and the Problematic of the Everyday World." *Human Studies* 21(4): 1–10.

Gramsci, Antonio. [1932] 1971. *Selections from the Prison Notebooks*. Edited and translated by Quintin Hoare and Geoffrey Nowell Smith. New York: International.

Granier, Jean. 1985. "Perspectivism and Interpretation." Pp. 190–196 in *The New Nietzsche: Contemporary Styles of Interpretation*, ed. David B. Allison. Cambridge, Mass.: MIT Press.

Grant, Judith. 1993 *Fundamental Feminism: Contesting the Core Concepts of Feminist Theory*. New York: Routledge.

Gray, John. 1992. *Men Are from Mars, Women Are from Venus: A Practical Guide for Improving Communication and Getting What You Want in Your Relationships*. New York: HarperCollins.

Green, Michelle. 1995. "The Feminine Mistake." *New York Times Book Review*, March 19.

Greer, Germaine. [1971] 2008. *The Female Eunuch*. New York: HarperCollins.

Grewal, Inderpal. 2005. *Transnational America: Feminisms, Diasporas, Neoliberalisms*. Durham, N.C.: Duke University Press.

Grewal, Inderpal, and Caren Kaplan, eds. [1994] 2006. *Scattered Hegemonies: Postmodernity and Transnational Feminist Practices*. Minneapolis: University of Minnesota Press.

Griffin, Susan. [1978] 1980. "Use." Pp. 52–54 in *Woman and Nature: The Roaring Inside Her*. New York: Harper Colophon.

Griffith, Alison I., and Dorothy E. Smith. 2005. *Mothering for Schooling*. New York: RoutledgeFalmer.

Griffith, Elisabeth. 1984. *In Her Own Right: The Life of Elizabeth Cady Stanton*. New York: Oxford University Press.

Grimes, Michael, Susan Mann, and James Shavor. 1998. "Gender and Intimacy: Do Race and Class Matter?" *Race, Gender, & Class* 5(2): 54-77.

Grimké, Sarah M. [1838] 2005. "Letter VIII from *Letters on the Equality of the Sexes and the Condition of Women*." Pp. 69–70 in *Feminist Theory: A Reader*, 2nd ed., ed. Wendy K. Kolmar and Frances Bartkowski. Boston: McGraw-Hill

Grimshaw, Jean. 1986. *Feminist Philosophers: Women's Perspectives on Philosophical Traditions*. Brighton, U.K.: Wheatsheaf.

_____. 1993." Practices of Freedom." Pp. 51–72 in *Up against Foucault: Explorations of Some Tensions between Foucault and Feminism*, ed. Caroline Ramazanoglu, New York: Routledge.

Grossman, Victor. 2007. "Unity—In Memory of Rosa Luxemburg." MRzine; www.mrzine.monthlyreview.org/grossman170106.html (retrieved Jan. 2, 2007).

Grosz, Elizabeth. 1994. *Volatile Bodies: Toward a Corporeal Feminism*. Bloomington: Indiana University Press.

Guerrilla Girls. 2001. Poster and Excerpt. Guerrillagirls.com; www.guerrillagirls.com/press/ourstory.shtml (retrieved May 9, 2011).

Guha, Ramachandra. 1999. "A Radical Environmentalism: A Third-World Critique." Pp. 281–289 in *Ecology: Key Concepts in Critical Theory*, ed. Carolyn Merchant. New York: Prometheus.

Gupta, Jyostna Angihorti. 2006. "Towards Transnational Feminisms: Some Reflections and Concerns in Relation to the Globalization of Reproductive Technologies." *European Journal of Women's Studies* 13(23): 23–38.

Gutiérrez, Ramón A. 1991. *When Jesus Came, the Corn Mothers Went Away: Marriage, Sexuality, and Power in New Mexico, 1500–1846*. Stanford, Calif.: Stanford University Press.

Guy, Donna. 1990. *Sex and Danger in Buenos Aires: Prostitution, Family, and Nation in Argentina*. Lincoln: University of Nebraska Press.

Guy-Sheftall, Beverly. 1995. *Words of Fire: An Anthology of African American Feminist Thought*. New York: New Press.

Halberstam, Judith. 1998. *Female Masculinity*. Durham, NC: Duke University Press.

_____. 2005. *In a Queer Time and Place: Transgender Bodies, Subcultural Lives*. New York: NYU Press.

_____. 2006. "Notes on Failure." Keynote address at "Failure: Ethics and Aesthetics," UCI Visual Studies Conference, March 3–4, Irvine, California.

Hall, Elaine J., and Marnie Salupo Rodriguez. 2003. "The Myth of Postfeminism." *Gender and Society* 17(6): 878–902.

Hall, Radclyffe. [1928] 2005. *The Well of Loneliness*. London: Wordsworth.

Hall, Stuart. 1997. "The Local and the global: Globalization and Ethnicity." Pp. 173–187 in *Dangerous Liaisons: Gender, Nation, and Postcolonial Perspectives*, ed. Anne McClintock, Aamir Mufti, and Ella Shohat. Minneapolis: University of Minnesota Press.

Halperin, David. 1995. *Saint Foucault: Towards a Gay Hagiography*. New York: Oxford University Press.

Halstead, Ted. 1999. "A Politics for Generation X." *Atlantic Monthly*, August.

Hanisch, Carol. [1969] 2000. "The Personal Is Political." carolhanish.org; www.carolhanisch.org/CHwritings/PIP.html (retrieved Aug. 15, 2011).

Haraway, Donna. [1985] 2005. "'A Cyborg Manifesto: Science, Technology, and Socialist-Feminism in the Late Twentieth Century.'" Pp. 384–393 in *Feminist Theory: A Reader*, 2nd ed., ed. Wendy K. Kolmar and Frances Bartkowski. Boston: McGraw-Hill.

_____. 1991. *Simians, Cyborgs, and Women: The Reinvention of Nature*. New York: Routledge.

_____. [1991] 2004. "Situated Knowledges: The Science Question in Feminism and the Privilege of Partial Perspective." Pp. 81–101 in *The Feminist Standpoint Theory Reader: Intellectual and Political Controversies*, ed. Sandra G. Harding. New York: Routledge.

Harding, Sandra.. [1986] 2005. "'From the Woman Question in Science to the Science Question in Feminism.'" Pp. 404–412 in *Feminist Theory: A Reader*, 2nd ed., ed. Wendy K. Kolmar and Frances Bartkowski. Boston: McGraw-Hill.

_____. 1991. *Whose Science? Whose Knowledge? Thinking from Women's Lives*. Ithaca, N.Y.: Cornell University Press.

_____. 1993. "Rethinking Standpoint Epistemology: 'What Is Strong Objectivity'?" Pp. 49–82 in *Feminist Epistemologies*, ed. Linda Alcoff and Elizabeth Potter. New York: Routledge.

_____. 1998. *Is Science Multicultural? Postcolonialisms, Feminisms, and Epistemologies*. Bloomington: Indiana University Press.

_____. 2004. *The Feminist Standpoint Reader: Intellectual and Political Controversies*. New York: Routledge.

_____. 2008. *Sciences from Below: Feminisms, Postcolonialities, and Modernities*. Durham, N.C.: Duke University Press.

Harris, Paisley Jane. 2003. "Gatekeeping and Remaking: The Politics of Respectability in African American Women's History and Black Feminism." *Journal of Women's History* 15(1): 212–220.

Hartmann, Betsy. 2002. "The Changing Faces of Population Control." Pp. 259–289 in *Policing the National Body: Race, Gender, and Criminalization*, ed. Jael Silliman and Anannya Bhattacharjee. Cambridge, Mass.: South End.

Hartmann, Heidi I. 1981. "The Unhappy Marriage of Marxism and Feminism: Towards a More Progressive Union." Pp.1–42 in *Women and Revolution: A Discussion of the Unhappy Marriage of Marxism and Feminism*, ed. Lydia Sargent. Cambridge, Mass.: South End.

Hartsock, Nancy. [1983] 2004. "The Feminist Standpoint: Developing the Ground for a Specifically Feminist Historical Materialism." Pp. 35–53 in *The Feminist Standpoint Theory Reader: Intellectual and Political Controversies*, ed. Sandra G. Harding. New York: Routledge.

_____. 1990. "Foucault on Power: A Theory for Women?" Pp. 157–175 in *Feminism/Postmodernism*, ed. Linda J. Nicholson. New York: Routledge.

Harvey, David. 1989. *The Condition of Postmodernity: An Enquiry into the Origins of Cultural Change*. Oxford: Blackwell.

Haug, Frigga. 1992. *Rosa Luxemburg and Women's Politics, Beyond Female Masochism: Memory-Work and Politics*. London: Verso.

Hayden, Dolores. 1982. *The Grand Domestic Revolution: A History of Feminist Designs for American Homes, Neighborhoods, and Cities*. Cambridge, Mass.: MIT Press.
Healey, Emma. 1996. *Lesbian Sex Wars*. London: Virago.
Heise, Lori. [1977] 1993. "The Global War against Women." Pp. 63–67 in *Feminist Frameworks: Alternative Theoretical Accounts of the Relations between Men and Women*, 3rd ed., ed. Alison M. Jaggar and Paula S. Rothenberg. Boston: McGraw-Hill.
Hekman, Susan. 2004. "Truth and Method: Feminist Standpoint Theory Revisited." Pp. 225–241 in *The Feminist Standpoint Reader: Intellectual and Political Controversies*, ed. Sandra G. Harding. New York: Routledge.
Hennessy, Rosemary. 2000. *Profit and Pleasure: Sexual Identities in Late Capitalism*. New York: Routledge.
Henry, Astrid. 2003. "Feminisms Family Problem: Feminist Generations and the Mother Daughter Trope." Pp. 209–231 in *Catching a Wave: Reclaiming Feminism for the 21st Century*, ed. Rory Dicker and Alison Piepmeier. Boston: Northeastern University Press.
_____. 2004. *Not My Mother's Sister: Generational Conflict and Third Wave Feminism* Bloomington: University of Indiana Press.
_____. 2005. "Solitary Sisterhood: Individualism Meets Collectivity in Feminism's Third Wave." Pp. 81–96 in *Different Wavelengths: Studies of the Contemporary Women's Movement*, by Jo Reger. New York: Routledge.
Herdt, Gilbert. 1993. *Ritualized Homosexuality in Melanesia*. Berkeley: University of California Press
Herman, Dianne. 1984. "The Rape Culture." In *Women: A Feminist Perspective*, ed. Jo Freeman. Mayfield.
Hernandez, Daisy, and Bushra Rehman. 2002. *Colonize This! Young Women of Color on Today's Feminism*. New York: Seal.
Hess, Beth, and Myra Marx Ferree, eds. 1987. *Analyzing Gender: A Handbook of Social Science Research*. Thousand Oaks, Calif.: Pine Forge/Sage
Hesse-Biber, Sharlene Nagy, Patricia Leavy, and Michelle Yaiser. 2004. "Feminist Approaches to Research as a *Process*: Reconceptualizing Epistemology, Methodology, and Method." Pp. 3–26 in *Feminist Perspectives on Social Research*, ed. Sharlene Nage Hesse-Biber and Michelle Yaiser. New York: Oxford University Press.
Heywood, Leslie, and Jennifer Drake, eds. 1997. *Third Wave Agenda: Being Feminist, Doing Feminism*. Minneapolis: University of Minnesota Press.
Higgenbotham, Evelyn Brooks. 1993. *Righteous Discontent: The Women's Movement in the Black Baptist Church, 1880–1920*. Cambridge, Mass.: Harvard University Press.
Hilferding, Rudolph. [1910] 2007. *Finance Capital: A Study in the Latest Phase of Capitalist Development*. London: Routledge.
Hill, Philip. 2009. *Lacan for Beginners*. Hanover, N.H.: Steerforth.
Hobson, John Atkinson. [1902] 1971. *Imperialism: A Study*. Ann Arbor: University of Michigan Press.
Hoganson, Kristin L. 1998. *Fighting for American Manhood: How Gender Politics Provoked the Spanish–American and Philippine–American Wars*. New Haven, Conn.: Yale University Press.
_____. 2001. "'As Badly Off as the Filipinos': U.S. Women's Suffragists and the Imperial Issue at the Turn of the Twentieth Century." *Journal of Women's History* 13(2): 9–33.
Hogeland, Lisa Marie. 1994. "Fear of Feminism: Why Young Women Get the Willies." *Ms.*, November/December.
Hole, Judith, and Ellen Levine. [1971] 1975. *Rebirth of Feminism*. New York: Quadrangle.
_____. 1979. "The First Feminists." Pp. 543–556 in *Women: A Feminist Perspective*, 2nd ed., ed. Jo Freeman. Palo Alto, Calif.: Mayfield.
Holley, Joe. 2007. "Obituary for Tillie Olson." *Washington Post*, January 5.
Holstein, James, and Jaber Gubrium, eds. 2008. *Handbook of Constructionist Research*. New York: Guilford.
hooks, bell. 1984. *Feminist Theory: From Margin to Center*. Cambridge, Mass.: South End.
_____. 1994. *Teaching to Transgress: Education as the Practice of Freedom*. New York: Routledge.
Hopkins, Sarah Winnemucca. 1883. *Life among the Paiutes: Their Wrongs and Claims*. Boston: Cupples, Upham.
Horkheimer, Max, and Theodor Adorno.[1944] 1972. *Dialectic of Enlightenment*. New York: Herder & Herder.
Horney, Karen. 1932. *Feminine Psychology*. New York: W. W. Norton.
_____. [1932] 2005. "'The Dread of Woman: Observations on a Specific Difference in the Dread Felt by Men and by Women Respectively for the Opposite Sex' from *Feminine Psychology*." Pp. 154–157 in *Feminist Theory: A Reader*, 2nd ed., ed. Wendy K. Kolmar and Frances Bartkowski. Boston: McGraw-Hill.
Howard, Dick, ed. 1971. *Selected Political Writings of Rosa Luxemburg*. New York: Monthly Review.
Hudis, Peter, and Kevin B. Anderson, eds. 2004. *The Rosa Luxemburg Reader*. New York: Monthly Review.

Huffman, D. J. 2002. " Making Sense of Third Wave Feminism: Its Multiple Movements and Their Theoretical Underpinnings." Master's thesis, University of New Orleans.

Huggins, Nathan. 1973. *Harlem Renaissance*. New York: Oxford University Press.

Hull, Gloria, Patricia Bell Scott, and Barbara Smith, 1981. *All the Women Are White, All the Men Are Black, but Some of us Are Brave*. Old Westbury, N.Y.: Feminist Press.

Humphreys, Margaret.1999. *Yellow Fever in the South*. Baltimore, Md.: Johns Hopkins University Press.

Hurston, Zora Neale. [1934] 2008. *Jonah's Gourd Vine*. New York: Harper Perennial.

_____. [1937] 2006. *Their Eyes Were Watching God*. New York: Harper Perennial.

Hutchinson, Earl Ofari. 1995. *Blacks and Reds: Race and Class Conflict, 1919–1990*. East Lansing: Michigan State University Press.

Incite! Women of Color against Violence. 2006. *The Color of Violence: The Incite! Anthology*. Cambridge, Mass.: South End.

_____. n.d. "Mission Statement"; www.incite-national.org (retrieved Dec. 12, 2010).

Irigaray, Luce. [1974] 1985. *Speculum of the Other Woman*. Translated by Leon Roudiez. New York: Columbia University Press.

_____. [1977] 1985. *This Sex Which Is Not One*. Translated by Catherine Porter. Ithaca, N.Y.: Cornell University Press.

Jackson, Cecile. 1993. "Women/Nature or Gender History? A Critique of Ecofeminist Development." *Journal of Peasant Studies* 20(3): 389–419.

Jacobs, Harriet. [1861] 2001. *Incidents in the Live of a Slave Girl*. Mineola, N.Y.: Dover.

Jacobs, Sylvia. 1981. *The African Nexus: Black American Perspectives on the European Partitioning of Africa, 1880–1920*. Westport, Conn.: Greenwood.

_____. 1995. "Give a Thought to Africa: Black Women Missionaries in Southern Africa." Pp. 103–123 in *We Specialize in the Wholly Impossible: A Reader in Black Women's History*, ed. Darlene Clark Hine, Wilma King, and Linda Reed. Brooklyn: Carlson.

Jaggar, Alison M. 1983. *Feminist Politics and Human Nature*. Lanham, Md.: Rowman & Littlefield.

_____. 1989. "Love and Knowledge: Emotion in Feminist Epistemology." Pp. 145–171 in *Gender/Body/Knowledge: Feminist Reconstructions of Being and Knowing*, ed. Susan R. Bordo and Alison M. Jaggar. New Brunswick, N.J.: Rutgers University Press.

Jaggar, Alison M., and Paula S. Rothenberg, eds. 1984. *Feminist Frameworks: Alternative Theoretical Accounts of the Relations between Women and Men*, 2nd ed. New York: McGraw-Hill.

_____. 1993. *Feminist Frameworks: Alternative Theoretical Accounts of the Relations between Women and Men*, 3rd ed. New York: McGraw-Hill.

Jayawardena, Kumari. 1986. *Feminism and Nationalism in the Third World*. London: Zed.

Jeffreys, Sheila. 1994. "The Queer Disappearance of Lesbian Sexuality in the Academy." *Women's Studies International Forum* 17(5): 459–472.

_____. 2003. *Unpacking Queer Politics*. Cambridge: Polity.

Jenkins, Richard. 1992. *Pierre Bourdieu*. London: Routledge.

Jervis, Lisa. 1998. "My Jewish Nose." Pp. 62–67 in *Adiós Barbie: Young Women Write about Body Image and Identity*, ed. Ophira Edut. Seattle: Seal.

Johnson, Georgia Douglas. [1929] 1996. "Safe." Pp. 26–32 in *Wines in the Wilderness: Plays by African American Women from the Harlem Renaissance to the Present*, ed. Elizabeth Brown Guillory. New York: Praeger.

Johnson, Merri Lisa, ed. 2002. *Jane Sexes It Up: True Confessions of Feminist Desire*. New York: Four Walls Eight Windows.

Jones, Colin, and Roy Porter, eds. 1994. *Reassessing Foucault: Power, Medicine, and the Body*. New York: Routledge.

Jones, Jacqueline.1985. *Labor of Love, Labor of Sorrow: Black Women, Work, and the Family from Slavery to the Present*. New York: Basic.

Jones, Mother (Mary). [1910] 2005. "'Girl Slaves of the Milwaukee Breweries." Pp. 124–125 in *Feminist Theory: A Reader*, 2nd ed., ed. Wendy K. Kolmar and Frances Bartkowski. Boston: McGraw-Hill.

"*Jyllands-Posten* Muhammad Cartoons Controversy." n.d.; http://europenews.dk/en/node/7143 (retrieved November 11, 2011).

Kamen, Paula. 1991. *Feminist Fatale: Voices from the "Twentysomething" Generation Explore the Future of the "Women's Movement."* New York: Donald I. Fine.

Kaminer, Wendy. 1995. "Feminism's Third Wave: What Do Young Women Want?" *New York Times Book Review*, June 4.

Kandal, Terry. 1995. "Gender, Race, & Ethnicity: Let's Not Forget Class." *Race, Gender, & Class* 2(2): 139–162.

Karl, Marilee. 1995. *Women and Empowerment: Participation and Decision Making*. London: Zed.

Karp, Marcell, and Debbie Stoller, eds. 1999. *The Bust Guide to the New Girl Order*. New York: Penquin.

Katherine, Amber L. 2000. "A Too Early Morning: Audre Lorde's 'An Open Letter to Mary Daly' and Daly's Decision Not to Respond in Kind." Pp. 266–296 in *Feminist Interpretations of Mary Daly*, ed. Sarah Lucia Hoagland and Marilyn Frye. University Park: Pennsylvania State University Press.

Katz, Jonathan Ned. 1976. *Gay American History: Lesbians and Gay Men in the U.S.A.; A Documentary History*. New York: Crowell.

Kauffman, Linda, ed. 1989. *Feminism and Institutions: Dialogues on Feminist Theory*. Cambridge, Mass.: Blackwell.

Keller, Evelyn Fox. 1992. *Secrets of Life, Secrets of Death*. New York: Routledge.

Kellner, Douglas. 1989. *Critical Theory, Marxism, and Modernity*. Baltimore, Md.: Johns Hopkins University Press.

Kelly, Joan. 1984. *History and Theory: The Essays of Joan Kelly*. Chicago: University of Chicago Press.

Kelley, Robin. 1990. *Hammer and Hoe: Alabama Communists during the Great Depression*. Chapel Hill, N.C.: University of North Caroline Press.

_____. 2003. *Freedom Dreams: The Black Radical Imagination*. Boston: Beacon.

Kemp, Alice Abel. 1994. *Women's Work: Devalued and Degraded*. Englewood Cliffs, N.J.: Prentice Hall.

Kempadoo, Kamala, and Jo Doezema, eds. 1999. *Global Sex Workers, Rights, Resistance, and Redefinition*. London: Routledge.

Kerr, Virginia. 1973. "One Step Forward—Two Steps Back: Child Care's Long American History." Pp. 150–167 in *Child Care, Who Cares? Foreign and Domestic Infant and Early Childhood Policies*, ed. Pamela Roby. New York: Basic.

Kessinger, Richard. 2008. "The Solipsism of Daily Experience and the Unequal Body: The Social Construction of Ableness." Master's thesis, University of New Orleans.

Khandker, Shahidur. 1998. *Fighting Poverty with Microcredit: Experience in Bangladesh*. New York: Oxford University Press for the World Bank.

Kimmel, Michael, and Matthew Mahler. 2003. "Adolescent Masculinity, Homophobia, and Violence." *American Behavioral Scientist* 46(10): 1439–1458.

King, Anthony, ed. 1991. *Culture, Globalization, and the World-System*. London: Macmillan.

King, Deborah. [1988] 1993. "Multiple Jeopardy: The Context of a Black Feminist Ideology." Pp. 220–236 in *Feminist Frameworks*, 3rd ed., ed. Alison M. Jaggar and Paula S. Rothenberg. Boston: McGraw-Hill.

King, Katie. 1990. "Producing Sex, Theory, and Culture: Gay/Straight Remappings in Contemporary Feminism." Pp. 82–101. *Conflicts in Feminism*, ed. Marianne Hirsch and Evelyn Fox Keller. New York: Routledge.

King, Ynestra. 1989. "The Ecology of Feminism and the Feminism of Ecology." Pp. 18-28 in *Healing the Wounds: The Promise of Ecofeminism*, ed. Judith Plant. Philadelphia: New Society; Ontario: Between the Lines.

_____. 1990. "Healing the Wounds: Feminism, Ecology, and the Nature/Culture Dualism." Pp. 106–121 in *Reweaving the World: The Emergence of Eco*feminism, ed. Irene Diamond and Gloria Orenstein. San Francisco: Sierra Club.

Kinsey, Alfred, Wardell Baxter Pomeroy, and Clyde Eugene Martin. [1943] 1975. *Sexual Behavior in the Human Male*. Bloomington: Indiana University Press.

Kinsey, Alfred, Wardell Baxter Pomeroy, Clyde Eugene Martin, and Paul Gebhard. [1953] 1998. *Sexual Behavior in the Human Female*. Bloomington: Indiana University Press.

Kirby, Jack Temple. 1987. *Rural Worlds Lost: The American South, 1920–1960*. Baton Rouge: Louisiana State University Press.

Kirk, Gwyn, and Margo Okazawa-Rey. [1998] 2001. *Women's Lives: Multicultural Perspectives*, 2nd ed. Boston: McGraw-Hill.

Kishwar, Madhu, and Ruth Vanita. 1984. *In Search of Answers: Indian Women's Voices from Manushi*. London: Zed.

Klein, Melanie. 1975. *Love, Guilt and Reparation: And Other Works, 1921–1945*. London: Hogarth.

Klein, Melissa. 1997. "Duality and Redefinition: Young Feminism and the Alternative Music Community." Pp. 207–225 in *Third Wave Agenda: Being Feminist, Doing Feminism*, ed. Leslie Heywood and Jennifer Drake. Minneapolis: University of Minnesota Press

Knott, Sarah, and Barbara Taylor. 2005. *Women, Gender, and the Enlightenment*. New York: Palgrave Macmillan.

Koedt, Anne. [1970] 2005. "'The Myth of the Vaginal Orgasm.'" Pp. 227–231 in *Feminist Theory: A Reader*, 2nd ed., ed. Wendy K. Kolmar and Frances Bartkowski. Boston: McGraw-Hill.

Kollontai, Alexandra. [1914] 2005. "'Working Woman and Mother.'" Pp. 126–130 in *Feminist Theory: A Reader*, 2nd ed., ed. Wendy K. Kolmar and Frances Bartkowski. Boston: McGraw-Hill.

Kolodny, Annette. 1980. "Dancing through the Minefield: Some Observations on the Theory, Practice, and Politics of a Feminist Literary Criticism." *Feminist Studies* 6(1): 1–25.

Komarovsky, Mirra. 1946. "Cultural Contradictions in Sex Roles." *American Journal of Sociology* 52(November): 184–189.

_____. 1953. *Women in the Modern World: Their Education and Their Dilemmas.* Boston: Little, Brown.

Koyama, Emi. 2003. "The Transfeminist Manifesto." Pp. 244–259 in *Catching a Wave: Reclaiming Feminism for the 21st Century*, ed. Rory Dicker and Alison Piepmeier. Boston: Northeastern University Press.

Kramarae, Cheris, and Paula A. Treichler, eds. 1985. *A Feminist Dictionary.* Boston: Pandora.

Krauss, Celene. 1994. "Women of Color on the Front Line." In *Unequal Protection: Environmental Justice & Communities of Color*, ed. Robert Bullard. San Francisco: Sierra Club.

Kristeva, Julia. [1977] 1980. *Desire in Language A Semiotic Approach to Literature and Art.* Translated by Leon Roudiez. New York: Columbia University Press.

_____. [1980] 1982. *Powers of Horror: An Essay on Abjection.* Translated by Leon Roudiez. New York: Columbia University Press.

Kropotkin, Peter. [1914] 2005. *Mutual Aid: A Factor of Evolution.* Boston: Extending Horizons/Porter Sargent.

Kuhn, Thomas S. [1962] 1970. *The Structure of Scientific Revolutions*, 2nd ed. Chicago: University of Chicago Press.

Labaton, Vivien, and Dawn Lundy Martin, eds. 2004. *The Fire This Time: Young Activists and the New Feminism.* New York: Anchor.

LaDuke, Winona. [1995] 2005. "'Mothers of Our Nations: Indigenous Women Address the World.'" Pp. 525–528 in *Feminist Theory: A Reader*, 2nd ed., ed. Wendy K. Kolmar and Frances Bartkowski. Boston: McGraw-Hill.

Lairap-Fonderson, Josephine. 2002. "The Disciplinary Power of Micro Credit: Examples from Kenya and Cameroon." Pp. 182–198 in *Rethinking Empowerment: Gender and Development in a Global/Local world*, ed. Jane Parpart, Shirin Rai, and Kathleen Staudt. New York: Routledge.

Landry, Donna, and Gerald MacLean. 1993. *Materialist Feminisms.* Cambridge, Mass.: Blackwell.

Landsman, Gail. H. 1992. "The 'Other' as Political Symbol: Images of the Indians in the Woman Suffrage Movement." *Ethnohistory* 39(1): 247–284.

Laslett, Peter. 1965. *The World We Have Lost.* London: Methuen.

Leacock, Eleanor Burke. 1972. "Introduction." Pp. 7–67 in Friedrich Engels's *The Origin of the Family, Private Property, and the State.* New York: International.

Leacock, Eleanor, and Helen I. Safa. 1986. *Women's Work: Development and the Division of Labor by Gender.* South Hadley, Mass.: Bergin & Garvey.

Leap, William L., and Tom Boellstorff. 2004. "Introduction: Globalization and 'New' Articulations of Same-Sex Desire." Pp. 1–22 in *Speaking in Queer Tongues: Globalization and Gay Language*, ed. William L Leap and Tom Boellstorff. Urbana: University of Illinois Press.

Learmonth, Anne. 2000. "Bread and Roses across the Pacific." *Hecate* 26(2): 69–87.

Lederer, Laura, ed. 1980. *Take Back the Night: Women on Pornography.* New York: William Morrow.

Lemert, Charles. 2004. *Social Theory: The Multicultural and Classical Readings.* Boulder, Colo.: Westview.

Lemert, Charles C., and Esme Bhan. 1998. *The Voice of Anna Julia Cooper: Including "A Voice from the South" and Other Important Essays, Papers, and Letters.* Lanham, Md.: Rowman & Littlefield.

Lengermann, Patricia, and Jill Niebrugge-Brantley. 1998. *The Women Founders: Sociology and Social Theory, 1830–1930.* Boston: McGraw-Hill.

Lenin, V. I. [1917] 1996. *Imperialism: The Highest Stage of Capitalism.* London: Pluto.

_____. 1920. "On Sex-Love." Translation by Sally Ryan. Marxists.org; www.marxists.org/archive/zetkin/1920/Lenin/zetkin1.htm (retrieved May 1, 2010).

_____. [1934] 1995. *The Emancipation of Women: From the Writings of V. I. Lenin.* New York: International.

Lerner, Gerda. 1979. *The Majority Finds Its Past: Placing Women in History.* New York: Oxford University Press.

_____. 1993. *The Creation of Feminist Consciousness.* New York: Oxford University Press.

Lessing, Doris. 1963. "To Room Nineteen." Pp. 278–287 in *A Man and Two Women.* NewYork: Simon & Schuster.

Levin, Murray. 1971. *Political Hysteria in America: The Democratic Capacity for Repression.* New York: Basic.

Levine, Irene. 1993. "Family as Mapped Realities." *Journal of Family Issues* 14(1): 82–91.

Lewis, Reina, and Sara Mills, eds. 2003. *Feminist Postcolonial Theory: A Reader.* New York: Routledge.

Li, Huey-li. 1993. "A Cross Cultural Critique of Ecofeminism." Pp. 272–294 in *Ecofeminism: Women, Animals, Nature*, ed. Greta Gaard. Philadelphia: Temple University Press.

Lim, Linda. 1985. *Women Workers in Multinational Enterprises in Developing Countries*. Geneva: International Labor Organization.

Lind, Amy, and Jessica Share. 2003. "Queering Development: Institutionalized Heterosexuality in Development Theory, Practice, and Politics in Latin America." Pp. 55–73 in *Feminist Futures: Re-Imagining Women, Culture, and Development*, ed. Kum-Kum Bhavnani, John Foran, and Priya Kurian. New York: Zed.

Longauex y Vasquez, Enriqueta. 1971. "Colonized Women: The Mexican-American Woman." Pp. 200–204 in *Writings from the Women's Liberation Movement: Liberation Now!* ed. Deborah Babcox and Madeline Belkin. New York: Dell.

Lopach, James, and Jean Luckowski. 2005. *Jeannette Rankin: A Political Woman*. Boulder: University Press of Colorado.

Lorber, Judith. 1994. *Paradoxes of Gender*. New Haven, Conn.: Yale University Press.

Lorde, Audre. 1980. "Uses of the Erotic: The Erotic as Power." Pp. 295–300 in *Take Back the Night: Women on Pornography*. ed. Laura Lederer. New York: William Morrow.

Lorde, Audre. 1984. *Sister/Outsider*. Trumansburg, N.Y.: Crossing.

Love, Heather. 2007. *Feeling Backward: Loss and the Politics of Queer Theory*. Cambridge, Mass.: Harvard University Press.

Lovell, Terry. 2000. "Thinking Feminism with and against Bourdieu." *Feminist Theory* 1(1): 11–32.

Lublin, Nancy. 1998. *Pandora's Box: Feminism Confronts Reproductive Technology*. Lanham, Md.: Rowman & Littlefield.

Luft, Rachel E., and Jane Ward. 2009. "Toward an Intersectionality Just Out of Reach: Confronting Challenges of Intersectional Practice." Pp. 9–37 in *Perceiving Gender Locally, Globally, and Intersectionally (Advances in Gender Research vol. 13)*, ed. Vasilikie Demos and Marcia Texler Segal. Bingley, U.K.: Emerald Group.

Lugones, Maria. 1997. "Playfulness, 'World'-Traveling, and Loving Perception." Pp. 147–159 in *Feminist Social Thought: A Reader*, ed. Diana Tietjens Meyers. New York: Routledge.

Lugones, Maria C., and Elizabeth V. Spelman. [1983] 2005. "'Have We Got a Theory for You! Feminist Theory, Cultural Imperialism, and the Demand for "The Woman's Voice"'." Pp. 17–26 in *Feminist Theory: A Reader*, 2nd ed., ed. Wendy K. Kolmar and Frances Bartkowski. Boston: McGraw-Hill.

Luke, Timothy. 1999. *Capitalism, Democracy, and Ecology: Departing from Marx*. Urbana: University of Illinois Press.

Luxemburg, Rosa. [1908] 2004. "The Dissolution of Primitive Communism: Introduction to Political Economy." Pp. 71–110 in *The Rosa Luxemburg Reader*, ed. Peter Hudis and Kevin Anderson. New York: Monthly Review.

_____. [1913] 1951. *The Accumulation of Capital*. New Haven, Conn.: Yale University Press.

_____. [1915] 1972. *The Accumulation of Capital: An Anti-Critique*. New York: Monthly Review.

_____. [1915] 2004. *The Junius Pamphlet: The Crisis in German Social Democracy*. Pp. 312–341 in *The Rosa Luxemburg Reader*, ed. Peter Hudis and Kevin Anderson. New York: Monthly Review.

Lyotard, Jean-François. 1984. *The Postmodern Condition: A Report on Knowledge*. Translated by Geoff Bennington and Brian Massumi. Minneapolis: University of Minnesota Press.

Maatita, Florence. 2005. "Que Viva La Mujer: Negotiating Chicana Feminist Identities." Pp. 23–38 in *Different Wavelengths: Studies of the Contemporary Women's Movement*, ed. Jo Reger. New York: Routledge.

Maccoby, Eleanor, ed. 1966. *The Development of Sex Differences*. Stanford, CA: Stanford University Press.

Macionis, John. [2002] 2011. *Society: The Basics*. Upper Saddle River, N.J.: Prentice Hall.

Mack-Canty, Colleen. 2005. "Third Wave Feminism and Ecofeminism: Reweaving the Nature/Culture Duality." Pp. 195–211 in *Different Wavelengths: Studies of the Contemporary Women's Movement*, edited by Jo Reger. New York: Routledge.

MacKinnon, Catharine. 1979. *Sexual Harassment of Working Women: A Case of Sex Discrimination*. New Haven, Conn.: Yale University Press.

_____. 1984. *Toward a Feminist Theory of the State*. New York: Academic.

_____. 1987. *Feminism Unmodified: Discourses on Life and Law*. Cambridge, Mass.: Harvard University Press.

_____. 1988. *Pornography and Civil Rights: A New Day for Women's Equality*. New York: Organizing against Pornography.

Magdoff, Harry. 1969. *The Age of Imperialism*. New York: Monthly Review.

Maguire, Patricia. 1984. *Women in Development: An Alternative Analysis*. Amherst: University of Massachusetts Center for International Education.

Manalansan, Martin F., IV, and Arnaldo Cruz-Malavé. 2002. "Introduction: Dissident Sexualities/Alternative Globalisms." Pp. 1–12 in *Queer Globalizations: Citizenship and the Afterlife of Colonialism*, ed. Arnaldo Cruz-Malavé and Martin F. Manalansan IV. New York: New York University Press.

Mandel, Ernest. 1970. *Marxist Economic Theory*. New York: International.

Mann, Susan A. 1986. "Family, Class, and State in Women's Access to Abortion and Day Care: The Case of the United States." Pp. 223–253 in *Family, Economy, & State: The Social Reproduction Process under Capitalism*, ed. James Dickinson and Bob Russell. London: Croom Helm.

_____. 1990a. *Agrarian Capitalism in Theory and Practice*. Chapel Hill: University of North Carolina Press.

_____. 1990b. "Common Grounds and Crossroads: Slavery, Sharecropping, and Sexual Inequality." *Signs: Journal of Women in Culture and Society* 14(4): 774-798.

_____. 2000. "The Scholarship of Difference: A Scholarship of Liberation?" *Sociological Inquiry* 70(4): 475–498.

_____. 2008. "Feminism and Imperialism, 1890–1920: Our Anti-Imperialist Sisters—Missing in Action from American Feminist Sociology." *Sociological Inquiry* 78(4): 461–489.

_____. 2011. "Pioneers of Ecofeminism and Environmental Justice." *Feminist Formations* 23(2): 1–25.

Mann, Susan A., and Douglas J. Huffman. 2005. "Decentering Second Wave Feminism and the Rise of the Third Wave." *Science & Society* 69(1): 56–91.

Mann, Susan A., and Lori R. Kelley. 1997. "Standing at the Crossroads of Modernist Thought: Collins, Smith and the New Feminist Epistemologies." *Gender & Society* 11(4): 391-408.

Mann, Susan A., and Michael. D. Grimes. 2003. "Common and Contested Ground: Marxism and Race, Gender, and Class Analysis." *Race, Gender, & Class* 8(2): 3–22.

Marcuse, Herbert. [1955] 1987. *Eros and Civilization: A Philosophical Inquiry into Freud*. Philadelphia: Psychology Press.

_____. 1964. *One-Dimensional Man: Studies in the Ideology of Advanced Industrial Society*. Boston: Beacon.

Margolick, David. 2001. *Strange Fruit: The Biography of a Song*. New York: HarperCollins.

Marshall, Barbara L. 2000. *Configuring Gender: Explorations in Theory and Politics*. Orchard Park, N.Y.: Broadview.

_____. 2008. "Feminism and Constructionism." Pp. 687–700 in *Handbook of Constructionist Research*, ed. James Holstein and Jaber Gubrium. New York: Guilford.

Marshall, Susan. [1989] 1995. "Keep Us on the Pedestal: Women against Feminism in Twentieth-Century America." Pp. 567–580 in *Women: A Feminist Perspective*, ed. Jo Freeman. Palo Alto, Calif.: Mayfield.

Martin, Jane Roland. 2001. "Mary Wollstonecraft, 1759–97." Pp. 69–72 in *Fifty Major Thinkers on Education: From Confucius to Dewey*, ed. Joy A. Palmer. London: Routledge.

Marx, Karl. [1848] 1972. "Manifesto of the Communist Party." Pp. 331–362 in *The Marx-Engels Reader*, 1st ed., ed. Robert Tucker. New York: W. W. Norton

_____. [1852] 1978. "The Eighteenth Brumaire of Louis Bonaparte." Pp. 594–617 in *The Marx-Engels Reader*, 2nd ed., ed. Robert Tucker. New York: W. W. Norton.

_____. [1867] 1967. *Capital, Volume I*. Moscow: Progress.

_____. [1882] 1986. *Ethnological Notebooks of Karl Marx*. Edited by Lawrence Krader. New York: Irvington.

Mattick, Paul. 1978. "Rosa Luxemburg in Retrospect." *Root and Branch* 6:1–14.

McCall, Leslie. (2005). "The Complexity of Intersectionality." *Signs* (30)3: 1771–1800.

McCall, Michal. 1996. "Postmodernism and Social Inquiry." *Symbolic Interaction* 19(4): 363–365.

McCaskill, Barbara, and Layli Phillips. 1996. "We Are All 'Good Woman'! A Womanist Critique of the Current Feminist Conflict." Pp. 106–122 in *"Bad Girls"/"Good Girls": Women, Sex, and Power in the Nineties*, ed. Nan Bauer-Maglin and Donna Perry. New Brunswick, N.J.: Rutgers University Press.

McClintock, Anne. 1995. *Imperial Leather: Race, Gender, and Sexuality in the Colonial Contest*. New York: Routledge.

McClintock, Anne, Aamir Mufti, and Ella Shohat, eds. 1997. *Dangerous Liaisons: Gender, Nation, and Postcolonial Perspectives*. Minneapolis: University of Minnesota Press.

McCormack, Thelma. 1978. "Machismo in Media Research: A Critical Review of Research on Violence and Pornography." *Social Problems* Vol.XXV 5(June): 552–554.

McHoul, Alec, and Wendy Grace. 1993. *A Foucault Primer: Discourse, Power, and the Subject*. New York: NYU Press.

McIntosh, Peggy. [1988] 2004. "White Privilege: Unpacking the Invisible Knapsack." Pp. 86–93 in *Women's Voices, Feminist Visions: Classic and Contemporary Readings*, ed. Susan Shaw and Janet Lee. Boston: McGraw-Hill.

McLelland, Mark. 2005. *Queer Japan from the Pacific War to the Internet Age*. Lanham, Md.: Rowman & Littlefield.

McMichael, Philip. 1996 . *Development and Social Change: A Global Perspective*. 1st ed. Thousand Oaks, Calif.: Pine Forge/Sage.

_____. 2008. *Development and Social Change: A Global Perspective.* 3rd ed.Thousand Oaks, CA: Pine Forge/Sage.
McNay, Louis. 1992. *Foucault and Feminism: Power, Gender and the Self.* Cambridge: Polity.
_____. 2000. *Gender and Agency: Reconfiguring the Subject in Feminist and Social Theory.* Cambridge: Polity.
McWhorter, Ladelle. 1999. *Bodies and Pleasures: Foucault and the Politics of Sexual Normalization.* Bloomington: Indiana University Press.
Mead, Margaret. 1928. *Coming of Age in Samoa: A Psychological Study of Primitive Youth for Western Civilization.* New York: Blue Ribbon.
_____. 1935. *Sex and Temperament in Three Primitive Societies.* New York: William Morrow.
_____. [1935] 2005. "'Sex and Temperament' from *Sex and Temperament in Three Primitive Societies.*" Pp. 157–162 in *Feminist Theory: A Reader,* 2nd ed., ed. Wendy K. Kolmar and Frances Bartkowski. Boston: McGraw-Hill.
Meeropol, Abel. 1939. "Strange Fruit." 78 rpm. Sung by Billie Holliday. Recorded April 20. Commodore.
Mellor, Mary. 1997. *Feminism and Ecology.* New York: NYU Press.
Memmi, Albert. [1957] 1991. *The Colonizer and the Colonized.* Boston: Beacon.
Mendoza, Breny. 2002. "Transnational Feminisms in Question." *Feminist Theory* 3: 295–314.
Merchant, Carolyn. 1981. *The Death of Nature: Women, Ecology, and the Scientific Revolution.* San Francisco: Harper & Row.
_____. 1989. *Ecological Revolutions: Nature, Gender, and Science in New England.* Chapel Hill: University of North Carolina Press.
_____. 1995. *Earthcare: Women and the Environment.* New York: Routledge.
_____. 2007. *American Environmental History: An Introduction.* New York: Columbia University Press.
Merchant, Carolyn, ed. 1999. *Ecology: Key Concepts in Critical Theory.* Amherst, N.Y.: Humanity.
Merrick, Beverly G. 1988. "Rosa Luxemburg: A Socialist with a Human Face." Feminist Theory Website: Rosa Luxemburg, www.cddc.vt.edu/feminism/Luxemburg.html.
Messer-Davidow, Ellen. 2002. *Disciplining Feminism: From Social Activism to Academic Discourse.* Durham, N.C.: Duke University Press.
Mies, Maria. 1986. *Patriarchy and Accumulation on a World Scale: Women in the International Division of Labor.* London: Zed.
Mies, Maria, Veronika Bennholdt-Thomsen and Claudia Von Werlhof. 1988. *Women: The Last Colony.* London: Zed.
Mies, Maria, and Vandana Shiva. 1993. *Ecofeminism.* London: Zed.
Mihesuah, Devon Abbott. 2003. *Indigenous American Women: Decolonization, Empowerment, Activism.* Lincoln: University of Nebraska Press.
Mill, Harriet Taylor. [1851] 1970. "Enfranchisement of Women." Pp. 89–122 in *Essays on Sex Equality,* ed. Alice Rossi. Chicago: University of Chicago Press.
Mill, John Stuart. [1869] 1970. "The Subjection of Women." Pp. 123–242 in *Essays on Sex Equality,* ed. Alice Rossi. Chicago: University of Chicago Press.
Mill, John Stuart, and Harriet Taylor. [1832] 1970. "Early Essays on Marriage and Divorce." Pp. 67–87 in *Essays on Sex Equality: John Stuart Mill and Harriet Taylor Mill,* ed. Alice Rossi. Chicago: University of Chicago Press.
Miller, James. 1993. *The Passion of Foucault.* New York: Simon & Schuster.
Miller, Leslie. 2008. "Foucauldian Constructionism." Pp. 251–274 in *Handbook of Constructionist Research,* ed. James Holstein and Jaber Gubrium. New York: Guilford.
Millett, Kate. 1970. *Sexual Politics.* New York: Ballantine.
Million Woman March. 1997. "Our Platform Issues," October 25; http: webspace.webring.com/people/wk/khandi_pages/mwm/platform-issues.htm (retrieved Aug. 22, 2001).
Minh-ha, Trinh. 1989. *Woman Native Other: Writing Postcoloniality and Feminism.* Bloomington: Indiana University Press.
_____. 1997. "Not You/Like You: Postcolonial Women and the Interlocking Questions of Identity and Difference." Pp. 415–419 in *Dangerous Liaisons: Gender, Nation, and Postcolonial Perspectives,* ed. Anne McClintock, Aamir Mufti, and Ella Shohat. Minneapolis: University of Minnesota Press.
Mitchell, Juliet. 1971. *Women's Estate.* London: Penguin.
_____. 1975. *Psychoanalysis and Feminism.* Harmondsworth, U.K.: Penguin.
Mohanty, Chandra Talpade. 1984. "Under Western Eyes: Feminist Scholarship and Colonial Discourses." *Boundary 2* 12(3)–13(1): 333–358.
_____. [1984] 2005. "'Under Western Eyes: Feminist Scholarship and Colonial Discourses' from *Third World Women and the Politics of Feminism.*" Pp. 372–379 in *Feminist Theory: A Reader,* 2nd ed., ed. Wendy Kolmar K. and Frances Bartkowski. Boston: McGraw-Hill.
_____. [2003] 2006. *Feminism without Borders: Decolonizing Theory, Practicing Solidarity.* Durham, N.C.: Duke University Press.

Moi, Toril. 1985. *Sexual/Textual Politics: Feminist Literary Theory*. London: Methuen.
_____. 1991. *French Feminist Thought: A Reader*. Oxford: Blackwell.
Molyneux, Maxine. 1985. "Mobilization without Emancipation? Women's Interests, the State, and Revolution in Nicaragua." *Feminist Studies* 11(2): 227–254.
Moore, Stephen. 1998. "Proposition 13: Then, Now and Forever." Cato.org; www.cato.org/pub_display.php?pub_id=5682 (retrieved Aug. 20, 2011).
Moraga, Cherríe, and Gloria Anzaldúa, eds. [1981] 1983. *This Bridge Called My Back: Writings by Radical Women of Color*. New York: Kitchen Table—Women of Color Press.
Morales, Aurora Levins. [1981] 1983. "... And Even Fidel Can't Change That!" Pp. 53–56 in *This Bridge Called My Back: Writings by Radical Women of Color*, eds. Cherríe Moraga and Gloria Anzaldúa. New York: Kitchen Table—Women of Color Press.
Morgan, Joan. 1999. *When Chickenheads Come Home to Roost: A Hip-Hip Feminist Breaks It Down*. New York: Simon & Schuster.
Morgan, Lewis Henry. [1877] 1964. *Ancient Society; or, Researches in the Lines of Human Progress from Savagery through Barbarism to Civilization*. New York: Henry Holt.
Morgan, Robin. 1977. *Going Too Far: The Personal Chronicle of a Feminist*. New York: Random House/Vintage.
_____. 1980. "Theory and Practice: Pornography and Rape." Pp. 134–140 in *Take Back the Night: Women on Pornography*, ed. Laura Lederer. New York: William Morrow.
_____. [1984] 1996. "Preface to the Feminist Press Edition." Pp. vii–xii in *Sisterhood Is Global: The International Women's Movement Anthology*, ed. Robin Morgan. New York: Feminist Press.
Morgan, Robin, ed. 1970. *Sisterhood Is Powerful: An Anthology of Writings from the Women's Liberation Movement*. New York: Random House.
_____. 1984. *Sisterhood Is Global: The International Women's Movement Anthology*. Garden City, N.Y.: Anchor/Doubleday.
Morrison, Toni. [1987] 1998. *Beloved*. New York: Plume.
Morton, Stephen. 2003. *Gayatri Chakravorty Spivak*. New York: Routledge.
Moser, Caroline. 1993. *Gender Planning and Development: Theory, Practice, and Training*. New York: Routledge.
Muñoz, José Esteban. 1999. *Disidentifications: Queers of Color and the Performance of Politics*. Minneapolis: University of Minnesota Press.
Murray, Alison. 2003. "Debt-Bondage and Trafficking: Don't Believe the Hype." Pp. 413–426 in *Feminist Postcolonial Theory: A Reader*, ed. Reina Lewis and Sara Mills. New York: Routledge.
Murray, Pauli. 1970. "The Liberation of Black Women." Pp. 87-102 in *Voices of the New Feminism*. ed. Mary Lou Thompson. Boston: Beacon.
Naples, Nancy A. 2002. "The Challenges and Possibilities of Transnational Feminist Praxis." Pp. 267–281 in *Women's Activism and Globalization*, ed. Nancy Naples and Manisha Desai. New York: Routledge.
Naples, Nancy A., and Manisha Desai. 2002. *Women's Activism and Globalization: Linking Local Struggles and Transnational Politics*. New York. Routledge.
Narayan, Uma. 1997. *Dislocating Cultures/Identities, Traditions, and Third World Feminism*. New York: Routledge.
Narayan, Uma, and Sandra Harding, eds. 2000. *Decentering the Center: Philosophy for a Multicultural, Postcolonial, and Feminist World*. Bloomington: Indiana University Press.
Nestle, Joan, Clare Howell, and Riki Wilchins, eds. 2002. *GenderQueer: Voices from Beyond the Sexual Binary*. New York: Alyson.
Nettl, Peter. 1969. *Rosa Luxemburg*. New York: Oxford University Press.
Newton, Esther, and Shirley Waltons. [1984] 2000. "The Misunderstanding: Toward a More Precise Sexual Vocabulary." In *Margaret Mead Made Me Gay: Personal Essays, Public Ideas*, ed. Esther Newton. Durham, N.C.: Duke University Press.
Nicholson, Linda J. 1990. *Feminism/Postmodernism*. New York: Routledge.
_____. 1997. *The Second Wave: A Reader in Feminist Theory*. New York: Routledge.
Norwood, Vera. 1993. *Made from This Earth: American Women and Nature*. Chapel Hill: University of North Carolina Press.
Nye, Andrea. 1999. "Luxemburg and Socialist Feminism." In *Rosa Luxemburg: Reflections and Writings*, ed. Paul Le Blanc. New York: Humanity.
Nyong'o, Tavia. 2009. "The Unforgiveable Transgression of Being Caster Semenya" Posted Sept. 8; http://bullybloggers.wordpress.com/tag/caster-semenya.
O'Brien, Karen. 2009. *Women and Enlightenment in 18th-Century Britain*. Cambridge: Cambridge University Press.
O'Brien, Mary. 1981. *The Politics of Reproduction*. London: Routledge & Kegan Paul.
O'Connor, James.1997. "Socialism and Ecology." *Capitalism, Nature, Socialism* 2(3): 1–12.
O'Neill, John. 1995. *The Poverty of Postmodernism*. New York: Routledge.

O'Reilly, Jane. 1971. "Click! The Housewife's Moment of Truth." In the preview issue of *Ms.*, published as an insert to *New York* magazine, Dec. 20.

O'Rourke, Meghan. 2011. "The Angry Muse." *New York Times Book Review*, April 3.

Oakley, Ann. 1974a. *Housewife*. New York: Pantheon.

_____. 1974b. *The Sociology of Housework*. New York: Pantheon.

Offen, Karen. 1988. "Defining Feminism: A Comparative Historical Approach." *Signs: Journal of Women in Culture and Society* 14(1) 128–152.

Olsen, Tillie. [1961] 1994. *Tell Me a Riddle*. New York: Dell.

Ong, Aihwa. 1987. *Spirits of Resistance and Capitalist Discipline: Factory Women in Malaysia*. Albany: State University of New York Press.

_____. 1991. "The Gender and Labor Politics of Postmodernity." *Annual Review of Anthropology* 20(1): 279–309.

_____. [1999] 2006. *Flexible Citizenship: The Cultural Logics of Transnationality*. Durham, N.C.: Duke University Press.

Orr, Catherine M. 1997. "Charting the Current of the Third Wave." *Hypatia: A Journal of Feminist Philosophy* 12 (3): 29–45.

Otto, Dianne. 1996. "Nongovernmental Organizations in the United Nations System: The Emerging Role of International Civil Society." *Human Rights Quarterly* 18(1): 107–141.

Painter, Nell Irvin. 1997. *Sojourner Truth: A Life, a Symbol*. New York: W. W. Norton.

Papandreou, Margarita Chant. 1988. "Causes and Cures of Anti-Americanism." Pp.152–154 in *Women on War: Essential Voices for the Nuclear Age*, ed. Daniela Gioseffi. New York: Simon & Schuster.

Parenti, Michael.1995. "Imperialism 101." Chapter 1 of *Against Empire* (San Francisco, City Lights); www.michaelparenti.org/Imperialism101.html (retrieved Sept. 28, 2007).

Parpart, Jane, Patricia Connelly, and Eudine Barriteau. 2000. *Theoretical Perspectives on Gender and Development*. Ottawa, Ontario: International Development Research Centre.

Parpart, Jane, Shirin Rai, and Kathleen Staudt, eds. 2002. *Rethinking Empowerment: Gender and Development in a Global/Local World*. New York: Routledge.

Parry, Benita. 1987. "Problems in Current Theories of Colonial Discourse." *Oxford Literary Review* 9(1–2): 27–58.

Parsons, Talcott. 1965. "The Normal American Family." Pp. 31–50 in *Man and Civilization: The Family's Search for Survival; A Symposium*, ed. Seymour M. Farber, Piero. Mustacchi, and Roger H. L. Wilson. New York: McGraw-Hill.

_____. 1966. *Societies: Evolutionary and Comparative Perspectives*. Englewood Cliffs, N.J.: Prentice Hall.

Parsons, Talcott, and Robert Bales, eds. 1955. *Family Socialization and Interaction Process*. New York: Free Press.

Pascoe, C. J. 2007. *Dude You're a Fag: Masculinity and Sexuality in High School*. Berkeley: University of California Press.

Patton, Cindy, and Benigno Sanchez-Eppler. 2000. *Queer Diasporas*. Durham, N.C.: Duke University Press.

Payne, Charles. 1995. *I've Got the Light of Freedom: The Organizing Tradition and the Mississippi Freedom Struggle*. Berkeley: University of California Press.

Pease, John, William H. Form, and Joan Huber Rytina. 1970. "Ideological Currents in American Stratification Literature." *American Sociologist* 5(2): 127–137.

Pels, Dick. 2004. "Strange Standpoints, or How to Define the Situation for Situated Knowledge." Pp. 273–289 in *The Feminist Standpoint Theory Reader: Intellectual and Political Controversies*, ed. Sandra G. Harding. New York: Routledge.

Phelan, Shane. 1997. "The Shape of Queer: Assimilation and Articulation." *Women & Politics* 18(2): 53–73.

Phillips, Anne. 1992. "Universal Pretensions in Political Thought." Pp. 10–30 in *Destabilizing Theory: Contemporary Feminist Debates*, ed. Michèle Barrett and Anne Phillips. Stanford, Calif.: Stanford University Press.

Phoco, Sophia, and Rebecca Wright. 1999. *Introducing Postfeminism*. New York: Totem.

Piercy, Marge. [1976] 1997. *Woman on the Edge of Time*. New York: Ballantine.

_____. 2005. *Sex Wars: A Novel of Gilded Age New York*. New York: Harper Perennial.

Piñeros, Marcela. 2001. "The Art of Being Third Wave: Coloring Outside the Lines." Unpublished manuscript, Florida International University.

Pitts, Leonard. 2008. "Feminism: Standing Up for the F-word." *Times-Picayune*, 9 Feb..

Piven, Frances Fox, and Richard A. Cloward. 1971. *Regulating the Poor: The Functions of Public Welfare*. New York: Pantheon.

_____. 1977. *Poor People's Movements: Why They Succeed, How They Fail*. New York: Pantheon.

Plumwood, Val. [1992] 1996. "Ecosocial Feminism as a General Theory of Oppression." Pp. 207–219 in *Ecology: Key Concepts in Critical Theory*, ed. Carolyn Merchant. New York: Humanity.

Pollitt, Katha. 1999. "Solipsisters." *New York Times Book Review*, April 18.

Portes, Alejandro. 1985. "The Informal Sector and the World-Economy: Notes on the Structure of Subsidized Labor." Pp. 53–62 in *Urbanization and the World-System*, ed. Michael Timberlake. New York: Academic.

Portes, Alejandro, and Saskia Sassen-Koob. 1987. "Making it Underground: Comparative Material on the Informal Sector in Western Market Economies." *American Journal of Sociology* 93: 30–61.

Prakash, Gyan. 1997. "Postcolonial Criticisms and Indian Historiography." Pp. 491–500 in *Dangerous Liaisons: Gender, Nation, and Postcolonial Perspectives*, ed. Anne McClintock, Aamir Mufti, and Ella Shohat. Minneapolis: University of Minnesota Press.

Puar, Jasbir. 2007. *Terrorist Assemblages: Homonationalism in Queer Times*. Durham, N.C.: Duke University Press.

Purdy, Laura. 1996. *Reproducing Persons: Issues in Feminist Bioethics*. Ithaca, N.Y.: Cornell University Press.

Queen, Carol, and Lawrence Schimel, eds. 1997. *Pomosexuals: Challenging Assumptions about Gender and Sexuality*. San Francisco: Cleis.

Quinn, Rebecca. 1997. "An Open Letter to Institutional Mothers." Pp. 174–182 in *Generations: Academic Feminists in Dialogue*, ed. Devoney Looser and Ann Kaplan. Minneapolis: University of Minnesota Press.

Radicalesbians. [1970] 2005. "'The Woman-Identified Woman.'" Pp. 239–242 in *Feminist Theory: A Reader*, 2nd ed., ed. Wendy K. Kolmar and Frances Bartkowski. Boston, McGraw-Hill.

Rainbow, Paul. 1984. *The Foucault Reader*. New York: Pantheon.

Ramazanoglu, Caroline, ed. 1993. *Up against Foucault: Explorations of Some Tensions between Foucault and Feminism*. New York: Routledge.

Randall, Margaret. 1974. *Cuban Women Now*. Toronto: Women's Press.

_____. 1981. *Sandino's Daughters: Testimonies of Nicaraguan Women in Suffrage*. Vancouver: New Star.

Redstockings. [1969] 2005. "'Redstockings Manifesto.'" Pp. 220–221 in *Feminist Theory: A Reader*, 2nd ed., ed. Wendy K. Kolmar and Frances Bartkowski. Boston, McGraw-Hill.

Reed, Evelyn. 1984. "Women: Caste, Class, or Oppressed Sex?" Pp. 132–136 in *Feminist Frameworks: Alternative Theoretical Accounts of the Relations between Men and Women*, 2nd ed., ed. Alison M. Jaggar and Paula S. Rothenberg. Boston: McGraw-Hill.

Reger, Jo, ed. 2005. *Different Wavelengths: Studies of the Contemporary Women's Movement*. New York: Routledge.

Rich, Adrienne. [1976] 1977. *Of Woman Born: Motherhood as Experience and Institution*. New York: Bantam.

_____. [1980] 2005. "'Compulsory Heterosexuality and Lesbian Existence' from *Blood, Bread, and Poetry*." Pp. 347–356 in *Feminist Theory: A Reader*, 2nd ed., ed. Wendy K. Kolmar and Frances Bartkowski. Boston: McGraw-Hill.

_____. [1984] 2003. "Notes toward a Politics of Location." Pp. 29–42 in *Feminist Postcolonial Theory*, ed. Reina Lewis and Sara Mills. New York: Routledge.

Rich, B. Ruby. 1986. "Review: Feminism and Sexuality in the 1980s." *Feminist Studies* 12(3): 525–561.

Richards, Ellen H. [1910] 1977. *Euthenics: The Science of Controllable Environment*. New York: Arno.

Richardson, Diane. 1996. "'Misguided, Dangerous and Wrong': On Maligning Radical Feminism." Pp. 143–154 in *Radically Speaking: Feminism Reclaimed*. eds. Diane Bell and Renate Klein. London: Zed.

Ritchie, Andrea J. 2006. "Law Enforcement Violence against Women of Color." Pp. 140–159 in *Color of Violence: The Incite! Anthology*. ed. Incite! Women of Color against Volence. Cambridge, Mass.: South End Press.

Ritzer, George. 2011. *Sociological Theory*, 8th ed.Boston: McGraw-Hill.

Roberts, Dorothy. 1998. *Killing the Black Body: Race, Reproduction, and the Meaning of Liberty*. New York: Random House.

Robinson, Cedric. 1983. *Black Marxism: The Making of the Black Radical Tradition*. London: Zed.

Roiphe, Katie. 1993. *The Morning After: Sex, Fear, and Feminism on Campus*. Boston: Little, Brown.

Roscoe, Will. 1991. *The Zuni Man-Woman*. Albuquerque: University of New Mexico Press.

Rose, Kalima. [1996] 1998. "Taking on the Global Economy." *Crossroads*, March 1996. Reprinted in 1998. Pp. 47–50 in *Women's Lives: Multicultural Perspectives*, ed. Gwyn Kirk and Margo Okazawa Rey. 1st ed. Mountain View, Calif.: Mayfield.

Rosenau, Pauline Marie. 1992. *Post-modernism and the Social Sciences: Insights, Inroads, and Intrusions*. Princeton, N.J.: Princeton University Press.

Rossi, Alice. 1970. *Essays on Sex Equality: John Stuart Mill and Harriet Taylor Mill.* Chicago: University of Chicago Press.

_____. 1974. *The Feminist Papers from Adams to de Beauvoir.* Toronto: Bantam.

Rostow, Walt. 1960. *The Stages of Economic Growth: A Non-Communist Manifesto.* Cambridge: Cambridge University Press.

Roth, Benita. 2004. *Separate Roads to Feminism: Black, Chicana, and White Feminist Movements in America's Second Wave.* New York: Cambridge University Press.

Rothfield, Philipa. 1990. "New Wave Feminism: Feminism and Postmodernism." In *Discourse and Difference: Poststructuralism, Feminism, and the Moment of History*, ed. Andrew Miller and Chris Worth. Clayton, Victoria, Aust.: Centre for General and Comparative Literature, Monash University.

Rowbotham, Sheila. 1975. *Hidden from History: 300 Years of Women's Oppression and the Fight against It.* London: Pluto.

_____. 1978. *Women's Consciousness, Man's World.* Baltimore, Md.: Penguin.

Rubin, Gayle. [1975] 2005. "'The Traffic in Women: Notes on the "Political Economy" of Sex.'" Pp. 273–288 in *Feminist Theory: A Reader*, 2nd ed., ed. Wendy Kolmar K. and Frances Bartkowski. Boston: McGraw-Hill.

_____. 1984. "Thinking Sex: Notes for a Radical Theory of the Politics of Sexuality." Pp. 267–391 in *Pleasure and Danger: Exploring Female Sexuality*, ed. Carole S. Vance. Boston: Routledge and Kegan Paul. [Reprinted as pp. 3–44 in *The Lesbian and Gay Studies Reader*, ed. Henry Abelove, Michèle Aina Barale, and David M. Halperin (New York: Routledge, 1993).]

Rubin, Lillian B. 1976. *Worlds of Pain: Life in the Working-Class Family.* New York: Basic.

_____. 1984. *Intimate Strangers: Men and Women Together.* New York: Harper Colophon.

_____. 1994. *Families on the Fault Line.* New York: HarperCollins.

Rupp, Leila J. 1994. "Constructing Internationalism: The Case of the Transnational Women's Organizations, 1888–1945." *American Historical Review* 99(5): 1571–1600.

_____. 1997. *Worlds of Women: The Making of an International Women's Movement.* Princeton, N.J.: Princeton University Press.

Rushin, Donna Kate. 1983. "The Bridge Poem." Pp.xxi–xxii in *This Bridge Called My Back: Writings by Radical Women of Color*, ed. Cherríe Moraga and Gloria Anzaldúa. New York: Kitchen Table—Women of Color Press.

Russell, Thaddeus. 2008. "The Color of Discipline: Civil Rights and Black Sexuality." *American Quarterly* 60(1): 101–128.

Ruth, Sheila. [1988] 1998. *Issues in Feminism: An Introduction to Women's Studies*, 4th ed. Mountain View, Calif.: Mayfield.

Said, Edward W. [1978] 2003. *Orientalism.* New York: Vintage.

Salih, Sara. 2002. *Judith Butler.* New York: Routledge.

Sanders, Mark. 2006. *Gayatri Chakravorty Spivak: Live Theory.* New York: Continuum.

Sandilands, Catriona. 1997. "Mother Earth, the Cyborg, and the Queer: Ecofeminism and (More) Questions of Identity." *NWSA Journal* 9(3): 18–40.

_____. 1999. *The Good-Natured Feminist: Ecofeminism and the Quest for Democracy.* Minneapolis: University of Minnesota Press.

Sandoval, Chela. [1991] 2003. "U.S. Third-World Feminism: The Theory and Method of Oppositional Consciousness in the Postmodern World." Pp. 75–99 in *Feminist Postcolonial Theory: A Reader*, ed. Reina Lewis and Sara Mills. New York: Routledge.

Sanger, Margaret. 1920. *Woman and the New Race.* New York: Truth.

Sargent. Lydia, ed. 1981. *Women and Revolution: A Discussion of the Unhappy Marriage of Marxism and Feminism.* Cambridge, Mass.: South End.

Sartisky, Joshua. 2006. "On Reading Zora Neale Hurston." Unpublished manuscript, Isidore Newman School, New Orleans.

Schechter, Patricia A. 2001. *Ida B. Wells-Barnett and American Reform: 1880–1930.* Chapel Hill, N.C.: University of North Carolina Press.

Schlafly, Phyllis. 1977. *The Power of the Positive Woman.* New Rochelle, N.Y.: Arlington House.

Schneider, Beth E. 1988. "Political Generations and the Contemporary Women's Movement." *Sociological Inquiry* 58(1): 4–21.

Schott, Linda. 1997. *Reconstructing Women's Thoughts: The Women's International League for Peace and Freedom before World War II.* Stanford, Calif.: Stanford University Press.

Schumpeter, Joseph. [1919] 1955. *Imperialism and Social Classes.* New York: Meridian.

Schweikart, Larry, and Michael Allen. 2004. *A Patriot's History of the United States.* New York: Sentinal Penguin Group.

Scully, Dana. 1990. *Understanding Sexual Violence: A Study of Convicted Rapists.* Boston: Unwin Hyman.

Sears, Alan. 2005. "Queer Anti-Capitalism: What's Left of Lesbian and Gay Liberation?" *Science & Society* 69(1): 92–112.
Seccombe, Wally. 1973. "The Housewife and Her Labour under Capitalism." *New Left Review* 83(January–February): 3–24.
_____. 1986. "Marxism and Demography: Household Forms and Fertility Regimes in the Western European Tradition." Pp. 23–55 in *Family, Economy and State: The Social Reproduction Process under Capitalism*, ed. James Dickinson and Bob Russell. London: Croom Helm.
Sedgwick, Eve. 1990. *Epistemology of the Closet.* Berkeley: University of California Press.
_____. 1992. "Identity Crisis: Queer Politics in the Age of Possibilities." *Village Voice*, June 39.
_____. 1993. *Tendencies.* Durham, N.C.: Duke University Press.
Segrest, Mab. 1994. *Memoir of a Race Traitor.* Cambridge, Mass.: South End Press.
Seidman, Steven. 2000. Queer-ing Sociology, Sociologizing Queer Theory. Pp. 434–455 in *Social Theory: Roots and Branches*, ed. Peter Kivisto. Los Angeles: Roxbury.
Self, Robert. 2006. "The Black Panther Party and the Long Civil Rights Era." Pp. 15–55 in *Search of the Black Panther Party: New Perspectives on a Revolutionary Movement*, ed. Jama Lazerow and Yohuru Williams. Durham, N.C.: Duke University Press.
Sen, Gita, and Caren Grown. 1987. *Development, Crises, and Alternative Visions: Third World Women's Perspectives.* New York: Monthly Review.
Senna, Danzy. 1995. "To Be Real." Pp.5–20 in *To Be Real: Telling the Truth and Changing the Face of Feminism*, ed. Rebecca Walker. New York: Anchor.
Sennett, Richard. 1998. *The Corrosion of Work: The Personal Consequences of Work in the New Capitalism.* New York: W. W. Norton.
Sennett, Richard, and Jonathan Cobb. 1972. *The Hidden Injuries of Social Class.* New York: Vintage.
Shah, Sonia, ed. 1997. *Dragon Ladies: Asian American Feminists Breath Fire.* Cambridge, Mass.: South End Press.
Shapiro, Laura. 1994 "Sisterhood Was Powerful." *Newsweek*, June 20.
Shaw, Stephanie. 1995. "Black Club Women and the Creation of the National Association of Colored Women." Pp. 443–447 in *We Specialize in the Wholly Impossible: A Reader in Black Women's History*, ed. Darlene Clark Hine, Wilma King, and Linda Reed. Brooklyn: Carlson.
Shiva, Vandana. 1989. *Staying Alive: Women, Ecology, and Development.* London: Zed.
Shohat, Ella. 1992. "Notes on the 'Post-colonial.'" *Social Text* 31/32: 100–115.
_____. ed. [1998] 2001. *Talking Visions: Multicultural Feminism in a Transnational Age.* Cambridge, Mass.: MIT Press.
Shorter, Edward. 1975. *The Making of the Modern Family.* New York: Basic.
Shulman, Alix Kates, ed. 1972. *Red Emma Speaks: Selected Writings and Speeches by Emma Goldman.* New York: Random House.
Shuttleworth, Russell P. 2004. "Disabled Masculinity: Expanding the Masculine Repertoire." Pp. 166–180 in *Gendering Disability*, ed. Bonnie G. Smith and Beth Hutchinson. New Brunswick, N.J.: Rutgers University Press.
Sidel, Ruth. 1973. *Women and Child Care in China.* Baltimore, Md.: Penguin.
Sidler, Michelle. 1997. "Living in McJobdom: Third Wave Feminism and Class Inequity." Pp. 25–39 in *Third Wave Agenda: Being Feminist, Doing Feminism*, ed. Leslie Heywood and Jennifer Drake. Minneapolis: University of Minnesota Press.
Siebers, Tobin. 2008. *Disability Theory.* Ann Arbor: University of Michigan Press.
Siegel, Deborah L. 1997a. "The Legacy of the Personal: Generating Theory in Feminism's Third Wave." *Hypatia: A Journal of Feminist Philosophy* 12(3): 46–75.
_____. 1997b. "Reading between the Waves: Feminist Historiography in a 'Postfeminist' Moment." Pp. 55–82 in *Third Wave Agenda: Being Feminist, Doing Feminism*, ed. Leslie Heywood and Jennifer Drake. Minneapolis: University of Minnesota Press.
Silliman, Jael, and Anannya Bhattacharjee, eds. 2002. *Policing the National Body: Race, Gender, and Criminalization.* Cambridge, Mass.: South End.
Simon, Reeva Spector, and Elanor Tejirian, eds. 2005. *The Creation of Iraq: 1914–1921.* New York: Columbia University Press.
Simpson, Helen. 2001. *Getting a Life: Stories.* New York: Knopf.
Singh, Nikhil Pal. 2004. *Black Is a Country: Race and the Unfinished Struggle for Democracy.* Cambridge, Mass.: Harvard University Press.
Sithole-Fundire, Sylvia, Anita Larsson, Ann Schlyter, and Agnes Zhou, eds. 1995. *Gender Research on Urbanization, Housing Planning, and Everyday Life.* Harare and Uppsala: Zimbabwe Women's Resource Center and Network and Nordic Africa Institute.
Sklar, Holly. 2009. "Imagine a Country." Pp. 307–316 in *Race, Class, and Gender in the United States*, ed. Paula S. Rothenberg. New York: Worth.

Sklar, Kathryn Kish, Anja Schuler, and Susan Strasser, eds. 1998. *Social Justice: Feminists in the United States and Germany: A Dialogue in Documents, 1855–1933*. Ithaca, N.Y.: Cornell University Press.

Smart, Barry. 1993. *Postmodernity: Key Ideas*. New York: Routledge.

Smith, Andrea. 2005. *Conquest: Sexual Violence and American Indian Suicide*. Cambridge, Mass.: South End.

Smith, Andrea, Beth Richie, Julia Sudbury, and Janelle White. 2006. "The Color of Violence: Introduction." Pp. 1–10 in *Color of Violence: The Incite! Anthology*, ed. Incite! Women of Color against Violence. Cambridge, Mass.: South End.

Smith, Andy. 1997. "Ecofeminism through an Anticolonial Framework." Pp. 21–37 in *Ecofeminism: Women, Culture, Nature*, ed. Karen J. Warren. Bloomington: Indiana University Press.

Smith, Barbara, ed. 1983. *Home Girls: A Black Feminist Anthology*. Lantham, N.Y.: Kitchen Table—Women of Color Press.

Smith, Dorothy E. 1987. *The Everyday World as Problematic: A Feminist Sociology*. Boston: Northeastern University Press.

_____. 1990. *The Conceptual Practices of Power: A Feminist Sociology of Knowledge*. Boston: Northeastern University Press.

_____. 1993a. "High Noon in Textland: A Critique of Clough." *Sociological Quarterly* 34(1): 183–192.

_____. 1993b. "The Standard North American Family: SNAF as an Ideological Code." *Journal of Family Issues* 14(1): 50–65.

_____. 1996. "Telling the Truth after Postmodernism." *Symbolic Interaction* 19(3): 171–202.

_____. 2004. "Comment on Hekman's "Truth and Method: Feminist Standpoint Theory Revisited." Pp. 263–268 in *The Feminist Standpoint Theory Reader: Intellectual and Political Controversies*, ed. Sandra G. Harding. New York: Routledge.

_____. 2005. *Institutional Ethnography: A Sociology for People*. New York: Rowman & Littlefield.

Smith, Joan, Immanuel Maurice Wallerstein, and Hans-Dieter Evers. 1984. *Households and the World-Economy*. Beverly Hills, Calif.: Sage.

Smith, Linda Tuhiwai. [1999] 2006. *Decolonizing Methodologies: Research and Indigenous Peoples*. New York: Palgrave.

Smythe, Cherry. 1992. *Lesbians Talk Queer Notions*. London: Scarlet.

Sneider, Allison L. 1994. "The Impact of Empire on the North American Woman Suffrage Movement: Suffrage Racism in an Imperial Context." *UCLA Historical Journal* 14: 14–32.

_____. 2008. *Suffragists in an Imperial Age: U. S. Expansion and the Woman Question, 1870–1929*. New York: Oxford University Press.

Snitow, Ann, Christine Stansell, and Sharon Thompson, eds. 1983. *Powers of Desire: The Politics of Sexuality*. New York: Monthly Review.

Snyder, Margaret, and Mary Tadesse. 1995. *African Women and Development: A History*. London: Zed.

Society for Disability Studies. n.d. "Mission Statement"; www.disstudies.org/abstract/mission (retrieved March 1, 2010).

Sokoloff, Natalie J. 1980. *Between Money and Love: The Dialectics of Women's Home and Market Work*. New York: Praeger.

Solway, Jacqueline S. 2006. *The Politics of Egalitarianism: Theory and Practice*. New York: Berghahn.

Somerville, Siobhan. 2000. *Queering the Color Line: Race and the Invention of Homosexuality in American Culture*. Durham, N.C.: Duke University Press.

Soper, Kate. 1993. "Productive Contradictions." Pp. 29–50 in *Up against Foucault: Explorations of Some Tensions between Foucault and Feminism*, ed. Caroline Ramazanoglu. New York: Routledge.

Sorisio, Carolyn. 1997. "A Tale of Two Feminisms: Power and Victimization in Contemporary Feminist Debate." Pp. 134–149 in *Third Wave Agenda: Being Feminist, Doing Feminism*, ed. Leslie Heywood and Jennifer Drake. Minneapolis: University of Minnesota Press.

Spelman, Elizabeth. 1988. *Inessential Woman: Problems of Exclusion in Feminist Thought*. Boston: Beacon.

Spivak, Gayatri Chakravorty. 1987. *In Other Worlds: Essays in Cultural Politics*. London: Methuen.

_____. [1985] 1988. "Can the Subaltern Speak?" Pp. 271–316 in *Marxism and the Interpretation of Culture*, ed. Cary Nelson and Lawrence Grossberg. Urbana: University of Illinois Press.

_____. 1989. "Naming Gayatri Spivak" (Interview). *Stanford Humanities Review* 1(1): 84–97.

_____. 1990. *The Post-colonial Critique: Interviews, Strategies, Dialogues*. London: Routledge.

_____. 1993. *Outside in the Teaching Machine*. New York: Routledge.

_____. [1992] 1997. "Teaching for the Times." Pp. 468–409 in *Dangerous Liaisons: Gender, Nation, and Postcolonial Perspectives*, ed. Anne McClintock, Aamir Mufti, and Ella Shohat. Minneapolis: University of Minnesota Press.

_____. [1999] 2006. *A Critique of Postcolonial Reason: Toward a History of the Vanishing Present*. Cambridge, Mass.: Harvard University Press.

Sprague, Joey, and Mark Zimmerman. 1993. "Overcoming Dualisms: A Feminist Agenda for Sociological Methodology." Pp. 255–280 in *Theory on Gender/Feminism on Theory*, ed. Paula England. New York: Aldine DeGruyter.

Spretnak, Charlene. 1978. *The Lost Goddesses of Ancient Greece: A Collection of Pre-Hellenic Myths*. Ann Arbor, MI: Moon Books..

_____. 1986. *The Spiritual Dimension of Green Politics*. Santa Fe, N.M.: Bear & Co.

_____. 1990. "Ecofeminism: Our Roots and Flowering." Pp. 3–14 in *Reweaving the World: The Emergence of Ecofeminism*, ed. Irene Diamond and Gloria Orenstein. San Francisco: Sierra Club.

Springer, Kimberly. 2002. "Third Wave Black Feminism?" *Signs: Journal of Women in Culture and Society* 27(4): 1059–1082.

Spurlin, William J. 2006. *Imperialism within the Margins: Queer Representation and the Politics of Culture in South Africa*. New York: Palgrave Macmillan.

Stacey, Judith. 1991. *Brave New Families*. New York: Basic.

Stanton, Elizabeth Cady. [1848] 2005. "'Declaration of Sentiments' from *The History of Women's Suffrage*." Pp. 71–73 in *Feminist Theory: A Reader*, 2nd ed., ed. Wendy K. Kolmar and Frances Bartkowski. Boston: Mc-Graw-Hill.1886.

_____. [1866] 1881. "Speech in 1866." P. 181 in *History of Women's Suffrage: 1861–1876*, Volume 2. ed. Elizabeth Cady Stanton, Susan Brownell Anthony, Matilda Joslyn Gage, and Ida Husted Harper. New York: Fowler and Wells.

_____. [1898] 1993. *Eighty Years and More: Reminiscences, 1815–1897*. Boston: Northeastern University Press.

_____. [1898] 2003. *The Women's Bible: A Classic Feminist Perspective*. Mineola, N.Y.: Dover.

Starhawk. 1979. *The Spiral Dance: A Rebirth of the Ancient Religion of the Great Goddess*. San Francisco: Harper.

Stein, Arlene. 1992. "Sisters and Queers: the Decentering of Lesbian Feminism." *Socialist Review* 22(1): 33–35.

_____. 1993. "Introduction." Pp. xi–xvii in *Sisters, Sexperts, Queers: Beyond the Lesbian Nation*, ed. Arlene Stein. New York: Plume.

Stein, Arlene, and Ken Plummer. 1996. "I Can't Even Think Straight: Queer Theory and the Missing Sexual Revolution in Sociology." In *Queer Theory/Sociology*, ed. Steven Seidman. Oxford: Blackwell.

Stein, Gertrude. [1903] 1950. *Things as They Are: A Novel in Three Parts*. Pawlet, Vt.: Banyan.

_____. [1922] 1984. "Miss Furr and Miss Skeene." Pp. 30–36 in *Women and Fiction: Volume 1*, ed. Susan Cahill. New York: New American Library.

_____. [1933] 1960. *The Autobiography of Alice B. Toklas*. Morrow, Ga.: P. Smith.

Stein, Leon. 1962. *The Triangle Fire*. New York: Carroll & Graf.

Steinem, Gloria. 1980. *Outrageous Acts and Everyday Rebellions*. New York: Macmillan.

Steinfels, Margaret O'Brien. 1973. *Who's Minding the Children? The History and Politics of Day Care in America*. New York: Simon & Schuster.

Stoler, Ann Laura. 1995. *Race and the Education of Desire: Foucault's History of Sexuality and the Colonial Order of Things*. Durham, N.C.: Duke University Press.

_____. 2002. *Carnal Knowledge and Imperial Power: Race and the Intimate in Colonial Rule*. Berkeley: University of California Press.

Stoller, Debbie. 1999. "Sex and the Thinking Girl." Pp. 74–84 in *The Bust Guide to the New Girl Order*, ed. Marcelle Karp and Debbie Stoller. New York: Penguin.

Stone, Chris. 2004. "Blood at the Root: 'Strange Fruit' as Historical Document and Pedagogical Tool." *OAH Magazine of History* 19(2): 54–56.

Stone, Lawrence. 1977. *The Family, Sex and Marriage in England: 1500–1800*. New York: Harper & Row.

Stryker, Susan. 2008. "Transgender History, Homonormativity, and Disciplinarity." *Radical History Review* 2008(winter): 145–157.

Sturgeon, Noel. 1997. *Ecofeminist Natures: Race, Gender, Feminist Theory, and Political Action*. New York: Routledge.

Swartz, David L. 1997. *Culture and Power: The Sociology of Pierre Bourdieu*. Chicago: University of Chicago Press.

Sweezy, Paul. 1965. *The Theory of Capitalist Development*. New York: Monthly Review.

Symington, Alison. 2005. "From Tragedy and Injustice to Rights and Empowerment: Accountability in the Economic Realm." Pp. 34–48 in *Defending Our Dreams: Global Feminist Voices for a New Generation*, ed. Shamillah Wilson, Anasuya Sengupta, and Kristy Evans. London: Zed.

Tannen, Deborah. 1990. *You Just Don't Understand: Men and Women in Conversation*. New York: Baltimore.

Taylor, Barbara. 2010. "Carers or Consumers?" *London Review of Books*, November 4.

Taylor, Dorceta E. 1997. "Women of Color, Environmental Justice, and Ecofeminism." Pp. 38–81 in *Ecofeminism: Women, Culture, Nature*, ed. Karen Warren. Bloomington: Indiana University Press.

_____. 2002. *Race, Class, Gender, and American Environmentalism*. General Technical Report PNW-GTR-534Portland, Ore.: U.S. Department of Agriculture, Forest Service, Pacific Northwest Research Station..

Taylor, Verta. 1989. "Social Movement Continuity: The Women's Movement in Abeyance." *American Sociological Review* 54(5): 761–775.

Temple, Kathryn. 2004. "Exporting Violence: The School of the Americas, U.S. Intervention in Latin America, and Resistance." Pp. 107–149 in *The Fire This Time: Young Activists and the New Feminism*, ed. Vivien Labaton and Dawn Lundy Martin. New York: Anchor.

Terborg-Penn, Rosalyn. 1998a. *African-American Women in the Struggle for the Vote, 1850–1920*. Bloomington: Indiana University Press.

_____. 1998b. "Enfranchising Women of Color: Woman Suffragists as Agents of Imperialism." Pp. 41–56 in *Nation, Empire, Colony: Historicizing Gender and Race*, ed. Ruth Roach Pierson and Nupur Chaudhuri. Bloomington: Indiana University Press.

Terrell, Mary Church. [1898] 1995. "The Progress of Colored Women." Pp. 60–74 in *Words of Fire: An Anthology of African American Feminist Thought*, ed. Beverly Guy-Sheftall. New York: New Press.

Thurow, Lester C. 1996. *The Future of Capitalism: How Today's Economic Forces Shape Tomorrow's World*. New York: William Morrow.

Tinker, Irene. 1976. "The Adverse Impact of Development on Women." Pp. 22–34 in *Women and World Development*, ed. Irene Tinker and Michele Bo Bramsen. Washington, D.C.: Overseas Development Council.

Toklas, Alice B. [1932] 1984. *The Alice B. Toklas Cookbook*. Guilford, Conn.: Globe Pequot.

Tompkins, E. Berkeley. 1970. *Anti-Imperialism in the United States: The Great Debate, 1890–1920*. Philadelphia: University of Pennsylvania Press.

Tong, Rosemarie Putnam. 1998. *Feminist Thought: A More Comprehensive Introduction*. 2nd ed. Boulder, Colo.: Westview.

_____. 2009. *Feminist Thought: A More Comprehensive Introduction*. 3rd ed. Boulder, CO: Westview.

Touraine, Allen. 1998. "Sociology without Society." *Current Sociology* 46(2): 119–143.

Tremain, Shelly, ed. 2005. *Foucault and the Government of Disability*. Ann Arbor: University of Michigan Press.

Trotsky, Leon. 1973. *Women and the Family*. New York: Pathfinder.

Troung, Thanh Dam. 1990. *Sex, Money and Morality: The Political Economy of Prostitution and Tourism in South East Asia*. London: Zed.

Truelove, Cynthia. 1987. "The Informal Sector Revisited: The Case of the Colombian Mini-Maquilas." Pp. 95–110 in *Crises in the Caribbean Basin: Past and Present*, ed. Richard Tardanico. Beverly Hills, Calif.: Sage.

Truth, Sojourner. [1851] 2005. "'Ain't I a Woman?'" Pp. 79 in *Feminist Theory: A Reader*, 2nd ed., ed. Wendy K. Kolmar and Frances Bartkowski. Boston: McGraw-Hill.

Tucker, Robert C. 1972. *The Marx-Engels Reader*. New York: W. W. Norton.

Turner, William. 2000. *A Genealogy of Queer Theory*. Philadelphia: Temple University Press.

Tyler, S. Lyman. 1973. *A History of Indian Policy*. Washington, D.C.: U.S. Department of the Interior, Bureau of Indian Affairs.

Tyrrell, Ian R. 1991. *Woman's World/Woman's Empire: The Woman's Christian Temperance Union in International Perspective, 1800–1930*. Chapel Hill: University of North Carolina Press.

Vance, Carole, ed. 1985. *Pleasure and Danger: Exploring Female Sexuality*. Boston: Routledge & Kegan Paul.

Varela, Maria. 1971. "Colonized Women: The Chicana." P.198 in *Liberation Now! Writings from the Women's Liberation Movement*, ed. Deborah Babcox and Madeline Belkin. New York: Dell.

Vogel, Lise. [1973] 1983. *Marxism and the Oppression of Women: Towards a Unitary Theory*. New Brunswick, N.J.: Rutgers University Press.

_____. 1981. "Marxism and Socialist-Feminist Theory: A Decade of Debate." *Current Perspectives in Social Theory* 2: 209–231.

_____. 1991. "Telling Tales: Historians of Our Own Lives." *Journal of Women's History* 2: 89–101.

_____. 1995. *Questions on the Woman Question: Essays in Feminist Theory*. London: Pluto.

Volion, Ashley Maria. 2010. "Everyday Lived-Experiences and the Domain of the Sexual as Explored by Four Physically Disabled Women." Master's thesis, University of New Orleans.

Voltaire. [1759] 2006. *Candide: or Optimism*. New Haven, Conn.: Yale University Press.

Wacquant, Loïc J. D. 1989. "Towards a Reflexive Sociology: A Workshop with Pierre Bourdieu." *Sociological Theory* 7(1):26–63.
Wagner-Martin, Linda, and Cathy N. Davidson. 1995. *The Oxford Book of Women's Writings in the United States*. New York: Oxford University Press.
Walker, Alice. 1980. "Coming Apart." Pp. 95–104 in *Take Back the Night: Women on Pornography*. ed. Laura Lederer. New York: William Morrow..
_____. 1982. *The Color Purple*. Orlando, Fla.: Harcourt.
_____. 1983. *In Search of Our Mothers' Gardens: Womanist Prose*. Orlando, Fla.: Harcourt.
Walker, Rebecca. 1992. "Becoming the Third Wave." *Ms.*, January–February.
Walker, Rebecca, ed. 1995. *To Be Real: Telling the Truth and Changing the Face of Feminism*. New York: Anchor.
Wallerstein, Immanuel. 1974. *The Modern World System: Capitalist Agriculture and the Origins of the European World-Economy in the 16th Century*. New York: Academic.
_____. 1979. *The Capitalist World-Economy: Essays*. New York: Cambridge University Press.
Walter, Natasha, 2004. "The Winners are Warlords, Not Women." *Guardian*; www.guardian.co.uk/afghanistan/comment;story/0,1325263,00.html (retrieved Sept. 25, 2007).
Ward, Kathryn. 1984. *Women in the World-System: Its Impact on Status and Fertility*. New York: Praeger.
Ward, Kathryn, ed. 1990. *Women Workers and Global Restructuring*. Cornell International Industrial and Labor Relations Report No. 17. Ithaca, N.Y.: ILR Press of Cornell University Press.
Warner, Michael. 1993. *Fear of a Queer Planet: Queer Politics and Social Theory*. Minneapolis: University of Minnesota Press
Warren, Karen J. 1997. *Ecofeminism: Women Culture Nature*. Bloomington: Indiana University Press.
Washington, Mary Helen. 1989. *Black-Eyed Susans and Midnight Birds: Stories by and about Black Women*. New York: Knopf Doubleday.
Washington, Sylvia Hood. 2005. *Packing Them In: An Archaeology of Environmental Racism in Chicago, 1865–1954*. Lanham, Md.: Lexington.
Waters, Mary-Alice, ed. 1970. *Rosa Luxemburg Speaks*. New York: Pathfinder.
Weber, Lynn. 2010. *Understanding Race, Class, Gender, and Sexuality: A Conceptual Framework*. New York: Oxford University Press.
Weber, Max. [1921] 1968. *Economy and Society*. Totowa, N.J.: Bedminster.
Weed, Elizabeth. 1997. "Introduction." Pp. vii–xiii in *Feminism Meets Queer Theory*, ed. Elizabeth Weed and Naomi Schor. Bloomington: Indiana University Press.
Wekker, Gloria. 2006. *The Politics of Passion: Women's Sexual Culture in the Afro-Surinamese Diaspora*. New York: Columbia University Press.
Wells-Barnett, Ida B. [1892] 1969. "Southern Horrors." In *On Lynchings*. New York: Arno.
_____. 1895. *The Red Record*. Chicago: Donohue & Henneberry.
_____. [1901] 2005 . "Lynching and the Excuse for It." Pp. 117–119 in *Feminist Theory: A Reader*, 2nd ed., ed. Wendy K. Kolmar and Frances Bartkowski. Boston: McGraw-Hill..
Welter, Barbara. 1973. "The Cult of True Womanhood: 1820–1860." Pp. 224–250 in *The American Family in Social-Historical Perspective*, ed. Michael Gordon. New York: St. Martin's.
West, Candace, and Don H. Zimmerman. 1987. "Doing Gender." *Gender and Society* 1(2): 125–151.
West, Traci C. 1999. *Wounds of the Spirit: Black Women, Violence, and Resistance Ethics*. New York: NYU Press.
Wexler, Alice. 1989. *Emma Goldman in Exile*. Boston: Beacon.
Wharton, Edith. [1905] 2000. *The House of Mirth*. New York: Oxford University Press.
White, Deborah Gray. 1985. *Ar'nt I a Woman? Female Slaves in the Plantation South*. New York: W. W. Norton.
Whitman, Walt. [1855] 2005. *Leaves of Grass*. New York: Oxford University Press.
Whittier, Nancy. 1995. *Feminist Generations: The Persistence of the Radical Women's Movement*. Philadelphia: Temple University Press.
Wilchins, Riki. 2002. "A Certain Kind of Freedom: Power and the Truth of Bodies—Four Essays on Bodies." Pp. 23–63 in *GenderQueer: Voices from Beyond the Sexual Binary*, ed. Joan Nestle, Clare Howell, and Riki Wilchins. New York: Alyson.
Wilkerson, Abby. 2002. "Disability, Sex Radicalism, and Political Agency." *NWSA Journal* 14(3): 33–57.
Williams, Raymond. 1998. *Keywords: A Vocabulary of Culture and Society*. London: Fontana.
Williams, Tennessee. [1958] 1976. *Four Plays*. New York: Signet.
Williams, Walter. 1986. *The Spirit of the Flesh: Sexual Diversity in American Indian Cultures*. Boston: Beacon.

Willing, Indigo Williams. 2005. "From Orphaned China Dolls to Long-Distance Daughters: A Call for Solidarity across Borders." Pp. 95–109 in *Defending Our Dreams: Global Feminist Voices for a New Generation*, ed. Shamillah, Anasuya Sengupta, and Kristy Evans. London: Zed.

Wilson, Shamillah, Anasuya Sengupta, and Kristy Evans, eds. 2005. *Defending our Dreams: Global Feminist Voices for a New Generation*. London: Zed.

Winant, Howard. 2007. "The Dark Side of the Force: One Hundred Years of the Sociology of Race." Pp. 535–571 in *Sociology in America: A History*, ed. Craig Calhoun. Chicago: University of Chicago Press.

Wintz, Cary D. 1996. *Remembering the Harlem Renaissance*. London: Francis & Taylor.

Woelfe, Gretchen. 2007. *Jeanette Rankin: Political Pioneer*. Honesdale, Pa.: Calkins Creek.

Wolf, Naomi. [1993] 1994. *Fire with Fire: The New Female Power and How It Will Change the 21st Century*. New York: Random House.

Wollstonecraft, Mary. [1792] 1975. *A Vindication of the Rights of Woman*. New York: W. W. Norton.

Wong, Nellie. [1981] 1983 "When I Was Growing Up." Pp.7–8 in *This Bridge Called My Back: Writings by Radical Women of Color*, ed. Cherríe Moraga and Gloria Anzaldúa. New York: Kitchen Table—Women of Color Press.

Woodhull, Victoria. [1873] 2005. "'The Elixir of Life; or, Why Do We Die?'" Pp. 95–97 in *Feminist Theory: A Reader*, 2nd ed., ed. Wendy K. Kolmar and Frances Bartkowski. Boston: McGraw-Hill.

Woodhull, Winnie. 2003. "Global Feminisms, Transnational Political Economies, and Third World Cultural Production. *Journal of International Women's Studies* 4(2): 76–90.

Woolf, Virginia. 1925. *Mrs. Dalloway*. New York: Harcourt.

_____. 1927. *To the Lighthouse*. New York: Harcourt.

_____. 1929. *A Room of One's Own*. New York: Harcourt.

_____. [1929] 2005. "Chapters 2, 5, and 6 from *A Room of One's Own*." Pp. 149–154 in *Feminist Theory: A Reader*, 2nd ed., ed. Wendy K. Kolmar and Frances Bartkowski. Boston: McGraw-Hill.

Wurtzel, Elizabeth. 1998. *Bitch: In Praise of Difficult Women*. New York: Doubleday.

Yamada, Mitsuye. 1979. "Invisibility Is an Unnatural Disaster: Reflections of an Asian American Woman." *Bridge, An Asian Perspective* 7(1): 11–13. Reprinted [1981] (1983) Pp. 35–40 in *This Bridge Called My Back: Writings by Radical Women of Color*. ed. Cherríe Moraga and Gloria Anzaldúa, New York: Kitchen Table—Women of Color Press.

_____. [1981] 2005. "'Asian Pacific American Women and Feminism.'" Pp. 365–367 in *Feminist Theory: A Reader*, 2nd ed., ed. Wendy K. Kolmar and Frances Bartkowski. Boston: McGraw-Hill.

Young, Iris Marion. 1981. "Beyond the Unhappy Marriage: A Critique of Dual Systems Theory." Pp. 43–69 in *Women and Revolution: A Discussion of the Unhappy Marriage of Marxism and Feminism*, ed. Lydia Sargent. Cambridge, Mass.: South End.

_____. 2005. *On Female Body Experience: "Throwing Like a Girl" and Other Essays*. New York: Oxford University Press.

Yuval-Davis, Nira. 1994. "Women, Ethnicity, and Empowerment." *Feminism & Psychology* 4(1): 179–198.

_____. 1997. *Gender and Nation*. London: Sage.

_____. 2006. "Human/Women's Rights and Feminist Transversal Politics." Pp. 275–295 in *Global Feminism: Transnational Women's Activism, Organizing, and Human Rights*, ed. Myra Ferree and Aili Tripp. New York: NYU Press.

Zalewski, Marysia. 2000. *Feminism after Postmodernism? Theorizing through Practice*. London: Routledge.

Zaretsky, Eli. 1976. *Capitalism, the Family, and Personal Life*. New York: Harper & Row.

Zeitlin. Irving M. 1981. *Ideology and the Development of Sociological Theory*. Englewood Cliffs, N.J.: Prentice Hall.

Zetkin, Clara. 1984. *Clara Zetkin: Selected Writings*. Edited by Philip Foner. New York: International.

Zita, Jacquelyn. 1994. "Gay and Lesbian Studies: Yet another Unhappy Marriage?" Pp. 258–276 in *Tilting the Towers: Lesbians Teaching Queer Subjects*, ed. Linda Garber. New York: Routledge.

Name Index

by Ashly Patterson

Subject Index

FEMINIST THEORY TIMELINE

1792	Mary Wollstonecraft	*A Vindication of the Rights of Women*
1838	Sarah Grimké	*Letters on the Equality of the Sexes and the Condition of Women*
1848	Elizabeth Cady Stanton	"Declaration of Sentiments," Seneca Falls Convention
1851	Sojourner Truth	"Ain't I a Woman?" (speech)
1851	Harriet Taylor Mill	"Enfranchisement of Women"
1861	Harriet Jacobs	Incidents in the Life of a Slave Girl
1869	John Stuart Mill	*"The Subjection of Women"*
1871	Josephine Butler	"Letter to My Countrywomen"
1872	Susan B. Anthony	Speech after Arrest for Illegal Voting
1873	Victoria Woodhull	"The Elixir of Life"
1884	Friedrich Engels	*The Origin of the Family, Private Property, and the State*
1892	Anna Julia Cooper	*A Voice from the South*
1895	Ida B. Wells-Barnett	*The Red Record*
1898	Charlotte Perkins Gilman	*Women and Economics*
1898	Mary Church Terrell	"The Progress of Colored Women"
1910	Emma Goldman	"The Traffic in Women"
1910	Mother (Mary) Jones	"Girl Slaves of the Milwaukee Breweries"
1913	Rosa Luxemburg	*Accumulation of Capital*
1919	Crystal Eastman	*On Women and Revolution*
1920	Margaret Sanger	*Woman and the New Race*
1923	Alice Paul	Equal Rights Amendment
1929	Virginia Woolf	*A Room of One's Own*
1932	Karen Horney	*Feminine Psychology*
1935	Margaret Mead	*Sex and Temperament in Three Primitive Societies*
1937	Zora Neale Hurston	*Their Eyes Were Watching God*
1952	Simone de Beauvoir	*The Second Sex*
1963	Betty Friedan	*The Feminine Mystique*
1969	Margaret Benston	"The Political Economy of Women's Liberation"
1969	Redstockings	"Redstockings Manifesto"
1970	Kate Millett	*Sexual Politics*
1970	Radicalesbians	"The Woman-Identified Woman"
1970	Shulamith Firestone	*The Dialectic of Sex*
1970	Pauli Murray	"The Liberation of Black Women"
1971	Boston Women's Health Book Collective	*Our Bodies, Ourselves*
1971	Gloria Steinem, ed.	*Ms.* magazine
1971	Juliet Mitchell	*Women's Estate*
1972	Charlotte Bunch	"Lesbians in Revolt"
1974	Andrea Dworkin	*Woman Hating*
1975	Gayle Rubin	"The Traffic in Women"
1975	Hélène Cixous	"The Laugh of the Medusa"
1976	Marge Piercy	*Woman on the Edge of Time*
1976	Michel Foucault	*History of Sexuality*
1977	Combahee River Collective	"A Black Feminist Statement"
1977	Luce Irigaray	*This Sex Which Is Not One*
1978	Mary Daly	*Gyn/Ecology*
1978	Nancy Chodorow	*The Reproduction of Mothering*
1978	Susan Griffin	*Woman and Nature*
1980	Iris Marion Young	"Throwing Like a Girl"
1980	Adrienne Rich	"Compulsory Heterosexuality and Lesbian Existence"
1980	Julia Kristeva	*Desire in Language*
1981	Angela Davis	*Women, Race, and Class*
1981	Cherríe Moraga and Gloria Anzaldúa, eds	*This Bridge Called My Back*
1981	Gloria T. Hull, Patricia Bell Scott, and Barbara Smith, eds.	*All the Women are White, All the Men are Black, But Some of Us Are Brave*
1981	Heidi Hartmann	"The Unhappy Marriage of Marxism and Feminism"

1982	Carol Gilligan	*In a Different Voice*
1983	Alice Walker	*In Search of Our Mothers' Gardens*
1983	Barbara Smith, ed	*Home Girls*
1983	Maria Lugones and Elizabeth Spelman	"Have We Got a Theory for You!"
1984	bell hooks	*Feminist Theory*
1984	Audre Lorde	*Sister/Outsider*
1984	Chandra Talpade Mohanty	"Under Western Eyes"
1984	Robin Morgan, ed.	*Sisterhood Is Global*
1985	Donna Haraway	"A Cyborg Manifesto"
1985	Gayatri Chakravorty Spivak	"Can the Subaltern Speak?"
1986	Sandra Harding	*The Science Question in Feminism*
1987	Dorothy Smith	*The Everyday World as Problematic*
1987	Gloria Anzaldúa	*Borderlands/LaFrontera*
1989	Kimberlé Williams Crenshaw	"Demarginalizing the Intersection of Race and Sex"
1989	Diana Fuss	*Essentially Speaking*
1989	Ynestra King	"The Ecology of Feminism and the Feminism of Ecology"
1990	Eve Sedgwick	*Epistemology of the Closet*
1990	Judith Butler	*Gender Trouble*
1990	Patricia Hill Collins	*Black Feminist Thought*
1991	Susan Faludi	*Backlash*
1993	Katie Roiphe	*The Morning After*
1993	Ruth Frankenberg	*The Social Construction of Whiteness*
1993	Maria Mies and Vandana Shiva	*Ecofeminism*
1994	Kate Bornstein	Gender Outlaw
1994	Naomi Wolf	*Fire with Fire*
1995	Anne McClintock	*Imperial Leather*
1995	Barbara Findlen, ed.	*Listen Up*
1995	Rebecca Walker, ed.	*To Be Real*
1995	Rene Denfeld	*The New Victorians*
1995	Winona LaDuke	"Mothers of our Nations"
1997	Leslie Heywood and Jennifer Drake, eds.	*Third Wave Agenda*
1997	Uma Narayan	*Dislocating Cultures*
1998	Dorothy Roberts	*Killing the Black Body*
1998	Judith Halberstam	*Female Masculinity*
1999	Aihwa Ong	*Flexible Citizenship*
1999	Joan Morgan	*When Chickenheads Come Home to Roost*
2000	Jennifer Baumgardner and Amy Richards	*Manifesta*
2000	Anne Fausto-Sterling	*Sexing the Body*
2002	Daisy Hernandez and Bushra Rehman, eds.	*Colonize This!*
2002	Joan Nestle, Clare Howell, and Riki Wilchins, eds	*GenderQueer*
2003	Julie Bettie	*Women without Class*
2003	Rory Dicker and Alison Piepmeier, eds.	*Catching a Wave*
2004	Astrid Henry	*Not My Mother's Sister*
2004	Vivien Labaton and Dawn Lundy Martin, eds.	*The Fire This Time*
2005	Andrea Smith	*Conquest*
2005	Inderpal Grewal	*Transnational America*
2005	M. Jacqui Alexander	*Pedagogies of Crossing*
2006	Incite! Women of Color against Violence	*Color of Violence*

SOURCE. Special thanks to Nicole S. Gillies and Jessie J. Jacobs for compiling this timeline.
NOTE: While most of these feminists authored many works, their most influential or groundbreaking texts are included here to illustrate the construction of different feminisms over time. Additional information on these authors is presented throughout the index.

CPSIA information can be obtained
at www.ICGtesting.com
Printed in the USA
BVOW04s1312040617
485975BV00002B/5/P